Microsoft® Internet Information Server™

UNLEASHED

Copyright © 1996 by Sams.net Publishing

FIRST EDITION

All rights reserved. No part of this book shall be reproduced, stored in a retrieval system, or transmitted by any means, electronic, mechanical, photocopying, recording, or otherwise, without written permission from the publisher. No patent liability is assumed with respect to the use of the information contained herein. Although every precaution has been taken in the preparation of this book, the publisher and author assume no responsibility for errors or omissions. Neither is any liability assumed for damages resulting from the use of the information contained herein. For information, address Sams.net Publishing, 201 W. 103rd St., Indianapolis, IN 46290.

International Standard Book Number: 1-57521-109-2

Library of Congress Catalog Card Number: 96-67957

99 98 97 96   4 3 2 1

Interpretation of the printing code: the rightmost double-digit number is the year of the book's printing; the rightmost single-digit, the number of the book's printing. For example, a printing code of 96-1 shows that the first printing of the book occurred in 1996.

Composed in AGaramond and MCPdigital by Macmillan Computer Publishing

Printed in the United States of America

Trademarks

All terms mentioned in this book that are known to be trademarks or service marks have been appropriately capitalized. Sams.net Publishing cannot attest to the accuracy of this information. Use of a term in this book should not be regarded as affecting the validity of any trademark or service mark. Internet Information Sesrver is a trademark of Microsoft Corporation.

President, Sams Publishing	*Richard K. Swadley*
Publishing Team Leader	*Dean Miller*
Managing Editor	*Cindy Morrow*
Director of Marketing	*John Pierce*
Assistant Marketing Managers	*Kristina Perry*
	Rachel Wolfe

Acquisitions Editor
Kim Spilker

Development Editor
Sunthar Visuvalingam

Software Development Specialist
Cari Skaggs

Senior Editor
Kitty Wilson

Production Editor
Kate Shoup

Copy Editors
*Kimberly K. Hannel,
Kate Shoup,
Colleen A. Williams*

Indexer
Gina Brown

Technical Reviewer
Kelly Held

Editorial Coordinator
Bill Whitmer

Technical Edit Coordinator
Lynette Quinn

Editorial Assistants
*Carol Ackerman
Andi Richter
Rhonda Tinch-Mize*

Cover Designer
Tim Amrhein

Book Designer
Gary Adair

Copy Writer
Peter Fuller

Production Team Supervisor
Brad Chinn

Graphics Image Specialists
*Dennis Sheehan
Brad Dickson*

Production
*Jeanne Clark
Bruce Clingaman
Sonja Hart
Susan Van Ness*

Overview

Introduction **xxiii**

Part I Introduction to the Internet Information Server

1. An Internet Overview **3**
2. An Internet Information Server Overview **29**

Part II Building Your Foundation for the Internet Information Server

3. A Windows NT Server Overview **47**
4. Choosing a Platform for Windows NT Server **75**
5. IIS Preparation and Installation **103**

Part III Administering Your Site

6. Using the Internet Server Manager **135**
7. Using the Internet Explorer **165**
8. Working with Microsoft Exchange **189**
9. Using DHCP, WINS, and DNS **205**
10. Advanced Security Issues **263**

Part IV Web Page Development

11. An HTML Primer **311**
12. Designing and Managing a Web Site with FrontPage **337**
13. Publishing on the Web with Microsoft Office **361**
14. Using Asymetrix Web3D and Corel's Web Designer **379**
15. Using Sausage Software's HotDog Pro **393**

Part V Advanced Web Page Development

16. The Internet Information Server SDK **427**
17. Unleashing the Power of VBScript **445**
18. Introduction to Windows NT CGI Programming **489**
19. Writing Java Applets **523**

Part VI Using Internet Information Server with Databases

    20   Interfacing Internet Information Server with ODBC Databases   **549**

    21   Building Dynamic Web Pages with SQL Server   **595**

Part VII Performance Tuning and Optimization Techniques

    22   The Performance Monitor   **623**

    23   Tuning the Server   **641**

Part VIII Appendixes

    A   Glossary   **685**

    B   HTML Reference   **713**

    C   The Registry Editor and Registry Keys   **761**

        Index   **799**

Contents

Introduction xxiii

Part I Introduction to the Internet Information Server

1 An Internet Overview 3
   A Little History, Please 5
      The Birth of ARPAnet and TCP/IP 6
      The Birth of the Internet 6
      The Internet Explosion 8
   Connecting to the Internet 9
      Defining Your Goals 10
      Defining Your Internet Service Requirements 12
      Choosing a Connection Type 13
      Choosing an Internet Provider or Internet Service Provider 17
   Using the Internet 20
      Publishing Data 21
      Collecting Data 25
      Selling Products 26
   Summary 27

2 An Internet Information Server Overview 29
   What Is the Internet Information Server? 30
      A Collection of Windows NT Services 30
      An Extensible Platform 33
   What Can the Internet Information Server Do for You? 35
      Internet and Intranet Publishing 36
      How Well Can the Internet Information Server Perform? 39
   Publicizing Your Web Site 40
      Directory Listings 41
      Newsgroups 42
   Summary 42

Part II Building Your Foundation for the Internet Information Server

3 A Windows NT Server Overview 47
   The Windows NT Design 48
      The Windows NT System Design Model 51
      The Windows NT Environmental Subsystem Design Model 54
   Additional Windows NT Features 56
      The New Technology File System 57
      Fault-Tolerant Capabilities 58
      Centralized Administration 61

Windows NT Server Concepts 65
    Workgroups Versus Domains 65
    Controllers Versus Servers 66
    Domain Models 68
Summary 73

4 Choosing a Platform for Windows NT Server 75

Choosing the Right Hardware 77
    Choosing a Processor Platform 77
    Choosing an I/O Bus 78
    Choosing a Disk Subsystem 82
    Easy Performance Gains 85
Hardware Upgrades 89
    System Memory Upgrades 89
    Hardware RAID Alternatives 91
    Adding Network Adapters 92
    Adding Processors 97
Choosing the Right Server Model 98
The Software Configuration 98
Summary 101

5 IIS Preparation and Installation 103

Determining Where to Install the Internet Information Server 104
    IIS on a Limited Budget 105
    IIS on an Unlimited Budget 105
    Choosing a Location for Your Data 106
IIS Preinstallation Requirements 106
    Installing the TCP/IP Protocol and Utilities 108
    Installing the Dynamic Host Configuration Protocol 112
    Installing the Windows Internet Name Service 114
    Installing the RIP for Internet Protocol Service 115
    Installing the Domain Name Server Service 115
    Installing the Simple Network Management Protocol 116
    Installing the Simple TCP/IP Service 118
    Installing the Microsoft TCP/IP Printing Service 118
The Remote Access Service 120
    Installing the Remote Access Service 120
    Configuring the Remote Access Service 126
    The Remote Access Administrator 126
    Using Remote Access as a Gateway to the Internet 128
Installing the Internet Information Server 129
Summary 132

Part III Administering Your Site

6 Using the Internet Service Manager 135
   - Basic Operations of the Internet Service Manager 136
     - Controlling the Internet Services 137
     - Managing Internet Information Server Sites 138
     - Using a View to Manage Multiple Sites 138
   - Configuring the WWW Service 139
     - Configuring the WWW Service 140
     - Configuring the WWW Service Directories 142
     - Logging WWW Activity 147
     - Limiting Access to Your WWW Site 149
   - Configuring the FTP Service 150
     - Configuring the FTP Service 151
     - Configuring the FTP Service Messages 152
     - Configuring the FTP Service Directories 153
   - Configuring the Gopher Service 156
     - Configuring the Gopher Service 156
     - Configuring the Gopher Service Directories 158
   - Logging Site Access with SQL Server 159
     - Building the Database 159
     - Assigning Permissions to Access the Database 161
     - Building the ODBC Data Source 161
   - Summary 163

7 Using the Internet Explorer 165
   - Installing Internet Explorer 167
   - Configuring Internet Explorer 168
     - Associating File Types 168
     - Configuring the Start and Search Pages 172
     - Configuring the Appearance 173
     - Configuring the Internet Connection 175
     - Configuring Internet Explorer Cache Settings 179
     - Configuring Internet Explorer Security 181
     - Configuring the Internet Explorer Character Set 184
     - Configuring the Rating System to Limit Access
       to Internet Sites 185
   - Using Internet Explorer 187
   - Summary 188

8	**Working with Microsoft Exchange 189**	
	Using Exchange Server on the Internet	190
	Installing the Internet Mail Connector	191
	Configuring the Internet Mail Connector	192
	Using the Internet to Connect Multiple Exchange Server Sites	199
	Microsoft Exchange Security Issues	200
	Protecting Your Server	200
	Protecting Your E-Mail Messages from Tampering or Theft	202
	Protecting Your Clients from Viruses	203
	Summary	204
9	**Using DHCP, WINS, and DNS 205**	
	Using the Dynamic Host Configuration Protocol	206
	The Design Goals for the Microsoft DHCP Protocol	207
	Planning Your DHCP Installation	209
	Installing the DHCP Server Service	221
	Managing Your DHCP Server with the DHCP Manager	221
	Managing the DHCP Databases	232
	DHCP Server Registry Keys	233
	Using the Windows Internet Name Service	234
	Design Goals for the WINS Service	235
	Planning Your WINS Installation	236
	Installing the WINS Service	241
	Configuring the WINS Service with the WINS Manager	241
	Managing Your WINS Clients	248
	Managing the WINS Databases	249
	Using the Performance Monitor to Monitor the WINS Server Service	250
	WINS Server Registry Keys	251
	Using the Domain Name System	254
	The Design Goals for the Microsoft DNS Service	254
	Planning Your DNS Installation	255
	The DNS Configuration Files	256
	Summary	261
10	**Advanced Security Issues 263**	
	Security and the Internet	264
	Application and Document Security Issues	264
	Firewalls, Proxy Agents, and Other Ways to Limit Access	270
	Security and Windows NT Server	275
	Using User Accounts to Limit Access	275
	Using NTFS to Protect Your Data	279

　　　　Setting Permissions on a Directory or File 280
　　　　Security and Dial-Up Networking 287
　　　　Configuring Windows NT Server as a Mini Firewall 290
　　Determining Who Is Using Your System 297
　　　　Configuring the System to Enable Auditing............................ 297
　　　　Auditing Directories and Files 299
　　　　Using the Windows NT Event Viewer 302
　　　　The Internet Information Server Logs..................................... 307
　　Summary 308

Part IV Web Page Development

　11　An HTML Primer   311
　　　What Is an HTML Document? 313
　　　　What Is a Markup Language? 313
　　　　HTML to the Rescue 314
　　　Basic HTML Styles 316
　　　　Changing Paragraph Attributes 318
　　　　Changing Text Attributes 320
　　　　Displaying Text Using a Fixed-Width Font 323
　　　　Creating Document Headers 324
　　　　Changing Page Attributes 325
　　　　Creating Numbered and Bulleted Lists 326
　　　　Additional List Styles 327
　　　　Miscellaneous Styles 329
　　　　Inserting Graphics 329
　　　　Creating Tables 332
　　　　Creating Hypertext Links 333
　　　Summary 335
　12　Designing and Managing a Web Site with FrontPage   337
　　　Installing FrontPage 338
　　　FrontPage Server 340
　　　Changing the Default Port of the FrontPage Server 341
　　　FrontPage Server Administrator 341
　　　　Installing Server Extensions 342
　　　　Managing Server Extensions 343
　　　FrontPage Explorer 345
　　　FrontPage To Do List 348
　　　Verifying Links 349
　　　FrontPage Editor 350
　　　　Designing Web Pages Using the FrontPage Editor 350
　　　Summary 358

13 Publishing on the Web with Microsoft Office 361
Microsoft Office and the Internet 362
Publishing on the Web with Microsoft Word 362
    Installing Internet Assistant for Word 363
    Creating an HTML Document with Word 364
Publishing on the Web with Microsoft Excel 368
    Installing Internet Assistant for Excel 369
    Publishing a Spreadsheet on the Web with Excel 370
Publishing on the Web with Microsoft PowerPoint 372
    Installing PowerPoint Internet Assistant 373
    Converting a PowerPoint Slide Show into HTML 374
Publishing on the Web with Microsoft Access 375
    Installing Internet Assistant for Access 376
    Publishing a Database on the Web with Access 376
Summary 378

14 Using Asymetrix Web3D and Corel's Web Designer 379
Using Asymetrix Web 3D 380
    How Does Asymetrix Web 3D Work? 381
    Creating Your Home Page with Web 3D 383
Using Corel's Web.Designer 387
    Using CorelWEB.DESIGNER 388
    Using CorelWEB.GALLERY 389
    Using CorelWEB.Transit 391
Summary 392

15 Using Sausage Software's HotDog Pro 393
Why Use HotDog Pro? 394
Getting Started with HotDog Pro 396
    Installing HotDog Pro 396
    The HotDog Pro Tutorial 397
    Customizing HotDog Pro 399
Working with Documents and Templates 410
    Creating an HTML Document 411
    Creating a Template from an HTML Document 421
    Publishing Your Documents 422
Working with Projects 422
Summary 423

Part V Advanced Web Page Development

16   The Internet Information Server SDK   427
    What Is an ISAPI Application? 428
        A CGI Application Versus an ISAPI Application 429
        A Few ISAPI Application Considerations 429
        The Basic ISAPI Interface 430
        An Internet Server Application Skeleton 439
    Summary 443

17   Unleashing the Power of VBScript   445
    Introduction to VBScript 446
    How VBScript Works 446
    Hello World! 447
        The Hello World! Dialog Box 448
        The Time Dialog Box 449
        The Date Dialog Box 449
    VBScript Operators 451
        The Addition Operator 451
        The Subtraction Operator 451
        The Multiplication Operator 451
        The Exponential Operator 451
        The Floating-Point Division Operator 451
        The Integer-Division Operator 452
        The String-Concatenation Operator 452
        The MOD Operator 452
        Boolean Operators 452
        The Equivalence Operator 454
        The Object-Reference Operator 454
        Comparison Operators 454
    VBScript Control Structures 455
        `Call` 455
        `Dim` 456
        `Do...While...Until...Loop` 457
        `Erase` 457
        `Exit` 458
        `For...Next` 458
        `For Each...Next` 458
        `Function` 459

If...Then...Else	460
Let	460
LSet	460
Mid	460
On Error	461
Private	461
Public	461
Randomize	461
Rem	461
RSet	462
Set	462
Static	462
Sub	462
While...Wend	463
VBScript Functions	**463**
Abs	463
Array	463
Asc	463
Atn	464
CBool	464
CByte	464
CDate	464
CDbl	464
Chr	464
CInt	464
CLng	464
Cos	464
CSng	465
CStr	465
CVErr	465
Date	465
DateSerial	465
DateValue	465
Day	465
Exp	466
Hex	466
Hour	466
InputBox	466
InStr	466
Int, Fix	467
IsArray	467
IsDate	467

IsEmpty	467
IsError	467
IsNull	467
IsNumeric	467
IsObject	467
LBound	468
LCase	468
Left	468
Len	468
Log	468
LTrim, RTrim, Trim	468
Mid	468
Minute	468
Month	468
MsgBox	469
Now	470
Oct	470
Right	470
Rnd	470
Second	470
Sgn	470
Sin	470
Sqr	470
Str	471
StrComp	471
String	471
Tan	471
Time	471
TimeSerial	471
TimeValue	471
UBound	471
UCase	472
Val	472
VarType	472
Weekday	473
Year	473
Applications of VBScript	**473**
Simple Calculator	473
Labeling an Image	484
Summary	**488**

18	Introduction to Windows NT CGI Programming 489	
	Introduction to CGI	490
	Benefits of an Interactive Web Site	491
	Applications of CGI	492
	CGI Basics	493
	How CGI Works	494
	CGI Issues	496
	Processing Time	497
	Multiple Instances of the Same Script	497
	Security	497
	CGI Environment Variables	499
	CGI Perl Scripts	503
	Perl Resources on the Internet	504
	CGI C Scripts	505
	"Content Type" Returned by CGI Applications	505
	A Few Things to Note About Developing CGI Applications	506
	Hello World!, CGI	506
	Hello World! CGI Script in Perl	507
	Hello World! CGI Script in C	509
	Accessing Environment Variables Available to CGI Scripts	511
	Accessing CGI Environment Variables from a C Program	511
	Accessing CGI Environment Variables from a Perl Script	513
	Using CGI to Provide Customized Content	514
	Setting Up a Feedback Form	519
	Summary	522
19	Writing Java Applets 523	
	Java Break	524
	Understanding Java	525
	Applets Work on Any Computer	525
	Object-Oriented Programming	526
	Secure and Robust	527
	What Can You Do with Java?	527
	Creating a Java Applet	528
	Parameters for the Marquee Applet	529
	The Marquee Applet's Code	530
	Imported Java	533
	Head of the Class	534
	The `init` Method	535
	Painting Applets	539
	Threads	542

Compiling Java Applets 544
Embedding Java Applets in HTML 545
    The `<APPLET>` Tag 546
    The `<PARAM>` Tag 546
Summary 546

Part VI Using Internet Information Server with Databases

20   Interfacing Internet Information Server with ODBC Databases   549
Installing Microsoft dbWeb 550
Using the Microsoft dbWeb Administrator 555
    Configuring dbWeb Preferences 556
    Creating the ODBC Data Source 561
    Creating the Database Schema 564
Creating a Custom Guest Book Using Microsoft dbWeb 589
Summary 593

21   Building Dynamic Web Pages with SQL Server   595
Using the Internet Database Connector 596
    Creating the Web Page Forms 597
Using the SQL Server Web Assistant 614
Summary 620

Part VII Performance Tuning and Optimization Techniques

22   The Performance Monitor   623
Using the Performance Monitor 624
    The Performance Monitor Toolbar 625
    Creating Charts 626
    Creating Logs 630
    Creating Reports 632
    Creating Alerts 635
Summary 640

23   Tuning the Server   641
Performance Tuning with the Performance Monitor 642
    Finding Processor Bottlenecks 643
    Finding Memory Bottlenecks 649
    Finding Disk Bottlenecks 654
    Finding Network Bottlenecks 658
    Finding IIS Bottlenecks 661
Configuring SQL Server 668
Summary 682

Part VIII Appendixes

- A Glossary 685
- B HTML Reference 713
  - How This Reference Is Structured 714
  - HTML Element List 715
    - \<A\> 715
    - \<ABBREV\> 716
    - \<ACRONYM\> 716
    - \<ADDRESS\> 717
    - \<APPLICATION\> 717
    - APPLET\> 717
    - \<AREA\> 718
    - \<AU\> 718
    - \<B\> 718
    - \<BANNER\> 719
    - \<BASE\> 719
    - \<BASEFONT\> 719
    - \<BDO\> 720
    - \<BGSOUND\> 720
    - \<BIG\> 720
    - \<BLINK\> 720
    - \<BLOCKQUOTE\> 721
    - \<BODY\> 721
    - \<BQ\> 722
    - \<BR\> 722
    - \<CAPTION\> 722
    - \<CENTER\> 722
    - \<CITE\> 723
    - \<CODE\> 723
    - \<COL\> 723
    - \<COLGROUP\> 724
    - \<CREDIT\> 724
    - \<DD\> 724
    - \<DEL\> 725
    - \<DFN\> 725
    - \<DIR\> 725
    - \<DIV\> 726
    - \<DL\> 726
    - \<DT\> 726
    - \<EM\> 726
    - \<EMBED\> 727

<FN>	727
<FIG>	727
<FONT>	728
<FORM>	728
<FRAME>	728
<FRAMESET>	729
<H1>	729
<H2>	730
<H3>	730
<H4>	730
<H5>	730
<H6>	731
<HEAD>	731
<HPn>	731
<HR>	732
<HTML>	732
<I>	732
<IMG>	732
<INPUT>	733
<INS>	734
<ISINDEX>	734
<KBD>	734
<LANG>	734
<LH>	735
<LI>	735
<LINK>	735
<LISTING>	736
<MAP>	736
<MARQUEE>	736
<MENU>	737
<META>	737
<NEXTID>	737
<NOBR>	738
<NOEMBED>	738
<NOFRAMES>	738
<NOTE>	739
<OL>	739
<OPTION>	739
<OVERLAY>	740
<P>	740
<PARAM>	740
<PERSON>	740

<PLAINTEXT> 741
<PRE> 741
<Q> 741
<S> 742
<SAMP> 742
<SELECT> 742
<SMALL> 743
<SPAN> 743
<STRIKE> 743
<STRONG> 743
<SUB> 744
<SUP> 744
<TAB> 744
<TABLE> 744
<TBODY> 745
<TD> 745
<TEXTAREA> 746
<TFOOT> 746
<TH> 746
<THEAD> 747
<TITLE> 747
<TR> 747
<TT> 747
<U> 748
<UL> 748
<VAR> 748
<WBR> 749
<XMP> 749

Defining Special Characters on Your Web Page 749
HTML Summary for the Internet Information Server and
the Internet Assistant for Word for Windows 754

C   The Registry Editor and Registry Keys   761
The Registry 762
The Registry Editor 764
Useful Registry Keys 767
System Service Configuration Registry Keys 768
NetBEUI Frame Protocol Configuration Registry Keys 787
Memory-Related Registry Keys 790
Miscellaneous Registry Keys 794

Index   799

Acknowledgments

Although an author might write the chapters himself, developing the book into a viable project is really a team effort. Therefore, I would like to thank my agent, Valda Hilley, for getting me involved in the project; Sams Publishing for the opportunity; and my family—my mother Antoinette Knowles and my two cats (Kit and Kat)—for their support. Special thanks go to Kim Spilker, Sunthar Visuvalingam, and Kitty Wilson of Sams Publishing. All these people helped to make this a better book. I also would like to thank Eric Beauchamp and Alex Sampera of WinBook Computer Corporation, for without their loan of a WinBook XP5 portable computer this book could not have been completed.

About the Authors

Arthur Knowles

Arthur Knowles is president and founder of Knowles Consulting, a firm specializing in systems integration, training, and software development. Art is a Microsoft Certified System Engineer. His specialties include Microsoft Windows NT Server, Windows NT Workstation, SQL Server, Systems Management Server, Windows 95, and Windows for Workgroups. Art is the author of *Microsoft BackOffice Administrator's Survival Guide* (Sams Publishing) and has served as a contributing author to several books, including *Designing and Implementing the Internet Information Server* (Sams Publishing), *Windows 3.1 Configuration Secrets*, *Windows NT Unleashed* (Sams Publishing), and *Mastering Windows 95*. He is the forum manager of the Portable Computers Forum on the Microsoft Network. You can reach Art on the Internet at webmaster@nt-guru.com or on his Web site at http://www.nt-guru.com.

Sanjaya Hettihewa

Sanjaya Hettihewa is an accomplished webmaster and consultant specializing in integrating Windows NT–based information systems on the Internet. He has been living in the Washington, D.C., area for the last six years and is a computer science major attending the University of Maryland. For the last two years, Sanjaya has done extensive research in setting up Internet information systems with Windows NT as well as exploring various ways of using Windows NT's unique features to publish information on the Internet. He is also the co-author of *Designing and Implementing Microsoft Internet Information Server* and a co-author of *FrontPage Unleashed*, *Microsoft Internet Explorer Unleashed*, and *Windows NT 3.51 Unleashed*, all by Sams and Sams.net Publishing. Sanjaya can be reached at http://www.NetInnovation.com/ (or, if you prefer the old-fashioned way, sanjaya@NetInnovation.com).

He wrote the following chapters for this book: Chapter 12, "Designing and Managing a Web Site with FrontPage," Chapter 13, "Publishing on the Web with Microsoft Office," Chapter 17, "Unleashing the Power of VBScript," and Chapter 18, "Introduction to Windows NT CGI Programming."

Sanjaya would like to dedicate his work on this book to his parents, Walter and Lakshmi Hettihewa, for all their love and support; without it, he could never have made it this far.

John J. Kottler

John J. Kottler (73157.335@compuserve.com or jay_kottler@msn.com) has been programming for 14 years and has spent the past 6 years developing applications for the Windows platform. In addition to Windows development, John has been programming multimedia applications for more than 2 years and has spent this past year developing for the Web. His knowledge includes C/C++, Visual Basic, Lotus Notes, PowerBuilder, messaging-enabled applications, multimedia and digital video production, and Internet Web page development. He has published numerous articles in a computer magazine, writing original programs and instructing developers on programming techniques. John has been recently published in Sams.net's *Netscape Unleashed* and *Web Publishing Unleashed* and Sams Publishing's *Programming Windows 95 Unleashed*. He was also a co-developer of the shareware application Virtual Monitors. A graduate of Rutgers University with a degree in computer science, he enjoys in-line skating, cycling, and playing digital music in his spare time.

He wrote the Chapter 19, "Writing Java Applets."

Tell Us What You Think!

As a reader, you are the most important critic of and commentator on our books. We value your opinion and want to know what we're doing right, what we could do better, what areas you'd like to see us publish in, and any other words of wisdom you're willing to pass our way. You can help us make strong books that meet your needs and give you the computer guidance you require.

Do you have access to CompuServe or the World Wide Web? Then check out our CompuServe forum by typing GO SAMS at any prompt. If you prefer the World Wide Web, check out our site at http://www.mcp.com.

> **NOTE**
>
> If you have a technical question about this book, call the technical support line at 800-571-5840, ext. 3668.

As the team leader of the group that created this book, I welcome your comments. You can fax, e-mail, or write me directly to let me know what you did or didn't like about this book—as well as what we can do to make our books stronger. Here's the information:

FAX: 317-581-4669

E-mail: opsys_mgr@sams.mcp.com

Mail: Dean Miller
       Comments Department
       Sams Publishing
       201 W. 103rd Street
       Indianapolis, IN 46290

Introduction

This book focuses on what Microsoft Internet Information Server is and how it can be used in the real world. It is designed for the intermediate to advanced reader. This book covers the basic concepts required for connecting your Microsoft network to the Internet. It includes information on daily maintenance, troubleshooting, and problem-solving areas. This book specializes in explaining some of the more arcane areas involved with the Internet. Special emphasis is on using the Internet Information Server to publish information on the World Wide Web.

This book will fulfill the following needs of readers (network administrators, network supervisors, upper management personnel, and so on):

- Introduces the Microsoft Internet Information Server and demonstrates how it can be used to enter the world of unlimited connectivity on the Internet.
- Prepares the reader to publish on the Internet using Microsoft Windows NT Server and the tools provided by the Internet Information Server. It also discusses various third-party tools you can use to build Web pages. It includes information to build Web pages that interact with the user—using VBScript or JavaScript—and to interact with your ODBC databases—using the Internet Database Connector or Microsoft dbWeb. This book includes information on how to customize your Web server using the IIS SDK and CGI scripts.
- Prepares the reader for advanced issues relating to Internet security. It describes how to use Windows NT Server as a mini-firewall to prevent unauthorized access to your network.

This book uses step-by-step procedures interspersed with figures captured from the actual tools. Icons point out information that will affect the reader's day-to-day duties.

Conventions Used in This Book

This book uses the following conventions:

- Menu names are separated from menu options by a vertical bar (|). For example, "File|Open" means "Select the File menu and choose the Open option."
- New terms appear in *italic*.
- Placeholders (words that stand for what you actually type) in regular text appear in *italic*.

- All code appears in monospace, as do filenames and directory names.
- Placeholders in code appear in *italic monospace*.
- When a line of code is too long to fit on only one line of this book, it is broken at a convenient place and continued to the next line. The continuation of the line is preceded by a code continuation character (➥). You should type a line of code that has this character as one long line without breaking it.

IN THIS PART

- An Internet Overview **3**
- An Internet Information Server Overview **29**

Introduction to the Internet Information Server

PART

I

An Internet Overview

IN THIS CHAPTER

- A Little History, Please **5**
- Connecting to the Internet **9**
- Using the Internet **20**

In this chapter you will look at a little (really, I kept it brief) history of how the Internet was created. Along the way you'll also learn just how popular the Internet has become by examining its rate of growth over the years. After your look back into history, you'll learn something about how you can connect to the Internet. There are a variety of options available; you'll look into several of them along with the associated costs of implementing them. This is not an all-inclusive listing, nor is it meant to be. Rather, it is being provided to give you some idea of what is available and an estimate of how much each option will cost you. You can be assured that the cost of your Internet connection, particularly a high-speed connection, will be the largest portion of your overall purchases.

Getting on the Internet is easy. Paying for it is not. The most common reason to want to get on the Internet is to host a World Wide Web (WWW) site, so in this chapter you will also learn about other ways to get your Web site on the Internet. Many service providers offer a Windows NT Server–based WWW server. Your Web site might even be hosted on a server running the Internet Information Server. You will look into some of these Web site hosting options a bit, this book assumes that you want to host your own site using the Internet Information Server (IIS).

Your first stop in building a Web site on the Internet is to learn a bit about what the Internet is and where it might be going. Your connection speed will really determine how many simultaneous clients you can support on the Internet, so your next stop is a look at some of the types of connections you can obtain. Then you will learn more about how to choose a provider to get you connected to the Internet. This is not something you want to take lightly. Although I can point out specific areas of concern, I cannot recommend any particular provider that will suit all of your needs. This is something you will need to research yourself.

> **TIP**
>
> Two good methods for finding a suitable service provider are to look at local computer magazines for local providers and to use the Internet for research into these providers. For example, I found my provider after a couple of months of research by using a local magazine called "Computer's Edge." This magazine, or an equivalent, can be found in your local computer store. Generally these magazines are free. Most of the advertisements include URLs (Universal Resource Locators) for the provider company's Web site and information about offered services and pricing structures.

The final section of this chapter takes a look at what you can do on the Internet with the Internet Information Server. I hope this will give you a better idea of the services you can offer to your clients.

A Little History, Please

The Internet is difficult to describe, simply because there is no single location that you can point to and say, "This is the Internet." So before you can really understand what the Internet is, you must first understand how the Internet was created. It all started in the late 1960s with the *Advanced Research Projects Agency* (ARPA) in the Department of Defense. This agency funded a study to link computer networks together so that they could reliably communicate with each other. This reliability requirement led to the development of a *packet-switched network protocol*, which provides the capability to pass data from the source computer to the destination computer through intermediary computers, rather than requiring a direct two-way connection. Let's look at this topic a little more closely. Assume that you have three computer networks that you need to link together, as shown in Figure 1.1.

FIGURE 1.1.
A sample packet-switched network.

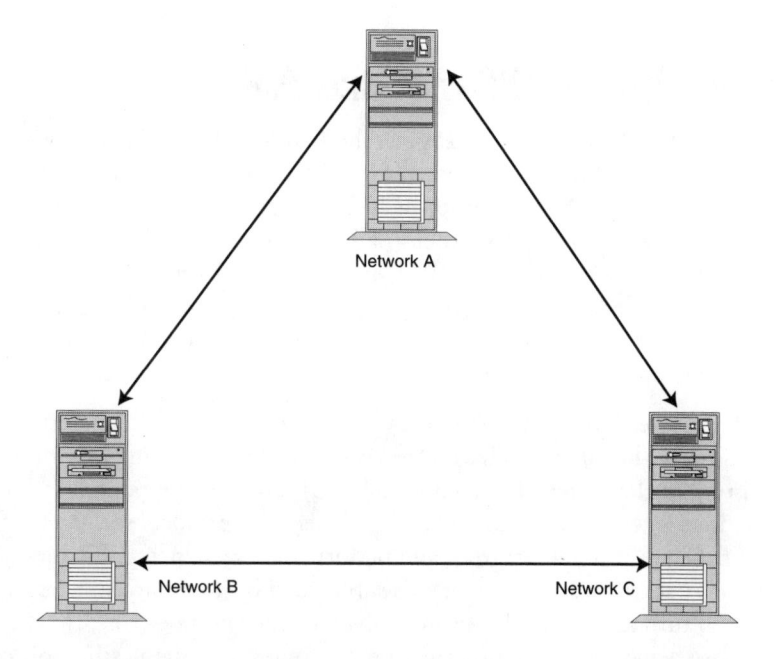

In a *circuit-switched network*, each connection from the source computer to the destination computer is a direct two-way connection called a *switch*. For example, if you wanted to send data from Network A to Network B, the path you would use would be switch AB. If you decided to send data from Network A to Network C, the path would be switch AC. This works fine as long as the physical connection, or switch, is active. But what happens if the connection between Network A and Network B fails? How can you get the data from Network A to Network B? In a circuit-switched network, you can't. But in a packet-switched network, you can. In a packet-switched network, the data is encapsulated inside of a *wrapper* that contains the destination computer's address. When a computer receives a packet that is not addressed to it, the packet is forwarded, or *routed*, to the next computer. This means that if the physical connection between Networks A and B has failed, but the connections between Networks A and C and Networks C and B are working, the packet can be sent from Network A to Network C. Network C can then forward the packet to Network B. The reply from Network B to Network A can follow the same route in reverse.

> **NOTE**
>
> The capability to route packets is one of the Internet's greatest strengths because it practically ensures that the data will arrive at the destination. However, it is also why you will sometimes encounter a slowdown when receiving data, because the route the data takes from source to destination can change drastically. A longer route means a longer delay.

The Birth of ARPAnet and TCP/IP

In 1970, ARPA created ARPAnet, the first packet-switched network, which connected the University of California at Los Angeles, the University of California at Santa Barbara, Stanford University, and the University of Utah in Salt Lake City. By late 1972, over 40 computers were connected using ARPAnet as a backbone. Later, ARPA was renamed *Defense Advanced Research Projects Agency* (DARPA), and research on network connectivity continued. In 1974, Vinton Cerf and Robert Kahn released the *Internet Protocol* (IP) and *Transmission Control Protocol* (TCP), which work in conjunction to provide a connection between computers. This is why the protocol is called TCP/IP rather than just TCP or IP.

IP is a lower-level protocol than TCP. Each node, sometimes referred to as a *host*, is assigned a unique 32-bit address. This address is formed by combining four numbers (each number consisting of three digits between 0 and 255) separated by periods (for example, my server's IP address is 206.170.127.65). TCP is a higher-level protocol and is used to handle large amounts of data, ensure data integrity, and perform data sequencing. If a message is too large to fit in a single packet, the message may be subdivided by TCP into smaller messages. These messages are in turn assigned a checksum and a sequence number, and are encapsulated in an IP layer before being sent to the destination computer. On the destination computer, these smaller messages are then passed to the TCP layer and combined back to their original format.

The Birth of the Internet

Although ARPAnet serviced many research centers, it was not the only network in town. In 1977 the University of Wisconsin decided to create a new network for the advancement of computer science technology. This idea eventually became CSnet. By the 1980s, CSnet was connected to ARPAnet using a gateway and the TCP/IP protocol. It was at this point, you could argue, that the Internet was born. After all, the idea of connecting disparate networks and communicating with a common protocol is what provides you and me with the capability to connect our networks (which may or may not use TCP/IP internally) to the Internet.

In the late 1980s, the National Science Foundation created NFSnet to support a small network of supercomputers. This network used state-of-the-art transmission capabilities to provide a high-speed backbone between central sites. While this was occurring, other changes were going on as well. In 1990, ARPAnet was replaced by NFSnet. Although CSnet was also absorbing smaller networks, by 1991 it too was finally replaced by NFSnet. NFSnet is in turn being slowly replaced with the very high-speed Backbone Network Service (vBNS), as shown in Figure 1.2, to provide even higher transmission capabilities.

FIGURE 1.2.
The NFSnet/vBNS core backbone.

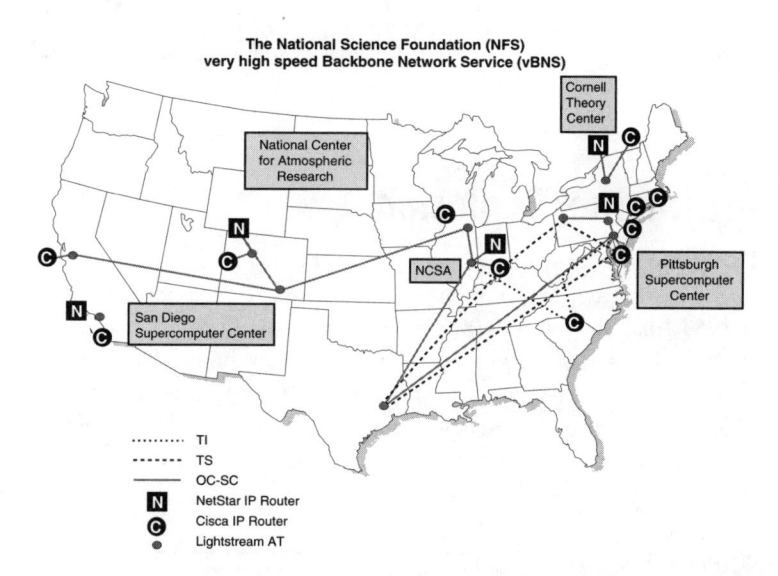

Just why do we need these higher transmission speeds? Well, it's because the Internet has taken the world by storm. In the early years of the Internet, transmission requirements were in the 2,000GB range, but by 1994 this figure had grown to 180,000GB, as shown in Figure 1.3; it continues to grow to this day.

FIGURE 1.3.
Internet growth in transmission requirements.

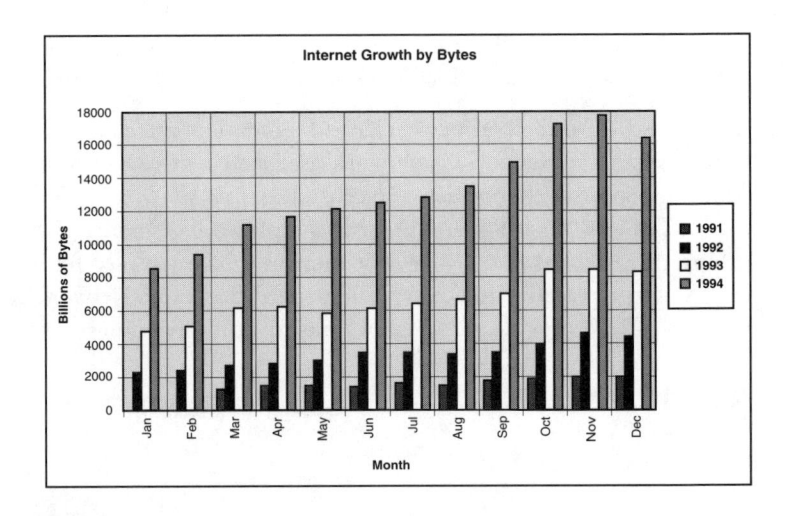

The Internet Explosion

The United States is the heaviest Internet consumer, as shown in Figure 1.4. The number of *hosts*, or computer components with assigned IP addresses, has grown from fewer than 1,000 in 1981 to almost 10,000,000 in 1996. Because of this demand for IP addresses, we will soon run out of 32-bit IP addresses. What will we do then? Well, we'll move to a 64-bit IP address. This should concern you—if not today, definitely tomorrow—because this move to a 64-bit IP address will also require new software implementations of the IP protocol. Can you imagine the confusion that will occur when this happens? I shudder at the thought, but maybe you are made of sterner stuff than I am.

FIGURE 1.4.
Growth of Internet hosts in the United States.

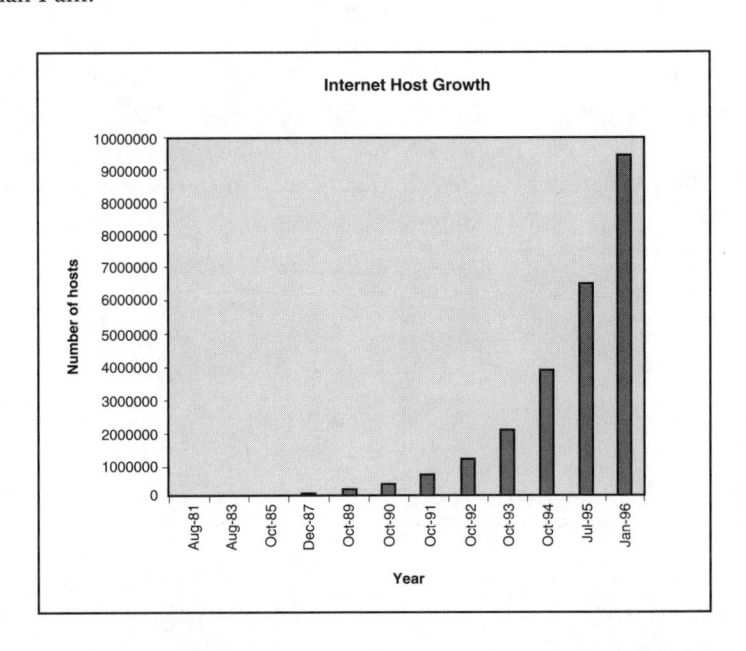

An Internet Overview
Chapter 1

Although the United States is the primary consumer of the Internet, it's not the only one. Other countries are also jumping on the bandwagon to get their networks on the Internet, as shown in Figure 1.5. In 1988 there were only 9 non-U.S. networks and 208 U.S. networks connected to the Internet. By 1995, there were 22,296 non-U.S. and 28,470 U.S. networks connected to the Internet.

FIGURE 1.5.
Worldwide Internet network growth.

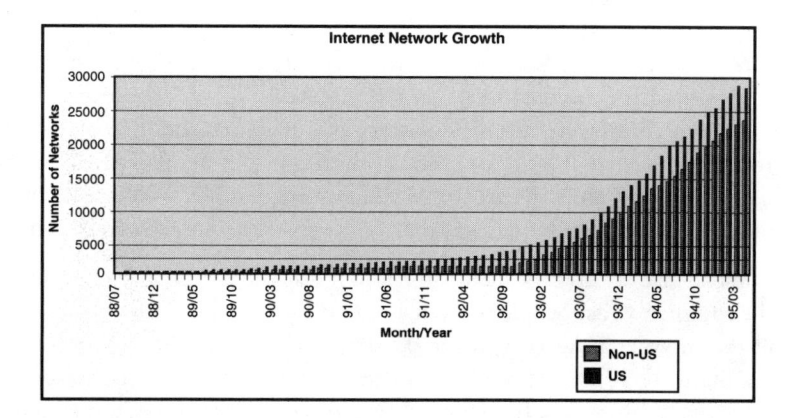

So what does all this really mean to you? Well, if you are not connected to the Internet now but you want to be connected sometime in the future, you should start making your plans to do so. Do it before the rules change, if at all possible.

> **NOTE**
>
> The statistics in this chapter and the rules for Internet conduct, can be found on the Merit Network Inc. home page at `http://nic.merit.edu`.

Connecting to the Internet

So you have decided that you want to connect to the Internet, but you have not decided how you will accomplish it. Will you need to connect just one computer, many computers, or possibly even your entire local area network? Will you need to support one-way or two-way network traffic? Do you need just a WWW site, or do you need full Internet services? If you only need a WWW site, will you use your own hardware or your Internet provider's hardware to host your site? How do you find an Internet provider? And what is the difference between an Internet provider and an Internet service provider? These are some of the questions I will either answer for you or, at the very least, give you enough information to get you started in your search for Internet connectivity.

Defining Your Goals

Before you begin talking to external agencies or going crazy on the Web in your search for connectivity solutions, let me offer a piece of advice: *Don't!* Don't solicit advice outside your company until you have some idea of the services you want to provide. Why? Because it is a cruel world out there. The information flow is staggering, and you can waste incredible amounts of time looking on the Internet and thinking about what you want. When you finally get everything connected, all your network clients can surf the Internet as well. As your network clients go surfing on the Internet, they can be eating up valuable network bandwidth, thus slowing down your entire network. These same network clients may spend so much time on the Internet that they might not even get the work they are paid for done on time. Between dealing with your numerous users and maintaining your WWW site instance, you'll probably run out of time to sleep, much less eat, unless you have an extremely competent staff to aid you.

You can also spend too much time looking at the wrong avenues to actually get connected to the Internet. Most people will tell you that the InterNIC is in charge of getting you connected to the Internet and that you should start your search there. (The InterNIC is the agency that maintains IP address allocations [to ensure routability of IP addresses] and domain name registration.) However, I'll save you some time by passing on some advice from the InterNIC: When the time comes for you to connect to the Internet, look at your requirements first. Then find an Internet provider, or Internet Service Provider, to fulfill them. Your provider will furnish the interface to the InterNIC. In essence, if you are not an Internet Service Provider, you do not need to worry about the InterNIC.

> **TIP**
>
> Tracking and providing the finite number of routable IP addresses are some of the InterNIC's primary concerns. Even though it is possible to obtain a small block of IP addresses from the InterNIC, the InterNIC may be unable to guarantee their routability. A routable IP address is a unique IP address guaranteed to be accessible by any host on the Internet. If your IP addresses are not routable, it means you may have problems finding external hosts, and external clients may have problems finding your hosts. For this reason, your first stop should be your Internet Service Provider, because the IP addresses assigned by it will be fully routable.

Instead of racing willy-nilly all over the place, take the time to write out your goals. Then determine how you will achieve them. Create a schedule for each milestone, then try to meet it. But don't push the schedule. Give yourself time to find the information you need for each step. It took me several months to find a local provider, but then again, I live in a rural area about 45 miles outside of the nearest large city. If you are located in a major city, you should be able to cut this time down to a couple of weeks.

Connecting the World to You

You can use Windows NT Server with the Internet Information Server to provide an Internet presence to the world, but not to your internal network clients (those on your LAN). In this configuration, you could create a separate network devoted to providing your Internet presence, or possibly just a single server to provide your presence on the Internet. In either of these configurations, there would be no direct connection from your computers connected to the Internet and your local area network. This lessens the risk for potential damage to your network from the Internet. The Internet is widely accessible by the public. As such, it often contains malicious programs or users that could wreak havoc on your network. Security is a big issue with Internet connectivity. Chapter 10, "Advanced Security Issues," addresses this subject in greater detail.

> **NOTE**
>
> Even though your server has no direct connection between the Internet and your LAN, you can still access the Internet (via a dial-up connection) to manage it. Most of the NT tools are RPC enabled, which means you can manage your server remotely. This can include managing the various services, adding users, or changing WWW, FTP, or Gopher content.

Your Internet presence could consist of three additional services:

- WWW Server—This is probably the main reason you want to use the IIS: to create a WWW site. Your site could be used to promote your ideas and your company products, and to provide technical support for your customers. It could even be used to sell products electronically. You will learn more about WWW capabilities in the section titled "Using the Internet" later in this chapter.

> **TIP**
>
> If all you want to provide is a WWW or FTP site, you may be better off putting your WWW server directly on the Internet provider's network. It could be a virtual server hosted on an Internet provider's computer, or it could be a server supplied and maintained by you. Each of these choices offers different financial options and should be discussed with your Internet provider.

- FTP Server—The *File Transfer Protocol* (FTP) server is used to exchange files over the Internet with FTP clients. Much like you use a communication program (such as Terminal) to transfer files using the Xmodem protocol, you can use the FTP protocol over the Internet.
- Gopher Server—This service provides a means to search and display large amounts of text. For example, you could use it to provide an online catalog.

Connecting You to the World

You can also use Windows NT Server and the Internet Information Server to connect your entire network to the world. If your network is small enough, you can use a single server that is connected to the Internet as your network router. You can also purchase a dedicated router that is connected to both the Internet and your internal network. A router is required, in either case, to bridge the gap between your network and the Internet. If this is your goal, you have additional implementation and security details to consider. In Chapter 5, "IIS Preparation and Installation," you learn more about the implementation issues, and Chapter 10 covers the additional security issues and offers some configuration ideas you can use to minimize your risk.

If you are providing full Internet access for your network clients, you may want additional services that are not offered with the Internet Information Server. If so, you will need additional software such as Microsoft Exchange to provide corporatewide e-mail. If you are providing full Internet connectivity for all your LAN clients, you will also need an IP address for each client. Remember that you cannot just make up your IP address. In order to provide a fully routable IP address (read: successful connectivity), you need an IP address provided by your Internet provider or the InterNIC. Even if you do obtain a block of IP addresses from the InterNIC, your Internet provider may decline to use them. This can leave you weeks to months behind your schedule to provide full Internet access. You should therefore assess your physical IP address requirements, but talk to your Internet provider before actually obtaining them or changing your network client configuration.

In any event, be prepared to update all your clients' network software. This may take a great deal of time, sometimes months, so allow for that in your schedule. A full migration to provide complete Internet access may also require additional on-site technical support personnel, and even classes for your network clients, so be prepared for this situation, too.

Defining Your Internet Service Requirements

Now comes the tough part. Before you finally talk with your Internet provider, you need to determine what Internet services you want. There is more to consider when connecting to the Internet than just providing WWW, FTP, or Gopher sites. Consider some of the following:

- Supported clients—Have you considered how many Internet clients you want to support? Your Internet connection will have a limited bandwidth, so it can support only a limited number of simultaneous connected users. The more users you want to support, the more money it will cost for the connection. You can assume that each supported client will consume at least 57.6Kbps (a standard 14.4Kbps modem connection) of your available bandwidth. So to calculate your required bandwidth, just multiply 57,600 by the number of simultaneous client connections you want to support. This will give you a rough estimate of your needs.

- IP addresses—For each host (a computer or peripheral) that you want to be visible on the Internet, you will need an Internet-routable IP address. Will your provider be able to fulfill your needs? Check this one out carefully before you sign on the dotted line. Some providers are too small to service large IP address allocations. Others charge extra for each additional IP address.

- Domain name—If you want your WWW site to have a specific name (such as my WWW site's www.nt-guru.com), you will need to obtain a *domain name*. Domain names are registered with the InterNIC and require that you have a static IP address and two *domain name service* (DNS) servers fully functional on your network at all times. Normally your Internet provider will register your domain name and provide the primary and secondary DNS servers. But it will also collect the additional fees!

- Hardware—Before you purchase any additional hardware, like a router, check with your Internet provider. Your provider may not support your intended hardware, or may offer a discount on hardware purchased directly from it as part of a service agreement.

- E-mail—Will you use an e-mail server provided by your Internet provider or use your own? If you use your own server, you may want to use one provided by the Internet provider as a backup. Otherwise, if your connection between the Internet provider and your network fails you may lose some mail.

Choosing a Connection Type

There are basically three established mechanisms for connecting to the Internet: a dial-up, a leased line, or frame relay. Each offers additional capabilities, at an additional cost. Prices vary from state to state and Internet provider to Internet provider. You'll learn more about the difference between an Internet provider and Internet service provider later in the section titled "Choosing an Internet Provider or Internet Service Provider." I can't offer standard pricing structures for you. Instead, you should discuss these with your Internet provider and possibly your phone company. I have provided some estimates based on information I obtained in my search for an Internet connection that may prove helpful to you.

CAUTION

If your site will be critical to the well-being of your company, you should consider obtaining two connections, possibly even from two different Internet providers. Why? Just in case the connection between your network and the Internet fails. If this occurs, you can use your backup connection to keep your system online.

Dial-up

A *dial-up connection* is by far the easiest to work with. It consists of an analog modem connected to your computer via a serial cable. Your analog modem is in turn connected to your plain old telephone system (POTS) jack. Analog modems are currently capable of achieving carrier rates of 28.8Kbps and, with 4:1 compression, they can obtain a throughput of 115.2Kbps. These types of connections are relatively inexpensive. Many major Internet providers will give you a local phone number to use and an unlimited access account for less than $20 a month. If you do not have a local phone number, though, prices can skyrocket. For example, a call outside of my local (that is, toll-free) area will cost me about a penny a minute. That doesn't sound like much, but when you add it up it's $14.40 a day, or $432.00 a month. If you can afford it, and you only need to support one to five simultaneous clients on your WWW site, a dial-up connection with an analog modem will suit you just fine.

56KB Leased Line

If you need to support more users, you might want to consider a 56KB *leased line*. Unlike a regular phone line, where calls are routed dynamically to their destination and that can offer many different endpoints (such as when you call your friend, then your mother, from the same phone), a leased line only has one routing and connection option. In essence, your leased line can connect to only one phone number. Many leased lines services are flat-rate services, but it really depends on the local phone company. In California, Pacific Bell will provide a leased line for around $1,000 to cover the installation and $125.00 per month. A 56KB leased line will provide twice the throughput of a 28.8Kbps modem, so it can support additional users.

There are additional hidden costs in this solution, however. Aside from the leased line charges, you will need to purchase supplementary equipment. You will need a CSU/DSU (Channel Service Unit/Data Service Unit) and a router. If you are connecting an existing Ethernet-based network, you may need an additional hub. A CSU/DSU can run from $300 to $1,500, and a router from $1,500 to $3,000. Sometimes the price of the equipment is included in your service contract with the Internet provider, or your provider might offer the equipment at a discount. In some cases, though, you may be required to purchase the hardware for your site and the Internet provider's site, so check this option out with care.

Frame Relay

When you need additional speed, you may want to consider *frame relay*. It comes in several flavors: from 56KB to 1.5MB, depending on your hardware, Internet provider, and phone company. With a frame relay connection, you do not own the entire line. Instead, you are purchasing a portion of its carrying capacity, or bandwidth. What makes frame relay so useful as an Internet connectivity solution is its capability for future growth. Depending on the hardware you choose (and, once again, you will need a CSU/DSU and router), you can start with a 56KB connection. As your needs grow, your provider and phone company can increase the bandwidth—at increased prices, of course. This is a good option to consider for midsize companies. To give you some idea of the associated costs involved, Table 1.1 summarizes Pacific Bell's current (which may be radically changed by the time you read this) pricing structure.

Table 1.1. Pacific Bell's frame relay pricing structure.

Speed	Monthly Fee	Installation Fee	Global Service Provider Fees
56Kbps	$525	$2,000	$125 per month; one-time installation fee of $400
128Kbps	$874	$2,259	$195 per month; one-time installation fee of $400
384Kbps	$1,324	$2,259	$295 per month; one-time installation fee of $400
1.536Mbps	$1824	$3,009	$445 per month; one-time installation fee of $400

1.5Mbps and Beyond

If you need higher bandwidths than those offered by frame relay, you'll want to consider some other choices. For example, you might want to use Fractional T1, T1, T2, or T3 connection options if your service provider supports the newer high-speed options, such as Switched Multimegabit Data Service (SMDS) or Asynchronous Transfer Mode (ATM) alternatives. The prices for these services vary significantly from vendor to vendor, so you should discuss the pricing with them directly. To give you an idea of what it could cost for service, Table 1.2 summarizes the offerings from Pacific Bell here in California.

Table 1.2. Pacific Bell's SMDS pricing structure.

Speed	Monthly Fee	Installation Fee	Global Service Provider Fees
56Kbps	$545	$2,001	$145 per month; one-time installation fee of $400
1.17Mbps	$1,624	$3,010	$395 per month; one-time installation fee of $400
4Mbps	$4,575	$6,500	$995 per month; one-time installation fee of $400
10Mbps	$5,500	$6,500	$1,995 per month; one-time installation fee of $400

continues

Introduction to the Internet Information Server

Part I

Table 1.2. continued

Speed	Monthly Fee	Installation Fee	Global Service Provider Fees
16Mbps	$6,400	$6,500	$2,995 per month; one-time installation fee of $400
34Mbps	$9,300	$6,500	$5,995 per month; one-time installation fee of $400

Fractional T1 is similar to frame relay in that you only lease a portion of the available bandwidth. Fractional T1 includes 24 64Kbps channels. You can start with one channel; then, as with frame relay, you can add bandwidth by adding channels and paying an additional fee to your service provider. If you choose to go the full route with a T1 (1.5Mbps) line, you will also need a DSU/CSU and router (in fact, you'll need similar equipment for any of the options discussed in this section). A T2 line falls in the midrange of the SMDS options with 6.3Mbps. Both T3 and ATM can achieve rates as high as 45Mbps. From what I have seen in the market, though, SMDS is slowly replacing the options for midrange Tx connections, so Tx connectivity may be unavailable in your area.

Integrated Services Digital Network

There are two types of *Integrated Services Digital Network* (ISDN) connections that you can use. The first is the *Basic Rate Interface* (BRI). A BRI consists of two 64Kbps bearer channels and one 16Kbps data channel. The second is the *Primary Rate Interface* (PRI), which consists of 24 bearer channels and one 16Kbs data channel. That's as big as a T1 line, offering 1.5Mbps. Although in California you may find that some ISDN bearer channels only offer a 56Kbps throughput, the missing 8Kbps per channel is combined and used for the 16Kbps data channel. In the future this will change so that even California residents can enjoy the full 64Kbps offered by ISDN, so for the rest of this discussion we will assume that a bearer channel offers 64Kbps. Two bearer channels can be combined to provide an effective carrier rate of 128Kbps. With compression, this can be quadrupled to 512Kbps. That is enough bandwidth to support a small (fewer than 15 users) network's Internet connection. It can also be enough bandwidth to support from 10 to 50 WWW simultaneous client connections.

An ISDN connection can be established using a digital modem connected to your server with your server acting as a router. You can also purchase an ISDN router, which combines the functions of a dedicated router and ISDN modem. ISDN routers often have four bearer channels that require a total of two ISDN BRI connections to obtain full efficiency. When connecting a small network to the Internet via ISDN, using an ISDN router is the preferred method because it provides additional network security.

It cost me $80 for the installation and $25 a month for a single BRI ISDN connection from Pacific Bell. My Motorola BitSURFER Pro cost an additional $400, and my Internet service provider charges $371 ($150 goes to PacBell as a data transport fee) a month for dedicated single-bearer channel ISDN access. The setup fees included $150 to convert the ISDN line to a dedicated line. To register my domain name cost an additional $100 setup fee with a $50 yearly fee. If you'd like to see what a single 64kbps connection can do, you can connect to my Web server at http://www.nt-guru.com. Dedicated dual bearer channel access would have cost me $550 a month. If you decide to use ISDN, make sure you to can obtain a dedicated connection, because this type of connection does not have any associated toll charges. Otherwise, you may find yourself paying more in phone company charges than you pay your Internet service provider!

Choosing an Internet Provider or Internet Service Provider

There is really nothing more important to the success of your Internet connectivity than your choice of an Internet provider, or *Internet service provider* (ISP). You may be wondering what the difference between an Internet provider and ISP is, as did I when I first started this quest. The answer is very simple. An *Internet provider*, sometimes also called a *Internet access provider* (IAP), only supplies you with a raw connection to the Internet. Everything else must be accomplished on your own. If you are a large commercial organization, an IAP may be just what you need. On the other hand, most of us prefer to work with an ISP because an ISP provides additional services, which can include the following:

- Domain name registration—Your ISP will, for a fee ($100 to the InterNIC and a monthly/yearly fee to the ISP), register your domain name with the InterNIC. It will also ensure that its domain name server (DNS) will equate your domain name with a routable IP address. Thus your clients can find you by entering
  http:www.*YourDomainName*.com
  rather than
  http:www.*YourISPDomainName*.com.*YourE-MailAddress* in their Web browser.

- Server hosting—If you cannot afford the high-speed Internet connectivity options, but you still need the bandwidth to support your clients, maybe putting your server on the ISP's network is the answer. Many ISPs offer the capability to place your hardware directly on their Internet backbone for a much lower fee (sometimes as little as $500 a month). You will have to watch this option carefully, however, because many ISPs also charge extra if you have more than a specific amount of traffic on your site. A very active WWW site can cause your monthly costs to soar!

- Virtual server—The step down the chain is a virtual server. A *virtual server* is a host (computer) that contains several sites. This server might have your domain, your next-door neighbor's domain, and many more. In essence, you are sharing resources (the computer's processor, disk storage, and Internet connection) and their associated costs. Because of this, you pay a lower fee to your ISP.

> **NOTE**
>
> The Internet Information Server can also support virtual domains. You can find out more about this capability in Chapter 6, "Using the Internet Service Manager."

- FTP drop box—An *FTP drop box* is a directory on your ISP's hardware where you can place files for clients to retrieve, or vice versa. These are generally included free with your initial service account as long as you stay below 5MB of total storage. If you go over that, you will be required to pay additional fees.

- News—The Internet contains many newsgroups. Each newsgroup can be considered a public bulletin board where users can meet to discuss their ideas. A newsgroup feed from your Internet provider will cost more and can run to over 90MB of data a day. Last but not least, the Internet Information Server does not include any software to exploit the newsfeed. If you want this option, you will need to find additional software.

- E-mail services—Many ISPs include e-mail accounts hosted on their servers. However, each additional e-mail account generally costs an additional fee (between $10–$20). This is perfectly reasonable for a small network, but may be more expensive than dedicated hardware and software at your company site for midrange to large networks. Again, you should discuss the options available to you with your service provider to find the best solution.

- Turnkey solutions—With the variety of hardware available today, incompatibilities are likely to arise with the equipment you use to connect to your service provider. For this reason, many service providers offer complete solutions. These can include a CSU/DSU, router, server, and possibly even software. If you purchase equipment directly from your service provider, they also often support it—that is, if your server hardware fails, the service provider will send someone out to repair it.

- Domain name or WWW page advertising—After you have your domain name and Web site, you have to find a way to tell the public about it. You can do this yourself, by registering your domain and Web site names at the appropriate places, or you can pay your service provider to do it for you. You will learn more about the options available to do this yourself in Chapter 2, "An Internet Information Server Overview."

- Professional WWW page development—Do you have the staff to create your own Web pages, or do you need a helping hand to get you started? If your answer is the latter, check with your service provider. It may offer Web page packages that include a virtual server, a domain name, and a WWW site designed and maintained by the service provider. You may also find that your service provider can offer Web page consulting services. If so, be prepared to pay between $50 and $100 per hour.

An Internet Overview

Chapter 1

Does Your ISP Measure Up?

Before you settle on a particular ISP to provide you with your Internet connection, there are a few inquiries you should make first. Consider the following questions as a starting point:

How long have you been in business?

If the company has not been in business for at least a year, you should reconsider doing business with it. The Internet is big business, and many companies are starting up to offer services but do not yet have much experience. Many of these same companies fold up within a year of opening their doors. If this were to happen to you, what would you do?

How long have you been providing Internet connectivity solutions?

Believe it or not, almost anybody can become an ISP. Many of these companies are marketing companies looking to provide a presence on the Web, and to make money at it by offering you a connectivity solution as well. But they really do not know much about providing customer service and support. The flip side of this is that your ISP may be a couple of techies with a server or two in the basement. They may know quite a bit about the Internet, but may not know much about customer service or technical support. In addition, their hardware may prove to be unreliable for a long-term connection. Again, if they haven't been in business for at least a year, keep on looking.

How large is your company?

This is one way to find out if your ISP is a basement ISP or a real company. If your ISP tells you there are fewer than 10 people in the company, I suggest you look around some more to find a reliable company. Smaller companies are more likely to collapse from disinterest, financial strain, or hardship, which can leave you in the lurch.

How many people do you have dedicated to providing technical support?

This is another test to see if your provider can really meet your needs. A reliable ISP will have several members on site to provide technical support. If your ISP tells you there are only one or two members available, this is a sign that you may want to look for another ISP. You should also check out your ISP's technical support by placing a few calls during the week to see how they respond.

How many network professionals do you have on site?

This is another technical support question. The idea here is to find out if the ISP has enough competent network professionals to address non-Internet-specific problems. The big question is, will there be someone ready to help when you need it, or will someone be given a manual and drafted to help you out? When you need help, you need it now. If your technical-support personnel are unfamiliar with the hardware and software, you are not going to get much help from them. You may even know more about the system than they do.

Can you supply me with any references?

References are important because they are a means of determining whether the ISP has performed well enough to at least make some of its customers happy. Obviously, the ISP will not give you a reference from anyone who had a bad experience. If it cannot supply any references, maybe its customers had only bad experiences.

What plans do you have for future growth?

Every company will tell you it plans to grow, but this isn't what you are really looking for. You want to find out what plans the company has to increase the scalability of its hardware. As previously noted, the Internet is growing at a phenomenal rate. Your ISP needs to keep up. Otherwise, as the ISP adds clients, your shared link, or bandwidth, to the Internet will deteriorate.

Assume for the moment that you have a 1.5Mbs T1 connection with your provider. Your provider has a 45Mbps T3 connection to the Internet. This T3 connection is the Internet backbone that all of your ISP's clients share. If your client has only 10 T1 clients, there is still enough capacity left in the backbone to support an additional 20 T1 clients. But when your ISP's client list grows beyond the capacity of the backbone, what happens to you? Well, you'll still pay for a 1.5Mbps connection, but you'll be getting less than that from it. Your provider must plan to increase its carrying capacity as the company grows. Without proper planning by the provider, you will pay the price.

What type of connection to the Internet do you have?

As I've mentioned, the ISP backbone's carrying capacity impacts the performance of your site. If your provider has a single T1 line or less as its backbone, it probably cannot service your needs. Look for someone with multiple T1 lines or their equivalent carrying capacity. I recommend avoiding anyone with less than a T3 (45Mbps) backbone.

Using the Internet

In the previous discussions you learned something about the history of the Internet and how to get connected, but you didn't learn much about what you can really do on the Internet. That is the subject for the rest of this chapter, because it is what really matters. If there was not some gain to made from the Internet, why bother with it at all, right? So let's look into what you can do on the Internet with Windows NT Server and the IIS. First, you can publish data on the Internet. Publishing uses any one, or all, of the services provided with IIS. You can use the WWW and FTP services to collect data. You can even use the WWW service to actually sell your company's products.

An Internet Overview
Chapter 1

Publishing Data

Publishing data, or content, is the most frequently selected reason for getting on the Internet and is how you create a presence on the Internet. If your content is particularly appealing, clients will flock to your WWW, FTP, or Gopher site. The big question is when and how to use each of these services. If you only want a repository for files that clients can upload or download, use the FTP service. To display large amounts of text online, use the Gopher service. To provide a GUI-driven application to play sounds or display graphics, animations, movies, and text, use the WWW service. In fact, the capabilities of a WWW server used in conjunction with a GUI Web browser far overshadow almost all other services provided with IIS. This book focuses its attention on the WWW server accordingly. You can use the WWW server to display just about anything, although you may need additional software to fully exploit your WWW server software. Let's consider a few examples to help illustrate these options.

Providing Technical Support

Let's assume for the moment that you are a computer manufacturer. You need to provide a simple, user-friendly interface to your customers for technical support. The reason you might choose to use the Internet Information Server to host a Web site is that after you create the HTML document, you can support any client computer that has a connection to the Internet and a Web browser. An HTML document is a hardware- and software- (since almost every platform has a Web browser designed for it) independent mechanism. The goal for this example is to provide a means for your customers to download a flash BIOS replacement. A Web page, such as that displayed in Figure 1.6, may just fit the bill. It includes enough information for the user to make a choice as to what to get. The description (Motherboard #1) specifies the type of motherboard, and it includes a built-in link (Award BIOS upgrade) to your FTP server to retrieve the file.

FIGURE 1.6.
Sample technical support WWW page.

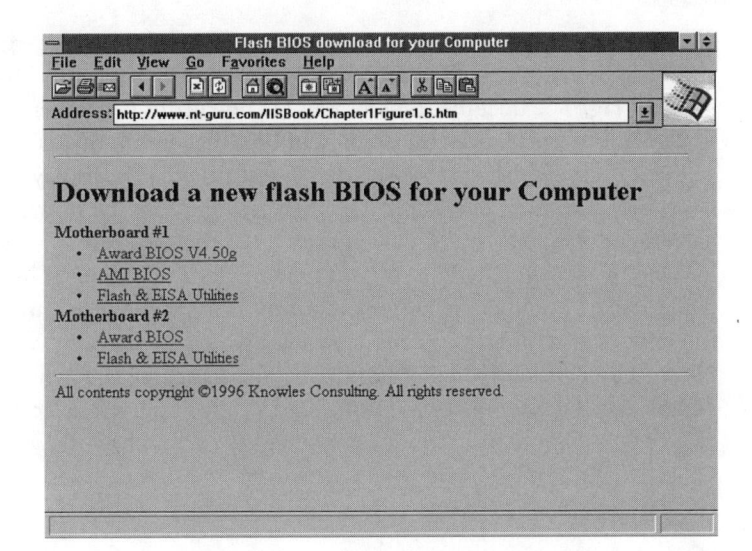

The code to create this Web page is simple. In fact, it's so simple you should take a look at it. The source for the document Chapter1Figure1.6.HTM can be found on the accompanying CD-ROM in the directory SOURCE\CHAP1. It can be created using any ASCII text editor, such as Notepad. You'll learn much more about HTML in Chapter 11, "An HTML Primer," which describes the basic syntax and usage of the HTML tags, but for now I would like to point out a few of the highlights:

```
<html>

<head>
<title>Flash BIOS download for your Computer</title>
</head>

<body>

<P>
<hr>

<h2>Download a new flash BIOS for your Computer</h2><br>

<B>Motherboard #1</B><br>
<UL><LI><A href="ftp://nt-guru.com/autoexec.bat">Award BIOS V4.50g</a>
    <LI><A href="ftp://nt-guru.com/autoexec.bat">AMI BIOS</A>
    <LI><A href="ftp://nt-guru.com/autoexec.bat">Flash & EISA Utilities</A>
    </ul>

<B>Motherboard #2</B>
<UL><LI><A href="ftp://nt-guru.com/autoexec.bat">Award BIOS</A>
<LI><A href="ftp://nt-guru.com/autoexec.bat">Flash & EISA Utilities</A>
</UL>

<hr>
All contents copyright &#169 1996 Knowles Consulting. All rights reserved.

</body>
</html>
```

What is important to notice here is that an *HTML* (Hypertext Markup Language) document is an ASCII document. It contains tags to format the text. Almost every tag has a corresponding end-tag. The document is started with an <html> tag and ended with an </html> tag. The <head> and </head> mark the document heading; within these tags you'll find the <title> and </title> tags, which enclose the document title that is displayed on the caption bar of your Web browser. The <body> and </body> tags delineate the body, or major component, of the document. The <h2> and </h2> tags mark the enclosed text as a level-two header. A <P> marks the end of a paragraph. The <B> and </B> mark text as bold, while <UL> and </UL> mark text as underlined. I could go on and on about this subject, but the only really important tags are the <LI>, <A href=ftp:// ...>, and </A> tags, which are used to create a link to your FTP server. When a user clicks on one of these items, the actual file is downloaded to his computer. In this sample, all of these choices will download a copy of my autoexec.bat file. But if this were a real Web page, it could just as easily download the actual flash BIOS update files.

An Internet Overview
Chapter 1

So simply by spending a few minutes with a text editor like Notepad, you can be on your way to creating a Web page for your customers to use. It only requires the user to know the domain name of your Web site, and then, when the page is retrieved, just one click of the mouse will download the BIOS upgrade. It can't get much easier than that.

Publishing a Product Catalog

Displaying a catalog of your products is quite similar to publishing data. You would create a table of contents Web page, or perhaps a search page, with links to actual document pages. Figure 1.7 displays a very simple sample page with a review of a WinBook XP5 computer. This page displays an image of the product (in this case a WinBook XP) and follows it with a review of the product. The background is set to white to make reading the large amount of text easier. The source for this example (`Chapter1Figure1.7.HTM`) can be found on the accompanying CD-ROM in the directory `SOURCE\CHAP1`.

> **NOTE**
>
> Don't be dismayed by the simple examples you are seeing in this chapter. In the latter half of this book, you will learn more than you'll want to know about how to create HTML documents.

FIGURE 1.7.
Sample WWW page with product information.

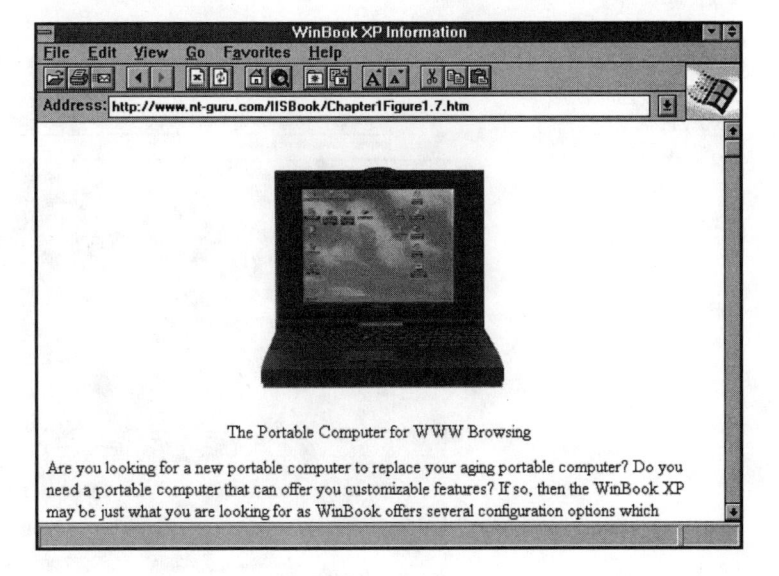

The previous example is a *static* example. By this I mean that you must physically create the Web page, and it must physically reside on your hard disk. To make a change to this page, you must edit the page in a text editor and then save it. This can be time-consuming. It can also cause a problem because a product catalog often changes rapidly. You may spend more time editing Web pages than you actually do selling products. So what can you do about it? You can create dynamic Web pages. A *dynamic* Web page is actually a template assembled by another program (such as an ISAPI extension or CGI script) from an external source. This external source could be a SQL Server database, for example. The database could have all of your product information (like a picture, price, and description). This information could be assembled into files on your Web server, which could then be displayed by your customers' Web browsers. Because this occurs dynamically every time a user requests the information, your catalog is as up-to-date as your database.

Publishing Very Large Amounts of Text

If you have an entire book or library of books, consider using the Gopher service. This particular service is designed to support text databases. You can search a Gopher site by keywords, or your menu structure could provide an index with hypertext links to the actual information, as shown in Figure 1.8. Notice in this figure that I am using the Internet Explorer (IE) Web browser. Rather than using a character-based application, I find the point-and-click capability is too nice a feature to give up, and the text is just as easy to read. You can use IE with your FTP sites, as well.

FIGURE 1.8.

The UCSD Gopher server's library index.

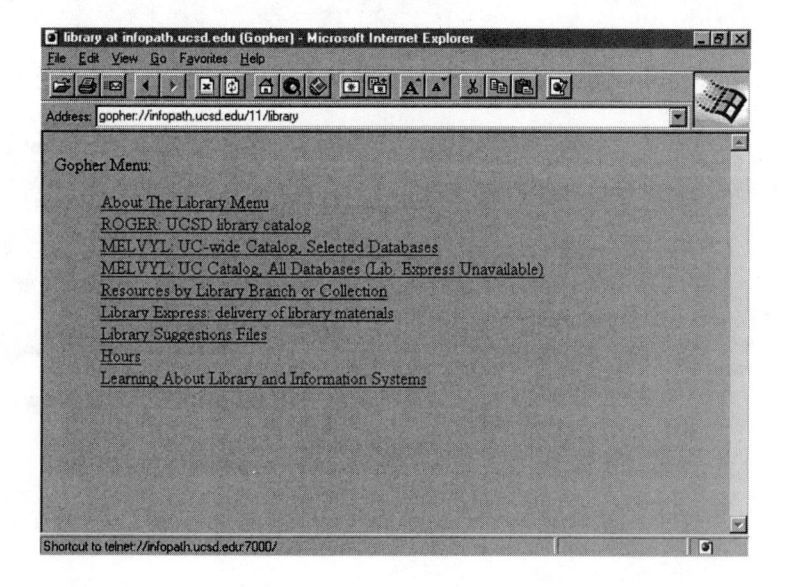

An Internet Overview

Chapter 1 25

Publishing large amounts of text with the Gopher service is fairly easy, but it doesn't provide any capabilities other than text retrieval. This is why many Gopher sites are being converted to Web sites. For example, although an encyclopedia is useful in text form, it's much more fun to use with audio-video pictures of animals at the zoo. The audio-video encyclopedia can convey more information, as well as emotional impact.

Collecting Data

There are several reasons why you might want to collect information from network clients that access your Web server. You may want to create an entry-order database for your roving salesperson, for example. Your salesperson could connect to the Internet from your client's office via a simple phone call to a local provider. Then he could access your Web site and choose from the menu to place an order. As each item is entered, your Web server can verify that the item is in stock. At the end of the order, your Web server could display an actual invoice form that your salesperson can print right in that same office with the client. In other words, you have turned your Web server into an online database.

You could also capture customer, or possible customer, information. Included with the Internet Information Server is a sample HTML page, as shown in Figure 1.9, that illustrates this capability. The information you collect could include such items as the user's name, address, phone numbers, marital status, or anything else the user is willing to tell you that strikes your fancy. After all, you can't force someone to visit your Web page and fill out all the forms if he doesn't want to, but you can entice him into doing so. Many sites include teasers, such as free gifts, when a user enters his customer information. As part of your form design, you can enforce a rule that specific fields must be filled out in order for the form to be submitted.

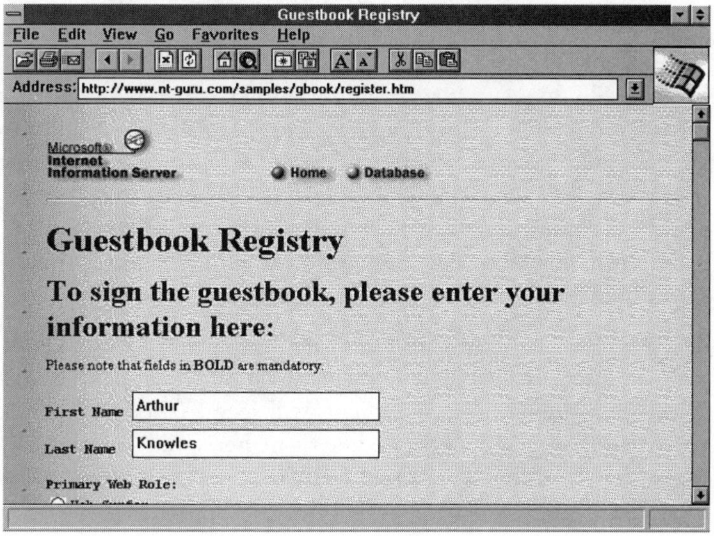

FIGURE 1.9.
Collecting customer information.

You might use this capability to collect information for a mailing list of potential customers. Your form could ask if the client is looking to purchase a house within 90 days, six months, or one year. The user could select radio buttons on the form to request further information from you about the services you could provide within that time frame. You may, for example, choose to keep the user informed, via e-mail, of special discounts for new home owners during the time period specified by the client on the submitted form. Then, a month or so before the person's selected time frame is up, you could generate a new mailing list to check that person's status. It might be just the right time for him to change from a potential customer to a new customer, and you might just sell another house.

Selling Products

Selling products directly on the Internet is a little bit different. Your first concern here has to be related to security. That means the *Secure Socket Layer* (SSL) is going to play an important part in your life. This is the most widely used support security mechanism for sensitive data. What's sensitive? Well, at the very least, your customer's credit card numbers should be considered sensitive information. I certainly wouldn't want my credit card numbers floating around the Internet. This means that your Web pages and forms may require some additional work, and you'll have to file for an SSL certificate. You'll learn more gory details of this and future security layers in Chapter 10.

For now, it's probably best just to note that selling products on the Internet is possible. I can't cover all the commercial possibilities or legal implications, but I can give you an glimpse or two now. It is possible for a client (or customer) to see a product he wants on his Web browser, order that product, and have it delivered to the doorstep of his house, all by filling out of a form and clicking a button.

There are two basic issues in selling merchandise on the Internet. First, how can you do it safely? Second, how will your users interact with your company? The first issue—safety—is addressed by using SSL to secure the communication channel between your server and the client. This provides the ability to encrypt data so you can obtain his credit card number without someone else on the Internet getting the credit card number, too. Keep in mind that the security of the data you collect should remain inviolate. That means you are responsible for keeping prying eyes away from this data. You should secure your server physically (that is, put it in a locked room) from intruders. You also need to keep the electronic thieves at bay, which you will look into a bit more in Chapter 10.

The second issue—how your users will interact with your company—directly translates to how you will use the available network bandwidth. The phrase "available network bandwidth" applies to how much time your clients will spend waiting to view any data you publish. While you might have a 1.5Mbps T1 line or higher-speed Internet connection, many of your customers will be using 14.4Kbps modems.

The longer it takes a user to download a Web page, the more frustrated that user gets, making it less likely that he will bother to visit that Web page again. If the people visiting your site don't stick around long enough to download your Web page, you aren't going to get any potential customers. If you want to supply an online catalog with pictures of your products, for example, then you should be frugal with your customers' available network bandwidth. You don't want to antagonize your customers by forcing them to download a 8" × 10" 24-bit picture when a 1" × 1.5" (or smaller) 8-bit picture will suffice. Giving the user the option to download an 8" × 10" 24-bit picture, maybe by clicking on the smaller image, is an acceptable use of your customers' available network bandwidth. However, because the practice of creating multiple pictures can be a bit tedious, you'll probably want to just use small pictures. In that case, you'll need to provide good textual descriptions to emphasize the product, since the small picture has less detail of the product than a large picture would.

Summary

In this chapter you have learned a little history about the Internet. The part you should remember is that the Internet is expanding rapidly. This expansion will affect you in the future, and you should prepare for it. You have also learned the available means to connect to the Internet, and a few things to prepare for your talks with your ISP. You have also taken a brief look into the possibilities you have with the Internet Information Server and publishing content on the World Wide Web. Chapter 2 looks at IIS in more depth, exploring the capabilities provided by the core services and how to extend your Web server's capabilities.

An Internet Information Server Overview

IN THIS CHAPTER

- What Is the Internet Information Server? **30**
- What Can the Internet Information Server Do for You? **35**
- Publicizing Your Web Site **40**

While there are currently other products available (such as those included with the Windows NT Resource Kit) that allow you to publish content on the Internet using Windows NT, none of them offer the same range of features as the Microsoft Internet Information Server (IIS). After reading this chapter, you may wonder if I work for Microsoft. I'm not a Microsoft employee, but I do like what the Internet Information Server can do. I think you will, too.

The idea of using the Internet to provide information is not new, but the concept of publishing content on the Internet is new. It is now possible for people who have no experience with HTML to create simple Web pages using their own word processor, such as Word for Windows, and a template, such as the one provided by the Internet Assistant. For a more professional-looking Web page, you can use dedicated programs like Sausage Software's HotDog Pro, SoftQuad's HotMetal, or Microsoft's FrontPage. These Windows applications do all the hard work of inserting HTML tags and formatting your documents for you.

Unlike the early years of the Internet, when only small amounts of information were made available, it is now possible to place huge amounts of information (including information from large internal databases) on the Internet for millions of users to view. Three changes have occurred to make this possible. First, the available bandwidth on the Internet has increased tremendously. Second, the Internet has changed to allow commercial enterprises. Finally, you no longer have to use UNIX or a derivative operating system to provide your Internet services.

This chapter starts with a look at what makes up the Internet Information Server. This includes the various components, as well as the possibilities to extend IIS to meet your specific needs. The chapter then moves on to look at what the Internet Information Server can do for you and how well it stacks up to the competition. Finally, you will take a brief look into publicizing your Web site so that potential customers can find you. After all, it does you little good to create an Internet Web site if no one knows how to find you, right?

What Is the Internet Information Server?

This question is not really as easy to answer as it seems. The Internet Information Server is more than just a port of a couple Internet services to Windows NT Server. Since IIS provides these services, a complete description of it practically requires a description of the collection of services provided by IIS. So this is where you will start to learn just what the Internet Information Server is. Once this is out of the way, you will learn more about what makes IIS different. This can really be summed up by just saying that IIS is an extensible platform. This extensibility provides many different methods to customize IIS to suit your individual needs.

A Collection of Windows NT Services

To begin, the Internet Information Server consists of three specific Windows NT services that are used to publish content (data) using the Transmission Control Protocol/Internet Protocol

An Internet Information Server Overview

Chapter 2

(TCP/IP) as the underlying transmission mechanism. These are a World Wide Web (WWW) server, a File Transfer Protocol (FTP) server, and a Gopher server. The key to understanding just how this works is to realize that IIS provides the servers of a client/server product. Without a client application, such as a Web browser like the Internet Explorer, the server doesn't do much good. The way a client/server application functions varies depending on the underlying transport mechanism. To get an idea of how the process functions, take a look at Figure 2.1. In this example, SQL Server illustrates how a client/server application functions.

FIGURE 2.1.
A sample client/server database model.

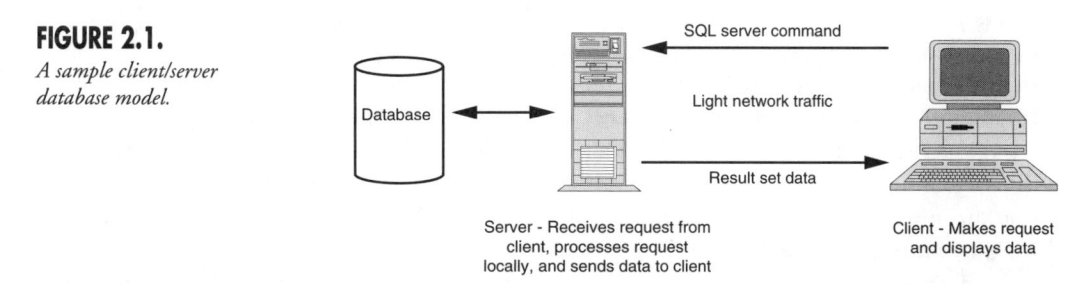

Server - Receives request from client, processes request locally, and sends data to client

Client - Makes request and displays data

The computer on the right executes an application such as Microsoft Access, which would be considered the client application. The computer on the left executes SQL Server, which would be considered the server application. In essence, the client application makes a request (for example, to retrieve a row of data). This request is then passed on to SQL Server over your network. Once SQL Server has received the request, it processes it, then passes just the data back to the client application for display. Only the commands from the client application to the server application and the data from the server application to the client application pass over the network. Now compare this with a monolithic database model, as shown in Figure 2.2.

FIGURE 2.2.
A sample monolithic database model.

Server - Database file located on network drive

Client - Accesses database file, processes file, and displays data

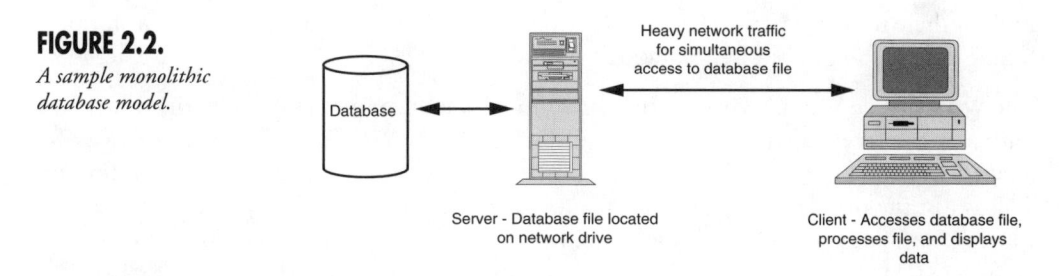

In this model, you can assume that the client computer is also running Microsoft Access instead of accessing a SQL Server database, although the database, or the file that contains the database, is stored on a network server. The database could just as easily be located on your local hard drive, but for comparison purposes I've placed the data on the file server. Instead of splitting the task between two separate applications, all the processing is performed by Microsoft Access. If you were to search a database, the entire contents of the database would have to be passed to Microsoft Access, which in turn would process the database row by row until it found the requested information. This places a heavy load on your network when compared to the client/server model shown in Figure 2.1.

One reason Internet services, such as FTP, WWW, Gopher, Archie, Finger, Telnet, RCP, RSH, and so on, use a client/server model is to lower the bandwidth requirements. You can think of the Internet as a very large wide area network (WAN), because that's essentially what it is. A WAN is a collection of computers that are not physically in the same location as your network (or local area network). Most WANs use very slow connections (56Kbps) to connect to your LAN. Some use higher-speed connections (up to 45Mbps). The connection speed determines how much information can be passed between the server application and the client application. Considering that most Internet connections by clients occur using 14.4kbps–28.8kbps (57.6kbps–115.2kbps with compression), there is a significant need to lower the bandwidth requirements as much as possible. After all, a 14.4Kbps connection is only 25% of the slowest WAN link in use today. If the bandwidth is not used appropriately to transmit the most important information first, the Internet client will just sit in front of his Web browser waiting for the complete page to appear. This is one reason why the client/server model is used, because it provides a mechanism for the client to obtain the text (the most important part) of a document first, followed by any graphical objects (which really just make the page look better, but usually contain no additional content).

WWW Publishing Service

The Microsoft WWW Publishing Service is a WWW server. It uses the Hypertext Transfer Protocol (HTTP) to communicate with its client application (a Web browser). This can be confusing, because people may refer to your WWW Publishing Service as a WWW server or an HTTP server; however, it really doesn't matter, because all of them perform the same task. Each of these responds to the client application requests. These requests are the basis for publishing information on the World Wide Web.

The World Wide Web is a content-rich environment. It encompasses the majority of network traffic on the Internet. It can be used to display (on your Web browser) text, static graphic images, animated graphic images, 3D worlds, and audio-video files, and to play audio files. This is just the tip of the iceberg. New features are being added to Web browsers constantly, which means you must add additional extensions to your Web server to support them.

Web browsers are no longer tied specifically to supporting Web servers, either. Today's Web browsers can be used to connect to FTP sites and Gopher sites, and can even access newsgroups. Future versions may encompass other Internet services as well. These services could include e-mail, telnet, remote shells, and so on. There's no telling exactly what the future will bring in the World Wide Web client/server arena.

FTP Publishing Service

Whereas the WWW Publishing Service is an HTTP server, the FTP publishing service is an FTP server. The FTP publishing service is much less complex than the WWW Publishing Service. The FTP publishing service is used primarily as a data repository. This repository can contain various types of files that users can upload or download to their systems using an FTP client application. It is similar to a communications program, such as Procomm for Windows, that you would use to access a bulletin board system (BBS). When you decide to download a file from a BBS, you have to specify a download protocol. Most often this is the ZMODEM protocol.

Gopher Publishing Service

The Gopher publishing service is used much less frequently than either the WWW or FTP publishing services. It is primarily used to publish very large amounts of textual data. If you had an encyclopedia to publish, for example, the Gopher publishing service would be a good choice to use as your publishing medium. The biggest benefit of the Gopher publishing service is that it can be searched with a relatively speedy response, and that the data can actually span multiple servers. While it is possible to perform similar processes with either the WWW or FTP publishing services, using the Gopher Publishing Service does require more work from you.

An Extensible Platform

The key to any, and I do mean any, project is the ability to extend the capabilities of the project based on user demands. Every project either grows to encompass new features and keep the customer satisfied, or it stagnates and dies. This is true of the Internet Information Server as well. The good news here is that IIS is so extensible that you may be overwhelmed by the possibilities. There is something for everyone. The software development kits available for IIS include legacy support, such as the Common Gateway Interface (CGI), as well as brand new APIs, which bring the power of OLE (using ActiveX objects) to the World Wide Web. While this chapter cannot cover all these possibilities in depth, it can give you a brief taste.

The Internet Information Server Software Development Kit

Depending on who you talk to and when, you may have heard of the Internet Server Application Programming Interface (ISAPI). This is a proprietary programming interface introduced with IIS as a replacement for CGI development tasks. You can create ISAPI applications to extend the functionality of the Internet Information Server just as you would a CGI application. The biggest difference between a CGI application and an ISAPI application is that a CGI application executes in a separate process, whereas an ISAPI application is really a dynamic link library (DLL) that executes in the same address space as the WWW Publishing Service. An ISAPI DLL is much faster than a CGI application that performs the same task. It also consumes fewer resources, which means you can service many more users.

> **CAUTION**
>
> There is a downside to ISAPI DLLs. Since they share the same address space as the HTTP server, it is possible that an errant ISAPI application could crash the WWW Publishing Service. Before you implement a new ISAPI application that you developed, be sure that it is thoroughly tested. If you will be using a third-party ISAPI application, make sure it has passed the Microsoft certification tests before you install it on your server.

So just what can you do with an ISAPI application? Well, you could create an online calculator, for example, where the user would see a calculator screen on his Web browser that he could interact with. The actual calculations would be performed on the WWW server, with the result being returned for display on the client's Web browser. This is a very simple task, which may not be challenging enough for you. So perhaps you should consider these possibilities:

- The Internet Information Server includes the ISAPI Internet Database Connector. This is a DLL that provides access to open database connectivity (ODBC) drivers. This means that your ISAPI applications can access any ODBC-compliant database, including SQL Server, Oracle, RBase, Access, Paradox, and dBASE, or any other database for which you have a 32-bit ODBC driver. Anything you can store in such a database can be displayed or downloaded on the client's Web browser.
- You could create an ISAPI filter that would be called whenever the WWW Publishing Service received an HTTP request. You could use this in much the same way that you would when you hook into the Windows operating system to control the behavior of the mouse to trap mouse messages, except in this case you would trap HTTP messages. You could use such a process to perform data encryption, data compression, user logging, or similar tasks.

ActiveX

ActiveX, formerly code-named Sweeper, is where the real heart-and-soul changes are going to be occurring in future products. ActiveX basically brings the power of OLE objects to the Internet. With ActiveX you will be able to create custom controls for Web browsers to enhance their functionality. If you currently have a custom control that you have developed, it should not be too difficult to migrate it to ActiveX. These same custom controls will be insertable into Visual Basic applications, which also implies the possibility of insertion into a Visual C++ application or any application environment that supports the OLE custom controls.

As another benefit, ActiveX introduces the OLE document objects concept. This will provide you the ability to create, or host, documents (a document in this context can be any object for which you have developed a custom control) in a frame within a Web browser. You could view a Word document, for example, inside a frame of your Web browser. Or you could go so far as to turn your Web browser into a full-fledged word processor as you do today with OLE automation. This technology is going to revolutionize the Web, and you can be a part of it.

ActiveX is such a huge topic that it requires its own book. I have space to point out two more potential items of interest. First, ActiveX supports two new scripting languages. The first is JavaScript, which is based on Sun Microsystems's Java language. Java is based on C++ and is used to provide interactive applications, commonly called applets, which can be integrated into your Web browser. The second is Visual Basic Script, which performs a similar function, but is based on Microsoft's Visual Basic. Both of these scripting languages have been trimmed down to remove potentially dangerous functions.

The Common Gateway Interface

The Common Gateway Interface has been around on the World Wide Web for quite some time. If you already have CGI applications, you can continue to use them. If not, you may want to consider writing some. If you are new to WWW development, you should decide whether to develop CGI or ISAPI applications. If your development skills are up to snuff, and you have been writing Windows applications using C++ for quite some time, there is really no contest. Use ISAPI, and start coding today.

On the other hand, if you are new to application development using C++, or you prefer C, FORTRAN, Pascal, or whatever, you may want to consider developing CGI applications. A CGI application is any application that supports the stdin (standard input) and stdout (standard output) interfaces, and can access environment variables. This can cover a lot of ground and can provide you with an easier transition. You can also use CGI in conjunction with the Perl scripting language instead of a compiled application, such as a C++ executable, to rapidly develop applications to extend your Web server's functionality. You will learn more about these in Chapter 17, "Unleashing the Power of VBScript," and Chapter 18, "Introduction to Windows NT CGI Programming."

What Can the Internet Information Server Do for You?

The most common reason to use IIS is to create a WWW or FTP site for your organization. How you will use IIS, however, may differ from site to site, as everyone has different needs. You could use it to create an Internet Web site or to create an intranet Web site. This is the subject of the next section, which examines how well IIS stacks up to the competition.

Internet and Intranet Publishing

The Internet is taking the corporate and home markets by storm. People everywhere are looking to leverage the Internet. The Internet services most commonly used include the World Wide Web and FTP. For the most part, these services have always been used externally; that is, they have been provided by sources outside the local area network. Even when a corporation begins to provide these services, they have been used to supply information to external users, sell products, or possibly even to provide technical support to customers. These services, however, have only been used to provide a means for external users, or Internet clients, to access these resources. But this policy is changing as third-party manufacturers add Internet capabilities to their products. Lotus Notes is one such application. It started as a groupware product used internally on the corporate LAN to facilitate user collaboration; however, it is now being enhanced to provide Internet support, as well.

You may be wondering why these groupware products are being enhanced to provide Internet functionality. The bottom line is that the Internet has become such a rich source of materials that it is becoming difficult to live without. If a tool does not provide Internet support, it is not nearly as useful as it could be. Take, for example, Lotus Notes. Your current version of Lotus Notes may have a great deal of corporate information in its proprietary database, but now that you plan to connect to the Internet, you want to share some of this information with your Internet customers. The current version of Lotus Notes provides this ability so that you can use this information within your corporate LAN as well as externally.

Although Lotus Notes is a powerful tool, not everyone has embraced it. One reason for this is the expense involved, and the functionality provided by Notes doesn't suit everyone's needs. But the tools you use today, such as a WWW browser, can now be used internally on your local area network to provide similar functionality. These tools are less developed than the current market of groupware products, but they are also less expensive to use. More important, however, is that they are also much easier to maintain, configure, and access from various operating system platforms. Almost every operating system in existence today provides a TCP/IP stack and associated tools. With the Internet Information Server and the current crop of Web browsers, you can do the following:

- Corporate directories—It is very simple to create a static Web page with document links to specific sections within a document. It is possible to put your entire office directory (user name, office location, phone number, and so on) on your Web server to provide access to the most up-to-date information.

- Corporate documentation—Most corporations include company documentation, such as employee handbooks, accounting procedures, EEO guidelines, and so on that could be placed on your Web server to provide instant access to the materials. The ecologically minded should think about how many trees you could save by placing such material on your LAN's Web server.

- Help desk—Many of you may already have proprietary software to aid in customer relations. This software is usually used to provide a means to track individual customer problems as you work on providing a solution. Yet the expense of such software is often higher than many smaller companies can afford. Even when a company can afford it, the software is often difficult to use and is not customizable. However, you can customize a forms-based Web page to your heart's content.

  This implementation could be used internally to provide a complete tracking mechanism just like the proprietary implementation. It could even be made available externally to your customers, who probably already have Internet access, so that they can avoid the (sometimes) long delays while waiting for a customer representative to answer the phone. They can obtain up-to-the-minute information with simple form submission using their customer tracking number. An informed customer is a happy customer. It's even possible to provide hooks to your FTP site within the customer response form so that customers can download the latest patch created specifically to solve their problem.

- Online inventory/order entry—Many corporations have an internal and external sales force that uses an online database. This database contains information on the current inventory, as well as information on customer orders. To access this information, you use a database front end, such as Microsoft Access or a custom application. It is possible, however, to use a Web-based form to query the database or place an order. You could use your Web browser to replace your current front end both for internal and external use.

  When your mobile sales force arrives at a client's office, he could either dial your server directly, or connect to the Internet via a local number and access your Web server. He could gain access to the company database so that when he places an order, via a form on your Web page, the order can be checked to verify that the requested items are in stock. If the items are in stock, the order can be passed to the appropriate department and shipped to the client. If the item is not in stock, an order can be sent to your supplier. This entire process could happen in real time, right at the customer's office.

- Database integration—There are many more possibilities for integrating your Web server and your online databases besides inventory or order-entry systems. It is also possible to create forms for ad hoc queries, create dynamic Web pages where the database formats its output in a standard HTML format, or create high-performance search engines. The possibilities are limited only by your imagination and your ability to write custom applications.

Intranet publishing is not suitable for every task, nor is it for everyone. To publish data internally requires additional resources. As with most products, there are pros and cons that you should be aware of before you commit your resources. These items are summarized in Table 2.1.

Table 2.1. The pros and cons of intranet publishing.

Pro	Con
An intranet is an excellent platform for publishing information internally.	Collaborative applications for intranets are not nearly as powerful as those offered by traditional groupware products such as Lotus Notes.
A Web browser is available for almost any operating system, unlike the proprietary clients used for traditional groupware applications.	Unlike a groupware product that has all the applications integrated into a single product, separate clients will need to be installed for Web browsing, using e-mail, and so on.
Web servers, especially IIS, do not require as much raw processing power or hard disk space as do traditional groupware products.	While it is quite easy to link an ODBC-compliant database to your IIS Web server, few tools are available to link other back-end components. It is possible to use the Software Development Kits (SDKs) provided with the BackOffice components, including IIS, to integrate your Web server; however, if your third-party product does not have such a development kit, you will be unable to link the information.
There are numerous Internet products you can use to access your data. These products generally operate together quite well.	Intranet publishing requires the TCP/IP protocol to use these tools. If your LAN uses another protocol, you may be forced to change to TCP/IP or install a gateway before these products will function properly. If you plan to access the Internet as well, you will also need to obtain routable IP addresses.
IIS is a scalable platform. As you need additional horsepower, you can migrate your system to another processor platform, or even add additional processors to improve performance.	There are no built-in replication services to distribute your data.

Pro	Con
With the availability of new HTML authoring tools, such as FrontPage, HotDog, and HotMetal, it is quite simple to create Web pages.	HTML by itself is not powerful enough to create client/server applications. While new standards, such as ActiveX, VBScript, JavaScript, and so on are available, they are still in their infancy. To use these tools will require custom development.

To sum up this discussion on intranet versus Internet publishing, I would like to point out one major benefit of intranets. If you start with an intranet publishing site, when the time comes for you to enter the world of Internet publishing, you will be ready. It takes very little to actually convert an intranet site to an Internet site. Specifically, you will need to consider the following:

- Routable IP addresses—These can be obtained from your Internet service provider or from InterNIC. If you think you may migrate to the Internet some day, you should follow the guidelines for intranets provided by InterNIC. You can find a wealth of information on this subject at http://www.internic.net.
- A domain name—If you plan to let users find your site using the form www.yourcompanyname.com, you will need to register your domain name with InterNIC. Your Internet service provider (ISP) may be able to perform this task for you.
- Security—The Internet is like a jungle. There are wild animals out there. To protect yourself, you will need to consider some hardware or software tools that you can use to prevent damage to your system. These include products such as routers, firewalls, and network isolation. Also, you will need to create policies based on common sense. For example, you should never execute an application downloaded from the Internet without checking it first for viruses.

How Well Can the Internet Information Server Perform?

The key factor on almost everyone's mind today is how well a particular product performs. If it is a poor performer, then your company suffers, which in turn means that you, too, may suffer for recommending the product. On the other hand, if the product performs well, everyone is happy, and you may even be rewarded for your product recommendation. The one key item, however, that most people seem to forget is that performance is relative. By this I mean that in order to determine a performance level, a product must be compared to another product that performs a similar function.

In an open throughput testing scenario, the Internet Information Server outperformed the Netscape Communication Server 1.12 for Windows NT on the same hardware platform (a Hewlett-Packard NetServer LS with an Intel Pentium 133MHz processor, 32MB RAM, a 1MB L2 cache, two 1GB hard drives, and a DEC 10/100MB Ethernet adapter) by four to one. It also outperformed the Netscape Communication Server 1.12 for BSD UNIX, which required 128MB RAM to complete the test, by three to one. When compared to Novell NetWare's Web Server version 2.0, the Internet Information Server surpassed it by two to one. These results are pretty impressive, considering that IIS requires fewer resources, which translates directly to providing faster client response times and the ability to handle larger peak loads than the competition.

> **NOTE**
>
> The complete whitepaper, from which this section is based, can be found on the Microsoft WWW site at `http://microsoft.com/infoserv/docs/Iisperf.htm`.
>
> Additional information concerning the benchmarks and testing procedures performed by Haynes & Company and Shiloh Consulting can be found at `http://microsoft.com/infoserv/haynes1.htm`. This information was based on a prerelease version of the Internet Information Server. The actual performance benchmarks may differ from those of the released product, although based on my experience, the released product generally improves performance rather than hindering it.

Similar results were obtained based on the number of connections per second. The average response-time results were even more impressive, which indicates that even for small Web sites, IIS is the best solution. But more importantly, IIS provides the means to use APIs to create custom solutions, such as dynamic Web pages, that outperform the competition, as well. When comparing the CGI to ISAPI on the same server using IIS, the ISAPI applications transferred almost five times as much data as a similar CGI application. When comparing ISAPI to NSAPI (the Netscape-proprietary APIs), ISAPI was almost three times faster.

What all this really means to you is that you can create a high-performance Web site that outperforms other platforms, including RISC servers such as Sun's SPARCServer-20 or Hewlett-Packard 9000 Model HP 200 workstations. This means you can get more bang for the buck, which is important to any company. It also means that you can achieve greater scalability and handle larger peak loads using the Windows NT Server and the Internet Information Server.

Publicizing Your Web Site

Once you have your WWW site designed and are ready to publish data on the Internet, there are a few additional items you need to take care of if you want people to find your site. If you have sufficient funds, check with your Internet service provider to see if they offer any plans to publicize your site. Many ISPs do have such plans, and it can make your life a lot easier to let them do the work for you. If your budget doesn't include funds for this purpose, then you can try to take care of it yourself. You can start by getting your site published in a directory listing or newsgroup.

Directory Listings

A directory listing is a service Internet users can use to search for an item by keywords. Usually the individual directory listing, such as Yahoo!, will index your entire Web site. This makes it easy for users to find your Web site, even when they cannot remember your site name. While you can submit your Web site to an individual directory listing service, it is much easier to submit your site to Submit It at `http://submit-it.permalink.com/submit-it/` because this uses a form-based approach to submit information about your WWW site. When you do, your site will be automatically submitted to a number of directory listing sites that include Apollo, ElNet Galaxy, Jump Station, Harvest, Infoseek, Lycos, Open Text, Web Index, New Rider's WWW Yellow Pages, Netcenter, Nikos, Pronet, Starting Point, WebCrawler, What's New Too, Whole Internet Catalog, World Wide Web Worm, Yahoo!, and Yellow Pages.com. You can expect a two- to four-week delay between the time you submit your site and it being available in these directory listings.

Other directory listing services are not included in Submit It's list. These include Excite at `http:www.excite.com`, NCSA's What's New page at `http://www.ncsa.uiuc.edu/SDG/Software/Mosaic/Docs/whats-new.html`, and the Open Market Commercial Sites Index at `http://www.directory.net`. The Webaholics Top 50 Links at `http://www.ohiou.edu/~rbarret/webaholics/favlinks/entries.html` is another good list to try. The lists here rotate constantly. There are numerous cool sites of the day and week, and pages that you can try to make. If you do, you'll be assured that some people will stop by to take a look at your site. And the more people that stop by, the more who will be told about your site. Word of mouth is still one of the most commonly used mechanisms people use to find hot sites on the Internet. Another possibility is to use a posting service such as PostMaster at `http://www.netcreations.com/postmaster/`. This service also uses a form to post information to 17 Web sites free of charge. For a fee of $500, you can post to a larger list of 300 different print and broadcast media contacts.

After these services, try Digital's Alta Vista engine at `http://www.altavista.digital.com`. It's a good bet that your site will already be listed, but if it's not, you can fill out a form and be on your way. Keep in mind that when you do go searching for your site, don't just stop with your home page. Look for all the pages you want to be sure Internet users will find. When you see your listing, check out the description for the page. If you do not like what you see, change your Web page. Many of these services will use the title of your Web page, plus a couple additional lines (generally the first couple lines on the page) as a teaser.

You should also check out the online malls, because many of them consist of links to other sites where you can post your link free of charge. Check the Index of Commercial Databases and Malls posted by the Multimedia Marketing Group at http://hevanet.com/online/com.html for a list. You can also try the Yellow Pages of the Entire United States on the WWW at http://www.telephonebook.com, which is made available by the American Business Information in Omaha, Nebraska. If you are not already listed, you can get a free listing by filling out a form.

Newsgroups

Publishing information about your Web site in a newsgroup (or an online BBS) is another way for members to notice that you have arrived on the Web. Before you try any postings in a newsgroup, however, keep in mind three rules:

1. Never post a message about a commercial Web site in a noncommercial newsgroup.
2. Keep your postings short and to the point. A paragraph or two should be sufficient.
3. Always read a few messages in the newsgroups in which you plan to post information about your Web site to make sure that the format and content are applicable.

Failure to follow these rules can mean that you may receive a lot of hate mail or flames, neither of which will do much to attract users to your Web site. The newsgroup for general announcements of a new Web site is comp.infosystems.www.announce. But if your Web site deals with a specific topic, look around to see what other newsgroups are good vehicles for your announcement.

Summary

This chapter touches on some of the basic concepts of the Internet Information Server. It describes some, but not all, of the possible uses to which you can put IIS within your organization. It also describes a bit about the available methods you can use to extend your Web server's functionality—ISAPI, ActiveX, JavaScript, VBScript, CGI, and Perl. In future chapters, you will get your hands dirty by learning how to develop some basic applications to demonstrate the functionality of these development tools. Although the amount of information can be daunting, there is something for everyone; you don't need to become proficient in all the available methodologies, but you can start slow and move up as your requirements grow.

In this chapter you got a peek at how you can use IIS internally within your company to publish information and use it as a stepping stone to full Internet access. You also had a chance to look at the basic performance characteristics of the Internet Information Server. You should remember that IIS takes advantage of the Windows NT architecture to provide a scalable platform that is more efficient (read faster) than other Web servers, including many RISC platforms that cost thousands of dollars more. Finally, this chapter describes some of the items you will need to address to publicize your Web site. With careful planning and attention to detail, your Web site could become one of the more popular Web sites available.

In the next chapter, you will learn more about Windows NT Server so that you can build a more efficient platform to host the Internet Information Server. This will provide you the additional knowledge to plan and build a truly awesome Web server.

PART II

Building Your Foundation for the Internet Information Server

IN THIS PART

- A Windows NT Server Overview 47
- Choosing a Platform for Windows NT Server 75
- IIS Preparation and Installation 103

A Windows NT Server Overview

IN THIS CHAPTER

- The Windows NT Design **48**
- Additional Windows NT Features **56**
- Windows NT Server Concepts **65**

Now that you've looked at some of the basics of the Internet Information Server, it's time to look at the operating system IIS runs on: Windows NT Server. The purpose of this chapter is to introduce you to some design features of Windows NT Server and to explain some of the buzzwords associated with Windows NT Server to give you a better understanding of the operating system and its capabilities. The goal for this chapter is to help prepare you to build an outstanding Web server using Windows NT Server and the Internet Information Server. For those of you who have not worked with Windows NT Server before, this chapter has a lot to offer. In this chapter you will learn why Windows NT Server is often considered one of the best network file and print servers available in today's market, and why you will soon be hearing more about Windows NT Server's WWW publishing capabilities. If some of the discussion is a bit too confusing or technical for you, take a look at another book of mine called *Microsoft BackOffice Administrator's Survival Guide*, as well as *Windows NT Server 4 Unleashed*, both by Sams Publishing, for more in-depth discussions of the material.

The Windows NT Design

The current version of Windows NT Server (version 4.0) includes some enhancements (discussed a bit later in this chapter), but the basic component model has stayed the same in each release. If you have been reading any of the literature produced by Microsoft about Windows NT Server, you've probably been confused by the scattering of buzzwords and how these buzzwords relate to your day-to-day activities as a webmaster. That's what you are going to look at here. Although I have not included all of these buzzwords, I have included those that I think will make the biggest difference in your life:

- Robust—When you hear this word used in conjunction with Windows NT, it simply means that Windows NT is designed not to crash when an application fails. Windows NT accomplishes this by using two specific features. First, all applications execute in their own address space (with the exception of 16-bit Windows applications). Second, all the operating system components are protected-mode components. Unlike Windows 3.*x*, Windows NT does not rely on any real-mode components (a real-mode application can access any memory or Input/Output [I/O] location arbitrarily, which can lead to a system crash) to interact with your computer hardware. These features are both good and bad, but it's the price we have to pay for an operating system that will not crash easily.

> **NOTE**
>
> It is possible to execute 16-bit Windows applications in separate address spaces by manually starting them from the command line with the START *ApplicationName* /SEPARATE switch, where *ApplicationName* is the name of a 16-bit Windows executable. As an alternative, you can change the program item's properties and enable the Run in Separate Memory Space option to execute the application in a separate address space.

Because Windows NT does not use the BIOS (a real-mode component) to access the hard disk controller, not all hard disk controllers will work with NT. If you want your unsupported hard disk and controller to work with NT, you will need a Windows NT device driver to support it. And since NT prevents applications from accessing the hardware directly, not all MS-DOS and Windows 3.x applications will work when running under NT. In such cases, a virtual device driver, or VDD, is required to support the hardware access.

- Fault Tolerant—This particular feature is so important that I have covered it in more detail later in this chapter. For now, you can just consider it to mean that when faced with a system failure, Windows NT Server provides the means to protect your data and to keep the server running if at all possible. It does this by detecting various software and hardware failures. If a hardware failure is detected, the redundant hardware will be used, if available, to continue providing access to your network server by your network clients. If a software failure occurs, Windows NT will attempt to resolve the failure and continue operating if possible.

- Secure—The good news about this particular feature is that Windows NT provides reliable methods to limit access to any computer resource. This includes access to the server and your data as well as access from one application to another application. There are two aspects to consider for this item. The first is related to limiting access to the network file server's shared resources and the server itself. This is accomplished through user identifications (a user ID) and password, or local or group identifiers (these topics will be covered in more detail in the section "User Management"). The second aspect is related to keeping your data secure from unauthorized access and is covered in the section "The New Technology File System."

- Scalable—When scalability is mentioned with Windows NT Server in the same breath, it generally refers to providing additional performance. Most people only consider adding resources, such as another CPU or disk channel (a disk controller and disk drives). But scalability refers to the ability of Windows NT to execute on different hardware platforms, such as the Intel 80x86 processors, the NEC MIPS processor, the DEC Alpha processor, and the IBM/Motorola PowerPC processor. Each of these different platforms can provide additional levels of performance.

- Symmetric Multiprocessing—Windows NT's internal design utilizes a symmetric processing model, which means that all processors can access system resources (memory, interrupts, and so on), and that any process/thread can execute on any processor. This is quite different from an asynchronous multiprocessing model, in which one processor is responsible for the operating system functionality and another processor is responsible for executing applications. With Windows NT, any process can execute on any processor. That allows you to make more efficient use of available processor resources.

- Multithreading—A *thread* is the minimum executable resource in Windows NT. The difference between a *thread* and a *process* is that a process is the container for an address space, while a thread executes within that address space. A process by itself is not executable; it is the thread that is scheduled and executed. Threads are unique because a single process can have more than one thread of execution. For instance, a multithreaded application can have one thread for user input (keyboard and mouse), another for printing, and another for file access. When you print a file, or even save a file, these threads run in the background and the user thread runs in the foreground. Your application continues to respond to your input, and you never see the hourglass as you do in Windows 3.*x*.

> **NOTE**
>
> Windows NT Server's ability to support multiple processors and multiple threads of execution is one of the main reasons that the Internet Information Server performs as well as it does. Don't overlook this capability when comparing IIS to other WWW server platforms.

- Compatible—This just refers to the ability to execute your legacy applications. These applications include your MS-DOS, 16-bit Windows, and OS/2 character-mode applications. The compatibility for a POSIX application does not include the ability to execute binary images. Instead the compatibility is limited to executing recompiled POSIX 1003.1–compliant applications. Each of these applications executes in a different environmental subsystem. Subsystems are discussed a bit later, in the section "The Windows NT Environmental Subsystem Design Model."

Along with the ability to execute your legacy application with Windows NT is the ability to use the Windows 95 user interface. This means that if you have applications designed specifically for Windows 95, they should run under Windows NT as well. This is a big benefit because Windows 95 includes the same Explorer interface to the file system, the Telephone Application Programming Interface (TAPI) to your modems, a desktop interface that includes the ability to create shortcuts, customize your display properties (even changing video resolution on the fly without rebooting the system), and various other enhancements as well. The biggest benefit occurs because you do not need to retrain your users to use Windows NT if they are already familiar with Windows 95.

- Integratable—This is one of the joys when working with Windows NT Server, because it means that you do not have to tear up your existing network. Instead, Windows NT Server can happily coexist with your UNIX, Novell, Banyan, and LAN Manager networks if you desire. It also includes the ability to migrate your existing Novell and LAN Manager networks to Windows NT networks over a period of time, or to even emulate an existing Novell server. More importantly though, you can integrate any of these network operating systems with the Internet (or Information Superhighway, as some people call it).

The Windows NT System Design Model

There is much more to the Windows NT design than can be explained in a few simple words. It is important for you to understand the under-the-hood features of Windows NT, because as a webmaster you will be responsible for supporting or developing applications that will interact with these components. The Internet Information Server, for example, relies on these key items to function. As you enhance your Web server with ISAPI DLLs or CGI applications, or attempt to tune Windows NT Server and the Internet Information Server, you will be interrelating with these components directly. As you've probably heard, a picture is worth a thousand words, and I'm going to put that theory to the test. Figure 3.1 is a basic picture of the Windows NT system design model and illustrates several of the system's more important features. I like to think of Windows NT as a mainframe operating system that has been scaled down a bit to run on your desktop. As such, it includes many of the features of a mainframe operating system. Specifically, I would like you to note that, like a mainframe operating system, Windows NT incorporates a split in the process hierarchy. This split includes a user mode (ring 3 on Intel CPUs) where your applications, the environmental subsystems, and services execute, and a kernel mode (ring 0 on Intel CPUs) where the core operating system executes.

This split architecture is used to prevent an errant application from bringing down the operating system. And just like a mainframe operating system, it cannot protect you from design flaws in the kernel, such as poorly written device drivers. Any error in the kernel is trapped, and if possible, an error handler will execute to maintain system integrity. However, if a device driver or other kernel component has an error that is unrecoverable, Windows NT will display a kernel core dump. I, and many others, often refer to this as the "blue screen of death," because what you will see on the screen is a blue background with white characters. This dump includes an error code, a device driver listing with address location, and a stack dump of the offending driver(s). Just to ease your mind a bit, core dumps are very infrequent with Windows NT Server. And if you use supported hardware and software, there is a good chance you will never even see one.

Part II — Building Your Foundation for the Internet Information Server

FIGURE 3.1.
The Windows NT design model.

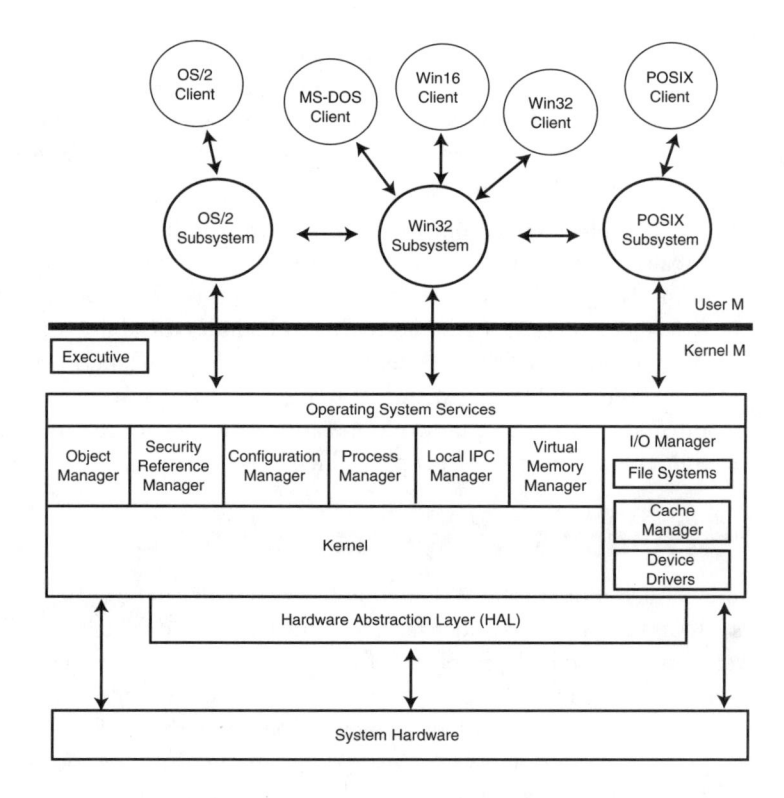

[Diagram: Windows NT architecture showing OS/2 Client, MS-DOS Client, Win16 Client, Win32 Client, and POSIX Client at the top, connected to OS/2 Subsystem, Win32 Subsystem, and POSIX Subsystem. Below the User M / Kernel M boundary is the Executive, containing Operating System Services (Object Manager, Security Reference Manager, Configuration Manager, Process Manager, Local IPC Manager, Virtual Memory Manager, I/O Manager with File Systems, Cache Manager, Device Drivers) and the Kernel. Below that is the Hardware Abstraction Layer (HAL) and System Hardware.]

> **WARNING**
>
> Development tools, such as Visual C++, interrelate with the operating system at very low levels during the build and debug stages. It is possible during one of these actions to hang the Win32 subsystem or the complete operating system. Therefore, if you will be developing applications for Windows NT Server, never do so on a production server. Always create a standalone network (server and workstations) for your development efforts to avoid any potential server downtime.

To continue the discussion of kernel components, take a closer look at Figure 3.1 and notice that the core operating system component is called the *executive* and includes many subcomponents. From left to right and top to bottom, these are

- Object Manager—As the name implies, this component is responsible for basic object management. These objects include the object name space (used to resolve an object name to an object handle for use by an application), resource sharing, some security related usage, and user visible events (like windows, processes, events, and files).

Although Windows NT is not an object-oriented operating system, everything in Windows NT is an object. And the object is the key to all the security features provided by Windows NT because an object (of which there are many) includes the basic data structures used by the Security Reference Manager to perform such actions as process tracking, file auditing, and user authentication.

- Security Reference Manager—This component is used in conjunction with the Object Manager to determine if a user or process has sufficient privilege to access or create an object. As an object is created, it is assigned a security descriptor, which can later be used to limit access to the object. If no security descriptor is explicitly assigned, the owner's (the owner is the person who created the object) security descriptor will be applied by default.

- Configuration Manager—This item is used to access the registry. You will learn more about the registry in Appendix C, "The Registry Editor and Registry Keys." For now you can consider the registry as the .ini file replacement for Windows 3.x. It is the storehouse for all configuration data for Windows NT.

- Process Manager—This component is responsible for managing (creating, terminating, suspending, and resuming) processes and threads executing on the system.

- Local IPC Manager—This component is the heart of the message-passing mechanism that enables Windows NT to be such a good distributed-computing operating system. It includes a fast and efficient mechanism, based on the industry standard remote procedure call (RPC) interface, to facilitate interprocess communication (IPC). This IPC mechanism passes messages between the various clients (MS-DOS, Win16, Win32, POSIX, and OS/2) and the environmental subsystem servers (Win32, POSIX, and OS/2) as well as between the environmental subsystems and the executive. Building on this interface also provides the ability to communicate between remote computers and provide full client/server functionality across the entire network.

> **NOTE**
>
> One of the interesting things produced by this mechanism is the ability to convert an RPC-enabled application to an LPC-enabled application. Where an RPC-enabled application is usually designed to operate on physically separate computers, or to provide a communication mechanism between applications on different environments (like a Windows application and a POSIX application), an LPC-enabled application is designed to operate on the same computer. An LPC-enabled application is an application that has both the client and the server applications executing on the same computer instead of on two computers. Simply changing the server name in the communication linkage to a single period will enable LPC instead of RPC for the transport mechanism. Also, LPC is faster than RPC for the same action. For instance, if you are

> using SQL Server to create dynamic WWW pages on your WWW server, you might want to configure your development WWW server to use a non-local SQL Server database by creating a named pipe with the format \\ServerName\Pipe\SQL\Query and use RPC. Then, when you have finished development, you can create a pipe with the format \\.\Pipe\SQL\Query and use LPC for increased performance (assuming that your WWW server and SQL Server are on the same computer).

- Virtual Memory Manager—This component is responsible for all memory manipulation, including, but not limited to, the virtual-to-logical-to-physical memory address translation, shared memory between processes, and memory-mapped files. Virtual Memory Manager also includes the management of your paging files because this is where your virtual memory, memory-mapped files (by default, although memory mapped files can use a different filename if the application supports it), and stop event debugging information is read/written.
- I/O Manager—This component is special because, unlike the other components that manage only one object type, the I/O manager contains several subcomponents. These subcomponents are all I/O related, but they have different tasks to accomplish. These subcomponents include the file system drivers (NTFS, FAT, HPFS, CDFS, and any third-party additions), the cache manager (which hooks in the file systems to cache all file access including network access), the device drivers (used to access system resources), and network device drivers.
- Kernel—This small component (about 60KB) is responsible for all process and thread scheduling, multiprocessor synchronization, and management of all exceptions (software generated) and interrupts (hardware generated). It is nonpageable (which means it always resides in physical memory) and nonpreemptive (no other thread of execution has a higher priority), but it is interruptable (so it can handle hardware-generated interrupts).
- Hardware Abstraction Layer (HAL)—The HAL is designed as the major interface to the hardware on the computer system. It is designed to isolate hardware-dependent code and is written in assembly language (unlike the other components, which are written in C) for maximum performance. Most executive components access the system hardware through interfaces provided by the HAL, but the kernel and I/O manager can access some hardware resources directly.

The Windows NT Environmental Subsystem Design Model

That pretty much takes care of the kernel-mode components. The user-mode components encompass everything else, including services (such as the LAN Manager Server, which is used to share resources on the network; the LAN Manager Workstation, which is used to access shared resources; and many others) and the environmental subsystems (such as the OS/2, POSIX, and Win32 subsystems). The reason these components are called environmental subsystems is because each of these subsystems creates a simulation of a particular operating system (the environment) that the applications (MS-DOS, Win16, Win32, and so on) execute under. What is important here is that each of these environmental subsystems execute in entirely different process address spaces and are therefore protected from each other. This means that if a POSIX application crashes, it has no effect on the other applications you may be running.

Nearly all these subsystems are completely isolated from each other and have no communication facilities between them except through supported RPC functions such as named pipes or sockets. There are two exceptions. First, the Win32 subsystem is responsible for all I/O interaction. This includes the mouse, the keyboard, and all rendering on the screen. Every subsystem must request such support from the Win32 subsystem (by using local procedure calls), which is why if the Win32 subsystem hangs, the entire system becomes unusable unless the Win32 subsystem can be restarted (possible, but very unlikely). Second, the Win32 subsystem also contains the support for your MS-DOS and 16-bit Windows applications. Both 16-bit and 32-bit Windows applications can pass messages back and forth to each other as well as make use of the standard OLE and DDE facilities.

The 16-bit Windows subcomponent is referred to as the *Windows on Win32* (WOW) layer and can be restarted without complications (as far as I have seen to date). These subcomponents use the Virtual 8086 mode of the Intel processor's hardware support to emulate an Intel 8086 (on RISC processors this emulation is entirely in software) and provide completely independent address spaces for the MS-DOS and 16-bit applications (if desired) to execute under. Figure 3.2 illustrates the MS-DOS virtual DOS machine (VDM) architecture, and Figure 3.3 illustrates the WOW architecture.

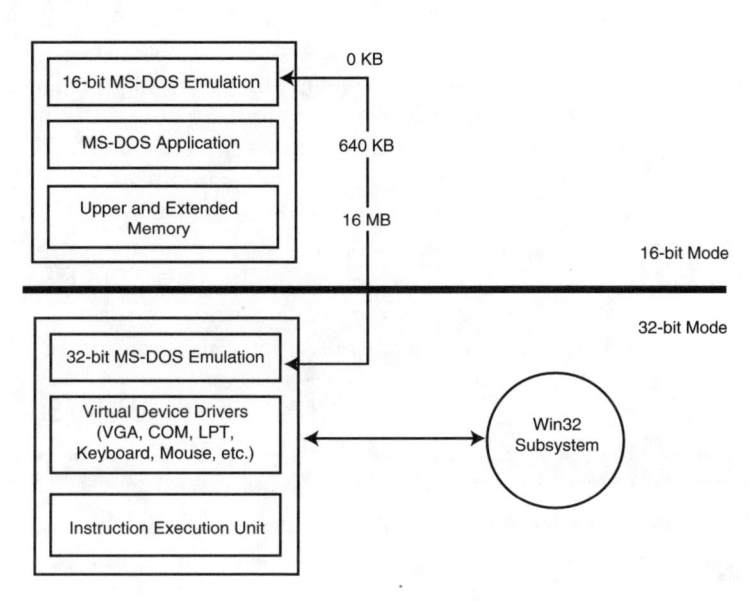

FIGURE 3.2.
The Virtual DOS Machine architectural model.

FIGURE 3.3.
The Windows on Win32 architectural model.

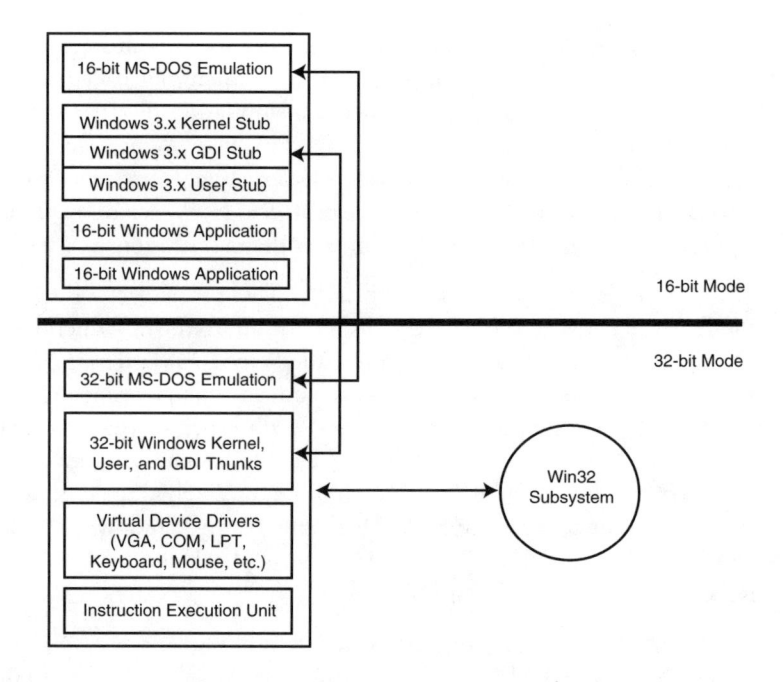

```
                    ┌──────────────────────────────┐
                    │  16-bit MS-DOS Emulation     │◄──┐
                    ├──────────────────────────────┤   │
                    │  Windows 3.x Kernel Stub     │   │
                    │  Windows 3.x GDI Stub        │◄──┤
                    │  Windows 3.x User Stub       │   │
                    ├──────────────────────────────┤   │
                    │  16-bit Windows Application  │   │
                    ├──────────────────────────────┤   │
                    │  16-bit Windows Application  │   │
                    └──────────────────────────────┘   │     16-bit Mode
─────────────────────────────────────────────────────────────────────────
                                                             32-bit Mode
                    ┌──────────────────────────────┐   │
                    │  32-bit MS-DOS Emulation     │◄──┤
                    ├──────────────────────────────┤   │
                    │  32-bit Windows Kernel,      │   │
                    │  User, and GDI Thunks        │◄──┘
                    ├──────────────────────────────┤         ┌──────────┐
                    │  Virtual Device Drivers      │◄───────►│  Win32   │
                    │  (VGA, COM, LPT,             │         │ Subsystem│
                    │  Keyboard, Mouse, etc.)      │         └──────────┘
                    ├──────────────────────────────┤
                    │  Instruction Execution Unit  │
                    └──────────────────────────────┘
```

The OS/2 and POSIX subsystems are similar, but less complicated because they are not built on the VDM concept. Instead, they just use the subsystem to directly support the application environment. It is important to note about the MS-DOS and WOW emulation that in order to directly support hardware access by an application, a virtual device driver must be available to support the emulation of the device and control access to it. This is why many MS-DOS disk utilities fail under Windows NT and why many Windows fax applications (which use virtual device drivers in enhanced mode) fail to execute under NT. It also explains why protected applications (which use a dongle hanging off the parallel port) fail, because the standard NT parallel port driver does not support access to the required I/O ports in the fashion the protected application expects. Another interesting thing about WOW applications is that by default they all run in a shared VDM. This provides the greatest level of compatibility, but if one WOW application fails, it can crash the entire WOW layer. In order to provide additional protection (at the expense of compatibility), each 16-bit application can run in its own VDM. This gives you the ability to preemptively multitask your 16-bit Windows applications, but prevents these same applications from making use of any shared memory (because they run in their own address spaces). This is one reason you cannot execute the 16-bit versions of Microsoft Mail and Schedule Plus in separate address spaces (they make use of shared memory).

Additional Windows NT Features

There is more to the Windows NT design than its user/kernel-mode architecture. Many other network operating systems incorporate similar architectural concepts. However, not every network operating system includes the New Technology File System, the additional fault tolerant features, and the centralized administration capabilities. These are the focus of the next discussion, where you will learn why they are so important to you in your role as a webmaster.

The New Technology File System

Windows NT includes a new file system called, appropriately enough, the New Technology File System, or NTFS. This file system includes several enhancements over existing file systems currently in use today on most network file servers. To begin with, it is entirely transaction based. Much like the transaction log that SQL Server uses to maintain data integrity, the NTFS file system utilizes a transaction log to maintain file system integrity. This does not mean you cannot lose data, but it does mean that you have a much greater chance of accessing your file system even if a system crash occurs. This capability stems from the use of the transaction log to roll back outstanding disk writes the next time Windows NT is booted. It also uses this log to check the disk for errors, instead of scanning each file allocation table entry as does the FAT file system. It has several other beneficial features:

- Security—The NTFS file system includes the ability to assign access control entries (ACEs) to an access control list (ACL). The ACE contains either a group identifier or a user identifier encapsulated in a security descriptor, which can be used to limit access to a particular directory or file. This access attribute can be used to provide the ability to grant or deny read, write, delete, execute, or ownership privileges of a directory or file. An ACL, on the other hand, is the container that encapsulates one or more ACEs. You will not be working with ACEs or ACLs directly unless you write your own application servers or IIS enhancements. For the most part, you will use File Manager or the Windows Explorer to set share-level, directory, or file-level access permissions to restrict access to your WWW server's data.

- Long Filenames—Long filenames are filenames that exceed the normal MS-DOS 8.3 limitation. These names can be up to 255 characters long, can be any mix of upper- or lowercase (although access to the file is not case sensitive except for applications executing in the POSIX subsystem), and can also include UNICODE characters if desired. One of the key features of NTFS is that it automatically generates an equivalent MS-DOS–compatible filename. It uses the first characters of the long filename as the base, adds a tilde, adds a sequence number, and uses the first three characters of the last file extension (the last word following a period). For example, if you had a long filename such as `Accounts Payable.July.1995.XLS`, the equivalent MS-DOS 8.3–compatible filename would be `ACCOUN~1.XLS`.

- Compression Support—This feature was introduced with Windows NT 3.51. It provides the ability to compress any NTFS file, directory, or volume, unlike MS-DOS compression packages, which create a virtual disk as a hidden file on your uncompressed host drive and which require you to compress all data on the compressed drive. Windows NT uses an additional layer in the file system to compress, or decompress, files on demand without creating a virtual disk. This is particularly useful for compressing either a partial disk (such as the directory containing your HTML documents or your FTP site directories), or just specific file types on a disk (such as graphics files). One thing you'll find with NTFS compression is that it is not designed for maximum compression as the MS-DOS compression schemes are; instead it is designed for reliability and performance.

Fault-Tolerant Capabilities

The primary purpose of a file server is to provide the ability to share resources. These can include CPU, file, and print resources. But what happens if you have a hardware failure? In many cases, this means your entire server and all the resources you share with it go down. And if you can't get everything back online quickly enough, your job may go down too. This is where the fault-tolerant capabilities come in to play to protect both your data and your job.

The previous section noted how an NTFS partition can provide data integrity at the file system level, but this may not be enough for mission-critical data. *Mission-critical data* is any data that is required to continue your business practice. For example, this could be a SQL Server database or the source code for your WWW pages. Windows NT Server provides three different options that can be used either separately or in conjunction which each other to safeguard your data:

- Disk Mirroring—This method works at the partition level to make a duplicate copy of your data. For every write to the primary partition, a second write is made to the secondary partition. If the fault-tolerant driver detects a device failure while accessing the primary partition, it can automatically switch to the secondary partition and continue providing you with access to your data.

- Disk Duplexing—This method works at the partition level as well, but also includes the ability to detect disk controller errors. It does this by using two separate disk controllers with separate disk subsystems. Should you have a failure to access data on the primary partition, or a hardware failure of the primary disk controller, access to your data can be maintained by using the redundant copy on the secondary controller and disk subsystem.

- Disk Striping with Parity—This option works by combining equally sized disk partitions on separate physical drives (a minimum of 3 to a maximum of 32 disk drives) to create one logical partition. Data is written to the disk in discrete blocks. Each of these blocks is referred to as a *stripe*. When data is written to the disk, an error correction code stripe is written as well. In the case of a disk failure, the data stripes can be combined with the error correction code stripe to rebuild the missing data stripe.

Chapter 3
A Windows NT Server Overview

> **TIP**
>
> The best types of disk subsystems are SCSI based because these types of subsystems support several important features. First, most SCSI controllers are bus masters (which means they have their own dedicated controller to transfer data to/from the disk to/from system memory. Second, most SCSI drives support command queuing (used to issue several commands to a disk) and bus detachment (meaning that while the disk is processing the request, it detaches from the SCSI bus so another SCSI peripheral can connect to the bus and possibly transfer data). Most SCSI controllers also include a dedicated CPU so that your system CPU does not have to watch over each byte of data transferred from the SCSI controller, as most IDE disk controllers do. That means your CPU can continue processing data and enhancing system throughput. One other important feature is that SCSI drives have spare sectors, which can be mapped to a failing sector (IDE drives have a similar feature, but do not support a specific command to replace a failing sector); the NTFS file system driver can take advantage of this.

The question is when do you use each of these techniques? Each technique provides increased data integrity, but at a cost. For instance, disk mirroring can be used to split a single disk into two partitions, using one partition to contain the primary data and the second partition to contain the copy (that is, the mirror) of the data of the primary partition. However, in order to create this copy, your disk controller must make two physical writes, one to each disk partition. And if the entire disk becomes defective, all your data is lost. To offset this problem, you might use two separate disk drives, but if the disk controller becomes defective, you again lose access to your data. Table 3.1 summarizes the capabilities of the fault-tolerant drivers.

Table 3.1. Summary of the fault-tolerant driver capabilities.

Fault Tolerant Driver	Pro	Con
Disk mirroring	May be used on a single physical disk with at least two equally sized partitions. Can be used to mirror separate physical disks on a single disk controller as well.	Does not protect against disk failure if a single disk is used. Does not protect against controller errors. Limits disk storage to half of system capacity. Performance hit for disk writes.

continues

Table 3.1. continued

Fault Tolerant Driver	Pro	Con
Disk duplexing	Used to mirror separate physical disks on separate physical disk controllers. Protects against disk failures and disk controller errors.	Requires twice the hardware (two disk drives, two disk controllers) to provide half of the storage capacity.
Stripe set with parity	Provides fault tolerance for single drive failure. Increases disk read performance.	Does not provide protection from disk controller errors. Does not protect against multiple disk failures. Requires percentage of disk partition to contain ECC stripe. Slight CPU performance degradation for disk writes to calculate ECC stripe.

My preference is to use striping with parity because it provides fault tolerance and increased performance (particularly if you also place the paging file on the striped set). However, if you need maximum data protection, use the disk duplexing option. Continuing with this basic premise of keeping your server functional during hardware failures, you might want to consider using one of these optional techniques:

- Uninterruptible power supply—This is used for two purposes. First, it protects against temporary power outages by providing a battery to supply AC power to the computer. In the case of a long-term power outage, the uninterruptible power supply service will shut down the server in a graceful fashion. Second, an uninterruptible power supply is used to filter your AC power. This is the most important feature because poor power (spikes, surges, low-line conditions) can cause more damage to your server's peripherals than anything else.

- Symmetric multiprocessing—When this feature is installed on a platform with multiple CPUs, both the performance of your server and its fault tolerance increase. Should one CPU fail, it will be disabled, but processing will continue on the other CPUs. On a uniprocessor computer, if the CPU fails, the entire server goes down.

- Multiple network adapters—Installing multiple network adapters provides several advantages. First, the adapters can be used to increase network performance by providing several channels for spreading the network load. Second, they can increase performance of a specific network transport by binding that transport to a single adapter. Conversely, by binding all the transports to all the network adapters, fault tolerance is increased. If a single adapter fails, it will be disabled and the load will spread among the additional adapters.

Centralized Administration

One of the major benefits of using Windows NT is the ability to manage your entire network from any NT Server, NT Workstation, Windows 95, or Windows 3.*x* workstation running in enhanced mode. I have divided these management tools into two sections: computer management and user management. Specifics on how to utilize these tools will be covered in later chapters. For now, I just want to mention what is available and why you will want to use it for your day-to-day system management.

Computer Management

Computer management includes all the administration tools used to configure either your local computer or a remote client computer. While I won't mention them all, I will point out the most useful tools:

- Event Viewer—This tool is seriously underrated; indeed, many administrators never even bother to use it. However, it is the first tool you should use to determine a Windows NT problem. It provides the ability to look at an NT computer and determine if any system, service, application, or security problems have occurred in the past. This tool is your first line of defense in isolating any system- or security-related problems. If you enable system auditing on a directory, for example, all of the information about who accessed the directory and when it was accessed will be contained within the security log.

> **NOTE**
>
> Every administrator should review all three logs on a daily basis to determine what type of problems may be accumulating. Not all problems are immediately flagged and sent to the administrator in an alert. Monitoring your system log can warn you of imminent failures. My portable computer, for example, has been reporting SCSIDISK bad partition warnings on a SCSI drive, indicating that this drive is getting ready to fail completely. You can also determine if a security breach has occurred by viewing the information contained in the security log.

- File Manager—As you might expect from its name, File Manager is responsible for creating network sharepoints (a shared directory) as well as manipulating your own files and directories as you may have done with the Windows 3.*x* File Manager. File Manager can be used to assign permissions to directories and files, to take ownership of existing directories or files, or to enable auditing of directories and files (for more information on this refer to Chapter 10, "Advanced Security Issues"). One other feature, which is included in no other tool, is the ability to view who currently has a specific file open.

- Internet Server Manager—This tool is used to configure your WWW, FTP, and Gopher servers on the network. It can also be used to control (stop, start, pause, and continue) the WWW, FTP, and Gopher server services on a local or remote computer.

- Print Manager—You can use this tool to create new printers by installing a printer driver, to connect to existing printers on the network, and to manage your local and remote print queues. The Print Manager is also used to assign permissions and to take ownership of existing printers on the network as well as to enable auditing of your printers.

- Remote Access Server (RAS) Administrator—This tool is used to completely control the remote access service on either a local or remote NT computer. The Remote Access Server Administrator is capable of starting the service, authorizing users to make use of the RAS connectivity features, and sending messages to connected RAS clients on a per-port basis. The remote access service can also be used to provide a cost-effective, wide-area network solution, particularly if you make use of either a 28Kbps modem or an ISDN connection.

TIP

Until you authorize a user to use the RAS service, he will not be authenticated if he connects and will not be able to access any network resource.

- Server Manager for Domains—Using this tool is the first step in controlling access to your domain. This tool is responsible for creating the computer account your NT Workstation clients will use to gain a trusted connection to your server. Without a computer account, the network client computer cannot be authenticated even if the user attempting to log on to the domain from the workstation has a valid user identification. Server Manager for Domains can also be used to control the services on a remote Windows NT client as well as determine who is connected and what resources they have in use. You can even disconnect such users if desired and, if installed, the FTP service can be monitored from the Server Manager for Domains as

well. A few additional capabilities are included to provide the configuration of the replication and alert services.
- Dynamic Host Configuration Protocol (DHCP) Manager—This tool is used to create DHCPs and configure scopes (that is, subnets) on your TCP/IP network. DHCP can be utilized to automate the assignment of IP addresses to network clients and, when their lease (or time-out) expires, retrieve the IP address for allocation to a new user. IP address reservations (a reassignment mechanism) can also be created with this tool.
- Windows Internet Naming Service (WINS) Manager—This tool manages all NetBIOS computer names to IP name resolution. It effectively performs the same task as a UNIX domain name server performs. A useful feature of WINS is the capability to replicate the database among several other WINS servers on the network automatically.

> **TIP**
>
> WINS is not designed to work with network clients that are not WINS aware, such as UNIX clients. However, there are two possible solutions. First, you can use the Microsoft domain name server service, which can be configured to interoperate with the WINS service to provide NetBIOS name resolution. Second, you can use a WINS proxy agent. A WINS proxy agent is either a Windows for Workgroups 3.11, a Windows NT Workstation, or Windows NT Server computer that will act as an intermediary between the WINS server and the client that is not WINS aware. The WINS proxy agent forwards the IP address to the client, based on the NetBIOS name the client is attempting to find. To enable the WINS proxy agent feature, check the WINS Proxy Agent check box in the TCP/IP-32 configuration dialog box on the Windows for Workgroups 3.11 computer, or the WINS Proxy Agent check box in the Advanced Microsoft TCP/IP Configuration dialog.

User Management

User management includes adding new users to the network and manipulating current user characteristics. Most of this is accomplished with User Manager for Domains, which is covered in detail in Chapter 10. For now I just want to introduce you to some of the features provided in the basic user management area in case you will also be using your IIS server as an Internet gateway for local or remote network clients. The tools you will be using include the following:

- User Manager for Domains—This is the heart of all user and group management. User Manager for Domains is used to enable system auditing on a global level and to create and manipulate local and global groups (local groups are unique to the computer they are created on while global groups are domainwide). It is used to create and manipulate user accounts, to configure system user policies (such as the minimum password length, the maximum password age, account lockout features, and so on), and to specify which computers the user can log on from and the time of day the user can be logged on to the system. You can also use User Manager to set up the user's profile, logon script, and any home directory if desired.

> **NOTE**
>
> Unlike Novell NetWare and other network operating systems, Windows NT Server does not provide the ability to limit the amount of file space a user can access. So be prepared to implement a system policy of notifying users who exceed your maximum disk quotas, backing up their data, and then deleting it when file space runs low. As an alternative, you can look into third-party add-ons for Windows NT Server, such as DiskQuota from New Technology Partners, to provide this functionality.

- User Profile Editor—This tool is used to create the initial user profile. A user profile is the environment in which the user works and includes all File Manager, Print Manager, and any other user-specific settings. A profile can be either user specific and non-sharable or sharable and non-user specific. It cannot be both. A sharable profile is called a mandatory profile and is used to restrict a group of users from changing their user environment, such as the .ini entries for Windows 3.x.

> **NOTE**
>
> One of the interesting features of profiles is the ability to use the same profile on more than one computer. As the user logs on from a different computer, his profile is used to configure the computer. He will see the same desktop and can use the same applications (as long as they are installed in the same directories on the local computer or are on a network sharepoint) he uses on his primary computer. But this will only occur if the user profile has been created and is available (shared) from a server that is accessible from the new location. Profiles are also server specific, unlike logon scripts, which can be replicated from server to server and can be executed from the server that authenticates the user.

- Logon Scripts—Logon scripts aren't really managed through a specific tool, although they are assigned (named) in User Manager for Domains. Basically, a logon script is a batch program that is executed when the user logs on to the domain and can include such capabilities as mapping sharepoints or printers, automatically checking the hard disk, running programs to keep track of a user's time on a project, or any other program that can be run from the command line.

Windows NT Server Concepts

Windows NT Server introduces several new concepts for you (the network administrator) to consider when designing your network. This section looks at the difference between workgroups and domains, and introduce the trust concept. Then it looks at the difference between the various Windows NT Server modes of operation. Following this discussion is an introduction to the various domain models supported by Windows NT Server. Next you'll learn about the System Management Server implementation methodologies. And by the time you have finished this section, you will be ready for the next chapter, where you will learn about implementing your network based on the concepts in this chapter.

Workgroups Versus Domains

When you install Windows NT Server, you have to decide whether your Windows NT Server is to be a domain member or a workgroup member. If you choose to be a member of a domain, your server will also have to be either a domain controller, backup domain controller, or server. If you choose to be a server, you also have the choice to be a workgroup member. If you make the wrong choice, your only supported option to change this decision is to reinstall Windows NT Server and lose any system settings you have already implemented. Because a Windows NT Server installation can be quite time-consuming, not to mention the loss of user accounts and other system configuration options that occur when you reinstall, you want to make sure that you do it right the first time. And that's where I come in, to help you make the best decision possible and limit your downtime.

What Is a Workgroup?

A workgroup is a casual affiliation of computers that are logically grouped into a single access point. This cuts down on the clutter when your users browse for resources on the network. Instead of seeing all the resources that are shared on the network, they will first see the shared resources of the workgroup they belong to. They will only see resources in other workgroups if they explicitly browse the other workgroup. Workgroups also cut down on the network traffic because each browse request requires that either a browse master (a computer that maintains a static list of computers that are online and belong to the workgroup) or the computer being browsed for shared resources responds with a list of the resources being shared.

All security in a workgroup is based on the local (the one sharing the resource) computer. This is a serious administrative chore because it requires that all workgroup computers have the same user accounts defined if you want to allow other computer users to access your shared resources transparently (without supplying a different user account and password) in a user-level access environment. A user-level access environment provides the ability to limit access to shared resources on an individual-user basis. Each individual user can have different access restrictions. In a large workgroup (more than five computers) environment, it is easier to only use share-level access to limit access to your shared resources. Share-level access uses an individual password for read-only access and another password for full access to your shared resources.

What Is a Domain?

A domain is similar to a workgroup in that it provides the same grouping ability as a workgroup. However, unlike a workgroup, a domain has a centralized user database that resides on the domain controller. All user logon authentication is based on this central user database. This makes your life as a network administrator much easier because you only have one user database to worry about, rather than one user database per computer (as the workgroup model uses).

Domains also include the ability to establish a secure, or trusted, connection. This concept of trust begins with the computer account assignment either when you install Windows NT or when you manually create the computer account with Server Manager for Domains. You cannot be a domain member without a computer account, although you can access shared resources on a domain if you are a workgroup member as long as you have a user account on the domain and there are no trust relationships defined for the domain.

> **NOTE**
>
> If you have a two-way trust relationship defined on your domain, you cannot apply the user account and password mapping of the workgroup authentication model. Even if you have a user account and a password on your domain controller, you cannot use it to access a shared resource. This occurs because you are not a trusted member of the domain (that is, you have no computer account on the domain) and will therefore be denied access to the shared resource.

A trust relationship provides the ability to use the user accounts and global groups defined in one domain (the trusted domain) in a completely different domain (the trusting domain). If this sounds a bit fuzzy, don't worry—it even confuses me on some days. You'll learn more about this in an upcoming discussion of the various domain models and in much more detail in the next chapter.

Controllers Versus Servers

When you install Windows NT Server you have three choices that basically define a specific mode of operation. Each of these operating modes provides different functional abilities and performance options. These choices include the following:

- Primary domain controller—The primary domain controller contains the master copy of the user database, which includes all your global groups, user accounts, and computer accounts. In addition, your primary domain controller is used to authenticate your users when they log on to the network or access a shared resource. Your primary domain controller also includes the tools you will use for centralized administration, such as User Manager for Domains, Server Manager for Domains, Dynamic Host Configuration Protocol Server, Windows Internet Name Service Server, and a host of additional tools.

- Backup domain controller—A backup domain controller is similar in function to a primary domain controller, but with one significant difference. A backup domain does not contain the master copy of the user database. Instead, the master database is replicated from the primary domain controller. This means that you cannot make any account changes (global groups, user accounts, or computer accounts) if the primary domain controller is unavailable. The primary reason for using a backup domain controller is to balance the load for authenticating users on the network. In addition, if a primary domain controller goes down, either inadvertently due to a hardware fault or purposely for, say, a hardware upgrade, you can promote a backup domain controller to a primary domain controller. This provides the ability to continue authenticating your users, and also provides continued network administrative capabilities.

- Server—A server's primary purpose is to provide optimum resource sharing. Since a server does not authenticate users logging on to the network and does not participate in the user database replication, it can devote all its resources to supporting your network clients. This means that if you have a choice, use a server as your Internet Information Server base platform for optimum efficiency. There is a tradeoff for this increased performance, however; you lose the domain administration tools. Instead of User Manager for Domains, for instance, you get a copy of User Manager.

TIP

Another reason to use Windows NT Server operating in server mode is to bypass the Windows NT Workstation limit of 10 simultaneous client user connections. Instead of using Windows NT Workstation, you can use Windows NT Server operating in server mode.

One major item to consider is that in order to create a domain, you must have at least a primary domain controller in your network. You can have one or more backup domain controllers if desired, although they are not required. Keep in mind that a backup domain controller can be useful if you have a primary domain controller failure, particularly since only a primary or backup controller can authenticate your Windows NT clients.

Domain Models

Microsoft has defined four basic domain models, which include the Single Domain Model, the Master Domain Model, the Multiple Master Model, and the Complete Trust Model. However, you should consider this a starting point when it comes time to plan your network implementation. (This is discussed in more detail in the next chapter). You do not have to limit yourself to a specific domain implementation; instead, you can stretch the basic domain model to fit your specific needs. So let's take a look at these different models so we can plan how to make the best network design possible.

The Single Domain Model

The single domain model, as shown in Figure 3.4, includes a primary domain controller and optionally one or more backup domain controllers and servers. It is the basis for all the other domain models. It is the simplest model that Microsoft has to offer and can perform well for you if you meet the following criteria:

- A small network with fewer than 300 users.
- Fewer than 15 servers.
- An administrative group, like an MIS department, that can administer the network.
- No wide area network (WAN).

These criteria do not form a hard and fast rule. You can play with the numbers for the maximum number of users and servers, as long as you keep in mind that the real issue is acceptable performance. If you have fast servers (single or dual CPU Pentiums, for example) and a high-performance backbone (100Mb/sec fiber optic, for instance), you will not see the same performance limitation as a company with 80386-based servers on a 10Mb/sec backbone.

The single domain model provides several benefits. It allows any network administrator to administer all the servers from any server or workstation on the network. Since there is only one user database defined that contains all the user accounts and local and global groups, resource administration is completely centralized. Because there is only a single domain, no trust relationships have to be created to access resources in other domains.

Of course, the single domain model has some limitations. For instance, browsing for resources is based on the domain, and as the number of computers in your domain increases, performance problems may arise. As the number of users in your domain grows, so does the list you have to search through to find an individual user account. And as you make changes to your accounts, either by creating or modifying user accounts and groups, these changes have to be replicated to every backup domain controller on the network. That can eat up a lot of your network bandwidth. Finally, if your company has multiple departments that do not want you to administer their network or have access to confidential files, you'll have to split up your domain and choose another domain model.

FIGURE 3.4.
The single domain model.

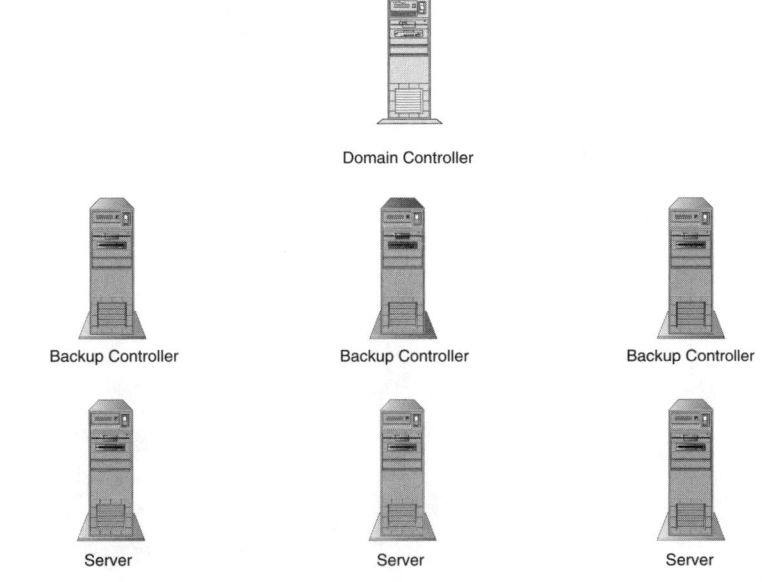

The Master Domain Model

The master domain model (see Figure 3.5) includes a single master domain with one or more resource domains that trust the master domain. The master domain contains all the user account and global groups; there are no user accounts or global groups defined in the resource domains. Since no user accounts exist on the resource domains, all logons and authentications are referred to the master domain.

> **WARNING**
>
> Because all user logons and authentications are processed by the master domain, no users will be able to log on to the network or access shared resources if the primary domain controller fails and you have not included at least one backup domain controller in the master domain.

The master domain model lets you split your network based on departmental resource allocations, yet still provides for centralized administration of your network. The master domain model is well suited for organizations that have the following specifications:

- Fewer than 1000 users.
- Fewer than 50 servers.
- An administrative group, like an MIS department, that can administer the network.

FIGURE 3.5.
The master domain model.

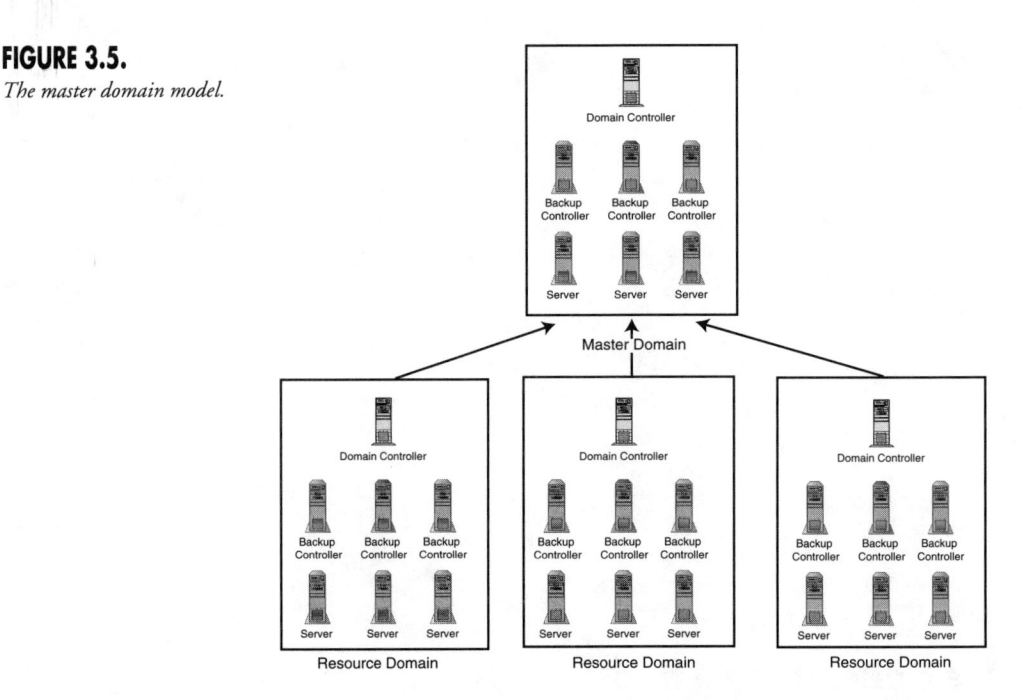

Notice, however, that while each resource domain trusts the master domain, they do not trust each other. This is because all the user accounts and groups are defined in the master domain, and since each resource domain trusts the master domain and users or groups can be granted access to the resource domain, no additional trust relationships are required. One of the other interesting capabilities of this model is that the central administration group can be limited to just creating user accounts in the master domain. The resource domain administrators can then determine who will be granted access to the resources on their domain by creating global groups that include user accounts from the master domain.

There are, however, a couple downsides to this model that you might want to keep in mind. For instance, a user list that includes 1000 users can be pretty intimidating to scroll through, and slow to browse. And replicating the entire user list to your backup controllers can generate enough network traffic to make your users scream, which is why I recommend that you do this after normal working hours. The limiting factors here are your network bandwidth and the speed of your servers. If your network bandwidth is insufficient to carry the user logon and authentication requests provided by your servers, or your servers cannot process the logon requests quickly enough, then your network performance as a whole will suffer. Consider, for example, a resource domain situated on a wide area network. All user logons and authentications will have to travel across the slow WAN link to the master domain, even when they are accessing resources on servers in their local resource domain.

The Multiple Master Domain Model

When you have more than 1000 users or 50 servers, you really need to think about how you can lessen your administrative burden and provide additional fault-tolerant capabilities. The multiple master domain model may just fit the bill. Like the master domain model, it includes resource domains. But instead of a single domain with all the user accounts defined in it, you have two or more domains that contain all the user accounts, as shown in Figure 3.6. Your MIS department can still administer the entire network as long as they have accounts defined in either of the master domains.

FIGURE 3.6.

The multiple master domain model.

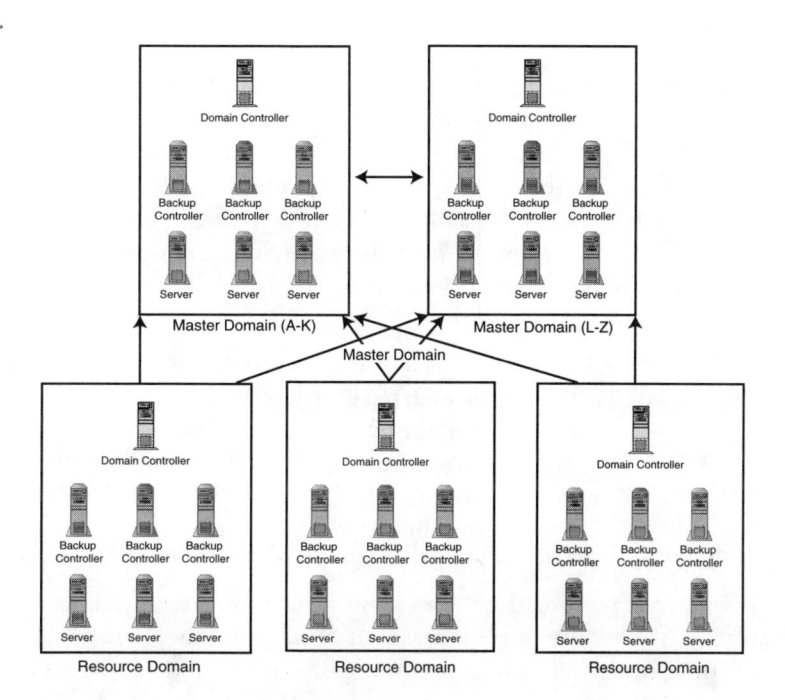

In the example shown in Figure 3.6 there are two domains that have split the user accounts between them. The master domain on the left includes all of the user accounts from A–K, while the master domain on the right includes user accounts from L–Z. Each of these master domains trusts the other, which essentially provides you with one user database, much as the master domain model provides. Continuing with this concept requires that each resource domain trust each master domain to provide all users access to all resources in the resource domains.

This increases your logon and user authentication capabilities because a single failure of a primary domain controller (assuming you do not have backup domain controllers) will only prevent half of your network users from logging on to the domain or being authenticated for resource access. If you have a WAN, you can also include a master domain on each side of the wire to give the local users fast access to their local resources, and still provide them the ability to access resources anywhere on the network.

However, while I have used this example to split user accounts alphabetically, you will find that this model will work better for large organizations if you split the user accounts by departments or divisions. Each of these departments would have a master domain with all the departmental user accounts. Departmental resource domains would then trust this departmental master domain. This would provide you (the administrator) the ability to create a global group that contains all your users to access a particular resource in only one domain rather than in two or more domains.

For example, suppose you want to create a global group called OFFICE that includes all the users to be granted access to the MSOFFICE sharepoint (which contains the Office installation files). If all of your departmental users are included in the departmental domain, then it is a simple matter of creating the group and including your users. But if you had multiple master domains that split up user accounts alphabetically, you would have to create an OFFICE global group in each of the master domains. Then, in your resource domain, you would have to create a local group that would contain the global groups defined in the master domain in order to accomplish the same task.

The Complete Trust Domain Model

The last domain model is the complete trust model. In this model all the domains trust each other, as Figure 3.7 demonstrates, with each domain having its own user database. This particular model is designed for corporations that do not have a centralized administration group or do not want to have a centralized group dictate who has access to their network resources.

In some cases corporations wind up with the complete trust domain model from lack of prior planning rather than any specific need. While this model works fine, it is much more difficult to administer. And as your network grows, it becomes very time-consuming to create additional trust relationships. You can express the number of trust relationships mathematically as $n(n-1)$ where n is the number of domains on the network. For instance, if you have 5 domains, as the example in Figure 3.7 shows, and decide to add another domain, you will have to create 30, or 6×5, trust relationships. If you have 20 domains, adding the 21st will require 420 trust relationships. And you thought your life as an administrator was difficult now!

FIGURE 3.7.
The complete trust domain model.

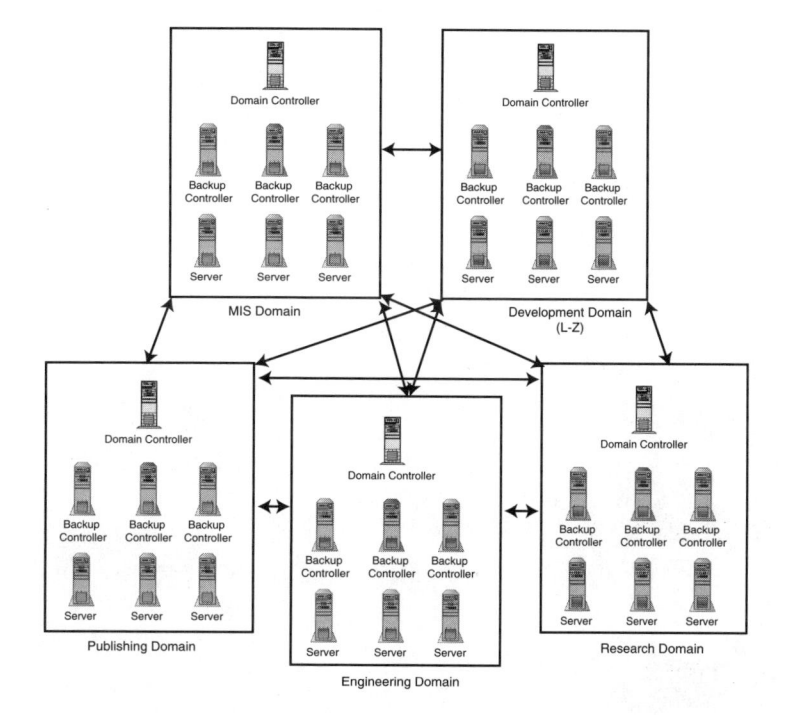

Summary

This chapter looks at some of the features provided by Windows NT Server and the system architecture to prepare you for actually working with Windows NT Server. Hopefully this will provide a fuller understanding of the Windows NT Server when you look at future troubleshooting and optimization techniques. We have also discussed some of the more important features of Windows NT such as the NTFS file system and what it can and cannot do, along with the fault-tolerant features. These fault-tolerant features can be implemented as part of your normal configuration, depending on your needs, available hardware, and budget. Finally, this chapter looks at some of the tools that are available to help you manage your network on a day-to-day basis.

In the next chapter you will learn more about hardware platform choices. Specifically, you will look into items to help you when building a platform to use as your WWW server. You will learn more about the I/O expansion bus, secondary-level cache options, processor considerations, and how other hardware choices can affect your performance. You will also learn a few tips for configuring your system, via software, to obtain better performance.

Choosing a Platform for Windows NT Server

4

IN THIS CHAPTER

- Choosing the Right Hardware 77
- Hardware Upgrades 89
- Choosing the Right Server Model 98
- The Software Configuration 98

This chapter focuses on how the choices you make, or that are made for you, affect the performance of your server. Windows NT Server is the foundation that the Internet Information Server (IIS) builds on to provide services to potentially thousands of Internet users, so you should be concerned about these choices. Performance and optimization rely on two key issues: the hardware and the software. How you use these components determines how well your Internet Information Server will perform.

Optimizing your Windows NT Server to provide the most efficient server performance can sometimes be a daunting task. So many options can overwhelm you at times. There is always the option of throwing money at bigger and better hardware, which will always increase some performance aspect, but that's not a very cost-effective solution. It's better to spend some time working with available tools first to determine how to best spend your money to increase performance.

This chapter begins by looking at some of the basic hardware choices. This section includes a discussion on items that can be useful in planning the initial hardware purchase of the platform you will use as your server. This chapter covers such items as the different processor platforms available for running Windows NT Server, the peripheral I/O expansion buses available on today's computers and when to choose them, and the various disk subsystems and how to best use them. Finally, the chapter covers the options that always increase the performance of your server as compared to the default system configuration provided by a standard Windows NT Server installation. I call these easy performance improvements because these solutions utilize the hardware you already have.

After the chapter explains these basic performance modifications, it examines how you can use some of the hardware-based solutions. You have options such as using hardware like a Redundant Array of Inexpensive Disks (RAID) solution, load-balancing your network by adding network adapters and adjusting the network bindings to increase performance, and using additional processors.

When the chapter finishes looking at some of the hardware choices, it looks into some of the software choices. This section determines whether you should use a domain controller or server as your IIS server platform choice, and why you want to choose between them. The chapter ends with a look at some of the basic software-configuration options to optimize your server.

> **NOTE**
>
> Throughout this chapter you will see references to the BackOffice system files. This is because I expect most of you will also be installing one or more of these components (SQL Server, Exchange Server, System Management Server, or SNA Server) as well as the Internet Information Server. So rather than list these items separately I have just combined them into a single product to make the reading a little easier to follow.

Choosing the Right Hardware

You can enhance server performance by choosing a faster processor (or using the scalability of Windows NT Server by installing it on an entirely different processor platform), using ISA-, EISA-, PCI-, or VLB-based peripherals (you will learn more about these later in the chapter), or using software RAID solutions. This section examines some options to help you obtain the maximum performance from your server without purchasing additional hardware. You can also use this section as a guide to help make future purchasing decisions.

Choosing a Processor Platform

Windows NT Server (version 4.0) has the capability to run on several different processor platforms. These include the Intel processor line and several different Reduced Instruction Set Computer (RISC) processors. You may currently use the MIPS, Alpha, or PowerPC RISC processors. The major differences between these platforms, aside from the purchase price, are twofold. First, the Intel processor line is the only processor line that can execute OS/2 16-bit character-mode applications. It is also the only processor line that can be used in a dual-boot mode to boot MS-DOS. If these are not real concerns, you can ignore these options and just consider the second difference: pure performance. Depending on the RISC processor line you choose, and the clock speed of the processor, one of these platforms may perform better for you than the Intel processors.

It is becoming very difficult to make a recommendation for a RISC processor over the Intel processor line because the Intel processor line keeps improving. For example, the DEC Alpha 275MHz processor is supposed to be about 265 percent faster in integer calculations and up to 600 percent faster in floating-point calculations than a 133MHz Intel Pentium. This means the Alpha will also be faster than a 200MHz Pentium. How do other lines compare (for example, the Intel-clone vendors, the Pentium Pro, or the SMP Pentium platform)? From what I've seen in actual performance, a dual Pentium 133MHz performs about as well as the DEC Alpha. Dual 150MHz or higher processors may be able to exceed the performance of an Alpha processor–based motherboard quite a bit. My server uses dual Pentium 166 MHz processors on a mixed Peripheral Component Interconnect (PCI) and Enhanced Industry Standard Architecture (EISA) bus.

If the primary job of a server is to share resources (generally processor, file, and printer resources, which is pretty much what your WWW and FTP servers do as well), the speed of the processor is not the most relevant issue. Processor performance is a concern, but not a major issue, because Windows NT and the add-on services (like IIS) are more processor-intensive than the same services on other network operating systems. This is due in part to the client/server design of Windows NT Server. This design requires additional overhead to pass messages between the client application (such as the WWW Publishing Service) and the server application (such as the Win32 environmental subsystem). Instead, you should be more concerned with your ability to send information over whatever channel you will be using. If IIS is used to build an intranet, the channel could be a network, in which case a 10Mb network adapter would be the limiting factor in how fast you could send information to your clients. In such a case, you could improve the situation by upgrading to a 100Mb network adapter. If you are using IIS to build an Internet site, your router could be used as a channel to provide your connection to the Internet. Router bandwidth starts at about 56Kbps, which is a far cry from the bandwidth offered by even a lowly 10Mb network adapter. If you need the increased bandwidth, it is possible to use routers that offer bandwidth up to 45Mbps. The primary issues you should be concerned with are the I/O bus performance of your server and the peripherals you choose, because they more noticeably affect your system's overall performance.

Choosing an I/O Bus

The next step after determining which processor platform you will use as your server is to determine the I/O bus architecture. As with processor platforms, several types of I/O buses are available; as summarized in Table 4.1, each has specific capabilities. The main thing to consider here is which bus will perform best for a particular function. For instance, how well will it perform for video, network, or small computer system interface (SCSI) adapters (these are the most common performance-oriented peripherals). These adapters must function at their peak. Adapters that are not performance intensive are items such as a sound card, a modem card, a parallel port, a mouse adapter, or even a joystick adapter.

Table 4.1. I/O expansion bus summary.

Type	Bus Width	Max. Bus Speed (MHz)	Max. Data Transfer Rate (MB/sec)
ISA (XT)	8	4.77	4.5
ISA (AT)	16	8.0	10
EISA	32	8.0	32
MCA	16	8.33–12.5	10–16
MCA	32	16	64
VLB	32	33–50	133–160
VLB	64	33	267
PCI	32	33	133
PCI	64	33	266
PCMCIA	16	N/A	2

> **TIP**
>
> Many Intel-based computers have an advanced BIOS setup option to increase the speed at which the I/O expansion bus operates. Increasing this bus speed above the default of 8MHz can increase performance. Most of today's peripherals are rated for a minimum of 12.5MHz, although some will operate at higher speeds.

> **WARNING**
>
> If you do increase the speed at which your I/O expansion bus operates, make sure you perform a reliability test before placing the unit in service, because not all adapters will operate reliably above 8MHz. Make sure when you perform this test that you check for full disk controller, network controller, video adapter, and communication port functionality.

There are several I/O bus types available on computers you have already purchased or that you will purchase in the near future. Each of these I/O buses has good points and bad points to consider. Choosing when and how to use them is where I can help. Consider the following as basic rules for the listed I/O bus:

- Industry Standard Architecture (ISA)—This is the original expansion bus that was introduced on the IBM (AT) personal computer. The original PC used an 8-bit I/O bus, which the AT computer extended to 16 bits, although the ISA standard includes both the 8- and 16-bit I/O buses. Most of today's peripherals are 16-bit peripherals and offer excellent value. If performance is not an issue, the ISA bus peripherals are the choice to make when purchasing. This bus should be used for your 8-bit expansion cards (filling up your 8-bit slots first) and your 16-bit expansion cards. It is a good choice for your sound cards, modem cards, and other peripherals, but try to avoid this expansion bus for your network, SCSI, and video cards unless you have no other option. It is an acceptable choice for secondary network and SCSI adapters.

> **NOTE**
>
> The ISA expansion bus is only able to directly access the first 16MB of system RAM. If you use a bus master controller (such as a SCSI disk controller), and if your system has more than 16MB of RAM, all disk access will have to be double buffered. *Double buffering* refers to data that must first be copied to a buffer within the adapter's addressable range (the first 16MB for a 16-bit adapter) and then copied to the application's data buffer. This copying of data from buffer to buffer will decrease overall performance. Although this is not a significant performance hit on most systems, on others it is very noticeable, depending on the system architecture.

- Enhanced Industry Standard Architecture (EISA)—This expansion bus is an extension to the ISA bus. It stretches the I/O bus to a full 32 bits and offers software configuration of peripherals through a configuration disk. An EISA expansion slot can also utilize ISA adapters because it utilizes a layered connection mechanism. An ISA adapter only fits halfway down this connection, thus enabling a connection to all the standard ISA expansion pins, while an EISA adapter fits all the way down and can reach the additional I/O and bus connectors. This bus is a good choice for network, video, and SCSI adapters. It performs well in most conditions and offers the ability to have several bus master adapters installed concurrently.

    A bus master adapter is one that has its own processor on it, and in most cases, one that has its own direct memory access (DMA) controller as well. The idea behind a bus master adapter is that it can use its own processor and DMA controller to pass data between the adapter and system memory, thus letting the processor on the motherboard continue to process data requests instead of spending time passing data between the system memory and the adapter. You can think of it as a poor man's multiprocessor platform.

> **TIP**
>
> Although many people talk about PCI and video local bus (VLB) as the buses to use on the desktop, they tend to forget about performance-oriented servers. These machines can make excellent use of the EISA bus to add additional network adapters, SCSI adapters (there are never enough SCSI channels), and even multiport communications boards, such as those from DigiBoard, to add functionality while maintaining performance. My recommendation for an I/O bus is to find a PCI/EISA bus combination, if you can. This will offer you the greatest level of performance and compatibility with a long-term growth potential.

- Microchannel Architecture (MCA)—IBM introduced this I/O bus as a replacement to the ISA expansion bus. It was designed for their new PS/2 line of computers. Although it offered increased performance compared to the ISA bus, it was completely incompatible with the ISA bus. This led to an increased cost of the adapters and a limited supply number of available peripherals for the consumer to purchase. This bus is a dead end and should be avoided for new purchases.
- Video Local Bus (VLB)—In order to increase performance of video adapters, a method was created to access an adapter by tying it directly to the system memory bus. This increased performance considerably, but limited it to supporting a maximum of three VLB adapters. The current implementation is a 32-bit-wide data bus with an extension to 64 bits on the way. This bus is an excellent choice for your primary video adapter, and in my limited testing, the same adapter in VLB and PCI

versions outperforms the PCI bus. Although it can be used for multiple purposes, such as a video adapter, disk controller, and network adapter, it is not the best choice for multiple adapters. Use it over an ISA bus for these purposes, but realize that you will not obtain optimum performance for simultaneous access. That is, in most cases, a video card as the only VLB adapter will perform better than if both a video card and disk controller are installed.

- Peripheral Component Interconnect (PCI)—This bus was designed to overcome the limitations of the ISA, EISA, MCA, and VLB expansion buses. It's designed to offer true plug-and-play functionality by automatically configuring the adapters (that is, no software-configuration program is needed), outperforming all other buses in data transfer rates, and offering more than three expansion slots. However, it has not lived up to the last item. Current implementations still limit you to three PCI expansion slots, which is why the PCI bus is usually paired with either the ISA, EISA, or even the VLB buses. It is an excellent choice for multiple adapters, such as your video card, SCSI (or Integrated Drive Electronics [IDE] disk controller) adapters, and network adapters. Keep in mind, though, that you will probably have only three PCI expansion slots, which can severely limit your performance options. If PCI is your choice as a primary I/O bus, try to find one that is paired with an EISA expansion bus. This gives you the ability to use the PCI bus for your video and two SCSI adapters while utilizing the EISA bus for network adapters. If you need to expand your disk subsystem again, you can always add SCSI adapters to the EISA expansion bus and still be able to maintain adequate performance, compared to a PCI SCSI adapter.

NOTE

Several new high-end servers from HP, Compaq, and other manufacturers have recently been making their way into the market and offer more than three PCI expansion slots. If your budget will support it, take a closer look at these types of servers to obtain the maximum possible performance.

- Personal Computer Memory Card Industry Association (PCMCIA)—This bus was originally designed to add memory components to hand-held and portable computers, but has since become an industry standard I/O bus. This bus is used to connect SCSI adapters, network adapters, video capture cards, miniature hard disk drives, and just about anything else, to portable computers. It is the first plug-and-play device to live up to the name under MS-DOS and Windows 95. Under Windows NT you will still need to choose an IRQ, I/O port, and possibly a memory address to configure the device driver. This is because Windows NT does not support the Card and Socket services that provide the plug-and-play functionality. Although this is not a high-performance I/O bus, it still performs relatively well.

> **TIP**
>
> If you need to demonstrate a Windows NT Server–based WWW server, such as with IIS, consider installing Windows NT Server on a portable computer. With today's hardware you can find Pentiums with disk drives in the 2.1GB range. Pentium-based portables (the low-end 75MHz models) give excellent runtime (2.5–3 hours), and the high-end 133MHz models, while offering limited runtime (1–1.5 hours), give excellent performance. I use my Toshiba T4600c portable and Windows NT for classes and demonstrations of the various BackOffice components. With the addition of supported PCMCIA network and SCSI adapters, it offers true plug-and-play capabilities. You can just plug your portable computer into your client's network and immediately be fully functional. Not only can you access their resources, but they can access yours as well. Combine this with a fully functional WWW site, and it makes an impressive demonstration. When you have finished your demonstration, you can pack it up and hit the road in minutes.

> **CAUTION**
>
> Avoid an architecture that has a mixture of more than two I/O buses (such as ISA, PCI, and VLB) for your server. Although these platforms offer the capability to use more types of peripherals on a single computer, these mixed bus types (VLB and PCI) do not perform as well. It is better to choose a platform with a dedicated ISA/PCI or ISA/VLB bus and use the faster bus for your video, disk, and network adapters.

Choosing a Disk Subsystem

The most important single component on your system, aside from the processor, is your disk subsystem. If your server cannot access the data fast enough to handle your client requests, it slows down the entire network as your clients wait to access data. On a dynamic WWW site, such as one produced with IIS and SQL Server, this poor performance means you will be notified sooner or later by your superiors, and it will rarely be a happy meeting. There are currently four types of disk subsystems on the market (see Table 4.2 for a summary), including the following:

- Antiquated Systems—If you have one of these in your server, you're in real trouble. Replace it immediately or suffer the consequences. Antiquated systems are based on the standard disk interface and are all part of the ST-506 family. They include Modified Frequency Modulation (MFM), Run Length Limited (RLL), Enhanced Run Length Limited (ERLL), and Enhanced Small Device Interface (ESDI). All these disk subsystems have since been replaced by more capable and less expensive versions. Computers using these types of disk subsystems should not be used as your primary WWW site. If you are connecting to the Internet on a full-time basis, they could be useful as domain name systems (DNS), WINS, or DHCP servers. The DNS, WINS, or DHCP services are not nearly as I/O intensive as a highly accessed WWW site, but they can still provide a useful service to your network by resolving NetBIOS names (such as the Microsoft Web site www.microsoft.com).

- Integrated Drive Electronics (IDE)—This drive interface is an outgrowth of the ST-506 interface and is designed to replace a dedicated (that is, smart) disk controller with a host (that is, dumb) adapter and a smart disk drive. In this particular scheme, the disk controller is just an interface between the host computer and the smart peripheral. You can add disk drives, tape drives, or even CD-ROM drives to a host adapter. The current limitation includes a maximum of four IDE peripherals in a single system. It accomplishes this by utilizing both the primary and secondary I/O addresses defined for ST-506 hard disk controllers (370-37F and 170-17F), and in some cases it actually provides separate interrupts for each I/O channel. The good news about IDE disk drives is that they are very inexpensive and can offer acceptable performance for a workstation computer. The bad news is that they are not fast enough for a server. The really bad news is that most IDE disk controllers are Programmed I/O (PIO) devices, which means that the host processor (on your motherboard) must transfer the data between the adapter and the system memory. This decreases the efficiency of your server and should be avoided if at all possible.

- Enhanced Integrated Drive Electronics (EIDE)—This is an extension of the current IDE standard and is designed to increase the data transfer rates. It does this by reading multiple sectors of the disk whenever a data access request is specified, as well as supporting various data transfer methods (from PIO to DMA). It also increases the maximum size of a disk drive from 512MB to 8GB, but you are still limited to a maximum of four IDE peripherals in a single system.

- Small Computer Systems Interface (SCSI)—This is my recommendation for a primary disk subsystem, although you can mix and match a SCSI system with any other subsystem mentioned earlier and use it as a secondary disk subsystem. SCSI is another expansion bus, not just a disk I/O bus like IDE. However, like IDE drives, the electronics for controlling the drive and accessing the data are located on the disk drive. You can add SCSI tape drives, SCSI scanners, SCSI printers, and any other SCSI devices to your SCSI host adapter. The standard SCSI interface offers a single disk channel, which can add up to 7 SCSI peripherals, while enhanced versions offer the capability to add up to 15 SCSI peripherals on two separate channels (7 on one channel and 8 on the other; the remaining SCSI ID on the first channel is used by the host adapter). Most SCSI adapters are also bus masters, which can increase performance quite a bit. Other factors include the capability to attach and detach the SCSI peripheral from the SCSI bus, so that another SCSI peripheral can access the bus while the first is processing a data request, queue multiple disk commands for later processing, and replace bad sectors with spare sectors on command.

> **NOTE**
>
> SCSI currently comes in several versions. There is the original SCSI I, which you should avoid when purchasing SCSI peripherals; SCSI II, which is the most used; SCSI III, which is on its way to becoming the new standard; FAST SCSI; and WIDE SCSI. FAST SCSI extends the data transfer rate from 10MB/sec to 20MB/sec, while WIDE SCSI extends the I/O interface from 8 bits to 16 bits. In some cases you can even find a combination of FAST WIDE SCSI (some call this ULTRA WIDE SCSI), which extends the data transfer rate from 40 to 60MB/sec. These types of SCSI adapters obtain their data transfer rates by combining multiple SCSI channels, where each channel can transfer data at 20MB/sec. To obtain the maximum transfer rate, you would need to place a SCSI drive on each channel and then stripe the disks to make a single large logical drive.

> **TIP**
>
> When adding a CD-ROM to Windows NT, always try to choose a SCSI II CD-ROM drive. These types of CD-ROM drives are the easiest to add to an NT system.

Table 4.2. Summary of disk subsystem characteristics.

Type	Data Transfer Rate (MB/sec)	Max. Number of Peripherals
MFM	2–4	2
RLL	2–4	2
ERRL	2–4	2
ESDI	20	2
IDE	3.3–8.3	2
EIDE	13.5–16.6	4
SCSI I	5	7
SCSI II	10	7
SCSI III	20	15
FAST SCSI	20	15
WIDE SCSI	20	15

Type	Data Transfer Rate (MB/sec)	Max. Number of Peripherals
FAST WIDE SCSI	40	15
ULTRA WIDE SCSI	60	30

Easy Performance Gains

Increasing the general performance of your Windows NT Server can be accomplished, for the most part, by applying some basic techniques. These techniques have to do with balancing the load of your disk subsystem to increase the I/O performance. You'll concentrate on using SCSI subsystems (because they provides the most benefit), but you could use other disk subsystems, such as IDE or EIDE, as well.

Let's look at this in a couple of steps. First there is the single disk subsystem, where there is only one disk controller with multiple disk drives. Second there is the multiple disk subsystem, where you have at least two disk controllers with one or more disk drives per controller. Finally, there is the ultimate disk subsystem where you have multiple disk subsystems with multiple disk drives per disk controller.

The Single Disk Subsystem

The single disk subsystem installation has limited performance-gain options. But that's not to say that there is nothing you can do; it just means that the options for increasing your server's performance are based on the number of physical disk drives you have installed on your system, and how much work you are willing to put in to obtain the maximum benefit. Let's begin with the minimum performance gain option, as it is also the easiest to perform.

This discussion starts with the assumption that you have one disk controller with two disk drives. Each disk drive is 500MB in size and can be an IDE, an EIDE, or a SCSI. Each drive has a single primary partition of 500MB. In this particular case, you have installed Windows NT Server to your C: drive in the WINNT directory (the installation default). This directory is called your SystemRoot. In fact, you have a special environment variable called SystemRoot that equates to the installation directory. For instance, in this example the SystemRoot environment variable is C:\WINNT. Because this drive is where all the system files and paging files are located, and where all the print jobs are spooled, it is a heavily used disk drive.

To help balance the load, you can do two things. First, install another paging file on the second disk (drive D:). This will provide Windows NT with the capability to use both paging files —the one on drive C: and the one on drive D:—when it needs to use virtual memory. If one disk is in use, the other disk can be used to access its paging file to fulfill the virtual memory request. Second, you can place all your BackOffice and support files on the second disk drive. You can even go so far as to split up your user sharepoints (or shared directories) between both drives so that the load is balanced equally. This will give you relatively good performance with minimum complexity.

> **NOTE**
>
> Windows NT Server makes heavy use of its paging file, and the most significant performance gain can be realized by placing your primary paging file on a striped set. The only alternative to paging to disk is to have enough physical memory installed on your system to avoid paging at all. If you have the funds available, a 256MB Windows NT Server can be an outstanding server. Adding processors can increase its capabilities even more as an application server. An application server is a server designed for the client/server environment (such as SQL Server) and not a file server that shares applications (such as Microsoft Office). An application server can make an ideal platform for dynamic WWW sites.

The alternate method of using two disk drives on a single disk controller to gain additional performance requires that you partition your hard disk drives into four equal sizes of 250MB each. You can do this before you install Windows NT Server, or you can partition it as part of the install process, which is the simplist method. If you have already installed Windows NT Server, you can back up your current NT Server installation and repartition, reformat, and reinstall NT and then restore your backed-up version, which is the toughest method. The idea here is to use two partitions (one on each physical disk) and create a striped set of 500MB. You could alternatively create four partitions with two partitions 150MB in size, and two partitions 350MB in size to create a 700MB striped set. A *striped set* is the creation of a single logical drive from two or more physical drives. The partitions on the separate physical drives are merged into a single drive by dividing the partitions into discrete blocks (512 bytes per block, usually). These blocks are then combined into a stripe. Multiple stripes are then combined to create the single logical drive. For more detailed information on striped sets and striped sets with parity, you may want to pick up a copy of my other book called *Microsoft Administrator's Survival Guide* by Sams Publishing.

> **NOTE**
>
> I would not recommend less than 150MB—and even that is cutting it close—for the system partition, because the free space available will dwindle as you install additional software. When this partition is filled, you will be required to back up, repartition, reformat, reinstall, and then restore your previous NT installation, which is a lengthy and tedious process, to say the least.

Of course, you cannot create the striped set until you have installed Windows NT, so your first task is to install NT to your first primary partition (drive C:). Once you have installed NT and created the second primary partition (drive D:), you may proceed to create the striped set (drive E:) with the Disk Administrator. Now you can follow a similar process, as mentioned earlier, to install your BackOffice software, and then create your paging files and user directories. In this case, however, you should create small paging files for your C: and D: drives (something in the 10MB to 30MB range) with your largest paging on your E: drive (possibly in the 100MB to 250MB range depending on your server load). Place the user directories on your D: drive and all other software on the E: drive (the striped set). This will give a moderate increase in system performance and an increased I/O capacity for your shared network files.

> **CAUTION**
>
> Because you are using a striped set without parity, there is no fault tolerance. Your only means of ensuring data integrity is your system backups. So be sure to schedule daily backups. And remember, in order to back up open data files (user files or SQL Server database devices), you must close them first. This can be accomplished by forcing all users off the system (do it gracefully by pausing the service, broadcasting a message to the users of your intentions, and then stopping the Server service) and shutting down SQL Server prior to running your backup.

The Multiple Disk Subsystem

This scenario builds on the previous performance optimizations by assuming that there are two disk controllers: one EIDE disk controller and single disk drive, which shipped with the computer; and an optional SCSI disk controller with at least two (preferably three to five) SCSI disk drives. In this case, let's install Windows NT Server to the EIDE drive (drive C:) and devote this drive completely to Windows NT and the BackOffice system files. The SCSI subsystem will be used to create a striped set, or if we have enough disk drives (at least three), a striped set with parity.

> **TIP**
>
> When creating a striped set or striped set with parity, the more drives you add, the better the performance you will achieve. This is because a striped set stripes the data to the disk drives in a sequential fashion. For instance, if you have three disk drives in a striped set, in theory you can read or write three times as much data. In actuality, the performance is not quite that scalable, but is still significant. A striped set with parity

> on a three-drive system will achieve only two reads/writes for the same logical drive because a complete stripe includes two data blocks with one ECC (error correction code) block. It is even more important for a striped set with parity to use more than three drives to obtain equal performance with a regular striped set.

Once the striped set (or striped set with parity) has been created (drive D:), you can install the BackOffice system files. These files should be installed on drive C: with all the data files (SQL Server devices, databases, and so on) installed to drive D: (the striped set). All the additional user data files and shared applications should also be installed to drive D: to take advantage of the increase in the I/O subsystem. This gives a significant increase in overall system performance and a noticeable improvement in I/O capacity for your shared network files and SQL Server databases.

The Ultimate Disk Subsystem

To obtain the ultimate in I/O performance without using a hardware RAID solution, you can use multiple disk controllers with multiple disk drives. In this example, let's assume there are three disk controllers: one EIDE disk controller with one disk drive (drive C:) and two SCSI disk controllers. One SCSI controller, SCSI 1, will have two disk drives (although more is better), while the other SCSI controller, SCSI 2, will have three or more disk drives. The single EIDE drive will once again become the SystemRoot partition, where Windows NT Server and all the BackOffice system files will be installed, along with a small system paging file.

The SCSI 1 disk controller and disk drives will be used to create a striped set, where the system paging file and alternatively the printer spool files will be installed as well. In this case, use of a striped set will increase system throughput without causing worry about data integrity because print jobs can be resubmitted should an error occur. If an error occurs on this striped set, the small paging file you created on the SystemRoot partition will be used to keep the system up and running.

All your user data files, shared applications, and SQL Server devices and databases will be installed on the striped set with parity, which you will create on the SCSI 2 disk controller. This will provide an additional level of fault tolerance for your data files and increased I/O performance. This will give you the best overall system performance and I/O capacity for your server.

> **TIP**
>
> If you use any of the earlier scenarios with multiple disk controllers in a multiprocessor platform, your performance will increase even more. This is because of the Windows NT symmetric processing model, where any processor can service interrupts and can thereby achieve an additional level of I/O concurrency over a uniprocessor platform.

> **TIP**
>
> In order to really get SQL Server to benefit from the increased I/O capabilities of your striped set with parity, you will need to make a few SQL Server configuration changes. Specifically, you will need to increase the `max async i/o` from its default of 32. The number will vary based on the number of disk drives and controllers you have available for the SQL Server installation.

Hardware Upgrades

The first rule in maximizing your Windows NT Server performance is to add system memory. The next rule to consider is a hardware RAID configuration to increase your I/O capacity. Then think about adding network adapters and load balancing your system. If your system is very CPU intensive (for example, running SQL Server, Systems Management Server, SNA Server, and Microsoft Mail on the same server), you may want to look at adding processors if your system is capable of being upgraded in this fashion. The following section looks at each of these options and explains some of the benefits each has to offer.

System Memory Upgrades

Memory upgrades can be divided into two types: secondary processor cache upgrades and main system memory upgrades. Your secondary (level 2) cache is used to hold a copy of main system memory that is frequently accessed, preread and hold sequential data requests from main memory, or buffer data writes to main memory. All these offer increased memory access times because cache memory operates in the 15-to-20 nanosecond range, while system memory operates in the 60 to 100 nanosecond range. Caches are used because the processor speed has exceeded the speed at which the main memory can be accessed. System memory is based on dynamic random access memory (DRAM) chips, which require a refresh cycle before they can be accessed again. This doubles or even triples, depending on the system architecture and wait cycles, the time between concurrent memory access rates. Secondary cache chips, on the other hand, are based on static random access memory (SRAM) chips, which do not require a refresh between concurrent data access cycles. My recommendation is to increase the size of your secondary processor cache based on the size of your system memory. Use a minimum of 256KB for a 16MB system, a 512KB cache for systems up to 64MB, and at least 1MB of cache for anything larger than 64MB, if possible. Not all systems have upgradable secondary caches.

> **TIP**
>
> Many Intel computers offer an advanced BIOS setup option to configure the secondary cache and main system memory refresh times and wait states. If you can, set your secondary cache to offer write-back functionality, which will buffer writes to system memory, because this will increase system performance. If data integrity is an issue, set your secondary cache settings to write-thru, which will pass all data writes directly to main memory and only cache memory read requests. If you decrease your refresh times and wait states, you may also increase system performance. Be careful about changing memory refresh rates and wait states, however, because not all memory chips are created equal and they may not be able to function reliably at faster speeds. If you start to see nonmaskable interrupts, which equate to an F002 blue screen error code under Windows NT, you have gone too far.

Upgrading your system memory offers three benefits. It cuts down the requests to page memory to disk, thereby increasing overall performance (memory access is in the nanosecond range, while disk access is in the millisecond range). The additional memory can be used by the Cache Manager to cache both local and network I/O requests, thereby increasing both local disk and remote disk data-access requests. Finally, you can increase the performance of your SQL Server by either pre-allocating a larger amount of system memory for SQL Server's use, creating the tempdb in RAM, or using both of these options. The tempdb is a temporary database used to process temporary tables created by SQL Server to help you answer a query or to sort your tables.

Windows NT can perform as well as, if not better than, most caching disk controllers with the addition of an equal amount of RAM. For instance, if you compare a caching controller with 16MB of RAM and Windows NT Server with an additional 16MB of RAM, you will find that the performance is about the same. This is because the caching controller is limited by the expansion bus to transfer the requested data, while the Cache Manager utilizes system memory and therefore accesses cached data based on the memory bus speed. If the caching controller only has 4MB of RAM, even the base installation of Windows NT (that is, 16MB of RAM and no caching disk controller) performs as well as, if not better than, the same system with a caching disk controller. Also consider that very few caching disk controllers are supported by Windows NT. These types of controllers require specific device-driver support in order to use the cache on the disk controller. Most device drivers for caching disk controllers just turn off the cache when used with Windows NT.

> **TIP**
>
> If you have an EISA-based computer, make sure the EISA memory setting, which is based on the EISA setup utility disk application, correctly identifies the amount of

physical memory you have installed in your system. If it does not, Windows NT will use the ISA setting (what the computer finds based on the BIOS setting), which may limit the amount of memory that Windows NT will use.

Hardware RAID Alternatives

If you have the budget when selecting a disk subsystem, nothing performs better than a hardware RAID system. A hardware RAID solution generally has an internal battery backed-up memory buffer, in case a power failure occurs during a disk write. This adds fault tolerance over a software-based RAID solution. It also has its own processor so that the overhead involved in calculating the ECC stripe is performed by the disk controller rather than by the host processor.

NOTE

Although there are several RAID levels currently in use with Windows NT Server, I'll discuss the use of a RAID 5 solution only, which includes RAID 0 (data striping), RAID 1 (disk mirroring), and RAID 5 (striping with parity). RAID levels 2, 3, and 4 are generally used by higher-end mainframes rather than with Windows NT. Each of these is just a slightly different variation of a striped set with parity.

Additional benefits of a hardware RAID solution include the capability to mirror these RAID drives either by using software with Windows NT or by striping multiple RAID drives because NT sees these RAID drives as a single logical drive. If you stripe a hardware RAID device, there is no need to use a stripe set with parity because this is already being performed on the hardware level. Another advantage of the hardware-based RAID solution is that most of them support hot swapping of a failed disk drive. *Hot swapping* is the capability to change a failed disk drive for a new working drive without powering off the entire computer system. After the drive is replaced, the RAID controller begins to rebuild the missing data stripes based on the available data stripes and ECC stripe in the background. Replacing a software-based RAID solution requires powering off the system to replace the drive. Then, once powered back up, you will need to use the Disk Administrator to regenerate the missing data.

TIP

When selecting your disk drives for a RAID solution, either hardware-or-software based, it is better to choose several small disk drives than a few large disk drives to build an equivalent logical drive. For example, suppose you want approximately a 5GB logical drive. You could select either six 1GB disk drives or three 2GB drives for a maximum logical drive of 4.8GB (RAID drives utilize one-fifth of the storage for the ECC stripe). Either solution gives the same logical drive size, but the unit based on the six 1GB drives generally outperforms the unit based on three 2GB drives.

Adding Network Adapters

Even if you have an optimized disk subsystem, multiple processors, and an abundance of physical RAM, your network server will not perform well if it has either a slow network adapter or too many network requests to handle. If you have only one network adapter installed on your server, it better be a 100MB FDDI or Fast Ethernet adapter if you want to get the data out to your network clients as quickly as possible. You may even want to use more than one for a couple reasons.

> **NOTE**
>
> Although I mentioned 100MB network adapters earlier, that does not mean you must use them to obtain increased performance. The same benefits can be achieved from techniques you'll learn about later for 10MB network adapters.

First, consider the network transports you will be using. If they are all bound to one network adapter, that adapter will be constantly changing modes to send out a broadcast name to find an associated resource when a network request is received. For example, assume you are looking for a NetWare-based SQL Server database that uses the IPX/SPX transport. In order to find this database, your server will probably send out name requests over the NetBEUI, TCP/IP, and IPX/SPX transport protocols (assuming that this is the default binding order you established) and all through the same adapter. After the SQL Server that contains the database has been found, all further requests will be routed just through the IPX/SPX protocol. The time it takes to switch modes and send out and process these name requests is wasted. This decreases the capability of your server to process additional requests over that same adapter, thereby decreasing overall network throughput.

What you can do to increase your network throughput is to change your default binding order to use the most-requested network transport. For example, let's assume you are using one adapter with multiple network transports (NetBEUI, TCP/IP, and IPX/SPX). Let's further assume that you have an integrated network with Windows NT Server, UNIX, LAN Manager, and Novell servers, along with Windows NT, Windows for Workgroups, and Novell clients. Approximately 75 percent of these clients use TCP/IP, 15 percent use IPX/SPX, and the remaining 10

Choosing a Platform for Windows NT Server

Chapter 4

percent using NetBEUI as their primary transport. In this case, you can achieve the best client support by changing the binding order for the Server service to TCP/IP, IPX/SPX, and then NetBEUI.

> **NOTE**
>
> The Server service is used by clients that access your server. This service provides the means to share your network resources. The Workstation service is used by your server to access other servers' shared resources (when the computer is a client, rather than a server).

You modify the binding order through the Control Panel Network applet, as shown in Figure 4.1. After you have selected the Bindings tab, the properties sheet shown in Figure 4.2 will be displayed. To change the binding order for the Server service, follow these steps:

FIGURE 4.1.
The Network dialog box.

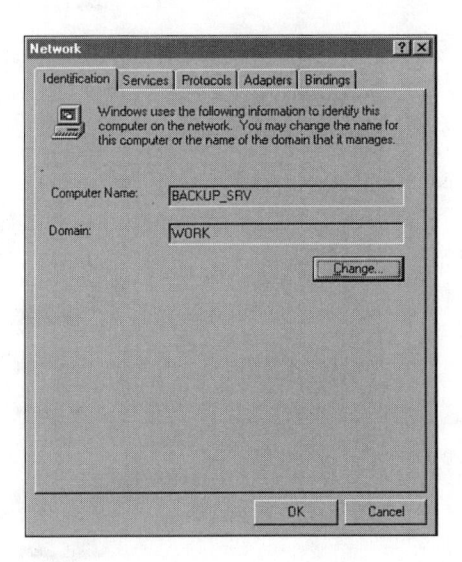

1. Expand the Server entry in the listbox. When you do, the network bindings for the service will be displayed. The properties sheet should look similar to what is displayed in Figure 4.3.
2. Notice that the uppermost binding is NWLink IPX/SPX Compatible Transport, because this is Microsoft's default binding order. At this point you want to select the WINS Client (TCP/IP) and then click on the upper arrow to move this protocol to the top, as shown in Figure 4.4. This will change the default binding order to TCP/IP, NWLink IPX/SPX Compatible Transport, NWLink NetBIOS, and then NetBEUI Protocol for the Server service.

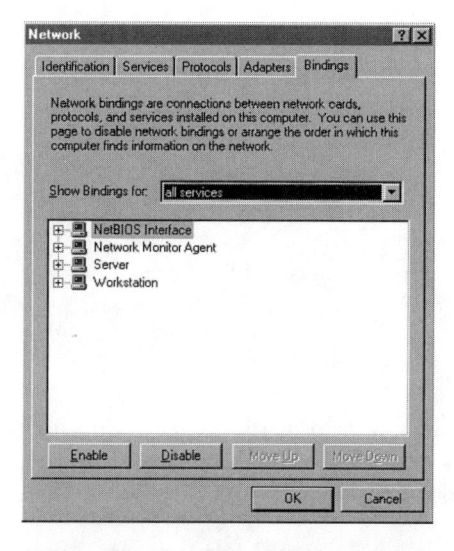

FIGURE 4.2.
The Bindings properties sheet.

FIGURE 4.3.
The Server service bindings for the Bindings properties sheet.

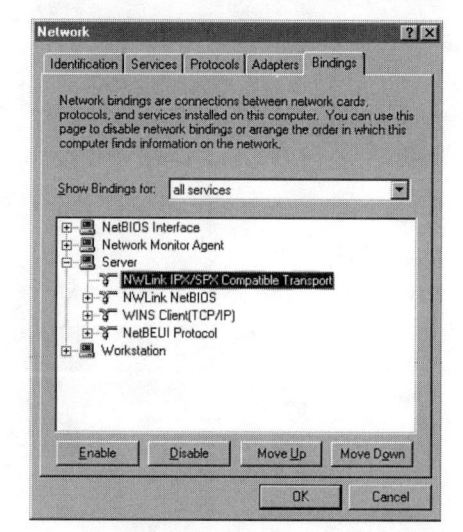

> **NOTE**
>
> If you are not using DHCP and WINS on your Windows NT Server, your binding listing may list TCP/IP instead of WINS Client (TCP/IP).

3. Repeat the earlier steps for the Workstation, NetBIOS Interface, and Remote Access Server service to change their binding order as well.

FIGURE 4.4.
The modified Server service bindings for the Bindings properties sheet.

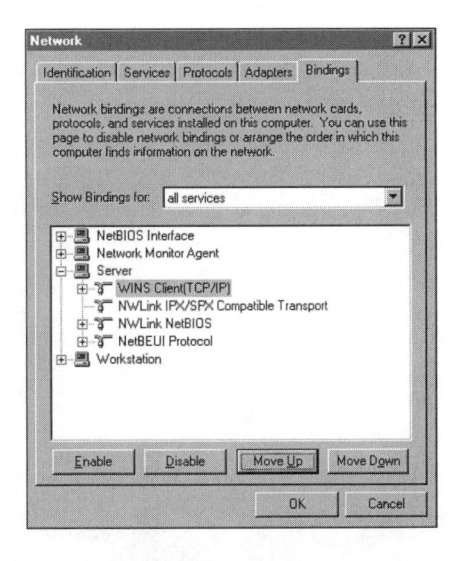

As an additional performance option, you can use multiple network adapters with each adapter being bound to a single network transport. You follow a procedure similar to the one outlined earlier, but instead of changing the binding order, you can just disable the bindings for the transports you do not want supported on the particular network adapter. Just follow these steps:

1. Select the appropriate protocol, then expand the item to display the binding for the protocol. In the example shown in Figure 4.5, I have selected the TCP/IP protocol.

FIGURE 4.5.
The WINS (TCP/IP) protocol bindings for the Bindings properties sheet.

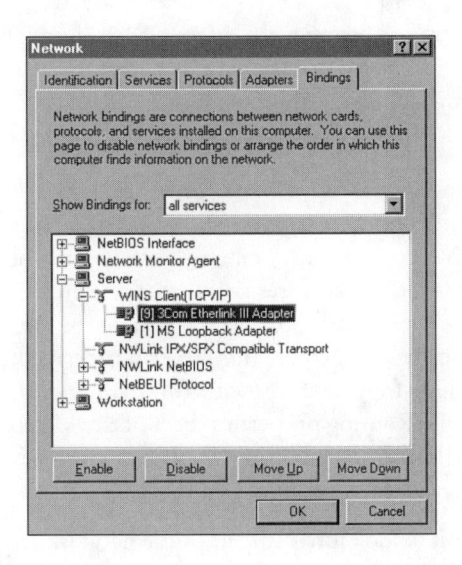

2. Select the network adapter for the appropriate transport protocol.

3. Click the Disable button. Figure 4.6 shows the disabled network transport protocol. Notice that next to the adapter is a little icon of a circle with a diagonal line through it indicating that the binding has been disabled.

FIGURE 4.6.

The disabled WINS (TCP/IP) protocol bindings for the Etherlink III network adapter in the Bindings properties sheet.

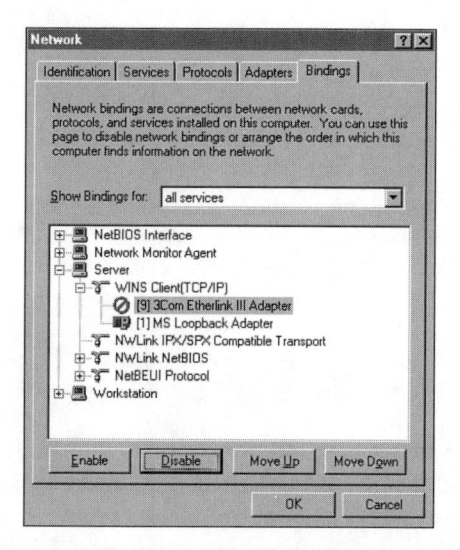

> **NOTE**
>
> In this example I have selected the Etherlink III adapter. Because this is my only physical network adapter, if I disable it I will only be able to share resources with the TCP/IP protocol for remote access clients. The Remote Access WAN Wrapper is a wrapper around a logical network adapter (that is, the modem).

If you want to increase network performance, you may want to use multiple network adapters to split your network into discrete components, commonly referred to as *segments*. This limits the impact that these network clients have on each other for accessing resources. Only if the network-client request requires access to a resource outside its default segment will it impact other network client users. However, if you do this on a TCP/IP-based network, each network adapter physically installed in your server must have its own IP address, and in order to route network requests from one segment to the other, you must check the Enable IP Forwarding check box in the Routing properties sheet of the Microsoft TCP/IP Properties dialog box. You access this dialog box by selecting TCP/IP Protocol in the Protocols tab of the Network dialog, then clicking the Routing tab of the TCP/IP Properties dialog.

Another reason to look into using multiple network adapters and modifying the network bindings is for security. Perhaps you want to use IIS to implement a WWW site, but you want to restrict access to your internal network. You could create a new subnet, which would contain all your servers that are physically connected to the Internet. Your servers (WWW, FTP,

Gopher, SQL Server, and so on) would be included on one side of a router and your network on the other. If your router filters all incoming traffic (from your subnet on the Internet), you can prevent a potential breach of security. If you are implementing IIS within your network instead of on another subnet, you can disable certain bindings (such as the NetBIOS Interface for the TCP/IP protocol) to limit access to your network from authorized clients. TCP/IP security issues are discussed in more detail in Chapter 10, "Advanced Security Issues."

Adding Processors

Windows NT Server is more processor intensive than other network operating systems, such as Novell NetWare or UNIX, on identical hardware platforms. So in most cases, adding a processor to a uniprocessor platform can make a significant difference in network throughput or an application server's performance (such as SQL Server). However, this performance increase is not quite twofold for a dual-processor system. As you increase the number of processors, this performance ratio decreases. As it stands now, four processors give the greatest multiprocessor benefit on standard Intel (Pentium) platforms. This is because most motherboard manufacturers use the Intel multiprocessor support chipset, which supports only four processors. Beyond that, it depends on the proprietary design of the system motherboard.

The problem with multiple processors is that the Windows NT design model requires all processors to have equal access to all system resources. That is what the symmetric multiprocessing model defines. The symmetric multiprocessing model means that the overhead involved in synchronizing access to hardware resources (such as an I/O port on a SCSI controller) increases as you add processors. Even problems with cache management will cause grief because each processor generally has its own secondary cache, and as a thread is moved from one processor to another, the cache must be flushed in order to ensure the integrity of system memory. All these little problems begin to build, until adding processors no longer increases performance or, at best, increases it a small fraction.

> **TIP**
>
> One of the interesting keys I've found in the registry is the key that specifies how many processors will be supported on a particular multiprocessor Hardware Abstraction Layer (HAL). If you look in
>
> `HKEY_LOCAL_MACHINE\SYSTEM\CurrentControlSet\Control\SessionManager`
>
> you will find the value *RegisteredProcessors*. This entry normally has a maximum setting of four processors for Windows NT Server or two for Windows NT Workstation. However, you can increase this value to support additional processors if your HAL can support them, and thereby increase performance on some platforms. The performance increase is based on the architecture of the particular platform. Some platforms will perform better than others, even if they have the same number of processors.

Choosing the Right Server Model

When you install Windows NT Server, you are given a choice between a domain controller or a server, but not both. In this case, a server means that Windows NT is operating in *server mode*, and therefore does not participate in *domain authentication*. This means that the server does not include a copy of the domain account database; instead it must refer all authentication requests to a domain controller. A domain controller can be either a primary or a backup. Only one primary domain controller (PDC), which contains the master copy of the domain account database, is available, but you may have multiple backup domain controllers (BDCs). The master copy of the domain database is periodically replicated from the PDC to each BDC. A PDC or BDC will use resources (processor, memory, storage, network) to update the account database or to respond to client authentication requests. Because server mode does not provide these services, the resources can be devoted to other tasks (such as the WWW Publishing Service) to improve performance.

The idea is to allocate as many resources as possible to improve IIS performance by choosing server mode. Other aspects of this choice may not have been previously considered. A server loses all domainwide administration tools (such as User Manager for Domains, Server Manager, and so on), but keeps the rest of NT Server's capabilities (such as fault-tolerant partitions, no user connection limit, and so on). This offers two important security considerations:

- The tools to manage your network, like User Manager for Domains, are not physically available on the server.
- No physical copy of the domain database is available on the server. A local account database is the only one available.

Both of these aspects can aid you in preventing unauthorized access to your server or network from users that connect to your server over the Internet. This should be a real concern because by connecting to the Internet, you are in essence connecting your network to probably the largest WAN in the world. There is no telling what is out there that might do you harm, but by taking some precautions you can limit the potential intrusions.

The Software Configuration

You can tune specific components in Windows NT Server in a couple ways, such as by using the provided Control Panel interfaces and the registry. A few of the Control Panel interfaces and what they will do for you are mentioned here, but the registry topics are in Appendix C, "Registry Editor and the Registry Keys." This is where the registry editor and the major keys of interest are described. For now, let's start with the Control Panel applets. The System Properties dialog includes the Performance properties sheet, as shown in Figure 4.7, which has two interfaces for modifying your system and directly affecting your performance.

The first option is the Application slider, as shown in Figure 4.7. This slider is used to set the runtime percentage of all applications running on your system. The default is to use Maximum setting, but this is a poor choice for a server. This setting steals processor cycles from your background processes (such as your Server service) to provide the best performance for the application you are currently using. This makes the application you are using perform well, but all other processes suffer. It is, however, an excellent choice for Windows NT Workstation because the goal is to provide optimum user interaction. I recommend that you use the middle setting if you plan to use this server interactively (maybe to create user accounts, add computer accounts, or other administrative duties). This will provide adequate response time, but steal fewer processor cycles from the background applications. For IIS optimum performance, you should set this to the None setting, which gives every process the same priority and distributes the processor time equally among them. This generally makes the server a very poor interactive partner because applications take a while to refresh the screen, and any network activity can bring your interactive usage to a crawl. However, this is not a major problem because you can perform all administrative duties from your desktop if you install the client-based administrative tools.

FIGURE 4.7.

The Control Panel System Properties dialog box Performance properties sheet.

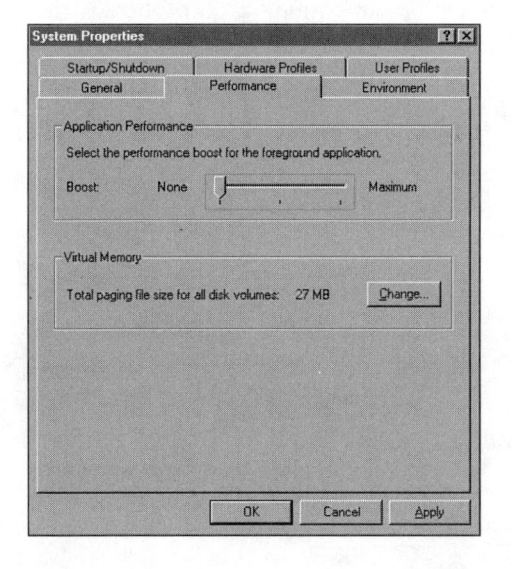

The second option is the Virtual Memory Change button, which will display the Virtual Memory dialog, as shown in Figure 4.8. In this dialog, you can create your paging files on a per-drive basis. You can also set the minimum and maximum sizes for your paging files. At a minimum, your paging files should total your physical memory plus 12MB, and your maximum should be approximately four times your physical memory size for optimum performance, although you can increase this value if needed (particularly if you do a lot of work with the computer interactively).

FIGURE 4.8.
The Virtual Memory dialog box.

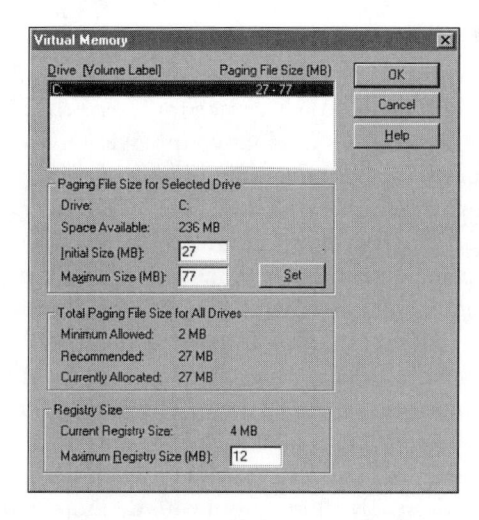

Changing the Server service properties in the Control Panel Network applet is the other commonly missed performance modification. The way to display this dialog is fairly simple, but it is hidden from casual modification. To get to it, run the Network applet, select the Service tab, and scroll down the Network Services list until the Server entry is visible. Then just double-click it, and the dialog box shown in Figure 4.9 is displayed.

FIGURE 4.9.
The Server dialog box.

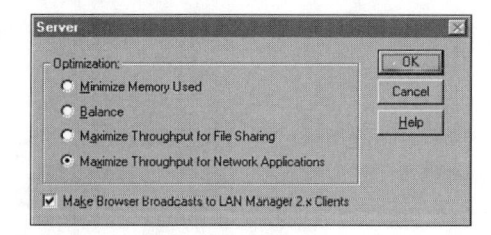

The Server dialog box has four optimization settings:

- Minimize Memory Used—This setting is best for servers with 10 or fewer clients connected to them, which is a very small network. In most cases, you can just use Windows NT Workstation as your server.
- Balance—This setting pre-allocates enough buffers for a maximum of 64 simultaneous network client connections. This is the default setting for networks that only support NetBEUI as their transport protocol.
- Maximize Throughput for File Sharing —This setting is best used for any network with more than 64 simultaneous network client connections. Not only does it pre-allocate buffers, but it also provides the capability to allocate additional buffers on an as-needed basis. It is the best setting to maximize your network clients' ability to share network resources such as directories, files, and printers.

- Maximize Throughput for Network Applications —This setting is also suggested for large networks with more than 64 simultaneous clients. However, this case has a trade-off. Rather than maximizing performance for resource sharing, as mentioned earlier, the performance optimization is for RPC buffers, which will increase the performance of an application server (like SQL Server and the Internet Information Server).

> **TIP**
>
> If you have installed multiple network providers, such as the Gateway Service for NetWare, you may also want to step through the Network Provider Search Order dialog accessed via the Networks button, shown in Figure 4.1, so that you can change the default search order to place the network you use most frequently at the top.

Summary

This chapter looks at some of the basic performance tuning issues and trade-offs. Tuning your server consists of several options. One of these options is to pick the right hardware platform and expansion bus to maximize performance of your peripherals. Another option is to optimize your disk subsystem to provide the maximum benefit for virtual memory usage and file sharing. Choosing the right server model to build a better application server, and configuring your application tasking options and the Server service to optimize processor timeslicing (the time each process can use before the next process will be scheduled for execution) and server response time are two other options. You can also upgrade your hardware by increasing the amount of physical memory or adding a hardware-based RAID solution, and balance the load of your network subsystem by adding additional network adapters, or increase processing performance by adding additional processors. The next chapter looks at some of the specific issues involved in preparing your Windows NT Server platform for a successful IIS installation.

IIS Preparation and Installation

IN THIS CHAPTER

- Determining Where to Install the Internet Information Server **104**
- IIS Preinstallation Requirments **106**
- The Remote Access Service **120**
- Installing the Internet Information Server **129**

Few Windows NT components can stand alone. They generally rely on one or more subcomponents to function properly. The Internet Information Server (IIS) is no different. It, too, requires additional components in order to function properly. Although it is possible to install IIS blindly (that is, without consideration of the consequences), you may wind up with a product that does not perform to your expectations or that has a security breach. In either case, the consequences could be quite severe. A competitor could gain access to proprietary data through your Internet connection, in which case you could lose your job.

> **WARNING**
>
> Internet security is a topic of such importance that an entire chapter is devoted to it. Before you install the IIS, I suggest you read Chapter 10, "Advanced Security Issues," to see what you can do about security issues that may affect you.

While Internet security is not the main focus of this chapter, performance considerations certainly are. The performance of IIS is affected by where you install IIS and the associated data you plan to publish with it. This chapter begins with where to install IIS. Once you have determined this, you will learn about the preinstallation requirements. Depending on where you plan to install IIS and how you plan to use it, this can be a pretty hefty list. This chapter walks you through the mechanics of installing various components and describes why you may want to use them. After you determine this, you can install the IIS and be publishing data for all your customers to see, hear, and interact with on the Internet.

Determining Where to Install the Internet Information Server

When planning your installation, you should first consider where to install the IIS and its related components. Do you have a limited budget? Or do you have sufficient funds to carefully plan your installation to obtain maximum performance? Will you place all your data on a single server? Will you use an external database for dynamic publishing? Will you connect to your server to update the data using your local area network (LAN)? Or will you use a dial-up connection? You need to consider all these items because they will make a difference as to how and where you will install IIS.

IIS on a Limited Budget

If you are on a limited budget, you may not have many choices. You'll probably have to install everything on a single server. Most publishers with a limited budget have a low-speed Internet connection that includes single ISDN BRI (Integrated Services Digital Network Basic Rate Interface) or modem connections. If this is the case, you should consider publishing only static data. If your server is fast enough (a 75MHz or higher Pentium), you may want to consider using an Access database if you plan to provide dynamic publishing capabilities.

With this configuration, you could use the Windows NT Server *Remote Access Service* (RAS) to provide your dial-up Internet connection. You could also use RAS for dial-in clients, and you could create a publishing site without ever connecting to the Internet. You do not have to connect to the Internet to publish data. You only need an Internet connection if you want to reach millions of Internet users. If you are providing local support, however, a non-Internet publishing service may be just what you need. You may be providing local technical support, for example, to your customers. These users could dial up your server for information, software upgrades, or whatever else and use familiar Internet tools (like the Internet Explorer) to access these services. In most cases, this would be less expensive and easier to maintain than a dedicated bulletin board system (BBS). As your client list grows, you could migrate to the Internet. This would certainly be easier than converting a proprietary BBS and all your data.

If you go this route, you should consider using Windows NT Server, operating in server mode, instead of a domain controller. This provides more efficient use of local resources without the overhead of a domain controller. I would recommend a domain controller instead of a server only if you also need to migrate a user account list (for your dial-in clients, for example) because anytime you upgrade a server to a domain controller, you will lose your account database. It's better to take the performance hit now than it is to have to re-enter each user account, password, and home directory, and reconfigure any file or directory permissions later.

IIS on an Unlimited Budget

An unlimited budget is unrealistic. However, it is quite possible that your budget is sufficient to build a high-performance publishing site. This can include using frame relay, T1, T2, T3, SMDS (Switched Multimegabit Data Service), or ATM (Asynchronous Transfer Mode) as your pipeline to the Internet. Your Internet connection is the main consideration in creating a high-performance publishing site because it doesn't matter how fast your servers are if they cannot quickly pump your data over your Internet connection. If this is the case, the budget for your hardware should be proportionally higher as well. In most cases, your yearly Internet connection fees will far outweigh your hardware purchases.

You should plan on having multiple Windows NT Server installations. You can use one or more domain controllers with one or more installations operating in server mode (which are referred to as servers for the rest of this chapter). These servers should be used as your IIS and SQL Server platforms because they provide the best all-around performance. All your installations should be connected to each other via a 100Mbps network segment for optimum network throughput and the fastest possible publishing site.

Choosing a Location for Your Data

You should carefully consider where you will place the data you plan to publish with one or more servers. You have two choices: You can place the data all on one drive or you can split it among multiple drives. If you can, use multiple drives. For best performance, consider using a striped set or striped set with parity. Both of these will increase your drive's ability to access your data, which in turn will decrease your clients' access times. If you have sufficient funds, consider a hardware RAID alternative, because this will increase your throughput even more.

You should also consider dividing your data based on the service and potential number of clients. If you will be providing a World Wide Web (WWW) and File Transfer Protocol (FTP) site that hundreds or thousands of users will access and a Gopher site that fewer than a hundred clients will access, devote your resources appropriately. Put your WWW and FTP data on your fastest drive and your Gopher data on your slowest drive. Your drives should also be NTFS (New Technology File System) rather than FAT (File Allocation Table) partitions because NTFS provides less wasted space due to large cluster size, faster access times, and increased security.

IIS Preinstallation Requirements

Because the IIS is based on providing Internet-related services, which in turn relies on the TCP/IP protocol as the network transport, you should first install the TCP/IP protocol, which will also install the utilities (such as arp, finger, hostname, ipconfig, nbtstat, netstat, ping, rcp, rexec, route, rsh, telnet, tftp, and tracert). You should *not* install the FTP service, however, because this will conflict with the IIS FTP Publishing service.

If you will be using the IIS as the basis for providing full-time Internet connectivity to your network clients, you may want to install a few additional services. Specifically, you want to include the following:

- Dynamic Host Configuration Protocol (DHCP)—This service provides dynamic IP address allocations to your network clients rather than statically configuring each client IP address. This can make life much easier for the network administrator. The network clients can be members of your LAN or even dial-up clients.

- Windows Internet Name Service (WINS)—This provides NetBIOS name resolutions. Rather than locate a computer service by its IP address, you can locate it by the computer name. The WINS service provides this option by maintaining a database of computer names to IP addresses.

- Domain Name Service (DNS)—This service also provides NetBIOS name resolution. Rather than being dynamic, like WINS, it utilizes a static list of computer names to IP addresses. The list is maintained in various configuration files, and it requires some additional work. You may ask why you should bother. The reasons are simple. First, you may need to have one or more DNS servers to fulfill your requirement with the InterNIC to maintain your own domain name. Second, e-mail name resolution is only supported via the use of an MX record type, which is not supported by WINS. If you plan on providing e-mail services (with Microsoft Exchange Server, for example) for your network clients, you must use DNS, and each client must have an MX record. Finally, DNS can be used with WINS to provide dynamic name resolution so that your clients that do not support WINS, which includes many non-Microsoft operating systems, can use DNS instead.

- Simple Network Management Protocol (SNMP)—If you have an SNMP-compatible monitor, such as Hewlett-Packard (HP) OpenView, you can use SNMP to monitor and configure, in many cases, your SNMP-capable hardware and software. This includes items such as hubs, routers, and most Windows NT services.

- Remote Access Service (RAS)—This service provides dial-out and dial-in connectivity services. You can use RAS to create a simple gateway to the Internet. In this configuration, you have one server connected to the Internet on your network, where each network client can access the Internet by routing their requests though the server. A more robust gateway can be created by using RIP for Internet Protocol.

- RIP for Internet Protocol—This service can create a software router. Although not as efficient as a hardware router, RIP is included free with NT Server. You can use RIP to combine multiple network segments into a single logical segment. It dynamically creates routing tables and is preferred over the static routing tables that must be created with the route utility.

NOTE

Even with the RIP for Internet Protocol installed, you must have Internet-routable IP addresses in order to use Windows NT Server as a gateway to the Internet. You cannot assign a random block of IP addresses for your LAN clients to use and expect it to work. Most likely these addresses are already in use on the Internet, which means you will have an IP address conflict and the connection attempt will fail. In order to obtain routable IP addresses, you must request these addresses from either your Internet Service Provider (ISP) or the InterNIC.

- Simple TCP/IP Service—This service provides support for TCP/IP clients that support the TCP/IP services Character Generator, Daytime, Discard, Echo, and Quote of the Day.
- Microsoft TCP/IP Printing—This service provides printing capabilities to UNIX-based print queues or from UNIX-based clients. When this service is installed, you can use Print Manager to connect to a UNIX-based print queue or to share a printer (in essence, this is the line printer daemon [lpd] service for Windows NT) and have a UNIX-based client connect to the shared printer. It will also install the line printer remote (lpr) and line printer queue (lpq) utilities, which print to a host running the lpd or check the status of a print job on an lpd server.

> **NOTE**
>
> In order to install the above services, you must be a member of the administrator's group on the computer on which you want to install the service.

Installing the TCP/IP Protocol and Utilities

If you did not install all the TCP/IP utilities during your initial Windows NT Server installation, you can add them through the Control Panel Network applet. Follow these steps:

1. Click the Protocols tab in the Network dialog box, shown in Figure 5.1.

FIGURE 5.1.
Installing a network protocol.

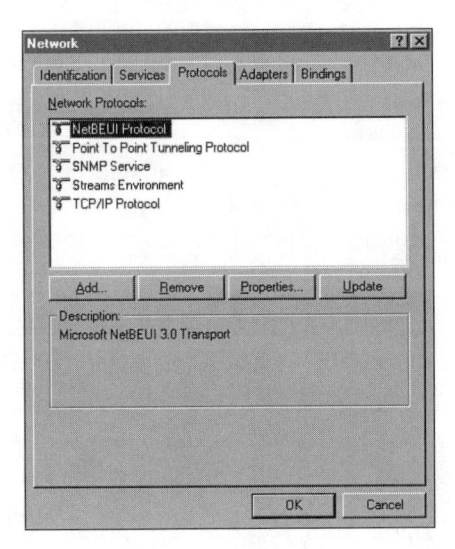

IIS Preparation and Installation
Chapter 5

2. Click the Add button to display the Select Network Protocol dialog box, shown in Figure 5.2.

FIGURE 5.2.
Installing the TCP/IP Protocol.

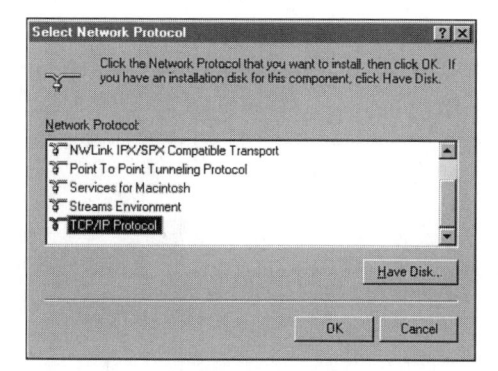

3. In the Network Protocol: field, select the TCP/IP Protocol and click the OK button. You will be prompted in the TCP/IP Setup dialog to use DHCP to allocate your IP address. If you have a DHCP server accessible by this computer, choose the Yes button; otherwise, choose the No button. This discussion assumes that no DHCP server is available.

> **NOTE**
>
> Your computer cannot be both a DHCP server and a DHCP client; it must be one or the other. If the computer is a DHCP server, you must manually configure the TCP/IP protocol, as described in step 6.

4. You will be prompted in the Windows NT Setup dialog box for the location of your Windows NT source files. Enter the drive and directory, and choose the Continue button.

5. At this point, the source files for the TCP/IP protocol and utilities will be copied to your computer. After the files have been copied, you may click the Close button in the Network dialog box if you have no additional services to install. Otherwise, choose the Services tab and install the additional services, as described in the following sections. This will display the Bindings Review and Configuration dialog box, which will perform an analysis of your network bindings.

6. The Microsoft TCP/IP Properties dialog box, shown in Figure 5.3, will be displayed so that you may specify your IP address, subnet mask, and default gateway. If you have more than one adapter, such as a multihomed system, enter steps 1 through 5 for

Building Your Foundation for the Internet Information Server

Part II

each adapter. If you want to assign multiple IP addresses to your adapter or you have multiple gateways, click the Advanced button to display the Advanced IP Addressing dialog where you can enter the earlier information.

FIGURE 5.3.
Specifying your IP address.

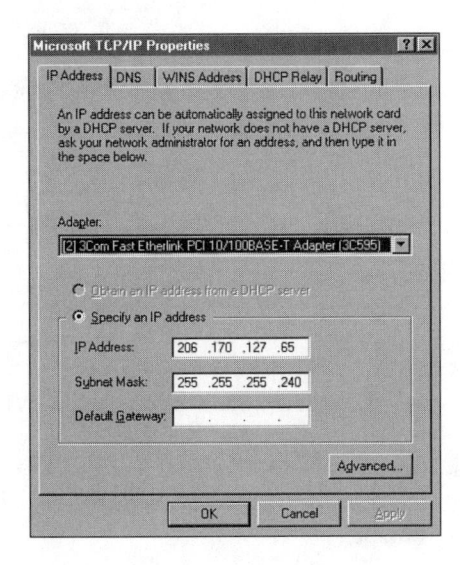

7. Choose the DNS tab, shown in Figure 5.4, and enter your hostname (the name of your computer), your Internet domain name, and the IP addresses of your DNS servers. If you have multiple Internet domains, enter your domain suffix search order.

FIGURE 5.4.
Specifying the TCP/IP DNS configuration.

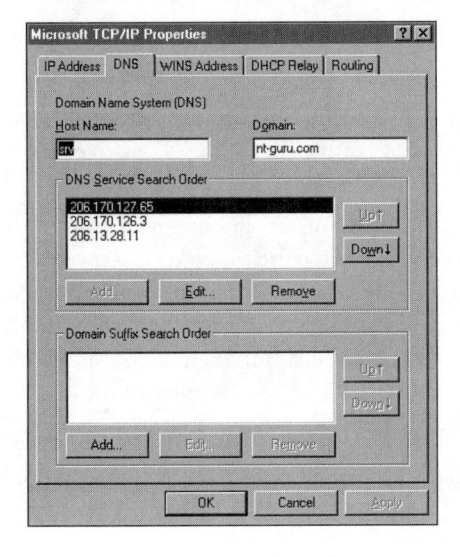

8. Choose the WINS Address tab, shown in Figure 5.5, where you may enter the following information:

   Primary WINS Server—This should be the IP address of the WINS server closest to you.

   Secondary WINS Server—This should be the IP address of an alternate WINS server. If you do not have more than one WINS server, enter the same IP address as your primary WINS server.

   Enable DNS for Windows Resolution—This option utilizes a DNS server in addition to a WINS server to provide name resolution.

FIGURE 5.5.
Specifying the TCP/IP WINS configuration.

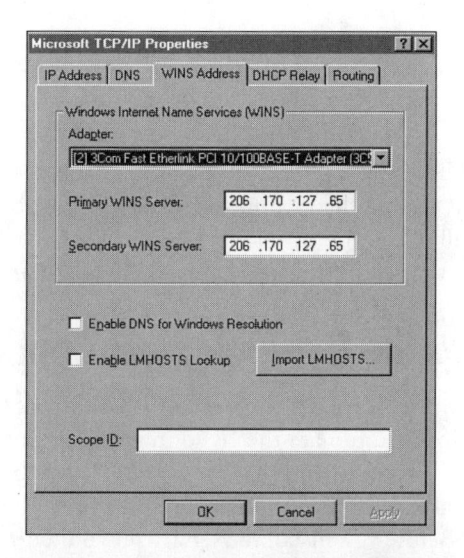

> **CAUTION**
>
> If you will be installing a DNS server on the same computer, you should not enable the Enable DNS for Windows Resolution check box.

Enable LMHOSTS Lookup—This option is useful if you do not have a DNS server or a WINS server available to provide name resolution. Instead, you may edit the LMHOSTS file located in the `SystemRoot\System32\Config\Etc` directory to provide a static computer name to IP address mapping. If you have an LMHOST file already configured, say on a network server, you can choose the Import LMHOSTS button to import the file to your computer.

Scope ID—This option provides a mechanism to register a unique NetBIOS name. Multiple computers that use a common scope ID will register broadcast traffic rather than ignore it. If you are unsure as to whether you need to configure your computer with a common scope ID, consult with your network administrator or Internet service provider.

9. If you have network clients on the other side of a router, with no corresponding DHCP server, that use either DHCP to allocate IP addresses or BOOTTP for diskless workstations, choose the DHCP Relay tab. In this tab, you may specify the IP addresses of your DHCP server, the number of seconds to wait before a retransmission, and the number of router hops to transmit the DHCP and BOOTTP requests over.

10. To enable forwarding of IP packets on your network, choose the Routing tab and click the Enable IP Forwarding check box. If you install the RIP for Internet Protocol, as described later in this chapter, the routes will be dynamically created. If not, you must create static routes using the route utility.

11. Finally, choose the OK button. You will then be prompted to restart your system. If you will not be adding any protocols or services, choose the Yes button. Otherwise, choose the No button and continue to add your protocols or services.

Installing the Dynamic Host Configuration Protocol

The DHCP Server service is also installed through the Control Panel Network applet. You can use this service to automate the IP address allocations to your local and remote network clients. I generally recommend that the DHCP Server be installed for even very small networks, because it makes administration easier and provides a means for expansion without a lot of grunt work. Before you install the service on your current server, however, check for the existence of other DHCP servers on the network. These could include other Windows NT Servers, a UNIX server, or possibly even a server provided by your Internet service provider. You want to avoid, at all costs, any conflicts with an existing scope. Creating and managing scopes is covered in Chapter 9, "Using DHCP, WINS, and DNS." To install the DHCP Server service, follow these steps:

1. Launch the Control Panel Network applet to display the Network dialog box and click the Services tab to display the Services page, shown in Figure 5.6.

IIS Preparation and Installation
Chapter 5

FIGURE 5.6.
Installing a network service.

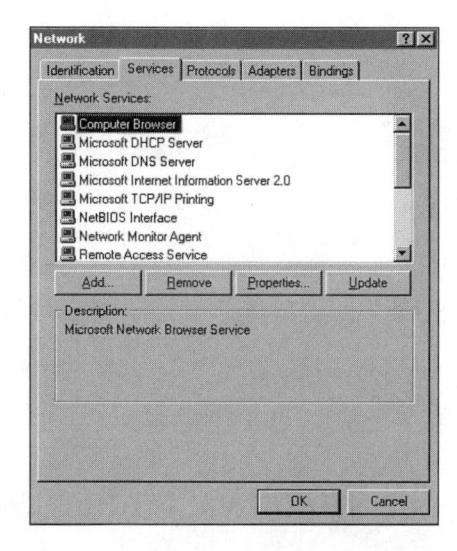

2. Next, click the Add button to display the Select Network Service dialog, shown in Figure 5.7.

FIGURE 5.7.
Installing the DHCP Server service.

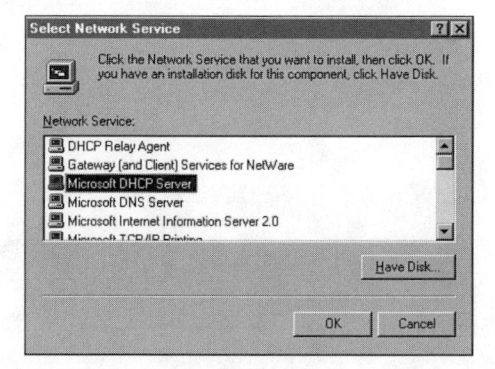

3. Select the Microsoft DHCP Server and click the OK button.

> **TIP**
>
> If you want to use SNMP to configure the DHCP Server service remotely, be sure to install the SNMP service as described in the section "Installing the Simple Network Management Protocol."

4. When prompted, enter the path to the distribution files and click the Continue button to copy the DHCP Server files to your computer.

5. Choose the Close button if you will not be installing any additional services, or repeat steps 2 through 4 for each additional service.

> **TIP**
>
> It is a good idea to install the additional service (such as WINS, DNS, RIP, SNMP, and Remote Access Service) at this point because it will save you some time. However, this is not required because you can install the services one at a time, as the following sections describe.

6. When prompted, restart your system to activate the DHCP Server service. If the service fails to activate, check your system event log for any error messages.

Installing the Windows Internet Name Service

Installing the WINS Server is quite similar to installing the DHCP Server service. While you can use the DHCP Server service and WINS separately, they function much better when used together. Managing your WINS is covered in Chapter 9. To install the WINS, just follow these steps:

1. Launch the Control Panel Network applet to display the Network dialog box and click the Services tab to display the Services page, shown in Figure 5.6.
2. Click the Add button to display the Select Network Service dialog box, shown in Figure 5.7.
3. Select the Windows Internet Name Service and click the OK button.

> **TIP**
>
> If you want to use SNMP to configure the WINS remotely, be sure to install the SNMP service as described in the section "Installing the Simple Network Management Protocol."

4. When prompted, enter the path to the distribution files and click the Continue button to copy the WINS files to your computer.
5. Choose the Close button if you will not be installing any additional services, or repeat steps 2 through 4 for each additional service.
6. When prompted, restart your system to activate the WINS. If the service fails to activate, check your system event log for any error messages.

Installing the RIP for Internet Protocol Service

If you are not familiar with TCP/IP routing, it is a good idea to install the RIP for Internet Protocol service even if you are not sure you will need it. This is because RIP can be used to build dynamic routing tables. This is preferred over building static routes with the route application because it lessens the administrative burden. To install RIP, follow these steps:

1. Launch the Control Panel Network applet to display the Network dialog box and click the Services tab to display the Services page, shown in Figure 5.6.
2. Click the Add button to display the Select Network Service dialog box, shown in Figure 5.7.
3. Select the RIP for Internet Protocol and click the OK button.
4. When prompted, enter the path to the distribution files and click the Continue button to copy the RIP for Internet Protocol files to your computer.

> **NOTE**
>
> Although you might expect the RIP for Internet Protocol to be installed in the Protocols page like the WINS service, it will be installed in the Services page. Don't let the name confuse you; RIP really is a service.

5. Choose the Close button if you will not be installing any additional services, or repeat steps 2 through 4 for each additional service.
6. When prompted, restart your system to activate the RIP for Internet Protocol service. If the system fails to activate, check your system event log for any error messages.

Installing the Domain Name Server Service

The DNS service is based on the UNIX BIND service. It provides a means to map computer names to IP addresses or IP addresses to computer names, much like the WINS service. The primary difference between WINS and DNS is that DNS uses a static mapping mechanism based on host files. Even if you plan on using WINS, you should install the DNS service because it can provide additional functionality when connecting to the Internet. Managing your DNS service is covered in Chapter 9. To install the DNS service, follow these steps:

1. Launch the Control Panel Network applet to display the Network dialog box and click the Services tab to display the Services page, shown in Figure 5.6.
2. Click the Add button to display the Select Network Service dialog box, shown in Figure 5.7.

3. Select the Microsoft DNS Server and click the OK button.
4. When prompted, enter the path to the distribution files and click the Continue button to copy the DNS Server files to your computer.
5. Choose the Close button if you will not be installing any additional services, or repeat steps 2 through 4 for each additional service.
6. When prompted, do not restart your system.
7. At this point, you should modify your host files, located in the SystemRoot\System32 \DNS subdirectory, as described in Chapter 9. After this has been accomplished, you may restart your system. After the system restarts, the DNS service should be activated. Even if the service is running, you should check the system event log for any error messages produced by the DNS service. Sometimes this is the only indication that you have incorrectly configured a record in one of your host files.

Installing the Simple Network Management Protocol

The SNMP service installation is similar to the installation of other services described in the preceding sections. You may not need to install this service, however, if you do not have an SNMP monitoring and configuration tool. This service only provides a means to monitor or configure your Windows NT services remotely from an SNMP console, such as HP OvenView or a similar product. Although the resource kit provides a simple command-line SNMP console, you will probably find it easier to use the Administration tools provided with Windows NT Server for remote administration. But just in case you really need the SNMP service, you can install it by following these steps:

1. Launch the Control Panel Network applet to display the Network dialog box and click the Services tab to display the Services page, shown in Figure 5.6.
2. Click the Add button to display the Select Network Service dialog box, shown in Figure 5.7.
3. Select the SNMP Service and click the OK button.
4. When prompted, enter the path to the distribution files and click the Continue button to copy the SNMP Service files to your computer.
5. Next, you should be prompted to configure the SNMP Service, shown in Figure 5.8, in the Microsoft SNMP Properties dialog box. Enter the name of the person to contact in case of problems in the Contact: field. You can use the Location: field to specify where the problem has occurred (in building A, for example) or a phone (or beeper) number for the person to contact (which you entered in the Contact: field). The Service field specifies the types of problems to monitor. You should ask your SNMP manager about these, because not every manager will want to see traps for each of these items.

FIGURE 5.8.
Configuring the SNMP contact and service properties.

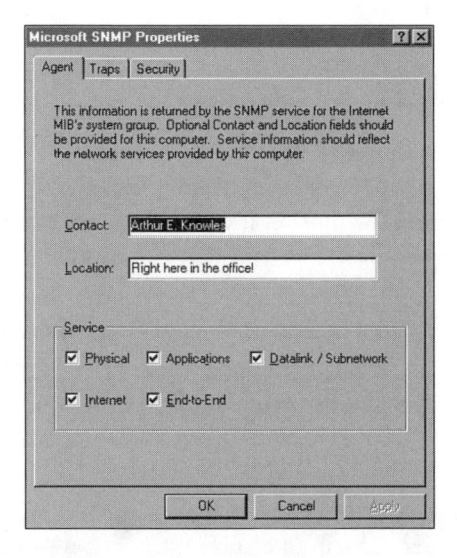

6. Before your SNMP Service will serve any useful purpose, you must configure where to send the information. The Traps page, shown in Figure 5.9, accomplishes this. You may specify the type of SNMP items you are concerned with, as well as their destination. If you are unsure of the type of SNMP information, just type `public` in the Community Name: field and click the Add button. When you do, the button will then be grayed out; however, the Add button under the Trap Destinations: field will be enabled. At this point, click the Add button and enter the IP or IPX addresses of the computer with the SNMP monitoring console.

FIGURE 5.9.
Configuring the SNMP traps properties.

7. If you want to limit the SNMP traps you will submit or receive, do so by choosing the Security tab. You should discuss this with your SNMP console manager to determine his requirements.
8. When you have finished configuring the SNMP service, choose the OK button to close the Microsoft SNMP Properties dialog.
9. Choose the Close button if you will not be installing any additional services to close the Network dialog, or repeat steps 2 through 4 for each additional service.
10. When prompted, restart your system. After the system restarts, the SNMP service should be activated. If not, check your system event log for any error messages.

Installing the Simple TCP/IP Service

Installing the Simple TCP/IP service is very straightforward. Just follow these steps:

1. Launch the Control Panel Network applet to display the Network dialog box, and click the Services tab to display the Services page, shown in Figure 5.6.
2. Click the Add button to display the Select Network Service dialog box, shown in Figure 5.7.
3. Select the Simple TCP/IP Services, and click the OK button.
4. When prompted, enter the path to the distribution files and click the Continue button to copy the DHCP Server files to your computer.
5. Choose the Close button if you will not be installing any additional services or repeat steps 2 through 4 for each additional service.
6. If you actually plan to use these services, and I hope you do since you have installed them, you will need to configure the Quotes file, which is located in the SystemRoot\Drivers\Etc subdirectory.
7. At this point, you may restart your system. After the system restarts, the Simple TCP/IP service should be activated. If not, check your system event log for any error messages.

Installing the Microsoft TCP/IP Printing Service

Installing the Microsoft TCP/IP Printing service is also straightforward and requires little user intervention. Just follow these steps:

1. Launch the Control Panel Network applet to display the Network dialog box and click the Services tab to display the Services page, shown in Figure 5.6.
2. Click the Add button to display the Select Network Service dialog box, shown in Figure 5.7.
3. Select Microsoft TCP/IP Printing and click the OK button.

IIS Preparation and Installation
Chapter 5

4. When prompted, enter the path to the distribution files and click the Continue button to copy the DHCP Server files to your computer.

5. When prompted, do not restart your system. Instead, launch the Control Panel Services applet, shown in Figure 5.10, and select the TCP/IP Print Server.

FIGURE 5.10.
Configuring the TCP/IP Print Server service.

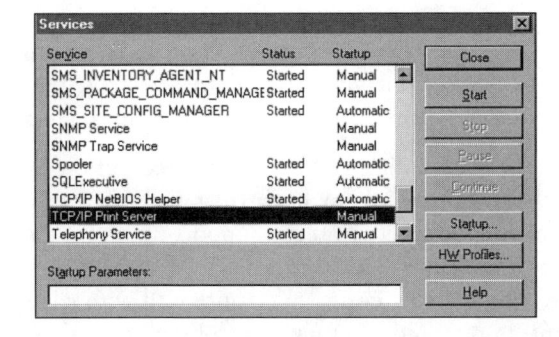

6. Next, click the Startup button to display the Service dialog, shown in Figure 5.11, to configure the Startup Type from Manual to Automatic. This will then start the TCP/IP Print Server service when the server starts instead of requiring you to manually start the service each time you power up the server.

FIGURE 5.11.
Configuring the TCP/IP Print Server service startup values.

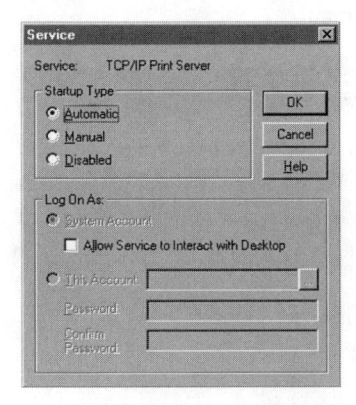

7. Choose the OK button to close the Service dialog. After this has been accomplished, you may click the Close button to exit the Services dialog.

8. Now all your services should be installed and configured, so you may restart your system. After the system restarts, the TCP/IP Print Server service should be activated. If not, check your system event log for any error messages.

The Remote Access Service

The Remote Access Service is a powerful tool that you can use to support your dial-in clients and provide complete network access to your network. You can also use the Remote Access Service to create a wide area network (WAN) or use it as an Internet gateway, if desired. Before you can use the software, you must install it. After installing the software, you have to grant access to your remote clients with the Remote Access Administrator. Otherwise, these clients will be able to connect, but will then be denied access to the network and forcibly disconnected. The Remote Access Administrator is also useful for managing your remote access clients.

One of the most interesting and powerful aspects of the Windows NT Server Remote Access Service is that it can utilize any of the installed network transports (NetBEUI, IPX/SPX, or TCP/IP) for your connection. It can support up to 256 simultaneous client connections on a single server. This can provide the means to create a serious communications server to support your entire sales force. It even works quite well with client/server applications because these applications do not send great amounts of data over the wire. If you were trying to provide application sharing over the wire, although it is possible, I would not recommend it. The Remote Access Service should be used to provide limited connectivity; that is, you should only share data files, not applications. Rather than share Microsoft Word for Windows, for example, you should install the application directly on the remote user's computer where it will execute quickly. However, the data files the user accesses may be on the server. This still provides adequate user performance.

> **NOTE**
>
> The Windows NT Workstation and Windows 95 Remote Access Service can support the NetBEUI, IPX/SPX, and TCP/IP protocols. MS-DOS and Windows 3.*x* Remote Access Service client software are limited to the NetBEUI protocol. If you want to use the IPX/SPX or TCP/IP transports, you will need additional third-party software, such as an Internet SLIP or PPP application, to provide your client with a TCP/IP connection to your Windows NT Server.

Installing the Remote Access Service

Installing the Remote Access Service is a multipart process if you want to get the most out of it, because Microsoft has configured the default settings to provide more reliable data communications on slower UARTs (Universal Asynchronous Receiver Transmitters), which is the hardware that is used for your serial port. To obtain a minimum connection of 38.4Kbps, you must have a 16450 or better UART. In reality, a 16450 will sometimes drop data, so a 19.2Kbps connection is a better selection. You will need a 16550 UART, which contains a 16-byte First In First Out (FIFO) buffer to obtain a speed of 57.6Kbps, and a proprietary UART from DigiBoard, Hayes, or another manufacturer to obtain a 115.2Kbps connection rate.

IIS Preparation and Installation
Chapter 5

Obtaining these higher data rates requires that you set the Maximum Speed field for the modem using the Control Panel Modems applet. I will point out the modifications that are needed at the appropriate time during our installation discussion. Before you install the Remote Access Service, you should install your multiport, X.25, or ISDN adapter. After the hardware has been added to the system, you will need to install the adapter device driver. This is accomplished by following these steps:

1. Launch the Control Panel Network applet to display the Network dialog box and click the Adapters tab to display the Adapters page, shown in Figure 5.12.

FIGURE 5.12.
Adding a network adapter.

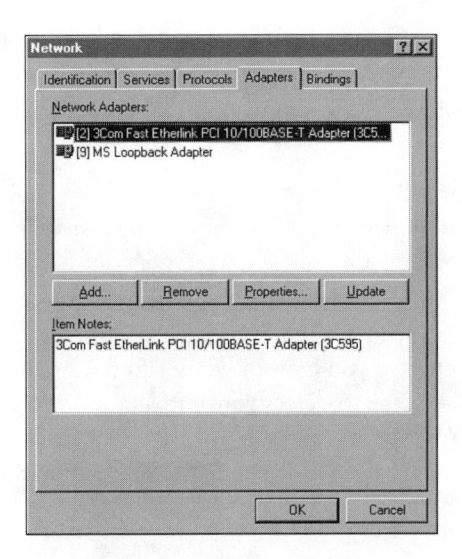

2. Click the Add button to display the Select Network Adapter dialog box, shown in Figure 5.13.

FIGURE 5.13.
Adding an adapter for use by the Remote Access Service.

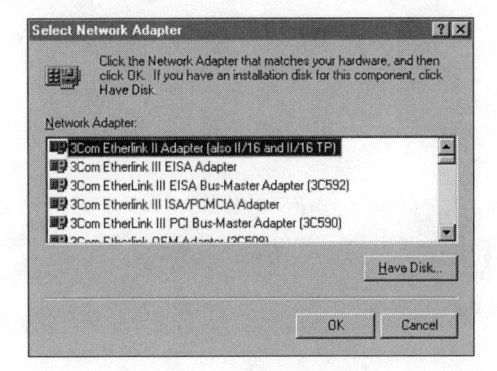

3. Scroll down through the list to find your adapter. If it is not listed, choose the Have Disk button and insert the OEM disk in your drive A:. Then choose the correct adapter from the list.
4. After installing the device driver and configuring it (if required), press the OK button. When prompted to restart your computer, select the Restart Now button and restart the server.

After the server has been restarted, you may install the Remote Access Service software. Use the Control Panel Network applet to perform this. Just follow these steps:

1. Launch the Control Panel Network applet to display the Network dialog box and click the Services tab to display the Services page, shown in Figure 5.6.
2. Click the Add button to display the Select Network Service dialog box, shown in Figure 5.7.
3. Select Remote Access Service and click the OK button.
4. When prompted, enter the path to the distribution files and click the Continue button to copy the Remote Access Service files to your computer.
5. The Install New Modem dialog box will appear (see Figure 5.14) and will attempt to automatically detect your modem. You should allow this if you do not know what type of modem you have or cannot find it listed in the Hardware Compatibility List. It will take time to detect your modem.

FIGURE 5.14.

The Install New Modem wizard.

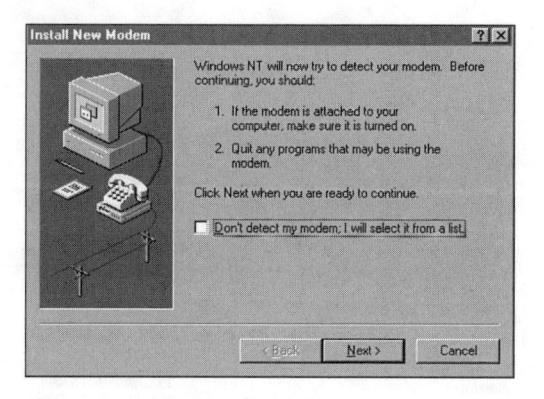

To manually select your modem, enable the Don't detect my modem: I will select it from a list check box, which will quickly bring you to another version of the Install New Modem dialog box (see Figure 5.15) where you may select the manufacturer, and then the specific modem, to install.

IIS Preparation and Installation
Chapter 5

FIGURE 5.15.
Installing a modem for use by the Remote Access Service.

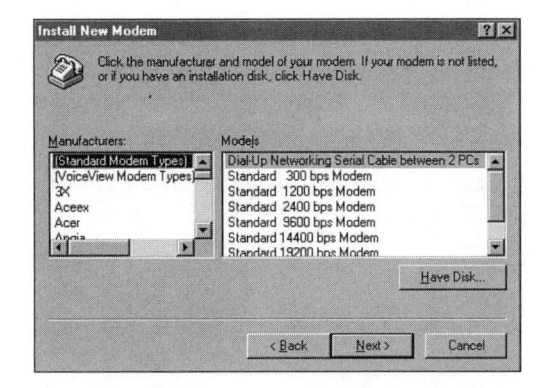

6. After selecting your modem, click the Next button and select the port to which the modem is attached. Then click the Next button, and the My Locations dialog will be displayed. (See Figure 5.16.)

FIGURE 5.16.
Specifying the location properties for use by the Remote Access Service.

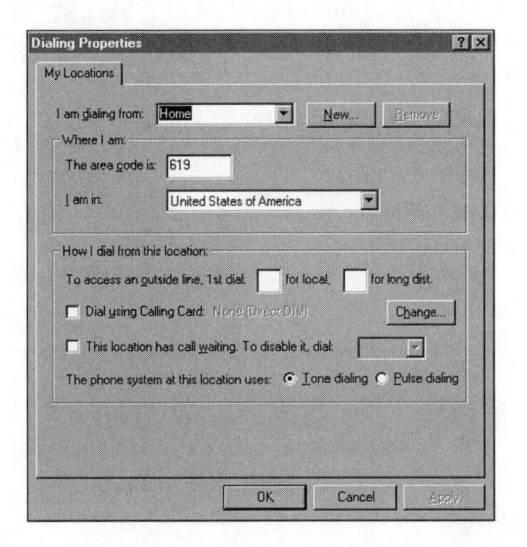

7. Choose your country from the I am in: drop-down listbox.
8. Enter the area code for the phone number you will use in the The area code is: field.
9. If your phone system requires that you dial a prefix (like 9) to access an outside line, enter that number in the To access an outside line, 1st dial: field.

10. Choose the appropriate phone-dialing type (Tone dialing or Pulse dialing radio button) in the The phone system at this location uses: field.
11. Click the Next button; you will be informed that your modem has been set up. Click the Finish button, and the Add RAS device dialog box will be displayed.
12. Select the modem you just installed in the RAS Capable Devices drop-down listbox. Then click the OK button to return to the Remote Access Setup dialog box.
13. Click the Configure button to display the Configure Port Usage dialog box. This dialog box offers you the capability to select how your RAS connection will be used. You can choose to support only dial in (Receive calls only), dial out (Dial out only), or both (Receive calls and Dial out).
14. After configuring your modem, click the OK button to return to the Remote Access Setup dialog box. Then click the Network button to display the Network Configuration dialog box. (See Figure 5.17.)

FIGURE 5.17.
Specifying the remote access service network configuration properties.

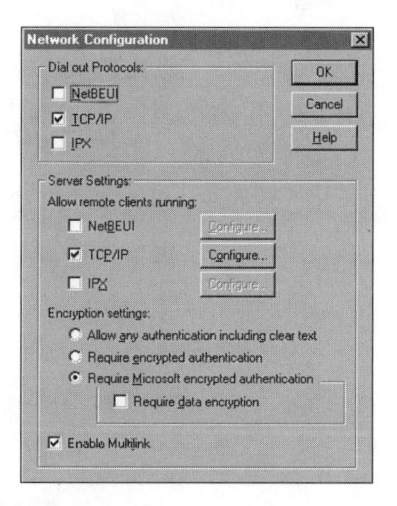

15. This dialog box will let you choose which protocols to support based on the protocols you have installed. You can choose to enable any (NetBEUI, IPX/SPX, or TCP/IP) protocol or only a single protocol for your dial-out and dial-in connections.
16. For each dial in (Server Settings field), you can choose to allow client access to your entire network or only to the server they connect to. You may additionally set a static range of IP addresses for your TCP/IP clients to use or use DHCP to assign IP addresses. I prefer to use DHCP to assign IP addresses. You can also specify a range of IP addresses that your dial-in clients cannot use. For your IPX/SPX clients, you can choose to allocate individual network numbers for each client or assign each IPX client the same network number. If you are integrating your Windows NT Server with a Novell NetWare network and will be providing access to it from your remote

connections, you should allocate network numbers. Just pick a number that is not currently in use, and enter this in the From: field. The To: field will be automatically entered based on the number of remote access ports you have installed. For both your TCP/IP and IPX/SPX connections, you may allow your dial-in clients to allocate a predetermined IP address or network address.

> **TIP**
>
> You may also set encryption settings for your dial-in clients in this dialog. The default is to require Microsoft encrypted authentication. This setting may prevent Point-to-Point Protocol (PPP) and Serial Line Internet Protocol (SLIP) connections from being authenticated if you are not using the Microsoft remote access client. To prevent this from happening, enable the Allow any authentication including clear text option. This option will still attempt to encrypt the password, but if all else fails, it will support a clear text password attempt. If you are really concerned about the security of your data when it is sent over the remote access connection, you may enable the Require data encryption setting, which will encrypt all data transmitted over the connection.

> **TIP**
>
> If you will be using more than one PPP connection to the Internet, check the Enable Multilink option, which will merge your separate datastreams into a single datastream and can increase throughput. If you will be using two 28.8Kbps modems, for example, and you connect each one to your Internet service provider—who also has to support multilink PPP connections—RAS will merge these two 28.8Kbps datastreams into a single 57.6Kbps datastream. This can double your network throughput.

17. After pressing the OK button, you will return to the Remote Access Setup dialog box. If you have additional ports to add, the quick and easy way is to press the Clone button. This will copy your current configuration to the next available port. Repeat this step for each port you want to install. If you have a different modem on a port, just select it and press the Configure button. You may then pick out the correct modem for it. If you choose another modem to properly configure it, remember to change the modem settings.

18. When all your modems have been installed and configured, click the OK button in the Remote Access Setup dialog box. Then click the Close button to exit the Network dialog box. You will be prompted to restart your computer. At this point, select the Restart Now button.

19. When the system restarts, be sure to check the system event log to look for any possible errors.

Configuring the Remote Access Service

After you have restarted your computer, you can then use the Control Panel Modems applet to configure your modem properties. These properties include the maximum speed at which your computer will transfer or receive data from the modem, whether to use the modem's built-in error correction and hardware compression, and the modem flow control type. These properties will be used by the Remote Access Service for dial-in clients. To dial-up an external RAS server you can use the Dial-Up Networking application, located in the Accessories program group on the taskbar, to connect to other Remote Access Service servers.

The first time you run the Dial-Up Networking application you will be prompted to create a phone book entry. In the New Phonebook Entry dialog box, enter a name for your connection in the Entry Name: field, a phone number to dial in the Phone Number: field, and a comment for the entry in the Description: field. If you have more than one modem, select it in the Dial using drop-down listbox. To use the Telephony service to configure your phone call (such as when an area code or number to access an outside line is used) properties, check the Use Telephony dialing properties.

You can also specify properties for the dial-up server you will connect to in the Server tab. You can specify the type and network protocols (and configure them as well), and enable software compression. If you want to automate your logon sequence, you can do it from the Script tab. You can specify your user authentication type (such as whether you want to encrypt your password or data) in the Security tab. Should you be using an X.25 connection, you can specify the network provider, address, and a few optional properties.

The Remote Access Administrator

The Remote Access Admin application is located in the Administrative Tools program group on your taskbar. You will use this application to grant access to your dial-in users, check the status of the communications port, send messages to your remotely connected users, and stop or start the Remote Access Service on your computer or a remote computer.

Preparing for Client Connectivity

Before your dial-in clients can access your network through the Remote Access Service, grant these users permission to connect through a dial-in connection. Choose Users|Permissions, and the Remote Access Permissions dialog will be displayed. For each user you want to provide dial-in access, follow these steps:

1. Select the user name in the Users: field.
2. Enable the Grant dial-in permission to user check box.

> **TIP**
>
> To quickly grant permission to all users to dial in to your network, click the Grant All button. To delete all user permissions, click the Remove All button.

3. Specify a callback option of No Call Back, Set By Caller, or Preset To. This option is used to provide one of two features. It can be used to enhance your system security by using the Preset to: field to always call a user back at a specific phone number, or it can be used to lower the bill of a remote user (such as a member of your sales department who travels a lot) by using the Set By Caller option. The user can then specify the phone number to call back so the client he is with will not have to pay the fees for the long-distance call. If you specify Preset To, be sure to enter a complete phone number, including any dial-out codes, calling-card codes, and so on.
4. Click the OK button, and you're done. Your remote access callers may now dial in to your network.

> **TIP**
>
> You can set these options using User Manager for Domains. Just select the user account; then click the Dial-in button to display the Dial-in Information dialog box where you can set these values for the user account.

Monitoring Remote Access Connections

To determine who is using your remote access connections, just double-click the server entry or choose Server|Communications Ports, which will display the Communications port dialog. If you have any connected users, the User: field will list the connected user, and the Started: field will list the time the user connected to your server. If you have an active connection, the following buttons will be enabled:

- Disconnect User—This button disconnects the selected user.
- Send Message—This button sends a message to the selected user.

> **NOTE**
>
> To send a message to a Windows 3.*x* or Windows 95 client, the windows messaging utility (`winpopup.exe`) must be running on the client computer.

- Send to All—This button sends a message to all connected users. It is extremely useful when you are about to bring down the server or restart the Remote Access Service because you can warn your connected users beforehand.

If you want to determine the compression ratios or errors that have occurred on the selected port, click the Port Status button.

Using Remote Access as a Gateway to the Internet

In order to use the Remote Access Service to connect to the Internet, you will need either a PPP or SLIP account from an Internet service provider. When you have obtained an account, simply create a phonebook entry with the Dial-Up Networking client. Then follow these steps:

1. In the Edit Phonebook Entry dialog box, click the Server tab to display the Server properties.
2. Choose the PPP:Windows NT, Windows 95 Plus, Internet selection in the Dial-Up server type drop-down listbox if you will be using a PPP connection to connect to the Internet service provider. If you will be using a SLIP account, choose SLIP Internet.
3. Disable the NetBEUI and IPX protocols in the Network Protocol group.
4. If you have a preassigned IP address or DNS IP address from your Internet provider, click the TCP/IP Settings button to enter this information.

> **NOTE**
>
> If you have a choice as to the type of connection your ISP provides, always choose a PPP connection. This connection type is more robust and offers additional functionality.

5. Click the OK button to return to the Edit Phonebook Entry dialog box.
6. Click OK to return to the Dial-Up Networking application main window.
7. Click the Dial button. The first time you dial your connection a dialog box will be displayed where you can specify the user name and password. Leave the domain name: field empty unless your ISP requires a specific domain name. To save the password so you do not have to enter this information the next time you want to use this connection, check the Save password check box.

After you have completed these steps, you can dial the connection by selecting it in the Phonebook entry drop-down listbox anytime in the future and clicking the Dial button to connect to the Internet. If you will be using your RAS connection as a gateway to the Internet so that your LAN clients can access the Internet through this same server, you have a bit more work to do. Specifically, you need to add the following values to the following keys in the registry:

Key:

HKEY_LOCAL_MACHINE\System\CurrentControlSet\Services\RasArp\Parameters

Value:

DisableOtherSrcPackets

Key:

HKEY_LOCAL_MACHINE\System\CurrentControlSet\Services\RasMan\PPP\IPCP

Value:

PriorityBasedOnSubNetwork

Both of these values are regular double words (REG_DWORD). DisableOtherSrcPackets should be set to 0, and PriorityBasedOnSubNetwork should be set to 1. The first entry specifies that network packets should use the IP address of the LAN client. This will ensure that the data is routed to the proper client. The second entry specifies that the network packets should be sent to the appropriate destination and adapter based on the individual subnet. This is usually required, for example, when your LAN has a subnet like 206.170.127.x and your RAS connection (or your ISP's subnet) is 206.170.126.x. If the PriorityBasedOnSubNetwork is not set to 1 (the default is assumed to be 0), all network traffic would be routed through your network adapter. When you set this value, however, your LAN traffic will be passed over your network adapter, and your Internet traffic will be passed over your RAS connection.

> **NOTE**
>
> There is one other critical part to this process that must be completed before your clients can use your server as a gateway to the Internet. Your ISP must create a routing table, and your server and client IP address must be added to their DNS servers (or your DNS server could be a client of their DNS server and replicate the information). If you experience problems transmitting or receiving data over the Internet and your ISP has performed the required steps, look at your routing table using the ROUTE PRINT command. You may need to modify this information (and your ISP should be able to help you through this step) in order to successfully use your computer as a gateway.

Installing the Internet Information Server

After all the work that you had to perform in the preceding sections to prepare for your Internet Information Server installation, you will be happy to know that installing IIS is going to be a piece of cake. To install IIS, just follow these simple steps:

1. On your desktop you will see a shortcut called Install the Internet Information Server. Just double-click this shortcut.
2. You will be greeted with the Microsoft Internet Information Server 2.0 Setup dialog box. Just click the OK button to continue.
3. Next, the dialog box shown in Figure 5.18 will be displayed. To specify a different installation directory from the default of SystemRoot\System32\INETSRV, click the Change Directory button. This will display the Select Directory dialog where you may specify a different location for your IIS installation.

> **NOTE**
>
> You should choose a different location for the Internet Information Server root directory, as I have done here. Your best choice is to choose an NTFS-formatted partition on a physically separate drive. This will cause less competition for the disk (the SystemRoot disk is heavily used) and enhance the performance of your IIS installation.

FIGURE 5.18.
Choosing the Internet Information Server installation options.

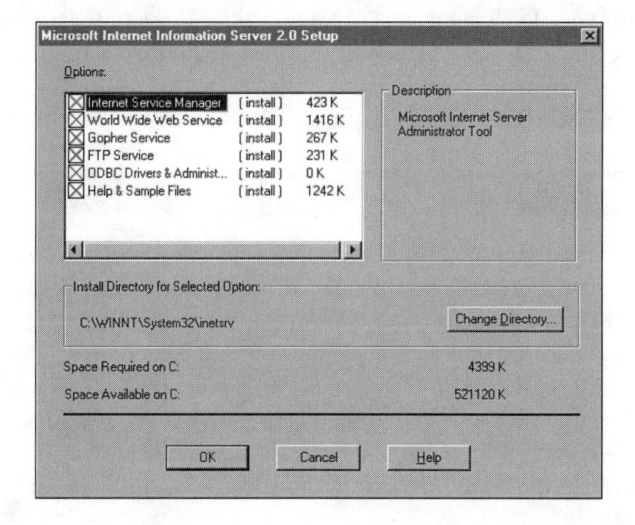

4. If you do not want to install all the IIS services, administration tools, help files and documentation, ODBC drivers, or the Internet Explorer, you may uncheck the specific items in the Options: field. I recommend, however, that you install all the options for now. When you no longer need them, you can easily execute the IIS setup program to remove specific components. You can also use this application to install components that you may have removed or not installed.

IIS Preparation and Installation
Chapter 5

5. When all your choices have been selected, click the OK button to proceed with the installation. If your installation directory does not exist, you will be prompted to create it.

6. The Publishing Directories dialog box, shown in Figure 5.19, will be displayed. In this dialog box, you may choose a directory to contain your data for the WWW, FTP, and Gopher services. You should seriously consider putting the data for each service on a separate physical drive (or a striped set, or striped set with parity), if at all possible, for maximum performance. To specify a different drive or directory, click the Browse button and choose a new location.

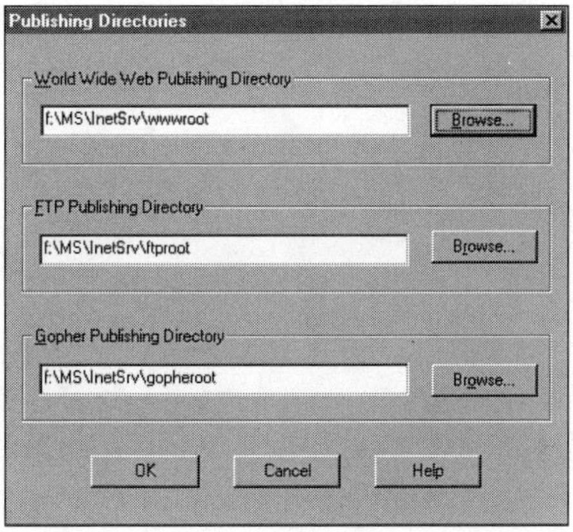

FIGURE 5.19.
Specifying the root directories for your publishing services.

7. When you have specified all your data locations, click the OK button to continue the installation. You will be prompted once again to create each directory, if they do not already exist.

8. The IIS files will be copied to your computer in the locations you specified, the publishing services will be started, and a new group will be created on the taskbar.

9. You will be prompted to install the ODBC drivers. The SQL Server driver is the default and the only driver. Select the driver, and choose the OK button.

> **NOTE**
>
> If you will be using a different ODBC driver, you will need to use the ODBC-32 Control Panel applet to install and configure the driver.

10. The Internet Explorer will then be installed and a shortcut will be added to the Microsoft Internet Server group on the taskbar. When this has been completed, a confirmation dialog will be displayed, informing you that IIS was successfully installed. Click the OK button to exit the setup application.

You are now ready to configure the IIS service, as described in Chapter 6, "Using the Internet Service Manager," install the data to be published on your server in the service's root directories, and begin to publish data on the Internet.

Summary

This chapter teaches you a bit about where you should install the IIS, and informs you about the preinstallation requirements for a successful IIS installation. The installation of the various components is part of this discussion. The chapter even shows you how to install and configure the Remote Access Service. Finally, the chapter coveres the basic IIS installation. In Chapter 6, you will learn how to configure IIS and begin publishing your content on the Internet.

PART III

IN THIS PART

- Using the Internet Service Manager 135
- Using the Internet Explorer 165
- Working with Microsoft Exchange 189
- Using DHCP, WINS, and DNS 205
- Advanced Security Issues 263

Administering Your Site

Using the Internet Service Manager

6

IN THIS CHAPTER

- Basic Operations of the Internet Service Manager 136
- Configuring the WWW Service 139
- Configuring the FTP Service 150
- Configuring the Gopher Service 156
- Logging Site Access with SQL Server 159

One nice aspect of Windows NT is that almost every service can be configured using an application specifically designed for it, and the Internet Information Server is no different. It includes a tool called the Internet Service Manager (see Figure 6.1), which is installed by default in the Microsoft Internet Service group.

This chapter focuses on managing your Internet Information Server sites using the Internet Service Manager. In this chapter you will learn how to control the basic operations of your IIS sites; how to configure the WWW, FTP, and Gopher services; and how to use the ODBC connector to log all of your IIS site activity to a database. Although it is possible to use any database that has an ODBC driver, this chapter concentrates on using the ODBC connector to connect to a SQL Server database.

FIGURE 6.1.
The Internet Service Manager.

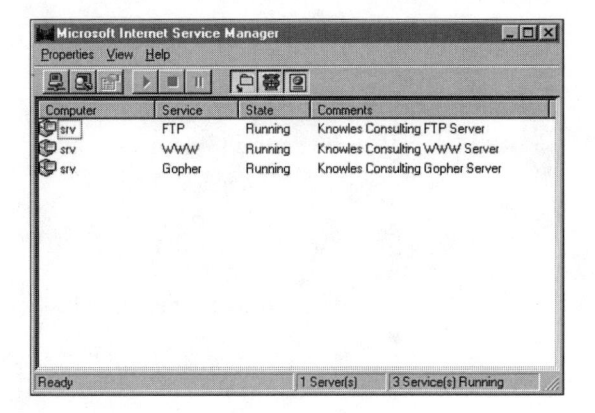

Basic Operations of the Internet Service Manager

The Internet Service Manager has a very simple set of controls. There are only three main menu commands: Properties, View, and Help. These commands are really all that is needed to manage your IIS services on a local or remote computer. Of these commands, only Properties and View offer real functionality. Although there are not many commands, a lot of care went into their design. This makes managing your IIS sites quite easy.

Let's start with a look at how you can use the Internet Service Manager to control your individual Internet services. After that, you will learn how to manage a single Internet Information Server site. Continuing with this theme, you will learn how to choose a view that will make finding the appropriate Internet services on multiple sites easier.

Controlling the Internet Services

One thing a site manager (that's you) needs is the ability to control the operating states of the individual Internet services. This can be performed on a local or remote server. Before you can control a service, however, that service must be added to the Internet Service Manager. This should be performed automatically the first time you execute the Internet Service Manager, because it will browse the network in an attempt to locate all available sites. If this should fail, however, choose one of the following options:

- Find All Servers—This option scans the entire network looking for IIS sites. This option is also activated by pressing Ctrl+F, or by clicking the Find Internet Servers button (second button from the left) on the toolbar.

- Connect to Server—This option displays the Connect to Server dialog, where you can specify the computer name of the server running the Internet Information Server. This option is also activated by pressing Ctrl+O, or by clicking the Connect to a Server button (first button on the left) on the toolbar.

After you have connected to the appropriate servers, the IIS services will be displayed in the main window of the Internet Service Manager. To start, stop, pause, or continue an IIS service on a connected server, follow these two steps:

1. Select the appropriate service by clicking the server name in the Computer column.
2. From the Properties menu, choose either Start Service, Stop Service, or Pause Service. If you prefer, you can use the Start Service, Stop Service, Pause/Continue Service buttons on the toolbar. These are the third, fourth, and fifth buttons, respectively.

> **NOTE**
>
> When you pause a service, the Properties | Pause Service menu will be in a checked state to indicate that the service is paused. To continue the service, just choose the Pause Service menu option once more, or use the toolbar Pause/Continue Service button.

Another way to control the state of the Internet services is to use Server Manager. This will display all computers in the domain. To control a service, choose Computer | Services from the menu to display the Services on *ComputerName* dialog box. Then scroll down the list until you find the appropriate service (FTP Publishing Service, Gopher Publishing Service, or WWW Publishing Service). Select the service, then click the Start, Stop, Pause, or Continue button.

> **NOTE**
>
> In order to control the state of a service, you must have administrative privileges on either the local computer or a remote computer.

Managing Internet Information Server Sites

Once you have more than a couple IIS sites on your network, managing them becomes more difficult. This is because you have to scroll through the lists of servers and services to check the state of each service. The Internet Service Manager makes this a little easier because it includes several commands to rearrange the display, allowing you to show the information you are most concerned with at the moment. These commands are accessible through the View menu command and include the following:

- Sort by Server—This command orders the display based on the computer name. This is the default sort order.
- Sort by Service—This command orders the display based on the type of service. This will change the order to FTP, Gopher, and then WWW.
- Sort by Comment—This command orders the display based on the service description.
- Sort by State—This command orders the display based on the execution state of the service. This is particularly useful for determining whether you have any services that are not executing. The default sort order is not alphabetical, however. Instead, the display will show stopped services at the top of the display, running services in the middle of the display, and paused services at the bottom of the display.

Using a View to Manage Multiple Sites

Another useful sorting method for managing multiple sites is to use the various view options accessible from the View menu. The default view is the Reports View. However, the Servers View and Services View offer benefits not available from the Reports View. First, you can see at a glance the state of the services. The state of each service is represented by the colors of a stop light: red for stopped, yellow for paused, or green for running. Second, you can expand or collapse the display to show just the type of services you want to see. Finally, the right mouse button will activate a pop-up menu to control the state or properties of the service, as shown in Figure 6.2.

FIGURE 6.2.

Using the Services View to manage your IIS sites.

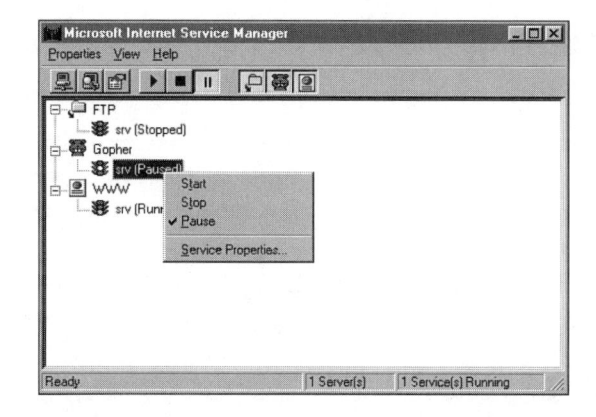

If you have many IIS sites, you may find that this view could use a little more room on the display to see the services of interest. If you want to remove a service from the display, you can choose the View|FTP, View|Gopher, or View|WWW commands, or you can choose the seventh, eighth, or ninth buttons on the taskbar, respectively. In either case, the commands toggle the current state. With the menu commands, a checked command signifies that the service is visible; if the command is unchecked, the corresponding service is removed from the display. The buttons work in a similar way: A depressed button represents a checked state, and a raised button represents an unchecked state.

Configuring the WWW Service

Before you make your WWW site available to the world, you should configure it to suit your individual needs. The default configuration provides some protection from Internet hackers, but if Internet security is your primary concern, you should take a look at Chapter 10, "Advanced Security Issues," to see what options are available to you. For the rest of this discussion, I'll assume you are just interested in the basic options for configuring your WWW Publishing service.

Configuring the WWW Publishing service can basically be broken down into four options. You can configure the general properties of the WWW service, specify the WWW directories and create virtual WWW servers, log the activity on your WWW site, and limit access to your WWW site. All of these options are obtained from the WWW Service Properties for *ComputerName* dialog box. This dialog is accessible by choosing Properties|Service Properties from the menu, clicking the Properties button on the toolbar (third button from the left), or right-clicking the service when in the Services View or Servers View. This dialog has four tabs, which are examined in detail in the following sections.

Configuring the WWW Service

The WWW Service properties sheet includes the following options:

- Connection Timeout—This option specifies the time, in seconds, before an inactive user's connection will be terminated. This ensures that even if the Web server fails to close a connection when a user exits the site, eventually it will be closed. The default is 900 seconds, or 15 minutes.
- Maximum Connections—This option specifies the maximum number of simultaneous users that can be connected to your Web server. The default is 1000.
- Anonymous Logon—This group box defines the user account and password for users that connect to your site using an anonymous logon. Most Web servers support the anonymous logon. If you want your site to support users that are not members of your domain, and most of us do, the access of those anonymous users will be based on the user account and password specified in the following fields:
    - Username—This field specifies either a local user account or a domain user account. By default, this account is called IUSER_*ComputerName*, where *ComputerName* is the name of the computer on which IIS was installed.

> **CAUTION**
>
> By default, this group is added to the Guests local group. If your server is a member of the domain, the account is also a member of the Domain Users global group. You should verify the privileges of the group to ensure that this account cannot be used to access secure network resources. Either move the user account to the Domain Guests global group or create a new group for the account. In either case, minimize the privileges associated with the user account or group. Chapter 10 describes this in more detail.

- Password—This field specifies the password to be used with the user account mentioned above. If you change the password here, you must also change the password using User Manager (for a server) or User Manager for Domains (for a domain controller).

> **TIP**
>
> It is a good idea to change the password for this account once in a while (every 30–45 days is recommended) to enhance the security of your site.

- Password Authentication—This group specifies the method to be used by users attempting to connect to your Web server. It has the following options:
    - Allow Anonymous—When this box is checked, any user may connect to your server using the anonymous logon procedure. When he does, the user account and password specified in the Anonymous Logon group are used to supply his account privileges. If this box is unchecked, anonymous logons are not allowed, and a valid user account and password must be supplied to obtain access to your WWW site.
    - Basic (Clear Text)—When checked, this option specifies that the password associated with a user account be transmitted in an unencrypted format.

WARNING

Using the Basic password authentication option opens the possibility of a serious security breach. An Internet user with access to a sniffer might be able to capture network packets sent to your site. This could provide him with a valid user account and password that he could use to access network resources.

- Windows NT Challenge/Response—When checked, this option specifies that the password be transmitted in an encrypted format when an anonymous logon is denied. That means that in order to secure your site to domain members only (such as for an intranet WWW site), and to support only encrypted passwords, you must also uncheck (disable) the Allow Anonymous and Basic (Clear Text) options.

NOTE

Currently, the only Web browser that supports the Windows NT Challenge/Response authentication mechanism is the Microsoft Internet Explorer version 2.0 (or higher).

- Comment—This option specifies a description to be displayed on the Internet Service Manager while in Reports View for the WWW Publishing service.

Configuring the WWW Service Directories

The ability to configure your WWW service's directories offers more than you might think at first glance. Not only can you configure a few basic operating characteristics, but you can also create virtual directories and virtual WWW servers. A virtual directory is a directory tree that is not physically attached to the parent WWW directory. By default, the parent WWW directory is `IISRoot`/wwwroot, where `IISRoot` is the directory where you installed the Internet Information Server (such as `F:\MS\InetSrv`). When you create a virtual directory, it is viewed by your WWW clients as a subdirectory of the parent WWW directory. A virtual directory can be physically present on the same server as the WWW Publishing service, or it can be on a remote computer.

A virtual server is a WWW server that does not exist as a physically separate entity. A physically separate entity, for example, could consist of a new computer with an assigned IP address (for the computer's network adapter), the WWW server software, and a registered domain name (so that users can find your site using the familiar form of `www.domainname.com`). It is totally self contained.

Alternatively, you can create a virtual server, which uses the WWW publishing service on your current computer. You will still need to assign an IP address to it and register the domain name, but the mechanism varies just a bit. Instead of assigning an IP address to a new network card, you can add it to your current network card. In essence, your WWW publishing service would now support two separate WWW sites. Each site would have its own root directory, which could be on the local server or on a remote server. Your clients would not know that the Web site was just one of many Web sites running on the same server. Pretty nifty, isn't it?

Configuring the WWW Service Basic Directory Properties

When you select the Directories tab on the WWW Service Properties dialog, the Directories properties sheet, shown in Figure 6.3, is displayed. This offers two basic configuration options. If you check the Enable Default Document option, you may specify an HTML document name in the Default Document field. Doing so specifies that this HTML document will be loaded as the default document when a client specifies a URL without a specific document name. A client could specify `http://www.nt-guru.com/Company Information`, for example, and the `Index.HTM` document would be loaded automatically. This is better than specifying `http://www.nt-guru.com/index.htm` because it provides a means for the client to navigate your Web site without having to know the name of each document.

FIGURE 6.3.

The Directory properties sheet.

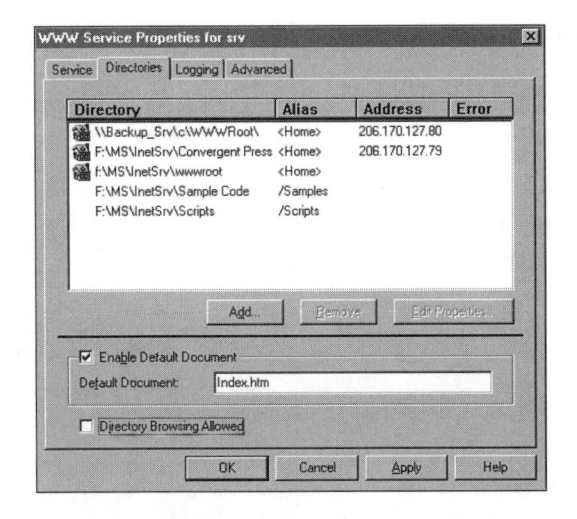

The other basic option is Directory Browsing Allowed. If this option is checked, a client can browse your entire Web site. The client's ability to browse your site, however, depends on the state of the Enable Default Document option. If this option is checked and the default document resides in the directory, the default document will be loaded into his Web browser. If the Enable Default Document option is unchecked, or if the option is checked but the default document is not resident in the directory, the client will see a list of files in the directory. This list is a hypertext list. If the user clicks on a document name, the document will be loaded.

The good news about this option is that the client will not be disappointed by seeing an error code on his Web browser. It can also be useful for intranets with a large number of documents, because it provides the ability to load a document without creating a master (or *index*) document. This lessens the administrative burden. The bad news about this option is that it opens the door for an unauthorized client to stop by and browse around, viewing information that he shouldn't. Maybe he got there by mistyping a URL, or perhaps an old employee told him about the URL. How he got there is not as important as the fact that he got there at all. To limit this type of problem, you can do one of the following:

- Disable the Directory Browsing Allowed option.
- Make sure that every subdirectory of the WWWRoot directory has a default document in it.
- Install IIS to an NTFS partition; then use File Manager or the Windows Explorer to set permissions on subdirectories with sensitive information. These permissions can be configured to limit access to only those domain members who require it. By default, then, any nonmember of this group will be denied access. This is the preferred method if you support directory browsing, because not only can you control access to the directories, but you can also audit them to determine who is accessing the directories, its subdirectories, and the files contained within them.

How to Create a Virtual Directory

Creating a virtual directory is not a difficult task. The only difference between a virtual server and a virtual directory is that only a virtual server may have an IP address and associated domain name. To create a virtual directory, just follow these steps:

1. In the Directories properties sheet, click the Add button to display the Directory Properties dialog box, shown in Figure 6.4.

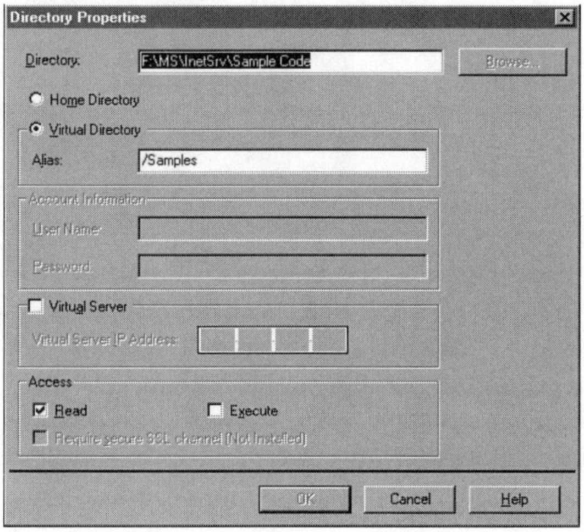

FIGURE 6.4.

Creating a virtual directory.

2. To create a virtual directory on the local computer, specify a directory name in the Directory field or click the Browse button to select a directory.

> **NOTE**
>
> If you use the Browse button, the Select Directory dialog box will appear. In it, you can choose an existing directory in the Directories listbox. To create new subdirectory, select an existing directory and enter the name of the subdirectory to create in the New Directory Name field. After you have entered the requested information, click the OK button. This will close the Select Directory dialog box. Your selected installation directory will then be displayed in the Directory field of the Directory Properties dialog box.

3. To create a virtual directory on a remote computer, specify a UNC filename (such as `Backup_Srv\C\WWWRoot`) in the Directory field.
4. If the Virtual Directory radio button is not enabled, click it to enable it.

5. Enter a name for the virtual directory, such as Samples, in the Alias field.
6. If the virtual directory will reside on a remote computer, enter a user name in the User Name field, along with a password for this user account in the Password field. This user name and password will be used to connect to the remote share.
7. In the Access group, specify the type of access your clients will use. By default, the Read check box is enabled, specifying that the client will have read-only access to the directory. If this directory will include executable code, such as a CGI script, enable the Execute check box as well. If you have an SSL certificate and have installed SSL on your Web server, the Require secure SSL channel check box will be available as well. This option can be used to provide a secure method for accessing the directory's contents.
8. Click the OK button to create your virtual directory and return to the Directories properties sheet.
9. Click the OK button to exit the Directories properties sheet.

How to Create a Virtual Server

Creating a virtual server is a lot like creating a virtual directory. In fact, a virtual server can use a virtual directory created on the local computer or a virtual directory on a remote computer. To create a virtual server, follow these steps:

1. Click the Add button in the Directories properties sheet to display the Directory Properties dialog box, shown in Figure 6.5.

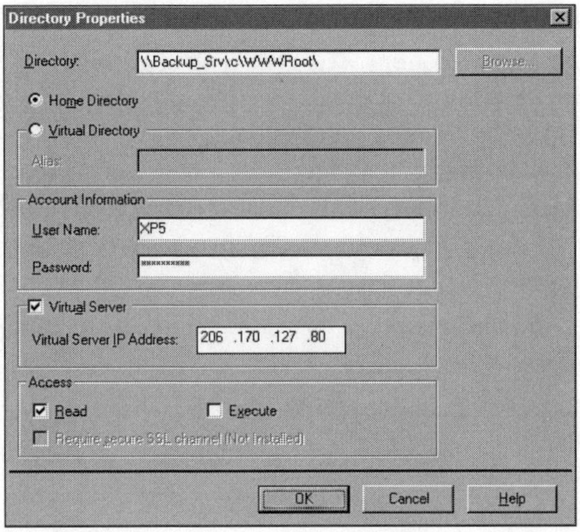

FIGURE 6.5.
Creating a virtual server.

2. To create the virtual directory to be used as the root directory for the virtual server on the local computer, specify a directory name in the Directory field or click the Browse button to select a directory.

> **NOTE**
>
> If you use the Browse button, the Select Directory dialog box will appear. In it, you can choose an existing directory in the Directories listbox. To create new subdirectory, select an existing directory and enter the name of the subdirectory to create in the New Directory Name field. After you have entered the requested information, click the OK button. This will close the Select Directory dialog box. Your selected installation directory will then be displayed in the Directory field of the Directory Properties dialog box.

3. To create a virtual directory to be used as the root directory for the virtual server on a remote computer, specify a UNC filename (such as `Backup_Srv\C\WWWRoot`) in the Directory field.
4. If the Home Directory radio button is not enabled, click it to enable it.
5. If the virtual directory will reside on a remote computer, enter a user name in the User Name field, and a password for this user account in the Password field. This user name and password will be used to connect to the remote share.
6. Click the Virtual Server check box to enable it.
7. Enter the IP address to be assigned to the virtual server in the Virtual Server IP Address field.
8. In the Access group, specify the type of access your clients will use. By default, the Read check box is enabled, specifying that the client will have read-only access to the directory. If this directory will include executable code, such as a CGI script, enable the Execute check box as well. If you have an SSL certificate, and have installed SSL on your Web server, the Require secure SSL channel check box will be available as well. This option can be used to provide a secure method for accessing the directory contents.
9. Click the OK button to create your virtual server and return to the Directories properties sheet.
10. Repeat steps 1 through 9 for each virtual server you want to create.
11. Click the OK button to exit the Directories properties sheet.

After you have added all of your virtual servers, you must add the IP addresses and subnet masks to your network adapter. This is accomplished by following these steps:

1. Open the Control Panel Network applet.
2. Click the Protocols tab to display the Protocols properties sheet.
3. You can display the Microsoft TCP/IP Properties dialog box in one of two ways. You can either double-click the TCP/IP Protocol entry or just click it once to select it and then click the Properties button.
4. Click the Advanced button to display the Advanced IP Addressing dialog box.
5. In the IP Address group, click the Add button to display the TCP/IP Address dialog box.
6. Enter an IP address and subnet mask in the IP Address and Subnet Mask fields. Then click the Add button. This will add the new IP address and subnet mask to the IP Address and Subnet Mask fields of the IP Address group.
7. Repeat steps 5 and 6 for each virtual server.
8. Click the OK button to exit the Advanced IP Addressing dialog box and return to the Microsoft TCP/IP Properties dialog box.
9. Click the OK button to return to the Network dialog box.
10. The Network Settings Change dialog box will be displayed. Click the Yes button to restart your computer. Once the server reboots, your virtual servers will be available.

> **NOTE**
>
> Before your virtual servers are available to the public, you must have registered your domain name. This means that the IP address and subnet mask you assigned must be the same as those assigned to your domain name. Your ISP should provide you with these. You ISP should also configure their DNS servers and set up the necessary routing tables so that clients will be able to find your virtual servers.

Logging WWW Activity

Logging your WWW activity is one way you can determine how active your site is, as well as determine whether someone is accessing data he should not have access to. There are two methods you can use to log your WWW site's activity. You can store the information in a standard text file, or you can store it in an ODBC database. If you use an ODBC database, you must create the database and then set up an ODBC data source name (DSN) using the ODBC Control Panel applet. Creating an ODBC database and setting up the DSN is discussed later in this chapter in the section titled "Logging Site Access with SQL Server." To enable logging, follow these steps:

1. Click the Logging tab in the WWW Service Properties dialog box to display the Logging properties sheet, shown in Figure 6.6.

FIGURE 6.6.
Configuring the WWW service to log activity.

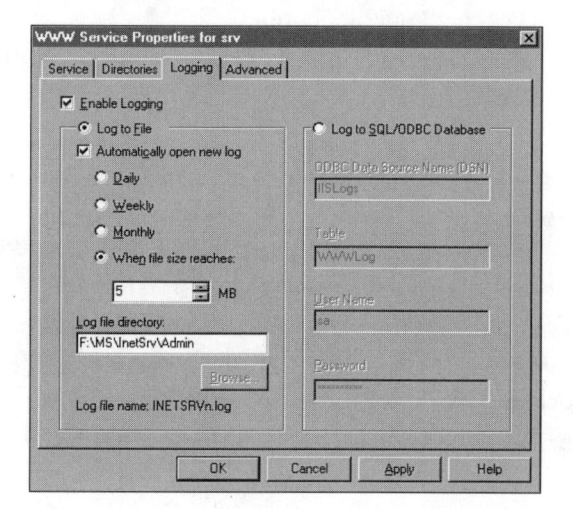

2. Click the Enable Logging check box.
3. To log your WWW site's activity to a text file, click the Log to File radio button. This will enable the following options:
    - Automatically open new log—This option specifies that a new log will be created based on one of the following criteria:
        - Daily—Every day.
        - Weekly—Once a week.
        - Monthly—Once a month.
        - When log file size reaches—Whenever the log file exceeds the size specified in the MB field.
    - Log file directory—This option specifies the location where the log file will reside.

4. To log your WWW site's activity to an ODBC database, click the Log to SQL/ODBC Database radio button. This will enable the following options:
    - ODBC Data Source Name (DSN)—Specifies the name of the data source to use to access the ODBC database.
    - Table—Specifies the table within the ODBC database to use for logging.
    - User Name—Specifies a user name to use to access the table within the ODBC database.
    - Password—Specifies a password for the associated user account.
 5. Click the OK button to close the WWW Site Properties dialog box and return to the Internet Service Manager.

Limiting Access to Your WWW Site

Almost everyone is concerned about the security of his WWW site. The Internet Service Manager does provide a limited means of securing your Web site against possible intruders, but these features are not too useful if you plan on providing site access to the public. But if you will be using IIS for an intranet, it is a very useful means of limiting access to sensitive data. To limit potential damage to your system from the public, however, I suggest you look at Chapter 10 to see how you can restrict access to your network. In the meantime, you can limit access to your Web server by following these steps:

 1. Click the Advanced tab in the WWW Service Properties dialog box to display the Advanced properties sheet (see Figure 6.7).

FIGURE 6.7.
Configuring the advanced WWW Publishing Service properties.

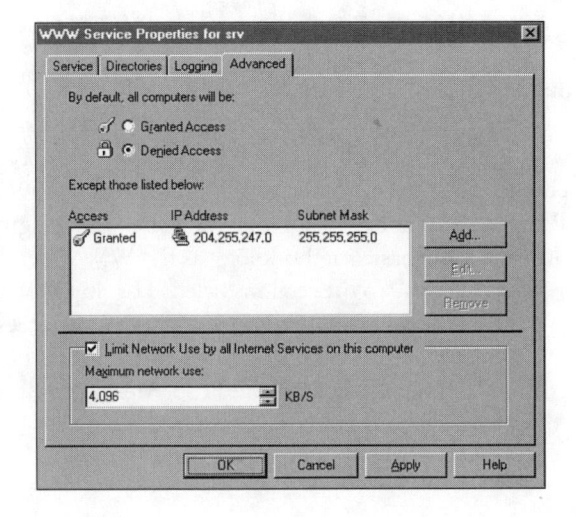

2. To limit access to a specific set of clients, click the Denied Access radio button. Then click the Add button to display the Grant Access On dialog box. To specify a single computer to give access to your Web site, click the Single Computer radio button and enter the IP address of the computer in the IP Address field. To specify multiple computers to give access to your Web site, click the Multiple Computers radio button and specify an IP address and subnet mask in the IP Address and Subnet Mask fields. Then press the OK button.

3. To grant access to all but a specific set of clients, click the Granted Access radio button. Then click the Add button to display the Denied Access On dialog box. To specify a single computer to deny access to your Web site, click the Single Computer radio button and enter the IP address of the computer in the IP Address field. To specify multiple computers to deny access to your Web site, click the Multiple Computers radio button and specify an IP address and subnet mask in the IP Address and Subnet Mask fields. Then press the OK button.

4. The IP addresses and subnet masks you specified in step 2 or step 3 will then be displayed in the Except those listed below listbox. Repeat step 2, or step 3, for each additional set of computers you want to deny, or grant, access to your Web site.

5. To limit the amount of network bandwidth used by your IIS services, click the Limit Network Use by all Internet Services on this computer to enable the check box. Then specify a value in the Maximum network use field.

6. Click the OK button to close the WWW Service Properties dialog box and return to the Internet Service Manager.

Configuring the FTP Service

Just as you need to configure your WWW Publishing Service before making it available to the public, you need to configure your FTP Publishing service as well. You have five configuration options. You can configure the general properties of the FTP service, specify the messages users will see when they connect to your FTP site, specify the FTP directories, log the activity on your FTP site, and limit access to your FTP site. The logging and limiting access properties sheets follow the same basic methodology as the WWW service. So rather than repeat this information, I will refer you to the sections titled "Logging WWW Activity" and "Limiting Access to Your WWW Site." All of these options, however, are accessed from the FTP Service Properties for *ComputerName* dialog box. This dialog is accessible by choosing Properties|Service Properties from the menu, clicking the Properties button on the toolbar (third button from the left), or right-clicking the service when in the Services View or Servers View.

Using the Internet Service Manager
Chapter 6 151

Configuring the FTP Service

The FTP Service properties sheet, shown in Figure 6.8, includes the following options:

FIGURE 6.8.
Configuring the basic FTP publishing service properties.

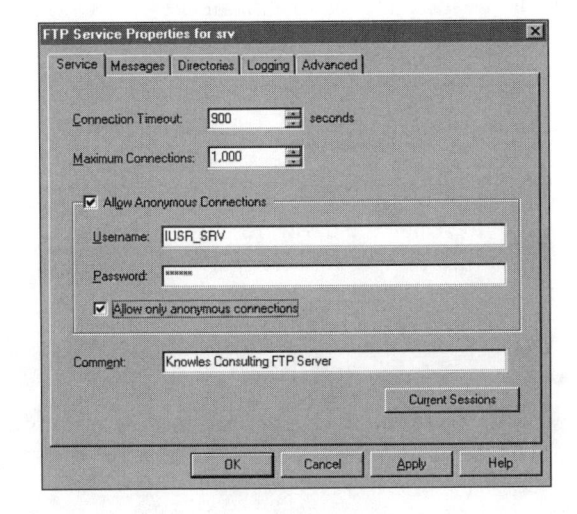

- Connection Timeout—This specifies the time, in seconds, before an inactive user's connection will be terminated. Connection Timeout is used to ensure that even if the Web server fails to close a connection when a user exits the site, eventually it will be closed. The default is 900 seconds, or 15 minutes.
- Maximum Connections—This specifies the maximum number of simultaneous users that can be connected to your Web server. The default is 1000.
- Allow Anonymous Connections—This check box enables you to specify a user account and password for users that connect to your site using an anonymous logon. Most FTP servers support an anonymous logon. If you want your site to support users that are not members of your domain, and most of us do, anytime a user logs on anonymously, his access will be based on the user account and password specified in the following fields:
    - Username—This field specifies either a local user account or a domain user account. By default, this account is called IUSER_*ComputerName* where *ComputerName* is the name of the computer on which IIS was installed.

> **CAUTION**
>
> By default, this group is added to the Guests local group. If your server is a member of the domain, the account is also a member of the Domain Users global group. You should verify the privileges of the group to ensure that this account cannot be used to access secure network resources. For additional information, refer to Chapter 10, which describes this in more detail.

- Password—This field specifies the password to be used with the user account. If you change the password here, you must also change the password using User Manager (for a server) or User Manager for Domains (for a domain controller).

> **TIP**
>
> It is a good idea to change the password for this account once in a while (every 30–45 days is recommended) to enhance the security of your site.

- Allow only anonymous connections—When this box is checked, only users that use an anonymous logon may connect to your FTP site.

> **WARNING**
>
> Since the FTP protocol does not encrypt passwords, an Internet user with access to a sniffer may be able to capture network packets sent to your site. This could provide him with a valid user account and password that he could then use to access network resources. It is therefore best to enable the Allow only anonymous connections check box.

- Comment—This specifies a description to be displayed on the Internet Service Manager while in Reports View for the FTP Publishing service.
- Current Sessions—Click this button to display the FTP User Sessions dialog box and see who is active on your FTP site.

Configuring the FTP Service Messages

When a user connects to your FTP site, you have the option to display a greeting message, an exit message, and an error message if the maximum number of clients are currently connected.

Not all FTP clients, however, will display these messages. Nor will all Web browsers. But it is still a good idea to specify them for those FTP clients that will support them. To do so, follow these steps:

1. Click the Messages tab to display the Messages properties sheet, shown in Figure 6.9.

FIGURE 6.9.
Specifying the FTP publishing service messages.

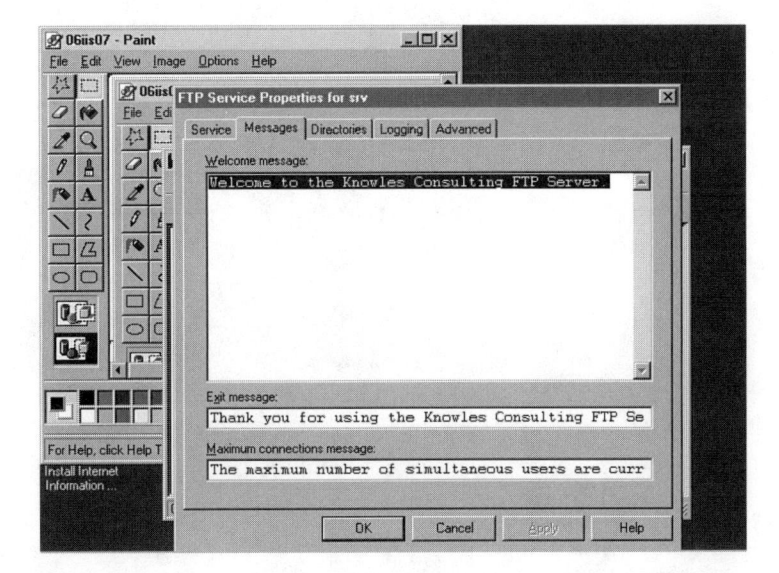

2. Enter a greeting message or a warning message (such as when the site is only for authorized users) in the Welcome message field.
3. Enter an exit message to be displayed when the user disconnects from your FTP site in the Exit message field.
4. To inform a user that he cannot connect to your FTP site because the maximum number of simultaneous clients have already connected, enter an error message in the Maximum connection message field.
5. Click the OK button to return to the Internet Service Manager.

Configuring the FTP Service Directories

Configuring the directories for the FTP service does not offer as much functionality as the WWW Publishing Service does. You cannot create a virtual server, though you can create virtual directories. When you select the Directories tab on the FTP Service Properties dialog, the Directories properties sheet, shown in Figure 6.10, will be displayed.

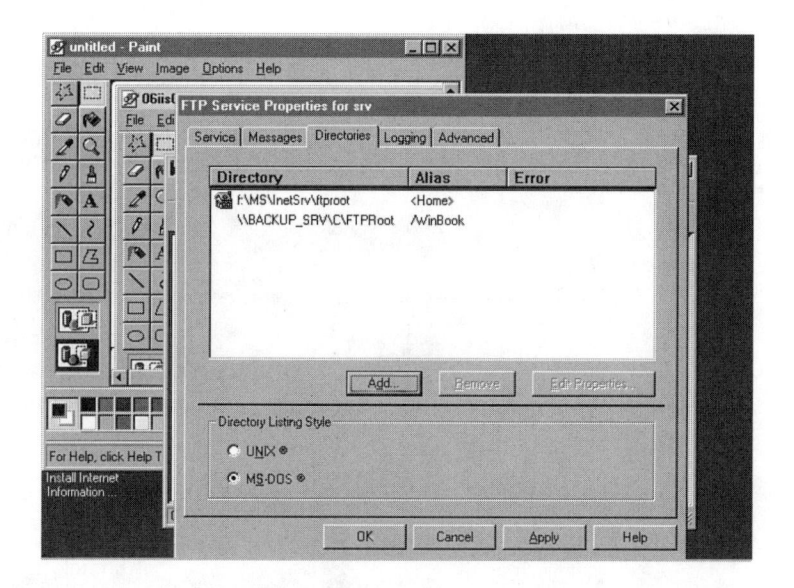

Part III *Administering Your Site*

FIGURE 6.10.
The FTP publishing service Directories properties sheet.

This offers two configuration options. You can specify that a directory listing will follow the UNIX or MS-DOS convention by enabling the UNIX or MS-DOS radio button, or you can create virtual directories.

Creating a virtual directory is pretty simple. The only determinate factor is deciding whether the virtual directory will reside on a local computer or a remote computer. To create a virtual directory, follow these steps:

1. In the Directories properties sheet, click the Add button to display the Directory Properties dialog box, shown in Figure 6.11.

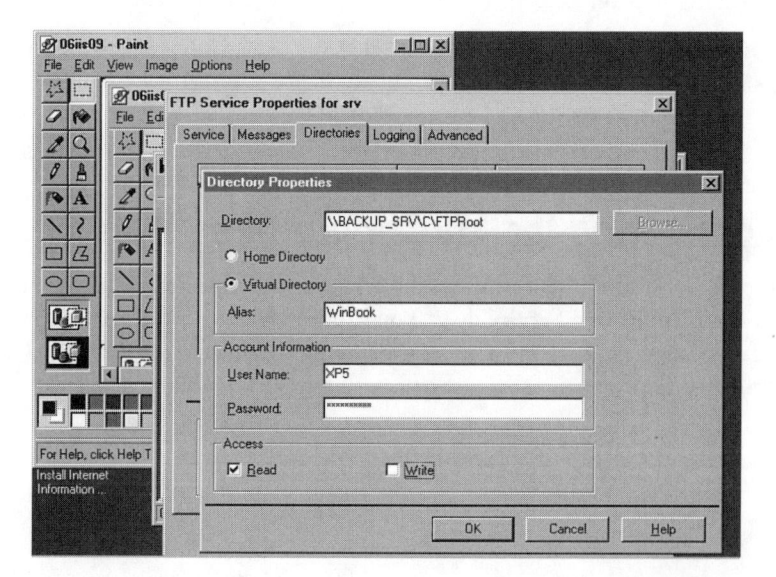

FIGURE 6.11.
Creating a virtual directory.

Using the Internet Service Manager

Chapter 6

2. To create a virtual directory on the local computer, specify a directory name in the Directory field, or click the Browse button to select a directory.

> **NOTE**
>
> If you use the Browse button, the Select Directory dialog box will appear. In it, you can choose an existing directory in the Directories listbox. To create a new subdirectory, select an existing directory and enter the name of the subdirectory to create in the New Directory Name field. After you have entered the requested information, click the OK button to close the Select Directory dialog box. Your selected installation directory will then be displayed in the Directory field of the Directory Properties dialog box.

3. To create a virtual directory on a remote computer, specify a UNC filename (such as `Backup_Srv\C\WWWRoot`) in the Directory field.
4. If the Virtual Directory radio button is not enabled, click it to enable it.

> **TIP**
>
> While you cannot create a virtual server, you can create multiple home directories by enabling the Home Directory radio button. This can provide your FTP site with multiple root directories, though your FTP clients will need to know the directory name in order to access them. They could use `ftp://ftp.nt-guru.com/WinBook` to access the files in the WinBook home directory, for example, instead of `ftp://ftp.nt-guru.com`, which would put them in the *IISRoot*/FTPRoot directory.

5. Enter a name for the virtual directory, such as `Samples`, in the Alias field.
6. If the virtual directory will reside on a remote computer, enter a user name in the User Name field, and a password for this user account in the Password field. This user name and password will be used to connect to the remote share.
7. In the Access group, specify the type of access your clients will use. By default, the Read check box is enabled, specifying that the client will have read-only access to the directory. If this directory will be used to upload files, enable the Write check box as well.
8. Click the OK button to create your virtual directory and return to the Directories properties sheet.
9. Click the OK button to exit the Directories properties sheet and return to the Internet Service Manager.

Administering Your Site

Part III

Configuring the Gopher Service

As with the WWW and FTP services, you should configure your Gopher site to suit your individual needs before you make it available to the world. You have four options when you configure your Gopher Publishing service: You can configure the general properties of the Gopher service; you can specify the Gopher directories; you can log the activity on your Gopher site; and you can limit access to your Gopher site. All of these options are obtained from the Gopher Service Properties for *ComputerName* dialog box. To access this dialog, choose Properties | Service Properties from the menu, click the Properties button on the toolbar (third button from the left), or right-click the service when in the Services View or Servers View. Gopher's logging and limiting-access properties sheets follow the same format as the WWW service's. So rather than repeat this information, I will refer you to the sections titled "Logging WWW Activity" and "Limiting Access to Your WWW Site."

The Gopher Service properties sheet, shown in Figure 6.12, includes the following options:

FIGURE 6.12.
Configuring the basic options of the Gopher properties service.

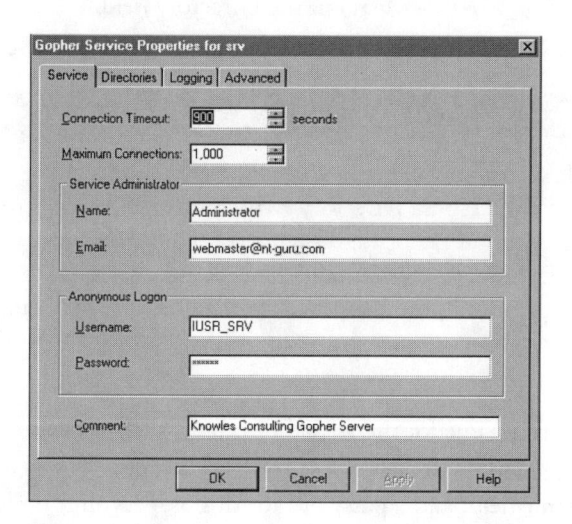

- Connection Timeout—This option specifies the time, in seconds, before an inactive user's connection will be terminated. This is used to ensure that even if the Gopher server fails to close a connection when a user exits the site, eventually it will be closed. The default is 900 seconds, or 15 minutes.

- Maximum Connections—This option specifies the maximum number of simultaneous users that can be connected to your Gopher server. The default is 1000.

- Service Administrator—A Gopher client can provide additional information to its user about the administrator of the gopher service. This information includes
    - Name—This field specifies a contact name or the administrator of the Gopher site.
    - Email—This field specifies an e-mail address for the contact name or administrator of the Gopher site.
- Anonymous Logon—This group box defines the user account and password for users that connect to your site using an anonymous logon. Most Gopher servers support the anonymous logon. If you want your site to support users that are not members of your domain, which most of us do, anytime a user logs on anonymously, his access will be based on the user account and password specified in the following fields:
    - Username—This field specifies either a local-user or a domain-user account. By default, this account is called IUSER ComputerName, where ComputerName is the name of the computer on which IIS was installed.

CAUTION

By default, this group is added to the Guests local group. If your server is a member of the domain, the account is also a member of the Domain Users global group. You should verify the privileges of the group to ensure that this account cannot be used to access secure network resources. For additional information, refer to Chapter 10.

- Password—This field specifies the password to be used with the user account mentioned above. If you change the password here, you must also change the password using User Manager (for a server) or User Manager for Domains (for a domain controller).

TIP

It is a good idea to change the password for this account once in a while (every 30–45 days is recommended) to enhance the security of your site.

- Comment—This option specifies a description to be displayed on the Internet Service Manager while in Reports View for the Gopher Publishing service.

Configuring the Gopher Service Directories

Of all the publishing services, Gopher has the fewest options for managing directories: It can only create virtual directories. Select the Directories tab on the Gopher Service Properties dialog to display the Directories properties sheet, shown in Figure 6.13.

FIGURE 6.13.
The Gopher publishing service Directories properties sheet.

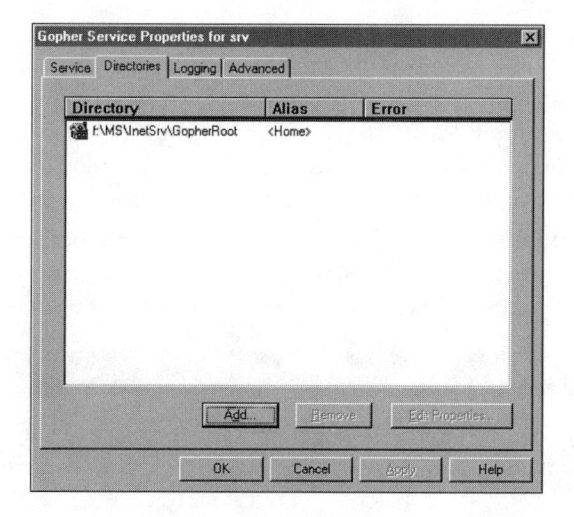

Creating a virtual directory can be accomplished by following these steps:

1. In the Directories properties sheet, click the Add button to display the Directory Properties dialog box, shown in Figure 6.14.

FIGURE 6.14.
Creating a virtual directory.

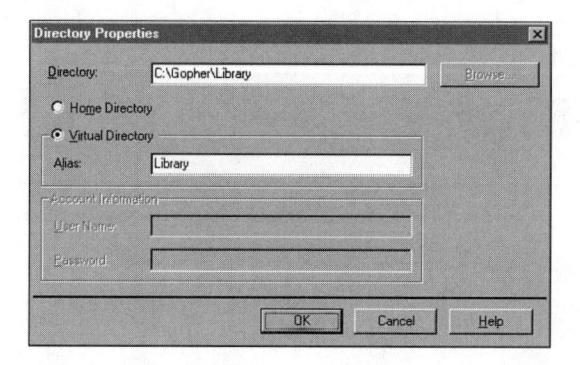

2. To create a virtual directory on the local computer, specify a directory name in the Directory field or click the Browse button to select a directory.

> **NOTE**
>
> If you use the Browse button, the Select Directory dialog box will appear. In it, you can choose an existing directory in the Directories listbox. To create new subdirectory, select an existing directory and enter the name of the subdirectory to create in the New Directory Name field. After you have entered the requested information, click the OK button to close the Select Directory dialog box. Your selected installation directory will then be displayed in the Directory field of the Directory Properties dialog box.

3. To create a virtual directory on a remote computer, specify a UNC filename (such as `Backup_Srv\C\WWWRoot`) in the Directory field.
4. If the Virtual Directory radio button is not enabled, click it to enable it.
5. Enter a name for the virtual directory, such as `Library`, in the Alias field.
6. If the virtual directory will reside on a remote computer, enter a user name in the User Name field and a password for this user account in the Password field. This user name and password will be used to connect to the remote share.
7. Click the OK button to create your virtual directory and return to the Directories properties sheet.
8. Click the OK button to exit the Directories properties sheet and return to the Internet Service Manager.

Logging Site Access with SQL Server

While you can use any ODBC database to log your IIS site's activity, this section will only describe how to use SQL Server because it is the most commonly used database engine. Configuring an IIS service to log the activity to an ODBC database is described in the section titled "Logging WWW Activity," so I will not repeat that here. What you will learn, though, is how to build the database to contain your logs, how to create a user account to access this database, and how to create an ODBC data source to access the logs from your IIS services.

Building the Database

The IIS services actually write their logging information to one or more tables. However, these tables must be contained within a database. While you can create the IIS table(s) in any database, I recommend that you create one specifically for the Internet Information Server. This can be accomplished by following these steps:

1. Create two new devices using the SQL Enterprise Manager. This is accomplished by going to the Server Manager window, expanding the registered SQL Server, selecting the Database Devices folder, right-clicking it, and then selecting New Device from the pop-up menu.
2. Specify a name for the new device (such as IISDatabaseDevice.DAT) in the Name field.
3. Specify the drive where the device should reside in the Location drop-down listbox. Next to the drop-down listbox is an unnamed field where you may specify the filename to be used for the device.
4. Specify the size of the device in the Size field. If you plan to have a very active Web site and don't plan to dump your database too often, you might want to start with 30MB.
5. Click the Create Now button to create the device.
6. Repeat steps 2 through 5 to create the log device, except use a name such as IISLogDevice.DAT and specify a size of 10MB.
7. Next, you will need to create the database. To do so, select the Databases folder, right-click it, and choose New Database from the pop-up menu.
8. In the New Database dialog box, specify the database name (such as IISLogs) in the Name field.
9. In the Data Device drop-down listbox, choose the device you created in step 2 (IISDatabaseDevice).
10. In the Log Device drop-down listbox, choose the device you created in step 6 (IISLogDevice).
11. Click the Create Now button to create the database.
12. After the database has been created, you can create the table(s) using the following script:
    ```
    USE DATABASE IISLOGS
    GO
    CREATE TABLE dbo.IISLog (    ClientHost varchar (255) NOT NULL ,
    username varchar (255) NOT NULL , LogTime datetime NOT NULL ,
    service varchar (255) NOT NULL , machine varchar (255) NOT NULL ,
    serverip varchar (50) NOT NULL , processingtime int NOT NULL ,
    bytesrecvd int NOT NULL , bytessent int NOT NULL , servicestatus int NOT NULL ,
    win32status int NOT NULL , operation varchar (255) NOT NULL ,
    target varchar (255) NOT NULL , parameters varchar (255) NOT NULL)
    GO
    ```

> **NOTE**
>
> This script will create one table called IISLog. If you want to create individual tables for each service, just change IISLog to WWWLog and run the script. Then change it to FTPLog, or GopherLog, and rerun the script to create the additional tables.

Assigning Permissions to Access the Database

After you have created the devices, the database, and the tables (as described in the preceding section), you will need to assign permission to access the database. You can use an existing user account or create a new one. The method you use depends on the security model of your SQL Server installation. The following will work for a standard or mixed model:

1. Expand the Databases folder using the SQL Enterprise Manager, and then expand the database you want to manage.
2. Select the Groups/Users folder, right-click it, and choose New User from the pop-up menu.
3. Enter a user account in the Name field. This is the name used by SQL Server for display purposes.
4. Specify a name in the Login field. This is usually the name of an existing SQL Server account (such as sa) or a domain account (such as IUSR_SRV).
5. Click the Add button. This will give the user account permission to access the database. Click Close.
6. Next, choose Object | Permissions from the top-level menu. Highlight the group or user for which you want to change the permissions. Click the Grant All button, and then the Set Button to give full permission for the user to access the objects (such as the tables you created) within the database.
7. Click the Close button to exit the dialog box and return to the SQL Executive Manager. You can either leave it running or close SQL Executive Manager, but you're done here.

Building the ODBC Data Source

The final step in using an ODBC database to store your IIS logs is to create the link between your ODBC client (the IIS services) and the ODBC server (SQL Server). This can be accomplished by performing the following steps:

1. Open the Control Panel ODBC applet, which will display the Data Sources dialog box.
2. Click the System DSN button to display the System Data Sources dialog box.

3. Click the Add button to display the Add Data Source dialog box.
4. Select the SQL Server entry in the Installed ODBC Drivers listbox. Then click the OK button.
5. The ODBC SQL Server Setup dialog box will appear. Click the Options button to expand the dialog box (see Figure 6.15).

FIGURE 6.15.

Creating an ODBC data source for IIS logging.

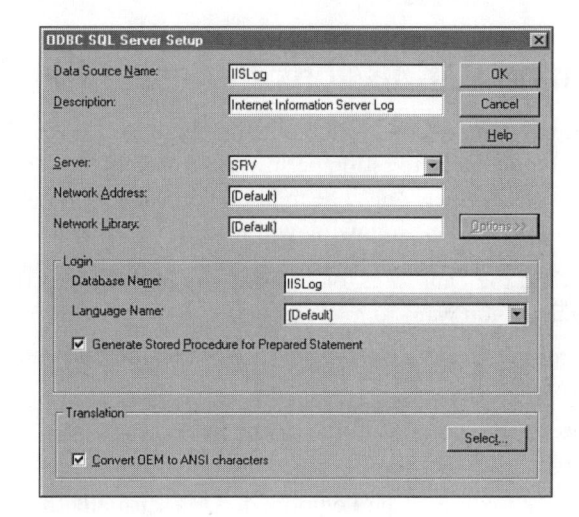

6. In the Data Source Name field, enter a unique name (such as IISLogs).
7. In the Description field, enter a comment to describe the DSN.
8. In the Server field, specify the SQL Server to which you want to connect.
9. In the Database Name field, enter the name of the SQL Server database you created (such as IISLogs).
10. Click the OK button to return to the System Data Source dialog box.
11. Click the Close button to return to the Data Source dialog box.
12. Click the Close button to return to the Control Panel.

That's all there is to creating an ODBC data source name. If you will be using a different ODBC database, just choose the ODBC driver in step 4 to match your ODBC-compliant database.

Summary

In this chapter you have learned how to manage your Internet Information Services using the Internet Service Manager, including how to manage the operating state of the services and use the various views to sort the IIS sites and services to make managing them easier. You have also learned how to configure the various options for each type of service. Your final stop was a look at how to use SQL Server, or another ODBC-compliant database, for your IIS service activity logging.

In Chapter 7, "Using the Internet Explorer," you will examine the Microsoft Internet Explorer to learn how it can be used to access your IIS sites. You'll also learn how to set the various configuration options to prepare you for those trying times with your network clients.

Using the Internet Explorer

IN THIS CHAPTER

- Installing Internet Explorer **167**
- Configuring Internet Explorer **168**
- Using Internet Explorer **187**

Administering Your Site

Part III

In order to obtain maximum performance from the Internet Information Server, you will need to use a Web browser that supports the complete feature set. Currently, the only Web browser to fit this bill is the Microsoft Internet Explorer. Luckily for you, this browser is included with Windows NT 4.0 and Windows 95. It is also available, at no charge from Microsoft, for Windows 3.*x*, as well as for Macintosh. You can download the Microsoft Internet Explorer from the Internet at `http://www.microsoft.com/ie`. Because Internet Explorer will also be used as the standard Web browser for The Microsoft Network, CompuServe, and AOL, the number of Internet Explorer users will soar in the next couple months.

All this simply means that Internet Explorer users should be your target audience for the Web pages you develop. This does not mean that you should ignore users of other Web browsers, such as Netscape Navigator; it is still a good idea to view your Web pages with these other browsers to make sure the content you want to provide is accessible. But you can take advantage of some of the Microsoft HTML extensions for the Internet Explorer, such as the `<MARQUEE>` tag, to customize the look of your Web pages and highlight special content areas. By the time this book is published, a new release of Internet Explorer (version 3.0) will become available. This version will include a new look and will support ActiveX controls, ActiveX scripts, ActiveX documents, new HTML tags, new security protocols, and a few additional options. For more information on ActiveX scripting, take a look at Chapter 17, "Unleashing the Power of VBScript."

As I write this chapter, Internet Explorer version 3.0 is still in beta form. However, it should be widely available by the end of 1996. If you are in charge of a corporate network, you should not rush to implement Internet Explorer version 3.0 at your site until some of the security-related issues have been completely worked out. The section of this chapter titled "Configuring Internet Explorer Security" covers the basic security options of Internet Explorer version 3.0. One of the main draws of Internet Explorer version 3.0 is the ActiveX components. With these components, it will be possible to download executable code or documents.

The potential to download an unfriendly application or document that could run amok on your network is quite high. The same could be said for Java applets supported by other Web browsers. Microsoft is implementing a means to digitally *sign* these executable enhancements to your Web browser. This means that it will be possible to hold accountable whoever created or provided the unfriendly element for your network. This accountability for possible damage is similar to that which you can currently obtain for any third-party software that you buy. What this means in the real world, however, is that you are still at risk. Accountability only means that you know who created or provided the enhancement. Your legal means for recuperating your losses may be another story.

As a WWW site administrator (webmaster) or developer, you will be left in the cold if you do not support Internet Explorer 3.0 and ActiveX controls and documents. So in order to help prepare you for your endeavors as a network administrator, webmaster, or developer, this chapter focuses on Internet Explorer 3.0 rather than the current retail version (Internet Explorer 2.0).

Using the Internet Explorer
Chapter 7

Installing Internet Explorer

The current version of Internet Explorer included with Windows NT 4.0, beta 2, is Internet Explorer 2.0. Microsoft will release Internet Explorer 3.0 as part of the retail Windows NT 4.0 product, or as an add-on product, so your installation procedure may vary. Version 2.0 is installed via the Control Panel Add/Remove Programs applet. It is normally installed automatically when you install Windows NT 4.0. However, if you performed a custom installation and chose not to include Internet Explorer, you can follow these steps to install it:

1. Launch the Control Panel Add/Remove Programs applet.
2. Select the Windows NT Setup tab to display the Windows NT Setup properties sheet.
3. Select the Accessories item; then click the Details button. This will display the Accessories dialog box.
4. Scroll down the Components listbox and check the Internet Jumpstart Kit item.
5. Click the OK button. This will return you to the Windows NT Setup properties sheet.
6. Click the OK button.
7. You will be prompted by the Add/Remove Properties - Copying Files - Files Needed dialog box to supply the path to the installation files. Enter the location of these files in the Copy Files From field and click the OK button.

NOTE

If the Add/Remove Programs setup application can find the files without your help, such as when the Windows NT CD-ROM is already in your CD-ROM drive or when the images located on a network server are accessible, the dialog box in step 7 will not be displayed.

8. At this point, the files will be copied to your computer and you will be prompted to reboot by the Systems Settings Change dialog box. Choose the Yes button to reboot and immediately start using Internet Explorer, or the No button to continue your current work session.

If you install Internet Explorer using a downloaded copy from the Internet, the installation should follow this sequence:

1. Copy the downloaded self-extracting archive file to a temporary directory.
2. Execute the self-extracting archive using File Manager, Windows NT Explorer, or another method of your choice.

3. The Microsoft Internet Explorer V3.0 Install Kit dialog box will appear. Click the Yes button to install, or the No button to cancel. For the sake of discussion, I'll assume you've chosen to install.

4. The installation files will be extracted from the archive and placed in the system's default temporary directory, as specified by your `TEMP=` environment variable.

5. Next, the Internet Explorer License Agreement dialog box will appear. This dialog box includes the legal agreement between you and Microsoft. It contains copyright information and rules that specify the usability and suitability of the application to be used by you. To install the product, choose the I Agree button. Choosing the I Disagree button will cause the installation to terminate.

6. Assuming you have chosen to install the program, the Copying Files dialog box will be displayed as it copies the files to your hard disk. By default, these files will be copied to the `Program Files\Plus!\Microsoft` Internet directory.

7. You will be prompted to reboot by the Systems Settings Change dialog box. Choose the Yes button to reboot and immediately start using Internet Explorer, or the No button to continue your current work session.

Configuring Internet Explorer

After you have installed Internet Explorer, it is possible to use it immediately. However, you'll get a lot more out of it by taking a few moments to configure. There are several options you can customize to make Internet Explorer look better, work better, and be safer to use by younger members of your family. In this section you will learn how each option works, as well as step through the process of configuring each option. When you are finished, Internet Explorer will be ready for use on the Internet.

> **TIP**
>
> If you are a network administrator responsible for rolling out many Internet Explorer installations, you should look into the Internet Explorer Administration Kit. This kit can be used to predefine the setup and configuration options for Internet Explorer 3.0.

Associating File Types

Associating a file type should be nothing new to you if you have used any version of Windows before. If not, a file association is nothing more than specifying the name of an application to use with a specific file extension. This file extension is used to launch the application when you

Using the Internet Explorer

Chapter 7   169

open a file with Internet Explorer. Once the application is executing, the file will be loaded into the application. If you do not have a file associated for a specific file type, you will be greeted with a dialog box to specify the application to run. If you choose not to specify an application to run, the hypertext link will fail.

> **TIP**
>
> One of the really neat things about file associations is how IE 3.0 works with OLE-enabled applications that support OLE automation, like Microsoft Word for Windows. If you open a Word document (*.DOC) on a computer with Word for Windows installed on it, Word will be loaded within the main IE 3.0 window. The IE 3.0 menu and toolbars will change, and you can work with the Word document right within IE 3.0. If you are using IE 2.0, or if the associated application does not support OLE automation, IE will load Word as a separate application, and then Word will load the document.

Normally, each application you install will also install the file associations for you. As you browse the WWW, however, you may encounter files for which you have no predefined association. To inform the Internet Explorer of the application to run when only a data file is selected, you need to add a new file association. You can view or edit your current file associations, or add a new file association, by using the following steps:

To view your current file associations, follow these steps:

1. Choose Options from the View menu. Then choose the File Types tab to display the File Types properties sheet, which is shown in Figure 7.1.

FIGURE 7.1.

Associating a file type with an application.

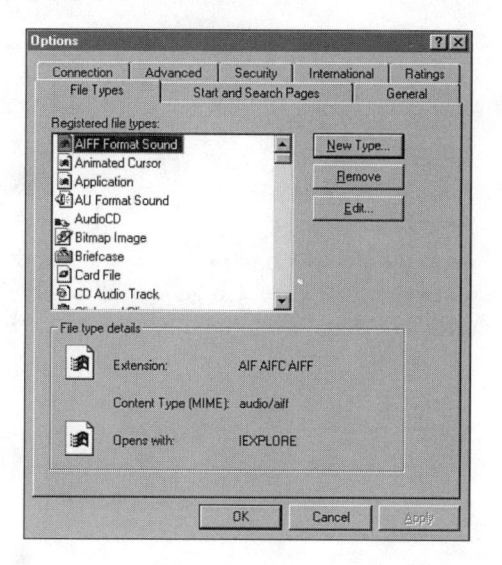

2. Scroll down the list of items displayed in the Registered file types listbox.
3. When you find the file type you are interested in, click the item in the listbox.
4. The File type details group will then display the relevant information about the file association. When you are finished, click the OK button to exit the Options properties sheet.

To edit a file association, follow these steps:

1. Choose Options from the View menu. This will display the File Types properties sheet, shown in Figure 7.1.
2. Scroll through the Registered file types listbox until you find the specific file type in which you are interested.
3. When you find the file type you are interested in, click the item in the listbox. The File type details group will update the display to show the current file extensions, MIME content type, and the application associated with the file association.
4. Click the Edit button to display the Edit File Type dialog box, which is shown in Figure 7.2.

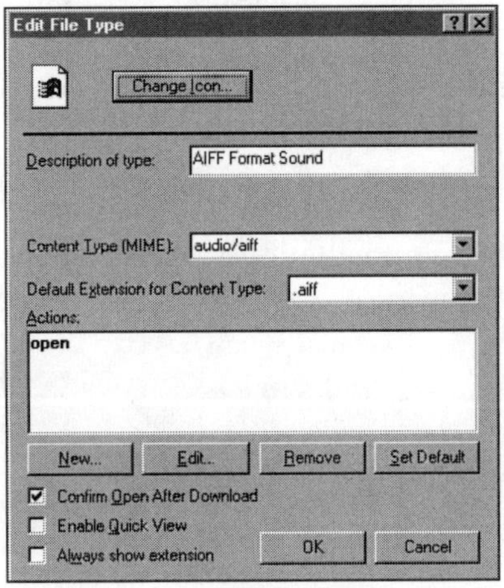

FIGURE 7.2.

Editing a file type association.

5. To specify a different icon to be displayed with the Windows Explorer, click the Change Icon button. The Change Icon dialog box will appear. Choose an icon in the Current Icon field and click the OK button to return to the Edit File Type dialog box.

> **TIP**
>
> If the icons displayed in the Change Icon dialog box are not acceptable, you can change the name of the icon bank in the File Name field either by manually specifying a path and filename or by using the Browse button to find a file on your computer. You can use any Windows application or DLL that has icons built into the file as a resource, or specify an icon file (*.ico).

6. Enter a comment in the Description of type field to display a better description of the type of file if the default is not acceptable.
7. Choose a MIME type for the file association in the Content Type (MIME) drop-down listbox. If there is no MIME type currently listed that fits the type of file, you can enter the information manually for a new MIME type.
8. Choose the file extension to be the default association in the Default Extension for Content Type drop-down listbox.
9. To change the function of the associated file type, do the following:
    1. Click the function (such as Open) in the Actions listbox.
    2. Click the Edit button. The Editing Action For Type dialog box will appear.
    3. You may then specify the application name and command-line parameters, whether the application responds to DDE commands, and the DDE messages to send to the application.
    4. When you are finished, click the OK button to return to the Edit File Type dialog box.
10. For increased performance, you can disable the Confirm Open After Download check box. This will allow files to load immediately, rather than displaying a dialog box each time a file is downloaded from the Internet with the specified file extension. The Confirmation dialog box requests user confirmation before the execution of the application and the loading of the associated file.

> **CAUTION**
>
> You should not disable the Confirm Open After Download check box unless you are 100-percent sure that no harm will come to your system. It is always a good idea to download any file, such as an executable file or any file that supports a macro language (such as Word for Windows), and scan it for viruses before loading or executing it.

11. Check Enable Quick View if you have a Windows Explorer viewer for the file type. This way, you can quickly display the document using the Windows Explorer rather than by loading the associated application.
12. Check the Always show extension check box to display the filename and file extension in any folder window.
13. Click the OK button to return to the File Types properties sheet.
14. Repeat steps 2 through 13 for each file association you wish to edit. When you have finished, click the OK button to close the Options dialog box.

Adding a new file association follows the same general steps as editing a file association, but with two basic differences. First, the name of the dialog changes to Add New File Type. Second, the dialog box is completely empty. You must specify the icon to display the associated file extension, the MIME content type, and the actions you want performed.

Configuring the Start and Search Pages

The Internet Explorer will load a default startup page each time it is executed. By default, this page is The Microsoft Network home page, located at http://www.msn.com. This is fine if you want to check out the MSN home page each time you launch Internet Explorer. However, I find this default startup page to be a bit of a nuisance for two reasons. First, if you are not already connected to the Internet, Windows NT will attempt to dial your default connection using the Dial-Up Networking service (see the section titled "Configuring the Internet Connection" for further information). Second, I have my own intranet and prefer to view the home page for my WWW site.

The Internet Explorer also has a default search page. This search page connects to the MSN site http://www.msn.com/access/allinone.htm. While I like this page because it includes shortcuts to several Internet directory listing services (such as Yahoo! and Lycos), it has the same disadvantages as described in the preceding paragraph. To change either of these options, follow these steps:

1. Connect to the Web site you want to use as your start page or your search page.
2. Choose Options from the View menu to display the Options dialog box.
3. Click the Start and Search Pages tab to display the Start and Search Pages properties sheet, shown in Figure 7.3.

FIGURE 7.3.
Specifying the default start and search pages.

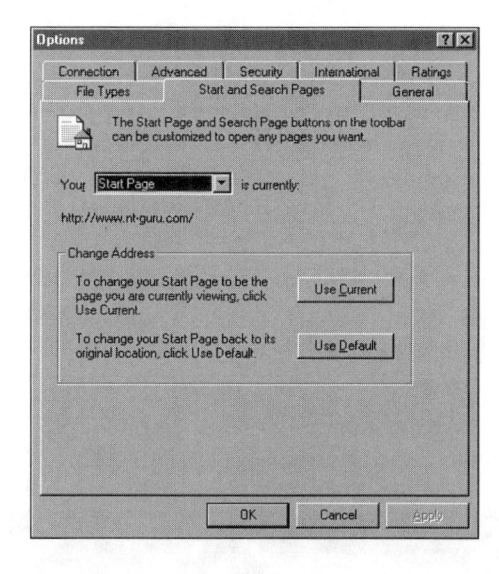

4. To change the start page, make sure that Your Start Page is selected in the drop-down listbox, then click the Use Current button.

5. To change the search page, make sure that Your Search Page is selected in the drop-down listbox, then click the Use Current button.

> **TIP**
>
> To return to the Internet Explorer default start or search page, select the appropriate page in the drop-down listbox, then click the Use Default button.

6. Click the OK button to update your changes and return to Internet Explorer.

Configuring the Appearance

As the old saying goes, "The clothes make the man." Appearance in your professional and personal life is everything. If you look like a bum, people will think you are a bum. Your Web site is no different. A good looking text-only Web site or a Web site with attention-grabbing graphics is what we all strive to create. What we often forget is that not every Web user will see all our nifty graphics. This often occurs because our client's Web browser cannot display the images. Their Web browser may be a text-only browser, or perhaps it cannot support the specific graphic format. Now Web sites incorporate audio-video and sound files that can be played on the client's Web browser automatically. The required Internet bandwidth to view or hear these files is increasing at a phenomenal rate.

This is why many Web browsers support a configuration option to disable graphic images. This can increase the performance of the Web browser to display the content (text and hypertext links) of the Web page. After all, downloading a graphic over a slow connection can be a time-consuming job. Downloading an AVI or sound file can be a nightmare. So as you develop your Web site, you should view it in text-only mode as well as in graphics mode. You may even want to change the default attributes for displayed text, background, and links just to see how your Web pages will look. If you are configuring multiple installations for your network clients, you may want to settle on a specific set of attributes. As a network administrator, you may even want to turn off some of these graphics options to limit the amount of network traffic. Changing these attributes is not a difficult task, and can be accomplished by the following steps:

1. Choose Options from the View menu to display the Options dialog box.
2. Click the General tab to display the General properties sheet (see Figure 7.4).

TIP

This properties sheet is also accessible from the Control Panel Internet applet.

FIGURE 7.4.
Changing the way Internet Explorer displays a Web page.

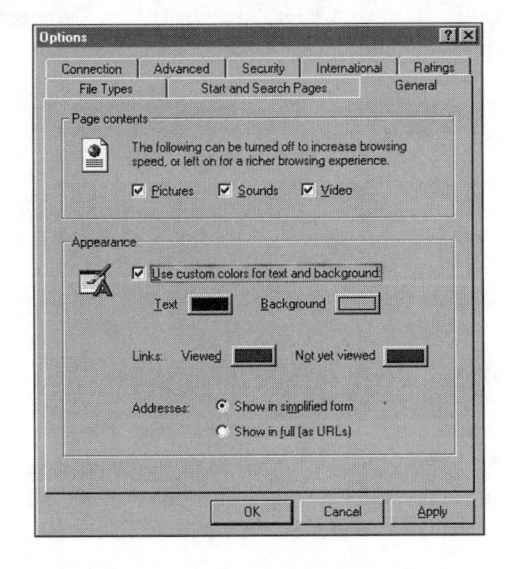

3. In the Page contents group, disable any of the following options to increase the speed at which Internet Explorer will display the page:

   - Pictures—This option specifies that graphic images (GIF or JPG) will be displayed when checked (the default), or skipped when unchecked.
   - Sounds—This option specifies that sounds will be played when checked (the default), or skipped when unchecked.

> **TIP**
>
> If you do not like the background sound of a particular site you visit often, you can disable the Sounds option before you visit the site.

   - Video—This option specifies that audio-video files will be downloaded and played automatically when checked (the default), or skipped when unchecked.

> **NOTE**
>
> Audio-video (AVI) files are notorious for eating up network bandwidth. If you have an intranet, or are using IIS as a gateway to the Internet, you may want to disable viewing of AVI files.

4. To change the default colors for the text and background, check the Use custom colors for text and background check box. Then click either the Text or the Background button to display the Colors dialog box, where you can choose a specific color.
5. To change the default colors for the hypertext links you have not viewed, or for those that you have already viewed, click the Viewed or Not yet viewed buttons, respectively. This will display the Colors dialog box, where you can choose a specific color.
6. To change the way Internet Explorer displays URLs on the status bar, enable either the Show in simplified form (the default) or the Show in full (as URLs) radio button. A simplified URL will appear as www.nt-guru.com, whereas a full URL will appear as http://www.nt-guru.com/.
7. Click the OK button to save your changes and return to Internet Explorer.

Configuring the Internet Connection

One of the most important Internet Explorer configuration options is the ability to specify how you will connect to the Internet. You can do so via a dial-up network connection or via a proxy server. If you are not physically connected to the Internet, Internet Explorer can make it

Administering Your Site

Part III

a little easier to access Internet resources. It does this by sensing whenever an Internet resource is requested (such as when you ping an Internet client), then using the Dial-Up Networking service to connect to the Internet. Once connected, you can access these Internet resources as if they were part of your local network.

Auto-dial is a great service if your internal network does not use TCP/IP. However, if you do use TCP/IP, using the auto-dial option is more of a problem than a solution because the auto-dial feature cannot determine whether you are trying to access a local or remote resource. In essence, if you use a TCP/IP-based client, the auto-dial attempts to dial up the Internet to access it. That means if you try and ping your server, the Dial-Up Networking services will be invoked in an attempt to resolve the IP address. You'll spend a lot of time pressing the cancel button to terminate the auto-dial attempt. I only recommend auto-dial when the internal network uses a network protocol other than TCP/IP, or when the computer is a standalone and not connected to a network at all. To configure the Internet Explorer to automatically connect to the Internet, follow these steps:

1. Choose Options from the View menu to display the Options dialog box.
2. Click the Connection tab to display the Connection properties sheet, shown in Figure 7.5.

TIP

This properties sheet is also accessible from the Control Panel Internet applet.

FIGURE 7.5.
Configuring Internet Explorer to connect to the Internet automatically.

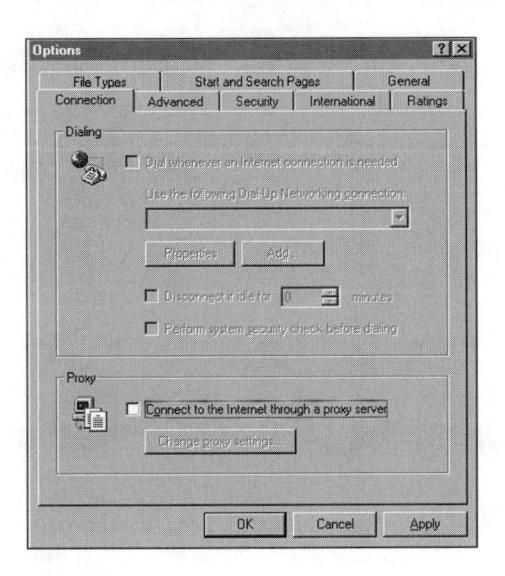

3. Check the Dial whenever an Internet connection is needed check box.

4. Select an existing Dial-Up Networking configuration to use in the Use the following Dial-Up Networking connection drop-down listbox.

5. If there are no Dial-Up Networking connections currently available, or if you need to create a new one for Internet use, click the Add button to specify the new connection parameters.

6. To change any existing properties for the specified connection, click the Properties button.

7. To specify a time, in seconds, to automatically disconnect when the system is not using the connection, check the Disconnect if idle for check box and enter a value in the field.

8. To prevent other Internet users from accessing your files or printers, check the Perform system security check before dialing check box. This will display a message if the bindings for the Server service are enabled for your Internet Dial-Up Networking connection. It will then offer to unbind them and prevent incoming file and print services from functioning.

9. Click the OK button to save your changes and return to Internet Explorer.

A *proxy server* is a computer on your network that acts as an intermediary between an Internet resource, such as a Web site, and your network client application (in this case Internet Explorer). You can think of a proxy server as a middleman. For example, when you purchase a steak at the local market, money passes from you, to the local store, to the rancher. You do not just go to a ranch and hack a steak off of a cow. Well, think of the proxy server as the market and the Internet resource as the rancher.

A proxy server also increases network security by preventing incoming or outgoing network traffic. This occurs because your network client connects to a specific (nonstandard) port on your proxy server to access an Internet resource. Your proxy server then connects to the Internet resource using the standard Internet resource port address assigned to the Internet service. Information from the Internet resource is then passed to the proxy server, which in turn passes the information to the connected client. This two-way data flow continues until the client disconnects from the Internet resource. By using nonstandard ports on the proxy server, you can prevent internal or external clients from accessing network resources.

However, Internet Explorer does not require that you use a proxy server for all network and Internet access. You can also configure the Internet Explorer by domain name, IP address, or port address to bypass the proxy server. This provides faster and more efficient access to intranet resources, which is a good thing considering that a proxy server, like any middleman, consumes

Administering Your Site

Part III

resources. Nothing in this world is really free; a proxy server provides increased network security at the cost of network bandwidth and time. To configure Internet Explorer to use a proxy server, follow these steps:

1. Choose Options from the View menu to display the Options dialog box.
2. Click the Connection tab to display the Connection properties sheet, shown in Figure 7.5.

TIP

This properties sheet is also accessible from the Control Panel Internet applet.

3. Check the Connect to the Internet through a proxy server check box, then click the Change proxy settings button.
4. The Proxy Settings dialog box, shown in Figure 7.6, will appear.

FIGURE 7.6.
Configuring Internet Explorer to use a proxy server.

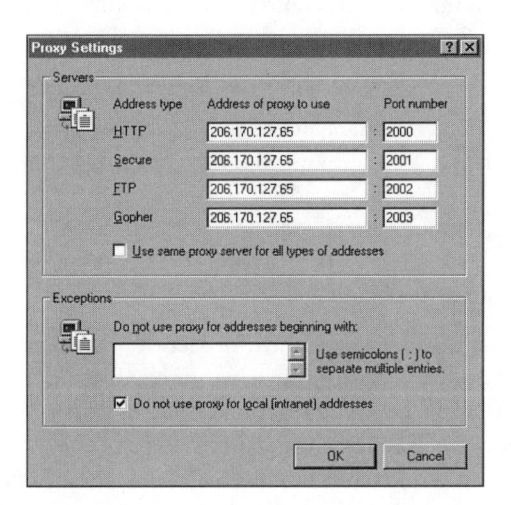

5. Enter a DNS name or IP address in the Address of proxy to use field for each type of Internet service (HTTP, Secure, FTP, Gopher) you want to use.

6. For each service type specified in step 5, enter the TCP/IP port you want to use in the Port number field.

> **TIP**
>
> If your proxy server uses a single port for all Internet services, fill out just the HTTP service entries. Then check the Use same proxy server for all types of addresses check box.

7. To bypass your proxy server for specific Internet resources, enter the DNS name, IP address, or TCP/IP port number in the Do not use proxy for addresses beginning with listbox. Each entry should be separated by a comma. To bypass a proxy for access to a specific computer or port, for example, you could enter `206.170.127.65,80`, which would bypass the proxy to access the computer with IP address `206.170.127.65` or to access any resource using TCP/IP port 80.
8. Click the OK button to save your changes and return to the Options dialog box.
9. Click the OK button to update your configuration and return to Internet Explorer.

Configuring Internet Explorer Cache Settings

To decrease the time it takes Internet Explorer to display a page on a Web site you visit frequently, a portion of your hard disk is used to cache the HTML page and in-line graphics. So when you access the Web site, a check is made to determine if it has changed. If the site has not changed, the information stored in the cache is used. If the page has changed, the information is downloaded and the cache is updated. The amount of disk space to use for this cache, as well as the update frequency, is configurable. To change any of the cache settings, follow these steps:

1. Choose Options from the View menu to display the Options dialog box.
2. Click the Advanced tab to display the Advanced properties sheet, shown in Figure 7.7.

> **TIP**
>
> This properties sheet is also accessible from the Control Panel Internet applet.

FIGURE 7.7.
Configuring Internet Explorer cache options.

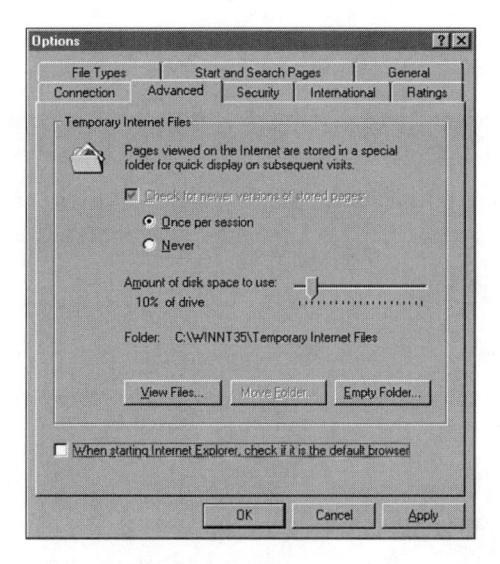

3. If you always want to use the copy of a Web page stored on your local hard drive regardless of whether it is outdated, disable the Check for newer versions of stored pages check box.

> **NOTE**
>
> Disabling the Check for newer versions of stored pages is not a recommended action because it can lead to stale (out-of-date) pages.

4. If you enable the Once per session radio button, Internet Explorer will determine whether the stored cache pages are outdated once per Dial-Up Networking session. If you enable the Never radio button, the Internet Explorer will not check the pages to see if they contain stale information.

> **NOTE**
>
> Enabling the Never radio button is not a recommended action because it can lead to stale (out-of-date) pages.

5. Move the slider on the Amount of disk space to use control to specify the percentage of your disk that can be used to cache Web pages.
6. To view the current contents of your cache, click the View Files button.
7. To change the location of your cached Web pages, click the Move Folder button.
8. To delete all of the cached files, click the Empty Folder button.
9. To disable the check that determines whether Internet Explorer is configured as the default Web browser, uncheck the When starting Internet Explorer, check if it is the default browser check box.
10. Click the OK button to save your changes and return to Internet Explorer.

Configuring Internet Explorer Security

In a world full of malicious system hackers, credit card fraud, unfriendly viruses, and poorly written applications, the Internet can be a dangerous place. Although abstinence is the only guaranteed option, Windows NT Server and Internet Explorer have options to help you limit the potential dangers of the Internet. In Chapter 10, "Advanced Security Issues," you will learn more about what Windows NT Server can do to lessen the danger involved in connecting to the Internet, but for now our focus is on what security features Internet Explorer has to offer.

> **WARNING**
>
> Internet security is a real problem not so much from what is occurring on the Internet today, but rather what may occur tomorrow. The first thing you should be concerned about is data snooping. Data snooping is where an Internet hacker traps information being sent between your computer and a remote site. If you send confidential information (such as your credit card number or user account and password) over an open connection, it is easy for a hacker to obtain this information and use it to your detriment. Another potential security problem is the fraudulent display of a secure site notice or a fraudulent security certificate. In both cases, you may think you are using a secure connection, but in reality you are not. The final cause of concern can arise either from a poorly written (but not malicious) ActiveX object or from a malicious ActiveX object. In the first case, the poorly written code simply may not function properly; in the second case, the ActiveX object may deliberately attempt to damage your system or pass confidential data to its originator.

There are three types of basic security Internet Explorer can provide for you. First, there is the option that warns you when you will be sending or viewing data over an open connection. This can occur when you enter data in a Web form, for example. Second, Internet Explorer can check the remote site's security credentials when you are sending or viewing data over a secure connection. You might encounter this type of connection when you purchase a product with a credit card from an electronic store. Finally, you can configure Internet Explorer to limit the active content that can be displayed on your Web browser. You will encounter active content anytime you download and activate an ActiveX object.

Of these three options, the last is the most important because you will encounter numerous Web sites with VBScript, JavaScript, or even ActiveX documents (such as Word or Excel) that are embedded in Web pages. Any of these might contain code that could damage your system. These problems do not necessarily occur from malicious developers; they could occur from poorly written applications. After all, ActiveX development is still in its infancy, and it will take a while for developers to learn how to write bullet-proof applications.

To modify Internet Explorer security options, follow these steps:

1. Choose Options from the View menu to display the Options dialog box.
2. Click the Security tab to display the Security properties sheet (see Figure 7.8).

TIP

This properties sheet is also accessible from the Control Panel Internet applet.

FIGURE 7.8.
Configuring Internet Explorer security options.

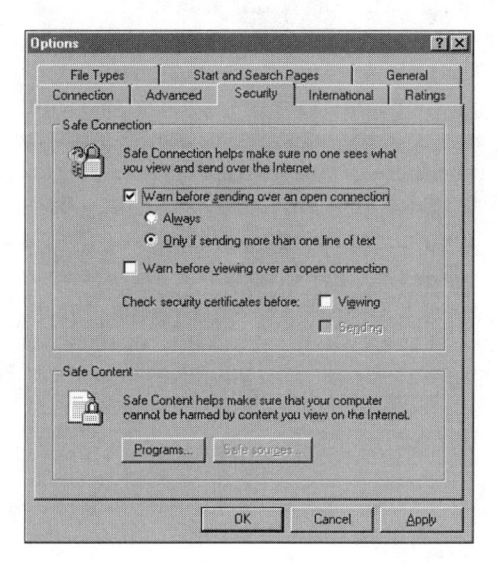

Using the Internet Explorer

Chapter 7

3. In the Safe Connection group you can specify the following options:
   - Warn before sending over an open connection—Checking this option and setting one of the following radio buttons will enable warnings for clear text transmissions.
     - Always—This radio button specifies that you should be warned every time you send clear text data over the Internet.

> **TIP**
>
> It is a good idea to choose the Always radio button so that you are warned each time you transmit information over the Internet. This helps you make sure that you do not send confidential information (such as your credit card number) over the Internet.

   - Only if sending more than one line of text—This option specifies that you be warned about sending clear text data over the Internet if the text is greater than a single line.
   - Warn before viewing over an open connection—This option specifies that you be warned whenever you view information over a clear text connection.
   - Check security certificates before—This option specifies that Internet Explorer check the security certificate to verify that the certificate is registered to the correct site and that it has not been tampered with. Internet Explorer will verify the certificate whenever the following occurs:
     - Viewing—If enabled, the certificate will be checked whenever you view data over a secure connection.
     - Sending—If enabled, the certificate will be checked whenever you send data over a secure connection.

4. To help protect you from active content damage, choose any of the following options:
   - Programs—This option allows you to specify the type of restrictions placed on Web pages with active content. The type can be one of the following:
     - Expert—This option is only recommended for ActiveX developers. A warning will be provided before any active content is displayed that could cause a security problem, but all active content is permissible.
     - Normal—This is the recommended option because it will automatically prevent security problems. However, some active content may not be displayed.

- None—This option is not recommend because it opens up the system to potential damage. No warnings will be displayed, and all active content is permitted.
- Safe Sources—This option allows you to specify, based on the ActiveX object's digital structure, those objects that are considered to be trusted and will not damage your system. Objects entered will not be checked for possible security violations. As such, you should place objects in this list with extreme care.

5. Click the OK button to save your changes and return to Internet Explorer.

Configuring the Internet Explorer Character Set

The Internet Explorer can support multiple languages. This can be beneficial to Web page developers who create international content. It is also very useful for your non-English-speaking Web clients because it provides a wider audience for your Web pages. You can also use this option to configure the default proportional-width and fixed-width fonts that will be displayed on the page. To configure the language and to display fonts, follow these steps:

1. Choose Options from the View menu to display the Options dialog box.
2. Click the International tab to display the International properties sheet, shown in Figure 7.9.

TIP

This properties sheet is also accessible from the Control Panel Internet applet.

FIGURE 7.9.

Configuring Internet Explorer for international use.

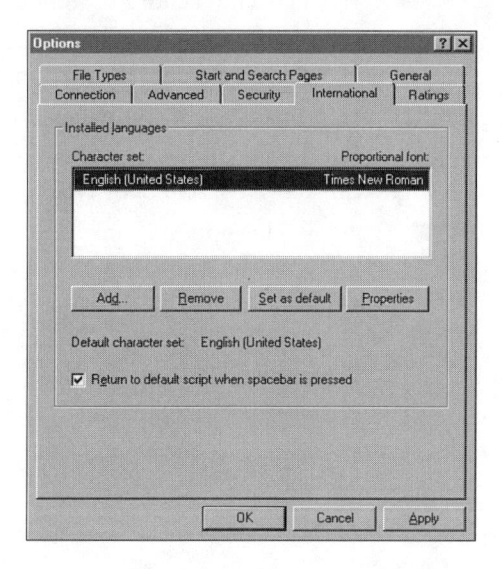

3. To add character sets, click the Add button and select the desired additional language from the list. Then click the OK button.
4. To change the default font for a character set, select the language in the Character set field and click the Properties button.
5. A Properties dialog box will appear. Choose the proportional font to be displayed from the Proportional Font drop-down listbox. Choose the fixed-width font to display from the Fixed-Width Font drop-down listbox. Choose a character-encoding sequence from the MIME Encoding drop-down listbox. Then click the OK button to return to the International properties sheet.
6. If you have installed multiple character sets, be sure to select one you want to use as the default and click the Set as default button. This will specify the default character set to be used with Internet Explorer.
7. To provide a hotkey to switch back to the default character set, check the Return to default script when spacebar is pressed check box.
8. Click the OK button to save your changes and return to Internet Explorer.

Configuring the Rating System to Limit Access to Internet Sites

New to Internet Explorer 3.0 is the rating system. This system uses the Platform and Internet Content Selection (PICS)–based rating system, and by default uses a rating system defined by the Recreational Software Advisory Council (RSAC). Web authors can obtain a RSAC rating to be applied to their Web site. For additional information check out the Web page at http://www.rsac.org. To enable ratings and specify the level of acceptance, follow these steps:

1. Choose Options from the View menu to display the Options dialog box.
2. Click the Ratings tab to display the Ratings properties sheet.

> **TIP**
>
> This properties sheet is also accessible from the Control Panel Internet applet.

3. Click the Set Ratings button. The Create Supervisor Password dialog box will be displayed. You must enter and confirm a new password in order to enable the rating system. When you have done so, click the OK button.
4. The Internet Ratings dialog box, shown in Figure 7.10, will be displayed.

FIGURE 7.10.
Configuring the Internet Explorer rating system.

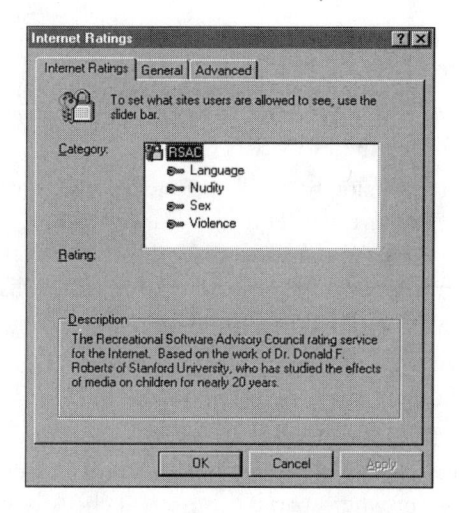

5. Click a Category item to display a slider control next to the Rating field.
6. Slide the control to select your restrictions. As each item is selected, the Description field will display a comment for each rating. The ratings are divided into four categories with five subtypes each:

    - Language—The five subtypes of this category are Inoffensive Slang, Mild Expletives, Moderate Expletives, Obscene Gestures, and Explicit or Crude Language.
    - Nudity—The five subtypes of this category are No nudity, Revealing Attire, Partial Nudity, Frontal Nudity, and Provocative Display of Frontal Nudity.
    - Sex—The five subtypes of this category are No sexual Activity Portrayed/Romance, Passionate Kissing, Clothed Sexual Touching, Nonexplicit Sexual Touching, and Explicit Sexual Activity.
    - Violence—The five subtypes of this category are No Violence, Fighting, Killing, Killing with Blood and Gore, and Wanton and Gratuitous Violence.

7. Click the General tab to specify that users can see unrated sites, to specify that a different PICS-based rating system be used, or to change the current password for the rating system.
8. Click the Advanced tab to specify that a user can view restricted sites by entering the supervisor password when prompted, and to choose a ratings bureau.
9. Click the OK button to update the rating options and return to Internet Explorer.

Using the Internet Explorer

Chapter 7

Using Internet Explorer

After you have configured Internet Explorer, you are ready to start using it to browse the Internet. To get the most out of the Internet Explorer, you can use the toolbar, shown in Figure 7.11, to quickly navigate from site to site.

FIGURE 7.11.
The Internet Explorer toolbars.

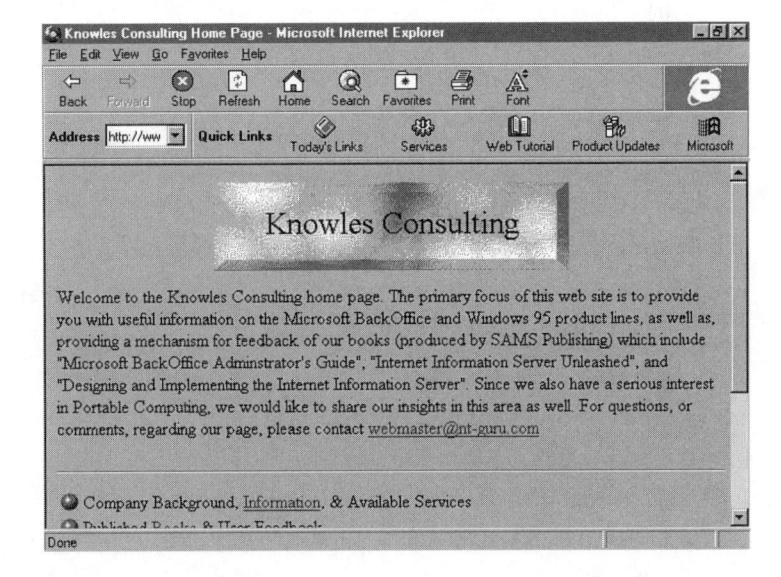

From left to right, and top to bottom, the toolbar buttons have the following functions:

- Back opens the previous Web page.
- Forward opens the next Web page.

> **NOTE**
>
> The Back and Forward buttons are applicable only when you have opened more than one Web page.

- Stop halts the downloading of a document, the attempt to activate a hypertext link, or the attempt to access an Internet service.
- Refresh updates the current Web page.
- Home displays the home page.
- Search searches the current Web page for a phrase or word.
- Favorites displays your list of favorite Web sites.
- Print prints the current page using the default printer.

- Font chooses the next font size in a rotating fashion. There are five sizes, and they rotate from smallest to largest.
- Address specifies the current address of a Web page, or you can enter an address of an Internet service to jump to.
- Quick Links provides an additional button bar with predefined links, which include the following:
    - Today's Links jumps to the Web site

        http://www.microsoft.com/links/links.asp

        which includes predefined links to topics of interest.
    - Services jumps to the Web site

        http://www.microsoft.com/lookup/services.asp

        which includes predefined links to useful references such as phone numbers, travel information, home references, and financial references.
    - Web Tutorial jumps to the Web site

        http://home.microsoft.com/tutorial/default.html

        and displays a hypertext Internet tutorial.
    - Product Updates jumps to the Web site

        http://home.microsoft.com/internet/center.asp

        and displays a list of hypertext links to Microsoft product updates.
    - Microsoft jumps to the Microsoft home page at

        http://www.microsoft.com/

To manually jump to a Web, FTP, Gopher, or other Internet site, simply enter a URL in the Address field. To access a WWW site, for example, you can enter www.nt-guru.com, and Internet Explorer will automatically add the resource type of http:// to build a fully qualified URL that will look like this: http://www.nt-guru.com. The same principle applies for the FTP, Gopher, and Telnet Internet resources. This makes browsing the Internet quite easy, because each site you visit will display hypertext links created by Internet Explorer, including the FTP and Gopher services, which are not specifically designed to build such links.

Summary

This chapter describes how to install Internet Explorer. You have learned how to configure Internet Explorer to meet your tastes and how to configure the more serious aspects of Internet Explorer to minimize potential security problems.

In Chapter 8, "Working with Microsoft Exchange," you will learn how to configure Microsoft Exchange Server to provide an Internet-based e-mail system. You can use the e-mail addresses you create with your Web pages to provide customer feedback or technical support, or to build e-mail lists.

Working with Microsoft Exchange

8

IN THIS CHAPTER

- Using Exchange Server on the Internet **190**
- Microsoft Exchange Security Issues **200**

There is one feature the Internet Information Server lacks—the capacity to send or receive electronic mail (e-mail) messages. Of course, this is probably by design. After all, Microsoft does include a product to accomplish this task. It is part of the Microsoft BackOffice suite and is called Microsoft Exchange Server. In this chapter, you will learn how to use Microsoft Exchange Server in conjunction with the Internet to provide an SMTP (Simple Mail Transfer Protocol) mail server.

An SMTP mail server is the backbone of Internet e-mail. If you want to allow users who access your Web site to send e-mail to your webmaster, capture information from a guest book, or send a message to your sales staff to follow up on leads from potential customers, you need to provide an SMTP e-mail address. An SMTP mail address uses the form `UserName@DomainName.com`, where `UserName` might be something like `webmaster` or `sales` and the domain name might be something like `nt-guru.com`. Providing Internet mail capabilities to all of your network clients, however, is not something you can do without associated risks, so this chapter also explains some of those risks and, I hope, shows you how to deal with them.

> **TIP**
>
> For best performance, Exchange Server should be installed on a server with no other duties. Exchange Server requires a lot of CPU horsepower and system resources to perform the duties of an enterprise mail server. Unless absolutely required, Exchange Server should not be installed on the same computer as the Internet Information Server. This will ensure that your computer's resources are applied toward your Internet services (such as the WWW, FTP, and Gopher publishing services) rather than your corporate e-mail services.

Using Exchange Server on the Internet

By itself, Microsoft Exchange Server will not provide you with the capability to create an SMTP mail server. Instead you must purchase an add-on product called the *Internet Mail Connector* (IMC). The IMC is used to create a gateway between Exchange Server and the Internet. When installed, the IMC uses the standard Internet Protocol port 25 to provide SMTP mail capabilities. If you are using a firewall with Exchange Server, you must enable this port for two-way access in order to send and receive Internet mail. In this section, you will learn how to install and configure the Internet Mail connector. You will also learn how to use the Internet Mail Connector to connect multiple Exchange Server sites using the Internet as a backbone.

> **NOTE**
>
> The Internet Mail Connector is included in the Enterprise edition of Exchange Server. If you would like more information on how to install and configure Microsoft Exchange Server, you might want to take a look at another book of mine called *Microsoft BackOffice Administrator's Survival Guide* by Sams Publishing.

Installing the Internet Mail Connector

Installing the Internet Mail Connector is a snap. It is simply a matter of running the setup program to install the files and update your Exchange Server installation. You perform this same basic process whether you purchase the Internet Mail Connector as a separate product or get it as an integral component when you purchase the Enterprise edition of Exchange Server. Just to make sure you do not have any problems installing the Internet Mail Connector, you can follow these steps:

1. Execute the `setup.exe` program located on the Exchange Server CD-ROM. Be sure to use the correct version of this program—your CD-ROM may contain several versions. The correct version will be located in the `\SETUP\PlatformName` directory, where `PlatformName` will be `I386` for Intel processors, `ALPHA` for DEC Alpha processors, or `MIPS` for NEC MIPS processors.
2. The Microsoft Exchange Server Setup dialog box appears. Click the Add/Remove button.
3. The Microsoft Exchange Server Setup - Complete/Custom dialog box appears, as shown in Figure 8.1.

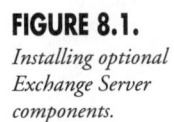

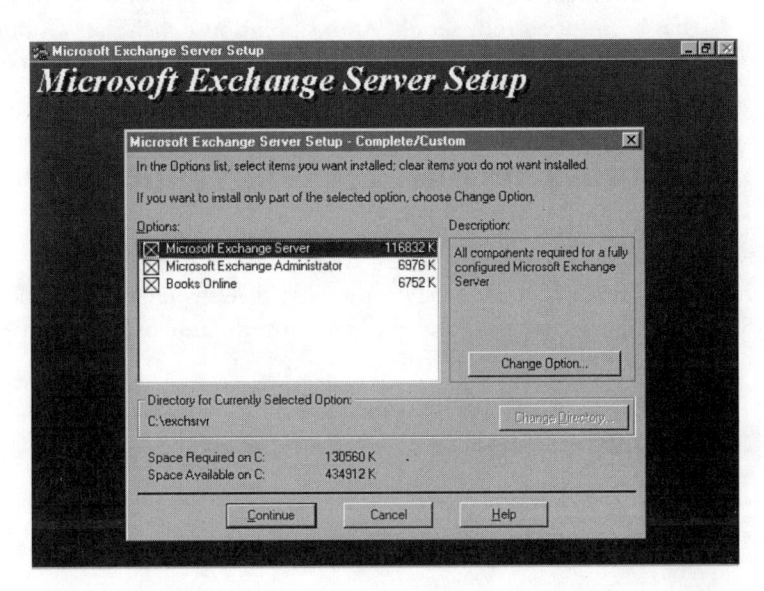

FIGURE 8.1.
Installing optional Exchange Server components.

4. Select the Microsoft Exchange Server item in the Options listbox. Then click the Change Option button. The Microsoft Exchange Server Setup - Microsoft Exchange Server dialog box, as shown in Figure 8.2, appears.

FIGURE 8.2.

Installing the Internet Mail Connector.

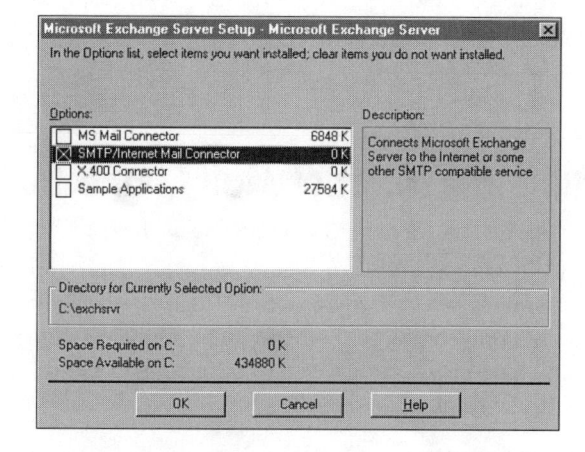

5. Check the SMTP/Internet Mail Connector check box. Then click the OK button.
6. You are then returned to the Microsoft Exchange Server Setup - Complete/Custom dialog box. Click the Continue button.
7. The Site Services Account dialog box then appears. Enter the password for the site (which you chose during your Exchange Server installation) in the Password field and click the OK button.
8. The Internet Mail Connector files are copied to your server, and Exchange Server is reconfigured. Then a message box is displayed informing you that Exchange Server has been successfully set up. At this point, just click the OK button to exit the setup program. You may then move on to the next section to configure the Internet Mail Connector.

Configuring the Internet Mail Connector

Configuring the Internet Mail Connector can be either very easy or very complex, depending on how you plan to make use of it. I know this does not sound very encouraging, but it is true. It's true because of the multitude of property sheets you have available to configure the service. So before you collapse from frustration (or information overload), just configure the following basic properties for the Internet Mail Connector:

- Specify the Administrator's mailbox. This mailbox is used by the Internet Mail Connector to send all error messages that occur.

- Specify MIME (multipurpose Internet mail extensions) or UUENCODE (a conversion scheme to convert 8-bit binary data to a 7-bit format) message encoding for outbound mail messages.

- Specify an SMTP address space. The SMTP address space is used to accept/reject all Internet mail if set to *@* or to accept mail from specific hosts and reject mail from all other hosts (based on their IP address).

- Specify a relay host or internal DNS server for message delivery. The relay host is usually an external host where all of your mail is sent to or received from. It is used for two reasons. First, it can be used internally as a single access point (such as when you have multiple Exchange Server installations but only one has a connection to the Internet) to which to forward all of your outbound mail. Second, it can be used to provide an additional level of fault tolerance (for example, when your e-mail server is down, the relay host will continue to receive e-mail from external clients). A DNS server is used to determine the IP address of the destination hosts and supply basic NetBIOS name resolution (such as when you need to convert the e-mail address of webmaster@nt-guru.com to the destination address of webmaster@206.170.126.65).

NOTE

Using a relay host based on an Internet mail server (such as those commonly used by Internet Service Providers) requires additional support considerations, generally adds additional complexities to the receipt of your e-mail, and is therefore not recommended unless you need the additional fault tolerance. If you choose to use a relay host, be sure to discuss your requirements with your ISP to determine their methodology for sending stored mail to your Exchange Server installation.

NOTE

If you will not be using a DNS server, you can map the IP addresses using the HOSTS file or WINS or by specifying the outbound servers in the Connections property sheet.

To configure the Internet Mail Connector to use these basic properties, follow these steps:

1. Launch the Microsoft Exchange Administrator, located in your Microsoft Exchange program group.
2. Expand the site folder (for my server, this is WORK, for example) so that the Add-Ins, Addressing, Connections, Directory Replication, Monitors, and Servers folders are displayed. (See Figure 8.3.)

FIGURE 8.3.
Preparing to configure the Internet Mail Connector.

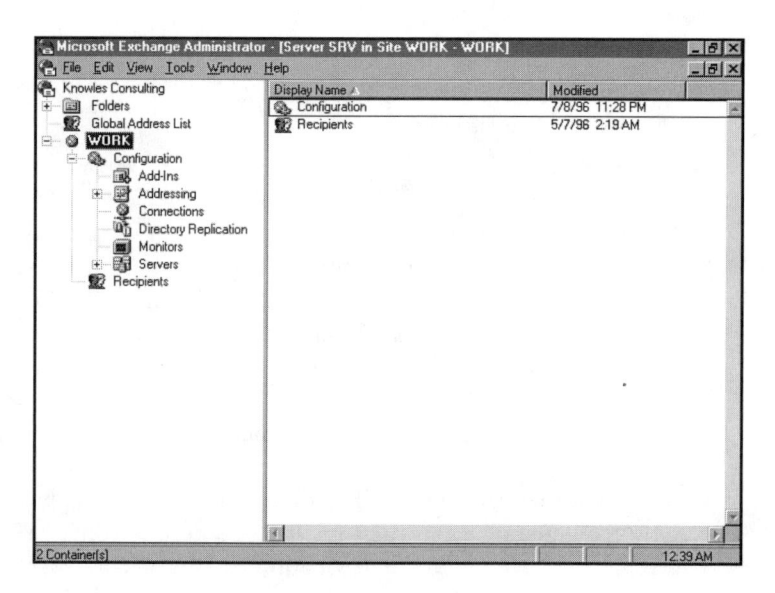

3. Select the Connections folder, and the installed connectors will be listed in the window on the right side. (See Figure 8.4.)

FIGURE 8.4.
The installed connectors in the WORK *site.*

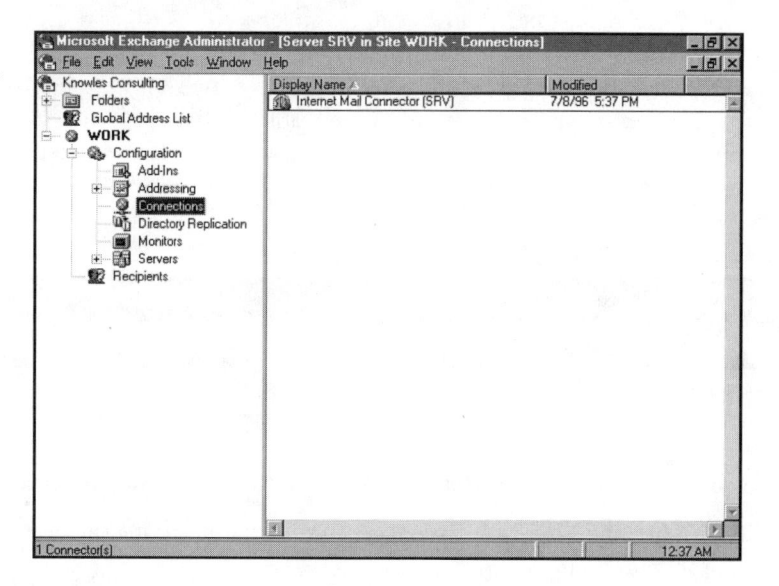

4. Select the Internet Mail Connector. Then choose Properties from the File menu, or just press the Enter key, to display the Internet Mail Connector Properties dialog box, as shown in Figure 8.5.

FIGURE 8.5.

Configuring the Internet Mail Connector's basic properties.

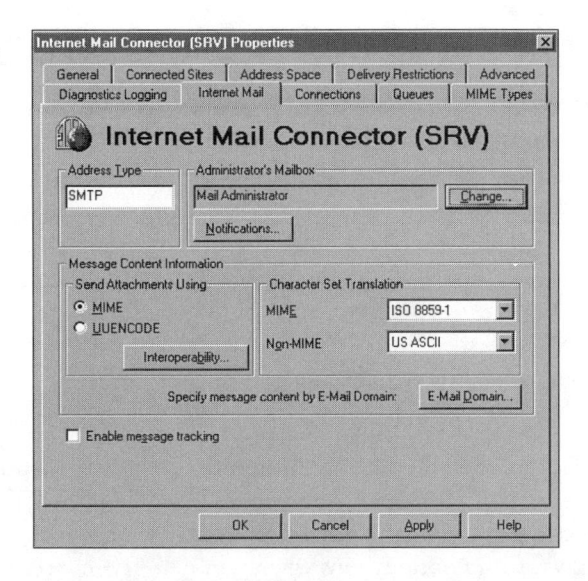

5. Click on the Change button. This displays the Administrator's Mailbox dialog box, where you may select an e-mail account to use for all administrative messages. After you select an account, click the OK button to return to the Internet Mail properties sheet.

> **NOTE**
>
> Some of the other interesting options, which not everyone will need to change, include the Address Type and Message Content Information group fields and the Enable message tracking check box. This check box is used to create a log file of the routes (or paths) of your e-mail messages to the destination host. The Message Content Information group includes two subgroups called Send Attachments Using and Character Set Translation. The Send Attachments Using subgroup is used to specify your outbound mail encoding scheme for embedded objects. This encoding scheme can be either MIME, the newer standard with richer content varieties, or UUENCODE, the older but more compatible scheme. When a message is sent, the character set may need to be translated based on the encoding scheme. This choice is configured in the Character Set Translation subgroup. If you would like to specify this information on a per–domain name basis, you can do so by clicking the E-Mail Domain button.

> **TIP**
>
> When connected to the Internet, some additional features of Exchange become more of a potential problem than a potential benefit. Having your internal e-mail clients send out-of-office (such as when you are on vacation) or automatically generated replies (such as when you need to time-stamp a message) is a nice feature. Sending confidential information (an address to reach you while you are vacation, perhaps) over the Internet, however, can be a possible security hazard. To prevent this from occurring, click on the Interoperability button to display the Operability dialog box. Then check the Disable Out Of Office responses to the Internet and Disable Automatic Replies to the Internet check boxes.

6. Click on the Notifications button to display the Notifications dialog box, shown in Figure 8.6. My personal preference is to be notified of all non-delivery (when a message could not be sent or received) events, which is accomplished by enabling the Always send notifications when non-delivery reports are generated radio button. You may, however, choose to limit the messages you will receive by enabling the Send notifications for these non-delivery reports radio button. Then you may choose from the following events:

- E-Mail address could not be found—Specifies that a message be sent to the mail administrator when either the sending or receiving party could not be located.

- Multiple matches for an E-Mail address occurred—Specifies that a message be sent to the mail administrator when there are multiple definitions for an e-mail address in either the sending or receiving party. The most common cause of this message is defining the same SMTP address for multiple Exchange Server recipients.

- Message conversion failed—Specifies that a message be sent to the mail administrator whenever an unknown mail format is received. This can often be corrected for future messages by updating the MIME mapping in the MIME Types tab.

- Destination host could not be found—Specifies that a message be sent to the mail administrator when the destination mail server could not be located. This can be caused for one of three reasons. First, the destination mail server could be down or otherwise unavailable. Second, the domain name server for the destination server could be down or otherwise unavailable. Third, there may be no definition in the HOSTS file in the `SystemRoot\System32\drivers\etc` subdirectory.

- Protocol error occurred—Specifies that a message be sent to the mail administrator whenever a transport protocol error occurs.

Working with Microsoft Exchange

Chapter 8

- Message timeout exceeded—Specifies that a message be sent to the mail administrator when a message could not be sent to the destination host. This type of failure is called a *timeout error* (these timeout choices can be specified in the Connections property sheet).

FIGURE 8.6.

Configuring the Internet Mail Connector message notification properties.

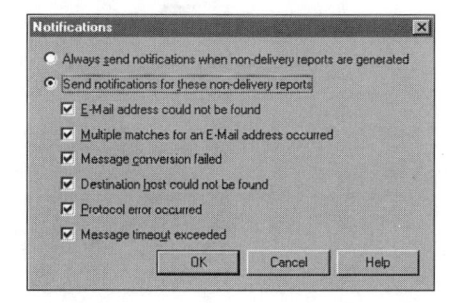

7. Click on the Address Space tab to display the Address Space property sheet, as shown in Figure 8.7.

FIGURE 8.7.

Specifying the SMTP address space.

8. Click on the New Internet button to display the SMTP Properties dialog box. Enter a value of *@* in the E-mail domain field. Leave the Cost field as 1. Then click the OK button.

9. Click the Connections tab to display the Connections property sheet, as shown in Figure 8.8.

FIGURE 8.8.
Using the Connections properties sheet to specify the SMTP address space.

10. In the Message Delivery field, choose the Use domain name service (DNS) radio button to use your DNS server for NetBIOS name resolution. Or choose the Forward all messages to host radio button and specify a name of the mail server to relay all of your outbound mail to, such as `ServerName` if another Exchange Server is used internally or `ServerName@DomainName.com` if using an external (Internet mail server) mail server.

> **TIP**
>
> I prefer to use the Microsoft DNS service included with Windows NT Server 4.0 rather than a relay host. Although this does add an additional level of complexity, I consider it a worthwhile effort because it keeps you in control. If you use a relay host, it is up to the administrator of that host to make sure that the DNS service on that site is properly configured. It's easier to use a relay host, but certainly not as satisfying.

11. Click the OK button to close the Internet Mail Connector Properties dialog box.

At this point you might think you are finished, but you're not. There are still two steps you need to accomplish before you can use the Internet Mail Connector. You need to add your DNS records to your DNS server and configure the Internet Mail Connector's service startup values. To configure your DNS service, follow these steps:

1. Open the file that defines your domain. Mine is `nt-guru.dom`, and the default file supplied with the Microsoft DNS service is `place.dom`, but yours will probably have another name. If you are unsure of the file to use, look in the boot file for a primary

entry with the domain name and associated filename (such as `primary nt-guru.com nt-guru.dom`). For additional information, refer to Chapter 9, "Using DHCP, WINS, and DNS."

2. If you left the comments in the file, look for the E-Mail Servers entry. If you did not leave the original comments, you can add the records anywhere in the file. Just make sure not to duplicate the records (in case someone else has already added them). The entries you need to add include an address record (A) and a mail record (MX) and will look like the following:

```
@            IN  MX   10     srv
srv          IN  A    206.170.127.65
```

Be sure to change the value of *srv* to the name of your computer hosting Exchange Server and the IP address (*206.170.127.65*) to the IP address assigned to your server. Otherwise you will not be able to send or receive e-mail from the Internet and I will wind up with a lot of non-delivery messages in my administrator's mailbox.

3. Repeat steps 1 and 2 for each DNS server you have hosting a separate Exchange Server installation. If you will only be using one DNS server, repeat step 2 for each Exchange server installation.

4. Save and close your file.

5. Stop and then restart your Microsoft DNS service using the Control Panel Services applet. Or enter NET STOP DNS, then NET START DNS, at a command console prompt.

To configure your Internet Mail Connector's service startup values, follow these steps:

1. Open the Control panel; then launch the Services applet.

2. Scroll down the list until you see the Microsoft Exchange Internet Connector entry in the Service listbox. Select the entry and click the Startup button to display the Service dialog box.

3. Choose the Automatic radio button in the Startup Type field.

4. Click the OK button to close the Service dialog box.

5. If you want to get started right away with the Internet Mail Connector, click the Start button to start the service. Then click the Close button to close the Services dialog box.

Using the Internet to Connect Multiple Exchange Server Sites

If your network has multiple sites in external locations (such as a WAN), you are probably using a proprietary means to connect your mail servers so that you can exchange e-mail with all of your network users. This proprietary connection method might be a router, a slow modem, or a similar product. As an alternative to proprietary (and costly) connection schemes, you can use your connection to the Internet to connect your external sites. There is a catch here, however, because you get nothing free. To create an SMTP mail system and connect two Exchange Server sites, you need multiple mail connectors. You can use one of three combinations: one X.400 and one Internet Mail Connector, the Microsoft Exchange Connector (which provides the Site Connector and Dynamic RAS Connector) and the Internet Mail Connector, or two of the same type of connectors (such as two Internet Mail Connectors).

> **NOTE**
>
> If you have the Enterprise edition of Exchange Server, or have purchased the Microsoft Exchange Connector, you can use the Site Connector (choose File|New Other|Site Connector) to connect multiple Exchange Server sites. This is a better choice than purchasing multiple Internet Mail Connectors. It is also a more efficient mechanism because it uses Windows NT Remote Procedure Calls over any supported transport protocol that supports NetBIOS or Windows sockets (TCP/IP, IPX/SPX, NetBEUI, and others) to connect the sites. The Site Connector is also required if you want to replicate directories with Exchange Server.

The basic idea is that you will use one Internet Mail Connector to send your SMTP mail to all external e-mail clients (those outside of your organization) and the other connector, whichever one it is, to connect your sites together. You would then set your external sites to forward their SMTP mail to the Exchange Server that provides the outbound SMTP mail service. All outgoing SMTP mail from the external site would be forwarded to this site for final transmission over the Internet. All incoming SMTP mail would be received on this site and then forwarded to the all the external sites (using the X.400 Connector, the Site Connector, or the Internet Mail Connector).

Microsoft Exchange Security Issues

The number-one service most users demand of the Internet is e-mail. E-mail has revolutionized communications in industry. This capability, however, also includes inherent risks that you must be prepared to deal with to minimize the potential problems that could occur. In this section you will examine some of these problems and the solutions you can apply to your Microsoft Exchange Server and Microsoft Exchange clients.

Protecting Your Server

Microsoft Exchange Server uses the Windows NT *Remote Procedure Call* (RPC) mechanism as the communication link between the server and client. It uses the Microsoft Challenge/Response security methodology built into the Windows NT RPC to authenticate client/server and server/server connections. Using this methodology, it is possible to not only encrypt the password associated with a user account, but to encrypt the entire communication stream. This means that it is possible to provide a secure means for a user to access his mailbox over the Internet, as well as replicate data between Exchange sites. (For more information on site replication and the Internet, refer to Chapter 11 of the *Exchange Administrator's Guide*). But there is more to protecting your server than just using a secure communications link. The following sections address these issues.

Preventing a Denial of Service

Have you considered what could occur if one of your network clients ticks off someone on the Internet? Suppose this problem occurred on an Internet news group. Your client may just have a nasty message reply (commonly called a *flame*) posted on the news group. If that's all that happens, consider yourself fortunate. Why fortunate? Because it is also possible that this ticked-off Internet user may be so upset, or just malicious enough, to decide to send a flood of e-mail to this network client of yours. There could be a series of small messages, a series of large messages, or possibly a series of huge messages that contain megabytes of junk embedded in them. Your server will have to deal with them all.

Because each message requires processing time and server storage, a flood of e-mail could cause what is commonly called a *denial of service*. In essence, this means your server could be overloaded, which would prevent all of your e-mail clients (not just the one user) from sending or receiving e-mail. To prevent such an occurrence from happening, you can perform one of the following actions:

- Warn your network clients about posting inflammatory messages on the Internet. Instigate a policy for users to inform you of high message traffic from an Internet user.
- Configure the Internet Mail Connector Message size parameter in the General tab of the Internet Connector Properties dialog box to limit the size of incoming and outgoing mail. This will prevent large messages from being received by your network client from an irate Internet user.
- Configure the Internet Mail Connector to reject messages sent from the irate Internet user. You do this from the Connections tab of the Internet Mail Connector Properties dialog box. Just enable the Accept or Reject by Host option; then click the Specify Hosts button. You can then specify the IP addresses of the host computers from which to reject messages.

Restricting Access to the Internet

Another problem that could occur with network clients who send or receive e-mail over the Internet is that they could send mail containing sensitive information to someone outside of the organization. This could occur, for example, when an e-mail message is received from an external user. Your very friendly network client, thinking that only someone who works for the company would ask for such information and have access to his e-mail account, sends the requested information back as a reply to the original message. He might not even have been aware that the originating e-mail message arrived from an external source. After all, how many network users do you know who check the properties for each e-mail address they receive?

The enhanced version of the Microsoft Exchange Client included with Microsoft Exchange Server attempts to avoid this possibility by displaying a *friendly name* (the actual name of the sender) along with the e-mail address at the top of each message. A message received from the Internet might appear as Arthur Knowles [webmaster@nt-guru.com]. The e-mail address within the brackets [] of the e-mail address is a sure sign that this message originated outside of the organization. Messages that are sent within the organization include only the friendly name, such as Arthur E. Knowles, which you define as the display name for the client mailbox.

To prevent such a possibility from occurring in your organization, you can limit the clients who are authorized to send e-mail over the Internet. You do this using the Delivery Restrictions tab on the Internet Connector Properties dialog box. You can specify individual clients to accept e-mail intended for the Internet in the Accept message from listbox or reject specific individuals in the Reject messages from listbox.

Preventing Auto-Replies to the Internet

One of the really nifty features of the enhanced Microsoft Exchange client is the capability to automatically send a reply to a received message. This is commonly used when a network client will be out of the office for a few days (such as when he is on vacation). It is an appropriate mechanism to inform colleagues at work that you will be unavailable until a specific date, and you might even go so far as to include private data (such as where you can be reached in an emergency). It is not necessarily a good idea, however, to send these types of replies to e-mail received from the Internet.

After all, do you want someone whom you may not know personally to receive private information? Do you want him to know that you will not be at your home for this length of time? Carelessly passing around information like this can lead to trouble. But again, it is easily solved using the Internet Connector Properties dialog box. Just select the Internet Mail tab. Under Message Content Information, choose Interoperability and check the Disable Automatic Replies to the Internet option.

Protecting Your E-Mail Messages from Tampering or Theft

Because anyone with a network packet sniffer can intercept packets sent over the Internet, you may want to ensure that e-mail messages you send cannot be read by just anyone. There are two encryption features you can use with Microsoft Exchange Server to ensure that your e-mail is secure from prying eyes. First, you can encrypt the data contained within a message;

second, you can sign a message digitally to verify the authenticity of the sender (to prevent someone else from sending messages in your name, for example).

Performing this task is a twofold process. First you must install the Microsoft Exchange Key Manager components on your Exchange Server. This is covered in Chapter 6 of the *Exchange Administrator's Guide*, so I will not step through all the details here. Second, you must configure your Microsoft Exchange clients using the Security tab of the Options dialog box (accessed by choosing Tools | Options from the menu). If you do not install the Key Manager, you cannot create the private and public keys for your network clients. Without these keys, the encryption options of the Security tab are disabled.

> **NOTE**
>
> Currently only the enhanced Microsoft Exchange client can support data encryption and digital signatures. If your clients will be sending e-mail to users who do not use the enhanced Microsoft Exchange client, they should not encrypt or digitally sign e-mail to that particular user. If they do, the recipient will not be able to read the message.

Protecting Your Clients from Viruses

In the early days of computing, viruses were transmitted primarily through the sharing of floppy disks. Although this should still be a concern for you, the primary vector for virus transmission has changed. Now, viruses are more easily transmitted by downloading files from an Internet WWW or FTP site. They can also be sent directly to you via e-mail as an embedded object. To prevent the spread of viruses in your organization, you should make sure to instigate a policy to protect your users. At the very least, you should follow these guidelines:

- At system startup, execute a virus-scanning utility such as those provided by the Norton Anti-Virus or McAffees Virus Scan.

- Do not directly activate embedded objects in a mail message that arrive from an external source (such as the Internet). Instead, save the attachment. Then run a virus scanner to verify the contents of the object. Only then should the object be opened.

- If a virus is found within an e-mail message, immediately notify the rest of your e-mail clients who may be the recipient of a broadcast message containing the object. If you want to be friendly about the situation, notify the sender of the e-mail message that a virus was found within the object (he might not have been aware that his system was infected when he attached the object to the message). If you want to take a stronger stand about the situation, configure the Internet Mail Connector (via the Accept or Reject by Host group options in the Connections properties sheet) to reject all e-mail messages from the sender of the infected e-mail message. You can reject all new messages from the sender until he proves to your satisfaction that he did not knowingly send you an infected message.

Summary

This chapter focuses on installing and configuring the Internet Mail Connector. It also describes some of the possible problems you might encounter using Microsoft Exchange and the Internet Mail Connector. For more information on harnessing the e-mail capabilities of Microsoft Exchange Server, consult *Microsoft BackOffice Administrator's Survival Guide* or *Microsoft Exchange Server Survival Guide*, also by Sams Publishing. You have learned some of the techniques you can employ to protect your server, prevent the flow of information to undesired parties, and protect your e-mail clients from viruses. In Chapter 9, you'll learn how to use the Dynamic Host Configuration Protocol (DHCP), Windows Internet Naming Service (WINS), and Domain Name Service (DNS) to make managing your network easier as well as to provide for maximum Internet connectivity.

Using DHCP, WINS, and DNS

IN THIS CHAPTER

- Using the Dynamic Host Configuration Protocol **206**
- Using the Windows Internet Name Service **234**
- Using the Domain Name System **254**

If you have a TCP/IP-based network and want to make your administrative life a little easier, there is nothing more important than the Dynamic Host Configuration Protocol (DHCP) and the Windows Internet Name Service (WINS). These two services provide the ability to automatically manage your client IP address allocations and NetBIOS name resolution, respectively. However, if you want to connect your network to the Internet or support clients that do not support the Microsoft implementation of DHCP and WINS, you will also be interested in the Microsoft domain name system (DNS). This version of DNS is WINS-aware. This gives you the ability to have your DNS service query the WINS for name resolution of any names not included in the static configuration files. You could also use the DNS service instead of DHCP and WINS, but I would not recommend it unless it's for a standalone server or Internet firewall because DHCP and WINS are much easier to administer.

All these services are client/server applications. You have a service running on your Windows NT Server domain controller, which is the server side of the component, and a service running on a network client, which is the client component. Currently the supported operating systems that have built-in DHCP and WINS client software include Windows NT Workstation, Windows 95, Windows for Workgroups, and MS-DOS (including Windows 3.1). The MS-DOS and Windows 3.1 network clients must use the Microsoft Network Client 3.0 as their network interface. All the various client platforms support the Microsoft DNS implementation, as well.

The goal of this chapter is to provide you with an understanding of these services so that you can properly implement the DHCP, WINS, and DNS services on your network. The chapter breaks down the discussion into design goals, installation, configuration, and management of these services, which will cover most of the administrative issues. Where prudent, the chapter includes specific discussions concerning interoperability with existing UNIX services, tips to get the maximum mileage from these services, and some of the possible problems (gotchas) that you want to avoid.

Using the Dynamic Host Configuration Protocol

The DHCP service is based on the Request for Comment (RFC) document 1541; it is not a newly invented mechanism by Microsoft for managing your IP address allocations. The Microsoft implementation varies a bit from the actual design goals, as specified in RFC 1541, but fulfills the basic design functionality quite well for your Microsoft network clients. There are a few concerns for interoperation with your existing TCP/IP-based clients that do not support DHCP, as well as some specific times not to use DHCP. Both of these will require that you maintain a LMHOST file on your Windows NT Server domain controllers, or install the DNS service and configure your network servers and clients properly.

> **NOTE**
>
> For your information, I have included RFC 1541 (and other RFCs mentioned in this chapter) on the accompanying CD-ROM in the SOURCE\RFC subdirectory as RFC1541.TXT. It is a rather interesting document, and I highly recommend that you read it for a fuller understanding of the DHCP service.

This chapter's discussion of the DHCP service will begin with some of the design goals of the service and then move on to planning your installation, installing the service, and using the DHCP Manager to administer the DHCP service. Administering your DHCP service consists of creating or deleting scopes and configuring individual scope properties. A *scope* is nothing more than a collection of IP addresses grouped into a single component for ease of administration. A scope can include all the IP addresses in a single subnet, if desired, or you can subdivide a subnet into multiple scopes. The final stops in this section are a look at DHCP database management, which will be required from time to time to improve performance, and a look at some of the registry keys that cannot be configured from the DHCP Manager.

The Design Goals for the Microsoft DHCP Protocol

As with every product a company introduces onto the market, there are definite goals the company must reach prior to releasing the product. Microsoft was no different than any other company in this regard, and had definite goals in mind for the implementation of DHCP for their operating systems. Their primary concern was making administration of a TCP/IP-based network easier to implement and maintain. This ease of administration makes it easier for the Microsoft Product Service Support (PSS) technical support groups, because TCP/IP is one of the most widely implemented protocols. The TCP/IP protocol is recommended for medium to large local area networks. TCP/IP is the preferred protocol for wide area networks, and is required for integration with a UNIX network or the Internet. Some of the goals that were actually met for Microsoft's DHCP implementation include the following:

- Centralized administration of your IP subnets. All of your IP addresses and their configuration parameters are stored in a central database located on your server.

- Automatic IP address assignment and configuration. As a client computer starts up and accesses the network for the first time, it is automatically assigned an IP address, subnet mask, default gateway, and WINS server IP address. If the client computer then moves between subnets, such as in the case of a portable computer, the original IP address and related configuration information is released back to the original pool of available IP addresses, and the client is assigned a new IP address and related configuration information at system startup.

- The return of unused IP addresses to the available pool of IP addresses. Normally IP addresses are allocated statically by a network administrator, and these IP addresses are stored on a piece of paper or a local database. This list can become outdated when clients move between subnets or new IP addresses are allocated and the list of IP addresses is not updated. This means that some IP addresses will be lost for reuse. However, DHCP utilizes a time-based mechanism called a *lease*, which a client must renew at regular intervals. If the lease expires and the client does not renew it, the IP address is returned to the pool of available IP addresses.

HOW A DHCP LEASE WORKS

A DHCP client computer will step through one of six transition states, as shown in Figure 9.1, in the process of establishing a valid IP address for use by the client computer. These transition states include the following:

Initialization—As the operating system starts, a DHCP client will broadcast a *discover* message on the network that may be received by all DHCP servers on the network. For each DHCP server that receives the discover message, an *offer* message will be returned to the client. Each offer message will include a valid IP address and relevant configuration information.

Selecting—At this point, each offer message will be collected by the client.

Requesting—The client will select an offer message, then send a *request* message that identifies the DHCP server for the selected configuration. The DHCP server will in turn send an *acknowledgment* message to the client, which contains the IP address that was initially sent in the offer message, along with a valid lease.

Bound—When the client receives the acknowledgment message, it stores the information locally on the computer (if a local storage mechanism, such as a hard disk, is available), completes the operating system startup, and may then participate as a network member with a valid IP address. This locally stored information is then used during subsequent system startups.

Renewing—When the lease has reached approximately 50 percent of its expiration time, the client attempts to renew the lease. If the lease is renewed (via an acknowledgment message from the DHCP server), the client enters the bound state once again.

Rebinding—When the lease has reached approximately 87.5 percent of its expiration time, the client attempts to renew the lease once again if it could not be renewed in the previous attempt. If this fails, the client will be assigned a new IP address by the DHCP server and enter the bound state once again. Only if the original DHCP server could not provide a valid IP address and lease will the client enter the initializing state to repeat the entire process.

FIGURE 9.1.

The six transition states of a DHCP client.

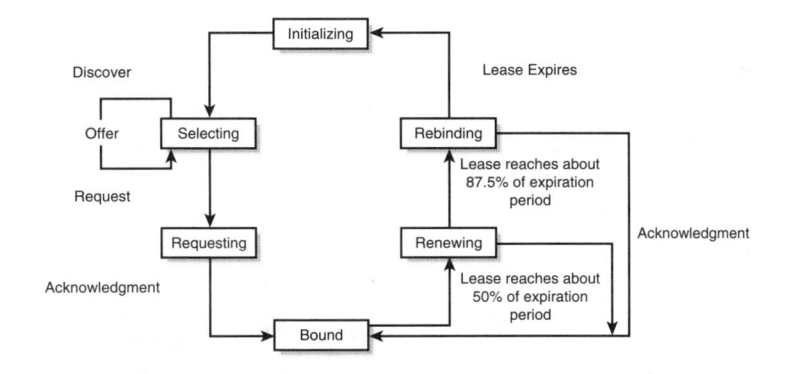

Planning Your DHCP Installation

If you have a small network with no UNIX-based interoperation required, you have a fairly easy DHCP server installation. But this does not mean you can just install the DHCP server components and forget about it. It just means there are fewer issues to contend with in your network installation. When you begin your planning, there are two types of network configurations to consider. The first, as shown in Figure 9.2, is a simple network with only one subnet. The second, as depicted in Figure 9.3, is a network with multiple subnets. The most common configuration is one with multiple subnets, and that is where most of this chapter's discussion is concentrated.

FIGURE 9.2.

A sample network with a single subnet.

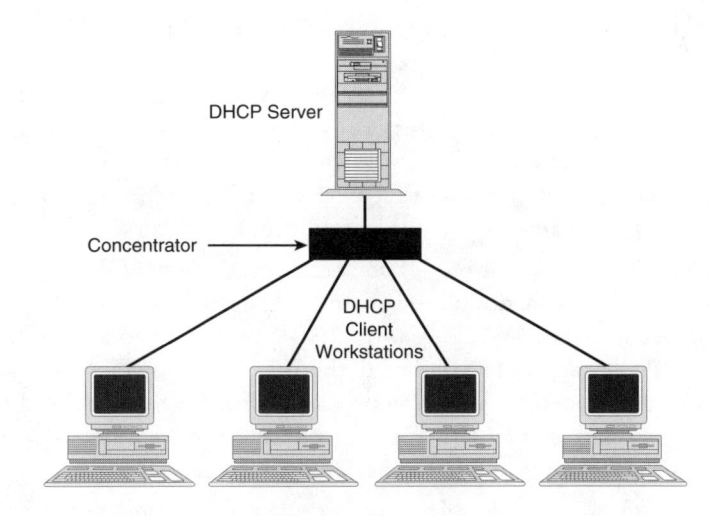

A single subnet is easiest to work with. All the DHCP and WINS servers will be located on the same subnet, so there is very little maintenance to be concerned with. Maintaining the LMHOST files will not be difficult unless you utilize many MS-DOS or Windows 3.*x* clients using the Microsoft Network Client 3.0 software. And because these computers are all on a single subnet, you can use the B-node node type for name resolution and bypass WINS configuration and LMHOST file maintenance altogether. But it will pay off in performance to use the same techniques described in this chapter for your network, just as if you did have multiple segments. It will also pay off if your network grows and must be divided into separate segments.

FIGURE 9.3.
A network with multiple subnets.

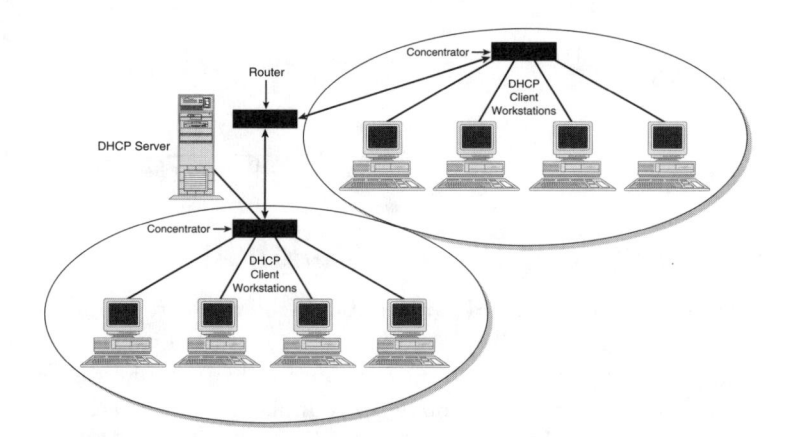

For a multiple-segmented network (one with subnets) you will have to do some planning before installing DHCP on your server and implementing DHCP for your clients. Some of the issues you will need to think about include the following:

- Routers—Your routers must support RFCs 1532, 1533, and 1541. These RFCs deal with the forwarding of packets required by the DHCP service. If your routers do not support these RFCs, your routers may discard the network packets required for DHCP operation. In this case, you may need a firmware upgrade. Consult your documentation to determine whether your routers support these specifications. If your routers do support these RFCs but you have connectivity problems, check your documentation to see if the default configuration passes or drops these packet types.

- WINS configuration—If you are planning to use DHCP to configure your WINS clients automatically, be sure to set options 44 and 46 (this is mentioned again in the section titled "Working with DHCP Scopes"). Option 44 specifies the WINS Server IP addresses to be assigned to the WINS client, while option 46 specifies the TCP/IP node type to be used. A *node type* specifies the mechanism the TCP/IP protocol uses to resolve NetBIOS name requests and to convert a NetBIOS name to a IP address. The following are the supported node types:
    - B-node—Resolves names using broadcast messages. This is the worst possible option because it can flood your network segment with broadcast messages, lowering your network's ability to carry data over the network and effectively lowering your network bandwidth on the segment. Broadcasts are also not forwarded by routers, so if the requested resource is on the other side of a router,

it will not be found. I would only recommend B-node for a very small network with a single subnet, and one that does not have a dedicated network administrator to maintain the network (using broadcasts can essentially eliminate the need to maintain an LMHOST file, or a WINS database, and for a small network there is very little network bandwidth eaten by the broadcasts).

> **NOTE**
>
> Another good reason to use B-node is that computers located on the same segment can still find each other, even if the WINS server or DNS server is down or otherwise unavailable.

P-node—Resolves names with a name server (WINS or DNS) using point-to-point communications. Point-to-point communications are based on IP address–to–IP address as the communication linkage. This is the most efficient mechanism, but should only be used on networks with a dedicated administrator that will religiously update the various LMHOST files on the network. If these files are not updated, the client may not be able to find a resource by name, or the resource computer may not be able to find the client.

> **NOTE**
>
> Unless you are a network client using Microsoft Network 3.0 software, updates should occur automatically if you are using WINS. Clients using Microsoft Network 3.0 software will need their IP addresses added to the LMHOST files of the DHCP servers or added to the configuration files for any DNS server on the network. The domain controller's TCP/IP configuration must also be configured to use the LMHOST file or DNS server.

M-node—Uses B-node first (broadcasts) to resolve the name, and then P-node (name queries) if the broadcast fails to resolve a name. This method works, but has the same problem as a B-node because it can flood the network with broadcasts.

H-node—Uses P-node first (name queries) to resolve the name, and then B-node (broadcasts) if the name service is unavailable or if the name is not registered in the WINS server's database. I recommend using this node type because it will first use a point-to-point connection to find a resource's IP addresses, and only if that fails will it use a broadcast to find the resource. This is the most efficient node type to use, and it practically guarantees that the resource will be found even if the LMHOST file or WINS database does not contain the requested resource's IP address.

> **NOTE**
>
> H-node is the default node type when configuring TCP/IP manually unless the WINS IP address field is left empty.

- Multiple DHCP servers—If you are planning to implement multiple DHCP servers, which is a good way to distribute load on a large network, each DHCP server must have a statically assigned IP address. These IP addresses must be excluded from the DHCP scope you create.

> **NOTE**
>
> You do not necessarily have to have a DHCP server on each subnet. Your router should be capable of forwarding DHCP requests across subnets. If your router does not support the RFCs mentioned previously, you should not use DHCP.

- Static IP addresses—Any static IP addresses, such as those used by other non-DHCP servers, non-DHCP computers, routers, and non-Microsoft Remote Access Software (RAS) clients that are using PPP (Point-to-Point Protocol) to connect to your network, must be excluded from the DHCP scope. If you forget to exclude these IP addresses, a name/address conflict is sure to occur, which could prevent your clients from communicating or even cause your network to crash (in the case of a router).
- DHCP server database replication—This feature doesn't exist in the current implementation, so if you install multiple DHCP servers to support a single segment, you will also have to split the DHCP scope into distinct IP ranges.
- DHCP server database backup—Because the DHCP database contains all the DHCP scopes for the server and the configuration parameters, it is a good idea to implement a backup policy. Normally, the DHCP database is backed up automatically, and this backup will be used if the original is corrupted. However, you should not rely on this mechanism as your only backup. Instead, back up the database regularly and then copy the files from the `SystemRoot\System32\DHCP\Backup\Jet` directory.

> **TIP**
>
> If you have a corrupted primary database file that is not detected by the DHCP service, you can force the backup copy to be used by editing the registry. Set the registry key
> `HKEY_LOCAL_MACHINE\SYSTEM\CurrentControlSet\Services\DHCPServer\Parameters\RestoreFlag`

to 1. Then restart the DHCP service by issuing `net stop dhcpserver` followed by `net start dhcpserver`.

- Lease expiration—The minimum lease expiration should be twice the maximum expected server downtime. For example, if you plan to upgrade the server on weekends, the expiration time should be at least four days. This will prevent a client from losing his lease and his IP address, which would prevent his computer from communicating on the network.

TIP

A good lease minimum should be based on your network turnaround. If you have many portable computer users, or frequent computer upgrades, or many users passing between subnets, you want a lease time of about two weeks. This will return the unused IP addresses to the pool of IP addresses, quickly making them available for reassignment. On the other hand, if you have a pretty static network, lease times of six months could be used. The one lease to avoid is an unlimited lease, because these addresses will never be released automatically and returned to the IP address pool.

If you are planning to implement your Microsoft DHCP server service in a mixed environment, such as with a third-party UNIX DHCP server service, you should be aware that not all of the DHCP configuration options are supported by the Microsoft client. Specifically, the Microsoft DHCP clients only use the configuration options specified in Table 9.1. Any other options received by the client are ignored and discarded.

Table 9.1. Microsoft DHCP client configuration options.

#	Name	Data Type	Description
1	Subnet mask	Subnet address	Specifies the TCP/IP subnet mask to be used by DHCP clients. Note that this value can only be set when you create a scope or when accessed from the DHCP Options|Scope Properties menu option.
3	Router	IP address array	Specifies a list, in order of preference, of router IP addresses to be used by the client. A locally defined gateway can override this value.

continues

Table 9.1. continued

#	Name	Data Type	Description
6	DNS servers	IP address array	Specifies a list, in order of preference, of DNS name servers for the client. Note that multihomed (a computer with more than one installed network adapter) can only include one IP address, not one IP address per adapter.
15	Domain name	String	Specifies the DNS domain name the client should use for DNS hostname resolution.
44	WINS/NBNS	Address array	Specifies a list, in order of preference, of NetBIOS name servers (NBNSs).
46	WINS/NBT node type	Byte	Specifies the node type for configurable NetBIOS clients (as defined in RFC 1001/1002). A value of 1 specifies B-node, 2 specifies P-node, 4 specifies M-node, and 8 specifies H-node. Note that on a multihomed computer the node type is assigned to the computer as a whole, not to individual network adapters.
47	NetBIOS scope ID	String	Specifies the Scope ID for NetBIOS over TCP/IP (NBT) as defined in RFC 1001/1002. Note that on a multihomed computer, the scope ID is a global resource and is not allocated on a per-network-adapter basis.
50	Requested address	IP address	Specifies that a client's preset IP address be used.
51	Lease time	IP address	Specifies the time, in seconds, from the initial IP address allocation to the expiration of the client lease on the IP address. Note that this value can only be set in the DHCP Options	Scope Properties menu option.

#	Name	Data Type	Description
53	DHCP message type	Byte	Specifies the DHCP message type where the message type is 1 for DHCPDISCOVER, 2 for DHCPOFFER, 3 for DHCPREQUEST, 4 for DHCPDECLINE, 5 for DHCPACK, 6 for DHCPNAK, and 7 for DHCPRELEASE.
54	Server identifier	IP address	Used by DHCP clients to indicate which of several lease offers is being accepted. The DHCP accomplishes this by including this option in a DHCPREQUEST message with the IP address of the accepted DHCP server.
58	Renewal (T1) time value	Long	Specifies the time, in seconds, from the initial IP address assignment to the time when the client must enter the renewal state. Note that this value cannot be specified manually because it is based on the lease time as set for the scope.
59	Rebinding (T2)	Long	Specifies the time, in seconds, from the time value initial IP address assignment to the time when the client must enter the rebinding state. Note that this value cannot be specified manually because it is based on the lease time as set for the scope.
61	Client ID	Word	Specifies the DHCP client's unique identifier.

The Microsoft DHCP client and server do not support option overlays, either. An *option overlay* is the process of using free space in the DHCP option packet to contain additional DHCP options. So if you are using a third-party DHCP server instead of the Microsoft DHCP server, make sure that your important configuration options are listed first and that they fit into the Microsoft 312-byte DHCP network packet allocation. The same consideration should be made if you are using the Microsoft DHCP server to support your third-party DHCP clients: Fit your most important configuration options first. And while you can use the additional configuration options (as listed in Table 9.2) to support your third-party DHCP clients, they will not be used by your Microsoft DHCP clients.

Table 9.2. Third-party DHCP client configuration options.

#	Name	Data Type	Description
0	Pad	Byte	Specifies that following data fields will be aligned on a word (16-bit) boundary.
2	Time offset	Long	Specifies the Universal Coordinate Time (UCT) offset time, in seconds.
4	Time server	IP address array	Specifies a list, in order of preference, of time servers for the client.
5	Name servers	IP address array	Specifies a list, in order of preference, of name servers for the client.
7	Log servers	IP address array	Specifies a list, in order of preference, for MIT_LCS User Datagram Protocol (UDP) log servers for the client.
8	Cookie servers	IP address array	Specifies a list, in order of preference, of cookie servers (as specified in RFC 865) for the client.
9	LPR servers	IP address array	Specifies a list, in order of preference, for line printer remote (as specified in RFC 1179) servers for the clients.
10	Impress servers	IP address array	Specifies a list, in order of preference, of Imagen Impress servers for the client.
11	Resource location servers	IP address array	Specifies a list, in order of preference, of RFC 887–compliant resource location servers for the client.
12	Hostname	String	Specifies the hostname (maximum of 63 characters) for the client. Note that the name must start with an alphabetic character and end with an alphanumeric character, and can contain only letters, numbers, or hyphens. The name can be fully qualified with the local DNS domain name.
13	Boot file size	Word	Specifies the default size of the boot image file in 512 octet blocks.
14	Merit dump file	String	Specifies the ASCII path of a file where the client's core dump may be stored in case of an application/system crash.

#	Name	Data Type	Description
16	Swap server	IP address	Specifies the IP address of the client's swap server.
17	Root path	String	Specifies a path (in ASCII) for the client's root disk.
18	Extensions path	String	Specifies a file that includes information that is interpreted in the same way as the vendor extension field in the BOOTTP response, except that references to Tag 18 are ignored. Note that the file must be retrievable via TFTP.
19	IP layer forwarding	Byte	Specifies that IP packets should be enabled (1) or disabled (0) for the client.
20	Nonlocal source routing	Byte	Specifies that datagram packets with nonlocal source route forwarding should be enabled (1) or disabled (0) for the client.
21	Policy filter masks	IP address array	Specifies a list, in order of preference, of IP address and mask pairs that specify destination address and mask pairs, respectively, used for filtering nonlocal source routes. Any source-routed datagram whose next hop address does not match an entry in the list will be discarded by the client.
22	Max DG reassembly size	Word	Specifies the maximum-size datagram that a client can assemble. Note that the minimum size is 576.
23	Default time to live	Byte	Specifies the time to live (TTL) that the client will use on outgoing datagrams. Values must be between 1 and 255.
24	Path MTU aging timeout	Long	Specifies the timeout, in seconds, for aging path maximum transmission unit values. Note that MTU values are found based on the mechanism defined in RFC 1191.

continues

Table 9.2. continued

#	Name	Data Type	Description
25	Path MTU plateau table	Word array	Specifies a table of MTU sizes to use when performing Path MTU (as defined in RFC 1191). Note that the table is sorted from minimum value to maximum value, with a minimum value of 68.
26	MTU option	Word	Specifies the MTU discovery size. Note that the minimum value is 68.
27	All subnets are local	Byte	Specifies whether the client will assume that all subnets in the network will use the same MTU value as that defined for the local subnet. This option is enabled (1) or disabled (0), which specifies that some subnets may use smaller MTU values.
28	Broadcast address	IP address	Specifies the broadcast IP address to be used on the client's local subnet.
29	Perform mask discovery	Byte	A value of 1 specifies that the client should use Internet Control Message Protocol (ICMP) for subnet mask discovery, while a value of 0 specifies that the client should not use ICMP for subnet mask discovery.
30	Mask supplier	Byte	A value of 1 specifies that the client should respond to ICMP subnet mask requests, while a value of 0 specifies that a client should not respond to subnet mask requests using ICMP.
31	Perform router discovery	Byte	A value of 1 specifies that a client should use the mechanism defined in RFC 1256 for router discovery. A value of 0 indicates that the client should not use the router discovery mechanism.
32	Router solicitation address	IP address	Specifies an IP address to which the client will send router solicitation requests.

#	Name	Data Type	Description
33	Static route	IP address array	Specifies a list, in order of preference, of IP address pairs that the client should install in its routing cache. Note that any multiple routes to the same destination are listed in descending order, or in order of priority. The pairs are defined as destination IP address/router IP address. The default address 0.0.0.0 is an illegal address for a static route and should be changed if your non-Microsoft DHCP clients use this setting.
34	Trailer encapsulation	Byte	Specifies with a value of 1 if the client should negotiate use of trailers (as defined in RFC 983) when using the ARP protocol. A value of 0 indicates that the client should not use trailers.
35	ARP cache timeout	Long	Specifies the timeout, in seconds, for the ARP cache entries.
36	Ethernet encapsulation	Byte	Specifies that the client should use Ethernet version 2 (as defined in RFC 894) or IEEE 802.3 (as defined in RFC 1042) encapsulation if the network interface is Ethernet. A value of 1 enables RFC 1042, while a value of 0 enables RFC 894 encapsulation.
37	Default time to live	Byte	Specifies the default TTL the client should use when sending TCP segments. Note that the minimum octet value is 1.
38	Keep-alive interval	Long	Specifies the interval, in seconds, for the client to wait before sending a keep-alive message on a TCP connection. Note that a value of 0 indicates that the client should only send keep-alive messages if requested by the application.

continues

Table 9.2. continued

#	Name	Data Type	Description
39	Keep-alive garbage	Byte	Enables (1) or disables (0) sending keep-alive messages with an octet of garbage data for legacy application compatibility.
40	NIS domain name	String	This ASCII string specifies the name of the Network Information Service (NIS) domain.
41	NIS servers	IP address array	Specifies a list, in order of preference, of IP addresses of NIS servers for the client.
42	NTP servers	IP address array	Specifies a list, in order of preference, of IP addresses of Network Time Protocol (NTP) servers for the client.
43	Vendor-specific info	Byte array	Handles binary information used by clients and servers to pass vendor-specific information. Servers that can not interpret the information ignore it, while clients that do not receive the data attempt to operate without it.
45	NetBIOS Over TCP/IP NBDD	IP address array	Specifies a list, in order of preference, of IP addresses for NetBIOS datagram distribution (NBDD) servers for the client.
48	X Window system font	IP address array	Specifies a list, in order of preference, of IP addresses of X Window font servers for the client.
49	X Window system display	IP address array	Specifies a list, in order of preference, of IP addresses of X Window system display manager servers for the client.
64	NIS + domain name	String	Specifies a list, in order of preference.
65	NIS + server	IP address array	Specifies a list, in order of preference.
255	End	Byte	Specifies the end of the DHCP packet.

Installing the DHCP Server Service

Installing the DHCP server service is accomplished through the Control Panel Network applet. This installation process is described in Chapter 5, "IIS Preparation and Installation," in the section titled "Installing the Dynamic Host Configuration Protocol." But before you install the service on your current server, check for the existence of other DHCP servers on the network. These could be other Windows NT Server servers or a UNIX server.

Managing Your DHCP Server with the DHCP Manager

Your interface for managing the DHCP service is the DHCP Manager. It is installed in the Network Administration Program Manager group, and to use it requires administrative privileges. With the DHCP Manager, you can do everything but stop or start the DHCP service. To stop or start the service, you need to use the Control Panel Service applet and specify the Microsoft DHCP service as the service to control. Alternatively, you can issue the `net stop dhcpserver` or `net start dhcpserver` commands from a console prompt.

The DHCP Manager's primary function is to work with scopes. This includes creating, deleting, activating, and deactivating scopes, and is discussed in the following section. When that discussion is concluded, you will learn how to manage your DHCP clients, including managing your client leases and reservations and setting individual DHCP properties for a reserved client that differ from those defined for the scope as a whole. And finally, you will learn about the DHCP database administration that will be required from time to time. This should provide you with a well-rounded education and prepare you for your duties as a network administrator managing your TCP/IP-based network.

Managing DHCP Scopes

Before you can use the DHCP server to assign IP addresses and relevant configuration options to your DHCP clients, you have to create a DHCP scope. A *scope* is the heart of your DHCP server service. It is based on an IP address range, or *subnet* if you prefer. Although a scope can only include a single subnet, within that subnet you can define the IP range to be used as the basis for your DHCP clients' IP address assignment, the subnet mask, any IP addresses to exclude from the scope, a lease duration, a name for the scope, and a comment that describes the scope. The following discusses how to create, delete, activate, and deactivate DHCP scopes. Next, you will learn about configuring global-, local-, or default-scope properties.

When you run the DHCP Manager for the first time, it will not have any scopes defined for it. However, it will include a listing in the DHCP server's window for the local machine. So before you start creating scopes, I suggest you add the additional DHCP servers on your network

Administering Your Site

Part III

to the DHCP Manager. When you do, your DHCP Manager will include a listing in the DHCP server window, as shown in Figure 9.4, for each DHCP server on your network. Not only will this provide you with the ability to manage your other scopes, but you can use these additional scopes as a reference point when creating new scopes.

FIGURE 9.4.
The Microsoft DHCP manager with multiple DHCP servers and scopes.

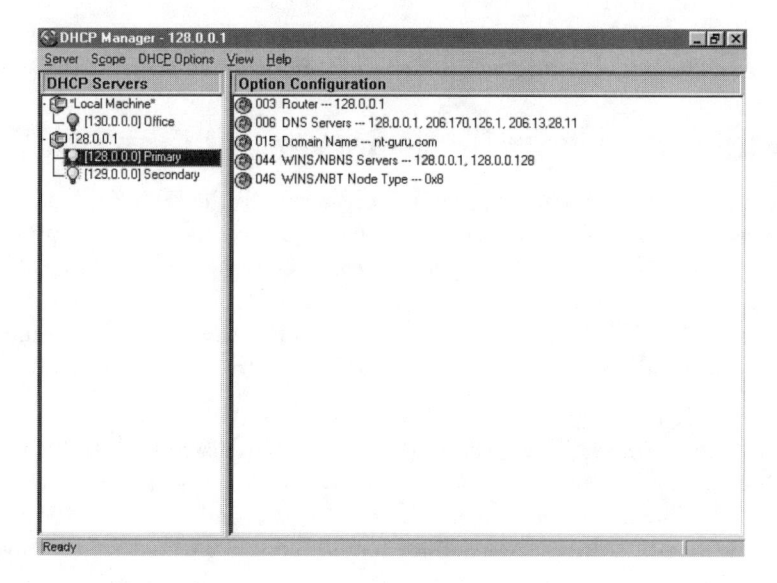

To add more DHCP servers to your local DHCP Manager, follow these steps:

1. Select Server|Add, or press Ctrl+A to display the Add DHCP Server on the Server List dialog.
2. Enter the IP address of the DHCP server in the DHCP Server field, and press the OK button. The IP address will then appear in the DHCP server window.

Repeat steps 1 and 2 for each DHCP server you want to add to your local DHCP Manager.

> **NOTE**
>
> Because the DHCP server service does not replicate its database and configuration information to other DHCP servers, you will have to configure the DHCP Manager on each server in order to manage all of the DHCP scopes from any computer with the DHCP Manager installed on it.

Working with DHCP Scopes

Working with DHCP scopes consists of four possible functions. You can create a scope, which is the beginning process to automating your DHCP client TCP/IP configuration. However, before you can use a newly created scope, you must activate it. Once you have an active scope, your DHCP clients can be assigned an IP address and relevant TCP/IP configuration information from the scope. When you have finished using a DHCP scope you can delete it, but you should deactivate it first. Deactivating a scope will not allow a client to renew its current lease, forcing it to obtain a lease from another DHCP scope. This is a means of migrating clients to a new scope without manual intervention.

To create a scope, follow these steps:

1. Select the DHCP server in the DHCP server window where you want to create the new scope. If you are creating a new scope on the computer running the DHCP server service, this entry will be `Local Machine`; otherwise, it will be an IP address.
2. Choose Scope|Create to display the Create Scope dialog, as shown in Figure 9.5.

FIGURE 9.5.
The Create Scope dialog.

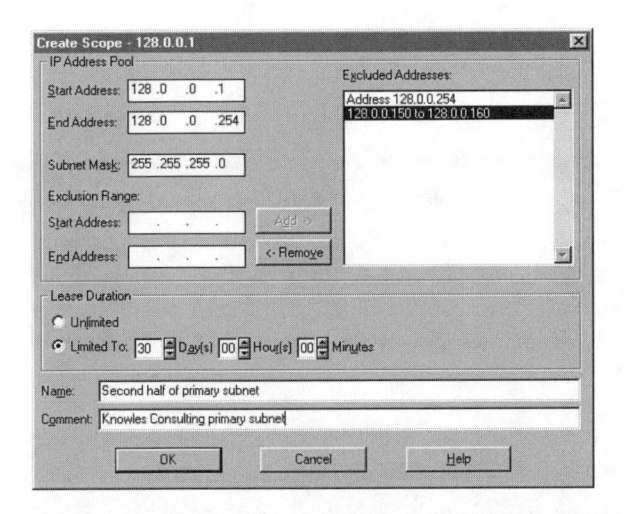

3. Enter the beginning IP address of your subnet in the Start Address field.
4. Enter the last IP address of your subnet in the End Address field.

> **TIP**
>
> If you are not planning to divide your subnet between two DHCP servers, enter the complete IP address range of your subnet. However, if you are planning to split your subnet, as I have, enter only half of your IP address range in the Start Address and End Address fields. This is easier to work with and will prevent complications with the second DHCP Manager's defined scope.

5. Enter the subnet mask to be assigned to your DHCP clients in the Subnet Mask field.
6. If your scope includes statically assigned addresses, such as those assigned to your network adapters in the computer or to the RAS, enter these addresses in the

Exclusion Range group. To exclude a single IP address, enter the IP address in the Start Address field, and press the Add button. To enter more than one consecutive IP address to be excluded, enter the beginning IP address in the Start Address field, enter the last IP address in the End Address field, and press the Add button. This will place the IP address range in the Excluded Addresses field.

> **TIP**
>
> To modify or remove an address range, select it in the Excluded Addresses field and press the Remove button. This will place it in the Excluded Range field, where you can modify it and later add it back to the Excluded Addresses field.

7. In the Lease Duration group, click either the Unlimited or the Limited To radio button to specify the lease type. If you click Limited To, the default, specify the length of time for your DHCP clients to keep their assigned IP address.

> **TIP**
>
> Choose your lease time based on the frequency at which your computers are upgraded, replaced, or moved between subnets. If you have a high movement of computers, choose a lease of approximately two weeks. If you have an extremely low movement of computers, choose a monthly, trimonthly, or biannual lease.

> **WARNING**
>
> Do not assign the unlimited lease type unless you are absolutely sure that no computers will ever be upgraded, replaced, or moved. This is because an unlimited lease will never be able to recover IP addresses that have been assigned to a DHCP client.

8. Enter a name for the scope in the Name field. Your name can be a floor or building location, or a description of the type of subnet. This name, along with the scope address, will be listed in the DHCP server window.
9. Enter a description for the scope in the Comment field.

> **TIP**
>
> To modify the scope properties of an existing scope, just double-click it. This will display the Scope Properties dialog, which, aside from its name, is identical to the Create Scope dialog. Once the Scope Properties dialog is displayed, you may change any of the options described previously.

10. Press the OK button. At this point you will be prompted with a message box to activate the scope. However, you should not activate the scope now unless all your default scope properties are correct.
11. Repeat steps 1–10 for each new scope to be created.

> **NOTE**
>
> Setting global-, local-, or default-scope properties is discussed in the following section.

Only after you have configured the scope, as described in the next section, should you activate it. To do so, choose Scope|Activate.

Before you delete a scope you should deactivate it. To do so, choose Scope|Deactivate. Once the scope lease time has expired and you are sure that no DHCP clients are using a lease from the scope, you may delete it. To delete a scope, follow these steps:

1. Select the DHCP server in the DHCP server window that contains the scope you want to delete. If you are deleting a scope on the computer running the DHCP server service, this entry will be `Local Machine`; otherwise, it will be an IP address.
2. Once the DHCP server has been connected to, the scopes for the server will be listed. Select the scope you want to delete.
3. Choose Scope|Delete. A warning message will be displayed, informing you that clients may still have active leases. Click OK and the scope will be deleted.
4. Repeat steps 1–3 for each scope to delete.

> **TIP**
>
> If you delete a scope with active clients, you can force the client to discontinue using his current lease and obtain one from another DHCP server by issuing the `IPCONFIG /RENEW` command at a command prompt. For a computer running Windows 95, you can use the `WINIPCFG` program. Click the Renew button to release the active lease and obtain a new lease.

Configuring DHCP Scope Options

Scope options are divided into two classes. You can have a global-scope setting, which applies to all scopes for the DHCP server, or a local-scope setting, which applies only to the current scope. Local-scope properties will override globally defined scope properties. This gives you the ability to define common properties, which apply to all scopes that you create, and then customize the scope properties for each individual scope you create. For example, say you define the global router setting to contain the IP addresses for your routers based on subnets.

That means that after you create a new scope, you can delete the first IP address entry on your list and tack it on at the end. In effect, that will change the order of router preference so that the router closest to the user will be used first. You can repeat this sequence to continue moving the router addresses for each subnet you create without having to type in each router address manually. To modify a scope property, follow these steps:

1. Select the DHCP server in the DHCP server window that contains the scope you want to modify. If you are modifying a scope on the computer running the DHCP server service, this entry will be `Local Machine`; otherwise, it will be an IP address.
2. Once the DHCP server has been connected, the scopes for the server will be listed. Select the scope you want to modify.
3. To set global properties for the scope, choose DHCP Options | Global. This will display the dialog shown in Figure 9.6. Otherwise, choose DHCP Options | Scope to set local properties.

NOTE

Aside from its name, the dialog displayed from selecting the DHCP Options | Scope menu option is identical to that from the Global menu option.

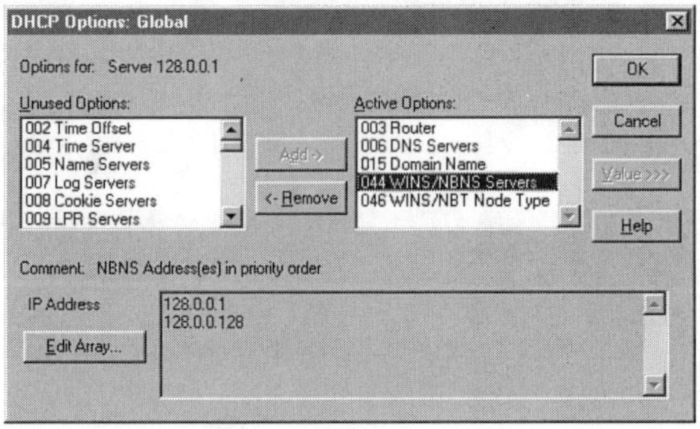

FIGURE 9.6.

The expanded DHCP options dialog.

4. Select the option in the Unused Options field that you want to modify, and then click on the Add button to move that option to the Active Options field.
5. Click the Value button to expand the dialog and display an edit field. Click the Edit button, if available, to modify the existing value.
6. Repeat steps 3–5 for each option you want to modify. When you are finished, click the OK button.

> **TIP**
>
> To modify an existing option, select that option in the Active Options field, then click the Value button to expand the dialog so that you can edit the entry.

Creating New DHCP Scope Options

Not only can you modify the predefined scope properties with the DHCP Manager, but you can also modify the name, unique identifier, and comment of existing configuration options. And if your DHCP clients can utilize them, you can even create new scope options to be assigned to your DHCP clients. However, just because you can modify an existing configuration option or create new ones doesn't mean you should do so arbitrarily. Instead, only do so if absolutely necessary. To change an existing configuration option default value, follow these steps:

1. Choose DHCP Options|Defaults to display the DHCP Options: Default Values dialog, which is shown in Figure 9.7.

FIGURE 9.7.
The DHCP Options: Default Values dialog.

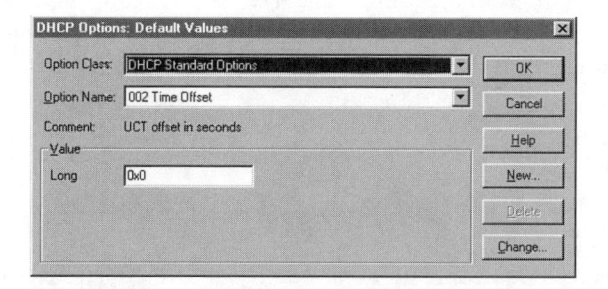

2. Select the class for the option you wish to modify in the Option Class drop-down listbox. The default is DHCP Standard Options.
3. Select the DHCP option in the Option Name drop-down listbox that you want to modify.
4. Specify the new value for the option in the Value field.

To change a configuration option's name, unique identifier, or description, follow these steps:

1. Repeat steps 1–3 from the preceding series of steps.
2. Click the Change button to display the Change Option Type dialog.
3. You may now change the name of the option in the Name field, the DHCP unique identifier number in the Identifier field, or the description in the Comment field.

> **WARNING**
>
> Changing the name or identifier may prevent a DHCP client from functioning properly. Only an expert who is aware of the consequences should modify any of these settings.

   4. Once all changes have been completed, click the OK button.
   5. Repeat steps 1–4 for each option you wish to change.

To add a new configuration option, follow these steps:

   1. Repeat steps 1–3 from the list of steps to change an existing configuration option default value.
   2. Click the New button to display the Change Option Type dialog.
   3. Enter a name for the new option in the Name field.
   4. Specify a data type in the Data Type field. This can be binary (an array of bytes), byte (an 8-bit unsigned integer), encapsulated (an array of unsigned bytes), IP address (an IP address in the form of 206.170.127.65), long (a 32-bit signed integer), long integer (a 32-bit unsigned integer), string (an ASCII text string), or word (a 16-bit unsigned integer). If the data type is an array of elements, enable the Array check box.
   5. Enter a unique number between 0 and 255 in the Identifier field.
   6. Enter a description in the Comment field for the new option.

> **WARNING**
>
> Adding a new configuration option as described here should only be performed by an expert who is aware of the consequences and who needs to support non-Microsoft DHCP clients that require the additional options.

   7. When all changes have been completed, click the OK button.
   8. Repeat steps 1–6 for each option you wish to add.

Managing DHCP Clients

Managing your DHCP clients consists of working with client leases and client reservations on the DHCP server and forcing the client to release or renew his lease on the client workstations. I'll talk more about the management options on the server in just a moment; for now, though, I'd like to discuss the options for the command-line program IPCONFIG.EXE. The syntax for IPCONFIG is

```
IPCONFIG [adapter] /all / /release /renew
```

where

`[adapter]`

is an optional component that is the specific adapter to list or modify the DHCP configuration. Use `IPCONFIG` with no parameters, as described below, to obtain the adapter names.

`/all` is used to list all configuration information. This includes the hostname, DNS servers, node type, NetBIOS scope ID, whether IP routing is enabled, whether the computer is a WINS proxy agent, and whether the computer uses DNS (instead of WINS) for name resolution. It also includes per-adapter statistics, which include the adapter name and description, the physical address (network adapter Ethernet address), whether the DHCP client is enabled, the IP address, the subnet mask, the default gateway, and the primary and secondary WINS server IP addresses.

`/release` is used to release the current DHCP lease. If specified for all adapters (or if there is only one adapter), TCP/IP functionality is disabled.

`/renew` is used to renew the lease. If no DHCP server is available to obtain a valid lease, TCP/IP functionality is disabled.

> **TIP**
>
> Use the `/renew` option to manually force a client to obtain a new lease from a new DHCP server or a new DHCP scope.

> **NOTE**
>
> Windows 95 does not include `IPCONFIG`. Instead, it includes a Windows GUI application called `WINIPCFG.EXE`.

If `IPCONFIG` is executed with no parameters, the current DHCP configuration is displayed. This can be useful for determining the installed adapters and IP addresses. For example, the following output is displayed on my WinBook XP:

```
Windows NT IP Configuration

Ethernet adapter Elnk31:

        IP Address. . . . . . . . : 128.0.0.254
        Subnet Mask . . . . . . . : 255.255.255.0
        Default Gateway . . . . . :
```

```
Ethernet adapter NDISLoop9:

        IP Address. . . . . . . . . : 129.0.0.1
        Subnet Mask . . . . . . . . : 255.255.255.0
        Default Gateway . . . . . . :
```

This listing shows that the WinBook XP includes two network cards. The first network card is a 3Com Etherlink III PCMCIA adapter. Its IP address is `128.0.0.254`, the subnet mask is `255.255.255.0`, and there is no default gateway. The second network adapter is the Microsoft Loopback adapter, which also has its own IP address (`129.0.0.1`) and subnet mask (`255.255.255.0`). This adapter is just a piece of software that emulates a network adapter. Since Windows NT Server requires a functioning network adapter to log you on to the computer, I have the Loopback adapter installed so I can log on in case the PCMCIA network card is not installed.

Managing Client Leases

Managing your DHCP client leases, for the most part, consists of informational displays. When you select an active scope and choose Scope|Active Leases, the Active Leases dialog (as shown in Figure 9.8) is displayed. In this dialog you can perform the following actions:

FIGURE 9.8.
The DHCP Manager Active Leases dialog.

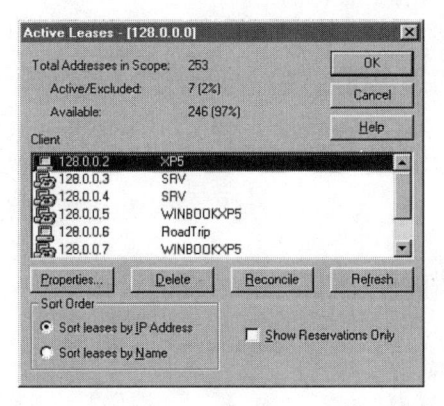

- View the active or reserved leases for the scope. By default, all the leases are displayed in the dialog. However, if you enable the Show Reservations Only check box, only the reserved leases will be displayed.
- View the Client Properties dialog, as shown in Figure 9.9. This is accomplished by selecting an IP address/computer name in the Client field and choosing the Properties button. This can be a very useful dialog because it will display the Media Access Control (MAC) adapter address in the Unique Identifier field. There are several Windows NT server applications, including the DHCP Manager (when reserving a lease, for example), that require a MAC address.

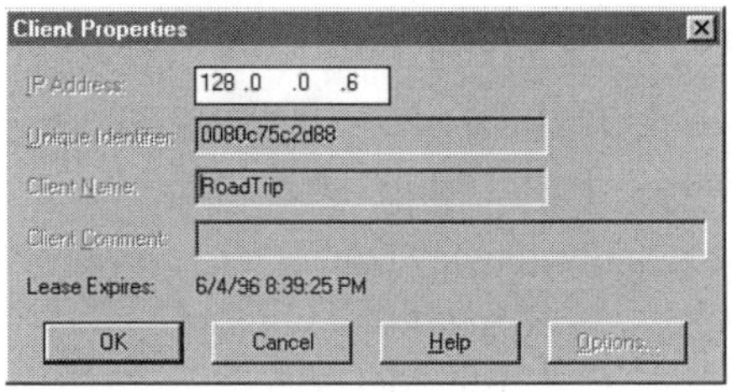

FIGURE 9.9.

A sample Client Properties dialog.

- Update the DHCP database after a restoration from a backup database copy. If your DHCP database has to be restored from a previous backup, either automatically updated by the system or manually updated by you, you should click the Reconcile button to update the database. This will add lease entries for any leases that are not in the database.

> **TIP**
>
> You can delete a lease by selecting the lease in the Client field and choosing the Delete button. However, this is not an action to be taken lightly. You may want to move a client to a reserved lease with a new IP address, for example. As soon as you delete the lease, reserve it as described in the next section, then force the client to establish a new lease by issuing the `IPCONFIG /RENEW` command on the client workstation (for a Windows 95 client, issue the command `WINIPCFG`, then click the Renew button). Otherwise, you could wind up with a duplicate IP address on the network if the original lease is used by another computer.

Managing Client Reservations

Client reservations can be more useful than your average lease because you can preassign an IP address for a DHCP client. You can also change the DHCP configuration options for a DHCP client with a reserved lease. This is a pretty powerful option because it gives you the ability to define global- and local-scope options for the majority of your DHCP clients when you create the scope. This option also allows you to specify DHCP options for those special DHCP clients that happen to be the exception to the rule. To create a reservation for a client, follow these steps:

1. Select the scope where you want the client reservation to occur.
2. Choose Scope|Add Reservations to display the Add Reserved Clients dialog.
3. Enter an IP address (which must fall within the IP address boundaries of your current DHCP scope) to be assigned to the client in the IP Address field.
4. Enter the MAC address for the client's network adapter in the Unique Identifier field.
5. Enter the client computer's name in the Client Name field.

6. Enter an optional description for the client computer in the Client Comment field.
7. Click the Add button.
8. Repeat steps 3–6 for each reservation you want to add to the scope.

Changing the configuration options for a reserved lease requires a little more work. To change a configuration option, follow these steps:

1. Select the scope you want to modify.
2. Choose Scope|Active Leases to display the Active Leases dialog.
3. Select the reserved lease you want to modify and click the Properties button. If there are too many leases to scroll through, enable the Show Reservations Only check box.
4. In the Client Properties dialog, click the Options button to display the DHCP Options dialog. This dialog is exactly the same as the other DHCP Option dialogs (except for its name).
5. Select the option in the Unused Options field that you want to modify, then click the Add button to move the option to the Active Options field. If the option to modify is already in the Active Options field, just select it.
6. Click the Value button to expand the dialog and display an edit field. In this expanded dialog, you may click an edit button, if present, to modify an existing value.
7. Repeat steps 4–6 for each option you want to modify. When you have finished modifying options, click the OK button.
8. Repeat steps three through seven for each reservation to modify. When you have completed modifying all reservations, click the OK button.

Managing the DHCP Databases

As your DHCP server operates day in and day out, the databases may grow as records are added or deleted. These databases are located in the SystemRoot\System32\DHCP directory and include DHCP.MDB (the DHCP database), DHCP.TMP (a temporary file created by the DHCP Server), JET*.LOG files (these files contain transaction records), and SYSTEM.MDB (contains structural information about the DHCP databases). This database growth affects the performance of the DHCP Server. So as your DHCP.MDB database approaches the 10MB limit, you should compact it. To do so, follow these steps:

1. Stop the DHCP server service from the Control Panel Services applet, or issue the net stop dhcpserver command from a console prompt.
2. From a console prompt run the JETPACK.EXE program, which is located in your SystemRoot\System32 directory. The syntax for this program is JETPACK *DatabaseName TemoraryDatabaseName*.

where

DatabaseName is the name of the database to compact, and can be a fully qualified pathname.

TemporaryDatabaseName is a name to use as a temporary database. It, too, can be a fully qualified pathname.

> **CAUTION**
>
> Do not compact the `SYSTEM.MDB` file. If you do, the DHCP server service will fail to start. If this occurs, restore your configuration from a previous backup or delete all of your files in the `SystemRoot\System32\DHCP` and `SystemRoot\System32\DHCP\backup\Jet` directories. Then expand the `SYSTEM.MDB` file from your source media and restart the DHCP server service. Finally, reconcile your database by selecting Scope|Active Leases and then clicking the Reconcile button.

3. Start the DHCP server service form the Control Panel Services applet or issue a `net start dhcpserver` command from a console prompt.

> **TIP**
>
> Since the potential for failure and data corruption is possible, you should back up your DHCP databases regularly, and definitely before you compact them. Just stop the DHCP server service temporarily and copy the files in the `SystemRoot\System32\DHCP` and `SystemRoot\System32\DHCP\backup\Jet` directories to another directory, or even another computer.

DHCP Server Registry Keys

Like most Windows NT services, the configuration information for the service is contained in the registry. For the most part, you should use the DHCP Manager to modify your configuration. These listed registry keys are not configurable from the DHCP Manager, and instead will require using the Registry Editor (`REGEDT32.EXE`). The Registry Editor can be a dangerous tool to use, and Appendix C, "The Registry Editor and Registry Keys," includes additional information about using it. If you are administering a remote computer with a configuration problem so severe that the service cannot be started, you can modify the registry and restore the database configuration remotely. Once these changes have been made, you can restart the service using Server Manager.

The registry keys are stored in the `HKEY_LOCAL_MACHINE\Systems\CurrentControlSet\Services\DHCPServer\Parameters` subkey. If you modify any of these keys (aside from the restore flag), you must restart the computer for your changes to be applied. The following are keys of interest:

- `APIProtocolSupport`—This key's value specifies the transport protocol to be supported by the DHCP server. The default is `0x1` for RPC over TCP/IP protocols. However, it can also be `0x2` for RPC over named pipe protocols, `0x4` for RPC over LPC (local procedure calls), `0x5` for RPC over TCP/IP and RCP over LPC, or `0x7` for RPC over all three protocols (TCP/IP, named pipes, and LPC).
- `BackupDatabasepath`—This key specifies the location of the backup copy of the DHCP database. The default is `%SystemRoot%\System32\DHCP\Backup`. For additional fault tolerance, you can specify another physical drive in the system. Note that you cannot specify a network drive because the DHCP Manager does not support remote drives for backup or recovery.
- `BackupInterval`—This key specifies the default backup interval in minutes. The default is 15.
- `DatabaseCleanupInterval`—This key specifies the interval, in minutes, for the time to remove expired client records from the database. The default is 86,400 (`0x15180`) seconds or 24 hours.
- `DatabaseLoggingFlag`—This entry specifies whether to record the database changes in the `JET.LOG` file. This file is used to recover the database if a system crash occurs. The default is `1` (enable logging), but if your system is extremely stable you can set this value to `0` to disable logging and slightly increase overall system performance.
- `DatabaseName`—This key specifies the database filename to be used by the DHCP server service. The default is `DHCP.MDB`.
- `DatabasePath`—This key specifies the location of the DHCP database files. The default is `%SystemRoot%\System32\DHCP`.
- `RestoreFlag`—This entry is used to specify whether the DHCP server should restore the DHCP database from its backup copy. Set this value to `1` to force a restoration, or leave it at `0` to continue to use the original database file. Note that if you change this value, you must stop and then restart the service for the changes to be applied.

Using the Windows Internet Name Service

The Windows Internet Name Service (WINS) can replace a domain name service to provide NetBIOS name resolution for computers using the TCP/IP protocol. WINS is based on the protocol specifications defined in RFCs 1001 and 1002, and can interoperate with any other NetBIOS name server that also supports these protocols. For those of you who want a fuller understanding of these protocols, I have included RFCs 1001 and 1002 on the accompanying CD-ROM in the `SOURCE\RFC` subdirectory as `RFC1001.TXT` and `RFC1002.TXT`.

This discussion of WINS will begin with some of the service's design goals and some of the concerns you may have while implementing WINS on your network. Then you'll learn about planning your WINS server installation, which will include some guidelines for the number of WINS servers and WINS proxy agents to install. Following that, you'll look at the actual installation steps required to install the service. Once that is out of the way, you'll move on to managing and configuring the WINS server with the WINS Manager. And since a major portion of WINS concerns client-related administration, you will learn how you can manage your WINS clients with the WINS Manager, along with some specific quirks for MS-DOS clients using the Microsoft Network Client software. The final stops will be a look at managing your WINS database, using the Performance Monitor to monitor your WINS server, and a brief look at some of the registry keys that control the WINS server behavior.

Design Goals for the WINS Service

The primary purpose of the WINS server service is to make an administrator's job easier by automating the process of mapping computer names to IP addresses for NetBIOS name resolution in a TCP/IP-based network. It can replace a UNIX DNS service, which uses a static text file (one or more host files) to define the computer name to IP address mapping. However, there is more to WINS than just automating the name resolution process. The WINS design also includes the following:

- Centralized management—Along with the WINS server, Windows NT Server also includes the WINS Manager. With the WINS Manager you can administer other WINS servers and set up replication partners. You'll learn more about replication partners in later sections of this chapter.

- Dynamic address mapping and name resolution—Every time a WINS client starts, or whenever the renewal time expires, the WINS client will register its name with the WINS server. When the WINS client terminates, such as when the computer shuts down, the name is released. This provides the capability for a client computer to change subnets or change its IP address and still be accessible from other computers, thus alleviating the manual modifications to host files required by a UNIX DNS service. These three stages (registration, release, and renewal) operate in the following manner:

    - Registration—A name registration request is sent to the WINS server to be added to the WINS database. The WINS server will either accept or reject a client name registration based on its internal database contents. If the database already contains a record for the IP address under a different computer name, the WINS server will challenge the registration. A challenge is a means of querying the current holder of the IP address to see if that address is still in use. If it is, the new client request is rejected. If the current holder of the IP address is not using the IP address, the new client request is accepted and is added to the database with a timestamp, a unique incremental version number, and other information.

- Release—Whenever a computer is shut down properly (meaning that it did not crash or have a power failure) by the user, it will inform the WINS server. The WINS server will then mark the name entry in the database as *released*. If the entry remains marked as released for a specific period of time, the entry will then be marked as *extinct*, and the version number is incremented. Version numbers are used to mark a record as changed so that changes to WINS partners will be propagated to all WINS servers.

  If a record is marked as extinct and a new registration arrives at the WINS server with the same name but a different IP address, then the WINS server will not challenge the registration. Instead, the new IP address will be assigned to the name. This might occur, for example, with a DHCP-enabled portable computer (or other DHCP-enabled computer) that is moved to a different subnet.

- Renewal—Periodically, when half of the renewal time has expired, a WINS client will re-register its name and IP address with a WINS server. If the renewal time expires completely, the name is released unless the client re-registers with the WINS server.

- Domainwide browsing—If you are using WINS servers, your clients (Windows NT, Windows 95, Windows for Workgroups, LAN Manager 2.*x*, and MS-DOS computers using the Microsoft Network Client 3.0) can browse for computer resources on a Microsoft network across a router without needing a domain controller on each side of the router.

- Reduction of broadcast traffic—A WINS server provides the capability to lower the number of broadcast messages. It does so by supplying an IP address when a name query message is received for a computer name from its local database on a WINS server or from its cache on a WINS proxy agent. Only if the name query request fails will a broadcast occur on the local subnet.

- Interoperation with non-WINS clients—WINS can interoperate with non-WINS clients to provide name resolution, but only if you have one or more WINS proxy agents installed on the subnet. A WINS proxy agent is a computer running the WINS client service that will capture a name query request from, for example, a UNIX client, obtain the IP address from the WINS server, then pass this back to the requesting non-WINS client.

Planning Your WINS Installation

For a small Microsoft-based network, all you really need to install are the DHCP and WINS services on each domain controller. This will provide the means to configure your TCP/IP-based network clients to fully interoperate with any other server or client on the network. This recommendation is based on the fact that a single WINS server can accommodate about 1,500 name registrations and 760 name query requests. In theory, this means you can use one WINS server, keeping a backup WINS server for every 10,000 clients. However, I prefer to use a WINS server for each logical grouping of computers, such as those within a workgroup or domain, to provide additional fault tolerance and load balancing.

> **NOTE**
>
> These name query requests can be routed to other WINS servers and WINS proxy agents, ensuring that a request will eventually be fulfilled. So if you enable replication of your WINS databases, each WINS server will have a complete listing of every WINS client name and IP address. This means that when a name query request is received, an IP address will be returned without broadcasting on the network. This mechanism provides the ability to reduce the amount of broadcast traffic on the subnet.

This logical grouping of computers should be based on the physical layout of your Windows NT Server domain controllers or servers. A logical group could be based on domain controllers or servers in separate physical buildings or floors. It could even be based on domain controllers on the other side of a WAN link or similar property. And for every three to five domain controllers or servers, I like to install the WINS service. This provides fault tolerance in case of required maintenance or a WINS server failure and limits the load on a single WINS server. At the very least, you should have a minimum of two WINS servers on your network supplying NetBIOS name resolution in preparation for a failure of the primary WINS server. You should also have a primary and backup domain controller to provide logon authentication in case of a primary domain controller failure.

This scenario works very well for Microsoft-based networks that use the Microsoft TCP/IP protocol stacks. But this scenario will fail if you use third-party TCP/IP protocol stacks that do not support WINS on your network clients. However, this does not mean that you cannot use WINS in this situation. It only implies that you also need to install WINS proxy agents. A WINS proxy agent should be installed on each subnet, as depicted in Figure 9.10, to provide a linkage between your non-WINS clients and the WINS servers. Your WINS servers should also share their database to provide complete coverage of the entire network. This sharing process is provided by WINS replication, which is discussed in detail a bit further on in this section.

> **NOTE**
>
> To support your non-WINS clients, you can create static mappings that will add a permanent computer name to IP address mapping in the WINS database.

FIGURE 9.10.

Supporting your non-WINS clients in a multiple subnet network with WINS servers.

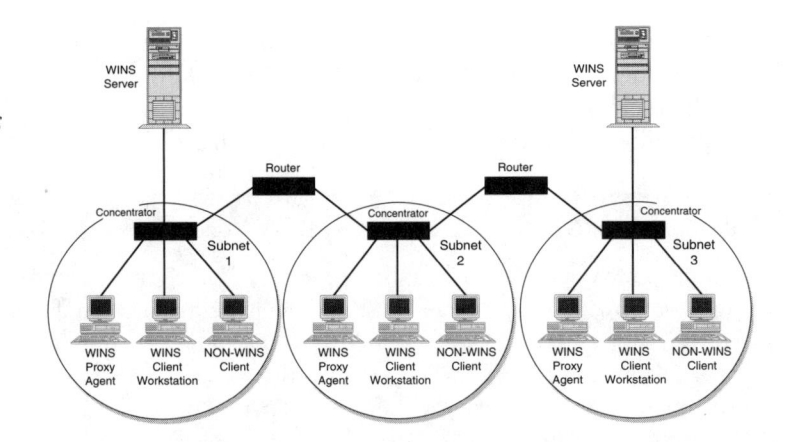

The reason you need to have one WINS proxy agent for each subnet is because broadcast messages are not passed across routers. And when a non-WINS client attempts to find another computer, it will use a broadcast message to obtain the IP address of the requested computer. If this computer is on the same subnet, the request will succeed; but if the computer is on a different subnet, the request will fail (unless you have domain controllers on both sides of the routers). This is where the WINS proxy agent comes into play, as shown in Figure 9.11.

In Figure 9.11, Client #1 is a WINS client, Client #2 is a non-WINS client, and Client #3 is a WINS proxy agent. Server #1 is a Windows NT domain controller running the WINS service. When the non-WINS Client #2 attempts to access WINS Client #1 by broadcasting to obtain Client #1's IP address, the request fails because Client #1 and Client #2 are on different subnets. However, the broadcast is intercepted by Client #3, who will then cache this name and IP address. Client #3 will also return the IP address for Client #1 to Client #2 so that a TCP/IP connection can be established. If another WINS client on a different subnet attempts to access Client #2 by issuing a name query request, the cached IP address for Client #2 that Client #3 has stored will be returned to the requesting client.

A WINS proxy agent will not store information obtained from a broadcast in the WINS server's database. This is why you must have a WINS proxy agent on each subnet that contains non-WINS clients. In this case, the WINS proxy agent can respond to name query requests from WINS clients or WINS servers, and will then broadcast on its local subnet to find the non-WINS client. Once the non-WINS client has been found, the IP address can be passed to the WINS client or server that issued the name query request.

When a WINS client requires access to another computer, it issues a name query request. This name query request can be routed to WINS servers, but this will only occur if the primary or secondary WINS server for the WINS client does not contain a registration for the requested computer. If the routed name query request cannot be resolved by any WINS server, the WINS client will then issue a broadcast message. Both broadcast messages and routed name query messages will eat network bandwidth that could be used to pass data. However, if your WINS servers have a complete listing of the computer names and IP addresses, the primary WINS server can then respond to the name query request, limiting the number of routed name query requests and broadcast messages.

FIGURE 9.11.
How a WINS proxy agent interoperates with non-WINS clients.

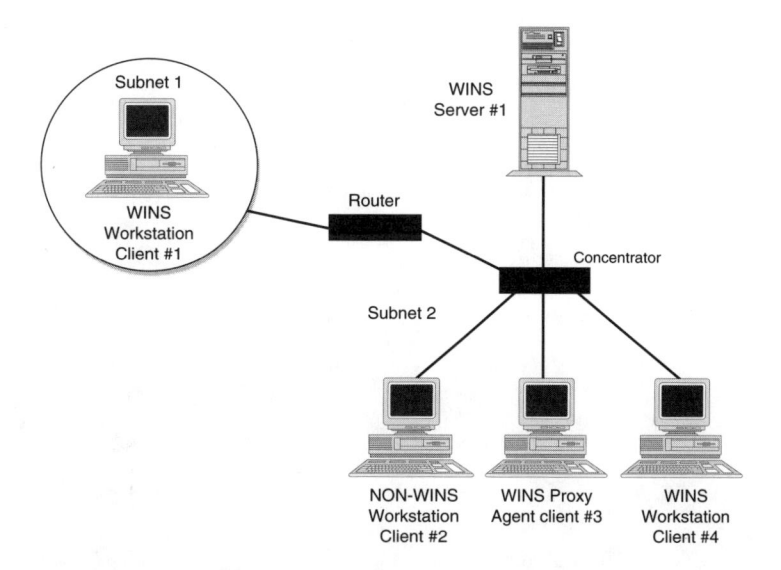

This leads to the next performance and planning tip, which is that every WINS server on a network should replicate its database to other WINS servers on the network so that every WINS server has a complete listing of every WINS client's name and IP address. This method will provide the fastest mechanism for resolving names to IP addresses, and limiting broadcast messages and routed name query messages. WINS servers provide two mechanisms for replication:

- Push partners—A push partner is a WINS server that will send update notifications to its pull partners. When the pull partner receives this update message, it will request the changes from the push partner. The push partner will then send a replica of its database to the requesting pull partner.

- Pull partners—A pull partner is a WINS server that will request updates from its push partner, and when the push partner responds, it will receive the database replica.

As you can see, the descriptions of push and pull partners are circular. In order to replicate the WINS database one way, one WINS server must be a push partner and the other must be a pull partner. To completely replicate a WINS database between two or more WINS servers, each WINS server must be a push and pull partner of the other(s). This is a two-way nonlinear chain, as shown in Figure 9.12, which can be used to replicate every WINS database to every other WINS database. But you can see from this example that some WINS servers receive update notifications from more than one WINS server, which can lead to increased network traffic.

FIGURE 9.12.
WINS server push and pull replication in a nonlinear chain.

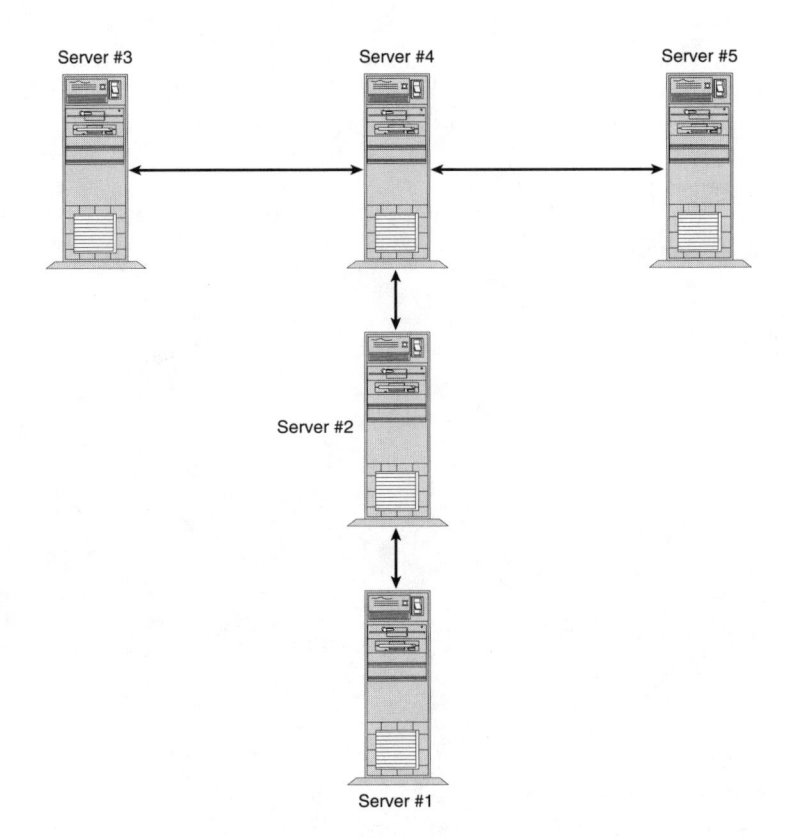

Although it's a bit slower, a better method is to create a linear chain (as shown in Figure 9.13) where only one WINS server is the push or pull partner of another WINS server. Only at a WAN link is the one pull- or one push-partner rule broken. Here, the WINS server at the LAN side is either a push or pull partner of a WINS server on the LAN, and it is also a push or pull partner of a WINS server on a WAN link. This leads to another point: How often should you replicate? My basic methodology is based on the distance between replication points and the speed of the link. For your local area network, 10 to 15 minutes is a good choice because the network throughput is quite high. For local heavily used WAN links, you should limit your replication period to between 30 and 60 minutes. Only lower the rate if you have a high turnover rate. For longer WAN links, choose a value between 45 and 90 minutes. And for intercontinental WAN links, replicate every 6 to 12 hours, scheduling it in the off-peak hours. The idea with all of these is the more heavily used the link, the higher the replication frequency (or the lower the number of scheduled minutes between replication attempts).

FIGURE 9.13.
WINS server push and pull replication in a linear chain.

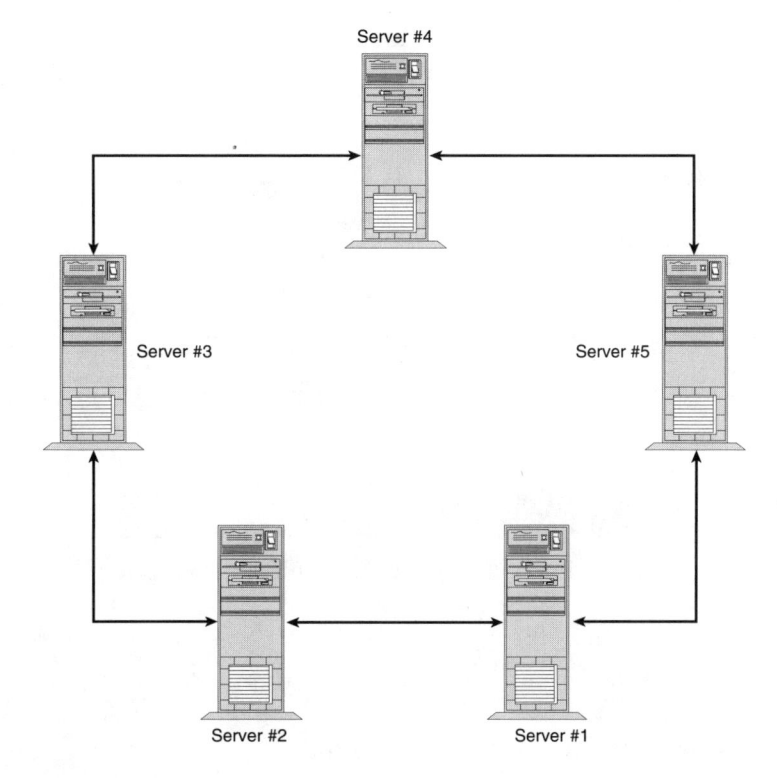

Installing the WINS Server

As with all the other built-in services, the installation process for the WINS server begins with the Control Panel Network applet. The steps to walk you through the installation of the WINS server are covered in Chapter 5 in the section titled, "Installing the Windows Internet Name Service."

Configuring the WINS Server with the WINS Manager

The first time you use the WINS Manager, it will display only the WINS server on the local computer. To add additional WINS servers to the WINS Manager, select Server|Add WINS Server, then supply the IP address or computer name in the Add WINS Server dialog. To delete a WINS server from your WINS Manager list, select it and then choose Server|Delete WINS Server. After adding your additional WINS servers to the local WINS Manager, you will need to configure the local WINS server for optimal performance. This includes setting your WINS server configuration, replication partners, and preferences. Each of these options performs a slightly different task.

Administering Your Site

Part III

The first recommended option is to choose Server | Configuration, which will display, as shown in Figure 9.14, the WINS Server Configuration dialog. In this dialog you can set the following options:

FIGURE 9.14.
The expanded WINS Server Configuration dialog.

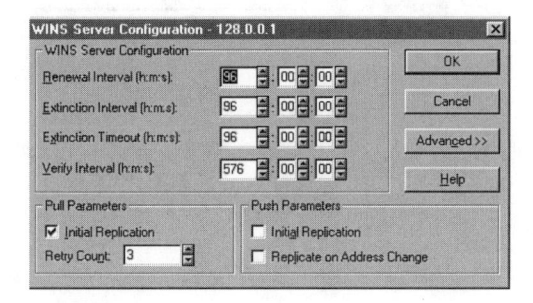

- Renewal Interval—This selection specifies how often a WINS client has to register its name with the WINS server. The default is four days.
- Extinction Interval—This item specifies the time interval between when a record is marked as released and when it is marked as extinct. The default, and maximum time, is four days.
- Extinction Timeout—This item specifies the time interval between when a record is marked as extinct and when it is scavenged from the database. The default is four days, and the minimum is one day.

NOTE

The extinction interval and extinction default for a fully configured WINS server is based on the renewal time and whether the WINS server has replication partners on the replication time interval.

TIP

You can manually scavenge the database by choosing Mappings | Initiate Scavenging. This process will remove outdated records from the database.

- Verify Interval—This entry specifies the time interval within which a WINS server must verify that old names owned by another WINS server are still valid. The default (24 days) is dependent on the extinction interval. The maximum is 24 days.
- Pull Parameters—The pull partner replication interval is set in the Preferences dialog, as described a little later on. However, if you want the replication to be triggered when

the WINS server starts, enable the Initial Replication check box and specify a number in the Retry Count box.

- Push Parameters—To configure push partner configurations, you may enable the following entries:
    - Initial Replication—If this setting is enabled, push partners will be informed that a change has occurred when the WINS server is started.
    - Replicate on Address Change—If this setting is enabled, push partners will be informed whenever an entry in the database changes or when a new entry is added.

- Advanced WINS Server Configuration—These options are accessed when you expand the dialog by choosing the Advanced button:
    - Logging Enabled—This option specifies that the WINS server will log database changes and inform you of basic errors in the system event log. The default is enabled.
    - Log Detailed Events—This option specifies that detailed events will be written into the system event log. It should only be used for a limited time, such as when you are troubleshooting WINS server problems, because it can consume considerable resources and will impact system performance. The default is disabled.
    - Replicate Only with Partners—This entry, if enabled, will only allow replication with push or pull partners. If it's disabled, you can replicate data from any unlisted WINS server. The default is to enable this setting.
    - Backup on Termination—This option will, if enabled, automatically back up the WINS database whenever the WINS server is shut down. However, it will not perform a backup when the entire system is shut down, such as when you shut down and restart the server from the Start|Shutdown menu. The default is enabled.
    - Migrate On/Off—This setting is used to enable or disable the treatment of static or multihomed records as dynamic whenever they conflict with a new registration or replica (data copied from another WINS server). This option should be enabled if you are upgrading a non-Windows NT system (such as a LAN Manager server) to Windows NT Server. The default is disabled.
    - Starting Version Count—This option specifies the highest database version number. Normally you will not need to change this value, but if you restore the WINS database from a backup because your primary database is corrupted, you should increment this value to a number higher than any other copy of the WINS server partners to ensure proper replication.

> **NOTE**
>
> The current value can be displayed by choosing View|Database from the menu. If you want to see the version numbers on other WINS servers, choose the WINS server before making the menu selection.

- Database Backup Path—This option specifies the full path to use for the backup copies of the WINS server database.

The next suggestion is to set your preferences for the WINS Manager and default settings for the WINS service. This is accessed by choosing Options|Preferences, which will display the dialog shown in Figure 9.15. In this dialog you can do the following:

FIGURE 9.15.
Specifying the WINS Manager preferences and WINS server defaults.

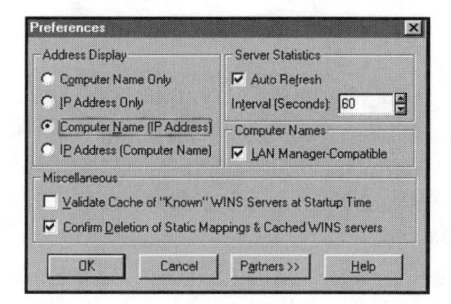

- Specify how the WINS Manager displays the names for the WINS servers it is connected to, and incidentally, the mechanism used for connecting to the service. These options are
    - Computer Name Only—If selected, this item specifies that just the computer name will be displayed. The connection to the WINS server will use named pipes.
    - IP Address Only—If selected, this item specifies that just the IP address of the computer will be displayed. The connection to the WINS server will use a TCP/IP socket.
    - Computer Name (IP Address)—If selected, this item specifies that the computer name will be displayed first and then the IP address, and that named pipes will be used to connect to the WINS server.
    - IP Address (Computer Name)—If selected, this item specifies that the IP address will be displayed first, followed by the computer name. The connection will use a TCP/IP socket to connect to the WINS server.
- Specify the refresh interval for updating the WINS Manager display. If you enable the Auto Refresh check box, you should also specify a value (number of seconds to wait before updating the display) in the Interval field.

Using DHCP, WINS, and DNS
Chapter 9 — 245

> **NOTE**
>
> The display will also be refreshed automatically whenever you initiate an action with the WINS Manager.

- Specify the NetBIOS name compatibility. If the LAN Manager–Compatible check box is enabled (the default setting), then NetBIOS names will be limited to 15 bytes to contain the name while the 16th byte will be used to contain a special code for static mappings. If you use other applications that require a 16-byte NetBIOS name, such as Lotus Notes, then this option should be disabled. The special codes are
    - `0x0`—Specifies that a NetBIOS name is used by the redirector.
    - `0x1`—Specifies that the NetBIOS name is used by the Master domain browser.
    - `0x3`—Specifies that the NetBIOS name is used by the Messenger service.
    - `0x20`—Specifies that the NetBIOS name is used by a LAN Manager server.
    - `0x1B`—Specifies the master browser name that clients and browsers will use to contact the master browser.
    - `0x1E`—Specifies that the NetBIOS name is used for a normal group.
    - `0x1D`—Specifies that the NetBIOS name is used for client name resolution when an attempt is made to contact the master browser for server lists.
    - `0x1C`—Specifies that the NetBIOS name is an Internet group name. An Internet group name contains the addresses of the primary and backup domain controllers for the domain. This name is limited to 25 addresses.
- Specify the miscellaneous support options. These are
    - Validate Cache of "Known" WINS Servers at Startup Time—If this option is enabled, whenever you start the WINS Manager it will attempt to connect to all WINS servers you have added. If a WINS server cannot be contacted, you will be prompted to remove the WINS server from the list of connected servers. The default is disabled.
    - Confirm Deletion of Static Mappings & Cached WINS servers—This option, if enabled (the default), will prompt you with a message box whenever you attempt to remove a static mapping or cached WINS server. I find the constant message boxes a bit annoying and normally disable this setting. However, before you do so, I suggest you become a bit more familiar with the WINS Manager.

If you click the Partners button, the dialog will expand and allow you to set defaults for the Partner Replication. These settings include

- New Pull Partner Default Configuration—The entries in this group are used to specify the default replication settings for new pull partners that you create for the currently selected WINS Server. These options include:

- Start Time—Specifies the time to start your WINS server database replication. There is no default, although I like to start at 12:00 a.m.
- Replication Interval—Specifies the interval for repeating the WINS server database replication. There is no default, although I generally choose a 15-minute interval for local area network WINS servers.
- New Push Partner Default Configuration—The entry in this group is used to specify the number of changes that have to occur in the WINS server database before a push notification will be sent to the push partners that you create for the currently selected WINS servers.
- Update Count—This entry specifies the number of changes that have to occur before a push notification is sent. There is no default, although I recommend a value of 1000.

Next, I suggest you set the replication settings for the local WINS server by choosing Server | Replication Partners, which will display the Replication Partners dialog, shown in Figure 9.16. Once the dialog has been displayed, click the Add button to add the WINS servers to be configured as the local push or pull partners. You can choose to replicate to any, or all, WINS servers in a nonlinear fashion, or you can choose to pull from one WINS server and push to another WINS server in a linear fashion. These techniques are described in more detail in the section titled "Planning Your WINS Installation." After you have added your WINS servers, you can do the following:

> **NOTE**
>
> To remove a WINS server from the WINS server list, select it and press the Delete key.

FIGURE 9.16.
Specifying the WINS server replication partners.

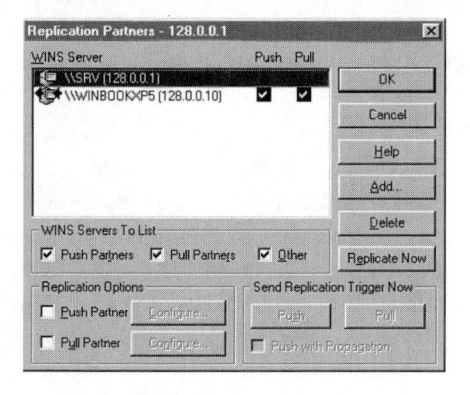

- Specify the WINS servers to display in the WINS server list by enabling or disabling the options in the WINS Servers To List field. These options are
    - Push Partners—If enabled, push partners of this WINS server will be displayed. The default is enabled.

- Pull Partners—If enabled, pull partners of this WINS server will be displayed. The default is enabled.
- Other—If enabled, any non-partner of this WINS server will be displayed. The default is enabled.
- Specify the individual settings for the currently selected WINS server to be a push, pull, or both partner in the Replication Options box. When you select a WINS server that is already configured as a push or pull partner, the Configure buttons will be enabled:
  - Push Partner—Enable the Push Partner check box to specify that the selected WINS server will be a push partner. You may then click the Configure button to display the Push Properties dialog, where you may view or set the Update Count.
  - Pull Partner—Enable the Pull Partner check box to specify that the selected WINS server will be a pull partner. You can then click the Configure button to display the Pull Properties dialog, where you may view or set the Start Time and Replication Interval.

> **TIP**
>
> If you specified the default values using the Preferences dialog, these settings will be automatically set for new push or pull partners. However, if you are configuring a push or pull partner across a WAN link, you should set higher values, as described in the section titled "Planning Your WINS Installation."

- Initiate a replication trigger immediately, rather than waiting for it to occur based on the replication times set in the Configuration dialog. To accomplish this, set the following values in the Send Replication Trigger Now group:
  - Push—Choosing this button will send a push trigger to the selected WINS server.
  - Pull—Choosing this button will send a pull trigger to the selected WINS server.
  - Push with Propagation—Enabling this check box will modify the Push message to indicate that changes sent to the selected WINS server are to be propagated to all other pull partners of the selected WINS servers.

> **TIP**
>
> By choosing the Replicate Now button, you can immediately send a complete replication to the selected WINS server.

Managing Your WINS Clients

Managing your WINS clients consists of creating static mappings, which are permanent computer names to IP address records, and viewing your current database records. Static mappings are added by choosing Mappings | Static Mappings, which will display the Static Mappings dialog (as shown in Figure 9.17). When you click the Add button, the Add Static Mappings dialog will be displayed. Here you may enter a computer name, IP address, and the type of static mapping that will be added to the WINS server database. The types of static mapping are listed in Table 9.3, which describes the special names that the WINS server uses and how WINS manages these names. Deleting a static mapping is made possible by selecting the mapping, then choosing the Delete button.

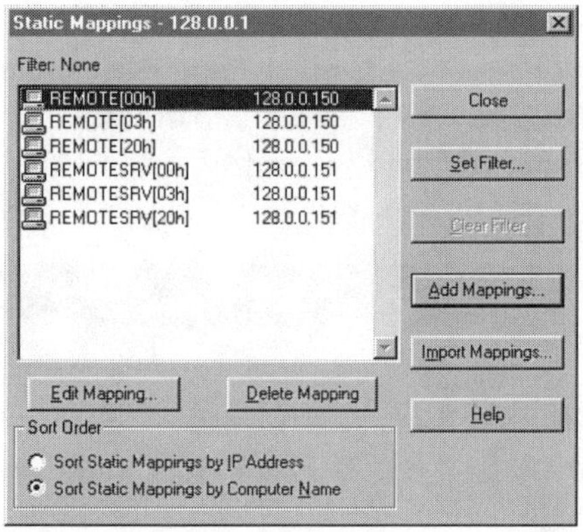

FIGURE 9.17.
The Static Mappings dialog.

> **TIP**
>
> You can import a series of static mappings by importing a host file from a DNS server to support your non-WINS computers.

Table 9.3. WINS server special names.

Name	Description
Unique	A unique name is a normal name, and implies that only one computer name will be associated with the IP address.
Group	A group name does not have an associated IP address. Instead, when a group name is registered with the WINS server and a name query request for this name is received, the WINS server returns the broadcast address (FFFFFFFF). The requesting client will then issue a broadcast message to find the requested computer.

Name	Description
Multihomed	A multihomed name has multiple IP addresses associated with it. A multihomed device contains two or more network adapters that can register each individual IP address associated with the computer by sending a special name registration packet. A multihomed group name can contain a maximum of 25 IP addresses.
Internet	An Internet name is a group name that contains domain controller IP addresses. WINS gives preference to the 25 addresses closest to the name registration request. When a request is received for the domain, the domain controller address and the additional 24 (maximum) IP addresses are returned to the client.

Managing the WINS Databases

Since your WINS server uses the same database format as the DHCP server (a modified Access database), it has the same basic issues as the databases for the DHCP server. As records are added and deleted, the database grows in size. The WINS databases are located in the SystemRoot\System32\WINS directory and include WINS.MDB (the WINS database), WINSTMP.MDB (a temporary file created by the DHCP server), JET.LOG files (this file contains transaction records), and SYSTEM.MDB (this contains structural information about the WINS databases). The database growth affects the performance of the WINS server. So as your WINS.MDB database approaches the 30MB limit, you should compact it. To do so, follow these steps:

1. Stop the WINS server from the Control Panel Services applet or issue the net stop wins command from a console prompt.

2. From a console prompt run the JETPACK.EXE program, which is located in your SystemRoot\System32 directory. The syntax for this program is

   JETPACK DatabaseName TemoraryDatabaseName

   where

   DatabaseName is the name of the database to compact, and can be a fully qualified pathname.

   TemporaryDatabaseName is a name to use as a temporary database. It, too, can be a fully qualified pathname.

CAUTION

Do not compact the SYSTEM.MDB file. If you do, the WINS server will fail to start. If this occurs, restore your configuration from a previous backup.

3. Start WINS from the Control Panel Services applet or issue a `net start wins` command from a console prompt.

> **TIP**
>
> Since the potential for failure exists with the compact utility, and since data corruption can occur on your `SystemRoot` partition, you should back up your WINS databases regularly. Definitely do so before you compact any WINS databases. This can be accomplished by choosing Mappings|Backup Database. Make sure to perform a full backup by disabling the Perform Incremental Backup option if you plan to use this copy to restore your configuration.

> **TIP**
>
> Before you back up or compact the database, you should choose the Mappings|Initiate Scavenging command to delete records that are no longer needed.

Using the Performance Monitor to Monitor the WINS Server

While the WINS Manager will display the same statistics as those used by the Performance Monitor, the WINS Manager can only display the statistics for the currently selected WINS server. However, if you use the Performance Monitor, you can monitor multiple WINS servers simultaneously. This can be an enormous benefit when you are comparing the performance of multiple WINS servers. Table 9.4 lists the available WINS server performance object counters that you may use to monitor your selected WINS server. For additional details on how to use the Performance Monitor, see Chapter 22, "The Performance Monitor."

Table 9.4. The Performance Monitor object counters for the WINS server.

Object Counters	Description
Failed Queries/sec	Total number of failed queries per second.
Failed Releases/sec	Total number of failed releases per second.
Group Conflicts/sec	The rate at which group registrations received by the WINS server result in conflicts with records in the database.
Group Registrations/sec	The rate at which group registrations are received by the WINS server.

Object Counters	Description
Group Renewals/sec	The rate at which group renewals are received by the WINS server.
Queries/sec	The rate at which queries are received by the WINS server.
Releases/sec	The rate at which releases are received by the WINS server.
Successful Queries/sec	Total number of successful queries per second.
Successful Releases/sec	Total number of successful releases per second.
Total Number of Conflicts/sec	The sum of the unique and group conflicts per second. This is the total rate at which conflicts are seen by the WINS server.
Total Number of Registrations/sec	The sum of the unique and group registrations per second. This is the total rate at which registrations are received by the WINS server.
Total Number of Renewals/sec	The sum of the unique and group renewals per second. This is the total rate at which renewals are received by the WINS server.
Unique Conflicts/sec	The rate at which unique registrations/renewals received by the WINS server result in conflicts with records in the database.
Unique Registrations/sec	The rate at which unique registrations are received by the WINS server.
Unique Renewals/sec	The rate at which unique renewals are received by the WINS server.

> **TIP**
>
> To get a feel for how well your WINS server is performing, you should monitor the total number of conflicts, registrations, and renewals, along with the failed queries and releases.

WINS Server Registry Keys

The WINS server also stores its configuration information in the registry, just as the DHCP server does. And once again, you may need to modify the registry in order to modify a configuration setting if that configuration setting cannot be set from the WINS Manager or if you are administering an inactive WINS server. This warning is being mentioned again because, if improperly used, the Registry Editor can damage your system beyond repair. Refer to Appendix C for additional information and tips on backing up your current registry before you attempt to use the Registry Editor (`REGEDT32.EXE`).

The primary registry keys are located in `HKEY_LOCAL_MACHINE\System\CurrentControlSet \Services\WINS\Parameters` and include

- `DbFileNm`—This item specifies the full pathname to the location of the WINS database file. The default is `%SystemRoot%\System32\WINS\WINS.MDB`.
- `DoStaticDataInit`—If this item is set to 1, the WINS server will initialize its database with records from one or more files in the `DataFiles` subkey. This initialization is performed at the time the process is executed and whenever a change to a key in the `Parameters` or `DataFiles` subkey occurs. If set to the default (`0`), this initialization will not occur.
- `InitTimePause`—If this entry is set to 1, the WINS server will start in the paused state. It will stay in this state until it has replicated with its partners (push or pull), or failed at least once in the replication attempt. If set to 1, the `WINS\Partner\Pull \InitTimeReplication` subkey should be set to 1 or removed from the registry for proper operation. A value of `0` (default) will disable this option. Note that the `InitTimeReplication` key value may be set by choosing Options | Preference and choosing the Advanced button to expand the dialog.
- `LogFilePath`—This item specifies the location for the WINS server log files. The default is `%SystemRoot%\System32\WINS`.
- `McastIntvl`—This value specifies the time interval, in seconds, for the WINS server to send a multicast and announce itself to other WINS servers. The minimum and default value is `2400` (40 minutes).
- `McastTtl`—This value specifies the number of times a multicast announcement can cross a particular router. The default is `6`, and the range is `1` to `32`.
- `NoOfWrkThds`—This value specifies the number of worker threads used by the WINS Server. The default is one per processor on the system, with a range of 1 to 40. Note that this value can be changed and placed in effect without restarting the WINS server.
- `PriorityClassHigh`—Set this entry to 1 to enable the WINS service to run in the high-priority class. This will prevent other applications and services that are running in lower priorities from preempting the WINS server. The default is `0`. Note that if you choose to enable this setting, you should monitor the system with the Performance Monitor to make sure the WINS server is not using too much processor time and that other applications and services are continuing to function properly.
- `UseSelfFndPnrs`—Set this option to 1 to enable or `0` to disable the WINS server from automatically finding other WINS servers and configuring them as push and pull partners. The default is `0`. If the push and pull partners are configured manually with

the WINS Manager, the partnership information will no longer be maintained automatically when a change occurs.

> **NOTE**
>
> If this option is enabled, the WINS service will only configure WINS servers as push and pull partners across routers if the routers support multicasting. Otherwise, only those WINS servers found on the local subnet will be automatically configured as partners.

> **TIP**
>
> Routers that support multicasting can be very useful because you are relieved of the burden of configuring your push and pull partners manually.

The following registry keys can be configured by choosing Server|Configuration and modifying the entries in the WINS Server Configuration dialog.

- `BackupDirPath`—This item specifies the full pathname to the location to be used to back up the WINS database.
- `DoBackupOnTerm`—If enabled (1), the WINS database is backed up whenever the WINS service is terminated. If disabled (0), the database is not backed up when the service is terminated. The default is 1. Note that the backup will not occur when the system is shut down. A backup only occurs when the service is manually stopped.
- `LogDetailedEvents`—If this item is enabled (1), verbose logging of WINS events will occur. The default is disabled (0).
- `LoggingOn`—If enabled (1), WINS messages will be placed in the event log. If disabled (0), no events will be placed in the event log. The default is 1.
- `RefreshInterval`—This specifies the time, in seconds, for the client to register its name with the WINS server. The default is `0x54600` (four days).
- `RplOnlyWCnfPnrs`—This enables (1) or disables (0) the ability to replicate a WINS server from a WINS server that is not a partner. The default is 1.
- `MigrateOn`—This enables (1) or disables (0) the treatment of unique and multihomed records as dynamic when a registration conflict is detected. The default is 0.
- `TombstoneInterval`—This specifies the time, in seconds, between when a client record is released and when it is marked as extinct. The default is `0x54600` (four days).
- `TombstoneTimeout`—This specifies the time, in seconds, between when a client record is marked as extinct and when it is scavenged from the database. The default is `0x54600` (four days).

- `VerifyInterval` — This specifies the interval within which the WINS server must verify that old names that it does not own are still valid. The default is `0x1FA400` (24 days).

The registry keys for partner replication are located in the `HKEY_LOCAL_MACHINE\System\CurrentControlSet\Services\WINS\Partners` key and include the following:

- `PersonaNonGrata` — This value is used to specify IP addresses for WINS servers from which you do not want to replicate data. This key may be very useful for administrators to block replication from WINS servers that are not under their control.
- `Pull\<IPAddress>\MemberPrec` — This specifies the preference order of addresses in an Internet group. Values can be `0` for low precedence, or `1` for high precedence. The default is `0`. Note that this entry appears under an IP Address (of a WINS server).

Using the Domain Name System

The primary purpose of a domain name system is to supply friendly computer names instead of an IP address to locate a resource. This process is often referred to as *NetBIOS name resolution*. The domain name system uses a hierarchical architecture. If a DNS server is unable to resolve an IP address at the local level, it will query other DNS servers at a higher level to resolve the name. If you do not mind maintaining multiple DNS servers and their associated configuration files, you could use DNS in place of DHCP and WINS. I prefer to use all three components working together because they complement each other to provide ease of administration, as well as maximum compatibility.

The Design Goals for the Microsoft DNS Service

You could use other DNS servers on your network, but they may not support the Microsoft WINS server. In such cases, you may lose the ability to manage a dynamic network. This is the real difference between the Microsoft DNS implementation and other DNS servers that run under Windows NT. The Microsoft implementation fully supports WINS, which in turn is aware of DHCP. If you use DHCP, WINS, and DNS together, you can achieve the following:

- Utilizing DHCP, your clients automatically allocate dynamic IP addresses. This allows you, the administrator, to provide dynamic IP addresses to your network clients as they move between subnets (as might be the case with clients who are consultants or temporary employees).

- Utilizing WINS, your clients automatically register their computer name and IP address every time they start up their computer. If the computer moves between subnets, this information is automatically updated, as well.
- Utilizing DNS, your clients can find any non-WINS-aware resources through the static mappings maintained in the configuration files. This also works in reverse. Any non-WINS-aware client who uses DNS to resolve names and who has a static mapping to your DNS service can locate a WINS client as long as the Microsoft DNS server is configured to use a WINS server for additional name resolution.

This combination of DHCP, WINS, and DNS provides additional benefits, as well. Dynamic address allocation also means dynamic address recovery. When a new IP address is allocated to a client on another subnet, the old address is released back to the DHCP scope's address pool. This can prevent the confusion caused by duplicate IP addresses on the network. The only thing DHCP and WINS will not do is make it easy for you to get on the Internet. One of the requirements for registering your domain (often your company name) with the InterNIC is that you maintain two or more DNS servers on your network so that clients who want to connect to your server, most likely to your WWW page, can find you. Because many Internet Service Providers (ISPs) don't know how to deal with or support DHCP and WINS, you might as well get accustomed to using a DNS server if you plan to connect to the Internet. But if you also use DHCP and WINS, you don't have to go through all of the hassle of modifying your configuration files every time you move or add a client to your network.

There are some additional benefits of using a DNS server, because it can provide some name resolution capabilities that WINS cannot. A DNS server includes e-mail name resolution by supporting the MX record type that associates an e-mail address with a hostname. And when a DNS server cannot resolve a name locally, it will refer the name query to another DNS server higher up the chain in an effort to resolve the name.

Planning Your DNS Installation

There are a few items to consider before you install a domain name system server on your network. If you plan to connect to the Internet, the most important of these is security. For this reason, I suggest you read Chapter 10, "Advanced Security Issues," and consider how this will affect your implementation. The other items are less serious, but equally important.

First, consider who will be in charge of maintaining the configuration files. This person will maintain a master copy of all shared configuration files. Everyone else will use a replicated copy of the master copy. Second, if you will have more than one person modifying any configuration file, be sure they are all trained to maintain the files in a standardized manner. Be certain this training includes a standard naming convention for filenames, hostnames, and verification of IP addresses.

> **CAUTION**
>
> A duplicate hostname or IP address on your network can cause serious problems. Make sure your administrators are aware of this, and that your registration plan includes the capability to register a name and IP address before it is reassigned. An access database could be used to maintain information (hostname, IP address, filename, and so on) about your network and could be queried to verify that the hostname and IP address are not in use.

To actually install the Microsoft DNS service, the step-by-step process described in Chapter 5 in the section titled "Installing the Domain Name Server Service" should come in handy. Installing the service is the easy part; configuring the service is the hard part, which you will learn about next.

The DNS Configuration Files

The configuration files used with the Microsoft DNS server can be replaced by those from a UNIX BIND installation if you are migrating or interoperating with a UNIX system. However, if you are using some outdated BIND commands, you may need to modify the files. These configuration files are divided into four basic types:

- BOOT—This file controls the startup behavior of the DNS server. It includes information on the default directory where the configuration files reside, the cache filename, the domain name that the DNS server will service, and the domain name for secondary DNS servers.
- CACHE—This file contains information for Internet connectivity.
- PLACE.DOM—This file contains information on hostnames within the domain. It also includes references to reverse lookup filenames and WINS servers.
- ARPA-###.REV—These files (there should be one per subnet) include information to resolve an IP address to a hostname.

BOOT

There are not very many commands supported in the BOOT file, so the syntax for the commands, as summarized in Table 9.5, is fairly easy to remember. The following is an example of a BOOT file for a simple network, such as the one in my office:

```
;   DNS BOOT FILE - Master configuration for DNS service
directory       %System32%\system32\dns
cache   .       cache
primary   nt-guru.com      nt-guru.dom
primary   127.in-addr.arpa      arpa-127.rev
primary   128.0.0.in-addr.arpa      arpa-128.rev
```

Table 9.5. Applicable commands for the BOOT file.

Command	Required	Description
;	No	Starts a comment. Avoid using unnecessary comments because the file is parsed line by line. Each comment added to the file slows down name resolution for any name not in the cache.
directory PathName	No	Describes the location of the DNS configuration files where PathName is a fully qualified pathname. The default, if not specified, is %SystemRoot%\System32\DNS. If the directory cannot be found, the DNS service will fail to start.
cache FileName	Yes	Describes the location of the cache file, which is used to find additional name servers where FileName is the name of the file. If the file cannot be found, the DNS service will fail to start.
Primary DomainName FileName	Yes	Specifies a domain name for which this DNS server is authoritative and a configuration filename that contains information for the domain.
Secondary DomainName HostList [FileName]	No	Specifies a domain name and associated IP address array from which to download zone information. If a filename is specified, the zone information will be downloaded and used if the domain DNS server, or alternate, cannot be located.

CACHE

The CACHE file is used for additional name resolution. When your DNS server cannot resolve a name, it queries the additional name servers listed in this file. If you are using this DNS server to resolve names on the Internet, your file should look similar to the following:

```
;    DNS CACHE FILE
;    Initial cache data for root domain servers.
;    YOU SHOULD CHANGE:
;       - Nothing if connected to the Internet.  Edit this file only when
;         update root name server list is released.
;            OR
;       - If NOT connected to the Internet, remove these records and replace
;         with NS and A records for the DNS server authoritative for the
;         root domain at your site.
```

```
;     Internet root name server records:
;         last update:    Sep 1, 1995
;         related version of root zone:    1995090100
; formerly NS.INTERNIC.NET
.                            3600000    IN    NS    A.ROOT-SERVERS.NET.
A.ROOT-SERVERS.NET.          3600000          A     198.41.0.4
; formerly NS1.ISI.EDU
.                            3600000          NS    B.ROOT-SERVERS.NET.
B.ROOT-SERVERS.NET.          3600000          A     128.9.0.107
; formerly C.PSI.NET
.                            3600000          NS    C.ROOT-SERVERS.NET.
C.ROOT-SERVERS.NET.          3600000          A     192.33.4.12
; formerly TERP.UMD.EDU
.                            3600000          NS    D.ROOT-SERVERS.NET.
D.ROOT-SERVERS.NET.          3600000          A     128.8.10.90
; formerly NS.NASA.GOV
.                            3600000          NS    E.ROOT-SERVERS.NET.
E.ROOT-SERVERS.NET.          3600000          A     192.203.230.10
; formerly NS.ISC.ORG
.                            3600000          NS    F.ROOT-SERVERS.NET.
F.ROOT-SERVERS.NET.          3600000          A     39.13.229.241
; formerly NS.NIC.DDN.MIL
.                            3600000          NS    G.ROOT-SERVERS.NET.
G.ROOT-SERVERS.NET.          3600000          A     192.112.36.4
; formerly AOS.ARL.ARMY.MIL
.                            3600000          NS    H.ROOT-SERVERS.NET.
H.ROOT-SERVERS.NET.          3600000          A     128.63.2.53
; formerly NIC.NORDU.NET
.                            3600000          NS    I.ROOT-SERVERS.NET.
I.ROOT-SERVERS.NET.          3600000          A     192.36.148.17
; End of File
```

> **TIP**
>
> An updated version of this file can be found at the InterNIC FTP site `ftp.rs.internic.net`. Log on anonymously, change to the `domain` directory, and download the file called `named.root`.

If this DNS server will not be used for Internet name resolution, you should replace the name server (NS) and address (A) records with the authoritative DNS server for your domain.

PLACE.DOM

This file is the heart of your DNS server's operation. It contains several record types, as summarized in Table 9.6, which are used to provide name resolution for the domain. Since the sample file that is included with the Microsoft DNS contains information for a non-existent domain, you should rename the file and modify it as appropriate for your domain. The following is a copy of my replacement file called `nt-guru.dom`. I use the naming convention *DomainName*.dom, and I recommend you do the same. This is particularly useful when administering multiple domains. The file contents I use in my replacement file are as follows:

```
@       IN  SOA      srv.nt-guru.com.  admin.srv.nt-guru.com.
↪( ;source host e-mailaddr
                                 1                              ;
↪serial number of file
                                 10800                          ; refresh interval
                                 3600                           ; retry interval
                                 604800                         ; expiration interval
                                 86400 )                        ; minimum time to live
@                   IN  NS       srv.nt-guru.com.               ;
↪name server for domain
srv                 IN  A        128.0.0.1                      ;
↪IP address of name server
@    IN  WINS 128.0.0.1 129.0.0.1                               ;
↪IP address of WINS servers
localhost           IN  A        127.0.0.1                      ; loop back
@                   IN  MX       10       srv                   ; e-mail server
srv     IN  A       128.0.0.1                                   ;
↪IP address of e-mail server
ftp                 IN  CNAME    srv                            ;
↪alias name for FTP service
www                 IN  CNAME    srv                            ;
↪alias name for WWW service
gopher              IN  CNAME    srv                            ;
↪alias name for Gopher service
```

The first entry in the file must be a start of authoritative (SOA) record. This record includes parameters that describe the source host (where the file was created), an e-mail address for the administrator of the file, a serial number (or version number) of the file, refresh interval (in seconds) used by secondary servers to determine when a revised file should be downloaded, retry time (in seconds) used by secondary servers that will wait before attempting to download the file in case of error, and expiration time (in seconds) used by secondary servers to determine when to discard a zone if it could not be downloaded. Your name servers (or DNS servers) for the domain should be listed, followed by their IP addresses. Next, include the local host identifier, which is used for loop-back testing, the name and address of any mail servers, and finally hostname aliases. A hostname alias is used to provide a host (such as my server SRV) with more than one hostname. This is particularly useful when you want your WWW site to be accessible in the commonly used format WWW.*DomainName*.COM (www.nt-guru.com, for example) rather than *ServerName*.*DomainName*.COM (srv.nt-guru.com, for example).

> **NOTE**
>
> When you specify a fully qualified domain name, it must be appended with a period. Otherwise, the domain name will be appended to the hostname for resolution and cause the name query to fail. For example, say I had specified my domain name as srv.nt-guru.com in line 7 instead of nt-guru.com. When trying to resolve the hostname srv.nt-guru.com, the domain name nt-guru.com would be appended once again (srv.nt-guru.com.nt-guru.com). Because there is no host by that name, the query would fail.

Table 9.6. Supported domain name records.

Identifier	Record Type	Description
A	Address	Specifies the IP address of the associated hostname.
CNAME	Class name	Specifies an alias for the associated hostname.
MX	Mail	Specifies the e-mail server hostnames.
NS	Name server	Specifies the DNS servers in the domain.
SOA	Start of authority	The first record in any configuration file; used to specify name.
WINS	WINS	Specifies the IP addresses of WINS servers that are used for additional name resolution.

ARPA-###.REV

This file is used for reverse lookups of hostnames within a domain. Instead of resolving a name to an IP address, a reverse lookup resolves an IP address to a hostname. For example, for my domain, which has only one subnet (128.0.0.0), the reverse lookup file is as follows:

```
@    IN   SOA      srv.nt-guru.com.     admin.srv.nt-guru.com.
( ;source host e-mailaddr
                            1                         ;
serial number of file
                            10800                     ; refresh interval
                            3600                      ; retry interval
                            604800                    ; expiration interval
                            86400 )                   ; minimum time to live
@            IN   NS       srv.nt-guru.com.          ;
name server for domain
@    IN   NBSTAT       nt-guru.com.                  ;
domain name to append for NBSTAT lookups
1        IN   PTR      srv.nt-guru.com.             ; SRV at 128.0.0.1
99       IN   PTR      winbookxp5.nt-guru.com.      ;
WinBook XP5 at 128.0.0.99
```

Once more, the first record should be an SOA record. The next record lists the name (or DNS) server for the domain, followed by an NBSTAT record, then the individual PTR records for each host in the domain. These records, and their usage, are summarized in Table 9.7. What most people find confusing are the PTR records. Instead of supplying a complete IP address (such as 128.0.0.1) for the host, you only supply the last digit of the IP address (such as 1), followed by the fully qualified hostname (host as well as domain name).

Table 9.7. Supported reverse lookup records.

Identifier	Record Type	Description
NBSTAT	NBSTAT	Specifies the domain name to append to any hostname found by an NBSTAT lookup.
NS	Name server	Specifies the DNS servers in the domain.
PTR	Pointer	Specifies an IP address for a host.
SOA	Start of authority	The first record in any configuration file; used to specify name.

Summary

The focus of this chapter is on implementing the DHCP, WINS, and DNS services on your network. It discusses the design goals for the services, basic planning issues, and the management options that are available for manipulating your DHCP and WINS clients.

The chapter also mentions specific issues for utilizing DHCP and WINS in a mixed Windows NT and UNIX environment and, where prudent, how to prepare for the possibility of a failure with the services database, some registry keys you can use to configure otherwise unconfigurable options, and some basic performance tips.

The next chapter looks at some of the security issues involved with connecting to the Internet and how you can configure your server to minimize unauthorized access to your network.

Advanced Security Issues

10

IN THIS CHAPTER

- Security and the Internet **264**
- Security and Windows NT Server **275**
- Determining Who Is Using Your System **297**

Security is a major issue with Internet connectivity. This chapter teaches you about some of these issues. You will start with a look at the two basic types of security: downloaded data and access limitations. Next you'll look into some of the capabilities provided with Windows NT Server to secure your data and your network. Your final stop will be a look into some of the tools you can use to determine who may be using your system, as well as who may be accessing your IIS site.

Security and the Internet

When you connect to the Internet, an entire world of information is available to you. Much of this information is provided by manufacturers to promote or support their products; other times it is provided by an individual to share ideas or provide a useful tool to other members of the online community. Sometimes, however, an object you download from the Internet is provided by someone who gets a sick enjoyment out of causing mental anguish or destroying data. You really need to watch what you download from the Internet, because you never know what it will do until after you try it. Sometimes, that's too late!

The flip side of accessing information on Internet sites is that an Internet client may be accessing your site as well. Not only can you access sites all around the world, but users from the entire world may be accessing your site too. Of course, this is another reason why you decided to get on the Internet in the first place: You want people all around the world to view your site. This opens up the possibility, however slight it may be, that an external user may attempt to access your site in unexpected—and dangerous—ways.

Because of the damage that can occur, you should seriously consider the possibilities. This section will look into two of these subjects. First you will learn about some of the security concerns involved with downloading objects from the Internet. Second, you will learn about some of the issues involved with having external users connect to your site. In both cases, you will learn about strategies you can implement to minimize damages.

Application and Document Security Issues

Most new Internet users love the Internet because they can find so much information, or applications, that they can download to their computer free. I will be the first to admit that this is an attractive capability. I will also be the first to mention that this can be a dangerous opportunity, too. Not everyone who provides files for you to download does it out of the goodness of his heart. Some people provide a file without cost only because they want to see how much damage to your system they can cause. This is not necessarily the intention of an Internet site administrator, although in some cases it could be. Take the following scenario, for example.

An Internet administrator creates a Web page to provide an easy-to-use interface to download a nifty shareware, or freeware, utility. This Web page has a hypertext link to an FTP site. This site could be local (on the same computer as the Web site) or remote (on someone else's FTP site). Now suppose some nasty person replaces the file on the FTP site with a copy of the utility that has been infected with a virus. The Web administrator may not even be aware that this has occurred, but he will be aware of it soon after he reads his e-mail from all the users who downloaded and executed the utility!

If you download a file from a private bulletin board system (like the Microsoft Network, CompuServe, or America Online), you have less to worry about because these services check files for possible viruses before making them visible to their members. So the safety factor is increased, but not necessarily eliminated. Public bulletin board systems and the Internet have a higher security risk that you must be prepared to deal with or you shouldn't be using them. This section addresses some of the types of problems that could occur, and what you can do to prepare yourself for such an eventuality.

Viruses and Trojan Horses

A *virus* is an application that contains code that is usually destructive to your computer system. A virus can also be embedded in a data object that supports a built-in macro language—a Word for Windows document template, for example. Some viruses are not destructive, but rather just cause the loss of a service (such as your ability to receive your e-mail) or user apprehension. A virus is a self-replicating snippet of code. Basically, a virus works like this:

1. An infected application is executed on your computer.
2. The infected application then either modifies the boot sector on your primary hard disk or infects other applications:

    - The boot sector on your hard disk contains 512 bytes of executable code, which is called the *master boot record* (MBR). This boot record is used to load the rest of the operating system. If the boot sector is replaced by a virus, as part of this replacement process the original boot sector is copied to a hidden file on your hard disk. After loading the infected boot sector, the rest of the virus's executable code is loaded, and then the virus loads the original boot sector. Because this process happens so quickly, and because the original operating system loads, you may not even be aware that your system has become infected. But any new disk that you load on your system may be infected with the virus. Thereafter any person who uses one of these disks to boot his system will also infect his boot disk.

    - If the virus is not designed to replace your boot sector, when it executes it often looks for other executable programs (most commonly *.EXE or *.COM files) and then infects them with a copy of the virus. Every executable program has a program header that tells the operating system what type of application it is (MS-DOS, 16-bit Windows, 32-bit Windows, OS/2, or POSIX), where the application should be loaded in memory, and where the starting point of the application's executable code begins. A virus may add its executable code to the original application, then change the application's header to point to the virus's startup code. After the virus loads into memory, it will load the application into memory and you will continue working as you normally would without realizing the virus is present.

> **TIP**
>
> Windows NT is somewhat protected from most viruses because direct hardware access by MS-DOS applications is not supported except through Windows NT device drivers. For this reason, it is less likely that an MS-DOS application will be able to infect the boot sector, or other applications, if the infected application is executed in a console window under Windows NT. If you boot your system from an infected floppy, however, it is possible that the boot sector could be infected because at this point Windows NT is not running to protect you. In most cases—in fact, in all that I have encountered to date—the next time you try to boot Windows NT it won't work. So if your system fails to boot, you should check it immediately for a boot sector virus. For more information, see the section titled "Recovering an Infected System" later in this chapter.

- A macro virus, such as the Prank macro virus found in a Word for Windows document in 1995, usually infects other data objects by hooking into a macro which is automatically executed whenever the document object is loaded into the source program. Thereafter, any new document that is created will be infected as well. Any user who opens one of these infected documents on a non-infected system will infect their system with the virus.

> **WARNING**
>
> One of the really nasty problems with a macro virus is that it is not platform specific. Most viruses are designed to infect a particular operating-system platform, like MS-DOS, but a macro virus is designed to infect the source application, such as Word. This means that the same macro virus could infect installations of the application that run under MS-DOS, Windows, Windows NT, Macintosh, OS/2, UNIX, or any other platform where the source application shares the same macro language capabilities.

3. If the virus is a malicious virus, one day the program may activate and wipe out all the data on your hard disk. If the virus is not malicious, you might just lose control of your system while a message is printed on the screen, or some similar action might take place. In most cases for a non-malicious virus, to regain control of your system you will be required to reboot it. This will not remove the virus, but will allow you (in

Advanced Security Issues

Chapter 10

most cases) to reboot your computer and try and clean your system using a write-protected bootable floppy disk and virus-scanning software.

A *trojan horse* is an application that is designed to be hidden from the user but to capture sensitive information (like a user account and password) that is then passed to another person for nefarious purposes. A trojan horse is very unlikely to occur under Windows NT, but it is possible. Windows NT requires that you use a specific mechanism to log onto the system. This is the familiar logon dialog box that is displayed when you press the Ctrl+Alt+Del key combination. This sequence is used only after the system has loaded.

If an MS-DOS trojan horse was activated at boot time to display the same logon dialog boxes, when the user pressed Ctrl+Alt+Del one of two things would occur:

1. The system would immediately reboot because the Ctrl+Alt+Del key combination is trapped by the system and is used to perform a warm boot.
2. If the Ctrl+Alt+Del combination was trapped by the trojan horse, the user account and password could be captured by the application. But then Windows NT would not load afterward.

In either case, you should readily notice if a trojan horse is present on your system. If either type of activity is noted, immediately notify your system administrator. It will then be up to the system administrator to take any corrective action that may be required.

Active Content Security Issues

Web browsers that can display active content, such as the Internet Explorer 2.0 or Netscape Navigator, incur additional security risks. These types of Web browsers can create interactive content by utilizing a scripting language, such as VBScript or JavaScript, that executes on the local computer. Even though most of the language constructs (such as direct I/O) that could cause damage to your system have been removed, the potential is still there for damage to your system or loss of confidential data.

Much of this risk is possible because these scripting languages are still in early stages of their life cycle. In an early release of Java-enabled Web browsers, for example, two potential security risks were identified and later corrected. In the first case it was possible for an invisible window to remain active on the client. This provided the capability for the invisible application to remain in contact with the host Web server and potentially pass data to the Web server. The Web browser user would not even be aware that this was occurring. In the second case, a Java application was able to access any computer on the network where the application was executing. This was a serious issue because it essentially provided a means for the application to bypass the network firewall.

Java-enabled Web browsers from Netscape have been on the market for a little longer than Web browsers from Microsoft that support VBScript or JavaScript, so some of the security leaks have been eliminated. The real problem, however, is that neither of these Web browsers has been available long enough to eliminate all possible problems. (Of course, it's doubtful that they ever will be able to eliminate *all* possible problems.) Consider the following capabilities of an active-content Web browser:

- ActiveX controls—An ActiveX control is a dynamic link library that executes in the context of the current user. Dynamic link libraries can be used to extend the functionality of an application and can call other functions in other dynamic link libraries.
- Scripting—Both VBScript and JavaScript are interpreted languages that are OLE enabled. They may load additional ActiveX controls or access additional applications using OLE.
- Object linking and embedding—OLE can be used to control the behavior of an OLE-aware application.

By creating an executable package (consisting of your HTML code and scripts) that is downloaded by the user and then executed, it may be possible to create applications that can damage the system. It may even be possible to access shared network resources. This could occur by building a series of dynamic link libraries that would be executed by either an ActiveX control, an interactive script, or a standalone application (like Word for Windows). It may even be possible to execute other functions in dynamic link libraries or even spawn a downloaded application using an OLE-enabled application (like Word for Windows) that could cause damage to your system.

It is really very difficult to say with 100% certainty whether this possibility could occur, simply because the products are either still in beta form or are newly released. In either case, they have not been completely tested to ensure that no security breach could occur, and I don't believe that would be entirely possible because the capability to extend the functionality of an application opens up the possibility that someone will do so with the intent to cause harm. One thing I have learned from my years of experience is that if it can be done, someone will find the way to do it.

Recovering an Infected System

When a computer system becomes infected with a virus, you are in trouble unless you can get rid of it. If your computer system uses the FAT file system, you have more options to remove a virus than if your system uses the NTFS file system. This is simply because there are not many tools that operate under Windows NT, and currently only a Windows NT application can access the NTFS file system. In this section you will learn a few methods for dealing with viruses that may have infected your system. They are as follows:

- **If Windows NT is active, try the following:**

  The easiest virus-removal process is to run a virus-scanning tool under Windows NT. Many MS-DOS– or 16-bit Windows–based tools will not work, but the Norton Anti-Virus and McAffee Virus Scan tools are available as native Windows NT applications. Each of these tools will scan each file on your hard disk, and if a virus is detected, it will either remove the virus or delete the infected file if the virus cannot be removed.

- **If Windows NT is not active, and your boot partition is a FAT partition, try the following:**

  Boot from a clean, write-protected, MS-DOS system disk. Execute your virus-scanning software. If it succeeds, reboot the computer and run a native Windows NT virus-scanning application to check your NTFS partitions for applications that may contain a virus.

- **If Windows NT is not active, you cannot boot NT, and your boot partition is an NTFS partition, try the following:**

  This generally occurs when you boot from an infected floppy disk and a boot sector virus replaces the boot sector on your hard disk. The first thing to try in this situation is the set of instructions described in the previous option.

  If that option fails to remove the boot sector virus, boot from a clean, write-protected, MS-DOS system disk. Then use the MS-DOS command FDISK /MBR, which will replace the master boot record (MBR). In some cases this will remove the infected boot sector, and Windows NT will then be able to boot normally.

  If after using the FDISK /MBR command the boot sector virus was removed but Windows NT will still not boot, you can try the emergency repair process. This is accomplished by booting your system using the original Windows NT installation disks. During the install process you are prompted to set up Windows NT or repair the current installation. Choose the repair option. When prompted, insert your emergency repair disk. Later you will be prompted as to the actions to take. Choose to verify the startup files, verify the boot sector, and compare the system files. This will restore the system configuration.

> **NOTE**
>
> The only time I have seen the repair process fail to replace the boot sector and system files is when Windows NT can no longer recognize the disk partition. Most times this can be corrected by using the FDISK /MBR option in conjunction with the repair disk

> process, but if this option fails your only other option is to wipe the disk (if it is a SCSI drive, you can low-level format it), repartition it, reformat it, and then reinstall Windows NT. Finally, you can restore your last Windows NT configuration using a previous backup.

Firewalls, Proxy Agents, and Other Ways to Limit Access

The first thought you should consider when planning your Internet Information Server installation is security of your data. As part of your plan, consider putting the IIS on a network segment that is isolated from your primary network. After all, if the whole world can access your network, there may come a time when someone will decide to try to access more than the information you are making freely available to the public. Preventing an external user from accessing unauthorized areas on your computer (or your entire network) or preventing your internal network clients from accessing external resources (such as Internet resources) is where you will enter the realm of firewalls, proxy agents, and other alternatives.

These topics are discussed in the following sections, but the idea is not to be an all-inclusive reference because there is just too much material to fit into a single chapter. Instead, the discussion is a general reference to describe the technologies that are involved in limiting access to your network. There is one sure statement I can make about this entire process of limiting access to your network, and that is… there is no 100-percent guarantee that you can prevent an expert from working his way into your system from the Internet. At best, you can be aware of an intrusion; at worst, the intruder could bypass all of your safeguards and do whatever he wants. These are unlikely propositions, but the longer you are connected to the Internet, the more likely they will become. It is therefore imperative that you do one of two things:

- Place your server that provides Internet connectivity on a standalone network. This is a guarantee that the worst an intruder can do is damage this particular server. He will not be able to worm his way into your internal network because there is no physical connection between the networks.

- If you cannot use a standalone server because you are also providing Internet connectivity to your network clients, consider a third-party firewall or proxy agent. At the very least, use the capabilities provided within Windows NT Server 4 to limit the damage that could occur. (See the section titled "Security and Windows NT Server" later in this chapter.)

Advanced Security Issues
Chapter 10   271

> **TIP**
>
> There is one other safeguard you can use that has absolutely nothing to do with limiting access to your computers. It's a pretty simple mechanism, but nonetheless is very important. Just make daily, weekly, and monthly backups of your server and your network client computers! If you have a backup, you can restore your previous configuration.

Using a Firewall to Restrict Access to Your Network

A *firewall* is an intermediary computer that stands between the Internet and your network. (See Figure 10.1.) A firewall basically performs the same task as the security guard at your office. The security guard will check your credentials at the door, and then either let you into the building or refuse you access. If your company allows visitors to enter the building, the guard may require that the visitor signs in to a log book and shows a proof of identity (like a driver's license) to verify that he is who he says he is. These two features—restricting access and logging access—are the fundamental functions that a firewall performs for your network.

FIGURE 10.1.
Using a firewall to protect your network.

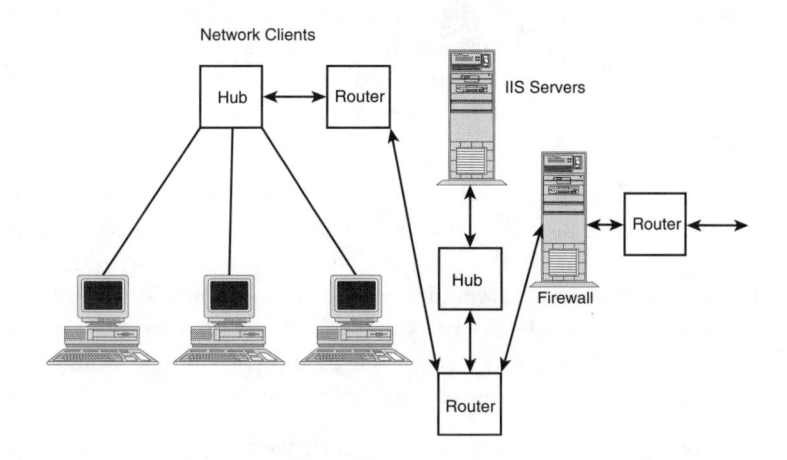

A firewall restricts access to your network by utilizing the information contained within a network packet. For Internet services, which use the TCP/IP protocol, this information can be divided into five basic components, as summarized in Table 10.1. These basic components include the protocol, destination IP address, destination IP port, source IP address, and source IP port.

Table 10.1. The five basic components used by a firewall in an Internet environment.

Component	Description
Protocol	Transmission Control Protocol (TCP) or User Datagram Protocol (UDP).
Destination IP address	Identifies the location of the computer receiving the data transmission.
Destination IP port	Identifies the application on the computer that will receive the data transmission.
Source IP address	Identifies the location of the computer initiating the data transmission.
Source IP port	Identifies the application on the computer that initiates the data transmission.

As a comparison, consider the way you make a phone call. First you pick up the phone, then you dial a 1 (or perhaps you dial 9 first to access an external line if you call from work), the area code, and finally the seven-digit phone number. When the other party hears the phone ring, she picks up the phone and you begin your conversation. You might say something like "Hello Valda, this is Art." If you want the party (Valda) on the other end of the phone to call you back, you exchange phone numbers. When you have finished your conversation, you hang up the phone.

In this example your area code could be considered as the source address, you would be considered as the source port, the other party's phone number would be the destination address, and Valda would be the destination port. The method you use to dial the number, initiate, and then end the conversation would be considered as the protocol. If your destination party's phone company supports caller ID and your destination party has the appropriate hardware, she can determine who is calling her before she picks up the phone. Some caller-ID hardware devices can even record the number of the calling party (you) and the duration of the call.

A firewall functions in a similar manner. By using the destination and source IP addresses and IP port information contained within the packet, the firewall can either accept or reject the packet. It can also accept or reject packets based on the protocol contained within the packet. The firewall can also log this activity, much as a caller-ID hardware device does, to determine who may be attempting to access the network.

Some firewalls go beyond the basic packet-filtering mechanism and utilize a network session as their key means to accept or reject network requests. A network session occurs at the user or application level rather than at the IP transport level. Each network session will utilize a different IP port, so each session is guaranteed to have a unique identifier consisting of the five basic components previously described. Session-based firewalls offer increased security and more efficient client activity–recording options, so if you are looking at purchasing a firewall, check to see if it supports session-based security.

Many people believe that a firewall is the only protection they need for their network. This is not true, however, because a firewall filters information. If you close the filter completely, you are secure, but this also prevents you from utilizing any of the Internet resources. If you open up the filter to provide access to the Internet, you are also creating a window of opportunity for someone to access your system. This follows the same analogy as the services provided by your security guard on the night shift. If he locks the building, he can prevent thefts from occurring. Of course, he also prevents any employee from entering the building and performing any work (such as cleaning the offices). By opening the doors of the building, the work can proceed. By making his rounds at night he can help prevent thefts from occurring by his presence, but he cannot prevent all occurrences because he cannot be everywhere at once. All a security guard can do for you is lessen the chance of a theft occurring. All a firewall can do for you is lessen the risk associated with an Internet connection. It cannot entirely remove all risk.

Using a Proxy Agent to Restrict Access to Your Network

A *proxy agent* is really another type of firewall. Rather than working at the packet level, it operates at the application level. This means that it also uses a network session as its primary means of denying access as a session-based firewall, but it includes one additional feature not provided by session-based firewalls: It can mask the address and IP port of the source computer from the destination computer. This can prevent unauthorized access to your network while still providing access to external users. Let's take a look at how this would work in theory.

Assume for the moment that your network includes a server running the Internet Information Server on one computer and a proxy agent on another computer, as shown in Figure 10.2. The IIS server and the proxy agent are both connected to a router, which in turn is connected to the Internet. Your network clients' only access to the Internet, however, is through the proxy agent, so all network traffic to or from these network clients and the Internet must go through the proxy agent.

FIGURE 10.2.
Using a proxy agent to protect your network.

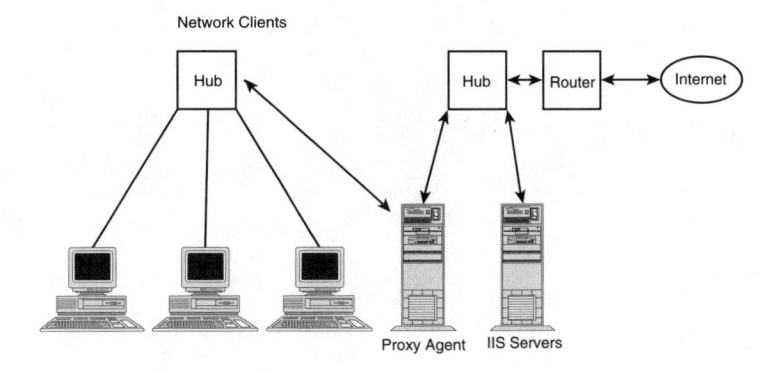

When you create your proxy agent, you also assign an IP port address for the proxy agent to monitor. You may assign one IP port address for all Internet services (such as WWW, FTP, or Gopher) or one port address for each Internet service. Your network clients will then connect to the port on your proxy agent. The proxy agent will then determine the destination IP address and IP port the client wants to use. If the connection is not authorized, it will be terminated. If the connection is authorized, the proxy agent will connect to the external source. As data is received from this external source, it is passed to the network client. Any requests from the network client will be passed to the external source through the proxy agent. In essence, the proxy agent masquerades as the destination computer to the network client and as the network client to the destination computer.

For an external user to gain access to your internal network, he will have to know the IP address of the client computer, the IP address of the proxy agent, and the IP port the proxy agent is monitoring. He will also have to be on the allowed access list (usually based on the external client's IP address). If any of these items are unknown, the external user cannot connect to the client on the other side of the proxy agent.

Using Multiple Network Protocols to Prevent Access to Your Network

A less expensive (and less secure) method to limit access to your network is to use different network protocols on your internal network and your IIS server. You could use the IPX/SPX protocol on your internal network, and both TCP/IP and IPX/SPX on your IIS server. (See Figure 10.3.) This way your network clients would be isolated from external Internet users, but they would still be able to access the shared directories on the IIS server. In this fashion you could provide a limited means of accessing data on an FTP site, for example.

FIGURE 10.3.
Using multiple protocols to protect your network.

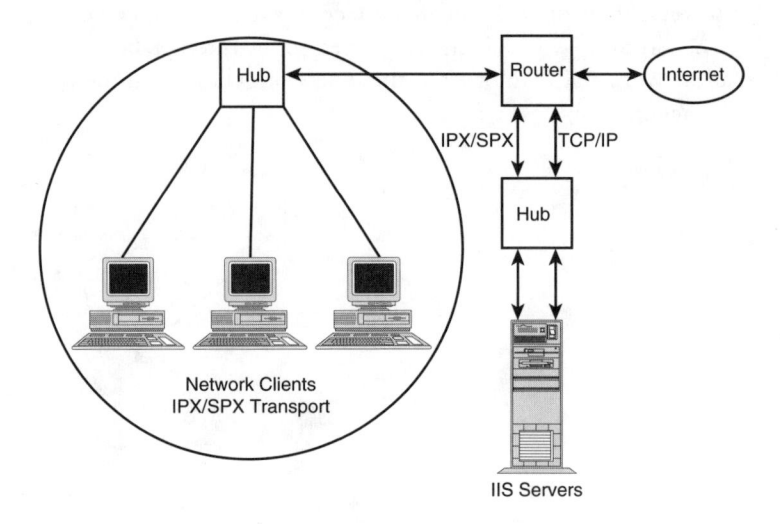

The only drawback to this solution is that your network clients would not be able to access the Internet. A solution does exist for multiple protocol–based networks, however. It is possible to use a *gateway* (another piece of hardware located between the network clients and the Internet connection) that would convert network requests from your clients using the IPX/SPX protocol to the corresponding TCP/IP protocol. This solution generally requires specially modified Internet utilities that are based on the IPX/SPX protocol rather than on the standard Internet protocols.

Security and Windows NT Server

By now you should be getting the idea that security is a very important issue with any computer connected to the Internet. With Windows NT Server 4, you have several tools in your arsenal that you can apply to limit access to your network and thereby limit the risks associated with the Internet. In this section you will look into four of the possibilities. The first item on the agenda is to examine your user-account policies. Your next stop will be a look at how you can use the NTFS file system. If you will be supporting dial-up networking clients or connecting to the Internet using a dial-up networking connection, there are a few configuration options you can apply to make it more difficult for someone to cause damage to your network. Your last stop is the most important; it will show you how to use the new security features in Windows NT Server to create a miniature firewall.

Using User Accounts to Limit Access

The starting point in securing your server—or your entire network—from unauthorized access is the user accounts that you create. These accounts will be created on your server if it is a standalone computer, or on your domain controller if you are supplying full Internet connectivity to your clients. These user accounts may be used differently depending on whether you are using the Internet Information Server to supply Internet or intranet services. This may be a bit confusing to some of you, so a more thorough discussion may help to clarify the situation.

When you are using IIS to create an intranet site, your network is usually physically secure. The possibility of someone connecting a packet sniffer to your network and capturing clear text password authentication is not very likely. If you use IIS to provide an Internet presence, however, this may change rapidly because anyone with a packet sniffer can capture network packets transmitted over the Internet. It is also possible that someone will go dumpster-diving in an attempt to locate a list of valid user accounts and their associated passwords. It may be that someone is doing this right now in an attempt to obtain a valid user account and password for your network. To prevent these possibilities you need to make sure of three things:

- Protect your user accounts and passwords. Do not leave any lists of user accounts and passwords where they can be easily found. Do not throw out any lists of user accounts and passwords. Instead, lock up any lists in a secure location (not your desk drawer, either) and, if you dispose of any lists, be sure to shred them first.
- Make sure your Internet Service Provider supports an encryption mechanism for any of your clients that will be connecting to your network over the Internet.
- Make sure your Internet tools support the Microsoft challenge-response authentication mechanism. If this is not possible, because currently only the Microsoft Internet Explorer 2.0 or higher supports this option, consider obtaining a security certificate and using the *Secure Socket Layer* (SSL) to provide access to your server for sites with sensitive data.

Configuring the IIS User Account

If you will be providing Internet access to your IIS site, you will want to make a few modifications to the user account that is created by the IIS setup program. By default, a user account called IUSR_*ServerName*, where *ServerName* is the name of your computer where IIS is installed, is created. This account is added to the Guests local group if you installed IIS on a standalone server. If your server is a member of a domain, the account is also a member of the Domain Users global group. My personal preference is to move the user account to the Domain Guests global group. If you have modified the privileges for the Domain Guests global group and you will have multiple IIS installations, create a new group, assign the IIS user accounts that are created to this new group, and make sure you remove the IIS accounts from all other global groups. If your IIS sites will be on standalone servers and you have not modified the Guest account, the default IIS user-account privileges should suffice.

> **NOTE**
>
> In order to use the Guest account on a domain, the account must be enabled. The default for the Guest account is for the account to be disabled. You can change this property by double-clicking the Guest account and clearing the Account Disabled check box.

If you create a new global group for the IIS user account, however, make sure that only the Log on locally privilege has been granted to the user account. This can be verified using User Manager (or User Manager for Domains) and choosing Policies | User Rights. This will display the User Rights Policy dialog box. Enable the Show advanced user rights check box so you can view all rights, not just the basic rights. Then in the Right drop-down listbox, select each right.

Advanced Security Issues
Chapter 10

As you do, the user accounts and groups that have been assigned the selected right will be displayed in the Grant To listbox.

Configuring the User Account Policies

Every network has certain rules for user accounts that can be used to provide additional security for your network. Windows NT Server is no exception. In User Manager (or User Manager for Domains) choose Account from the Policies menu to display the Account Policy dialog box. (See Figure 10.4.)

FIGURE 10.4.
Setting user account policies with User Manager.

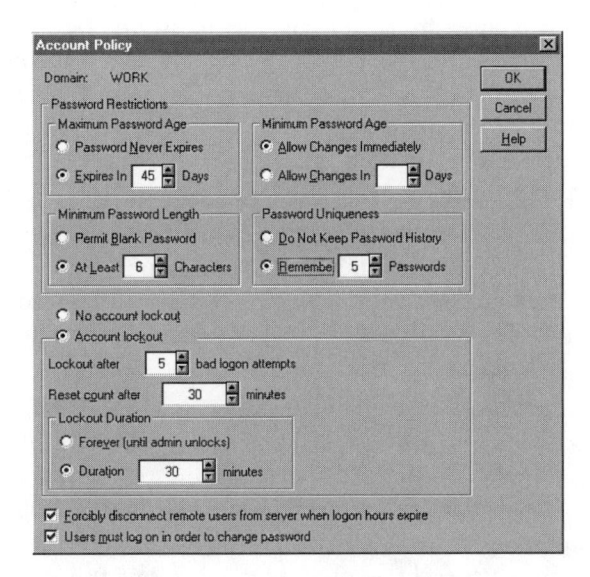

In the Account Policy dialog box, you can set the following options:

- Maximum Password Age—You can require that a user change his password every so often by specifying a number in the Expires in *x* Days edit field. This is a good idea to implement because it requires that the user change his password and prevents a potential breach of network security.

- Minimum Password Age—By specifying a number in the Allow Changes In *x* Days edit field, you can limit the time period during which the user can change his password. This provides two useful benefits. First, it provides some administrative relief by requiring that a user employ a specific password for a period of time. Second, it provides some network security by preventing a user from setting his password back to a previous password immediately if you have the Password Uniqueness option enabled.

- Minimum Password Length—This option has a tradeoff that you need to consider before implementing. First, you need to consider that the smaller the password length, the easier it is for the user to remember. However, it also makes it easier for a network hacker to gain access to your network by repeatedly guessing the password for a particular user account. The larger password lengths offer increased network security, but probably will require more intervention from you because your network users will forget their passwords. To specify the minimum length of a password, enter a number in the At Least *x* Characters edit field.

You should require a minimum password length of eight characters. This is a good balance between the ease of user management and potential security breaches.

- Password Uniqueness—Specifying a number in the Remember *x* Passwords edit field prevents a user from using an older password based on the history list. The *history list* is a record of the user passwords. The number you enter here is used to specify the number of passwords that should be recorded. Any password included in this record cannot be employed by the user when it is time to choose a new password based on the maximum password age.

- Account Lockout—This is your best weapon to fight system hackers because it specifies how many times a user can enter the wrong password to access an account before the user account is disabled. This option prevents a hacker from repeatedly attempting to specify a password for a user account to gain access to your network. On the down side, it also can lock out your users who forget their passwords during a logon sequence.

  You can specify the number of logon attempts before an account lockout occurs in the Lockout after *x* bad logon attempts edit field. This count is based on the Reset count after *x* minutes edit field. This duration specifies the time frame to determine the count of bad logon attempts. If the number of attempts occurs within the time frame you specify here, the account is locked out. In the Lockout Duration group, you can specify whether the account is locked out for a specific period of time by entering a number in the Duration field, or until an administrator reactivates it by selecting the Forever radio button.

- Forcibly disconnect remote users from server when logon hours expire—You can enable this check box to force any connected user off the network and close any shared network files (like a SQL Server database) so that you can make system backups.

- Users must log on in order to change password—You can enable this check box to require that the user log on before he can change his password. This option can prevent a user from using an expired password to gain access to the network for an idle account.

The security of your network is only as good as the policies you implement. You need to balance the aggravation your users encounter due to these policies with reasonable security measures. A good balance between the ease of user management and potential security breaches is to specify a value of 45 to 60 days for the maximum password age, for example. This requires that users change their passwords occasionally to help prevent a hacker from gaining access to your network by using an easily remembered password that never changes.

Using NTFS to Protect Your Data

The *New Technology File System* (NTFS) is another item in your arsenal that, if properly utilized, can aid you in your goal to prevent unauthorized access to your data. You can think of NTFS as your personal security system. In action it is similar to the numerous code-key door-lock systems in use on doors in secure areas. In order to open the door, you must first supply a code, use a badge with a preset code, or wait for someone on the other side of the door to escort you in. All access to this secure area is monitored by security cameras and logged by a security guard. If someone attempts to break in, an alarm is sounded, the guards run to the source of the alarm, and the culprit is taken into custody.

With Windows NT Server, an alarm can be created by using the Performance Monitor in Alert view (see Chapter 22, "The Performance Monitor"). By monitoring the Server object counters Errors Logon and Errors Access Permissions, you can be alerted if the frequency of bad logons or data access attempts are occurring in real time. When informed of the event, if the culprit is a local network client, you certainly can physically confront him face to face. If the culprit is a remote user, although you cannot take him into custody you can kick him off of the system. The key to being able to determine who is using your system and what they are doing, however, is based on system resource auditing. Auditing directory or file access is supported only on an NTFS partition. For more specific information on how to configure your system and use this auditing information, refer to the section titled "Determining Who Is Using Your System" later in this chapter. I also recommend that you set permissions on all of your directories and files contained on NTFS partitions because it can help eliminate additional security risks. For more information on how to set directory and file permissions, see the following section titled "Setting Permissions on a Directory or File."

During the Internet Information Server setup process, the default root installation directory for your WWW, FTP, and Gopher services is `SystemRoot\System32\InetSrv`. Keeping this directory as the root installation directory is not such a good idea, for at least two reasons.

- First, this directory is accessible from the Windows NT hidden administration shares `ADMIN$` and `C$`. Although you can delete the sharepoint for the `C$` administrative share, deleting the `ADMIN$` sharepoint will cause numerous problems with remote administration of the server.

- Second, if your boot partition has a data error, it's possible to lose not only your Windows NT installation but your Internet service's data as well. It is a much better choice to create a new root directory on another physical drive, such as `D:\InetSrv`. By creating a new root directory, you can control access by deleting the root administration share (`D$`, for example). You also increase your recoverability options in case your boot partition fails. In the worst case, you can reinstall Windows NT Server and have your Web site back up and running in a couple of hours.

> **TIP**
>
> Wherever you install the Internet Information Server files, you should choose an NTFS partition if you have one available. You can then assign permissions to the executable files, as well as all of the root directories for your content files.

Another item in your arsenal is to consider using the fault-tolerant capabilities of Windows NT to limit the downtime that could occur in case of a disaster. You can use a stripe set with parity for increased performance and improved fault tolerance, a mirrored set for additional data redundancy, or both. For maximum fault tolerance, create a mirrored set for your `SystemRoot` partition to protect you against boot partition errors and a striped set with parity for the partition used as your IIS root directory. But just because you are using a fault-tolerant partition, don't think that you do not need to make system backups.

Plan on daily, weekly, and monthly backups in case all other methods fail. This way, if you install Windows NT Server as a standalone server you have a way to restore your site. This restoration can occur on the same physical computer that failed (after you replace the failed hardware) or on another computer on your network.

Setting Permissions on a Directory or File

You can prevent unauthorized access to a network resource by setting permissions on a directory or one or more files. Directory- and file-level permissions are divided into the following incremental possibilities:

- No Access—This permission level prevents any access to the selected directory or files. This includes the parent directory, any subdirectories, and all the files.

> **CAUTION**
>
> Use the No Access option with care because it is exclusive of all other privileges. If you set permissions for directories or files with No Access permissions by user or group, all users or group members are denied access. This occurs even if a different group, which includes selected users of the first group, provides access.
>
> Suppose that you have a group called ChangeAccess that includes the users Bob, Valda, and Mary. You have another group called ExcludeAccess that includes Mary, Joe, and Sally. If you assign the No Access share privilege to the ExcludeAccess group and then assign Change access to the ChangeAccess group, Joe, Sally, and Mary are denied access to the data in the directory, whereas Bob and Valda have change access to the sharepoint.

Advanced Security Issues
Chapter 10

- Add—This is an interesting permission level because it denies the user the capability to list the contents of a directory or file. The only thing a user with this permission setting can do is create a subdirectory or file. After he creates the file or subdirectory, he cannot make any changes to it.

> **TIP**
>
> I have found two good reasons to use the Add permission setting. The first is if you want to create an anonymous drop box. You might want to allow users to send you a data file but prevent some users from seeing it, for example. This is particularly useful for an FTP directory because you can then scan the file with a virus scanner before moving the file to another directory where your users can only read files. This can prevent an Internet user from replacing a file with an infected version. The second good use for this setting is as a backup directory. You can let users drop confidential data files into this directory for backup but prevent any users (including the owner) from accessing it, for example. The only catch for this type of permission setting is that you have to delete directories or files after using them so that the users can add them again later. This is because the user has a one-time option to add a directory or file but cannot replace an existing one.

- Add and Read—This permission is similar to the Add permission, but it also includes the capability to list the directory contents, open a data file, or execute an application.
- Read—Provides read-only access to the parent directory, any subdirectories, and files in a shared directory. Users can connect to the sharepoint, list the directory contents, change subdirectories, read files, and execute applications, but they cannot create subdirectories, add files, or make changes to any data files in the shared directory.
- Change—This permission level includes all the functionality of read access. Users can create subdirectories, add files, and make changes to data files. They also can delete subdirectories and files.
- Full Control—Not only does this level provide the capabilities of the Change share-level permission, it also lets users change the subdirectory- and file-level permissions.
- Special Directory Access—This is a user-specified accumulation of the permissions specified from the list of Read, Write, Execute, Delete, Change Permissions, or Take Ownership and applies only to directories.
- Special File Access—This is a user-specified accumulation of the permissions specified from the list of Read, Write, Execute, Delete, Change, or Take Ownership permissions and applies only to files.

> **NOTE**
>
> The capability to change subdirectory- and file-level permissions applies only to network sharepoints that have been created on NTFS partitions.

> **TIP**
>
> Use the Special Directory Access or Special File Access permission if one of the default settings does not provide the restrictions you want. You might want to give someone the capability to use a source code revision program to which you assign the Read, Write, and Delete special file permissions, for example. This assignment lets users make changes to the source code but does not enable them to change any permission settings, take ownership of the files, or execute applications contained in the directory. If you combine this assignment with the special directory permissions, you can even restrict the user from listing or accessing subdirectories.

Table 10.2 summarizes the directory- and file-level permissions. Table 10.3 contains explanations of these abbreviations.

Table 10.2. Directory- and file-level permissions.

Permission	Directory/Subdirectory-Level Access	File-Level Access
No Access	None	None
Add	(A)	(A)
Add and Read	(L) (R) (W) (E)	(L) (R) (W) (E)
Read	(L) (R) (E)	(L) (R) (E)
Change	(L) (R) (W) (E) (D)	(L) (R) (W) (E) (D)
Full Control	(L) (R) (W) (E) (D) (P) (O)	(L) (R) (W) (E) (D) (P) (O)
Special Directory Access	User Specified	Not Specified
Special File Access	Not Specified	User Specified
List	(L)	(L)

Table 10.3. Directory and file permission attributes.

Attribute	Description
A	Creates a directory or a file once, but you can't make any changes thereafter.
D	Deletes subdirectories and files.
E	Executes applications.
L	Lists subdirectories and files.
O	Takes ownership of subdirectories and files on NTFS partitions.
P	Changes permissions on subdirectories and files on NTFS partitions.
R	Reads files but makes no changes.
W	Creates subdirectories and files as well as modifies existing files.

To set permissions on directories, follow these steps:

1. Select the directories by using File Manager.
2. Choose Permissions from the Security menu to access the Directory Permissions dialog box. (See Figure 10.5.)

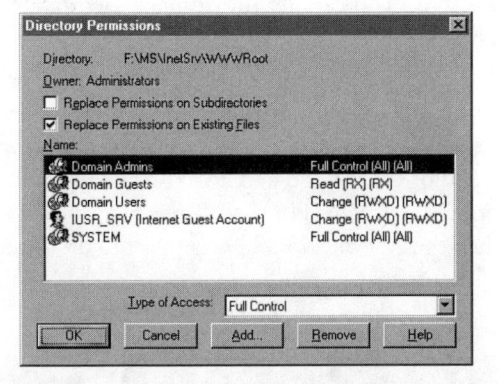

FIGURE 10.5.
The Directory Permissions dialog box.

> **TIP**
>
> As a shortcut to the Security|Permissions menu option, you can click the Permissions toolbar button.

3. Click the Add button. The Add Users and Groups dialog box appears. (See Figure 10.6.)

FIGURE 10.6.
The Add Users and Groups dialog box.

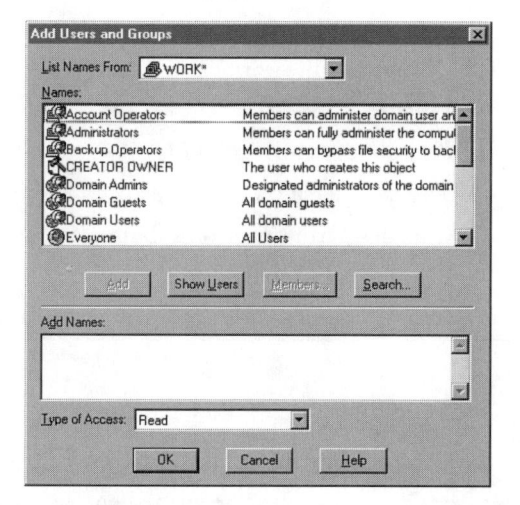

4. By default, the domain you logged onto is displayed in the List Names From drop-down listbox. You can use the domain user database from any domain with which you have established a trust relationship. You also can use the local database for a Windows NT Server computer operating in server mode.
5. By default, only groups are listed in the Names drop-down listbox. If you want to include user accounts, click the Show Users button. This adds all your user accounts to the end of the list. To add an existing group or user, just double-click on the group or user name displayed in the Names drop-down listbox, or select a group or name and click the Add button. This copies the user account or group to the Add Names box. If you mistakenly add a name to the Add Names box, you can highlight the name and then press the Delete key to remove it.

TIP

To display individual user accounts, select a group name in the Names box and click the Members button. If you select a local group and click the Members button, the Local Group Membership dialog box appears, which includes local user accounts and global groups defined in the local group. If you then select a global group and click the Members button, the Global Group Membership dialog appears, which includes a list of users defined in the global group. In either of these dialog boxes, you can select an individual user account (or global groups in the Local Group Membership dialog box) and click the Add button to add users or global groups to the Add Names box in the Add Users and Groups dialog box.

Advanced Security Issues
Chapter 10

6. After you place the user accounts or groups in the Add Names box, you need to select the directory permission level from the Type of Access drop-down listbox. This can be No Access, Add, Add and Read, Read, Change, or Full Control.

7. Click the OK button to return to the Directory Permissions dialog box. All the user and group accounts now are displayed in the Name box of the dialog box.

8. If you want to replace the permissions on all subdirectories of the directory you are setting permissions on, make sure to enable the Replace Permissions on Subdirectories check box. If you do not want to replace the permissions on files currently contained in the directory, be sure to disable the Replace Permissions on Existing Files check box.

9. Click the OK button to assign the directory-level permissions you selected.

10. After you see a confirmation dialog box, click the OK button to continue.

To modify an existing user or group directory-level permission, follow these steps:

1. In the Directory Permissions dialog box, select the user account or group name listed in the Name box.

2. In the Type of Access drop-down listbox, select the Share permission level. This can be No Access, Add, Add and Read, Read, Change, Full Control, Special Directory Access, or Special File Access. If you specify Special Directory Access, the dialog box shown in Figure 10.7 appears. If you select Special File Access, the dialog box shown in Figure 10.8 is displayed. In these dialog boxes, you can specify the exact permission settings you want.

FIGURE 10.7.
The Special Directory Access dialog box.

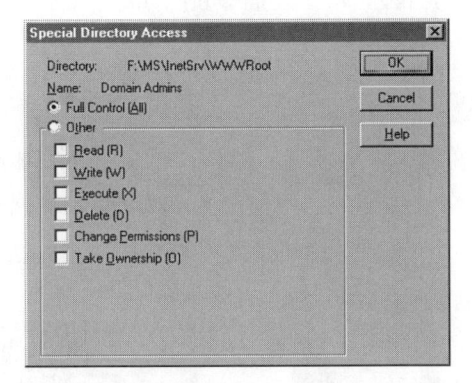

3. Repeat these steps for each user account or group for which you want to change the permissions.

FIGURE 10.8.
The Special File Access dialog box.

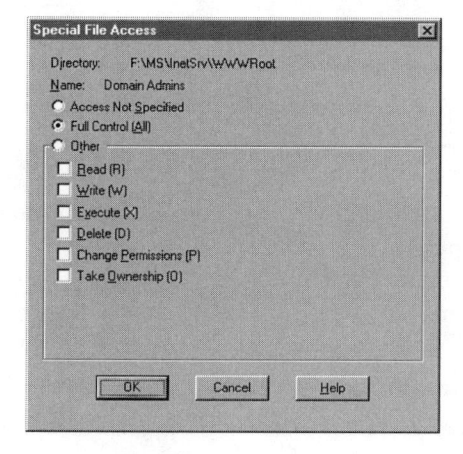

To delete an existing user or group permission, follow these steps:

1. In the Directory Permissions dialog box, select the user account or group name listed in the Name box.
2. Click the Remove button.
3. Repeat these steps for each user account or group you want to delete.

To set file permissions, you follow the same basic steps as outlined earlier, with two basic differences. First, when you select files instead of directories, the File Permissions dialog box appears, as shown in Figure 10.9. If you select Special Access in the Type of Access drop-down listbox of the File Permissions dialog box, the Special Access dialog box shown in Figure 10.10 is displayed.

FIGURE 10.9.
The File Permissions dialog box.

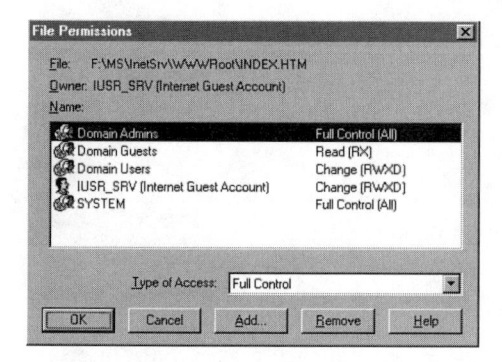

One other interesting feature you can select from the Security menu is Owner. If you select directories or files and then the Security | Owner menu option, you can take ownership of these directories or files. In essence, you replace all the permission settings with those from your current user account. This can be useful if you need to assume ownership of orphaned directories or

Advanced Security Issues
Chapter 10

files so that you later can give this ownership to another user. You can give ownership back to a user by assigning permissions for that user and specifying the Take Ownership permission setting. Then have the new user take ownership by using File Manager. After he takes ownership, only he will be able to access the directories or files. Or, you can just assign permissions using his user account.

FIGURE 10.10.
The Special Access dialog box.

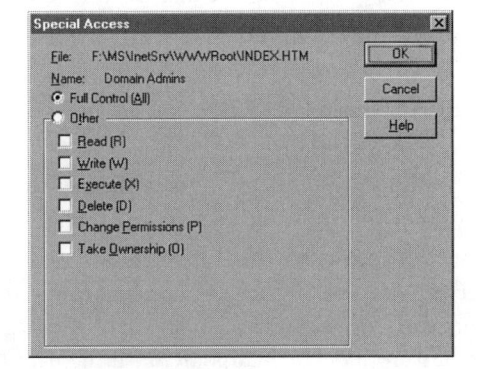

Security and Dial-Up Networking

The Windows NT dial-up networking service does not provide a high level of security for your network. There are, however, at least two choices you can make that can improve the situation. First, you can configure your dial-out and dial-in connections to use encryption. Second, you can choose to allow all network clients to access either just the computer that is providing the dial-up networking connection or the entire network. The choice as to which encryption setting to use, and whether to provide full access to your network, will be determined by your requirements.

If you are supporting dial-in connections for both remote clients that must access the entire network and those that don't, set up multiple dial-in connections on two or more modems. Each of these remote clients can then access the appropriate modem using a specific phone number that you provide, thus lessening the chance of a security breach. To configure your dial-in connection to enable or disable full access to the network, follow these steps:

1. Open the Network Control Panel applet.
2. Select the Services tab to display the Services properties sheet.
3. Select the Remote Access Service. Then click the Properties button to display the Remote Access Setup dialog box.
4. Select the appropriate connection; then click the Network button. This displays the Network Configuration dialog box.
5. In the Server Settings group, click the Configure button next to the appropriate network protocol under the Allow remote clients running title. This displays the RAS

Server *Protocol* Configuration dialog box, where *Protocol* is NetBEUI, TCP/IP, or IPX/SPX.

6. In the Allow Remote *Protocol* clients to access field, where *Protocol* is NetBEUI, TCP/IP, or IPX/SPX, check either the Entire network radio button to grant access to all computers on your network or the This computer only radio button to limit access to just the server providing the dial-in connection.
7. Click the OK button to return to the Network Configuration dialog box.
8. If you will be supporting multiple network protocols, repeat steps 5 through 7 for each additional protocol. When you are finished, click the OK button to return to the Remote Access Setup dialog box.
9. For each additional connection to configure, repeat steps 4 through 8. Then click the OK button to return to the Network dialog box.
10. Click the OK button to close the Network dialog box. You will then be prompted by the Network Settings Change dialog box to restart your system. Click the Yes button to restart your system so that the changes will be applied when the system restarts, or the No button to defer the update until the next time the server is restarted.

To modify your dial-in connections to require password or data encryption for increased security, follow these steps:

1. Open the Network Control Panel applet.
2. Select the Services tab to display the Services properties sheet.
3. Select the Remote Access Service. Then click the Properties button to display the Remote Access Setup dialog box.
4. Select the appropriate connection; then click the Network button. This will display the Network Configuration dialog box.
5. In the Server Settings group, click one of the following options to specify your encryption requirements:
    - Allow any encryption including plain text—Specifies that any supported (either MS-CHAP, SPAP, or PAP) encryption method be allowed. A connection will be attempted using the Microsoft password encryption (MS-CHAP) first, then the standard Internet encryption method (SPAP), followed by a plain text (PAP) authentication.
    - Require encrypted authentication—Specifies that a connection will be attempted using the Microsoft password encryption (MS-CHAP) first; then, if that fails, the standard Internet encryption method (SPAP) will be used.
    - Require Microsoft encrypted authentication—Specifies that a connection will be attempted using only the Microsoft password encryption (MS-CHAP) method. If this item is selected, you can also enable the Require data encryption check box to encrypt your data as well as your password.

> **NOTE**
>
> Many Internet Service Providers support Microsoft encryption, so you should try this option first. If it fails, try the Require encrypted authentication. Only if both methods fail should you enable the Allow any encryption including plain text check box.

6. Click the OK button to return to the Network Configuration dialog box.
7. If you will be supporting multiple network protocols, repeat steps 5 and 6 for each additional protocol. When you are finished, click the OK button to return to the Remote Access Setup dialog box.
8. For each additional connection to configure, repeat steps 4 through 7. Then click the OK button to return to the Network dialog box.
9. Click the OK button to close the Network dialog box. You will then be prompted by the Network Settings Change dialog box to restart your system. Click the Yes button to restart your system so that the changes will be applied when the system restarts, or the No button to defer the update until the next time the server is restarted.

To configure your dial-out connection (such as when you are using Windows NT Server as a gateway to the Internet), follow these steps:

1. Launch the Dial-Up Networking applet by choosing Dial-Up Networking from the Start|Accessories menu. This displays the Dial-Up Networking dialog box.
2. To create a new connection, click the New button to display the New Phonebook Entry dialog box.
3. Enter a unique name in the Entry name field for the connection.
4. Enter a description in the Comment field for the connection.
5. Specify the phone number to dial in the Phone number field.
6. Specify a modem connection to use in the Dial using drop-down listbox.
7. To use the telephony settings for the modem (recommended), check the Use Telephony dialing properties check box.
8. Select the Server tab to display the Server properties sheet.
9. Choose PPP—Windows NT, Windows 95 Plus, or Internet in the Dial-Up server type drop-down listbox.
10. Enable the TCP/IP check box in the Network protocols field and disable the NetBEUI and IPX/SPX compatible check boxes.
11. Select the Security tab to display the Security properties sheet.
12. In the Authentication and encryption policy group, specify your encryption requirement. This can be one of the following:

- Allow any encryption including plain text—Specifies that any supported (either MS-CHAP, SPAP, or PAP) encryption method be used to encrypt the password. A connection will be attempted using the Microsoft password encryption (MS-CHAP) first, then the standard Internet encryption method (SPAP), followed by a plain text (PAP) authentication.
- Require encrypted authentication—Specifies that a connection will be attempted using the Microsoft password encryption (MS-CHAP) first; if that fails, the standard Internet encryption method (SPAP) will be used.
- Require Microsoft encrypted authentication—Specifies that a connection will be attempted using only the Microsoft password encryption (MS-CHAP) method. If this item is selected, you can also enable the Require data encryption check box to encrypt your data as well as your password. You may also enable the Use current username and password check box to attempt to connect using the username and password of the active account. This option is rarely used with an ISP, but is often used by clients that will connect directly to your server.

NOTE

Many Internet Service Providers support Microsoft encryption, so you should try this option first. If it fails, try the Require encrypted authentication. Only if both methods fail should you enable the Allow any encryption including plain text check box.

13. Click the OK button to create the new phonebook entry and return to the Dial-Up Networking dialog box.

At this point you are ready to connect to the Internet by just clicking the Dial button on the Dial-Up Networking dialog box. The connection you will dial will be displayed in the Phonebook entry to dial drop-down listbox. If you want to dial a different connection, just choose it before you click the Dial button.

Configuring Windows NT Server as a Mini Firewall

Windows NT Server 4.0 adds two new features that you can use to build a miniature firewall. The first new feature includes PPTP (Point to Point Tunneling Protocol), which can be used to support multiprotocol *virtual private networks* (VPNs). Basically PPTP can be used to provide a secure method of accessing your network over the Internet. It does this by tunneling your network transport protocol (TCP/IP, IPX/SPX, or NetBEUI) over a PPP connection. This also encrypts your network communication linkage so that only the server and network client can make any use of the embedded network packets. To use this option, however, your Internet Service Provider must also support the PPTP protocol. So check with your service provider(s) before you reconfigure all of your clients to use PPTP. The second feature is the capability to accept or reject specific Internet protocols and specific IP ports that use TCP (Transmission Control Protocol) or UDP (User Datagram Protocol).

To really use these options to obtain the maximum benefit requires that your system fit one of two models. It can be either a standalone server or a multihomed server. Both of these configurations should use a dedicated router connected to a network adapter in the server. (A *multihomed server* is just a server with more than one network adapter.)

The reason you need to use one of these two models is because the security and PPTP filtering options, which you will step through shortly, are bound to a specific network adapter. If you have only one network adapter in your computer, use the dial-up networking service to provide an Internet gateway, and attempt to restrict access using the TCP/IP security features. This will apply to all computers that are connected to your server. For a standalone server, this does not matter because you want to support only specific ports and protocols. But for a server acting as an Internet gateway, it matters quite a bit because your server's primary purpose is to provide file and print services to your network clients, and its secondary purpose is to act as an Internet gateway and pass packets from your clients to the Internet and vice versa. Your server will not be able to function in both capacities if you use the security features of the TCP/IP protocol and have only a single network adapter.

It would be possible to configure a server with a single network adapter to support multiple protocols such as IPX/SPX and TCP/IP. This way, your network clients would still be able to access the file and print services on the server. If you use the TCP/IP security features to block specific IP ports or protocols, the single network adapter will still affect your network clients' ability to access the Internet service. The TCP/IP security features may also prevent your Internet clients from accessing your IIS services. You will need to be very careful as to which ports and protocols you decide to block if you do not want to have a negative impact on your network functionality.

To configure your server to accept only PPTP packets or to enable the TCP/IP security features, follow these steps:

1. Open the Network Control Panel applet to display the Network dialog box.
2. Select the Protocols tab to display the Protocols properties sheet.
3. Select the TCP/IP Protocol; then click the Properties button to display the dialog box shown in Figure 10.11.

FIGURE 10.11.
The Microsoft TCP/IP Properties dialog box.

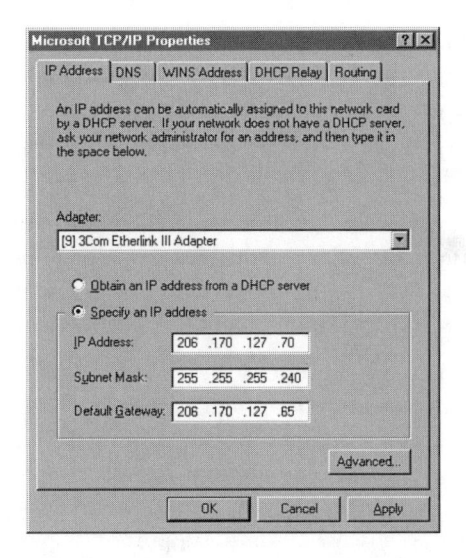

4. Click on the Advanced button to display the dialog box shown in Figure 10.12.

FIGURE 10.12.
The Advanced IP Addressing dialog box.

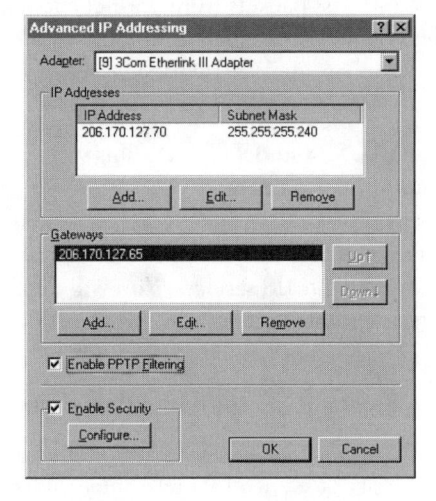

5. Select the adapter to configure in the Adapter drop-down listbox.
6. To accept only PPTP packets on the adapter, check the Enable PPTP Filtering check box.

> **NOTE**
>
> By enabling the PPTP Filtering check box, you disable all other network protocols for the selected adapter.

7. Repeat steps 5 through 6 for each adapter you want to configure to accept only PPTP network packets.
8. To enable the advanced TCP/IP security features, check the Enable Security check box. Then click the Configure button to display the dialog box shown in Figure 10.13.

FIGURE 10.13.
The TCP/IP Security dialog box.

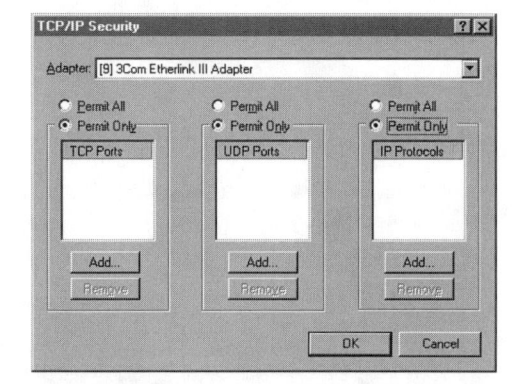

9. Select the adapter to configure in the Adapter drop-down listbox.
10. For the TCP Ports, UDP Ports, or IP Protocol, enable the Permit All (the default) radio button to accept all IP ports or protocols to pass through the network adapter, or enable the Permit Only radio button.

    If you select the Permit Only radio button, click the Add button to display the Security Add dialog box for each item.

    In the TCP Port, UDP Port, or IP Protocol field, enter the port or protocol to disable for the specified network adapter. Then click the Add button to add the specified port to the list.

> **NOTE**
>
> Table 10.4 lists the more common IP port addresses and protocols that you may want to disable on the specified network adapter.

11. Repeat step 10 for each additional port or protocol to disable.
12. Repeat steps 9 through 10 for each additional adapter to configure the options for TCP/IP security.
13. Click the OK button to return to the Advanced IP Addressing dialog box.
14. Click the OK button to return to the Network dialog box.
15. Click the OK button to close the Network dialog box. You are then prompted by the Network Settings Change dialog box to restart your computer. Click the Yes button for your changes to go into effect after the system restarts, or the No button to defer your changes until the next system restart.

Table 10.4. Common IP ports and TCP/IP protocols.

Port	Protocol	Description	Note
	ICMP	Internet Control Message Protocol	Used to send error, or test, messages from a local computer to a remote computer. Commonly used to ping Internet hosts. Disabling this protocol will prevent external hosts from probing your network to see what hosts may be available; however, it will also prevent your network clients from pinging external Internet hosts.
	MBONE	Multicast Backbone	This protocol is used to tunnel multicast packets through routers that do not support multicast routing. (*Multicast* is the capability to send a single packet to multiple destinations on the Internet. It is often used for live performances, such as radio broadcasts or video feeds.) The threat occurs from the fact that you do not know the protocol and service of the internal IP packet.
21	TCP	File Transfer Protocol (FTP)	This port should be disabled only if you want to prevent your network clients from accessing external FTP sites. If you want to disable your FTP server, it is best to disable the FTP Publishing service in the Control Panel Services applet.
23	TCP	Telnet	Used for remote terminal sessions. There is no Telnet server included with Windows NT Server, so this should not be a concern unless you have installed a third-party Telnet server.

Port	Protocol	Description	Note
25	TCP	Simple Mail Transfer Protocol (SMNP)	Used by e-mail servers to send/receive e-mail over the Internet.
53	TCP or UDP	Domain Name System (DNS) service.	If this port is not blocked for external Internet access, it may be possible for an external DNS server to update the name servers on your network. In addition, your internal DNS servers may share information (such as your host names) that you would prefer to remain only within your internal network.
70	TCP	Gopher	This port should be disabled only if you want to prevent your network clients from accessing external Gopher sites. If you want to disable your Gopher server, it is best to disable the Gopher Publishing service in the Control Panel Services applet.
79	TCP	Finger service	Used to obtain information about a user on a specified host. Commonly used to probe networks; however, Windows NT Server does not provide a finger server.
80	TCP	World Wide Web (WWW) service	This port should be disabled only if you want to prevent your network clients from accessing external Web sites. If you want to disable your Web server, it is best to disable the WWW Publishing service in the Control Panel Services applet.

continues

Table 10.4. continued

Port	Protocol	Description	Note
111	TCP or UDP	Port Mapper	Used by remote procedure call (RPC) applications to obtain the IP port of a service.
119	TCP	Network News Transfer Protocol (NNTP)	
123	UDP	Network Time Protocol (NTP)	
210	TCP	Wide Area Information Servers (WAIS)	An add-on to the Gopher service. Not provided with Windows NT Server, but may be obtained from third parties.
161, 162	TCP or UDP	Simple Network Management Protocol (SNMP)	Used by SNMP management consoles to monitor or configure services as well as trap errors. It is a good idea to disable the SNMP port unless you need to allow external access to your system or access an external system using SNMP.
513	TCP	Remote Login (rlogin) service	Used by the remote login, remote copy, remote shell, and other remote services. This should be a concern only for users who have installed either a third-party service or one of these services from the Microsoft Windows NT Resource Kit.
1525	UDP	Archie	An add-on to the Gopher service. Not provided with Windows NT Server, but may be obtained from third parties.

2049	UDP	Network File System (NFS)	Provides the capability to remote mount a file system. This can be a potentially dangerous situation, but will only occur with Windows NT Server if you also install a third-party NFS server because the base package does not include this functionality.
6000+	X11	X graphical interface	Each Xserver can use a port above 6000. The first Xserver would use port 6000, the second port 6001, and so on.
6667	TCP	Internet Relay Chat (IRC)	Used to support text-based online chats.

Determining Who Is Using Your System

Determining who may have accessed your system in the past, or who may be accessing your system now, is very important to anyone connected to the Internet. One of the best methods to determine whether a security breach has occurred or is occurring is to use the security logs created by Windows NT and the Internet Information Server. To determine who may be accessing your system or attempting to access restricted data files, however, the system must be configured to audit events. To restrict access to your sensitive files or enable auditing of your files requires that you use File Manager (or the Windows Explorer). To view your system events requires that you use the Windows NT Event Viewer, but to view your IIS event logs you can use a text editor (like Notepad) if you configured the service to write a text file, or you can use an ODBC front-end (like Access) to view your logs that were created on an ODBC-compliant database.

Configuring the System to Enable Auditing

If you want to be able to determine who is using your shared network resources, or even who is abusing their privileges on your network, you need to enable the auditing features provided in Windows NT Server. Auditing is divided into several categories, however, and is not enabled in a single application.

Part III — *Administering Your Site*

To audit a system event related to account usage or modification and the programs running on your server, launch User Manager for Domains and choose Audit from the Policies menu to display the Audit Policy dialog box. (See Figure 10.14.)

FIGURE 10.14.

Enabling system auditing with User Manager.

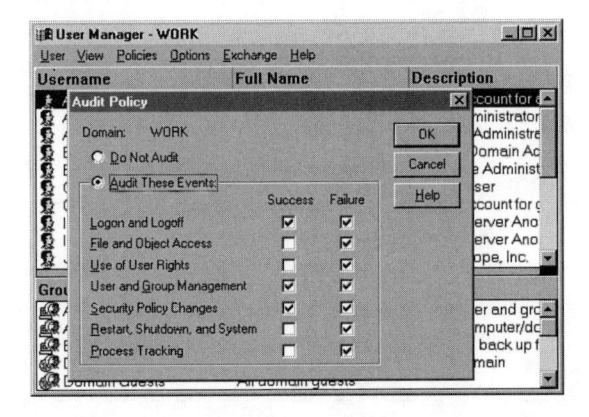

To audit any event, you first need to enable the Audit These Events radio button in the Audit Policy dialog box (even if you select no options here to audit) and then choose the application's audit options. To audit the use of files, use File Manager; for printer auditing, use Print Manager. Both of these have an Auditing option on the Security menu that displays a dialog box similar to the Audit Policy dialog box. There, you can specify the events to audit.

When you select an event to be audited, it is entered into the security log, which you can view with the Event Viewer. You can select to audit the successful use of a privilege, failure to obtain access (which indicates a security violation attempt), or both.

You can audit the following events:

- Logon and Logoff—Determines who has logged on to or off of your network. I recommend that you enable both these check boxes (Success and Failure) to determine who may be using your network.
- File and Object Access—Works with other applications that have been used to specify auditing. You can use File Manager to enable auditing of a directory, for example. You can enable the Success or Failure events for the File and Object Access in order to record any access to the audited directory.
- Use of User Rights—Provides the capability to audit any use of a user right, other than logon and logoff, such as the capability to log on as a service.
- User and Group Management—Gives you the capability to track any user account or group management—whether a new user is added, an existing user password is enabled, or new users are added to a group, for example.

Advanced Security Issues
Chapter 10

If you have constant problems with a particular user account or group being modified and cannot determine who is making these changes, you should enable both Success and Failure for this option. This can help you determine who may be making the changes. I've seen a few problems caused by personnel who have been granted administrative privileges but who are not trained in their use, for example. By using this option, you can determine who needs additional training, or even who should have his administrative privileges revoked.

- Security Policy Changes—Helps you determine who may be making changes to your system-audit policies, user-right policies, or trust relationships. Enable this option for both Success and Failure to determine who may be modifying your network policies. This is a good idea particularly if you have several administrators and find that things have been changing without anyone admitting responsibility.
- Restart, Shutdown, and System—Enables you to determine who may be shutting down your servers or performing any event that affects system security or the security log.
- Process Tracking—Determines which applications are executing on your system.

> **CAUTION**
>
> Auditing the Success events for Process Tracking can fill up your security log in a matter of minutes. Only enable this event for Success when absolutely necessary.

Auditing Directories and Files

If you want to monitor who is using your network resources or if you are concerned about users who consistently attempt to bypass your security restrictions, you can use the auditing features to determine who is doing what with your shared directories or files. Suppose you have an HTML document as a template on your server that is used by many users on your network. Each user should save his copy of the data file under a different name, but suppose someone inadvertently saves his version of the file, replaces the original on the network, and then, to hide his mistake, deletes the file. If you have enabled auditing of the file, you will know which user modified or even deleted it. You then can have a serious talk with him about network security. Another possible use of security auditing is to identify an Internet user who may be trying to access restricted data using a stolen user account and password, or maliciously deleting files on your FTP site.

> **NOTE**
>
> Auditing is available only on NTFS partitions.

You can view this auditing information by using the Event Viewer and examining the security log. This is covered later in this chapter in the section titled "Using the Windows NT Event Viewer." For now, just take a look at what is required to enable auditing of directories and files with File Manager. The first thing to consider is that in order to enable auditing at the system level, you have to use User Manager for Domains and choose Policies | Auditing to turn on the auditing features. (Refer to the section titled "Configuring the System to Enable Auditing" in this chapter.)

> **NOTE**
>
> I still prefer to use File Manager for my security-related tasks, so this is the tool I will describe how to use. The only difference between File Manager and the Windows Explorer is the means you use to gain access to the Permissions or Auditing dialog boxes. For the Windows Explorer, you can just right-click a directory or file to display a Properties dialog box. Then you just choose the Security tab to display the Security properties sheet. To set permissions on the selected directories, just click the Permissions button. To enable auditing, click the Auditing button. To take ownership, click the Ownership button.

After you enable systemwide auditing, you can follow these steps to audit your directories on your server:

1. Select the directories you want to audit with File Manager. Choose Auditing from the Security menu. The Directory Auditing dialog box appears. (See Figure 10.15.)

FIGURE 10.15.
The Directory Auditing dialog box.

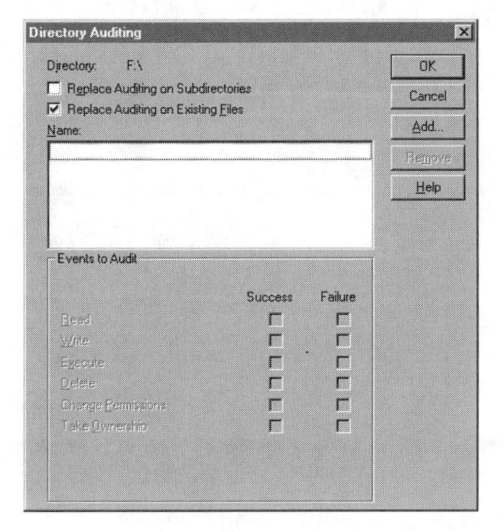

Advanced Security Issues
Chapter 10 301

2. Select the users or groups you want to audit. To accomplish this task, click the Add button; the Add Users and Groups dialog box appears. (See Figure 10.16.)

FIGURE 10.16.
The Add Users and Groups dialog box.

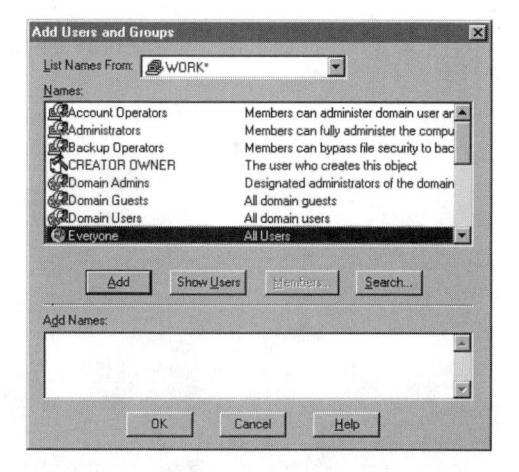

3. By default, the domain you logged on to is displayed in the List Names From drop-down listbox. You can use the domain user database from any domain with which you have established a trust relationship, however. You also can use the local database for a Windows NT Server computer operating in server mode or a Windows NT Workstation.

4. By default, only groups are listed in the Names box. If you want to include user accounts, click the Show Users button. This adds all your user accounts to the end of the list. To add an existing group or user, just double-click the group or user name displayed in the Names list or select a group or name and click the Add button. This copies the user account or group to the Add Names listbox.

> **TIP**
>
> The easiest way to begin this process is to select the Everyone group. This enables the auditing of every user for the selected directories. If you are concerned only about network users who remotely connect to the resource, select the Network group instead.

5. After you complete your user and group selections, click the OK button to return to the Directory Auditing dialog box.

6. Now you must determine which events to audit. Do this by checking the boxes in the Success or Failure column. Normally, I audit all Failure events, but only the Take Ownership and Change Permissions Success events (as shown in Figure 10.17).

FIGURE 10.17.
Enabling directory auditing.

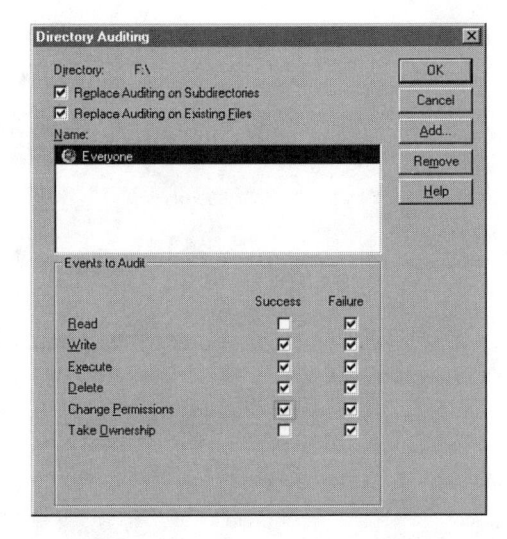

7. If you want to replace the auditing information for all the subdirectories of the parent directory, make sure to enable the Replace Auditing on Subdirectories check box. If you do not want to replace auditing on the files in directories, clear the Replace Auditing on Existing Files check box.
8. Now click the OK button to change your current auditing settings.
9. After you receive a confirmation message box, just click the OK button to continue.

To audit files, you follow the same procedure as outlined here. (The dialog box displayed will not have the Replace Auditing on Subdirectories or Replace Auditing on Existing Files check boxes, however.)

Using the Windows NT Event Viewer

Use the Event Viewer to display status events that occur on your computer. These events are divided into three categories. Each category is contained in a specific log. The *system log* includes events related to the operation of the operating system, the *application log* includes application-specific events, and the *security log* includes auditing events. Of these three, the most important to you is the security log because it can be used to determine whether someone is attempting to access restricted data or whether someone is trying to break into your system by guessing passwords for a known user account. The next log of concern is the system log because it can show, by service, the anonymous logon requests that have occurred on your system. It can also display other publishing-service events. Events are further divided into types that have specific icons associated with them. Table 10.5 summarizes the event types for each log category.

> **NOTE**
>
> You should use the Event Viewer to view your logs on a daily basis for your file servers, and at least once a week for a workstation. If you do not review your logs in this time frame, you might be unaware of system errors that could propagate to a system failure, and you will not be aware of possible attempts to violate the security of your network.

Table 10.5. Event icons and types.

Icon	Type	Description
Stop Sign	Error	Indicates a serious problem that prevents an application, system service, or device driver from functioning properly. Also indicates when a malfunction has been noticed by an application, system service, or device driver.
Exclamation	Warning	Indicates a problem that is troublesome but noncritical to the operation of the operating system or application. Warnings often can propagate errors over time, and therefore should not be ignored.
I Sign	Informational	Does not indicate a problem. This is just a status code to inform you that an application, system service, or device driver is functioning properly.
Key	Success Audit	Informational events to indicate the success of a security modification or usage of a security-related operation. These event entries are based on the audit events you have selected with User Manager for Domains, File Manager, Print Manager, Clipbook Viewer, Registry Editor, and any other application that supports auditing.
Lock	Failure Audit	Informational events to indicate the failure of a security-related operation. These event entries are based on the audit events you have selected with User Manager for Domains, File Manager, Print Manager, Clipbook Viewer, Registry Editor, and any other application that supports auditing.

Viewing Events

To view the events that have occurred on your system, you first need to select the log to view. Access this information from the Log menu. You can select the application, security, or system log to view. Each event in a log is broken down into components that describe the event. Table 10.6 summarizes these event components. To get the details of an event, just double-click its name and the Event Detail dialog box appears, as shown in Figure 10.18. What is important to note here is that the description contains a textual message in the Description box that describes the error condition, and if the event has any associated data with it, it is included in the Data box. This data list often contains information that you or Microsoft technical support can use to isolate and solve the problem.

FIGURE 10.18.
The Event Detail dialog box.

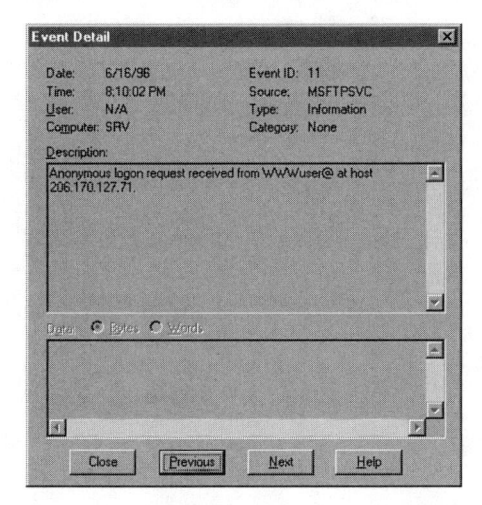

Table 10.6. The event components.

Component	Description
Icon	A quick indicator to the type of event.
Date	The date the event occurred.
Time	The time the event occurred.
Source	The name of the application, system service, or device driver that reported the event.
Category	A general classification of an event type. In most cases, categories are used only in the security log.
Event ID	An event number specific to the event source and associated with a specific error message.

Advanced Security Issues
Chapter 10 305

Component	Description
User	An event can be associated with a specific user that triggered the event. In most cases, this is used only in the security log.
Computer	An event can be associated with a specific computer that triggered the event. In most cases, this is the name of the host (the computer where the log resides) computer.

Filtering Events

One of the problems you will notice over time is that so many events occur on your system that finding the trouble spots can be quite time-consuming. And, if it takes too much of your time, you probably will stop checking for these problems. Eventually, a problem will grow into a system-related failure that could cause you to lose your job. I would like to help you avoid that. The easiest way to minimize the amount of data overload is to use the Event Viewer's filtering capabilities.

Follow these steps:

1. Choose Filter Events from the View menu to display the Filter dialog box shown in Figure 10.19.

FIGURE 10.19.
The Event Viewer Filter dialog box.

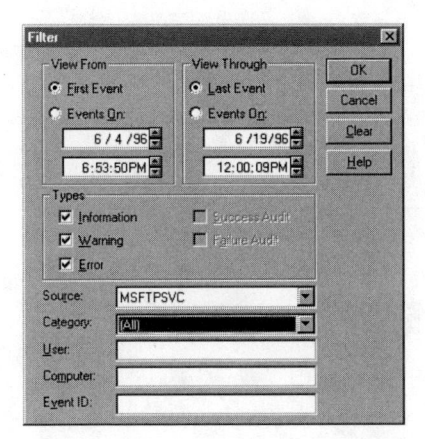

2. In the View From section, select the Events On radio button. Then specify a date and time.
3. In the View Through section, select the Events On radio button. Then specify a date and time.
4. In the Types section, select the type of event to report. For a quick look, I suggest looking only for warning and error conditions.

5. In the Source drop-down listbox, select the event source to view. This is useful for limiting the report to a specific application, system service, or device driver to determine how often the error has occurred.
6. In the Category drop-down listbox, select the event categories to view. In most systems, there will be only security-related categories, or possibly no subcategories. If you have categories, you can further limit the report to a particular category by selecting it from the list.
7. In the User field, enter the user account you want to use to further limit the report. This can be useful when you are checking events in the security log and have noticed a potential violation. By limiting the report to just this user, you can determine how often the user has attempted to violate your system security.
8. Enter the computer name in the Computer field to further limit events to just events that have occurred on the specific computer.
9. If you are looking for a specific event, enter the event number in the Event ID field. This can be useful to determine how often a specific event has occurred in the past.
10. After you finish entering all your filtering characteristics, click the OK button to engage the filter. When a filter has been engaged, the title bar of the Event Viewer changes to include the word "Filtered."

> **NOTE**
>
> After a filter has been specified, it remains in effect until you change it. If you enabled the Save Settings on Exit option, the next time you launch Event Viewer, the filter also remains in effect.

To remove a filter that you have created using these steps, just choose the View|All Events menu option, and all the events are displayed in the logs. Select a menu option to refresh the screen.

Archiving Events

Instead of throwing away the events in your event logs when you fill them up, you should archive them. This gives you the ability to load them at a later date for comparison with current logs to isolate any potential problems. You also can use these logs with Excel or any database that can import a comma-separated value or ASCII text file. Use this imported data to spot trends that can indicate a network trouble spot or hardware-related failure.

> **TIP**
>
> You can set the maximum size of the log by choosing the Log|Log Settings menu option to display the Log Settings dialog box. In this dialog box, you also can specify that you want the log to automatically wrap and overwrite events on an as-needed basis, to overwrite events after a specific number of days, or to manually clear the log to free space for further events.

To archive a log, follow these steps:

1. Choose Log Type from the Log menu, where Log Type is the Application, Security, or System log.
2. Choose Save As from the Log menu to display the Save As dialog box. In the Save File As Type field, select Event Log Files (*.EVT) to save the event file as a binary file that can be reloaded later into the Event Viewer. Or, select Text Files (*.TXT), which is a standard ASCII text file, or Comma Delim Text (*.TXT), a comma-separated value text file.
3. Enter a filename in the File Name field and click the OK button. If the drive or directory is not the one you want, change it before clicking the OK button.

The Internet Information Server Logs

Although you can use the Windows NT Event Viewer to look at the security and system logs, these logs do not contain as much information about who is doing what with your Internet services as do the Internet Information Server logs. Your IIS logs contain the following fields:

- Clienthost—Specifies the IP address of the connected client.
- Username—Specifies the name supplied by the user to log onto the specified service.
- Logtime—Specifies when the user started the connection in MM/DD/YY HH:MM:SS time format.
- Service—Specifies the service to which the user connected. This will be MSFTPSVC for the FTP Publishing service, W3SVC for the WWW Publishing service, or GopherSvc for the Gopher Publishing service.
- Machine—Specifies the IIS server on which the service is executing.
- ServerIP—Specifies the IP address of the server on which the service is executing.
- Processingtime—Specifies the time the client was connected.
- Bytessent—Specifies the number of bytes sent to the client.

- Bytesreceived—Specifies the number of bytes sent by the client.
- Servicestatus—Specifies a service-specific status code.
- Win32Status—Specifies a Windows NT 32-bit API-specific status code.
- Operation—Specifies the service operation type for the client request.
- Target—Specifies the data object name requested by the client.
- Parameter—Specifies any additional command parameter.

By saving these logs and reviewing them at least once a week, you can obtain performance characteristics such as how many users visited your site. You can also use these logs to determine whether someone was trying to access data on your site that he does not have access rights to by looking for user logon failures. If you see several of these from the same IP address, you may want to prevent that IP address from logging onto your site by configuring the advanced options for the service as described in Chapter 6, "Using the Internet Service Manager."

Summary

This chapter covers a lot of material, and it has only touched on some of the complex security issues. One key concept you should remember is that a security policy needs to be in place both to protect you from data you download from the Internet and to limit access to your network. You have learned how you can configure Windows NT Server to function as a mini firewall as part of your policy of limiting access, and how to further protect your data by using the NTFS file system and applying permissions to directories and files. Finally, you have learned about some of the tools you can use to enable system auditing, set auditing on directories and files, and then use the Event Viewer so you can see if anyone is accessing those files on which you enabled auditing. In Chapter 11, "An HTML Primer," you will learn about the Hypertext Markup Language (HTML) in preparation for creating your own Web pages.

IN THIS PART

- An HTML Primer **311**
- Designing and Managing a Web Site with FrontPage **337**
- Publishing on the Web with Microsoft Office **361**
- Using Asymetrix Web3D and Corel's Web Designer **379**
- Using Sausage Software's HotDog Pro **393**

Web Page Development

PART IV

An HTML Primer

IN THIS CHAPTER

- What Is an HTML Document? **313**
- Basic HTML Styles **316**

Part IV

This chapter teaches you how to create basic Hypertext Markup Language (HTML) documents using an American Standard Code of Information Interchange (ASCII) editor, such as Notepad. The purpose is to give you the skills to build a Web page. This chapter is not a complete tutorial because the subject matter is too broad to cover in a single chapter. If you need additional help creating your Web pages, the following chapters should be helpful because you will look into some of the better Web page editors currently available on the Internet and in the retail market. A Web editor can write your HTML documents for you using a point-and-click interface. You don't even need to know any HTML to create the documents.

> **TIP**
>
> For a complete description of HTML syntax and more information on writing HTML documents that will fully exploit the HTML specification, check out Laura Lemay's *Teach Yourself HTML in 14 Days* by Sams.net Publishing.

You will need to know HTML, however, if you have to debug an HTML document. Perhaps the editor is not supplying the correct tags, or perhaps the editor is using a tag designed for a Web browser other than the Internet Explorer (IE). In either case, to solve the problem will require you to know something about the structure of an HTML document. After all, it is very difficult to solve a problem if you cannot recognize the error when you see it. Appendix B, "HTML Reference," includes additional information on HTML tags supported by the Internet Information Server (IIS).

> **NOTE**
>
> For the most part, the figures in this chapter were captured using IE 1.5 for Windows NT. However, IE 2.0 for Windows 95 was used occasionally to capture a screen when IE 1.5 could not support a particular HTML tag. I cannot stress enough the importance of testing your HTML documents on various Web browsers to determine how your documents will appear onscreen. Even the same Web browser on different operating systems may display your document differently than you expect. The samples provided on the CD-ROM in the SOURCE\CHAP11 directory were coded for use with IE 1.5 on Windows NT.

What Is an HTML Document?

Before you actually begin building an HTML document, it is a good idea to understand what an HTML document really is. It's not a difficult concept, but it can be confusing to someone who has never worked in the Web-publishing field. This is what you are about to embark on as you publish content on the World Wide Web (WWW). The word *World* is an important concept behind WWW publishing because it plays a significant part in the design philosophy of publishing Web documents.

If you were creating a document for your boss, you could use any word-processing program. As long as your boss had the same word processor, he could read, print, or modify the document. On the Web, however, you cannot be sure that everyone will use the same Web browser. This is where HTML comes into play.

What Is a Markup Language?

HTML is based on the Standard Generalized Markup Language (SGML) concept, which is used in publishing to describe a document's content. An SGML document is an ASCII document (or plain text file) that uses tags to describe how the document's content will be displayed. Suppose that you want to highlight a word in a sentence. With Word for Windows, you would press Ctrl+B before the word to enable the bold-text function and Ctrl+B after the word to disable the bold-text function. In SGML you could use a set of tags: one tag to enable text bolding and another to disable text bolding. The tags might look like <BOLD> to enable text bolding, and </BOLD> to disable text bolding. Anything that appeared within these tags would have the bold attribute.

> **TIP**
>
> Since these HTML tags are plain ASCII text, almost any Web browser on any platform (Windows NT, Windows 95, Macintosh, MS-DOS, UNIX, and so on) can see the content of your HTML document. Because not all Web browsers support every HTML tag, your content may not be displayed entirely as you intended; however, the core of your document will be visible. The platform independence offered by HTML allows you to reach the widest possible audience.

> **NOTE**
>
> In an SGML tag pair, the ending tag is always the same as the beginning tag, except that it has a / in front of the tag. Our previous example uses <BOLD> as the beginning tag and </BOLD> as the ending tag. The two tags and any content within the tags are referred to as an *element*. Sometimes an element is referred to as a *container* because the tag pair acts on the data contained between the two tags.

Marking text before and after with language elements (tags) determines how the document will be displayed, hence the term *markup language*. The SGML language is very strict. Every tag must have an associated end tag. However, this is not true for HTML. Most tags have an end tag, but not all of them. An SGML document is also divided into three parts. The first consists of the SGML declaration, the second is the document-type declaration (DTD), which describes the acceptable structure of the document, and the final component is the document instance. In order for an SGML document (the document instance) to be valid, it must follow the rules as specified in the DTD. The DTD is a lexical description of the tags and all acceptable tag attributes. If a tag is used without the corresponding end tag, this will be found by the SGML parser. You might consider this similar to the process that a C compiler goes through as it examines your source code. If you have forgotten an ending parenthesis, the C compiler will generate an error message.

This ability to parse a file to determine if it contains any errors is what makes SGML so useful to publishers. After all, how would you like it if someone forgot to include an end italic tag in the first chapter of this book so that all the chapters were printed in an italic font? Of course, with an SGML document and SGML parser, this could not happen by mistake. An SGML document is also portable. Anyone with an SGML editor and the appropriate DTD could edit, view, or print the document.

HTML to the Rescue

The primary reason why you do not use SGML to edit your documents with Word for Windows is because SGML can be a pain to work with. I'm not knocking SGML, because what it does is important to publications and it does its job very well, but it can be much too complex to use for everyday tasks. Luckily, you can use a subset of the SGML convention: HTML. Because HTML utilizes a much smaller set of tags, it is much easier to work with. It is not for the faint of heart because if you do not code your document properly (that is, follow the rules exactly), your client's Web browser may not show the page correctly. In fact, HTML does not ensure that your document will appear the same on every Web browser because different computer systems have different display capabilities. However, it does ensure that the original content and intent will remain.

One of the best tools you can use is a Web editor, which includes an HTML parser that ensures that your HTML documents follow the rules. You will look at a few of these in the following chapters. For now though, let's look at the components of an HTML document. A typical HTML document is divided into two components: the *head* and the *body*. Both are enclosed in an <HTML> </HTML> tag pair. Anything outside of these two tags would create an illegal HTML document. Many programmers create skeleton code that can be used as a foundation to build fully functional programs. A skeleton HTML document would look like this:

```
<HTML>
<HEAD>
<TITLE>Skeleton HTML Document</TITLE>
</HEAD>

<BODY>
Insert your custom HTML code here!
</BODY>
</HTML>
```

If you opened the document with a Web browser, it would look like Figure 11.1. It doesn't look like much, but it does illustrate several key points. First, it includes the required information: the <HTML>, <BODY>, </BODY>, and </HTML> tags, which create a valid HTML document. None of the rest is required, but an HTML document without anything else would be boring! Therefore, it also includes the <HEAD>, <TITLE>, </TITLE>, and </HEAD> tags, which are used to place a document description (that is, title) on your Web browser's caption bar. The text between the <BODY> and </BODY> tags is the HTML document content that you want to display. Every document you create can be based on the skeleton code in this example. In the next sections, I will show you how to use some of the basic tags to make your content look more appealing.

FIGURE 11.1.

The skeleton HTML document displayed in a Web browser.

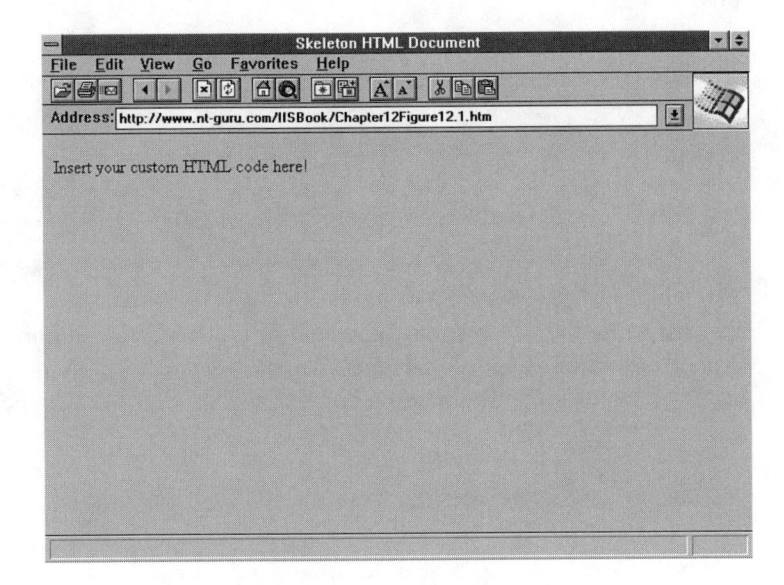

> **TIP**
>
> Every HTML document you create should include a descriptive title. Why? Because most Web browsers will use the document title as the default name whenever a user chooses to save the document or to add it to the list of favorite places to visit. A title based on your URL (uniform resource locator) is less likely to be used by a reader to find your site again. Various WWW automatons also will search out Web sites to index their content. A descriptive title is more likely to provide information to a user in his search, which means the user will be more likely to visit your site.

Basic HTML Styles

Because most HTML documents are text based, it makes sense to begin the discussion with the basic HTML styles available to manipulate text. Before you get too involved, however, I should point out a few quirks concerning text manipulation and HTML. Let's assume that you have a tabbed table to display your favorite Web sites, such as

```
WWW Site Description               URL
--------------------               --------------------
Knowles Consulting                 http://www.nt-guru.com
The Microsoft Network              http://www.msn.com
Microsoft Corporation              http://www.microsoft.com
```

If you just place this text in the body of your HTML document, do you think it will appear as it is in the example? Well, if you do, you are mistaken. Instead, it will look something like Figure 11.2.

FIGURE 11.2.
An incorrectly formatted tabbed table displayed on a Web browser.

So what happened? Well, two things. First of all, the default font in an HTML document is a proportional font. Proportional fonts are easier to read and appear more natural to the reader, but a proportional font also makes it difficult to align text properly. Second, an HTML

document attempts to collapse all whitespace (or nonprinting characters) into a single space. In the previous example, this means everything just runs together, making it almost impossible to read. Obviously, this is an unacceptable method of displaying your content. But what can you do about it? There are three possible solutions.

First, you can add a paragraph tag <P> to the beginning and </P> to the end of each sentence to force a line break at the end of each sentence. If you do, the display will look like Figure 11.3. Although it's better than the previous example, it still doesn't appear correctly on the screen.

FIGURE 11.3.
Displaying a tabbed table with a proportional font.

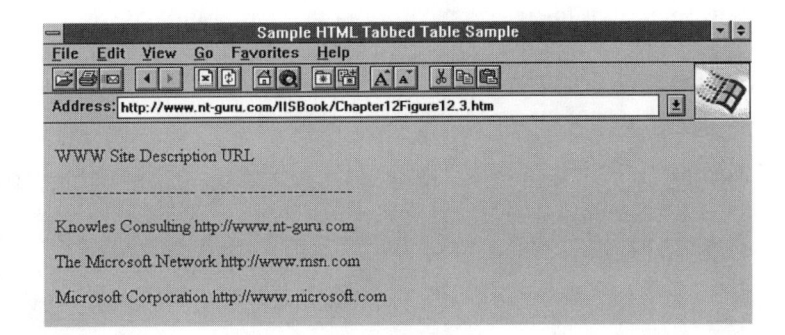

Second, you can use one of the HTML tags to force the text to be displayed in a fixed-width font, as shown in Figure 11.4. This example looks quite a bit better. It is easy to read and appears just as the original source code does. This example makes use of the <LISTING> and </LISTING> tags and drops the paragraph <P> </P> tags in each sentence. If you leave the <P> and </P> tags, they will also be displayed on the screen.

> **NOTE**
>
> Most Web browsers will force a paragraph break whenever they encounter a <P> tag even if no corresponding </P> tag is present. Although the </P> tag is not really required, nor in some cases is it even considered part of the HTML specification (depending on which version you are looking at), I recommend that you use it for consistency.

FIGURE 11.4.
Displaying a tabbed table with a fixed-width font.

```
                    Sample HTML Tabbed Table Sample
 File  Edit  View  Go  Favorites  Help

 Address: http://www.nt-guru.com/IISBook/Chapter12Figure12.4.htm

 WWW Site Description     URL
 ----------------------   -----------------------
 Knowles Consulting       http://www.nt-guru.com
 The Microsoft Network    http://www.msn.com
 Microsoft Corporation    http://www.microsoft.com
```

The solution is to create a table with each item displayed within a table column, as shown in Figure 11.5. This is the best option because it utilizes a proportional font, which makes it easier for the reader. Unfortunately, this option makes it more difficult for the HTML document developer, or in this case, you.

FIGURE 11.5.
Displaying data within a table using a proportional font.

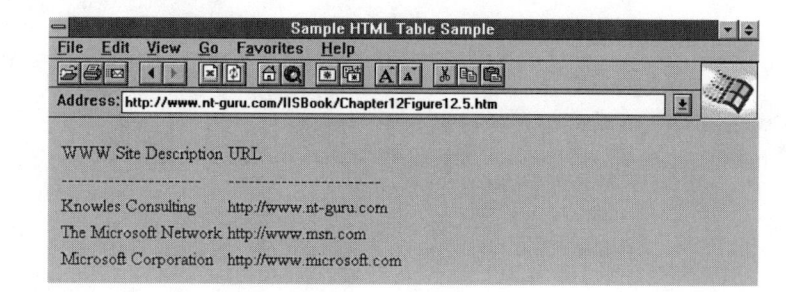

```
                    Sample HTML Table Sample
 File  Edit  View  Go  Favorites  Help

 Address: http://www.nt-guru.com/IISBook/Chapter12Figure12.5.htm

 WWW Site Description    URL
 ---------------------   ----------------------
 Knowles Consulting      http://www.nt-guru.com
 The Microsoft Network   http://www.msn.com
 Microsoft Corporation   http://www.microsoft.com
```

The rest of this section explores the options available to format your HTML documents. You will learn how to change paragraph and text attributes, create document headers, change page attributes, create numbered and unnumbered lists, insert graphics, create tables, and create hypertext links.

Changing Paragraph Attributes

Most word processors provide a means to format paragraphs of text within your document. A word processor commonly allows you to align text on the left page boundary, the right page boundary, or center the paragraph on the page. You can also indent a paragraph or justify the paragraph so that the paragraph margins on the page are as even as possible. HTML also provides this ability, as shown in Figure 11.6.

An HTML Primer
Chapter 11

> **NOTE**
>
> To make the discussions a little easier to follow, I have also displayed the source code in Figure 11.6 for each paragraph formatting option as well. I will continue to do so with future HTML examples when applicable. The actual samples can be found on the accompanying CD-ROM in the \SOURCE\CHAP11 subdirectory.

FIGURE 11.6.
Aligning paragraphs on the screen.

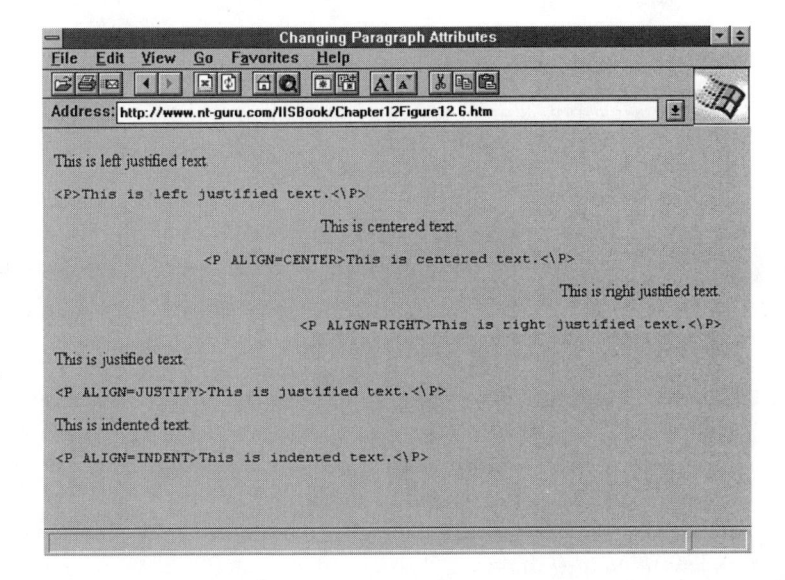

```
                     Changing Paragraph Attributes
File  Edit  View  Go  Favorites  Help
Address: http://www.nt-guru.com/IISBook/Chapter12Figure12.6.htm

This is left justified text.
<P>This is left justified text.<\P>
                            This is centered text.
                <P ALIGN=CENTER>This is centered text.<\P>
                                          This is right justified text.
                    <P ALIGN=RIGHT>This is right justified text.<\P>
This is justified text.
<P ALIGN=JUSTIFY>This is justified text.<\P>
This is indented text.
<P ALIGN=INDENT>This is indented text.<\P>
```

You may notice that not all attributes are supported. The indent and justify options do not seem to appear properly on the screen with IE 2.0. Even though the justify attribute is supposed to be an accepted attribute according to the documentation I have found, it certainly does not appear to function properly. The indent attribute is not supported by IE 2.0, although it may be for IE 3.0. One of the reasons you should test your HTML documents on a variety of Web browsers is because not all Web browsers support the HTML 2.0 specification or the HTML 3.2 draft. Unless you actually test your Web pages on the appropriate Web browsers, you really have no idea what the pages will look like on them.

> **TIP**
>
> Create sample HTML documents such as the ones I have created to test the Web browsers you want to support. No one really expects you to support them all. If you are only going to support a single browser, your Web page should note this on the page. Or include a shortcut to the Web browsers you do support on your Web page so your clients will be able to view your Web pages in all their splendor.

The basic structure for paragraph alignment is

`<P ALIGN= CENTER¦LEFT¦RIGHT¦JUSTIFY¦INDENT...</P>`

There are other variations depending on which HTML specification you are using. You can also use the `<CENTER>` and `</CENTER>` tags to center text or graphics on the screen, although this tag may disappear from future versions of HTML. You should use the `<P ALIGN=CENTER>` and `<\P>` tags if you want to maintain future HTML source code compatibility.

Changing Text Attributes

Plain text is boring, so most people like to spice it up. To make a word stand out on the screen, make it bold. To call attention to a term you are defining, italicize or underline it. Figure 11.7 illustrates the HTML commands you can use to modify the way your text will appear on the screen. Most Web browsers will look similar onscreen, but then again, maybe not. Keep in mind that HTML tags define a logical, not physical, representation. It is up to the Web browser to determine how the text will appear onscreen.

If you look closely at Figure 11.7, you should note the `<EM>` `</EM>` and `<STRONG>` `</STRONG>` tag pairs. These tags are used to emphasize text and to strongly emphasize text, respectively. The HTML specification states that the `<EM>` tag displays on the screen with a distinct difference from the `<STRONG>` tag. However, in my experience the `<EM>` tag generally displays as italic text, while the `<STRONG>` tag displays text in bold. I prefer to use the `<I>` `</I>` and `<B>` `</B>` tag pairs when I want to display italic or bold text rather than to use the `<EM>` `</EM>` or `<STRONG>` `</STRONG>` tag pairs. I prefer the consistency of using specific tags so I have a better idea of how the text will be displayed.

FIGURE 11.7.
Changing text attributes.

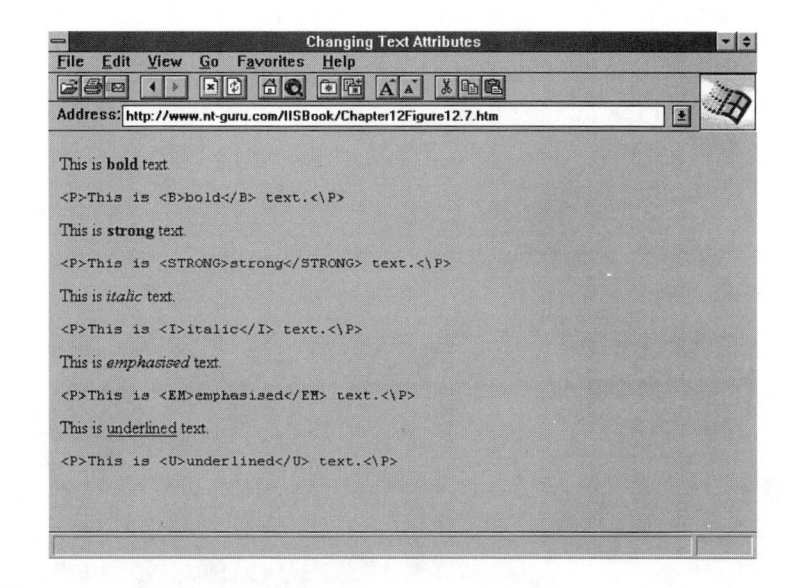

[Screenshot showing browser window titled "Changing Text Attributes" displaying:

This is **bold** text.
`<P>This is <B>bold</B> text.<\P>`

This is **strong** text.
`<P>This is <STRONG>strong</STRONG> text.<\P>`

This is *italic* text.
`<P>This is <I>italic</I> text.<\P>`

This is *emphasised* text.
`<P>This is <EM>emphasised</EM> text.<\P>`

This is underlined text.
`<P>This is <U>underlined</U> text.<\P>`]

Other tags that may prove useful to you, shown in Figure 11.8, include the `<CITE>` and `</CITE>` tags. This pair of tags is used to display citations (usually used in legal documents). Most Web browsers will display this as italic text. You can also use `<STRIKE>` and `</STRIKE>` to display text with a strikeout character, although this tag pair is being replaced with the `<S>` and `</S>` tags. You can use `<KBD>` and `</KBD>` to display text the user should type in exactly as shown on the screen. The `<CODE>` and `</CODE>` tags are used to display source code on the screen. You can use `<TT>` and `</TT>` to display teletype text on the screen. The `<KBD>`, `<CODE>`, and `<TT>` tags all use a fixed-width font.

FIGURE 11.8.
Additional text attribute tags.

[Screenshot showing:

This is the way a *cite* appears.
`<P>This is the way a <CITE>cite</CITE> appears<\P>`

This is ~~strikeout~~ text.
`<P>This is <STRIKE>strikout</STRIKE> text.<\P>`

This is **keyboard** text.
`<P>This is <KBD>keyboard</KBD> text.<\P>`

This is code text.
`<P>This is <CODE>code</CODE> text.<\P>`

This is teletype text.
`<P>This is <TT>teletype</TT> text.<\P>`]

Web Page Development
Part IV

You can also change the size of the font displayed on the screen using the `<FONT>` and `</FONT>` tags. The full tag is `<FONT SIZE=FontSize COLOR="DisplayColor" FACE="TypeFace">`, where `FontSize` is a number from 1 to 7 or the + and - (to increase or decrease the size by one). `DisplayColor` is either Black, Maroon, Green, Olive, Navy, Purple, Teal, Gray, Silver, Red, Lime, Yellow, Blue, Fuchsia, Aqua, or White. `TypeFace` is a specific font family to use. Both COLOR and FACE are IE 2.0 extensions, so if you do not use IE as your Web browser, you may want to avoid using these extensions. Figure 11.9 displays examples of the various fonts and colors you can use.

FIGURE 11.9.
Specifying a font size.

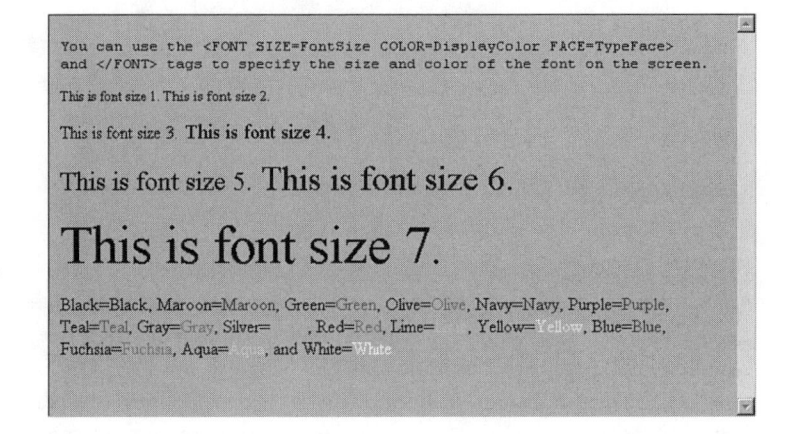

> You can use the `<FONT SIZE=FontSize COLOR=DisplayColor FACE=TypeFace>` and `</FONT>` tags to specify the size and color of the font on the screen.
>
> This is font size 1. This is font size 2.
>
> This is font size 3. This is font size 4.
>
> This is font size 5. This is font size 6.
>
> This is font size 7.
>
> Black=Black, Maroon=Maroon, Green=Green, Olive=Olive, Navy=Navy, Purple=Purple, Teal=Teal, Gray=Gray, Silver=   , Red=Red, Lime=   , Yellow=Yellow, Blue=Blue, Fuchsia=Fuchsia, Aqua=   , and White=White

Depending on your Web browser, you may find additional HTML tags you can use to specify text attributes. Be aware that the supported tags seem to change quite rapidly. If you want to keep up-to-date, then you will need to do three things:

1. Use the manufacturer's WWW pages to find information on the HTML tags and extensions that your particular Web browser supports. For the MS Internet Explorer, check the Microsoft home page at `http://www.microsoft.com`. For Netscape Navigator, check the Netscape home page at `http://home.netscape.com`. The HTML 2.0 specification and 3.0 draft can be found at `http://www.w3.org`.

2. Check for and download the latest version of the Web browser from the manufacturer. You should check at least once a month. If you have the time, try once a week. You never know when an update will be available.

3. Create a link for your customers to download the latest version of the Web browser and place it on your home page. This way, your customers will be able to take advantage of the tags and extension you use.

Displaying Text Using a Fixed-Width Font

As previously mentioned, there are several HTML tag pairs you can use to display text onscreen using a fixed-width font. They include the `<KBD>`, `<CODE>`, and `<TT>` tags. However, while you can use these tags to display large amounts of text, they are designed for small amounts of text. If you have a large amount of text that you want to display onscreen, you should use the `<PLAINTEXT> </PLAINTEXT>`, `<LISTING> </LISTING>`, or `<PRE> </PRE>` tag pairs. These are unique in that they will display anything within the enclosed tags onscreen; however, this also is implementation dependent. The `<LISTING>` tag assumes that a maximum of 132 characters can be displayed onscreen, while the `<PLAINTEXT>` tag does not make this assumption. I used the `<PLAINTEXT> </PLAINTEXT>` tag pair around the previous sample HTML source code so that you could see onscreen the behavior of the text-attribute tags.

While I used the tags for consistency on individual sentences, you could use them to enclose a paragraph or even an entire document. Depending on your Web browser, you may find that these tags are not supported. The reason behind this is simple. HTML is an evolving specification. Previous versions utilized these tags; however, the current specification based on RFC 1866 does not mention it. As such, many Web browsers have dropped support for it. Therefore, you should use the `<PRE> </PRE>` tag pairs if you want to maintain maximum compatibility in the future. If your customers are using archaic Web browsers, you can either recommend that they upgrade their software or you can use the old tag pairs with the understanding that your future customer's Web browsers may not support the tag. You really cannot please everyone all the time. I prefer to use the newer tags, and I recommend that you do so as well.

> **NOTE**
>
> Even the same version of the Web browser may have different display characteristics depending on the operating system. For example, IE 2.0 on Windows 95 does not support the `<PLAINTEXT> </PLAINTEXT>` or `<PRE> </PRE>` tags to display embedded HTML tags. Instead, I had to use the `<LISTING> </LISTING>` tags to capture Figure 11.9. Why? Because IE 1.5 under Windows NT does not support the COLOR keyword in the `<FONT>` tag.

The basic format of these tags is

```
<LISTING WIDTH="MaxNbrOfCharacters"> </LISTING>
<PLAINTTEXT> </PLAINTEXT>
<PRE WIDTH=MaxNbrOfCharacters> </PRE>
```

MaxNbrOfCharacters is the maximum number of characters to be displayed on the screen. One particular quirk you should be aware of is that some Web browsers will decrease the font size

Web Page Development

Part IV

in order to fit the characters on the screen. You should test your Web pages at different resolutions with your Web browser to determine if the effect is acceptable. If not, you should reformat your text if possible.

Creating Document Headers

Most people break their documents into sections when they write. This section of the chapter, for example, uses a level *d* heading to describe the contents and make it easier for the reader to find information. You can do the same with HTML by using the header tags. There are seven defined header levels, shown in Figure 11.10, starting with <H1> </H1> and ending with <H7> </H7>. As you can see, each header level utilizes a different-size font. Levels 1 through 6 use a bold font, and by the time you reach level 7 you are back to the default font size and characteristics. Once again, you really can't expect the headers to display this way on all Web browsers, but you can expect that each header level will be displayed with a noticeable difference.

FIGURE 11.10.
The seven HTML header levels.

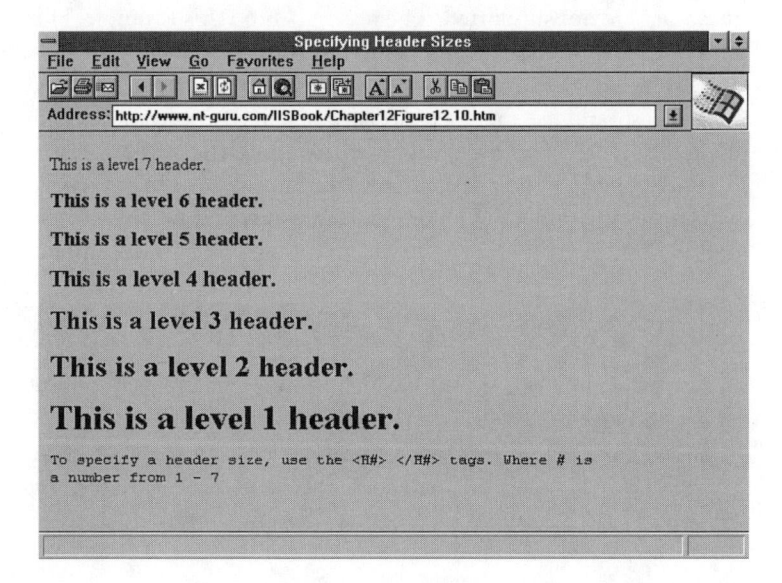

You may specify additional information when you define your headers. You can align them on the left side of the page, the right side, center them, or even justify them. The basic syntax is <H# ALIGN=LEFT|RIGHT|CENTER|JUSTIFY NOWRAP> </H#>, where # is a value from 1 to 7. There may be additional options depending on your Web browser, but this will do for a start. If printing your Web pages is a concern, be aware that if you center a header that utilizes a large font, a page break may be generated after the header.

> **NOTE**
>
> You should not use any additional text attribute tags, such as <B>, <I>, <EM>, <STRONG>, and so on, within a header tag because this can cause undefined behavior.

Changing Page Attributes

One of the coolest features of HTML is the ability to specify a picture to be used as a background for your document. It works the same way that a tiled background does for your desktop. Basically, the image is duplicated multiple times to fill the screen, and your document text and images will appear layered on top of the background. You can also specify the default background color and colors for your links. Although IE 1.5 does not seem to support color-related tag extensions, it does work fine with background bitmaps.

A background bitmap must be either a Graphical Interchange Format (GIF) or Joint Picture Experts Group (JPEG) file, and you should keep it as small as possible. The smaller the file, the quicker the user can get back to reading your document content. You see, it works like this: The background color is set, then the background image is loaded, then the text is loaded, and finally any images embedded within the document will be displayed by the Web browser. If your backgrounds are too large, the user will probably give up in disgust and move on to a new Web site. It also makes little sense to specify a background color if you also use a background image that will fill the screen when tiled, as shown in Figure 11.11, unless your image is an irregular (that is, not square) shape. Otherwise, the image will completely overlay the background. If you actually load the sample file (Chapter11Figure11.11.HTM), you will see a red flash as the background color is set, followed by the background image overlaying the background color.

FIGURE 11.11.
A tiled background image.

I am particularly fond of using background images because it's an easy way to build a great-looking page with minimal user impact. You can use a small pattern, such as a square marble image, to create a high-visibility document that the user will say, "Wow! That looks nifty." Word will spread to other users who will then come to visit your pages.

Use <BODY> to specify the page background and color. The basic syntax is <BODY BACKGROUND=*PathName* BGCOLOR=*BackGroundColor*> </BODY> where *PathName* is a relative URL to your background (/images/picture.gif, for example) and *BackGroundColor* is either Black, Maroon, Green, Olive, Navy, Purple, Teal, Gray, Silver, Red, Lime, Yellow, Blue, Fuchsia, Aqua, or White.

Another neat tag to use is the <BGSOUND SRC="*PathName*" LOOP="*NbrOfIterations*"> </BGSOUND>, where *PathName* is a relative URL that points to the location of your sound file and *NbrOfIterations* is a number or the keyword infinite to play continuously. There are two considerations when using this option. First, the size of the audio file will cause a delay in displaying the document. If the wait is too long, the user will go elsewhere. Second, there is currently no way to turn off the ability to play a sound in most Web browsers. Not everyone will appreciate listening to the same sound over and over (if you use the infinite option). So, use this option with care, or if you want to play a sound, create a link to let the user play it if he desires.

Creating Numbered and Bulleted Lists

The HTML specification includes the ability to create both numbered and bulleted lists, as shown in Figure 11.12. If you want to use fancy bullets, you can load images or specify a different bullet character in your HTML source. An HTML editor can make this job a lot easier. The basic format is <OL> </OL> for an ordered (numbered) list and <UL> </UL> for an unnumbered (bulleted) list. Within these tags you may specify the list items using the <LI> and </LI> tags and an optional list header using the <LH> and </LH> tags.

FIGURE 11.12.
Creating numbered and bulleted lists.

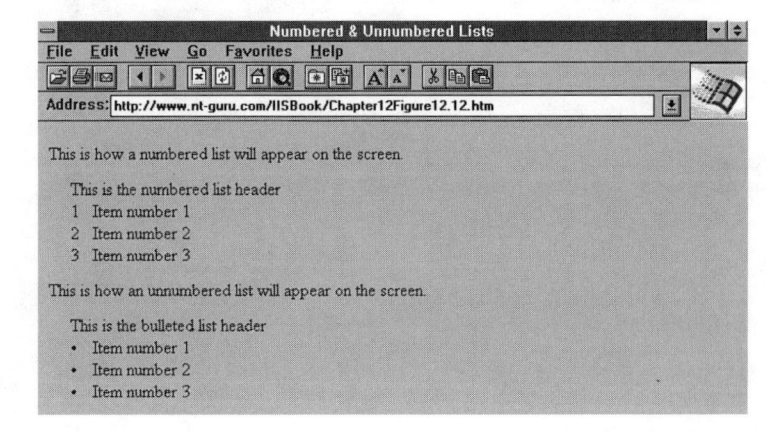

The actual source code for this Web page is as follows:

```
<HTML>
<HEAD>
<TITLE>Numbered & Unnumbered Lists</TITLE>
</HEAD>

<BODY>
<P>This is how a numbered list will appear on the screen.</P>
<OL>
<LH>This is the numbered list header</LH>
<LI>Item number 1
<LI>Item number 2
<LI>Item number 3
</OL>
<P>This is how an unnumbered list will appear on the screen.</P>
<UL>
<LH>This is the bulleted list header</LH>
<LI>Item number 1
<LI>Item number 2
<LI>Item number 3
</UL>
</BODY>
</HTML>
```

For readability, I always start each item on a separate line. However, this is not required. The same effect could be generated by creating a single paragraph (or line) of text. I think you will agree that the previous example is much easier to read than the following:

```
<HTML><HEAD><TITLE>Numbered & Unnumbered Lists</TITLE></HEAD><BODY>
➥<P>This is how a numbered list will appear on the screen.</P><OL>
➥<LH>This is the numbered list header</LH><LI>Item number 1
➥<LI>Item number 2<LI>Item number 3</OL><P>This is how an unnumbered
➥list will appear on the screen.</P><UL><LH>This is the bulleted list
➥header</LH><LI>Item number 1<LI>Item number 2<LI>Item number 3</UL>
➥</BODY></HTML>
```

As with most other textual tags, you can specify the alignment. The basic syntax for lists is `<OL ALIGN=LEFT¦RIGHT¦CENTER¦JUSTIFY> </OL>` or `<UL ALIGN=LEFT¦RIGHT¦CENTER¦JUSTIFY> </UL>`.

Additional List Styles

If you have a brief amount of information to display within a list, you can use the `<MENU> </MENU>` tags. These tags are recommended for lists of items that have fewer than 40 characters each. The idea is that the Web browser can use a more compact font to display the material, although this too is implementation dependent. A similar tag is used to display directories. A directory will appear as a single column of items (another list). To create a directory, use the `<DIR> </DIR>` tags. Each item within a menu or directory is preceded with the `<LI>` tag. To create a menu of items, you could use something similar to the following:

```
<MENU>
<LI>First menu item.
<LI>Second menu item.
</MENU>
```

To create a directory list, say of files in your File Transfer Protocol (FTP) site, you could use the following:

```
<DIR>
<LI>autoexec.bat
<LI>config.sys
</DIR>
```

The only difference between these tags and those for numbered or bulleted lists is that these tags do not precede the list with either a bullet or a number. While I may not find much use for these tags unless I am creating custom bullets, I do find the definition-list tag pair quite useful. This set of tags is often utilized to create a dictionary or glossary of terms for your Web page. Here's the way it works: The outer body utilizes the <DL> </DL> tags while the term utilizes a <DT> tag and the definition utilizes a <DD> tag. Suppose you wanted to display a glossary for your Web page for new users. You could use something similar to the following, which would look something like Figure 11.13:

```
<DL>
<DT><B>HyperText Transmission Protocol (HTTP)</B>
<DD>Is the common protocol, or language, used by World Wide Web (WWW)
➥servers and web browsers as the communication link between client
➥and server.
<DT><B>HyperText Markup Language (HTML)</B>
<DD>Is a set of rules which utilize ASCII based tags used to format text,
➥display objects, and create links within a document, or web page.
</DL>
```

FIGURE 11.13.
A sample glossary for your Web page.

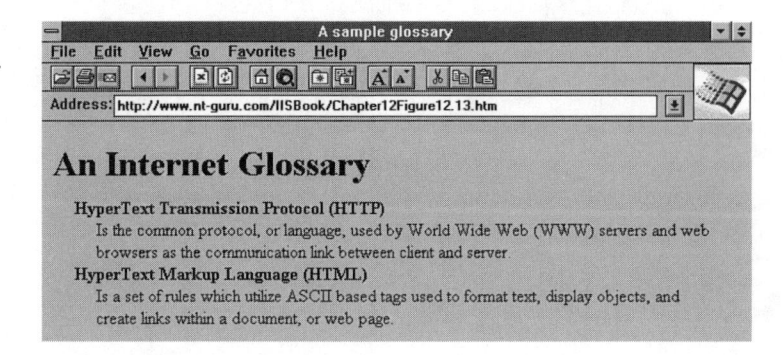

You also might find it useful to change the size of the font for the term, rather than bold it as I have done in the previous example. It's also possible to create an index at the top of your page with links to the respective terms and definitions. A later section of this chapter, "Creating Hypertext Links," looks at an example that illustrates this particular method.

Miscellaneous Styles

A few additional HTML tags may be useful in your endeavors to design the perfect Web page. To create a visual line break, for example, you can use the horizontal rule tag <HR>. If you are quoting a source on your Web page, you can use the <BLOCKQUOTE> </BLOCKQUOTE> tags. The text enclosed within these tags often appears surrounded by single quote marks or as an indented paragraph of italic text. Another cool tag pair is <ADDRESS> </ADDRESS>. This set of tags is most commonly used to highlight your name, address, or e-mail address. I often include contact information such as this on the bottom of the page. To give you an idea how these tags will display your text onscreen, take a look at Figure 11.14.

FIGURE 11.14.
Horizontal lines, quoted material, and addresses.

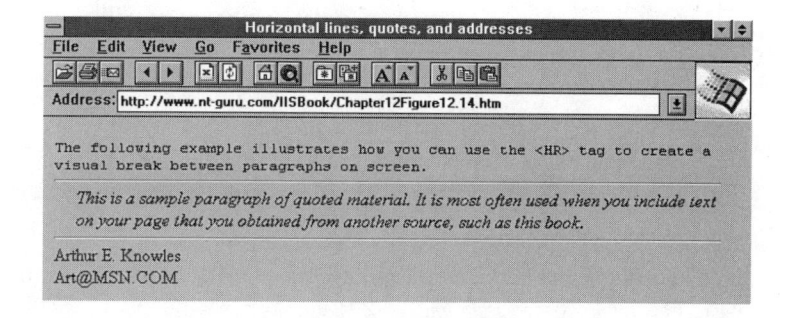

If you look at the source code for this example, you will see another new tag within the <ADDRESS> </ADDRESS> tags. This tag is the line break tag <BR>. It starts a new line without creating extra vertical space, such as when you start a new paragraph. I prefer to use it at the end of a sentence, as shown in the following; however, you can place it anywhere within your text:

```
<ADDRESS>
Arthur E. Knowles<BR>
Art@MSN.COM
</ADDRESS>
```

Inserting Graphics

What makes today's Web browsers fun to work with is the graphics. There is really no doubt about it. Graphics are an integral part of a Web page and without them life is really boring. The good news is that it's very easy to insert graphics into your Web page. You should keep the following rules in mind when using graphics in your documents:

- Never use a 24-bit graphic image. These images, while very nice to view, are too large. They take an inordinate amount of bandwidth to download, and for most users the wait just isn't worth it. If you do decide to provide 24-bit images, place them on your

FTP site. The user can then choose whether to download them. Be aware that not every Web browser can display 16-bit or 24-bit images. Most only support 8-bit (or 256-color) bitmaps in GIF or JPEG formats.

- Don't go overboard. While graphics are nice, keep it simple. Too many graphics cause the reader to collapse from image overload. If your client is using a modem as his Internet connection, too many graphic images may try the client's patience. A modem is not a fast connection mechanism, and the client may decide to stop waiting for his slow modem to download all the images and move on to another site.

- Use GIF, instead of JPEG, graphics. Unless you are 100 percent sure that your customer's Web browser will support JPEG graphic files, stick to the GIF format. Otherwise, your customers may not think you actually know how to create a Web page because all they will see is the crossed-out square that is normally displayed for a missing graphic image.

- Always have a text alternative. If you are using an image as a link, remember that not everyone has a Web browser that supports graphic images. The user might have even disabled image viewing entirely in order to decrease access times. So always include a textual reference.

Having said all that, to insert an image on your Web page you can use the `<IMG> </IMG>` tag pair. The basic syntax is

```
<IMG SRC="ImageURL" ALT="TextAlternative" ALIGN=LEFT | RIGHT | MIDDLE | TOP |
BOTTOM | TEXTTOP | ABSBOTTOM | ABSMIDDLE | BASELINE> </IMG>
```

`ImageURL` is a URL that points to the image to be displayed, and `TextAlternative` is a text description to be used if the graphic cannot be displayed. The Microsoft Internet Explorer can also display video animation. If you choose to do so, the alternate version is as follows:

```
<IMG SRC="ImageURL" ALT="TextAlternative" ALIGN=LEFT | RIGHT | MIDDLE | TOP |
BOTTOM | TEXTTOP | ABSBOTTOM | ABSMIDDLE | BASELINE
DYNSRC="VideoURL" START=FILEOPEN | MOUSEOVER CONTROLS
LOOP=number|INFINITE|-1 LOOPDELAY=number > </IMG>
```

In this case, a static image, as defined by the SRC element, will be used if the browser does not support video files. The actual video file is referenced by the DYNSRC element, and the location of the video clip is defined by `VideoURL`. The START element specifies that the image will begin to play when the file is opened; however, if you use the MOUSEOVER option, the video will discontinue playing whenever the mouse is over the image. The CONTROLS option is used to specify that a set of video controls (stop, start, and so on) should be displayed to control the flow of the video clip. The LOOP element is used to control how many times the video clip will play. If INFINITE or -1 is selected, the image will play continuously. The LOOPDELAY element is used to define how long in milliseconds the video clip will pause before restarting.

An HTML Primer

Chapter 11 331

> **TIP**
>
> Be nice to your customers. If you have a large graphic, video image, or file for them to download when they click on a link, place a notice of the object size next to it. This will let the user know just how long it will take to download and will prepare them for the wait.

I wish that this book could display live video because this option is one of the coolest I've seen. It can be used to create a marquee of moving textual content that you can use instead of a static banner and display any type of animation, including 3D effects. Chapter 17, "Unleashing the Power of VBScript," will look into this when it covers Asymetrix's WEB 3D. To give you an idea of how to place an image and some sample code (Chapter11Figure11.15.HTM), see Figure 11.15, which displays the IIS logo in several areas on the screen.

FIGURE 11.15.
Displaying images on your Web page.

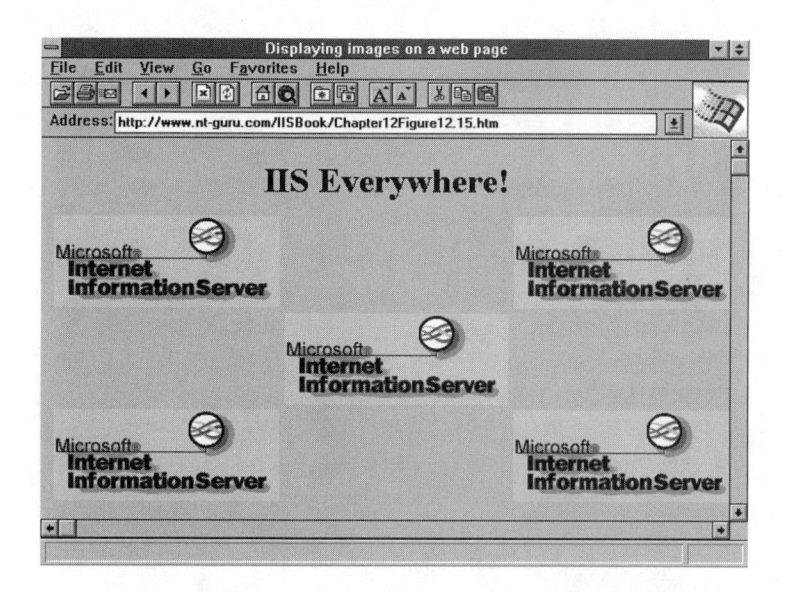

Now, if you look at the sample source code, you will notice that I did not use the ALIGN keyword to align the objects on the screen. Instead, I created a 3×3 table (tables are discussed in more detail in the next section, "Creating Tables") with an image inserted in the four corners and the center element of the table. I wanted the images to create an X-shaped display. The ALIGN keyword is used to relatively align an image. It is not an absolute alignment of the viewing area. The actual placement of the image will depend on the text or other images on the screen. If you want to place an image in a specific location, the best way to do so is to divide your page into logical grouping with a table. Then place each element within a specific column and row, as I have done.

Another cool use for inline graphics is to create custom horizontal rules, banners, mastheads, or even bullet lists. Figure 11.16 demonstrates the creation of custom bullets in a menu list. This looks a lot better than the standard bullet, and you can be pretty sure that the user will see it this way unless he has images disabled or is using a text-based Web browser.

FIGURE 11.16.

Creating custom bulleted lists.

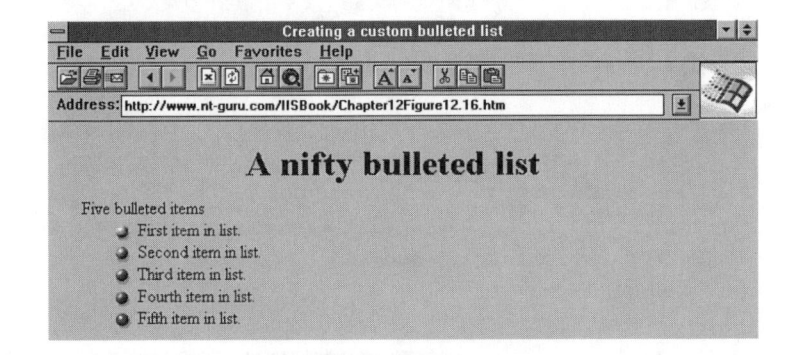

Creating Tables

As previously mentioned, tables are a useful method for breaking up your Web pages into discrete sections. While you cannot be assured that this will work in every case, it will work for Web browsers that support the HTML table definitions as described in the HTML 3.0 draft. This includes the Internet Explorer and Netscape Navigator. Although these Web browsers do not support the full HTML 3.0 draft at this time, they do support the basic implementation that consists of the <TABLE> </TABLE> tag pair. Within this tag pair you can include a table header, specified with the <TH> </TH> tags. A row is defined using the <TR> </TR> tag pair. An individual column in a row is defined with the <TD> </TD> tag pair. To create a 2×3 table, for example, you could use the following HTML code:

```
<H1 ALIGN=CENTER>A sample 2 x 3 table.</H1>
<TABLE ALIGN=CENTER BORDER>
<TH>This is the table header for the first column.</TH>
<TH>This is the table header for the second column.</TH>
<TH>This is the table header for the third column.</TH>
<TR>
<TD ALIGN=LEFT>This is the first column in the first row.</TD>
<TD ALIGN=CENTER>This is the second column in the first row.</TD>
<TD ALIGN=RIGHT>This is the third column in the first row.</TD>
</TR>
<TR>
<TD ALIGN=LEFT>This is the first column in the second row.</TD>
<TD ALIGN=CENTER>This is the second column in the second row.</TD>
<TD ALIGN=RIGHT>This is the third column in the second row.</TD>
</TR>
</TABLE>
```

This will create the table shown in Figure 11.17. The first line creates a header that will be centered on the screen and displayed before the table. The next line begins the definition for the table. It specifies that the table should be centered on the screen and that the table should have a border around each table element. The following three lines create the table column headers. The subsequent line with the <TR> tag is used to specify the beginning of the first table row. The next three lines, prefaced with the <TD ...> tag, define the first three columns of the table. The data displayed within these columns are left, right, and center aligned within the column. The very next line, with the </TR> tag, defines the end of the first row. The next five lines define the second row of data, followed by the ending table definition. That's all there is to creating tables!

FIGURE 11.17.

Creating a 2×3 table with table and column headers.

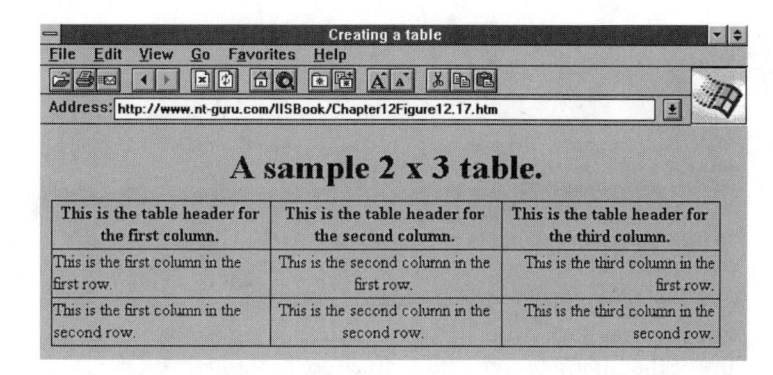

The basic syntax for each of these table elements is as follows:

```
<TABLE ALIGN=LEFT|RIGHT|CENTER|JUSTIFY BORDER> </TABLE>
<TH ALIGN=LEFT|RIGHT|CENTER|JUSTIFY|CHAR CHAR=UserSpecifiedCharater
 VALIGN=TOP|MIDDLE|BOTTOM|BASELINE BGCOLOR=DisplayColor> </TH>
<TR ALIGN=LEFT|RIGHT|CENTER|JUSTIFY|CHAR|DECIMAL CHAR=UserSpecifiedCharater
VALIGN=TOP|MIDDLE|BOTTOM|BASELINE> </TR>
```

The BORDER option specifies that the table should have a border surrounding each cell. The *UserSpecifiedCharacter* option is used in conjunction with the ALIGN=CHAR option to specify the horizontal alignment of data. It defaults to a decimal point if no other character is specified. The *DisplayColor* option can be either Black, Maroon, Green, Olive, Navy, Purple, Teal, Gray, Silver, Red, Lime, Yellow, Blue, Fuchsia, Aqua, or White. The VALIGN option is used to specify the vertical alignment of items within the table cell.

Creating Hypertext Links

I saved the best for last. No HTML document is complete without a link to another document. In HTML terms, a link is defined within an *anchor*. An anchor, <A> </A>, is a relative reference to another object. It can include text or images, and, when selected, it will send the user to the specified location. An anchor can either include an HREF, which is a URL to a destination, or a NAME, which is a reference to a specific hypertext link within the associated document. The basic syntax is as follows:

```
<A HREF="PathName"> URLDescription </A>
<A NAME="PathName#LinkName> URLDescription </A>
```

The `PathName` is a relative URL to the HTML document, and `URLDescription` is the hypertext link that will be displayed on the screen. For a NAME entry, `LinkName` specifies a hypertext link within the associated document. With a NAME anchor, the document will be loaded by the Web browser, then a jump will be made to the specified location within the document specified by `LinkName`.

When you create an anchor, you may specify a graphic image to be loaded by including the <IMG> tag between the beginning <A> and </A> tags. A link to the IIS Web page, for example, would look like the following:

```
<A HREF="http://www.microsoft.com/infoserv"><IMG ALIGN=LEFT SRC="/samples/images/
➥h_logo.gif"></A>
<P ALIGN=CENTER>The Internet Information Server (or IIS) is a new set of tools to
provide Windows NT Server with a WWW, FTP, and Gopher server.
To find out more about the <A HREF="http://www.microsoft.com/infoserv">
Internet Information Server</A> click on the picture to the left, or the link
<A HREF="http://www.microsoft.com/infoserv">here</A></P>
```

The previous code would appear onscreen as shown in Figure 11.18. You can create a URL for any of the Internet services as defined in Table 11.1. Of course to make all of this work properly, you must also have an application associated with the specific service. For example, if you select a URL that includes the `mailto:` URI, then your e-mail client will be launched. If you choose a `news:` URI, then a newsgroup reader will be launched. Unfortunately, news is not supported in version 1.5 of the Internet Explorer for Windows NT, but it does work fine with the Internet Explorer 2.0 for Windows 95 as long as you also have a user account on The Microsoft Network.

FIGURE 11.18.
Creating a hypertext link.

Table 11.1. Acceptable Internet services types.

Uniform Resource Identifier	Description
http	Hypertext Transfer Protocol. This is the most widely used mechanism to retrieve a file and requires that the destination include an application (WWW server) that understands the HTTP protocol.
https	Hypertext Transfer Protocol Secure. A variation on the previous example that includes a secure connection mechanism.
file	Local file access. This option will load a local file.
ftp	File Transfer Protocol. Commonly used to access an FTP server to download a specified file.
mailto	E-mail. Commonly used to load and execute an e-mail form from the host computer on the local computer.
news	Usenet newsgroups. Commonly used to access Internet newsgroups.
wais	Wide area information service. Commonly used to search a Gopher site.
gopher	Commonly used to access large text servers.
telnet	Commonly used to access a telnet server on a remote host.

Summary

Wow, this is an intense chapter, and it only teaches the basics of HTML programming. In future chapters you will learn about using ActiveX, Visual Basic Scripting, CGI, and Perl programming to create custom forms. If you would like additional information on the HTML specification, take a look at Appendix B, "HTML Reference." It includes as much of a description of the current HTML 3.0 specification as I could find on the Internet in an easily digestible format. Keep in mind that HTML is a moving target. It changes rapidly, and the only way to keep up is to use the Internet as an information resource.

This chapter teaches the basics about text manipulation (headers, paragraphs, and so on). It also shows how to create lists, embed images, and create links and tables, all with your standard ASCII editor. In the next chapter, you will take a look at the Internet Assistant for Word for Windows and see how it can make the creation of HTML documents a little easier.

Designing and Managing a Web Site with FrontPage

12

IN THIS CHAPTER

- Installing FrontPage **338**
- The FrontPage Server **340**
- Changing the Default Port of the FrontPage Server **341**
- The FrontPage Server Administrator **341**
- The FrontPage Explorer **345**
- The FrontPage To Do List **348**
- Verifying Links **349**
- The FrontPage Editor **350**

FrontPage is a powerful Web site development tool. Not only can it be used to edit Web pages, but it also can be used to manage your Web site. The next few sections demonstrate how FrontPage can be used to develop and manage the contents of a Web site. More information about FrontPage can be obtained from Microsoft's Web site.

> **NOTE**
>
> The Microsoft FrontPage Web site can be found at
> `http://www.microsoft.com/frontpage/default.htm`

Installing FrontPage

Installing FrontPage is as easy as downloading it from Microsoft's Web site and running the file `setup.exe`. When the FrontPage installation program is executed, it will display a dialog box similar to the one shown in Figure 12.1. Use this dialog box to specify the directory in which FrontPage should be installed. Three optional FrontPage components also can be selected to be installed using the same dialog box. It is recommended that you make sure the Client Software component is checked. The Client Software component consists of the FrontPage Explorer and Editor. Select the Personal Web Server check box if you would like the FrontPage server to be installed on your system. If your Web server is compatible with FrontPage Server Extensions, you do not have to install the FrontPage Web Server. Visit the FrontPage Web site for the most up-to-date list of Web servers supported by FrontPage. At the time of this writing, FrontPage Server Extensions are compatible with the Netscape Commerce Server, Netscape Communications Server, and WebSite. However, by the time you read this, FrontPage will support several other Web servers including Internet Information Server by Microsoft.

> **NOTE**
>
> If you select to install the Personal Web Server component, be sure no other Web server is running on port 80 of your system. If another Web server is using port 80, the FrontPage Web server might have problems binding to port 80 of your server. If you would like to install the FrontPage server for testing purposes and have already installed a server such as Internet Information Server, there is a way to get the FrontPage server to use a different port. In the latter case, stop the other server for the duration of the installation process. After FrontPage is installed and its port is changed, you can continue to use the previous server as you did earlier.

FIGURE 12.1.
The FrontPage component selection dialog box.

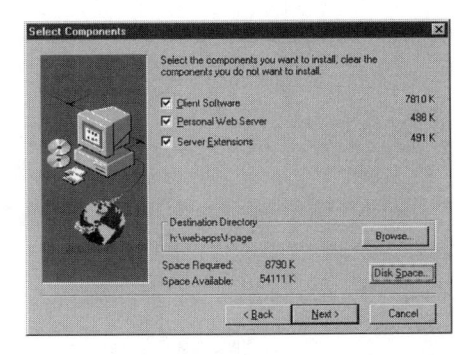

If you wish to install FrontPage extensions for your Web server, place a check mark by the Server Extensions check box. Afterwards, click the next button to continue.

Use the Select Program Folder dialog box, shown in Figure 12.2, to select the folder in which FrontPage should be installed. When FrontPage is installed, the string of text you specify in Figure 12.2 will become a branch of the Windows NT Start menu. The scroll-down list can be used to install FrontPage into an existing Start Menu folder.

FIGURE 12.2.
The Select Program Folder dialog box.

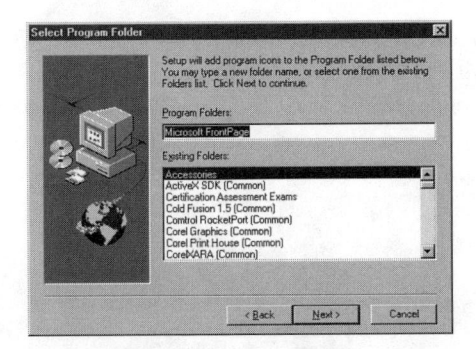

When all the files are copied, the installation program will display a dialog box identical to the one shown in Figure 12.3. FrontPage is now installed on your system. Before the installation program terminates, it might check the IP address of your system and display a confirmation dialog box. As soon as FrontPage is installed on your system, the FrontPage Explorer can be started by checking the check box in Figure 12.3.

FrontPage consists of several separate programs. Depending on the components you selected in Figure 12.1, the FrontPage installation program will install various FrontPage applications and insert them into a Start Menu folder, as shown in Figure 12.4.

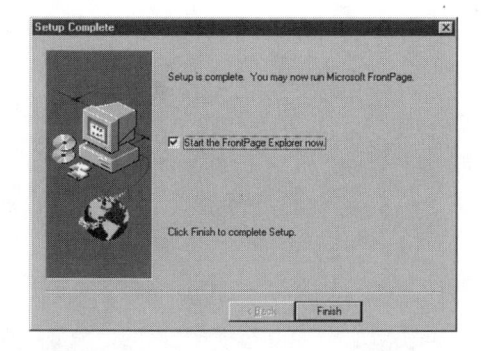

FIGURE 12.3.
The Setup Complete dialog box.

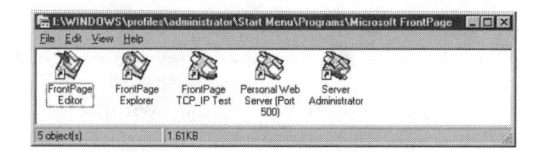

FIGURE 12.4.
FrontPage application icons.

The FrontPage Server

If your Web server is not compatible with Windows NT, you can use the FrontPage server to experiment with FrontPage and create a Web site. After creating Web pages, they can be transferred to the production Web server. The FrontPage server looks similar to Figure 12.5. It can be launched from the Windows NT Start menu. You may need to edit several configuration files to configure the FrontPage server if you wish to run it on a port other than port 80.

FIGURE 12.5.
The FrontPage server.

Changing the Default Port of the FrontPage Server

By default, the FrontPage server is installed on port 80. If you have another Web server running on port 80, this can cause problems because both servers cannot share the same port. As described shortly, this problem can be solved by changing the default port of the FrontPage server by editing several configuration files. Note that the following instructions are based on FrontPage 1.1. If you are using a later version of FrontPage, refer to its documentation for the most up-to-date information about changing the default port of the FrontPage Web server. If you've already installed server extensions for the FrontPage server, invoke the FrontPage Server Administrator application and select Uninstall to remove server extensions from the FrontPage server. Once the port number of the FrontPage server is changed, you can reinstall server extensions for the FrontPage server. The port used by the FrontPage server can be changed by editing the file H:\FrontPageWebs\Server\conf\httpd.cnf, assuming you installed the FrontPage server in the H:\FrontPageWebs directory. As shown in Figure 12.6, to change the port of the FrontPage server, locate the line containing the server port information and type in the new port number.

FIGURE 12.6.
The default port of the FrontPage server can be modified by editing the httpd.cnf *file.*

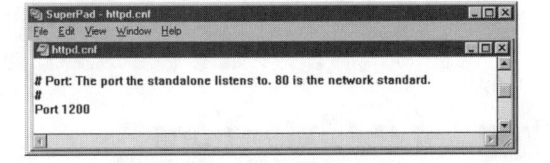

> **CAUTION**
>
> When changing the default port of a Web server, selecting a port below 1024 can potentially cause problems in the future.

You can now install server extensions for the FrontPage server and start it in a different port. If you had another Web server running on port 80, that Web server can be restarted and used as usual.

The FrontPage Server Administrator

The FrontPage Server Administrator is used to manage server extensions installed on various Web servers managed with FrontPage. It also can be used to make sure Web server extensions are installed properly as well as to enable and disable authoring on a server. The next few sections discuss how FrontPage Server Administrator can be used to manage and administer server extensions. When it is first invoked, the FrontPage Server Administrator dialog box will list

Web servers that can be authored with FrontPage, as shown in Figure 12.7. By default, if you selected to install the FrontPage server, only contents of the FrontPage server can be managed using FrontPage Explorer. As you will learn shortly, it is easy to manage and author the contents of a Web site using FrontPage Explorer. However, FrontPage server extensions have to be installed on a server before it can be managed using FrontPage Explorer. Therefore, it is recommended that you install FrontPage server extensions for your Web server as shown in the next section. Make sure FrontPage supports your Web server before attempting to install FrontPage server extensions on your Web server. If your Web server is not supported by FrontPage, you can still use the FrontPage server to design and manage the contents of your Web site. In the latter case, skip the following section and proceed to the "Managing Server Extensions" section.

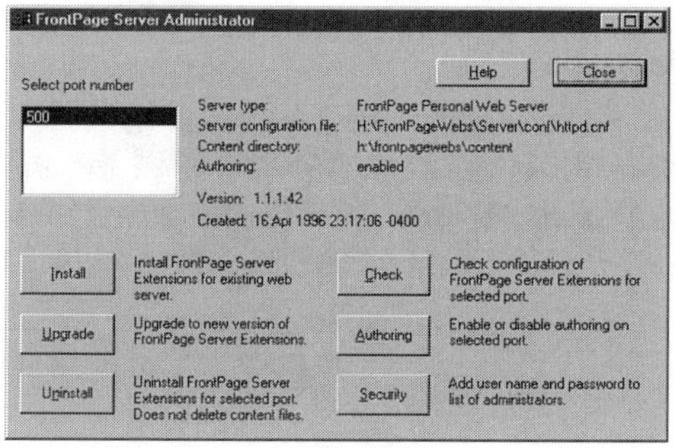

FIGURE 12.7.
The FrontPage Server Administrator dialog box.

Installing Server Extensions

It is easy to install server extensions for additional Web servers as long as they are supported by FrontPage. Click the Install button in the dialog box shown in Figure 12.7 to install server extensions for an existing Web server. You then will be presented with a dialog box similar to the one shown in Figure 12.8. Use this dialog box to select the type of your Web server and press OK to continue. Note that for the purpose of this demonstration, FrontPage server extensions will be installed on a WebSite Web server that is configured to run on port 200. (Again, when changing the port number of a secondary Web server running on your server, do not follow my example and use a port number below 1024. Always use port numbers above 1024 to avoid potential conflicts.)

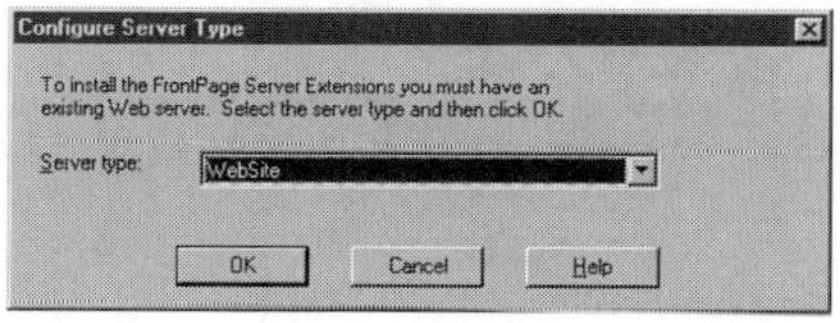

FIGURE 12.8.
The Configure Server Type dialog box.

FrontPage then will gather information about your Web server and display a confirmation dialog box similar to the one shown in Figure 12.9. Simply press the OK button to continue and FrontPage will install server extensions for the Web server selected earlier. If you are installing FrontPage server extensions on a WebSite Web server and have it configured for multiple domain names, enter multiple domain name information when asked for it. Otherwise, leave the dialog box asking for multiple domain name information blank and press the OK button to continue.

FIGURE 12.9.
The Confirmation Dialog dialog box.

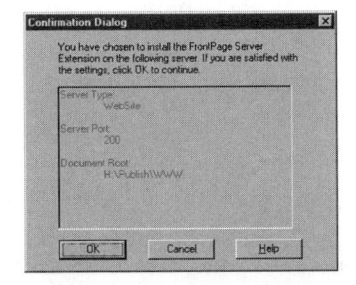

After server extensions are installed for a new Web server, its port will be added to the FrontPage Server Administrator dialog box, as shown in Figure 12.10. Server extensions and authoring settings of each server then can be configured by selecting the server port you wish to administer and following the directions in the next section.

FIGURE 12.10.
The FrontPage Server Administrator dialog box after you install server extensions for an additional Web server.

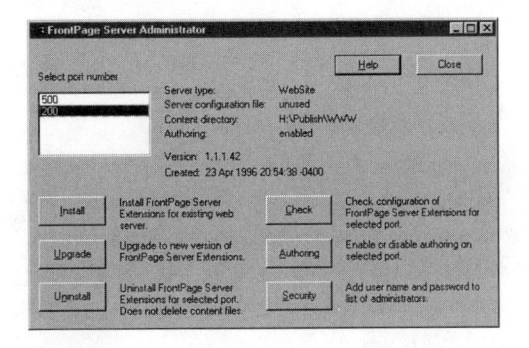

Managing Server Extensions

The Upgrade button of the dialog box shown in Figure 12.10 can be used to upgrade server extensions of a Web server to the server extensions of the current version of FrontPage. This feature is particularly useful after upgrading to a newer version of FrontPage. When the Install button is pressed, a dialog box identical to the one shown in Figure 12.11 will ask for confirmation to upgrade the server extensions of the Web server selected.

FIGURE 12.11.
The server extensions upgrade dialog box.

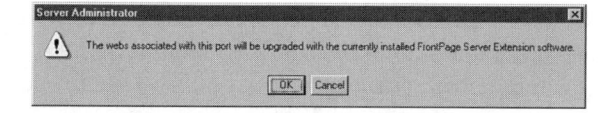

The Uninstall button can be used to uninstall server extensions from a Web server. When the Uninstall button is pressed, a dialog box similar to the one shown in Figure 12.12 will ask for confirmation before proceeding to uninstall server extensions from the Web server selected. As mentioned in Figure 12.12, this action will not delete the contents of a Web site. Only FrontPage server extensions will be removed.

FIGURE 12.12.
The server extensions uninstall dialog box.

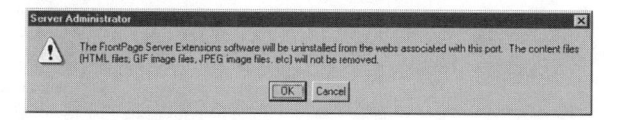

The Check button can be used to verify whether server extensions for a Web server have been installed properly. When the Check button is pressed, if a dialog identical to the one shown in Figure 12.13 is not displayed, it means the server extensions have not been installed properly; in which case, you might want to try and reinstall FrontPage server extensions using the Install button.

FIGURE 12.13.
The Check button of the FrontPage Server Administrator can be used to check the status of server extensions installed on a Web server.

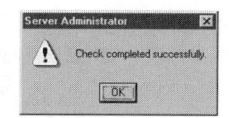

The Authoring button can be used to control whether a Web server's content can be authored using FrontPage. When the Authoring button is pressed, a dialog box similar to the one shown in Figure 12.14 will confirm that you wish to change authoring settings on the Web server selected.

FIGURE 12.14.
The Enable/Disable Authoring dialog box.

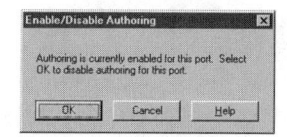

The Security button is used to administer various security settings of FrontPage server extensions. It can be used to assign a password to a Web of documents managed by FrontPage as well as to limit which computers can manage a Web site using FrontPage server extensions.

When the Security button is pressed, a dialog box similar to the one shown in Figure 12.15 will be displayed. This dialog box can be used to specify a user name and a password that can be used to author a Web site managed with FrontPage.

FIGURE 12.15.
A user name and password can be used to make sure unauthorized persons do not make changes to your Web site using FrontPage.

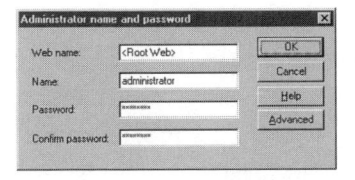

The Advanced button in the dialog box shown in Figure 12.15 can be used to specify which computers can use FrontPage to manage the contents of a Web site. If your Web site will only be managed by computers in your own domain, it is recommended that you change the default setting to match your domain name's IP address. Note that this dialog box accepts numeric Internet IP addresses. Your IP address can be found by executing the FrontPage TCP_IP Test icon. This icon can be found in the FrontPage Start Menu folder shown in Figure 12.4. When it is executed, it will display your IP address, as shown in Figure 12.16.

FIGURE 12.16.
The FrontPage TCP/IP Test application can be used to find the IP address of your computer.

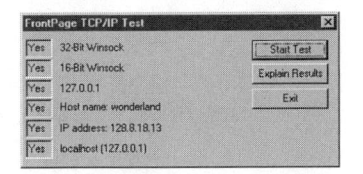

If you would like to make sure no other computers can make modifications to your Web site using FrontPage, you might want to enter your IP address in the dialog box shown in Figure 12.17. Even if you do not specify an IP address in Figure 12.17, FrontPage still requests a user name and a password before users are allowed to make changes to your Web site. When specifying an IP address, it has to be a numeric IP address that has four numbers (1-256) separated by periods. A wildcard character (*) can be used instead of a digit. For example, `128.*.*.*` allows all computers whose IP addresses begin with 128 to administer a FrontPage Web site.

FIGURE 12.17.
Internet address restriction dialog box.

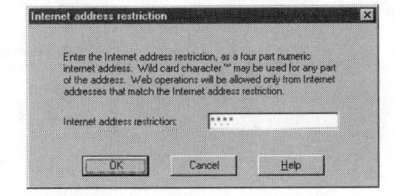

The FrontPage Explorer

FrontPage Explorer is a powerful utility that can be used to view your Web site from a different perspective. Although it is possible to view the contents of a Web site using File Manager or Windows NT Explorer, these applications were not meant to be used to view the contents of a Web site. For example, when you look at your document root directory using a utility such as Windows NT Explorer, you will most likely see several directories and files. However, you will not be able to find out information such as what these files are, what is in these files, or if they have any URLs that point to your Web site or other Web sites. Most importantly, there is no way to find out if hyperlinks at your Web site actually work at all without checking them individually.

FrontPage Explorer solves all these problems by enabling Web site developers to look at Web sites they create in a new perspective. This section will demonstrate how FrontPage Explorer can be used to effortlessly manage the contents of a Web site. When it is first invoked, FrontPage Explorer looks similar to the window in Figure 12.18. Select File | Open Web from the dialog box shown in Figure 12.18 to invoke the Open Web dialog box shown in Figure 12.19. After selecting a Web using the Open Web dialog box, you can manage it using FrontPage Explorer.

FIGURE 12.18.
FrontPage Explorer.

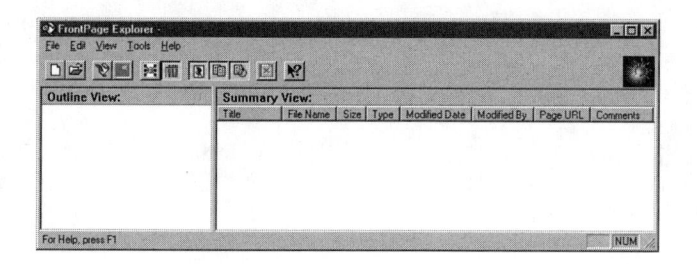

After invoking the Open Web dialog box, type in the address of your server as shown in Figure 12.19. If the server you wish to manage is installed in a different port than port 80, specify its port name by preceding the port number with a colon. Afterwards, click the List Webs button in Figure 12.19 and you will see various Webs installed on the Web server you selected. Select <Root Web> as shown in the Open Web dialog box and press OK to continue. You then will have to type in a user name and password to administer the Web you selected in Figure 12.19.

FIGURE 12.19.
The Open Web dialog box.

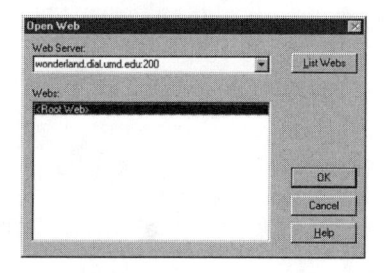

FrontPage Explorer then will extract information about the Web selected in Figure 12.19 and display the information graphically, as shown in Figure 12.20. After you install FrontPage, it defaults to the Summary View. Select View | Link View from the menu bar to see the Link

View. As you can see in Figure 12.20, the Outline View pane lists various home pages and the Link View pane graphically displays various URLs that are part of the Web page selected in Outline View. If you wish to edit a Web page shown in Link View, simply double-click it. You then will be able to edit it using FrontPage Editor. Note the plus and minus buttons that appear in the upper-left corner of some Web pages. Also note how the Web tree of the page selected in Figure 12.20 is expanded and how there is a minus sign in the upper-left corner of this page. If a Web page has a plus sign in its upper-left corner, it means that document has URLs that link to other Web pages. If you click the plus sign, the plus sign will change into a minus sign and you will see all the URLs in that page, as shown in Figure 12.20.

FIGURE 12.20.
FrontPage Explorer can be used graphically to view the contents of a Web site.

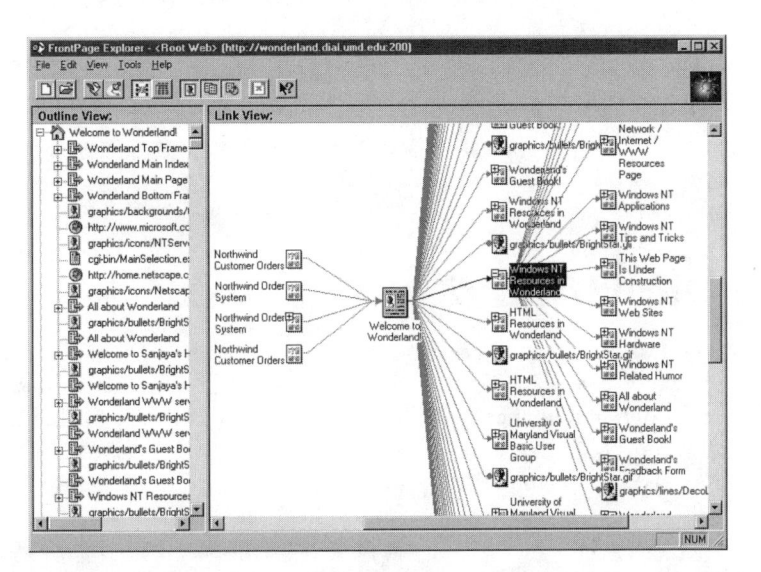

Although the graphical view shown in Figure 12.20 is useful for viewing how Web pages in a Web site are connected to each other, it does not give much information about various files at a Web site. More detailed information about a Web site can be obtained by selecting View | Summary View from the main menu. As you can see in Figure 12.21, Summary View is ideal for obtaining detailed information about a Web site. Note that the various columns in Summary View can be sorted by clicking the description label at the top of each column. This feature is powerful. For example, certain Web pages at your Web site may use graphics files that are too large to be transferred over a POTS link in a reasonable period of time. Such graphics files can be easily singled out by clicking the Size column and sorting files based on their file size.

As you can see in Figure 12.21, FrontPage Explorer is a powerful tool that can be used to graphically manage the contents of a Web site. FrontPage Explorer can be used to exploit capabilities of FrontPage because it is integrated with various components of FrontPage, such as the To Do List and the program that verifies URLs of Web pages. Be sure to spend some time with FrontPage Explorer to become more familiar with it and realize its potential.

FIGURE 12.21.
Summary View can be used to obtain detailed information about various files at a Web site.

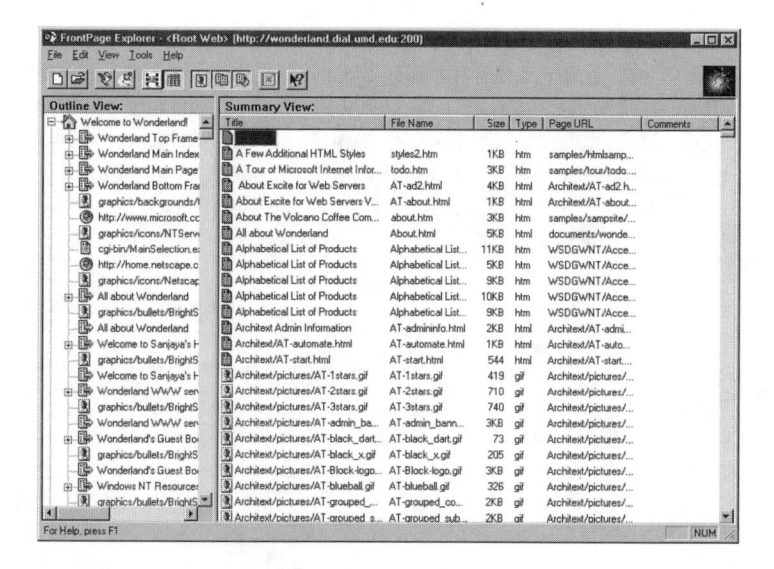

The FrontPage To Do List

The FrontPage To Do List can be used to keep track of various tasks that have to be done as shown in Figure 12.22. Because it is integrated with other components of FrontPage, such as the program that checks for broken links, the FrontPage To Do List is ideal for keeping track of various tasks that have to be done to maintain a Web site. The FrontPage To Do List can be invoked by selecting Tools | Show To Do List from the main menu.

FIGURE 12.22.
The FrontPage To Do List.

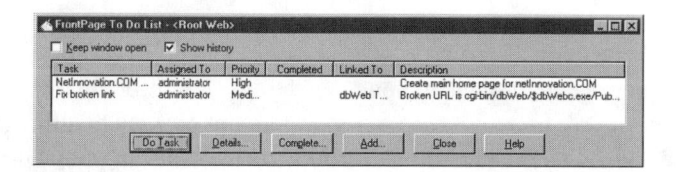

New tasks can be added to the To Do List by clicking the Add button. When the Add button is pressed, a dialog box similar to the one shown in Figure 12.23 will be displayed to gather information about the task being added to the To Do List. As shown in Figure 12.23, this dialog box can be used to type in the name and description of a task along with its level of priority.

FIGURE 12.23.
Adding a task to the FrontPage To Do List.

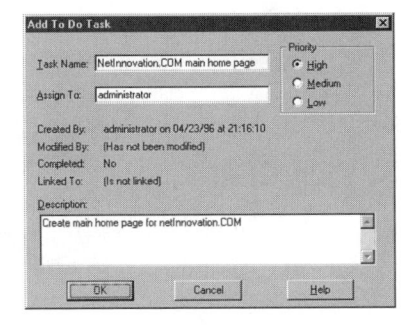

Verifying Links

After setting up a Web site, it is inevitable that at some point the Web pages are going to have broken URLs for objects that no longer exist. It is important that you check your Web site periodically for broken links. An application that can be used to verify links at a Web site is included with FrontPage. This utility can be invoked by selecting Tools | Verify Links from the main menu. As you can see in Figure 12.24, the Verify Links utility can be used to locate invalid URLs of a Web site as well as Web pages that contain them.

FIGURE 12.24.
FrontPage can be used to verify URLs of a Web page.

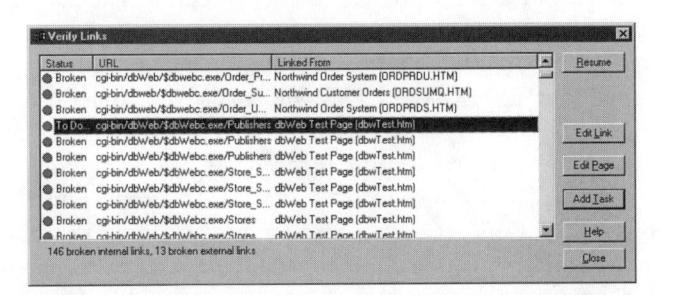

If you want, you can add a broken link to the To Do List so you can take care of it another time. Refer to Figure 12.22 for an example of a broken link added to the To Do List. Invalid URLs can be added to the To Do List by clicking the Add Task button in Figure 12.24. It is also possible to immediately correct broken links by clicking the Edit Link button and correcting the URL, as shown in Figure 12.25. Also, the Edit Page button can be used to edit the Web page containing the broken URL.

FIGURE 12.25.
FrontPage can be used to verify URLs of a Web page.

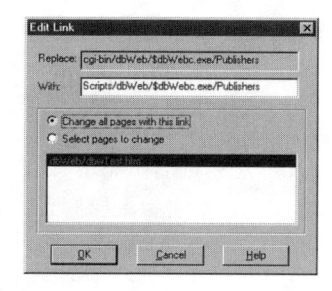

The FrontPage Editor

The FrontPage Editor is a powerful WYSIWYG HTML editor that can be used to create Web pages with tables, frames, and other HTML 2.0 enhancements. The purpose of this section is not to comprehensively cover all aspects of the FrontPage Editor. However, a few key features of it will be discussed shortly to provide you an overview of some of its capabilities.

Designing Web Pages Using the FrontPage Editor

The FrontPage Editor is a powerful HTML editor that can be used to create and edit Web pages. Although it is possible to invoke the FrontPage Editor as a standalone application or through the FrontPage Explorer, it is recommended you first open an existing Web and then open the FrontPage Explorer. This will enable you to use features of FrontPage Explorer to create and edit Web pages. It is recommended that you spend some time and become familiar with FrontPage Explorer because it can be used to view Web pages at a Web site in a more natural manner, and you can edit Web pages by simply double-clicking them. The next few sections will help you get started with FrontPage. Before proceeding to the next section, bring up FrontPage Explorer, select a Web, and then select Tools | Show FrontPage Editor from the main menu. Doing this will enable you to save Web documents edited with FrontPage into an existing Web.

Document Attributes

Various document formatting attributes of a Web page can be defined using the FrontPage Editor. For example, when creating a new document, you might want to assign colors to various elements of the Web page. This can be done by selecting Edit | Properties from the main menu. You then will be presented with a dialog box similar to the one shown in Figure 12.26. This dialog box can be used to assign a title to a Web page to customize its appearance.

Text in a Web page can be formatted by first selecting the text using the mouse and selecting Format | Characters from the main menu. By using a dialog box identical to the one shown in Figure 12.27, you then will be able to format the text you selected. The Choose button can be used to change the color of the text selected. This feature is handy for emphasizing a paragraph or heading. After selecting various text formatting options, press the OK button to apply them to the text selected.

FIGURE 12.26.
The Page Properties dialog box.

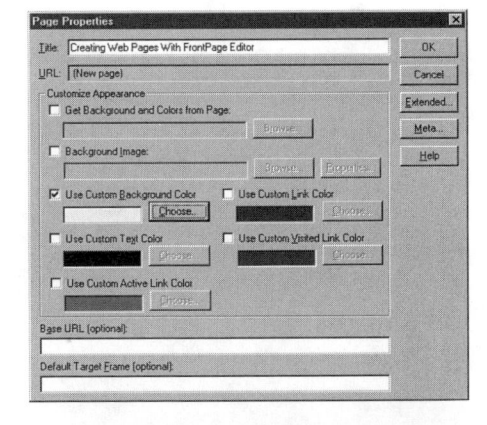

FIGURE 12.27.
The text formatting dialog box.

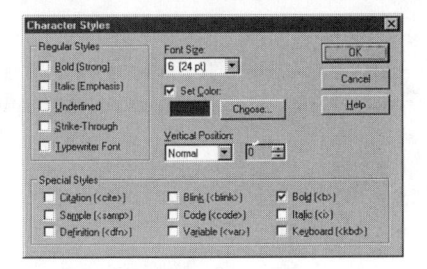

Frames

Frames can make a Web site easier and more interesting to navigate when they are used properly. It's easy to create a multiframe Web page with FrontPage. In order to create a Web page with frames, select File | New from the main menu. You then will be presented with the dialog box shown in Figure 12.28. Use the scroll-down list in this dialog box to select the Frames Wizard, as shown in Figure 12.28, and press OK to continue.

FIGURE 12.28.
The Frames Wizard can be used to create a Web page with frames.

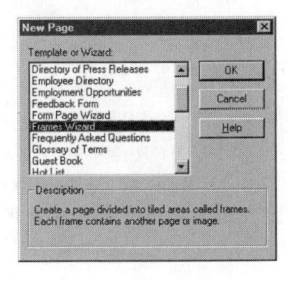

The next dialog box, shown in Figure 12.29, can be used to create a multiframe Web page using a custom grid or frames template. Generally, you should select to create a multiframe Web page using a custom grid if you are familiar with Frames and have an unusual frame set in mind. If not, select to create a Web page using a frames template. After selecting the Pick a template radio button, click the Next button.

FIGURE 12.29.
The frame creation technique dialog box.

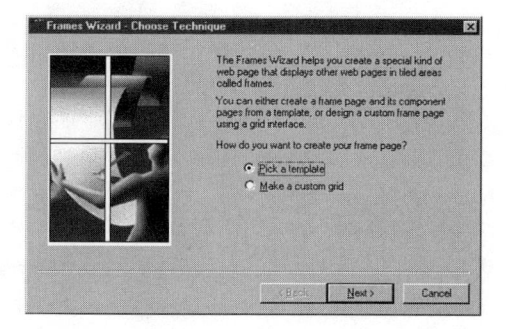

You then will see a dialog box similar to the one shown in Figure 12.30. This dialog box can be used to select the layout of various frames on your Web page. Select a layout you like and press the OK button to continue. When selecting the layout of frames, be considerate toward users who might browse your Web site with 640×480 resolution monitors. After creating a frame set, take a look at it after resizing your Web browser window to 640×480 pixels to make sure everything is legible.

FIGURE 12.30.
The frame layout selection dialog box.

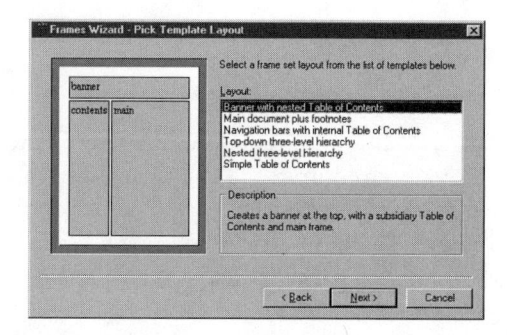

When creating Web pages with frames, be aware that some Web browsers do not support frames. Although the percentage of users using technologically challenged Web browsers is going down, you should make sure a user browsing your Web site with an older browser can still view the contents of your Web site. A Web page that will be shown to users whose browsers do not support frames can be specified using the dialog box shown in Figure 12.31.

Designing and Managing a Web Site with FrontPage

Chapter 12 353

FIGURE 12.31.
Alternate content page URL for Web browsers that do not support frames.

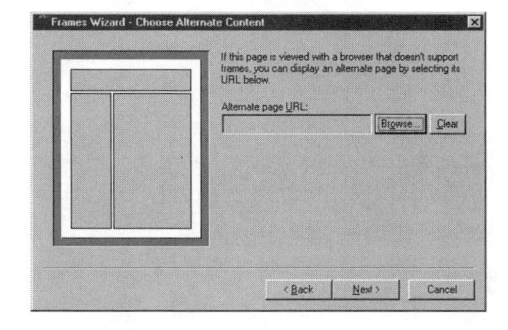

FrontPage will finally ask you for the title of your multiframe Web page and its filename as shown in Figure 12.32. Fill in the information requested and click the Finish button to continue. FrontPage then will create your multiframe Web page.

FIGURE 12.32.
Page information dialog box.

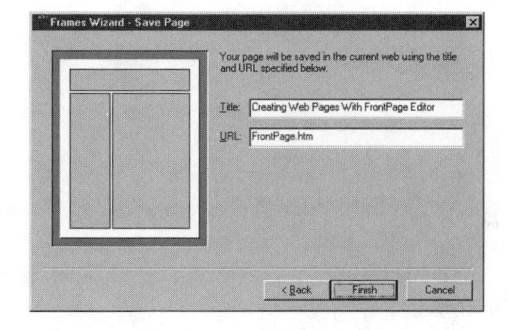

If you go back to FrontPage Explorer, you will see the multiframe Web page that was just created, as shown in Figure 12.33. Note how the Web page that was just created is broken down into three separate Web pages. Each of these Web pages holds the contents of a frame. A frame can be edited by selecting and double-clicking the corresponding file in the Link View pane of FrontPage Explorer.

FIGURE 12.33.
A multiframe document just created when viewed with FrontPage Explorer. Various frames can be edited by double-clicking them.

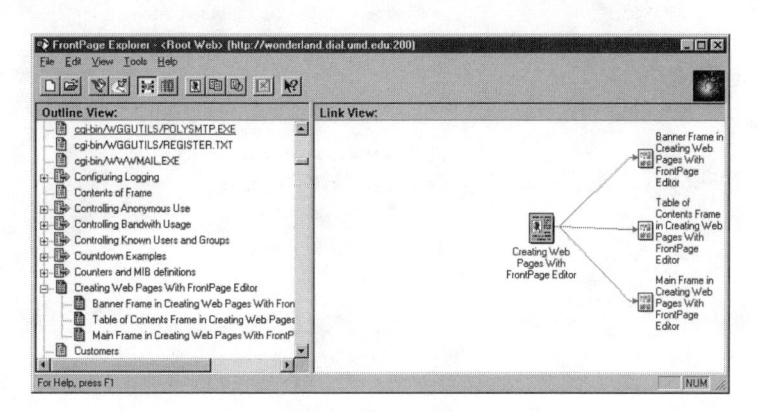

Tables

The table menu option can be used to add tables to a Web page. The following example illustrates how a table can be inserted into a Web page. Select Table | Insert Table to insert a table into a Web page. You then will see a dialog box similar to the one shown in Figure 12.34. This dialog box can be used to specify the number of columns and rows in a table as well as several other attributes.

FIGURE 12.34.
The Insert Table dialog box.

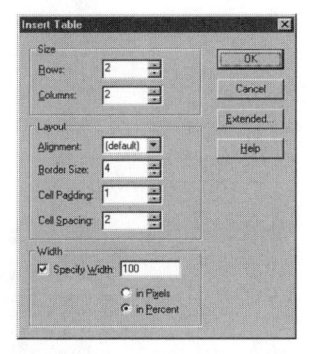

After a table is created, text and images can be inserted into various cells the same way text and images are inserted into regular Web pages. Images can be inserted by selecting Insert | Image from the main menu. By default, the columns of a two-column table have equal width. As shown in Figure 12.35, this is not ideal for some cases. The image in Figure 12.35 is cut off because the left column takes up too much space. This can be fixed by placing the mouse pointer on the left column and clicking the right mouse button. You then will see the pop-up menu shown in Figure 12.35.

FIGURE 12.35.
The right mouse button can be used to format cells in a table.

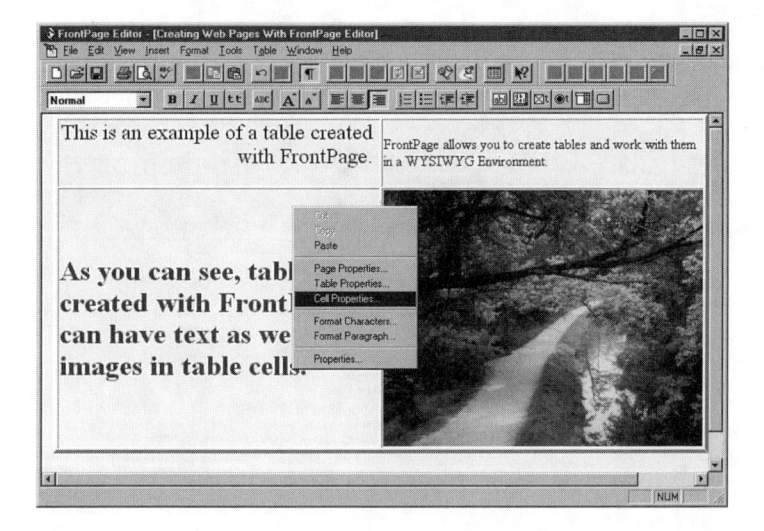

Select Cell Properties to change the width of the left column. You then will see a dialog box that can be used to define the width of a column, as shown in Figure 12.36. In order to reduce the width of the left column, a lower percentage value can be specified for the width of the column. A cell width value of 30 percent is used in this example to reduce the size of the left column.

FIGURE 12.36.
Cell Properties dialog box.

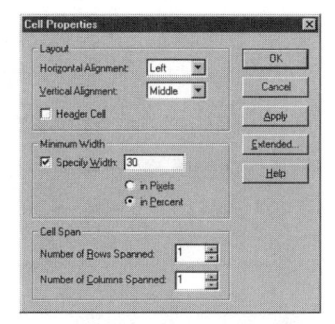

See Figure 12.37 for the result of the modification made in Figure 12.36. Note how the entire image now can be displayed on the window when the width of the left column is reduced. Tables are useful for formatting the contents of a Web site. As demonstrated in this example, the right mouse button can be used to format cells of a table and have more control over the contents of a table cell.

FIGURE 12.37.
Table after its left column size is reduced.

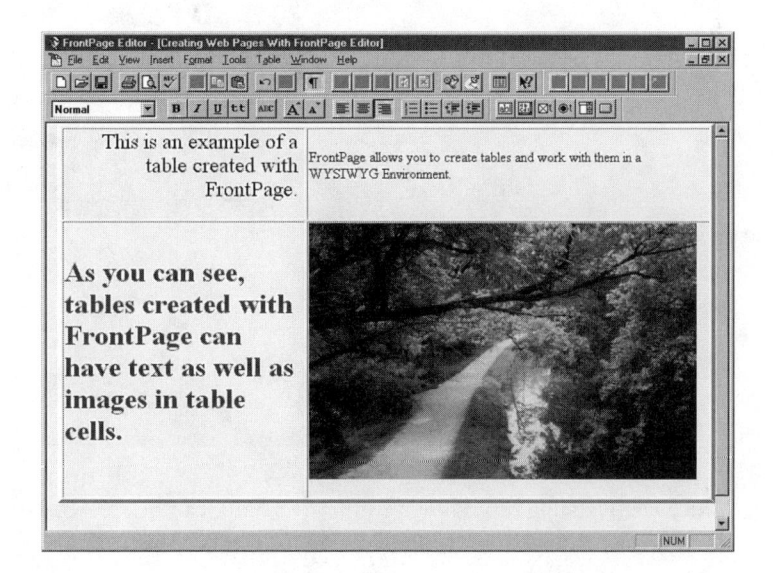

FrontPage Scripts

FrontPage scripts can be used to effortlessly add CGI programs to a Web site. For example, if you would like to set up a guest book at your Web site, one can be set up with FrontPage in just a few minutes. Setting up a guest book is as simple as selecting File | New from the main menu and selecting the Guest Book option, as shown in Figure 12.38.

FIGURE 12.38.
Selecting the Guest Book template.

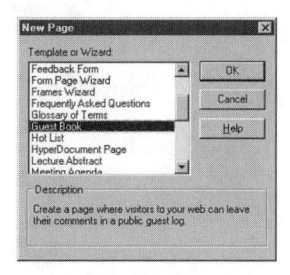

The Guest Book template then will be loaded into the FrontPage Editor as shown in Figure 12.39. You can edit the Guest Book page as you want by changing the font and maybe adding a few images. Afterwards, select File | Save from the main menu to save the Guest Book Web page.

FIGURE 12.39.
Editing the Guest Book Web page.

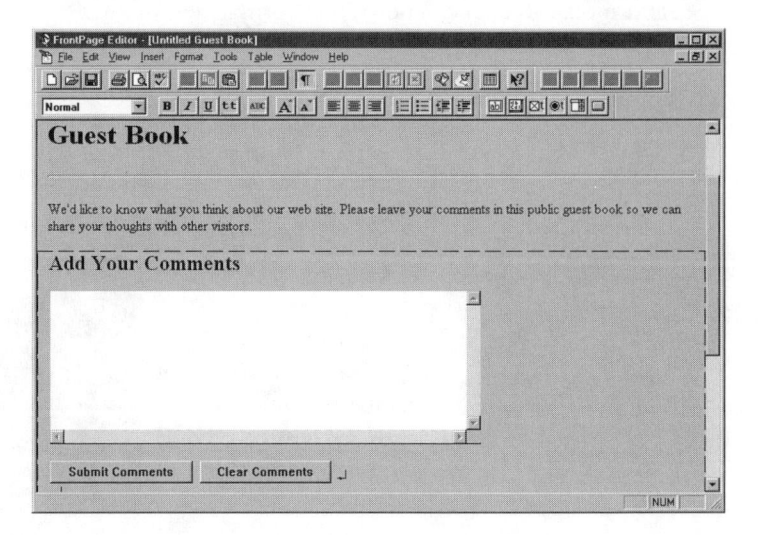

The Save As dialog box, shown in Figure 12.40, can be used to save the guest book Web page and give it a title. After typing in a title for the Web page and a filename for the Guest Book, click the OK button to save the file.

FIGURE 12.40.
Saving the Guest Book Web page.

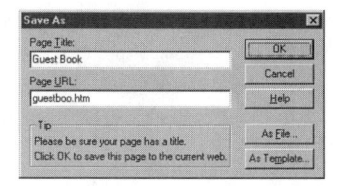

Users now can connect to your Web server and sign your guest book using the filename specified in Figure 12.40. See Figure 12.41 for an example of how a user can connect to your Web server and sign the guest book.

FIGURE 12.41.
The Guest Book setup using the FrontPage Editor is immediately functional.

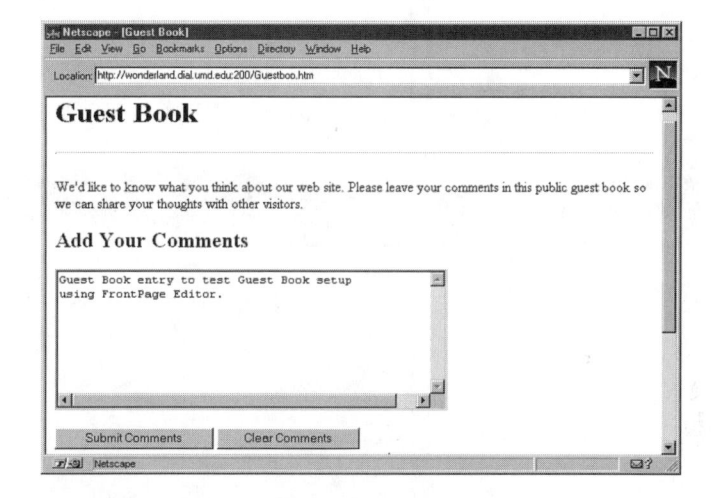

After a user types in a guest book entry and presses the Submit Comments button, the information is sent to a FrontPage CGI (Common Gateway Interface) program for processing. After the information is processed, FrontPage will display a message as shown in Figure 12.42. This message also has a link to go back to the previous page.

When a user either clicks the link to go back to the previous page or manually goes back and reloads the Guest Book Web page, the entry that was just added will be displayed as shown in Figure 12.43. As you can see from this example, CGI applications that are built into FrontPage are powerful. For example, a guest book can be set up using FrontPage—without writing a single line of CGI code—in about five minutes. Experiment with other FrontPage CGI scripts and incorporate them into your Web site to make it more interactive.

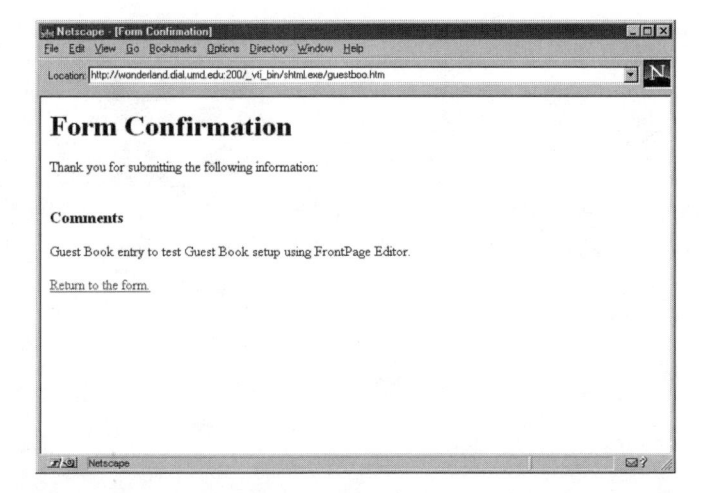

FIGURE 12.42.
The Guest Book entry confirmation message.

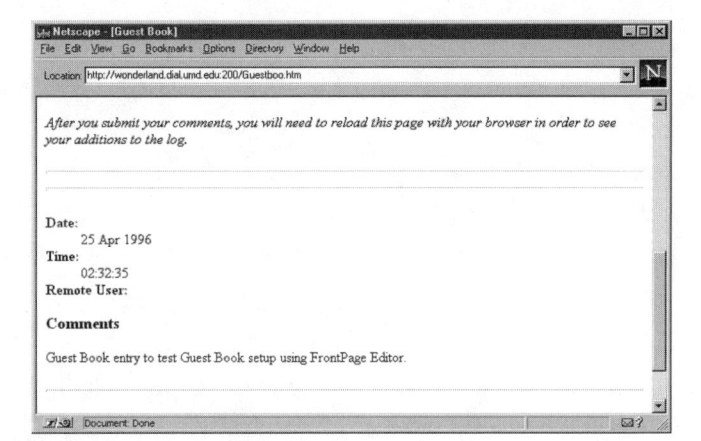

FIGURE 12.43.
The Guest Book entry confirmation message.

Creating Web Pages Using Templates

Web pages also can be created using predefined document templates. In order to create a document using a predefined template, select File | New from the main menu and select a template that best resembles the page you wish to create. Experiment with various FrontPage templates and become more familiar with using them. You then will be able to save time by using templates to create routine Web pages.

Summary

FrontPage is a powerful, yet easy-to-use Web page development application that can be used to manage the contents of a Web site. Because FrontPage is part of Microsoft Office, it is likely that it will be integrated with various Microsoft Office applications in the future. Because FrontPage can be used to create interactive Web pages without writing CGI programs or worrying about details of HTML, it is an ideal application to use to easily create a Web site.

Publishing on the Web with Microsoft Office

IN THIS CHAPTER

- Microsoft Office and the Internet **362**
- Publishing on the Web with Micosoft Word **362**
- Publishing on the Web with Microsoft Excel **368**
- Publishing on the Web with Microsoft PowerPoint **372**
- Publishing on the Web with Microsoft Access **375**

Various Microsoft Office applications can be used to publish information on the Internet. This capability is particularly useful for effortlessly publishing existing MS Office documents on the Web. There are many advantages to using Microsoft Office Internet Assistants to create content for your Web site. One of the most significant benefits is the capability to enable those who create content to publish it on the Internet without waiting for someone else to convert it into HTML. For example, the person who puts together a sales report is probably not a Web developer. Having someone else convert the sales report into an HTML file is not only a waste of resources but can also be time consuming. On the other hand, using Internet Assistant for Microsoft Word or Excel, the person who created the sales report can easily publish the information on the Internet or an intranet without waiting for someone else to go through the sales report and add a few funny HTML tags here and there.

Visit the Microsoft Office Web site for more information about using various Internet Assistants to publish content on the Internet.

> **NOTE**
>
> The Microsoft Office Web site is located at
>
> `http://www.microsoft.com/msoffice/`

Microsoft Office and the Internet

The next few sections will demonstrate how Microsoft Word, Excel, PowerPoint, and Access documents can be published on the Web using various Internet Assistants. Internet Assistants are special add-on programs that can be downloaded from Microsoft's Web site. These applications are designed to seamlessly integrate with various office applications and extend their functionality by allowing office documents to be saved as HTML documents. Note that most Internet Assistants covered in later sections require Microsoft Office for Windows 95.

> **NOTE**
>
> Microsoft's Internet tools for Microsoft Office Web page can be found at
>
> `http://www.microsoft.com/MSOffice/MSOfc/it_ofc.htm`

Publishing on the Web with Microsoft Word

Microsoft Word is a feature-rich word processing application. Internet Assistant (IA) for Microsoft Word can be used to effortlessly publish Word files on the Internet. As you will be shown shortly, it can also be used as a WYSIWYG HTML editor. At the time of this writing, in addition to various standard HTML 2.0 tags, Internet Assistant for Word also supports various HTML enhancements such as tables, table cell colors, TrueType fonts, and font colors.

Internet Assistant is not part of Microsoft Word. Before using it to create content for the Web, Internet Assistant for Microsoft Word has to be downloaded from Microsoft's Web site.

> **NOTE**
>
> Microsoft Internet Assistant for Word download site:
>
> ```
> http://www.microsoft.com/msword/internet/ia/ia95/chcklist.htm
> ```

Installing Internet Assistant for Word

After downloading the Internet Assistant for Word from Microsoft's Web site, simply execute the executable file and specify a directory where IA for Word should be installed. Note that it is recommended you close all applications before installing IA for Word, because the installation program might need to copy several shared DLL files. When IA for Word is installed, you might get a few message boxes similar to the one shown in Figure 13.1. Simply press the Ignore button to proceed installing IA for Word. Later, if you encounter problems running IA for Word, remove applications from the Windows NT start folder, reboot NT, and then install IA for Word soon after logging in.

FIGURE 13.1.
Shared DLL files that are open and being used by other applications cannot be replaced by the Internet Assistant for Word installation program.

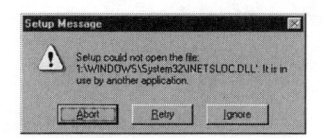

After IA for Word is installed, you will see a message box similar to the one shown in Figure 13.2. At this point, you can launch Microsoft Word and begin creating documents for the Web using Microsoft Word.

FIGURE 13.2.
Immediately after IA for Word is installed, Microsoft Word is capable of creating content for the Web.

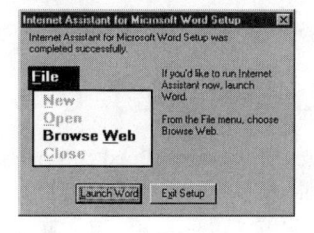

Creating an HTML Document with Word

Once IA for Word is installed, creating HTML documents is as easy as creating Word documents. This section demonstrates how various features of IA for Word can be used to create an HTML document with TrueType fonts, inline images, a table, and various other HTML attributes. In order to begin creating an HTML document, select File and New from the main menu. You will be presented with a dialog box similar to the one shown in Figure 13.3. Note the HTML document template that has been added by the IA for Word installation program.

FIGURE 13.3.
The HTML document template can be used to create HTML files with Internet Assistant.

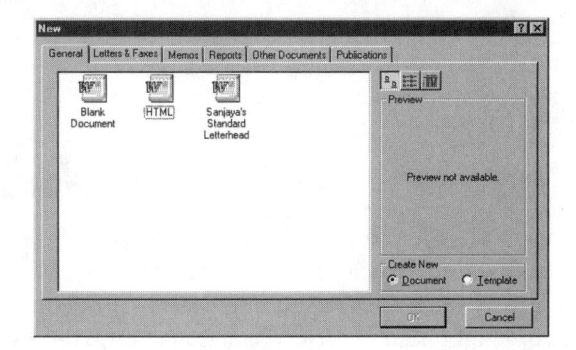

From the dialog box shown in Figure 13.3, select the HTML document template and press the OK button. You are now ready to start creating an HTML document using Microsoft Word. Before continuing to create a document, you might want to select Tools | Customize from the main menu to customize the toolbar. Because you will be shown how to add TrueType fonts to HTML files shortly, you might want to make sure the Font button shown in Figure 13.4 is added to your toolbar.

FIGURE 13.4.
The Microsoft Word toolbar can be customized with useful HTML attributes such as TrueType fonts.

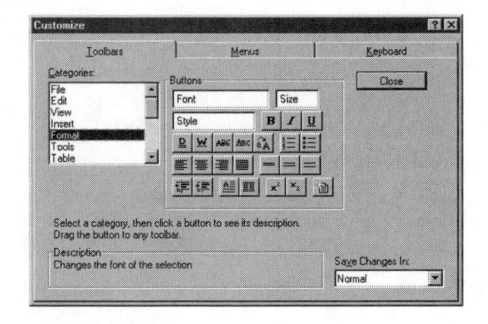

Background Images and Text Colors

HTML documents created with Word can be customized with a background image and various text attribute colors. This can be done by selecting Format | Background and Links from the main menu. By using a dialog box similar to the one shown in Figure 13.5, you will be able to specify various text attributes, colors, and a background image.

When using background images and special text colors, always use either a light-colored background and dark-colored text, or light-colored text with a dark background. Otherwise, users browsing your document will not be able to read the text. Before putting a document created with Microsoft Word on the Internet, use a Web browser to preview the documents to ensure that they are legible.

FIGURE 13.5.
The Background and Links attribute specification dialog box.

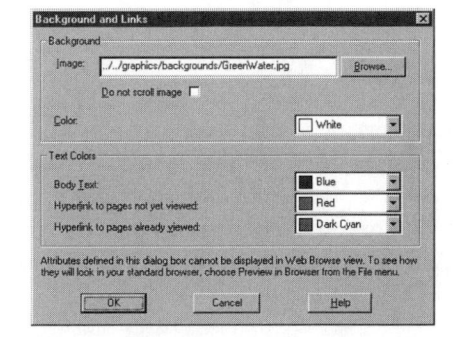

If you wish to specify a background image, click the Browse button to bring up the Insert Picture dialog box shown in Figure 13.6. This dialog box is handy for selecting backgrounds because it displays a preview of the background image on the right column. After selecting the image you wish to use, click the OK button. It is recommended that you work with a directory structure identical to that of the production Web server to make sure directory path names are compatible between the production server and the development environment in which you work.

FIGURE 13.6.
The Insert Picture dialog box can be used to add a background image to an HTML document.

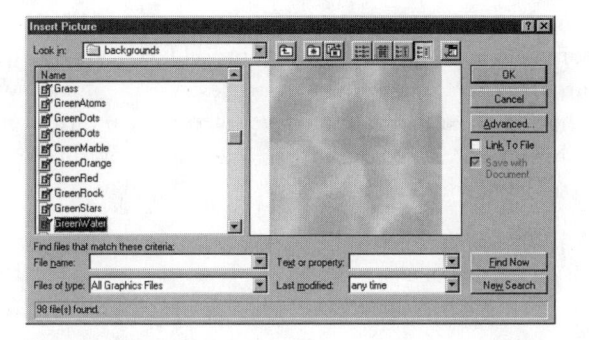

Using TrueType Fonts

Micrososft Word supports TrueType fonts in HTML documents. In order to change the font of some text, select the text and select Format | Font from the menu bar. You will then be able to specify a TrueType font typeface for the selected text using a dialog box similar to the one shown in Figure 13.7. This dialog box can also be used to specify the size and color of the selected typeface. Note that not all Web browsers support TrueType fonts.

FIGURE 13.7.
The Font specification dialog box.

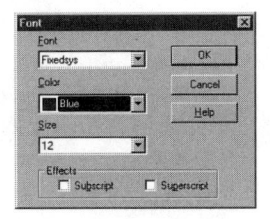

Inserting Tables

HTML documents created with Word can also have tables. Inserting a table into an HTML document is as easy as inserting a table into a Word document. Simply select Table | Insert Table, and you will see the dialog box shown in Figure 13.8. This dialog box can be used to specify the number of rows and columns the table should have. Table columns and rows can be inserted, deleted, and merged if it becomes necessary to make changes to a table after it is created.

FIGURE 13.8.
The Insert Table dialog box.

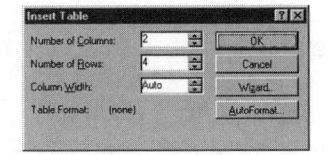

Inserting Inline Images and Video

Inline images and video clips can be inserted to an HTML document by selecting Insert | Picture from the main menu. The dialog box shown in Figure 13.9 can then be used to select an image or video clip to insert into a Word HTML document. When adding an image, use the data entry field for Alternative Text to describe the image. Web browsers such as Internet Explorer show this text in a balloon if a user rests the mouse pointer on the image. If you click the Browse button shown in Figure 13.9, a dialog box similar to the one in Figure 13.6 can be used to select an image.

FIGURE 13.9.
The inline picture insertion dialog box.

Publishing on the Web with Microsoft Office
Chapter 13

Formatting Table Cells

It is easy to format table cells of an HTML document. Simply select the cell(s) you wish to format and click the right mouse button. You will then see a pop-up menu similar to the one shown in Figure 13.10. This menu can be used to specify various cell formatting attributes. For example, if you wish to change the background of a cell, select it and click the Background Color option of the pop-up menu shown in Figure 13.10. You will then be able to define a background color for the selected cell using a Background Color dialog box similar to the one in Figure 13.11.

FIGURE 13.10.
The right mouse button can be used to format cells in a table.

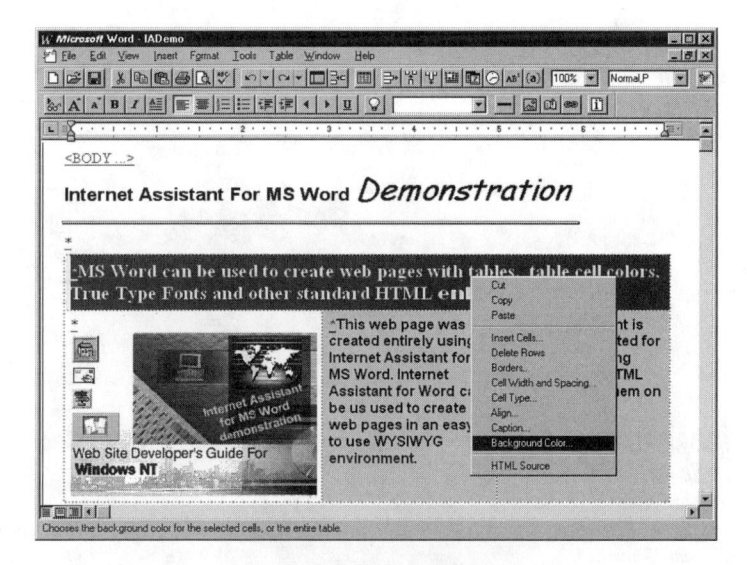

FIGURE 13.11.
The Background Color dialog box can be used to assign a color to one or more selected table cells.

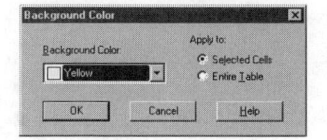

Publishing an HTML Document with Microsoft Word

Attractive HTML documents can be created with MS Word using various tips and procedures discussed earlier. An example of an HTML document created with various standard HTML 2.0 extensions such as tables and TrueType fonts is shown in Figure 13.12. After creating an HTML document with Word, publishing it on the Internet is as easy as saving the document as an HTML file.

HTML documents created with Microsoft Word can be viewed with any Web browser. The HTML document shown in Figure 13.12 looks similar to the Web page in Figure 13.13 when it is viewed with Internet Explorer. As you can see in Figure 13.13, the inline image and text in the table is appropriately formatted by IA for Word. As demonstrated in previous sections, IA for Word is a powerful Web publishing tool that can be used to leverage the power of Word to the Internet and create richly formatted Web pages.

FIGURE 13.12.
An HTML document created with Microsoft Word.

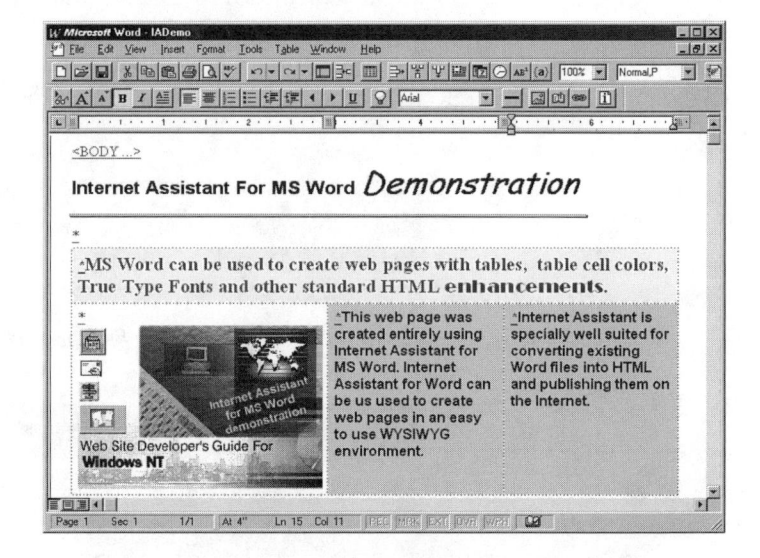

FIGURE 13.13.
A Web browser, such as Internet Explorer, can be used to view HTML documents created with Microsoft Word.

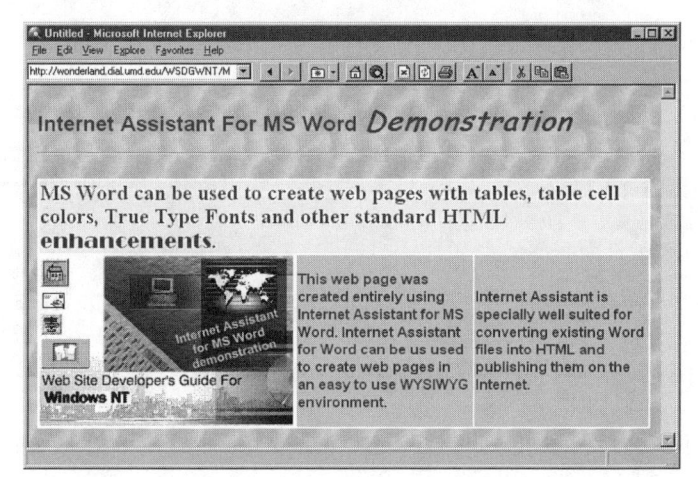

Publishing on the Web with Microsoft Excel

Internet Assistant for Excel can be used to effortlessly convert Excel spreadsheets into HTML documents so they can be published on the Web. You might want to visit the Microsoft Excel

Web page to obtain the most up-to-date information about Excel and how it can be used to create content for the Web. The next few sections illustrate how the Excel spreadsheet shown in Figure 13.14 can be converted into HTML and published on the Web.

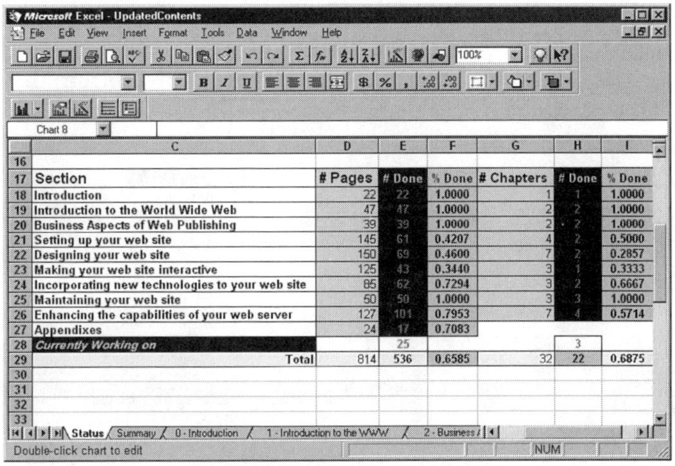

FIGURE 13.14.
Shortly, you will be shown how to convert this spreadsheet into HTML.

Incidentally, the spreadsheet shown in Figure 13.14 was actually used when this book was being written. Internet Assistant for Excel was used to regularly update the contents of the spreadsheet in Figure 13.14 to an HTML file so my acquisitions editor could monitor the progress of the book. The HTML file was stored in a secure Web server directory protected with a password. This is an example of how IA for Excel can be used to share information with selected users using a secure Web server.

> **NOTE**
>
> Use the following URL to reach the Microsoft Excel home page:
>
> http://www.microsoft.com/msexcel/default.htm

Installing Internet Assistant for Excel

Internet Assistant for Excel can be installed by following a few simple steps after downloading it from Microsoft's Web site.

> **NOTE**
>
> Internet Assistant for Microsoft Excel download site:
>
> http://www.microsoft.com/msexcel/Internet/IA/default.htm

The following are the steps you need to follow to install Internet Assistant for Excel:

1. Download Internet Assistant for Excel. This file is named HTML.XLA.
2. After downloading it, place it in the \EXCEL\LIBRARY directory if you are running a stand-alone version of Excel, and \MSOFFICE\EXCEL\LIBRARY if you are running the Microsoft Office version of Excel 7.0.
3. Start Microsoft Excel and select Tools | Add-Ins from the main menu. You will then be presented with a dialog box similar to the one shown in Figure 13.15.

FIGURE 13.15.
The Microsoft Excel tool Add-Ins dialog box.

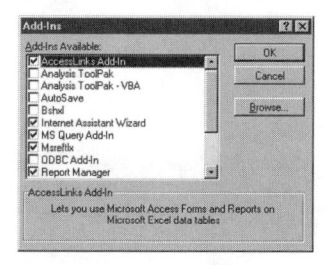

4. Locate the tool Internet Assistant Wizard, place a checkmark beside it, and click the OK button.

Internet Assistant for Microsoft Excel is now installed and ready for use.

Publishing a Spreadsheet on the Web with Excel

Internet Assistant for Excel can be used to effortlessly convert a spreadsheet into HTML. As shown in Figure 13.16, simply highlight the area of a spreadsheet you wish to convert into HTML and select Tools | Internet Assistant Wizard from the main menu.

FIGURE 13.16.
The selected area of a spreadsheet can be converted into HTML using Internet Assistant for Excel.

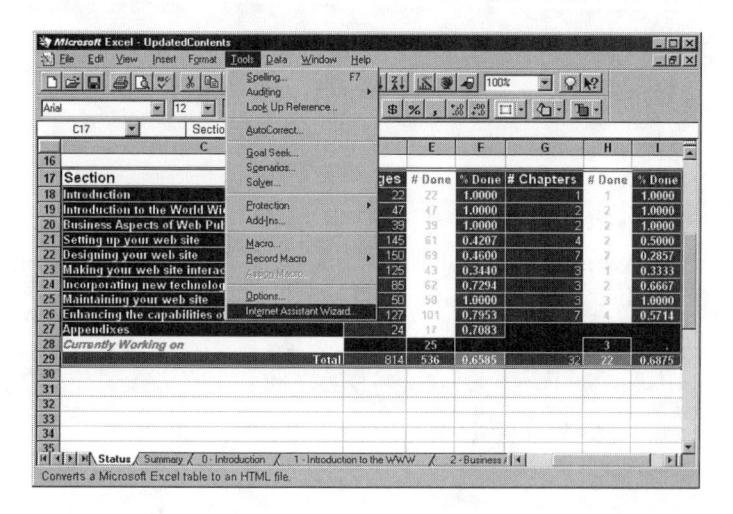

After the Internet Assistant Wizard menu option is selected, a dialog box similar to the one shown in Figure 13.17 will be displayed to confirm the area selected in Figure 13.16. At this point, you can change the area selected to be converted into HTML.

FIGURE 13.17.
Step 1 of Internet Assistant Wizard for Excel confirms the area selected in Figure 13.16.

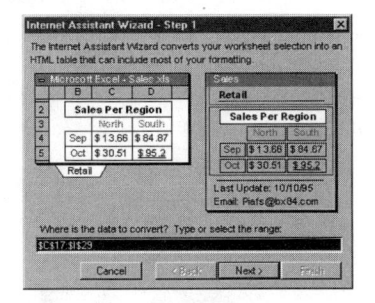

The next dialog box (see Figure 13.18) will ask if you'd like to create a new HTML file or would like the data to be inserted into an existing HTML document. Note that if you select to have the data inserted into an existing file, the file should contain the string `<!--##Table##-->`. Internet Assistant for Excel will then insert the data from the spreadsheet where it encounters the string `<!--##Table##-->`.

FIGURE 13.18.
The target HTML file selection dialog box.

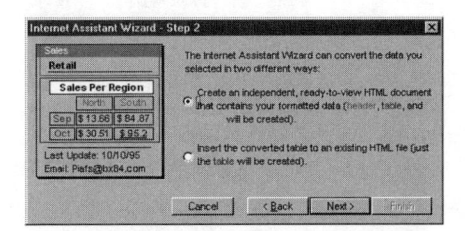

If you selected the option to create a new HTML file, a dialog box similar to the one shown in Figure 13.19 will be presented to you. This dialog box can be used to customize the HTML file created by IA for Excel.

FIGURE 13.19.
The HTML file customizing dialog box.

The next dialog box will ask if you'd like to preserve as much formatting as possible. Select this option if you'd like the HTML file created by IA for Excel to resemble the original Excel spreadsheet as much as possible. Use the other option only if you notice other browsers having problems with some of the enhanced HTML tags used by IA for Excel. If your users use Internet Explorer or Netscape, using the option to preserve as much formatting as possible will produce the best results. Afterwards, provide the HTML filename of the new file and the spreadsheet you selected in Figure 13.16 will be saved as an HTML file. After the HTML file is saved, it can be viewed with a Web browser as shown in Figure 13.20. Compare the HTML document in Figure 13.20 with the Excel spreadsheet in Figure 13.14 and note how they closely resemble each other. As illustrated in this example, it is quite easy to publish Excel spreadsheets on the Web using Internet Assistant for Excel.

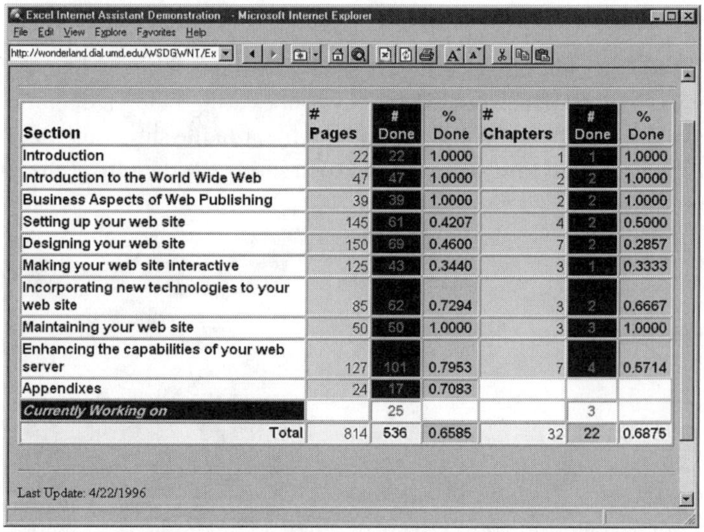

FIGURE 13.20.
The spreadsheet in Figure 13.14 after it is converted into HTML.

Section	# Pages	# Done	% Done	# Chapters	# Done	% Done
Introduction	22	22	1.0000	1	1	1.0000
Introduction to the World Wide Web	47	47	1.0000	2	2	1.0000
Business Aspects of Web Publishing	39	39	1.0000	2	2	1.0000
Setting up your web site	145	61	0.4207	4	2	0.5000
Designing your web site	150	69	0.4600	7	2	0.2857
Making your web site interactive	125	43	0.3440	3	1	0.3333
Incorporating new technologies to your web site	85	62	0.7294	3	2	0.6667
Maintaining your web site	50	50	1.0000	3	3	1.0000
Enhancing the capabilities of your web server	127	101	0.7953	7	4	0.5714
Appendixes	24	17	0.7083			
Currently Working on		25			3	
Total	814	536	0.6585	32	22	0.6875

Last Update: 4/22/1996

Publishing on the Web with Microsoft PowerPoint

PowerPoint is a powerful presentation tool that can be used to create slide show presentations on the Internet using Internet Assistant for PowerPoint. The next few sections illustrate how easy it is to create a PowerPoint presentation and save it as an HTML file. For the purpose of this demonstration, you will be shown how to convert the slides in Figure 13.21 into HTML. Visit the Microsoft PowerPoint Web page for the most up-to-date information about PowerPoint and Internet Assistant for PowerPoint.

> **NOTE**
>
> Microsoft PowerPoint Web page:
>
> http://www.microsoft.com/mspowerpoint/default.htm

FIGURE 13.21.
You will learn shortly how to convert these two slides into HTML.

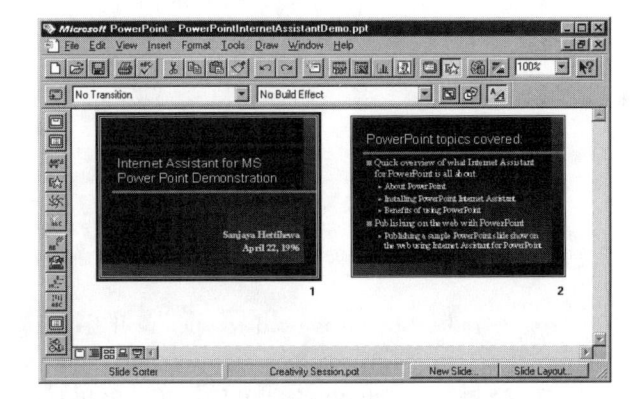

Installing PowerPoint Internet Assistant

Internet Assistant for PowerPoint can be downloaded from Microsoft's Web site. After downloading it, copy it to a temporary directory and execute the executable file. This will decompress the PowerPoint distribution file. Once the distribution file is decompressed, execute the file IA4PPT95.EXE to install Internet Assistant for PowerPoint. Before executing this file, make sure PowerPoint is not running. The installation program will then install IA for PowerPoint and terminate with a message similar to the one shown in Figure 13.22.

> **NOTE**
>
> Internet Assistant for Microsoft PowerPoint download site:
>
> http://www.microsoft.com/mspowerpoint/Internet/ia/default.htm

FIGURE 13.22.
PowerPoint Internet Assistant installation program.

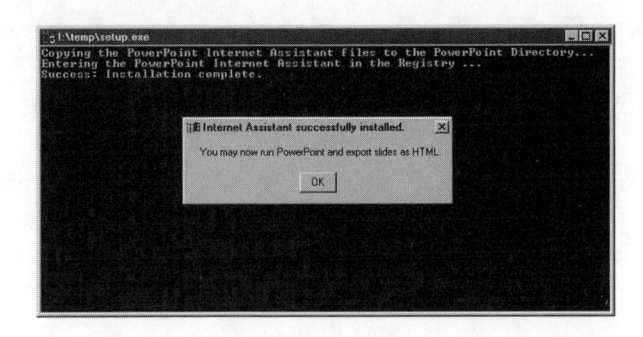

Converting a PowerPoint Slide Show into HTML

PowerPoint slides can be easily converted into HTML by selecting File | Export as HTML from the main menu. After selecting Export as HTML, a dialog box similar to the one shown in Figure 13.23 will be presented to obtain information about the output that should be generated by IA for PowerPoint.

FIGURE 13.23.
The HTML Export Options dialog box.

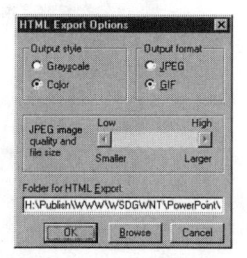

The Output style radio button is used to specify if IA for PowerPoint should output the slides in color or grayscale format. It is recommended that you select slides to be exported in color unless your slides contain only a limited number of colors and you are concerned about the size of slide files.

The next radio button is used to specify the file format of the exported PowerPoint slides. Generally, use the JPEG format for natural photograph-looking slides that do not have too many sharp edges; use the GIF format for all other slides.

If you are using the JPEG format, the slide bar in Figure 13.23 can be used to define the image quality of JPEG files. Higher image quality results in larger files and lower image quality results in smaller files. You might want to experiment with various settings to determine the ideal level of quality for your slide presentation if you are concerned about bandwidth and file sizes. Note that this is not an issue in an intranet environment where there is usually an abundance of available network bandwidth.

Finally, specify the folder that will contain the HTML version of the PowerPoint presentation and click the OK button to begin the conversion. IA for PowerPoint will then export the slide show presentation and display a message similar to the one shown in Figure 13.24.

FIGURE 13.24.
The HTML conversion dialog box.

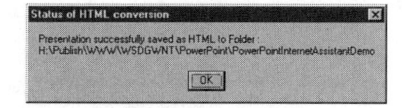

The PowerPoint presentation can now be viewed using a Web browser as shown in Figure 13.25. Note that the first page contains an index of all slides of the presentation.

FIGURE 13.25.
HTML slide presentation index.

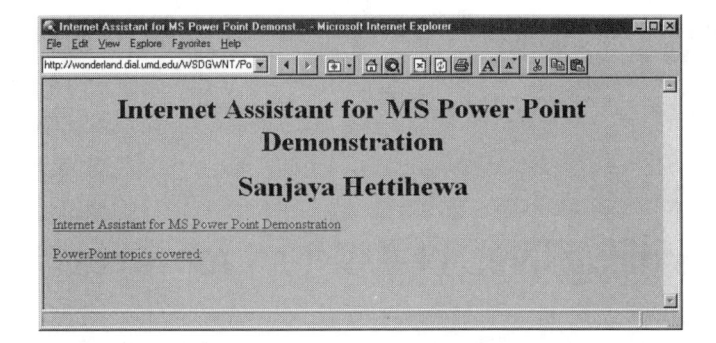

The index shown in Figure 13.25 can be used to view individual PowerPoint slides as shown in Figure 13.26. Note the navigation aids at the bottom of the slide. These navigation aids are automatically created by IA for PowerPoint to make it easier for users to browse a PowerPoint presentation using a Web browser.

FIGURE 13.26.
PowerPoint slides exported as HTML files can be viewed with a Web browser.

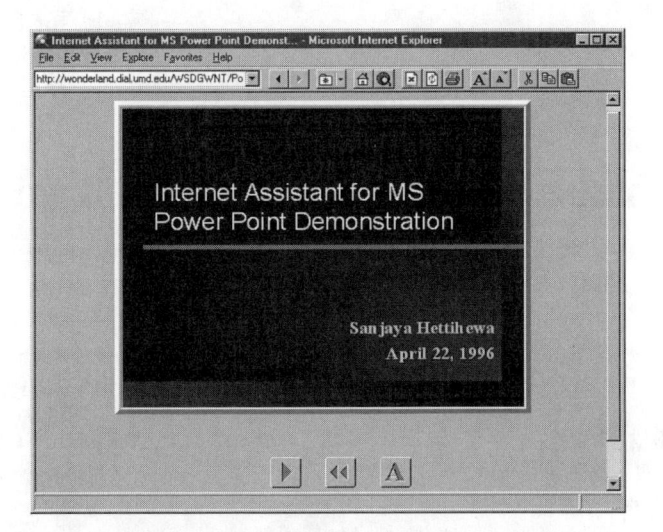

Publishing on the Web with Microsoft Access

An Internet Assistant is also available for Microsoft Access. As you will be shown shortly, information in a Microsoft Access database can be easily published on the Web using Internet Assistant for Access. Visit the Microsoft Access Internet tools Web page for the most up-to-date information about publishing Access databases on the Internet.

> **NOTE**
>
> The Microsoft Access Internet tools Web page:
>
> `http://www.microsoft.com/msaccess/it_acc.htm`

Installing Internet Assistant for Access

Internet Assistant for Microsoft Access can be downloaded from Microsoft's Web site. After downloading it, execute the executable file and allow the installation program to detect the Microsoft Access directory. After it detects the directory Access is installed in, click the large Install button to install IA for Access.

> **NOTE**
>
> Microsoft Internet Assistant for Access download site:
>
> `http://www.microsoft.com/msaccess/internet/ia/default.htm`

Publishing a Database on the Web with Access

The next few sections illustrate how a Microsoft Access database can be published on the Web using IA for Access. In order to publish an Access database, load the database into Access and select Tools | Add-ins | Internet Assistant from the main menu (see Figure 13.27). Internet Assistant for Access will then begin a welcome message. Click the Next button, and a dialog box similar to the one shown in Figure 13.28 will be displayed.

FIGURE 13.27.
The Internet Assistant for Access can be invoked from the Tools menu.

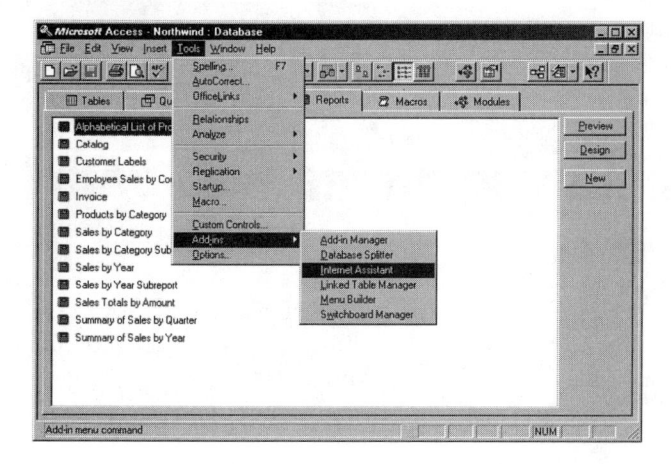

Internet Assistant for Access can be used to export any combination of Microsoft Access tables, queries, reports, and forms into HTML. This is done by selecting the object type and names of objects in that type using a dialog box similar to the one shown in Figure 13.28. Note that one or more object types and object names can be selected. For example, you might want to select several reports and several tables.

FIGURE 13.28.
Various Microsoft Access objects can be selected to be exported into HTML.

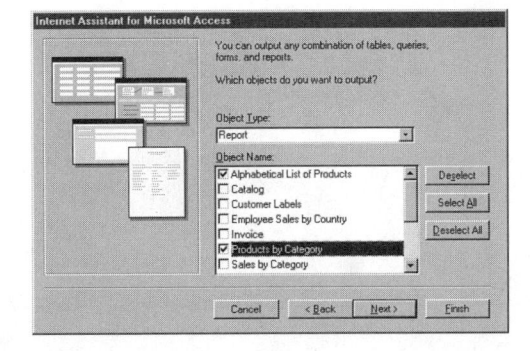

After selecting various objects to export as HTML files, click the Next button to continue. IA for Access will then present you with a dialog box similar to the one in Figure 13.29 and ask you for a template. A template can be used to enhance the appearance of data exported by IA for Access by adding a background image, navigation buttons, and various graphics to its output. Various templates included with IA for Access can be browsed by clicking the Browse button. Note that templates with filenames ending with the suffix _r are used for reports and those without _r for data sheets. When several object types are selected, select the template without the _r suffix and IA for Access will apply the correct template based on its filename.

FIGURE 13.29.
A template can be used to format HTML output generated by Internet Assistant for Access.

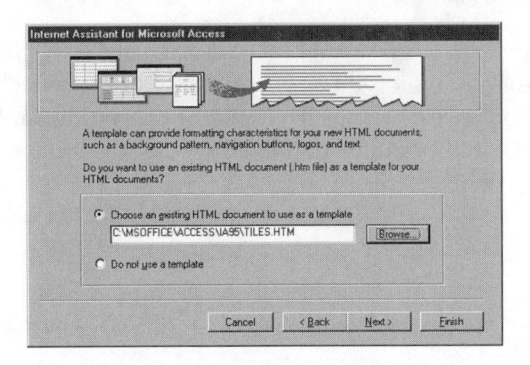

After selecting a template, type in a directory that will contain the exported HTML files. After typing in the directory, click the Finish button to export selected objects as HTML files. IA for Access will then export selected objects and let you know when it has finished creating the HTML files. The exported data can then be viewed using a Web browser as shown in Figure 13.30.

FIGURE 13.30.
Data exported by IA for Access can be viewed with a Web browser.

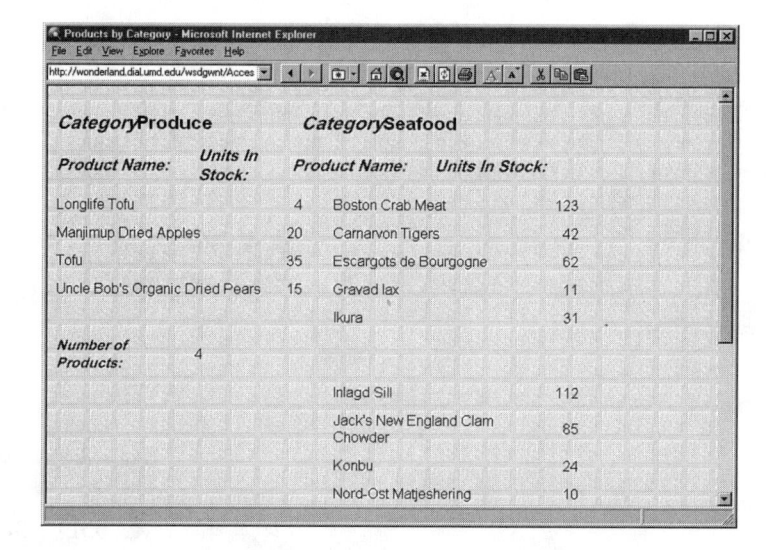

Note that IA for Microsoft Access might not always copy all the graphic files that are part of the HTML files it creates into the target HTML directory. Use a Web browser to look at HTML files that IA for Access creates. If you see any broken images, look at the source code to locate graphic files it refers to and copy them to the target HTML directory. These graphics files are located in the \MSOFFICE\ACCESS\IA95 directory (assuming you installed Office 95 into the \MSOFFICE directory). If you do not feel like doing this, you might want to copy all the graphic files from the \MSOFFICE\ACCESS\IA95 directory to the target HTML directory.

Summary

Microsoft Office is a powerful suite of productivity applications. Various Internet Assistants available for Microsoft Office can be used to effortlessly publish content for the Internet. These Internet assistants are especially useful for converting large amounts of Microsoft Office files into HTML so they can be published on the global Internet or a local intranet.

Using Asymetrix Web3D and Corel's Web Designer

14

IN THIS CHAPTER

- Using Asymetrix Web3D **380**
- Using Corel's Web. Designer **387**

When you create your initial Web site, your goal is to publish content on the Internet and to get it up and running as quickly as possible. This usually means that the design is strictly functional and text based. If you have a dedicated graphic-design staff, you may also have graphic banners, buttons, backgrounds, rules, or images. If you do not have a dedicated graphic-design staff, however, you have a lot of work ahead of you to create these graphical objects. You can use any graphical application, such as CorelPHOTO–PAINT, which can export GIF or JPEG file formats to create these objects. The alternative to spending days or weeks creating these images is to use a tool specifically designed for Internet WWW site development.

In this chapter you will explore two of these tools to add pizzazz to your site. The first of these tools is Asymetrix Web 3D, which can be used to create three-dimensional static objects such as a banner or button, and animated objects such as a helicopter or a banner where each character of text drops from the top down one at a time until the entire text message is displayed. The second tool is Corel's Web.Designer, which includes three tools to help get you up and running on the Web as quickly as possible. The first tool is CorelWEB.DESIGNER, which is a basic Windows HTML editor. CorelWEB.DESIGNER also includes several HTML templates. The next tool is called CorelWEB.GALLERY, which is a collection of prebuilt banners, buttons, rules, special characters, and clip art. The final tool in the package is CorelWEB.Transit, which is used to convert documents you already have (like Word for Windows documents) into HTML pages.

Although there are many other tools available to help you in your Web page development, I chose Web 3D and Corel's Web.Designer for two reasons. First, they are inexpensive. Each of these tools costs less than $100. Second, these tools demonstrate the basic types of tools that are available: special effects (like Web 3D) and quick development (like Corel's Web.Designer). Both Web 3D and Corel's Web.Designer also include clip art, or templates, to save you some development time.

Using Asymetrix Web 3D

As the name implies, Asymetrix Web 3D can be used to render a three-dimensional object in a two-dimensional picture. This picture is referred to as a *snapshot* within the application context. A snapshot can be exported as a GIF or JPEG bitmap image. The application, however, does much more than just create static 3D images. It can be used to build animated objects exported as an audio-video interleave (AVI) file. It includes several prebuilt templates that you can use as a starting point for building a very impressive Web page. It also includes many prebuilt objects (such as backgrounds, banners, buttons, and rules) that you can incorporate into your Web pages.

You should be aware of a couple items before you run amok with Web 3D:

- Rendering 3D objects is very resource intensive. For example, when I rendered a 3D revolving welcome sign consisting of 61 frames into an AVI file, it required over 90 percent of both of my 166MHz Pentium processors, maxed out my disk drives, and used about 50MB of paging file space. And it still took over an hour to create the finished AVI file. Rendering simpler static objects requires fewer resources, but is still very time-consuming.

- When you have completed the design of your image, you will need to export the snapshot to either a GIF or JPEG file. You can use this snapshot image as a simple background, but if you want to use the various objects as inline graphics, as a hot-linked button (to jump to another URL, for example), or as an image map, then you will need another graphics application to cut out the individual objects. Finally, you'll need to create the HTML document to include the various objects you created.

- Too many graphical objects on a single Web page may require more Internet bandwidth than your user has patience for, particularly on a 14.4Kbps modem connection. Rather than waiting for the nifty Web site to be displayed on his Web browser, your user may just cancel the update and move on to another site. To avoid this, keep the number of graphics on your Web site low and try to minimize the size of the individual images.

- Not everyone uses a Web browser that can display a background. In this case, the default background will be a light gray rather than the background image you selected. If the user has disabled image rendering on his Web browser, or if his Web browser is incapable of displaying inline images, then all your fancy work is for naught. Be sure to provide text-only alternatives for any banners, buttons, or image maps so your users can navigate through your Web site.

If you keep these items in mind, you, too, can create some pretty spectacular Web pages that incorporate 3D graphics. The two areas of a Web page that you really want to stand out, and that can really benefit from a 3D object, are your home page banner and your shortcut buttons. Usually these are strictly text on an opaque background, so the completed images are relatively small and do not consume a great deal of your user's Internet bandwidth.

How Does Asymetrix Web 3D Work?

Web 3D utilizes a mathematical model of an object to render a 2D picture that appears to exist in three dimensions. There are many other applications, such as AutoDesk 3D Studio, that can create 3D images. The basic process to create a 3D image follows:

1. A wireframe image is generated. In effect, this is a connect-the-dots image, as shown in Figure 14.1.

FIGURE 14.1.
A wireframe representation of a cube.

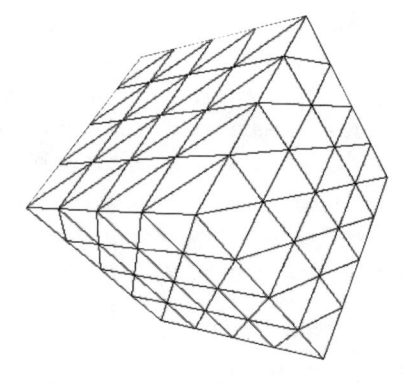

2. After the wireframe image has been created, a *surface* (the texture and color of the image's exterior) can be applied. This creates an object that appears to be solid, as shown in Figure 14.2, yet still does not appear very realistic.

FIGURE 14.2.
A wireframe representation of a cube with a surface applied.

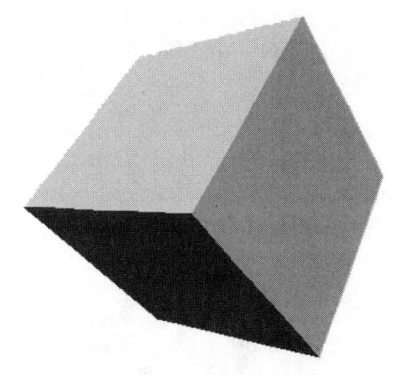

3. To apply the finishing touches to the object, lights and shadows are applied. This dramatically improves the illusion of three-dimensionality, as shown in Figure 14.3.

FIGURE 14.3.
A completed representation of a cube with a surface, lights, and shadows applied.

Although these steps seem simple in principle, in reality they are quite complex. That is why it may take hours to generate a finished 3D image. However, this should not deter you from creating 3D text banners, buttons, or other images because the computer will do the tough work of rendering the image for you. What you should be aware of with rendered images is that the higher the color depth, the more realistic the image will appear. The downside to a more realistic image is that it is also much larger in size. This is the reason the publisher asked me to submit the images for this chapter in a 256 (8-bit) color palette instead of a 16 million (24-bit) color palette.

Creating Your Home Page with Web 3D

When you are searching for that special look for your home page, you can use Web 3D's templates. Three of my favorite designs include the Neon style, which provides a flashy color display; the Glass Bubbles style, which provides a futuristic display; and the Polished Wood style, which gives a bit of elegance to your home page.

Creating a home page based on a template can be accomplished by following these steps:

1. Select File | New from the menu, then press Ctrl+N, or click the New button on the toolbar to create a new scene window.

2. If the current catalog is not the WEB3D catalog, open it using the File | Open command. In the List files of type drop-down listbox, choose Catalogs (*.cat). The WEB3D catalog can be found in the WEB3D\WEBSTYLE subdirectory. Then click the Styles tab to display the available templates.

3. Click the template of your choice in the Catalog window; then drag it over the Scene Preview window and drop it in place. The Scene Preview window will then display the template with the default objects, as shown in Figure 14.4.

Web Page Development

Part IV

FIGURE 14.4.
Creating a home page using a Web 3D template.

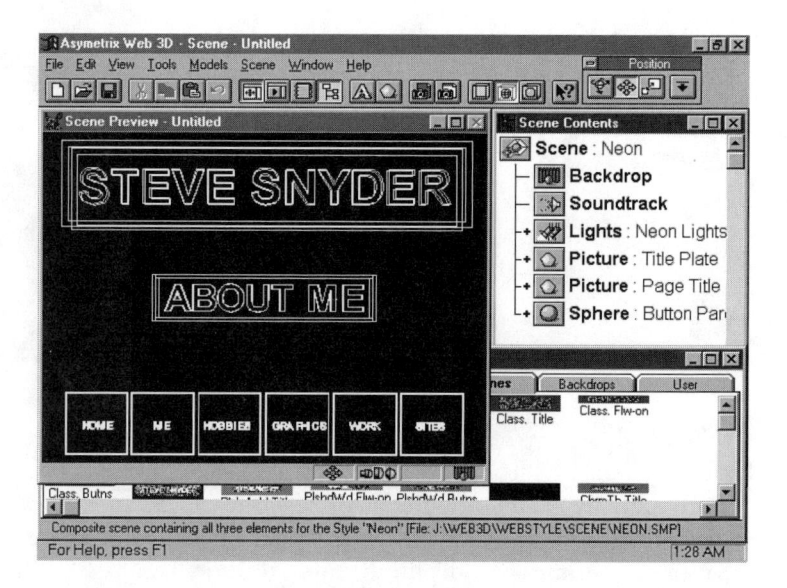

4. Maximize the Scene Contents window. Double-click the icon next to the Picture: Title Plate entry. This will expand the scene and display the individual element list of the composite entry.

> **TIP**
>
> When designing a 3D image, the key ingredients are lighting, shadows, and reflections. These properties are applied based on the common Lights entry in the Scene Contents window. An individual item may also have a Lights entry, which will override the common setting. However, if you override this common light setting, your objects appear out of place with the rest of the objects. It is best to use a common setting, such as that defined within a scene (or template), to provide a more uniform model.

5. Double-click the Text: Steve Snyder entry. This will display the Modify Text Model dialog, shown in Figure 14.5, where you may modify the text, model name, font, font size, font justification, and other properties.

FIGURE 14.5.
Modifying an object's text in a default Web 3D template.

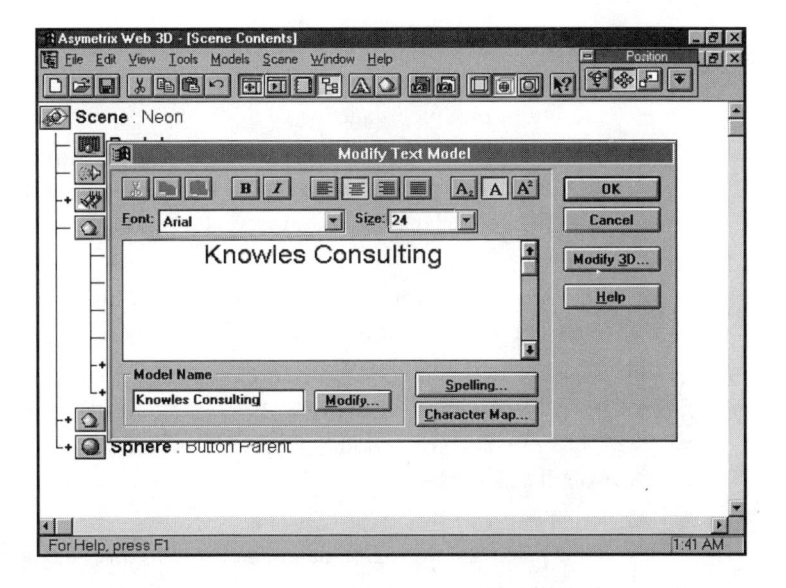

6. Click the OK button after you have finished your modifications. The Scene Preview window will then update the display with your changes.

7. To change the properties for the text face, back, sides, or bevels, expand the text entry by double-clicking on the icon next to the text entry. Then double-click the All Faces, All Backs, All Sides, or All Bevels text description to display the Modify Surface and Color dialog box. Within this dialog box, you may change the name, the color object, the highlight characteristics, or the effects of the object. When you have completed your changes, click the OK button to update the Scene Preview window.

8. For each additional object you want to modify in the template, repeat steps 5 through 7. To delete an object, just select it in either the Scene Preview or Scene Contents window and press the Delete key. Choose Models | Create Text Models to insert a new text object, Models | Create Picture Model to insert a new object based on a graphic image, or Models | Create Simple Model to insert a new circle, cone, square, or other basic geometric object.

9. Finally, you need to render the image and create your output file. This is accomplished by choosing Scene | Generate Snapshot, which will display the Generate Snapshot dialog box (see Figure 14.6). In this dialog box, you may specify how realistic the image will be by choosing an entry in the Style drop-down listbox. A style may be one of the following:

- Wireframes—No shadows, no reflections, no dithering, no custom color palette, and no fog. In essence, this creates an image consisting of lines with no surface and is an unusable image for Web pages.
- Solid Models—No shadows, no reflections, no dithering, no custom color palette, no fog. Although similar to the wireframe style, this option does create a solid image that may be used for Web graphics, but the overall quality is very poor.
- Realistic—No shadows or true reflections. This style creates a suitable image for Web page graphics and renders quite rapidly.
- Realistic w/Shadows—No true reflections. This style creates more realistic images suitable for Web page graphics.
- Ray Traced—No shadows. This style creates a more realistic image with higher overall quality.
- Ray Traced w/Shadows—Displays shadows, true reflections, dithering, custom color palettes, and fog. This image is the highest quality, but also takes the most time to render.

FIGURE 14.6.
Modifying snapshot properties to create your final image.

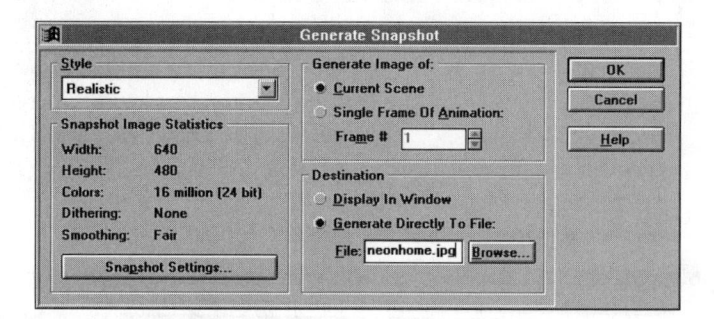

> **TIP**
>
> To create an image suitable for use in your Web page, select the Generate Directly To File radio button in the Destination group and enter a filename in the File edit field.

10. Click the Snapshot Settings button to display the Snapshot and Animation Settings dialog box, where you may specify the image size, quality, default color palette, special effects, or animation settings. Click the OK button to return to the Generate Snapshot dialog box.

11. When you are satisfied with your snapshot options, click the OK button in the Generate Snapshot dialog box to render the image. While this is happening, I suggest you relax and drink a cup of coffee (or a pot of coffee, if you chose a ray-traced style).

12. When the image has been created, you may then import it into your favorite bitmap editor and cut out the individual components you want to use in your Web pages. The final product will look similar to the one shown in Figure 14.7 after you have created the HTML document.

FIGURE 14.7.

The completed home page using the Neon *template.*

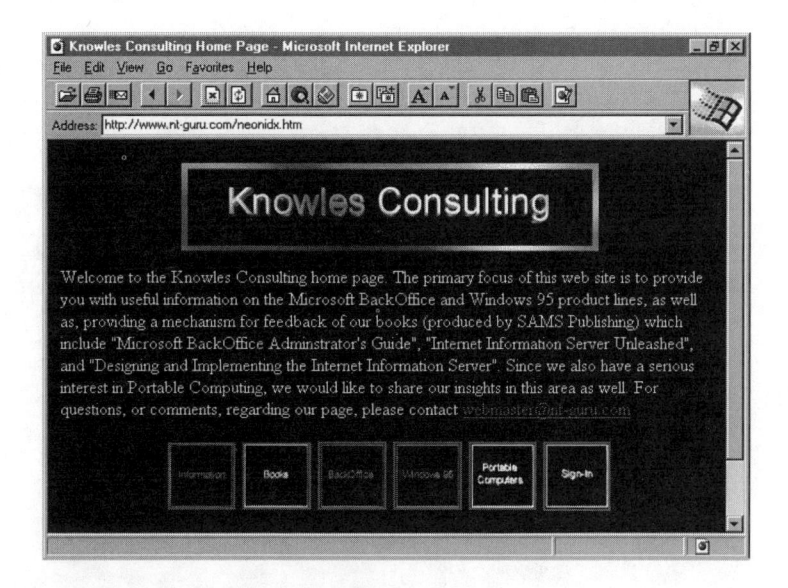

Using Corel's Web.Designer

Corel's Web.Designer is a new product recently introduced to the market. It is so new, in fact, that I bought Corel's Web.Gallery package on CD-ROM only to find out later that Corel is seriously considering the Internet market and is developing other products for Web developers as well. If you look at their product offerings you'll find design tools, database tools, and conversion tools.

Web.Designer is really three separate products on a single CD-ROM. It includes CorelWEB.DESIGNER, a WYSISIG HTML editor; CorelWEB.GALLERY, a collection of Web-ready clip art; and CorelWEB.Transit, a document conversion tool. In this section, you will get a sneak peek at each of these products to see what they can offer you in your desire to get up and running on the World Wide Web.

Using CorelWEB.DESIGNER

The first thing you should know about CorelWEB.DESIGNER is that it is not designed to build Web pages that use the HTML 3.0 tags or the HTML 2.0 tag extensions by Netscape or Microsoft. Nor is it designed specifically to support the Internet Information Server. It is a basic HTML 2.0 editor. I expect this to change with future versions. However, just because CorelWEB.DESIGNER does not support the HTML extensions and the Internet Information Server directly does not mean that it is a worthless product. It works very well as a Web-page forms editor, as you can see in Figure 14.8. It also includes an HTML text editor so that you can add HTML-specific tags that are not supported directly by CorelWEB.DESIGNER. It even includes a built-in spell checker so you can avoid potentially embarrassing spelling errors.

FIGURE 14.8.

Using CorelWEB.DESIGNER to build a Web form.

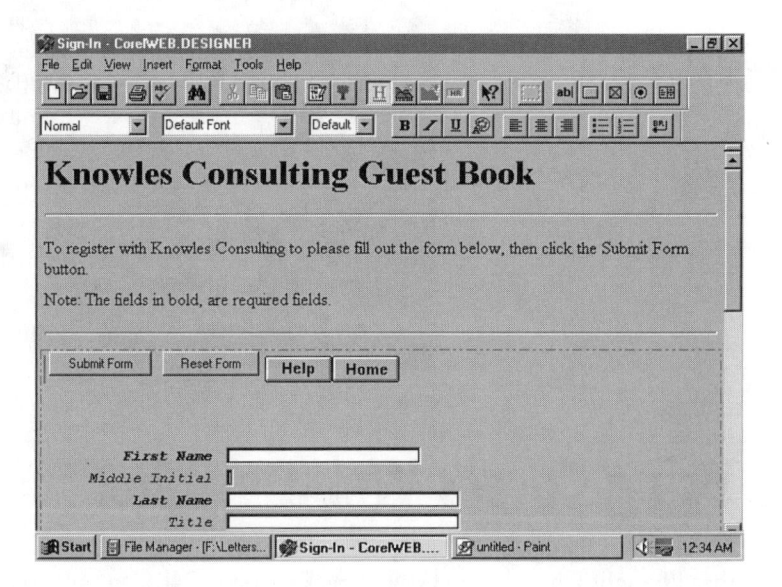

What I like most about CorelWEB.DESIGNER is the user interface. It is a very simple interface with button shortcuts to most of the functions you will want to use to develop the majority of your Web pages. You can insert text, lists, hypertext links, and images. You can even create image maps from any image you insert into your document. You can change paragraph styles, paragraph alignment, fonts, font sizes, and font attributes (bold, italic, and so on) just as you would with any Windows-based word processor. I like the HTML templates included with CorelWEB.DESIGNER. There are over a hundred different templates that you can use to get a head start on your Web page development. These include artistic templates, business templates, form templates, and even humorous templates. I also like the capability to use whatever names I want for my form input fields (unlike with Microsoft FrontPage), which makes form development for dbWeb a lot easier.

Using Asymetrix Web3D and Corel's Web Designer

Chapter 14

What I do not like, however, is the lack of support for HTML 3.0 and the HTML 2.0 extensions. I also dislike the lack of support for IIS virtual directories. However, I can't fault Corel alone for this, because no product I have used to date supports the Internet Information Server virtual directory structure. All WYSIWYG HTML editors that I have tried have been designed to support one root directory with all subdirectories as physical subdirectories under the root directory. What this means to you is that you will need to manually insert the relative URLs into your HTML documents rather than use the Browse button to create them. You can avoid this problem by making sure that your virtual directory structure matches your physical directory structure.

Using CorelWEB.GALLERY

CorelWEB.GALLERY includes more than 7,500 different images that you can use in your Web pages. These images include arrows, backgrounds, banners, bullets, buttons, clip art, capital letters, dividers (or rules), icons, photos, and themes (which include groups of matching banners, buttons, dividers, and so on that you can use to build a homogenous Web page). These images are either in a GIF or JPEG file format. Regardless of the original file format, you can export them to BMP (Windows or OS/2), JPEG, GIF, PCX (Paintbrush), TGA (Targa), or TIF bitmap file formats.

Many of these objects, like the buttons shown in Figure 14.9, include built-in captions so the objects are ready to be used as inline graphics without any additional effort. There are also blank objects, such as buttons and banners, that you can import into your favorite graphics application. You can then add any text to the object to create a custom object.

FIGURE 14.9.
A sample of the buttons included with CorelWEB.GALLERY.

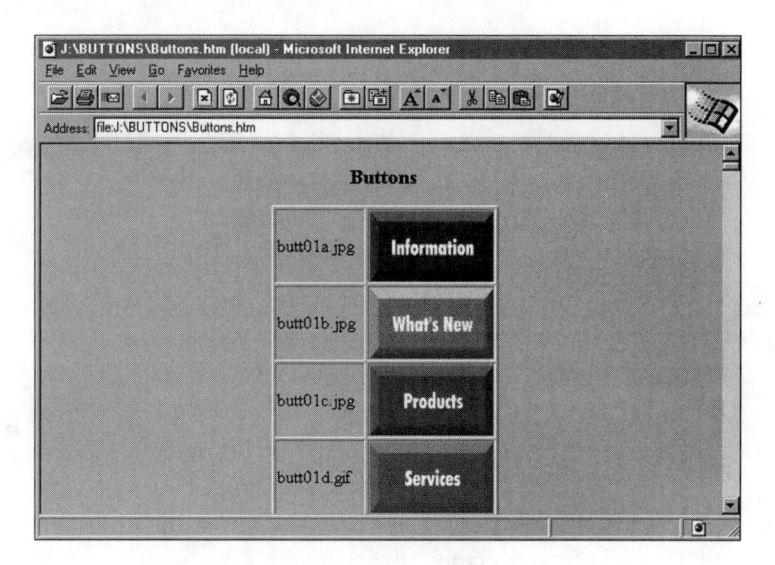

Creating a custom object may be just the ticket for your Web page. I found this to be very useful while experimenting with the design for my home page, as shown in Figure 14.10, because it provided me with the ability to create a custom banner. I also created custom bullets to provide a more interesting bulleted list. This was accomplished by exporting the bullet from Web Gallery, importing it into CorelPHOTO–PAINT, modifying the bullet background to match the background of my Web page, saving the final image, and then inserting the image as a custom bullet in my HTML document.

FIGURE 14.10.

Creating a custom banner from an empty banner object.

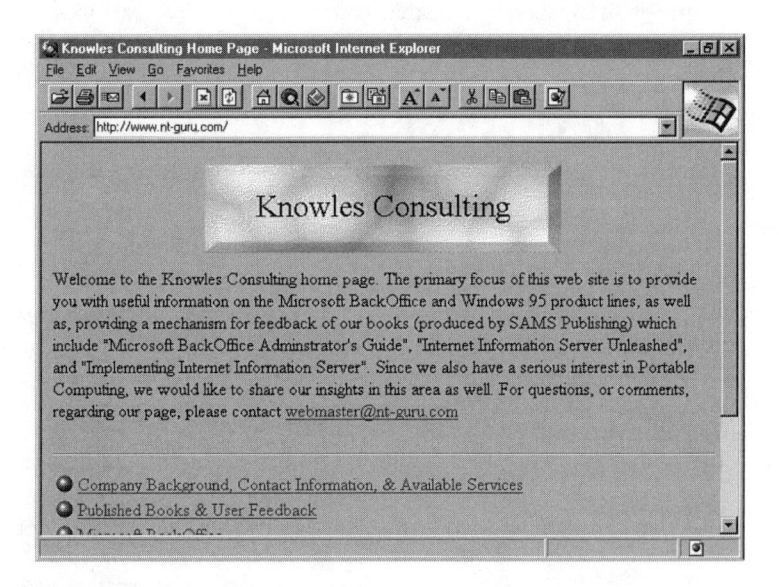

By using these customized objects, I was able to provide a unique look to my document while still keeping the required Internet bandwidth to a minimum. Because my Internet connection uses a single 56Kbps (224Kbps with software compression enabled) ISDN connection, this is an important consideration. If you have the available bandwidth, however, you may be able to take advantage of the numerous other graphic objects provided with Web Gallery. The icons, in particular, can be very useful. If you are creating an intranet application, for example, your Web pages can use these icons to provide a custom interface that your users are more comfortable with than standard text links or text-based buttons. After all, most users have been taught to click icons in their Windows applications, so icons in your Web pages are much more intuitive to the user.

Whichever items you choose to use from Web Gallery, you can be assured that by using them, you will be able to create a custom look for your Web pages without having to spend days or weeks designing them. Your first Web page can be created within a single day, possibly within a couple hours. This time savings is what using a clip-art gallery is all about, particularly because not all of us are graphically inclined.

Using Asymetrix Web3D and Corel's Web Designer

Chapter 14

Using CorelWEB.Transit

Out of all the tools provided by Web.Designer, the CorelWEB.Transit is what prompted me to purchase the package. This tool provides you with the ability to convert Microsoft Word, Corel WordPerfect, Lotus AmiPro, and any Rich Text file to an HTML file. Embedded images will be converted to GIFs (the default) or JPG files. This opens up the potential to publish many documents that you already have on the Internet. You can even customize the behavior of the CorelWEB.Transit conversion process to convert your document styles, paragraph attributes (left, right, and center justification), and font attributes (bold, italic, and so on); set up heading levels; insert address fields and e-mail addresses; and much much more. However, none of these options needs to be assigned to perform a quick conversion. For most of us, the defaults operate quite well. To give you a quick idea of how simple it is to publish your documents on the Internet, here are the steps I used to convert a review of the WinBook XP portable computer to an HTML document:

1. Launch CorelWEB.Transit, and the dialog box shown in Figure 14.11 will appear.

FIGURE 14.11.
The CorelWEB.Transit dialog box.

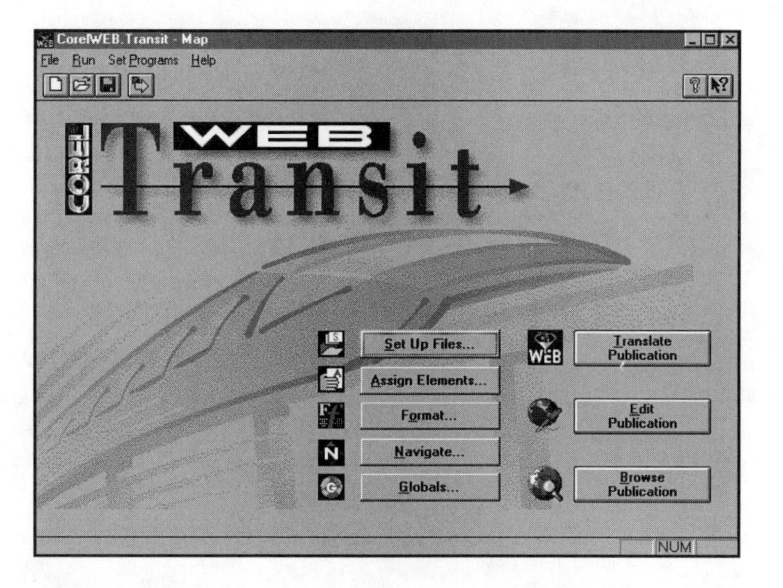

2. Click the Set Up Files button, and the Set Up Files dialog box will appear.
3. Specify the document to be converted in the Select Source File field.
4. Specify the location for the output files in the Output directory field.
5. Specify a name for the output file in the HTML File field.
6. Specify the HTML document title in the Web page title field.
7. Click the OK button to return to the main window.
8. Click on the Translate Publication button, and the document will be generated.

You can find a slightly modified version of this document on my Web site at

`http://www.nt-guru.com/PortableComputing/WinBook/XP/WinBookXP.HTM`

The modifications I performed were minor. I moved the table of contents to after the document title. I created a table where I could insert the picture of the laptop, the company information, and the review specifications so I could control the layout of these items. I right-justified the other images, and made all of the GIFs transparent GIFs to mimic the original file as closely as possible. The total conversion time was about 15 minutes.

> **NOTE**
>
> If CorelWeb.Transit is not powerful enough for you, you can upgrade it to HTML Transit. HTML Transit can upgrade multiple documents in a single session, create master documents with hypertext links, create hypertext indexes, and much more.

Summary

This chapter focuses on two products you can use to provide a custom look for your Web page without a lot of effort. The goal here is not to promote a specific product, as there are other products that perform similar functions just as well. The idea is to provide you with a little exposure to the types of tools that are available and how you can use them to customize your Web page with a little, rather than a lot, of effort. This can give you a head start in creating a Web page that has more user appeal than just a plain text-based Web page. That means that if the user likes it, he'll be back.

In the next chapter you will learn about Sausage Software's HotDog Pro. HotDog Pro is a Windows-based Web editor that you can use as an aid in creating and managing a Web site. It provides many functions, such as an HTML syntax checker, that are not included in the Microsoft Internet Assistant.

Using Sausage Software's HotDog Pro

IN THIS CHAPTER

- Why Use HotDog Pro?   **394**
- Getting Started with HotDog Pro   **396**
- Working with Documents and Templates   **410**
- Working with Projects   **422**

One of the most helpful items for a new HTML document developer is a tool that can help him over the rough spots as he learns all of the intricacies of HTML coding. HotDog Pro is just such a tool. HotDog Pro is not only for beginners, however, because it provides features that the expert HTML document developer may want as well. It includes multiple-language support for its spelling checker, an HTML syntax checker, and even limited project-management capabilities. This chapter explores HotDog Pro, beginning with an in-depth look at its features to understand why you may want to use it. Then I move on to the basics of HotDog Pro, such as how to install it and customize it to fit your needs. You'll then look into using HotDog Pro to create documents. Finally, you'll get a brief introduction on this tool's project-management capabilities.

> **TIP**
>
> This chapter discusses the retail version of HotDog Pro. A shareware version called HotDog, with slightly fewer features, is available on Sausage Software's Web site at `http://www.sausage.com`.

Why Use HotDog Pro?

In Chapter 12, "Designing and Managing a Web Site with FrontPage," you looked at the Microsoft Office Internet Assistants, which are available to the public free when downloaded from the Internet. Microsoft Office Internet Assistants provide a means to use familiar tools that you may already own to produce materials for your Web pages. So why should you consider using HotDog Pro? First of all, not everyone has Microsoft Office. You can purchase HotDog Pro for less than $50, whereas Microsoft Office costs between $300 and $400, depending on whether you purchase the standard or professional version. This can be a significant savings, and by itself may make the purchase of HotDog Pro worthwhile. There are, however, some additional compelling reasons to use HotDog Pro over other products. These features include the following:

- Ease of use: HotDog Pro is designed to make it easy for the novice HTML developer to produce Web pages. However, its advanced features make it a productive tool for hard-core HTML enthusiasts as well. There is something for everyone in HotDog Pro!

- Compatibility: HotDog Pro is a Windows application that will execute under Windows 3.*x*, Windows 95, and Windows NT. It provides some of the Windows 95 user interface, such as tabbed dialog boxes, under all versions of Windows. More importantly, the application executes under all versions of Windows without any problems. There is no need to worry about which version of the Internet Assistant template, spreadsheet, or whatnot you are using with the correct version of Word, Excel, or other application. HotDog Pro is a fully self-contained application.

- Customizability: HotDog Pro is fully customizable. You can specify how the application will appear onscreen and how the application will behave. You can configure the button bar and application font, create or modify document templates, assign or change shortcut keys, and take advantage of numerous other options that are described later in this chapter in the section titled "Customizing HotDog Pro."

- Project management: In addition to editing and publishing individual documents, HotDog provides the capability to group multiple documents into a project. You can perform search-and-replace operations on multiple documents, edit individual documents within a project, or even add documents to a project. When all changes have been completed, you can publish the entire project on your Web server with the push of a single button.

- Multiple HTML format support: HotDog Pro can be customized to use HTML 2.0 tags, HTML 3.0 tags, Netscape-specific tag extensions, or Microsoft Explorer–specific tag extensions. This makes it quite easy to support different Web browsers. HotDog Pro provides menus and buttons to insert the most common types of tags into your document, as well as tag tables that can be customized to insert a partial or complete tag sequence into your document. As the HTML standard changes, you can use the multiple-file search-and-replace function to update any nonstandard tags to their new formats.

- HTML syntax checker: This feature provides the capability to check an HTML document for syntactical correctness, which in my opinion is one of the biggest benefits of HotDog Pro. There is nothing worse than a document with an incorrect tag, or a missing end tag, to cause you embarrassment or grief. This option alone is worth the purchase of HotDog Pro. An additional benefit of this option is the capability to color-code HTML tags so that you know when you are using nonstandard HTML extensions within your document.

- Spell checker: HotDog Pro includes a standard American English language dictionary plus dictionaries for British English, German, Italian, and French. These dictionaries can be used by international content providers to avoid common spelling errors.

- External tools: HotDog Pro includes HotFTP and MapThis. HotFTP is a Windows-based File Transfer Protocol (FTP) application that is far superior to the Windows NT character-mode FTP client. MapThis is used to perform the difficult work of mapping graphical object boundaries for image maps into NCSA or CERN formatted text files.

Getting Started with HotDog Pro

HotDog Pro is one of the easiest applications I've had the pleasure to use. I'm sure you, too, will find it to be as useful as it is easy to use. Before you can use HotDog Pro, however, you have to install it. If you are a new HTML developer, going through the tutorial may be beneficial before you start using the application. On the other hand, you may want to jump right into customizing the application after you have installed it so you can start producing content right away. Let's get started on the features of HotDog Pro you will be examining.

Installing HotDog Pro

Installing HotDog Pro could not be made much easier than it already is. If you are using Windows NT 4.0 or Windows 95 as your HTML development platform, as soon as you insert the CD-ROM you'll be greeted with an installation dialog box. This dialog box is displayed because the CD-ROM includes an autorun script. An autorun script is a file (called `autorun.inf`) in the root directory of your data CD. This file specifies an application to execute whenever Windows NT 4.0 or Windows 95 is notified that a new CD has been inserted into your CD-ROM player. If you are using Windows 3.*x* or earlier versions of Windows NT, you will need to execute the `setup.exe` application located in the root directory of the CD-ROM.

> **NOTE**
>
> HotDog Pro requires Windows enhanced mode to operate. Therefore, it may not run on any software emulation that does not support the 80386 instruction set. This includes some of the older versions of Windows NT for RISC platforms.

After the setup program has been launched, just follow these steps:

1. The Registration Details dialog box appears. Enter your name and company information in the User Name and Company Name fields, respectively. Then press the OK button.

2. The Select Destination Directory dialog box appears next. Choose the default (`C:\HTDOGPRO`) or change this to the drive and directory of your choice. Then press the OK button.

> **NOTE**
>
> Although the installation program accepts long filenames, I found that when I used long filenames the installation program failed to create a Program Manager group on a Windows 95 installation. So it is better to stick to the MS-DOS 8.3 filename limitations unless you are willing to create your own Program Manager group.

3. The Select Components to Install dialog box appears. For most users, the default options will suffice. However, if you want to skip the tutorial, additional dictionaries, or other optional components, uncheck the appropriate check boxes. Then press the OK button to continue the installation.

4. Next, you are prompted to have the setup program create backup copies of any files it replaces. Choose Yes to back up these files, or No to skip the backup. If you choose Yes, you will then be prompted to choose a directory to contain the backed-up files. The default is `C:\HTDOGPRO\BACKUP`. After you choose whether or not to back up, HotDog Pro files will be copied to your hard drive.

5. Next, the Create HotDog Program Group dialog box appears. Click the Yes button if you want to create the group, or the No button if you do not want to create a Program Manager group. For this discussion, I'll assume you choose the Yes button.

6. The Select Folder dialog box appears. In the Folder Name field, enter a name if the default group name (HotDog Pro) is unacceptable, or select an available group from the list shown below on the screen. Then click the OK button to create the group.

7. Finally, the Installation Complete dialog box appears. Here you are prompted to run HotDog Pro now, or exit the setup program. Either option will terminate the setup program. So if you are in a hurry to get started, as I was, choose the Yes button. Otherwise, choose the No button.

The HotDog Pro Tutorial

When you first execute HotDog Pro, you are greeted with a cute dialog box. (See Figure 15.1.) It provides you with the following five options:

- Don't show this screen again: Check this option to disable the Welcome dialog box from appearing the next time you start HotDog Pro.

FIGURE 15.1.
The HotDog Pro Welcome dialog box.

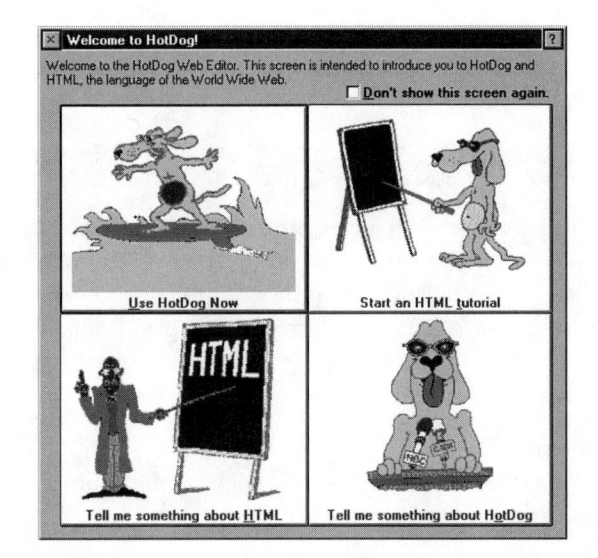

- Use HotDog Now: Click this button to exit the dialog box and start working with HotDog Pro.
- Start an HTML tutorial: Click this button to display the HotDog Pro HTML tutorial. This is a help file that describes the basics to create an HTML document, insert HTML links, and insert graphic images into your HTML document. It also includes an HTML overview and the HTML tag reference. The examples demonstrate both the tag structure and the associated application shortcuts, and are a good place to start for someone unfamiliar with HTML documents.
- Tell me something about HTML: Click this button for a description of HTML. It describes the basic structure of an HTML tag and includes a discussion concerning the various HTML flavors that are available.
- Tell me something about HotDog: Click this button for a working description of HotDog Pro. This option provides you with additional links to an HTML overview, application features, system requirements, and manufacturer-specific information.

All of these options, except for the Don't show this screen again check box, are available from the application's built-in help system (just choose Help | Contents). So I recommend that you enable the Don't show this screen again check box on the Welcome to HotDog! dialog box to speed up the loading of the application.

Using Sausage Software's HotDog Pro

Chapter 15

Customizing HotDog Pro

The major benefits of HotDog Pro are gained by customizing the application to suit your individual needs. You can customize the button bar, define the application's behavior, and create shortcut keys. Of these three customizable options, I find that the capabilities to create shortcut keys and define the application's behavior to be most beneficial. Creating custom shortcut keys can be used to provide faster access to menu commands. This can save time for a skilled, more proficient user. Defining the application's behavior, however, is useful to everyone. With HotDog Pro you can specify how the application interacts with you, such as by setting display preferences. You can also specify the style of HTML code to be used within your document. There is a pretty wide range of options available to make HotDog Pro suit almost everyone.

Customizing the Button Bar

The HotDog Pro button bar, as shown in Figure 15.2, provides easy access to the application's major menu functions. While the button bar is fully customizable, the other bars are not customizable at all. These other bars include the elements bar, the documents bar, and the status bar. These bars can be disabled if desired so they are not displayed on the screen, but again, they are not customizable.

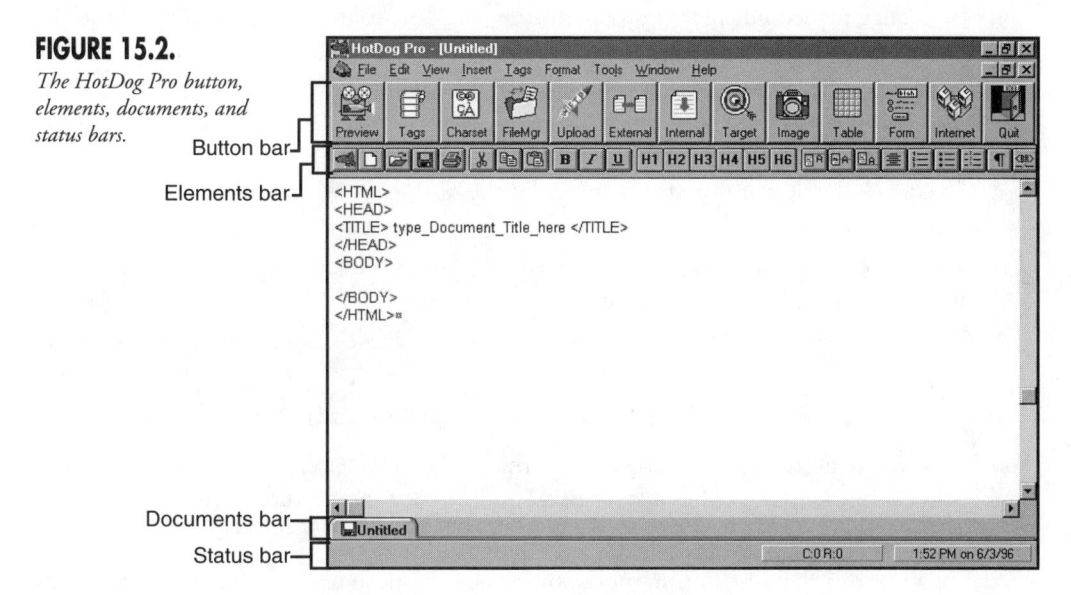

FIGURE 15.2.
The HotDog Pro button, elements, documents, and status bars.

To modify button properties on the button bar, follow these steps:

1. Choose Customize Button Bar from the Tools menu to display the Customize Button Bar dialog box, shown in Figure 15.3.

FIGURE 15.3.
Modifying the properties of a button on the button bar.

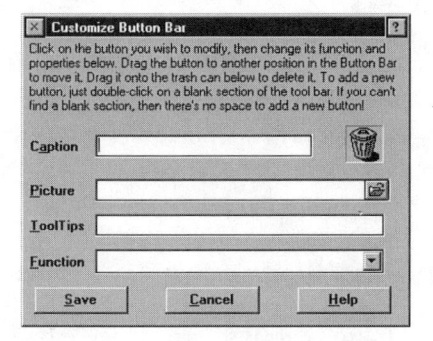

2. Click an existing button, and the Caption, Picture, ToolTips, and Function fields will be populated with the button's current information.
3. To change the button's caption, enter a new description in the Caption field.
4. To change the icon displayed on the button, click the folder icon at the end of the Picture field. This will display the HotDog Pro—Select Picture dialog box, where you can specify any icon (*.ico) or bitmap (*.bmp) filename. After you have specified a new file, click the OK button to return to the Customize Button Bar dialog box. The new filename will then be displayed in the Picture field.
5. To change the description displayed under the button when the mouse is over the button, enter a new description in the ToolTips field.
6. To change the menu command that is executed when the button is clicked, choose a menu command from the Function drop-down listbox.
7. Click the Save button to update the button bar. Click the Cancel button to disregard your modifications.
8. Repeat steps 1 through 7 for each button you want to modify.

To add a new button to the button bar, repeat the above steps, except when you reach step 2, double-click a blank spot on the button bar. The new button will then be inserted into the location of the blank spot when you click the Save button.

To delete a button, click the button on the button bar; then drag it over the trash can in the Customize Button Bar dialog box and drop it. This will leave a blank spot on the button bar.

To move a button to a different location, you must first display the Customize Button Bar dialog box. Then just click and hold the mouse button, which will display a white rectangle (or *button outline*, if you prefer) to illustrate the button. Next, drag the outline to the new location on the button bar, and then drop it. The button will then be moved to its new location.

Customizing Application Shortcut Keys

Are you a touch typist? If so, customizing the shortcut keys may be one of the ways you can maximize the performance of HotDog Pro and increase your productivity. You do not have to be a touch typist, however, to benefit from shortcut keys. Even a hunt-and-peck typist, such as I, can use the shortcut keys to access any menu command with a single keystroke. This means you can insert HTML tags or formatting commands with a single keystroke. If you are a touch typist, you can crank out HTML documents quite rapidly. If you are not, just saving the time it takes to manually type the HTML tags, or access them from the menu, will prove to be a useful feature. To add a shortcut key sequence to HotDog Pro, follow these steps:

1. Choose Shortcut Keys from the Tools menu to display the Customize Shortcut Keys dialog box. (See Figure 15.4.)

FIGURE 15.4.
Creating shortcut keys.

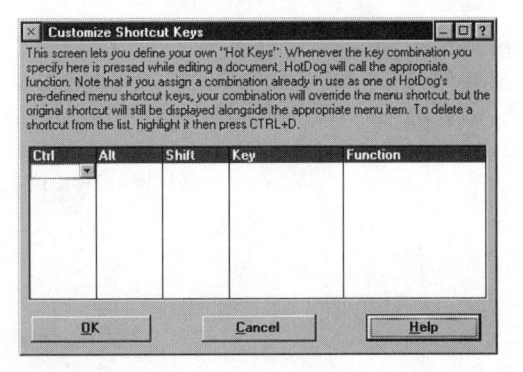

2. To specify a Ctrl+key sequence, choose CTRL from the drop-down listbox in the Ctrl column.
3. To specify an Alt+key sequence, choose ALT from the drop-down listbox in the Alt column.
4. To specify a Shift+key sequence, choose SHIFT from the drop-down listbox in the Shift column.

> **NOTE**
>
> Key-column sequences are cumulative. So, if you specify an entry for the Ctrl, Alt, and Shift columns, you must press all three of these keys plus the key you specified in the Key column to activate the function. This can be a pretty hefty set of keys, so it is best to limit your key sequence to no more than three keys (such as Ctrl+Shift+C).

5. Next, choose a key from the drop-down listbox in the Key column. This key can be a special key (such as the Insert, left-arrow, or pause key), a number, a letter, a function key, or a number-pad key. In fact, from what I have been able to determine, you can use almost any key on your keyboard.
6. Specify a function to execute when the shortcut key is pressed by choosing an entry in the drop-down listbox in the Function column.
7. Repeat steps 2 through 6 for each shortcut key you want to create. When all shortcut keys have been entered, click the OK button.

Customizing the Application's Behavior

There are numerous options for HotDog Pro that you can configure to suit your individual tastes and needs. In fact, there are so many options that I have summarized them in Table 15.1 rather than stepping you through each one. The subheads of the table give the name of the tabbed dialog box, the first column names the actual option, and the second column specifies a description for the option. To set one of these options, follow these steps:

1. Choose Options from the Tools menu to display the Options dialog box, as shown in Figure 15.5.

FIGURE 15.5.
Customizing the behavior of HotDog Pro.

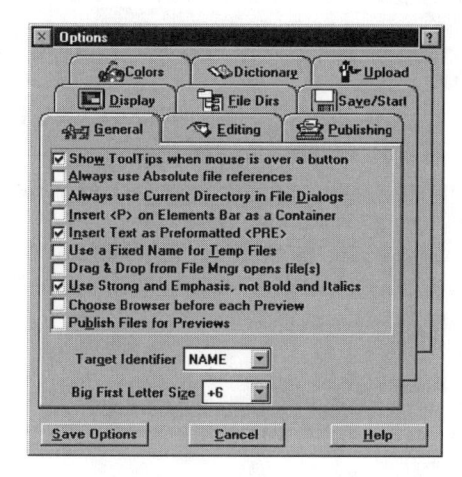

Using Sausage Software's HotDog Pro

Chapter 15

2. Click a tab to display the appropriate dialog box.
3. Change the options as desired.
4. Click the Save button to save your changes, or the Cancel button to disregard your changes.

Table 15.1. The customizable options for HotDog Pro.

Option	Description
General Tab	
Show ToolTips when mouse is over a button	Specifies that a description for the button will be displayed when the mouse cursor is over a button.
Always use Absolute file references	Specifies that a file reference will use the complete path and filename to the location of the reference (such as F:\WWW\GRAPHICS\Button.GIF) rather than a relative pathand filename (such as ..\GRAPHICS\Button.GIF). Note that while this is a useful option for a locally (on the computer where HotDog Pro is installed) hosted WWW server, it may cause a problem for a remotely hosted server when an attempt is made to locate the file.
Always Use Current Directory in File Dialogs	Overrides the directory location defaults as specified in the File Dirs tab and will use the last directory location as the default.
Insert <P> on Elements Bar as a Container	Specifies that the paragraph (<P>) tag be treated as a tag pair (<P>...</P>).
Insert Text as Preformatted <PRE>	Specifies that inserted text be treated as preformatted text. Note that to insert text as a normal part of your document you need to disable this option.
Use a Fixed Name for Temp Files	Specifies that a fixed filename will be used when you preview a document. Note that this should only be required for browsers that do not support DDE commands. After each preview option, you will have to refresh the display in your Web browser to update the contents.

continues

Table 15.1. continued

Option	Description
General Tab	
Drag & Drop from File Mngr opens file(s)	Specifies that files dragged from File Manager and dropped on a HotDog Pro window will open the files. Disabling this option may improve performance on slower computers. Note that when this option is disabled you can use the HotDog Pro File Manager to drag and drop files to accomplish the same tasks.
Use Strong and Emphasis, not Bold and Italics	Specifies that the HTML tags <STRONG> and <EMPHASIS> will replace the <B> and <I> tags when you choose the bold or italic menu, elements bar, or shortcut key options. Note that this is the preferred method and should only be changed for HTML documents that will be used by Web browsers that do not support the <STRONG> or <EMPHASIS> tags.
Choose Browser before each Preview	Specifies that HotDog Pro will prompt you for the Web browser to use each time you preview a document. This is a useful feature if you will be supporting multiple Web browsers.
Publish Files for Previews	Specifies that an HTML document will be published (that is, moved to your Web server) before being previewed on your Web browser.
Target Identifier	The HTML 3.0 specification utilizes the ID element to specify a target location (such as <A ID="*LocationName*">), whereas previous versions of HTML used a NAME element in an anchor tag (such as <A NAME="*LocationName*">). To use the old format, specify NAME in the drop-down listbox.
Big First Letter Size	Specifies the size for the Big First Letter option. This is often referred to as a drop

Option	Description
	caps option, where the first capital letter in a paragraph is a larger size than the rest of the text in a paragraph. The size is specified in a relative format +1 to +6, or -1 to -6.

Editing Tab

Option	Description
Default Font Name	Specifies the default display font.
Default Font Size	Specifies the size of the default font to be displayed.
Color tags after XX seconds idle	Specifies that HTML tags will be colorized after the number of seconds you specify. The minimum time is 0, the maximum time is 60 seconds. Note that to color tags, the Quick Color option must be enabled as well.
Quick Color	Specifies that HTML tags in the edit window will be color coded. This color coding is only used to highlight different types of HTML tags for easier readability. The color coding will not be used by published documents displayed on a Web browser. Nonstandard HTML tags, such as Microsoft or Netscape extensions, will be set to a different color than the base HTML tags.
Convert Extended Characters while typing	Specifies that extended characters (most commonly used by European users) will be converted to the appropriate HTML tag. HotDog Pro could convert the copyright symbol (©) to &copy, for example, while you type. Note that this option may slow down the application, so it may be better to perform this operation when you publish files instead. (See the Convert Extended Characters to HTML codes in the Publishing Tab section later in this table.)

continues

Table 15.1. continued

Option	Description
Editing Tab	
Popup Menu with right mouse button	Specifies that the right mouse button will display an object menu when selected. Note that this option performs the same function as a right mouse click on a computer running Windows 95, Windows NT 4.0, or prior versions of Windows or NT that normally do not support this option.
Tags in lowercase	Specifies that HTML tags be entered in lowercase rather than uppercase (the default). HTML tags are not case sensitive, so this choice is only for readability.
Show spaces	Specifies that spaces will be displayed onscreen while editing.
Show Paragraph Marks	Specifies that paragraph marks be displayed onscreen while editing.
Tab Indent	Specifies the default tab width, in inches.
Undo Depth	Specifies the number of buffers to be used for undo operations. Higher numbers require additional memory. The minimum is 0, the maximum is 99, and the default is 10.
Publishing Tab	
Remove All Carriage Returns	Specifies that all CRLF (carriage return line feed) pairs be changed to LF only.
Publish as UNIX text file	Specifies that all CRLF pairs be changed to LF only when the document is published.
Convert Extended Characters to HTML codes	Specifies that extended characters be converted to the appropriate HTML tag when you publish a document.
Replace \ with / in filenames	Specifies that the normal directory designator \ be replaced with the HTML directory designator / when the document is published.

Option	Description
Extension for Published Documents	Specifies the published document extension. By default this is .PUB, which is a reminder to change the extension when the document is published. Note that it is best to change this to the .HTM extension so that you can use the default association for your Web browser and preview the document by double-clicking on it in File Manager. It also removes one more step when you publish the document on your Web server.
Replace Words During Publishing	Specifies a set of words to be converted. You may use GP-But\BUTTON.GIF in your document, for example, to specify a relative path to your button. During the publishing phase the GP-But could be automatically changed to ..\GRAPHICS\BUTTONS, which specifies the relative location of your buttons.
Display Tab	
3-D Windows	Specifies that the windows will be displayed using the Windows 95 user interface rather than the more traditional Windows 3.x interface.
Rounded Tabs	Specifies that tabs on a tabbed dialog will use rounded corners rather than the square corners of the Windows 95 user interface.
Fast Draw	This option may be used to reduce flickering of screen updates on slower systems, but in turn will use additional system resources.
Word Wrap	Specifies that text lines wider than the screen be automatically wrapped to the next line.
Icons Only	Specifies that only the icon be displayed for buttons on the button bar.
Text Only	Specifies that only the text description of a button be displayed on the button bar.

continues

Table 15.1. continued

Option	Description
Display Tab	
Icons and Text	Specifies that both text and icons be displayed on each button on the button bar.
Refresh document on each keypress	Specifies that the document will be updated after each keypress. Note that use of this option may cause an additional performance degradation on slow computers.
File Dirs Tab	
Preview Browser	Specifies the location of the Web browser to use for a document preview. Note that when this option is enabled, the icon on the button bar will change to the icon of your Web browser.
Documents	Specifies the location of your HTML documents.
Published Files	Specifies the location of your HTML documents in the published format (that is, after any character translation may have occurred).
Graphics Files	Specifies the location of your graphics files.
AutoSave Files	Specifies the location for automatically saved copies of your documents.
.INF Files	Specifies the location of the HotDog Pro initialization files.
Templates	Specifies the location of your HTML document templates.
Temporary Files	Specifies the location to be used for temporary files.
Save/Start Tab	
AutoSave every *XX* minutes	Specifies how often to automatically save your documents, in minutes, where *XX* is the amount of time to wait between saves.

Option	Description
Show Handy Hints when HotDog starts	Specifies whether to display the Handy Hints dialog every time at application startup.
Create Backup Files when saving	Specifies that a backup copy of your document be created with a .BAK file extension whenever a document is saved.
Restore Last Session when HotDog starts	Specifies that the current windows and associated documents be reopened whenever the application starts. This provides the capability to quickly return to your last session status without having to manually open the appropriate files.
Open New Document when HotDog starts	Specifies that the application always open a new document when the application starts.
Colors Tab	
Foreground Color	Specifies the application foreground color.
Background Color	Specifies the application background color.
Default Tag Color	Specifies the default color for HTML tags when used in conjunction with the Quick Color option of the Editing dialog.
Tag Type	Specifies the default HTML tag format to use. This can be Microsoft, Netscape, or HTML 3.0. Note that for optimum usage, you should set this value to Microsoft when designing HTML documents for the Internet Explorer.
Tag Type Color	Specifies the default color for HTML tags you specified in the Tag Type option. This is useful to display any HTML extension tags in a different color than the standard HTML tags.
Dictionary Tab	
Custom Dictionary	Specifies a path and filename to be used for additions to the standard dictionary. Note that if you already have a default dictionary created with Word for Windows, you can use it with HotDog Pro.

continues

Table 15.1. continued

Option	Description
Dictionary Tab	
Standard Dictionary	Specifies the dictionary to use for standard spelling comparisons. This can be `american.vtd` for an American English, `brit.vtd` for a British English, `french.vtd` for a French, `german.vtd` for a German, and `italian.vtd` for an Italian dictionary.
Upload Tab	
Default Web Server	Specifies the name of your Web server, such as `ftp.nt-guru.com`.
Directory on Server	Specifies the default directory on your Web server to store the HTML documents.
Default Login Name	Specifies a user name to use when logging on to your server via the HotFTP FTP client.
Password	Specifies the password to use with the user name specified.
HotFTP Location	Specifies the location of the HotDog Pro FTP client.

Working with Documents and Templates

By now, you should have HotDog Pro customized to your satisfaction and be ready to actually start creating your HTML document. In this section you will learn how to create an HTML document, create a template from an HTML document, and publish your completed HTML document on your Web server. This section focuses on individual document management, and the next section focuses on multiple-document management (or projects). Before you can work with multiple documents, however, you need to learn how to work with individual documents contained within a project. This follows the old adage that says you need to learn how to walk before you can run, which is why we will start with the basics and then move on to the more advanced features.

Creating an HTML Document

Creating an HTML document is the meat of this chapter. Everything else just leads up to this point. When you first run HotDog Pro, the default document (shown in Figure 15.6) will be displayed. This default document is based on the Normal template (we'll talk more about templates in the section "Creating a Template from an HTML Document"). After your default document loads, it's time to customize it to create your finished Web page. Creating a Web page includes such steps as defining the basic properties for the document, adding the document's basic text, and finally adding any HTML tags and associated text. In the following sections, you will look further into creating a Web page using these steps.

FIGURE 15.6.
Creating an HTML document.

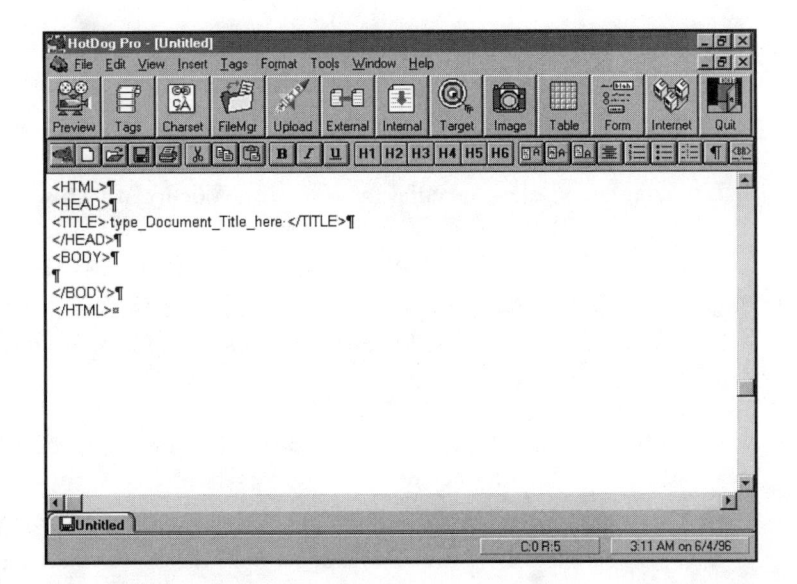

Defining the Document Properties

Every HTML document you create will have content unique to it, even if it is only the document title. HotDog Pro makes entering this information easy. Just choose Document from the Format menu, press Ctrl+D, or click the Document button on the button bar. This will display the Format Document dialog box, shown in Figure 15.7, with the Document Information tabbed dialog box (the default), where you may specify the following information:

FIGURE 15.7.
Specifying the general document properties.

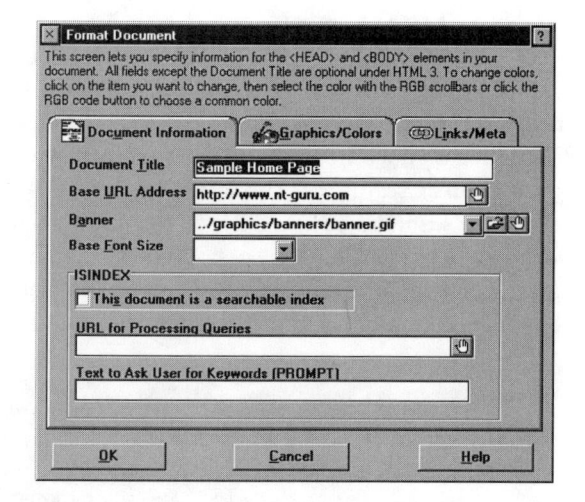

- Document Title—Specifies the title of the document. This title will be displayed on the caption bar of most Web browsers.
- Base URL Address—Specifies the location of the HTML document.
- Banner—Specifies either an image (GIF or JPEG) to insert into the document as a document banner, or builds an external link to an image. To insert an image, click the folder icon. This will display the HotDog Pro—Select Image File dialog box where you specify a filename. To insert an external link, click the hand icon. This will display the Build External Link dialog box, where you specify the resource type, host address, port, path, filename, target, and description.
- Base Font Size—Specifies the default font size for the document.
- This document is a searchable index—Specifies that this document is a searchable document.
- URL for Processing Queries—Specifies the URL to which the search queries will be forwarded.
- Text to Ask User for Keywords (prompt)—Specifies a replacement for the default prompt, `This is a searchable index. Enter search keywords:`, with the message you specify.

If you want to specify additional characteristics for the document, click on the Graphics/Colors tab. This will display the dialog box shown in Figure 15.8, where you can display the following information:

FIGURE 15.8.
Specifying the document colors.

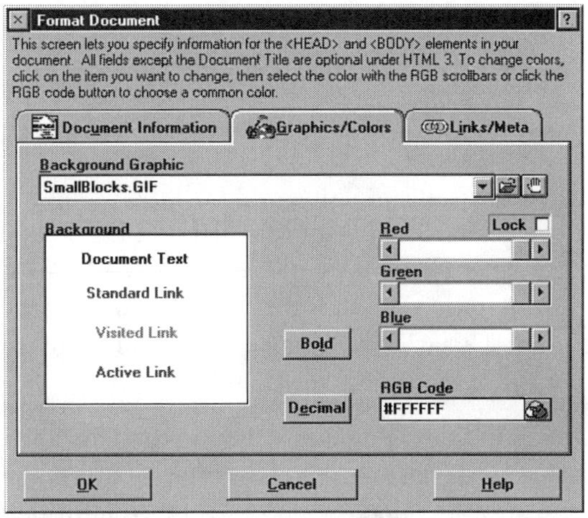

- Background Graphic—Specifies an image to be used as a background image. This image will be tiled across the Web browser.

> **CAUTION**
>
> A background image will prevent anything else from displaying on the Web browser until the image has been downloaded. Therefore, any background image you use should be as small as possible. It should also be a non-interlaced graphic for best results. On the aesthetic side, you might want to consider how the color of your background will affect the readability of the text.

- Background—Specifies the background color of the Web page.

> **NOTE**
>
> Unless your background graphic is a transparent graphic, it makes little sense to use a background color. This is because the background image will be layered over the background.

- Document Text—Specifies the color of regular text on your Web page.
- Standard Link—Specifies the color of a hypertext link that has not been accessed.

- Visited Link—Specifies the color of a hypertext link after it has been accessed.
- Active Link—Specifies the color of a hypertext link while it is being activated and the new document loads.

To change the display color of a link, you can use one of three methods. You can click an entry in the bitmap (such as the Document Text), then change the Red, Green, or Blue sliders until the desired color is achieved. You can click the RGB color icon at the end of the RGB Code field and select a color from the Color dialog box. Or you can specify an RGB entry in decimal or hexadecimal notation in the RGB field. To change from decimal to hexadecimal, click the Decimal button. This will then toggle the button state to Hex. I prefer to use the RGB color icon, because this is the easiest way to select a color.

The final option in this dialog box is the Links/Meta tab. This dialog box has two listboxes for entering link or meta information. This type of information is used to associate links between this document and other documents or to embed information about the document which cannot be performed in any other way. Unless you have a specific need to use these fields, you are better off leaving them alone.

Once you have finished entering the document properties, click the OK button. The HTML document will then be updated to include the information you specified.

Entering Text in a Document

Entering text in your document is a matter of typing it in. Formatting your text, however, is a little more complicated. To format your text, you can use one of the following methods:

- Highlight your text, then choose one of the elements bar buttons (such as the B button to make the text bold, the H1 button to make the text a level-one header, or the Center button to center the text).
- Highlight your text and choose an option (such as Bold) from the Format menu.
- Manually enter your HTML start tags, your text, and then the HTML end tags.
- Use one of the other HotDog Pro methods (choose a menu option, select a tag from the tag dialog box, and so on) to insert an HTML tag pair, then enter your text between the tag pairs.

Using Sausage Software's HotDog Pro

Chapter 15

415

> **TIP**
>
> To insert a special character, such as the copyright symbol, select Special Characters from the View menu, click the Charset button on the button bar, or press F7. This will display the Entity list, where you can scroll through the available special characters until you find the one you want. Then just double-click it to insert it into the document.

Inserting HTML Tags in a Document

This is where most of the real work occurs with HotDog Pro. There are so many different HTML tags and methods to insert into your document that it can be a bit confusing. However, no matter which method you use, once you've inserted the tag or tag pair you will have to insert your text. To make this easier to understand, I have divided this section into five basic types.

Using the Tag Dialog Box to Insert an HTML Tag

The most versatile method for inserting a tag is to select it from the Tags dialog box. Just follow these steps:

1. Select Tags from the View menu, click the Tags button on the button bar, or press F6. Any of these will display the Tags dialog box, as shown in Figure 15.9.

FIGURE 15.9.
Inserting an HTML tag from the Tags dialog box.

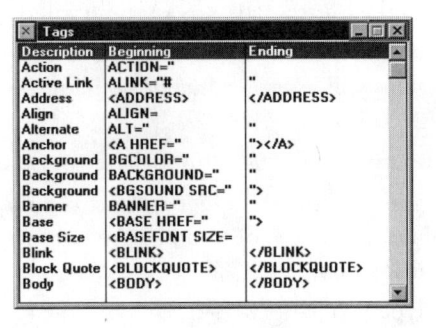

2. Click the scrollbar until the tag you want to insert is visible. Then double-click the tag. This will place it into the document at the current insertion point.

3. Repeat step 2 for each tag you want to insert. When you have finished inserting tags, you can close the Tags dialog box by selecting View | Tags, clicking the Tags button on the button bar, or pressing F6.

> **TIP**
>
> If the tag does not insert all of the available options you want, you may change this behavior by selecting Tag Information from the Edit menu. This will display the Edit Tag Information dialog box, where you can modify the tag to include the additional options. You can even add new tags.

Inserting a Hypertext Link in a Document

Most, if not all, of your HTML documents will include hypertext links to either a location within the same document or to an external document. The format will vary a bit between a link to an internal or external location. However, the method you will use to create these links is quite similar. To make this a little easier, we'll start with how to insert an internal link, then move on to inserting an external link.

To insert a link to an internal point within a document, follow these steps:

1. Move the cursor to the location in your document where you want to jump.
2. Choose Hypertext Target from the Insert menu, press Ctrl+G, or press the Target button on the button bar. Any of these will display the Enter Target ID dialog box.
3. Enter a unique (within the document) identifier in the edit field and press the OK button. This will insert an anchor point at the current insertion point (where the cursor is).
4. Move the cursor to the location where you want the hypertext link to be inserted.
5. Choose Jump Within this Document from the Insert menu, press Ctrl+K, or press the Internal button on the button bar. Any of these will display the Select Hypertext Target dialog box.
6. In the Hypertext Target ID field, select the identifier you want to jump to.
7. Enter a comment in the Description of Link field to identify the link.
8. Press the OK button to create the link.

Using Sausage Software's HotDog Pro

Chapter 15

To insert a link to an external document or service, follow these steps:

1. Move the cursor to the location in your document where you want the link to be created.
2. Choose Jump to Document on Another System from the Insert menu, press Ctrl+H, or click the External button on the button bar. Any of these will display the Build External Hypertext Link dialog box, as shown in Figure 15.10.

FIGURE 15.10.

Inserting a link to an external document.

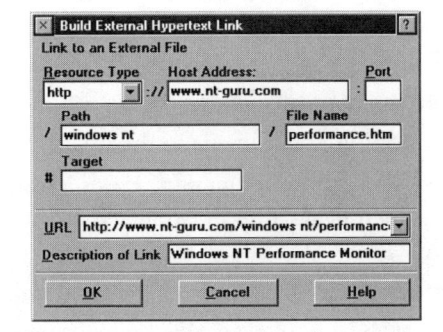

3. Select the appropriate type of link (such as http for a WWW document) in the Resource Type drop-down listbox.
4. Specify the name of the host to which you wish to link (such as www.nt-guru.com) in the Host Address field.
5. If the resource requires a specific TCP/IP port, such as when a proxy agent is used for additional security, enter this number in the Port field.
6. Specify the path to the external document (such as windows nt/performance) in the Path field.
7. Specify the filename you are linking to (such as performance.htm) in the File Name field.
8. If the link will jump to a specific location within the external document, specify the location identifier in the Target field.
9. Specify a comment in the Description of Link field to identify the link.
10. Press the OK button, and the link will be created and inserted at the current insertion point of your document.

Inserting a Graphic Image in a Document

Inserting an image into your document follows a procedure similar to that for inserting a hypertext link into your document. You can insert an image as a static resource, meaning that it is just there for show, or you can insert it as a hypertext link. If you insert it as a hypertext link, when the user clicks it he will jump to the link destination. To insert an image or an image link, follow these steps:

1. Move the cursor to the location in your document where you want the image to be inserted.
2. Choose Image from the Insert menu, or click the Image button on the button bar to display the Insert Image dialog box.
3. Enter the location of the image in the Image File field.
4. Enter the URL of the document to execute when the image is selected in the Document to Launch field. If no document is entered, then the image will be a static resource.
5. Enter a comment in the Alternate Description field to describe the image or link.
6. Click the OK button to create the link and insert it into your document.

> **TIP**
>
> Use the Image Advanced option on the Insert menu to specify additional information about an image. You may specify that the image is an image map or a figure, whether the image is low resolution or high resolution, the image width and height, image border, image alignment, and how much whitespace will be displayed around the image.

Inserting a Table into a Document

Creating tables with HTML can be a real pain. HotDog Pro can make it a lot easier for you. You might be surprised at just how easy it can be to insert a table. Keep in mind, however, that if you insert just a blank table, it will be up to you to populate the rows and columns.

To insert a completed table, follow these steps:

1. Move the cursor to the location in your document where you want the table to be inserted.

2. Choose Table from the Insert menu, press Ctrl+T, or click the Table button on the button bar. Any of these will display the Create Table dialog box (see Figure 15.11).

FIGURE 15.11.

Inserting a table into a document.

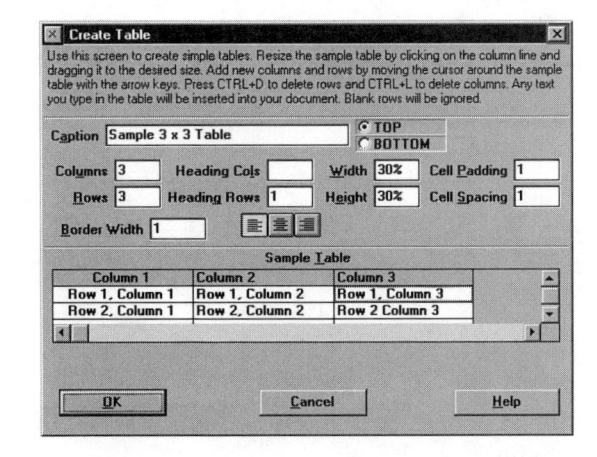

3. To specify a description for the table, enter it in the Caption field. To place the caption at the top of the table, click the TOP radio button. To place the caption at the bottom of the table, click the BOTTOM radio button.
4. Specify the number of columns in the table in the Columns field.
5. Specify the number of rows in the table in the Rows field.
6. Specify the number of heading columns in the Heading Cols field.
7. Specify the number of heading rows in the Heading Rows field.

> **NOTE**
>
> When you specify the size of your table, be sure to include the number of heading rows and columns. For example, if you want to insert three rows with three columns, each with a single header row, you really need to create a table with four rows and three columns.

8. Specify the width of the table in an absolute (generally measured in pixels) value or as a relative value (a percentage of the Web browser's displayable area) in the Width field.

9. Specify the height of the table in an absolute or relative value in the Height field.

> **TIP**
>
> It is usually better to specify relative rather than absolute values. A relative value will give the Web browser more leeway to determine how the table should be displayed for optimum results.

10. Specify the vertical distance between cells of the table in the Cell Padding field.
11. Specify the horizontal distance between cells of the table in the Cell Spacing field.
12. Specify the size of the table border in the Border Width field.
13. Specify a table alignment by clicking the left, center, or right justification button.
14. For each cell in the table where you want to enter text, double-click the cell, then enter your text.
15. When you have entered all of your text, click the OK button to insert the table at the current insertion point.

The table height, table width, cell padding, cell spacing, and border width are optional components that, if not specified, will be determined by the Web browser.

> **TIP**
>
> One of the features that makes using HotDog Pro so worthwhile is the way it manages tables. If you create a table in the fashion described in this section, you can later select the entire table, click the Table button to display the Create Table dialog box, and modify the table without losing any of your data. You can add columns, change the table width, change the table alignment, or use any other option in this dialog box.

Inserting an Internet Command in a Document

If you want to insert a hypertext link to an Internet service, HotDog Pro makes this a snap as well. The basic method requires the following four steps:

1. Move the cursor to the location in your document where you want the link to be inserted.
2. Choose Launch an Internet Service from the Insert menu, press Ctrl+Y, or click the Internet button on the button bar. Any of these will display the Create HyperText Link dialog box, as shown in Figure 15.12.

FIGURE 15.12.
Inserting a link to an Internet service in a document.

3. Click the button of the appropriate service (such as Let the User send Mail to someone) to launch (or in this case e-mail a message). This will display a service-specific dialog box.
4. Enter the requested information in the dialog box and press the OK button. The appropriate link will then be inserted into your document.

Creating a Template from an HTML Document

If you will be creating multiple HTML documents, either for yourself or for clients, it is a good idea to create a template. A template is used to create a skeleton HTML document that you can modify as needed. You may want to have a home page button on every document you create, for example. If you create a template that includes the button and the link, every page you create will have this predefined hypertext link to your home page. You can create templates that even include themes. A *theme* might be, for example, a specific color scheme or document layout.

The basic method for creating a template is as follows:

1. Create the basic document. When you create the document, make sure the document properties are correctly set. These properties include the document title, banner, background, base URL, document background, link colors, and link and meta information. If you have any buttons (such as the home page button), copyright information, or other standard items you wish to add, do so now.
2. When the basic framework has been completed, choose Make Template from Document from the Tools menu. This will display the Create Template dialog box. Enter a unique name to describe the template, press the OK button, and the template will be created.

Publishing Your Documents

Publishing your documents is one of the easiest tasks you will perform with HotDog Pro. It only requires the push of a single button to publish your documents, but in order to succeed you must first make sure HotDog Pro is properly configured. So keep the following in mind when it's time to publish your documents:

- Because most Web browsers use the .HTM file extension, you should too. This means that you should either change the default extension of .PUB to .HTM before you upload your documents or be sure to rename them after you upload your documents to your Web server. This is performed in the Publishing tab of the Options dialog box.
- If you do not have a network drive mapped to your Web server, you will need to use the HotFTP client to upload your files to your Web server. This means you must specify the appropriate URL, directory, user name, and password in the Upload tab of the Options dialog box.
- If you have a mapped network drive, you can specify the location for published files in the File Dirs tab of the Options dialog box.

To actually publish your document, just make sure the active document is the document you want to publish, then choose either File | Publish Document or press the Publish button on the button bar.

Working with Projects

A project provides the ability to group many HTML documents into a single manageable unit. You can create multiple projects, each with different properties. You can use projects to support several different clients, each with their own Web server. Or you can use a project to divide a large Web site into several smaller, and easier to manage, subsets. It's really up to you to determine if you will use the project management features, though I do recommend them.

The starting point, of course, is to create a project. This is accomplished by choosing Project Manager from the File menu. This will display the Project Manager dialog box, where you can specify the name of the project, the project directory, the Web server, the Web server directory, the user name and password, and the document files within the project.

Thereafter you can use the File | Open Project to access all the files defined within the project with one easy step. But more importantly, you'll have the ability to check all of the internal and external links contained within the project. The Project Manager Links dialog box provides you with the ability to examine individual links, or to check all links within a project to verify that the link is correctly formed. This can prevent a flood of e-mail to you about a hypertext link that has been broken.

Summary

In this chapter you have learned a bit about HotDog Pro. From this discussion, you should have gotten a glimpse into its capabilities, perhaps enough to interest you in trying out the shareware version to see how well it suits your needs. HotDog Pro is an easy-to-use tool that can help both the beginner and expert alike in their HTML document development efforts.

In the next chapter, you'll take a look at the Internet Information Server Software Development Kit (SDK). While the SDK itself is too much to cover in a single chapter, you will get a glimpse into the possibilities that are available to extend the Internet Information Server's capabilities by creating ISAPI applications. You'll also learn why ISAPI is the preferred method for developing custom applications.

IN THIS PART

- The Internet Information Server SDK **427**
- Unleashing the Power of VBScript **445**
- Introduction to Windows NT CGI Programming **489**
- Writing Java Applets **523**

Advanced Web Page Development

PART

V

The Internet Information Server SDK

16

IN THIS CHAPTER

- What Is an ISAPI Application? **428**

The Internet Information Server SDK (Software Development Kit) is still under construction. By the time you read this, however, it should be available as a finished retail product. So what you need to keep in mind here is that some of the information contained in this chapter may be a little outdated by the time you read it, particularly because this chapter was written using an early beta of the SDK. Having given you fair warning, let me tell you a little about what it contains.

The Internet Information Server SDK is strictly for developers, who will use it in one of two ways:

- To create interactive HTML documents using the ActiveX components, which include Visual Basic Scripting, JavaScript, and OLE (object linking and embedding) controls and documents. Because many of you will be creating HTML documents with active content, you may want to look at Chapter 17, "Unleashing the Power of VBScript," for more in-depth information.
- To create ISAPI (Internet Server Application Programming Interface) applications to extend the capabilities of the Internet Information Server.

This chapter focuses on the latter aspect: how to use the IIS SDK to create ISAPI applications. You will start your exploration of the ISAPI interface by defining an ISAPI application. Then you will look into the ISAPI interface and ISAPI-specific functions. Finally, you will look at a skeleton ISAPI application that you can use to build your own ISAPI applications. In order to successfully build an ISAPI application and to understand the following discussions, you must be a proficient Win32 developer. You need to be familiar with the Win32 API, to understand the basic issues in a multithreaded environment (data coherency is one of these issues), and be able to develop a dynamic link library.

What Is an ISAPI Application?

An ISAPI application is a Windows NT dynamic link library (DLL). The primary purpose of ISAPI is to provide an alternative interface to the more commonly used *Common Gateway Interface* (CGI). For more information on CGI development, take a look at Chapter 18, "Introduction to Windows NT CGI Programming." A *CGI application* is an external application that executes in a separate process from the Web server and is commonly used to provide services not provided by the HTTP (or Web) server or defined by the HTML specification. You can use a CGI application to interface to a SQL Server database, to save data from an HTML form, or even to insert a counter on your Web page (such as the hit counters we have seen on too many Web pages lately).

Because CGI applications have been around for quite a while, you may be asking yourself why you need (or should care about) another methodology to provide similar functionality. You're probably wondering just what the difference is between ISAPI and CGI. After all, both extend your Web server's capabilities by creating custom extensions, and both allow you to write extensions using your favorite C or C++ compiler. Well, the main difference between these two interfaces can be summed up in one word: performance!

A CGI Application Versus an ISAPI Application

A CGI application executes as a separate process. This means that each time the application is called, it must be loaded into memory, passed the client parameters, and executed. Then it must pass the client data back to the HTTP server. If the application is called multiple times by different clients simultaneously, multiple copies of the application will be resident in memory at the same time, which consumes system resources. An ISAPI application, however, is quite a bit different than a CGI application, as illustrated by the following:

- Rather than executing as an external application in a separate process, an ISAPI application is a native Windows NT application that executes in the same address space as the HTTP server. This is possible because the ISAPI application is a dynamic link library rather than an external program, and it executes as an integral part of the HTTP server.
- A dynamic link library can be loaded or unloaded at will. This means that if the additional functionality provided by the DLL is no longer required, it can be unloaded from memory to conserve system resources. When the service is needed again, it will be reloaded.
- An ISAPI application is a multithreaded shareable image. This means that only one copy of the DLL will be loaded into memory, and this one copy can support multiple simultaneous client requests. Again, this conserves system resources and improves response time.

A Few ISAPI Application Considerations

Although a dynamic link library has its good points (described in the preceding section), it also has a downside that you must consider: Because a dynamic link library executes in the same address space as the parent application, an errant dynamic link library (such as one that references memory indiscriminately) can cause the parent application to fail! That means a poorly written ISAPI application can cause your Web server to choke, spew, and die a cruel and unnatural death. You should prepare yourself for this eventuality by implementing the following suggestions:

- Never perform development or testing on a production server. It may cost you more to maintain a duplicate of your production environment, but this is a necessary requirement if maintaining your server's operation is critical to your business.

> **TIP**
>
> It is possible to lower the costs associated with ISAPI development by creating a standalone server with all of your development tools and required databases installed on it. You can even use an Access database (or any ODBC database) instead of a SQL Server database to lower costs. However, final testing before installing the ISAPI application on the production server should be performed in an environment that mimics the production environment as closely as possible. This means that if your production server uses an external SQL Server database, your final testing should also use an external (not necessarily the same SQL Server database as your production server) SQL Server installation rather than a local or remote Access database.

- Never install a third-party ISAPI application on your production server without thoroughly testing the ISAPI application on a different server (such as your duplicate test environment).

- Stress test the ISAPI application using multiple connections from multiple Web browsers (including the Internet Explorer, Netscape Navigator, and any others you may have available) to make sure your ISAPI application functions as expected.

- If you develop your own ISAPI applications, make use of the structured exception handling provided by the Win32 API. These exception APIs include the `try except` and `try finally` statements. The `try except` statements are used to capture any exception (such as an invalid memory reference) that occurs in the `try` block and then execute the statements in the `except` block (so you can determine the type of exception and then remedy the situation). The `try finally` statements are used to ensure that no matter what happens in the `try` block (including an exception), your code in the `finally` block will execute (so you can clean up your application by releasing allocated memory, for example).

Even if you do not follow the suggestions described in the preceding section, there is a little extra insurance I can provide for you. If you will stop by my Web site at http://www.nt-guru.com/IIS, you can pick up a copy of my IIS service-monitoring application. This application just monitors the operating state of the IIS publishing services. If it detects a service that is not responding either because it has hung up or has terminated, my service-monitoring application will attempt to restart it. This application cannot solve all of your problems, but it can help keep your IIS services up and running. This will make your Web clients a little happier because they will be able to connect to your site and view all of the wonderful content you are providing.

The Basic ISAPI Interface

If you have performed any Windows or Windows NT development in the past, you may already be aware of the multitude of interfaces (or requirements to implement a desired function) defined by the Windows or Windows NT API. An *ISAPI application*, also commonly called an *Internet Server Application* (ISA), is no different. It too requires that you use a specific interface. The first part of this interface, which is optional, is that the application must support the basic definition of a dynamic link library. This means it can include a function called DLLMain that will be called when the application is loaded or unloaded by the operating system (Windows NT Server). This function is used to provide specific ISA initialization and cleanup.

After the application is loaded into memory, the HTTP server calls the GetExtensionVersion function to obtain version-specific information. If the version numbers are acceptable, the HTTP server then calls the HttpExtensionProc function each time a client makes a request requiring this ISA. Normally, this request by the client is executed whenever a URL, in the form of

```
http:\\www.DomainName.com/scripts/ExtensionName.DLL?Parameter
```

is selected by the client. You can substitute your own domain name, ISA name, and parameters for the values DomainName, ExtensionName.DLL, and Parameter in the URL, respectively. For example, your URL might appear as

```
http://www.nt-guru.com/scripts/skeleton.dll?NoFunction
```

> **NOTE**
>
> The DLLMain, GetExtensionVersion, and HttpExtensionProc functions must be exported in order for the extension to function properly.

To give you a better idea of this required interface, take a look at Figure 16.1, which illustrates the basic ISA architecture.

As you can see in the figure, there is one address space within which the HTTP server and the Internet Server Applications execute. The HTTP server communicates with the ISA using an *extension control block* (ECB). A pointer to the ECB is passed to the HttpExtensionProc function each time a client makes a request. It is up to the HttpExtensionProc function to parse the ECB structure and determine the request by the client and to perform the appropriate processing. The HttpExtensionProc function is similar to the main function of a C application used as a CGI extension, but instead of receiving its input using stdin, as a C application does, the HttpExtensionProc function uses the ECB structure to retrieve its data. Also, instead of using stdout to send the processed data back to the client, the HttpExtensionProc function uses the WriteClient or ServerSupportFunction functions. Within the HttpExtensionProc function, you can use any Win32 API. This provides a means to extend the HTTP server to perform almost any task. Microsoft dbWeb, for example, is an ISAPI application. Microsoft dbWeb is used to provide an ODBC interface to the HTTP server so that your clients can insert, delete, update, or query, your ODBC-compliant databases using their Web browser.

FIGURE 16.1.
The Internet Server Application interface.

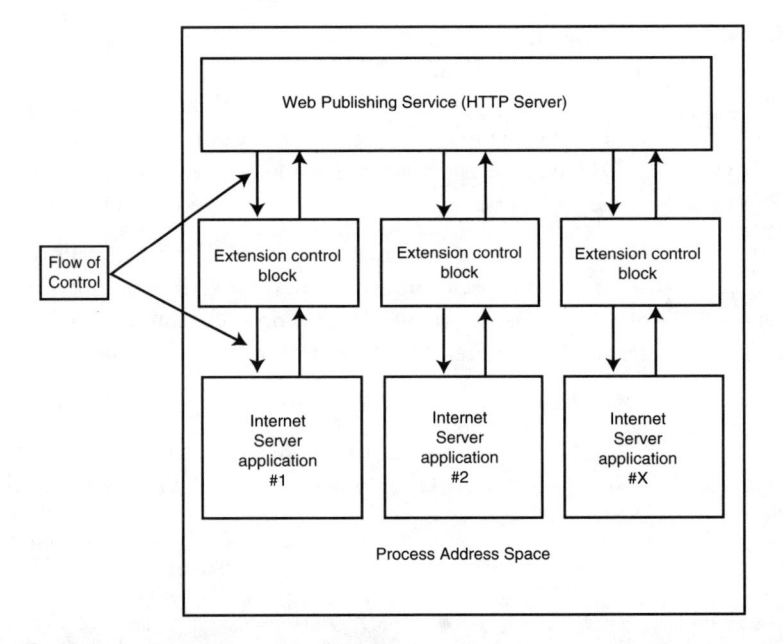

Following are the six functions defined for an ISA:

- `GetExtensionVersion`—Provides version-specific information to the HTTP server.
- `HttpExtensionProc`—Performs the real work of the ISA extension.
- `GetServerVariable`—Provides access to predefined environment variables.
- `ReadClient`—Obtains additional data from the client when the ECB data buffer cannot contain all the data.
- `WriteClient`—Sends data back to the client.
- `ServerSupportFunction`—Provides general-purpose functions as well as HTTP server-specific functions to the ISA.

Let's look into these so you can get a better understanding of their structure and function.

The `GetExtensionVersion` Function

The `GetExtensionVersion` function is used to inform the HTTP server of the suitability of the extension. In essence, when the function is called by the HTTP server, it is passed a pointer to an `HSE_VERSION_INFO` structure. This structure contains the major and minor versions of the HTTP server that the extension supports, along with a text description of the server extension. The ISA must populate the `HSE_VERSION_INFO` structure with this version information when called by the HTTP server. This function is used to prevent an outdated ISA from being loaded on a non-compatible HTTP server. The function definition is as follows:

```
BOOL WINAPI GetExtensionVersion (HSE_VERSION_INFO *pVer);
```

The `HSE_VERSION_INFO` structure in `httpext.h` is defined as

```
typedef struct _HSE_VERSION_INFO {
   DWORD dwExtensionVersion;
   CHAR  lpszExtensionDesc[HSE_MAX_EXT_DLL_NAME_LEN];
} HSE_VERSION_INFO, *LPHSE_VERSION_INFO;
```

Currently the `HSE_MAX_EXT_DLL_NAME_LEN` definition is set to a value of 256 characters, which provides you with a 255-character name space because you must leave room for the string's null terminator. When this function is called, it must populate the `HSE_VERSION_INFO` structure and return `TRUE` (1) if successful or `FALSE` (0) if unsuccessful. The `dwExtensionVersion` element can be populated using the `HIWORD` and `LOWORD` macros. The major version number is contained in the high word, and the minor version number is contained in the low word of the `dwExtensionVersion` element.

The `HttpExtensionProc` Function

Whenever the client (the Web browser) makes a request requiring the ISA, the `HttpExtensionProc` function of the ISA is called and passed a pointer to an ECB structure. The ECB structure is defined in the header `HTTPEXT.H` as `EXTENSION_CONTROL_BLOCK` and has the elements summarized in Table 16.1. The `HttpExtensionProc` is defined as follows:

```
DWORD WINAPI HttpExtensionProc (EXTENSION_CONTROL_BLOCK *pEcb);
```

Table 16.1. The extension control block format.

Element	Type	Used for	Description
cbSize	DWORD	Input	Specifies the size of the ECB structure.
dwVersion	DWORD	Input	Specifies the IIS version number that this extension supports. The major version number is contained in the high word, and the minor version number is contained in the low word. You can use the HIWORD and LOWORD macros to obtain the major and minor version numbers.
ConnID	HCONN	Input	A unique number assigned by the HTTP server. This number should not be modified.
dwHttpStatusCode	DWORD	Output	Specifies the status of the current completed transaction to be returned to the HTTP server.

continues

Table 16.1. continued

Element	Type	Used for	Description
lpszLogData	CHAR	Output	A null-terminated string of HSE_LOG_BUFFER_LEN (currently defined as 80 characters) to be inserted into the HTTP server log.
lpszMethod	LPSTR	Input	Specifies a null-terminated string containing the method used by the client for this transaction. This is the same value as the CGI variable REQUEST_METHOD.
lpszQueryString	LPSTR	Input	Specifies a null-terminated string containing the query information. This is the same as the CGI variable QUERY_STRING.
lpszPathInfo	LPSTR	Input	Specifies a null-terminated string containing the extra path information given to the client. This is the same as the CGI variable PATH_INFO.
lpszPathTranslated	LPSTR	Input	Specifies a null-terminated string containing the translated path. This is the same as the CGI variable PATH_TRANSLATED.
cbTotalBytes	DWORD	Input	Specifies the total number of bytes received from the client. This is the same as the CGI variable CONTENT_LENGTH.
cbAvailable	DWORD	Input	Specifies the available number of bytes, out of the total as defined by cbTotalBytes, contained within the buffer pointed to by lpbData.
lpbData	LPBYTE	Input	Specifies a pointer to a buffer, of size cbAvailable, containing the data sent by the client.
lpszContentType	LPSTR	Input	Specifies a null-terminated string containing the type of data sent by the client. This is the same as the CGI variable CONTENT_TYPE.

It is up to the HttpExtensionProc function to parse the ECB to determine what the client is requesting. This information will be contained in the ECB lpszQueryString element. Any additional data will be contained in the buffer pointed to by the lpbData element. If the buffer is too small to contain all the data as defined by the cbTotalBytes element, the HttpExtensionProc can retrieve the additional data using the `ReadClient` function. When the `HttpExtensionProc` has completed its processing, it must send the resulting data (in HTML format) to the client using the `WriteClient` or `ServerSupportFunction` function. It must return a status code to the HTTP server upon completion. The status code can be one of the following:

- HSE_STATUS_SUCCESS—This status code specifies that the ISA completed its task successfully and that the HTTP server can disconnect and free up system resources by unloading the ISA.
- HSE_STATUS_SUCCESS_AND_KEEP_CONN—This status code specifies that the ISA completed its task, but that the HTTP server should keep the ISA active in memory if the client supports persistent connections.

> **NOTE**
>
> The HSE_STATUS_SUCCESS_AND_KEEP_CONN status code should only be used if the ISA has sent a keep-alive header to the client.

- HSE_STATUS_PENDING—This status code specifies that the ISA has queued the request for processing and that it will inform the HTTP server when the request has completed using the `ServerSupportFunction` with the dwHSERequest parameter set to HSE_REQ_DONE_WITH_SESSION.
- HSE_STATUS_ERROR—This status code specifies that the ISA encountered an error while attempting to complete its task and that the HTTP server can disconnect and free up system resources by unloading the ISA.

The `GetServerVariable` Function

The `GetServerVariable` function is used to obtain information about the connection or information about the HTTP server. The function is defined as follows:

```
BOOL WINAPI GetServerVariable (HCONN hConn, LPSTR lpszVariableName,
➥LPVOID lpvBuffer, LPDWORD lpdwSizeofBuffer);
```

The function parameters are defined as follows:

- hConn—Specifies the connection handle.
- lpszVariableName—Specifies the name of the desired CGI variable. These variable definitions are summarized in Table 16.2.
- lpvBuffer—Specifies a pointer to a buffer to contain the data defined by the CGI variable.
- lpdwSizeOfBuffer—Specifies the size of the buffer pointed to by lpvBuffer. When the function returns, this parameter contains the length of the data returned, including the null terminator.

Table 16.2. The GetServerVariable variable definitions.

Variable Name	Definition	Note
ALL_HTTP	All HTTP headers that are not parsed into one of the other listed variables in this table.	
AUTH_PASS	Specifies the password supplied by the client.	The password will be a null-terminated string.
AUTH_TYPE	Specifies the authorization type in use.	If the user has been authenticated by the server, the return value will be Basic. Otherwise, the entry will not be present.
CONTENT_LENGTH	Specifies the number of bytes the script can expect to receive from the client.	
CONTENT_TYPE	The content type of the information supplied in the POST request.	
GATEWAY_INTERFACE	Specifies the revision level of the CGI specification.	
HTTP_ACCEPT	Returns special-case HTTP header information.	
PATH_INFO	Additional path information as given by the client.	This value will contain the trailing part of the URL after the script name, but before the query string (if any query string was supplied).
PATH_TRANSLATED	The same as PATH_INFO, but without any virtual pathname translation.	
QUERY_STRING	Specifies the information after the ? in a script query.	
REMOTE_ADDR	Specifies the IP address of the client.	
REMOTE_HOST	Specifies the hostname of the client.	
REMOTE_USER	Specifies the user name supplied by the client and authorized by the server.	

Variable Name	Definition	Note
REQUEST_METHOD	Specifies the HTTP request method.	
SCRIPT_NAME	Specifies the name of the script being executed.	
SERVER_NAME	Specifies the name of the server (or IP address) as it should appear in self-referencing URLs.	
SERVER_PORT	Specifies the TCP/IP port on which the request was received.	
SERVER_PROTOCOL	Specifies the name and version of the request.	Usually HTTP/1.0.
SERVER_SOFTWARE	Specifies the name and version number of the Web server under which the IIS extension is executing.	

The ReadClient Function

The ReadClient function is used to obtain additional data from the client when the entire block of data will not fit into the buffer pointer by lpdData in the ECB block. The definition of the function is as follows:

BOOL ReadClient (HCONN *hConn*, LPVOID *lpvBuffer*, LPDWORD *lpdwSize*);

The function parameters are defined as follows:

- hConn—Specifies the connection handle.
- lpvBuffer—Specifies a pointer to a buffer. This buffer will be used to contain the data returned by the read request.
- lpdwSizeOfBuffer—Specifies the size of the buffer pointed to by lpvBuffer. When the function returns, this parameter contains the length of the data returned.

The WriteClient Function

The WriteClient function is used to send data to the client. The definition of the function is as follows:

```
BOOL WriteClient (HCONN hConn, LPVOID lpvBuffer, LPDWORD lpdwSize,
➥DWORD dwReserved);
```

The function parameters are defined as follows:

- hConn—Specifies the connection handle.
- lpvBuffer—Specifies a pointer to a buffer. This buffer will be used to contain the data sent to the client. Normally, this will be a series of HTML tags and data.
- lpdwSizeOfBuffer—Specifies the size of the buffer pointed to by lpvBuffer. If a null-terminated string is to be sent to the client in its entirety, this value should be set using the value returned by the function call strlen(lpvBuffer). When the WriteClient function returns, this parameter contains the length of the data sent to the client.
- dwReserved—Specifies that the parameter is reserved for future use.

The ServerSupportFunction Function

The ServerSupportFunction is used to send data back to a client in much the same way as the WriteClient function does. However, it provides additional functions to inform the HTTP server about the status of the operation, which the WriteClient function cannot do. The function definition is as follows:

```
BOOL ServerSupportFunction (HCONN hConn, DWORD dwHSERequest, LPVOID lpvBuffer,
➥ LPDWORD lpdwSizeofBuffer, LPDWORD lpdwDataType);
```

The function parameters are defined as follows:

- hConn—Specifies the connection handle.
- dwHSERequest—Specifies the type of request to be sent to the client. This can be a custom request type, which uses a value greater than that defined by HSE_REQ_END_RESERVED, or it can be one of the following general-purpose predefined values:
    - HSE_REQ_SEND_URL_REDIRECT_RESP—Specifies that a 302 (URL redirect) message be sent to the client. This is similar to specifying URI:<URL> in a CGI script header. If this value is used, the lpvBuffer should point to a null-terminated string containing the URL.
    - HSE_REQ_SEND_URL—Specifies that the data associated with a URL be sent to the client as if he explicitly selected the URL. The lpvBuffer should point to a null-terminated string containing the URL.
    - HSE_REQ_SEND_RESPONSE_HEADER—Specifies that a complete HTTP server response header be sent to the client. The application should append additional information, such as the content type, content length, a \r\n (carriage return–line feed pair), and any other additional information. The skeleton example

source code, later in this chapter in the section titled "An Internet Server Application Skeleton," uses this operation to send basic HTML data to be displayed on the Web browser.

- `HSE_REQ_MAP_URL_TO_PATH`—Specifies that the `lpdvBuffer` will contain a logical pathname when the `ServerSupportFunction` is executed, and that the `lpdvBuffer` will have a physical pathname corresponding to the logical name upon completion.

- `lpvBuffer`—Specifies a pointer to a buffer containing the null-terminated status string (such as `Error 402-Payment required`) to be returned to the client. If this value is `NULL`, the default status code (`200 OK`) will be sent to the client.

- `lpdwSizeOfBuffer`—Specifies the size of the buffer pointed to by `lpvBuffer`. If a null-terminated string is to be sent to the client in its entirety, this value should be set using the value returned by the function call `strlen(lpvBuffer)`. When the `ServerSupportFunction` function returns, `lpdwSizeOfBuffer` contains the length of the data sent to the client.

- `lpdDataType`—This specifies a pointer to a zero-terminated string of data to be appended to the header. This is an optional string, and if this field is `NULL`, the header will be terminated with a \r\n.

An Internet Server Application Skeleton

To make things a little easier for you in your efforts to develop an ISA to perform a specific task, I have created a basic skeleton framework for you. The source code, including the Visual C++ 4.0 makefile, can be found on the CD-ROM in the \SOURCE\CHAP16 subdirectory. It is printed here to give you an idea of the functional requirements. Basically, an ISA can be divided into three components. The first is an optional application header (shown in Listing 16.1). The second is a required application definition (shown in Listing 16.2). The third is a required application definition file (shown in Listing 16.3), which is used to define the procedures to export. An exported procedure can be called by another application (such as the HTTP server) by name. This export list is what makes it possible for the HTTP server to execute your ISA.

The source code should be self-explanatory, but I would like to mention two things. First, the `DLLMain` function is not required to build an ISA, but it can be used to perform per-process or per-thread initialization or cleanup when called. You might use this function to allocate and deallocate process or thread resources, or you might use it to maintain state information. You can even use it to report performance data that the Performance Monitor could display. There are numerous possibilities, but if you do not use this function, none of these possibilities will be available. Second, if you look at the `HttpExtentionProc` definition in the `Skeleton.C` code listing, you will see a bare-bones ISA. This function retrieves the query string sent by the client, and then sends this information back to the client along with a very basic HTML

Advanced Web Page Development
Part V

document (header, title, and body). This HTML document is created on the fly, so to speak, by the function. If you create an ISA, it will be up to your ISA to create a properly formatted HTML document to display on the Web browser.

Listing 16.1. The source code for `Skeleton.H`.

```
//--------------------------------------------------
// THIS CODE AND INFORMATION IS PROVIDED "AS IS" WITHOUT WARRANTY OF
// ANY KIND, EITHER EXPRESSED OR IMPLIED, INCLUDING BUT NOT LIMITED TO
// THE IMPLIED WARRANTIES OF MERCHANTABILITY AND/OR FITNESS FOR A
// PARTICULAR PURPOSE.
//
//
//     Skeleton.H              -    Sample skeleton code to create an Internet
//                                  Server Application (ISA)
//                                  multithreaded processor intensive application.
//
//
// Copyright (c) 1996         -    Knowles Consulting. All rights Reserved.
//
//--------------------------------------------------

#define    ISA_DESCRIPTION    "Skeleton Internet Server Application"
#define    ISA_TITLE          "<head><title>Skeleton \
 Internet Server Application \
                                Document Title</title></head>\n"
#define    ISA_HEADER         "<h1>Skeleton Internet Server Application \
 Document \
                                Header</h1>\n"
#define    ISA_CALL           "<b>This ISA was called passed the '%s' \
                                QueryString.</b>"
#define    ISA_DO_NOTHING     "This is the body of your document. In this \
 case, \
                                the skeleton application does nothing other
 than \
                                print this basic message on your web browser.
 You \
                                could do much more, but to do so you will have
 to \
                                write the code. You can't get everything for \
                                free. :)"
#define    ISA_CONTENT        "Content-Type: text/html\r\n\r\n"
#define    ISA_BODY_BEGIN     "<body>"
#define    ISA_BODY_END       "</body>"
#define    ISA_HR             "<hr>"
```

Listing 16.2. The source code for `Skeleton.C`.

```
//--------------------------------------------------
// THIS CODE AND INFORMATION IS PROVIDED "AS IS" WITHOUT WARRANTY OF
// ANY KIND, EITHER EXPRESSED OR IMPLIED, INCLUDING BUT NOT LIMITED TO
// THE IMPLIED WARRANTIES OF MERCHANTABILITY AND/OR FITNESS FOR A
// PARTICULAR PURPOSE.
//
```

```c
//
//      Skeleton.C              -       Sample skeleton code to create an Internet
//                                      Server Application (ISA)
//                                      multithreaded processor intensive application.
//
//
// Copyright (c) 1996      -       Knowles Consulting. All rights Reserved.
//
//————————————————————————————————————

#include <windows.h>
#include <httpext.h>
#include <stdio.h>
#include <string.h>
#include "Skeleton.H"

// This function is not required to build an ISA, although it is a
// good idea to include it and perform your initialization and cleanup
// as required by your ISA.
BOOL WINAPI DllMain (HANDLE hModule,ULONG ulReason, LPVOID lpReserved)
    {
    switch (ulReason)
        {
        case DLL_PROCESS_ATTACH:
            { // Insert process specific initalization here
            }
        case DLL_THREAD_ATTACH:
            { // Insert thread specific initalization here
            }
        case DLL_PROCESS_DETACH:
            { // Insert process specific cleanup here
            }
        case DLL_THREAD_DETACH:
            { // Insert thread specific cleanup here
            }
        }

    return (TRUE);
    }

BOOL WINAPI GetExtensionVersion (HSE_VERSION_INFO *pVer)
    {
    pVer->dwExtensionVersion = MAKELONG(HSE_VERSION_MINOR, HSE_VERSION_MAJOR);
    // Note: Be sure to change ISA_DESCRIPTION in the Skelaton.H header file
➥to define your ISA
    if ((lstrcpyn (pVer->lpszExtensionDesc, ISA_DESCRIPTION,
➥HSE_MAX_EXT_DLL_NAME_LEN)) != NULL)
        {
        return (TRUE);
        }
    else
        {
        return (FALSE);
        }
    }
```

continues

Listing 16.2. continued

```
DWORD WINAPI HttpExtensionProc (EXTENSION_CONTROL_BLOCK  *pEcb)
    {
    DWORD dwStatus = HSE_STATUS_SUCCESS;
    CHAR szBuff[4096];
    CHAR szTemp[80];
    DWORD dwLen;

    // Assign your basic document attributes here
    // Note: These values are defined in Skeleton.H
    wsprintf( szBuff, ISA_CONTENT ISA_TITLE ISA_BODY_BEGIN ISA_HEADER ISA_HR);

    // Insert code to perform the real work here and replace the sample code.
    sprintf (szTemp, ISA_CALL, pEcb->lpszQueryString);   // Build temporary
➥string with query string
    strcat (szBuff, szTemp);                              // Inserts query
➥ string passed
    strcat (szBuff, ISA_HR);                              // Inserts
➥ horizontal rule
    strcat (szBuff,ISA_DO_NOTHING);                       // Inserts do
➥ nothing text
    strcat (szBuff,ISA_BODY_END);                         // Inserts </body>
➥ tag
    dwLen = lstrlen(szBuff);                              // Gets length of
➥ buffer
    //    Sends a completed response header
    if (!pEcb->ServerSupportFunction(pEcb->ConnID,
➥HSE_REQ_SEND_RESPONSE_HEADER, NULL, &dwLen, (LPDWORD) szBuff ))
        {   // If an error occured sending the response header, then sets
➥status code. to error
        dwStatus = HSE_STATUS_ERROR;
        }

    // Returns status code
    return (dwStatus);
    }
```

Listing 16.3. The source code for Skeleton.DEF.

```
LIBRARY      Skeleton

DESCRIPTION      'Internet Server Application Extension DLL'

EXPORTS
    DllMail
    GetExtensionVersion
    HttpExtensionProc
```

Summary

This chapter begins with a definition of an ISAPI application. You have learned some of the differences between a CGI application and an ISAPI application, and why you may want to develop ISAPI applications instead of CGI applications. You have also learned that not every aspect of ISAPI is a bed of roses, and you have been introduced to some of the possible pitfalls associated with ISAPI development. To gain a better understanding of how an ISAPI application works, you have looked into the basic ISAPI interface and the associated ISAPI functions. Your final stop was a look at actual working code to build a functional ISAPI application. You can use this application as a skeleton framework to build your own ISAPI applications. In Chapter 17 you will learn how to create CGI applications for the Internet Information Server. This may be of particular interest to readers who already have quite a few CGI applications developed for other HTTP servers and just want to get them up and running with the Internet Information Server.

Unleashing the Power of VBScript

17

IN THIS CHAPTER

- Introduction to VBScript **446**
- How VBScript Works **446**
- Hello World! **447**
- VBScript Operators **451**
- VBScript Control Structures **455**
- VBScript Functions **463**
- Applications of VBScript **473**

VBScript is Microsoft's scripting language for the Internet. Similar in functionality to JavaScript, VBScript has been designed to leverage the skills of millions of Visual Basic programmers to the Internet. Although JavaScript is a powerful scripting language, it is not as easy to learn and use as VBScript. VBScript can be used to easily create active Web pages. Since VBScript is supported by Microsoft, in the near future you will also see a great deal of VBScript/Windows NT/95/MSOffice Backoffice integration, unlike JavaScript. VBScript code is lightweight, fast, and has been optimized to be transmitted via the Internet. You should spend some time with VBScript and learn how it can be used to enhance a Web site by making it easier and more exciting to navigate. By the time you read this, you can expect to see VBScript supported by several other Web browsers in addition to Internet Explorer—specifically, browsers from Oracle, Spyglass, and NetManage.

Introduction to VBScript

VBScript is a subset of Microsoft Visual Basic and is upwardly compatible with Visual Basic for Applications (VBA). VBA is shipped with MS Office applications to make it easier for developers to build custom solutions using MS Office applications. The ability to provide scripting, automation, and customization capabilities for Web browsers is a major feature of VBScript. If you are already familiar with Visual Basic, very shortly you will be able to leverage your skills to the Internet using VBScript. Even if you are not familiar with another programming language, after reading this chapter you will be able to create active Web pages using VBScript. However, familiarity with a programming language will make it easier for you to grasp various concepts such as recursion, type casting, and Boolean arithmetic. Visit the Microsoft VBScript home page for the most up-to-date information about VBScript.

> **NOTE**
>
> Visit the Microsoft VBScript information Web site for the latest information about VBScript:
>
> http://www.microsoft.com/VBScript

How VBScript Works

VBScript programs are defined between two HTML tags. Browsers that support VBScript read the VBScript program contained between the two HTML tags and execute it after checking for any syntax errors. VBScript works as shown in Figure 17.1.

FIGURE 17.1.
How VBScript works.

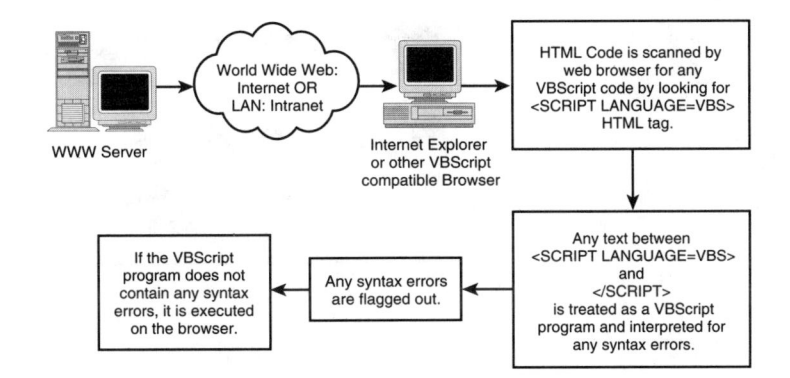

As you can see in Figure 17.1, a VBScript program is part of a regular HTML file and is enclosed between two HTML tags, `<SCRIPT LANGUAGE=VBS>` and `</SCRIPT>`. When a Web browser that supports VBScript encounters the `<SCRIPT LANGUAGE=VBS>` HTML tag, all text between that tag and `</SCRIPT>` is treated as a VBScript program and is interpreted for syntax errors. If any syntax errors are detected, they are flagged by the VBScript interpreter, as shown in Figure 17.2.

FIGURE 17.2.
Syntax errors in VBScript programs are flagged by the VBScript interpreter.

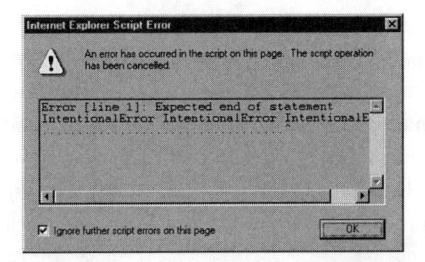

If the code does not contain any syntax errors, it is executed on the Web browser. In order to hide VBScript code from technologically challenged Web browsers, VBScript code can be enclosed in two HTML comment tags as shown here:

```
<SCRIPT LANGUAGE=VBS>
<!-- To hide VBScript code from technologically challenged browsers
… VBScript code …
!-->
</SCRIPT>
```

Hello World!

Writing the classic Hello World! application with VBScript is very easy. For the purpose of this example, you will be shown how to create a Web page similar to the one in Figure 17.3. This Web page will have three buttons. The first button will display a message box with a greeting, the second button will display the current time, and the third button will display today's date.

FIGURE 17.3.
The classic Hello World! application written with VBScript.

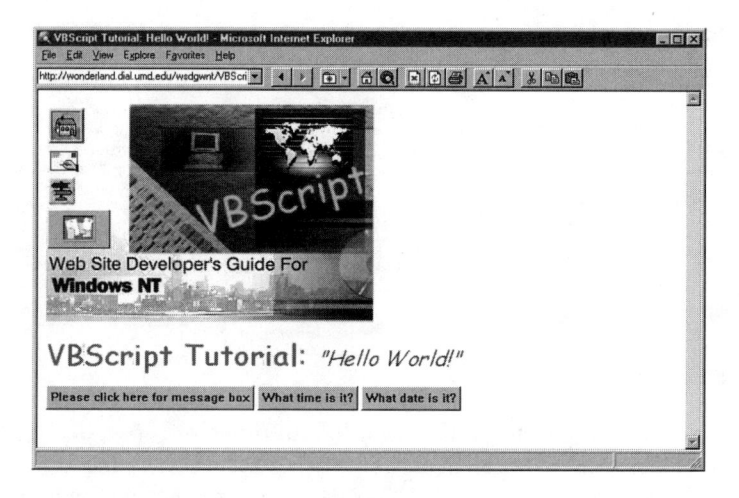

Various key elements of the Hello World! VBScript program are outlined next.

The Hello World! Dialog Box

As shown in Figure 17.4, the Hello World! dialog box is shown each time a user clicks on the `Please click here for message box` button in Figure 17.3. If you look at the HTML page the VBScript program is in, you will see that the command button associated with the Hello World! dialog box is named `BtnHello` (`NAME="BtnHello"`). As you can see from the following listing, the `OnClick` event is associated with the `BtnHello` subroutine. Each time a user clicks on the `Please click here for message box` button in Figure 17.3, the Web browser invokes the `BtnHello_OnClick` subroutine and any VBScript code defined in that subroutine is executed.

The `BtnHello_OnClick` subroutine is a very simple VBScript subroutine. The first three lines create strings displayed by the dialog box in Figure 17.4. Note how the string concatenation operator (&) is used in line 4 to merge two strings into one and assign the result to a variable. The result is then displayed in a message box, as shown in Figure 17.4:

> **NOTE**
>
> Line numbers in various code segments are not part of the VBScript code. The line numbers are only there for reference purposes.

```
1: Sub BtnHello_OnClick
2:   titleString = "Web Site Developer's Guide for Windows NT"
3:   helloString = "Hello world! Welcome to the fun filled "
```

```
4:     helloString = helloString & "world of VBScript programming!"
5:     MsgBox helloString, 0, titleString
6: End Sub
```

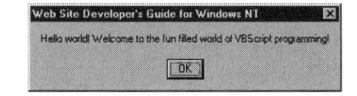

FIGURE 17.4.
The Hello World! dialog box.

The Time Dialog Box

The `BtnTime_OnClick` subroutine is very similar to the `BtnHello_OnClick` subroutine. The only difference is the fact that rather than concatenating two strings, it concatenates a string with the result of a function. The `time` function returns the current time. As shown in Figure 17.5, line 3 of the following program listing displays the current time in a dialog box:

```
1: Sub BtnTime_OnClick
2:     timeString = "So, you want to know the time? The time is " & time
3:     MsgBox  timeString , 0, "Time Dialog Box"
4: End Sub
```

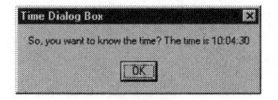

FIGURE 17.5.
The Time dialog box.

The Date Dialog Box

The Date dialog box displays the current date in a dialog box, as shown in Figure 17.6. As you can see in line 2 of the following code listing, the result of one function (`date`) can be used as an argument of another function (`DateValue`).

```
1: Sub BtnDate_OnClick
2:     dateString = "Today's date is " & DateValue(date)
3:     MsgBox  dateString , 0, "Date Dialog Box"
4: End Sub
```

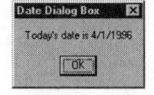

FIGURE 17.6.
The Date dialog box.

For your reference, the full source code of the Hello World! application appears in Listing 17.1.

Listing 17.1. The Hello World! Web page.

```
<!--
(C) 1996 Sanjaya Hettihewa (http://wonderland.dial.umd.edu)
All Rights Reserved.
```

continues

Listing 17.1. continued

```
!-->

<HTML>
<HEAD>
<TITLE>VBScript Tutorial: Hello World!</TITLE>
</HEAD>

<BODY BGCOLOR="#FFFFFF" TEXT="#0000FF"
      LINK="#B864FF" VLINK="#670000" ALINK="#FF0000">

<IMG SRC="vbscript.jpg"><P>

<B><FONT FACE="Comic Sans MS" SIZE=6 COLOR=RED>
VBScript Tutorial: <FONT></B>
<I><FONT FACE="Comic Sans MS" SIZE=5 COLOR=BLUE>
 "Hello World!" </I><P><FONT>

<form>
<INPUT TYPE=BUTTON VALUE="Please click here for message box"
       NAME="BtnHello">
<INPUT TYPE=BUTTON VALUE="What time is it?"
       NAME="BtnTime">
<INPUT TYPE=BUTTON VALUE="What date is it?"
       NAME="BtnDate">
</form>
<SCRIPT LANGUAGE=VBS>
<!-- To hide VBScript code from technologically challenged browsers

Sub BtnHello_OnClick
 titleString = "Web Site Developer's Guide for Windows NT"
 helloString = "Hello world! Welcome to the fun filled "
 helloString = helloString & "world of VBScript programming!"
 MsgBox helloString, 0, titleString
End Sub

Sub BtnTime_OnClick
 timeString = "So, you want to know the time? The time is " & time
 MsgBox  timeString , 0, "Time Dialog Box"
End Sub

Sub BtnDate_OnClick
 dateString = "Today's date is " & DateValue(date)
 MsgBox  dateString , 0, "Date Dialog Box"
End Sub
!-->
</SCRIPT>

</BODY>

</HTML>
```

Unleashing the Power of VBScript
Chapter 17

VBScript Operators

VBScript supports several operators for various string, Boolean, and number-manipulation tasks. Various operators supported by VBScript are listed in the following sections.

The Addition Operator

Syntax: `<operand1> + <operand2>`

The addition operator can be used to add two operands together. If both operands are numeric, the result of the addition operator will also be numeric. However, if they are strings, VBScript will instead do a string concatenation instead of a numeric addition. To avoid ambiguity, it is recommended that you use the string concatenation operator (&) when joining strings, and use the addition operator (+) when adding numeric expressions.

The Subtraction Operator

Syntax: `<operand1> - <operand2>`
Syntax: `-<OperandToNegate>`

The subtraction operator is used as a unary minus and the binary subtraction operator. When used as the binary subtraction operator, it subtracts `<operand2>` from `<operand1>` and returns the resulting value. When used as the unary minus, it negates the numeric operand it is used with.

The Multiplication Operator

Syntax: `<operand1> ^ <operand2>`

The multiplication operator takes two numeric operands, multiplies them, and returns the resulting value.

The Exponential Operator

Syntax: `<operand1> ^ <operand2>`

Returns the resulting value of `<operand1>` raised to the `<operand2>` power.

The Floating-Point Division Operator

Syntax: `<operand1> / <operand2>`

The division operator is used to divide `<operand1>` from `<operand2>`. Both `<operand1>` and `<operand2>` have to be numeric expressions, and the resulting value is a floating-point number.

The Integer-Division Operator

Syntax: `<operand1> \ <operand2>`

The integer-division operator is somewhat similar to the floating-point division operator. The integer-division operator returns an integer number after dividing `<operand1>` by `<operand2>`. A few examples of the integer division operator are listed next.

```
( 23 \ 4 ) = 5
( 4 \ 23 ) = 0
( 4 \ 2 ) = 2
( 5 \ 2 ) = 2
```

The String-Concatenation Operator

Syntax: `<operand1> & <operand2>`

The string-concatenation operator can be used to join `<operand1>` and `<operand2>` together.

The MOD Operator

Syntax: `<operand1> MOD <operand2>`

The MOD operator is somewhat similar to the integer-division operator. The only difference is that it returns the remainder of `<operand1>` divided by `<operand2>`. A few examples of the MOD operator are listed next.

```
( 23 MOD 4 ) = 3
( 4 MOD 23 ) = 4
( 4 MOD 2 ) = 0
( 5 MOD 2 ) = 1
```

Boolean Operators

VBScript supports a number of Boolean operators. The best way to explain how Boolean operators work is with a truth table. See Figure 17.7 for truth tables of a number of useful VBScript Boolean operators. Various useful VBScript Boolean operators are listed next, along with how they can be used in VBScript programs.

The AND Operator

Syntax: `<operand1> AND <operand2>`

The AND operator returns TRUE if both `<operand1>` and `<operand2>` are true. If not, it returns FALSE. The AND operator can be used with expressions and functions that return a Boolean value.

FIGURE 17.7.
Truth tables of VBScript Boolean operators.

AND				
TRUE	AND	TRUE	=	TRUE
TRUE	AND	FALSE	=	FALSE
FALSE	AND	TRUE	=	FALSE
FALSE	AND	FALSE	=	FALSE

OR				
TRUE	OR	TRUE	=	TRUE
TRUE	OR	FALSE	=	TRUE
FALSE	OR	TRUE	=	TRUE
FALSE	OR	FALSE	=	FALSE

XOR				
TRUE	XOR	TRUE	=	FALSE
TRUE	XOR	FALSE	=	TRUE
FALSE	XOR	TRUE	=	TRUE
FALSE	XOR	FALSE	=	FALSE

NOT				
	NOT	TRUE	=	FALSE
	NOT	FALSE	=	TRUE

The OR Operator

Syntax: `<operand1> OR <operand2>`

The OR operator returns TRUE if either `<operand1>` or `<operand2>` is true. The OR operator can be used with expressions and functions that return a Boolean value.

The NOT Operator

Syntax: `NOT <operand>`

The NOT operator can be used to negate a Boolean value. The NOT operator can be used with expressions and functions that return a Boolean value.

The XOR Operator

Syntax: `<operand1> XOR <operand2>`

The XOR operator is very similar to the OR operator. The only difference is that in order for the XOR operator to return TRUE, `<operand1>` or `<operand2>` has to be true. However, they both can't be true at the same time. The NOT operator can be used with expressions and functions that return a Boolean value.

The Equivalence Operator

Syntax: `<operand1> Eqv <operand2>`

The equivalence operator can be used to determine if `<operand1>` is equal to `<operand2>`. If either `<operand1>` or `<operand2>` is NULL, then the resulting value will also be NULL. The truth table of the equivalence operator is listed next:

```
TRUE  Eqv TRUE  = TRUE
FALSE Eqv TRUE  = FALSE
TRUE  Eqv FALSE = FALSE
FALSE Eqv FALSE = TRUE
```

(TRUE *may be replaced with binary 1 and* FALSE *may be replaced with binary 0.*)

The Object-Reference Operator

Syntax: `<operand1> IS <operand2>`

The object-reference operator is used to compare two object-reference variables. If `<operand1>` refers to the same object as `<operand2>`, the object-reference operator returns TRUE. Otherwise, it returns FALSE.

Comparison Operators

VBScript supports several comparison operators. These comparison operators can be used to compare strings as well as numbers. Various comparison operators that can be used in VBScript programs are listed next.

The Equal Operator

Syntax: `<operand1> = <operand2>`

Returns TRUE if both `<operand1>` and `<operand2>` are equal to each other. However, if either `<operand1>` or `<operand2>` is NULL, the equal operator will return NULL.

The Unequal Operator

Syntax: `<operand1> <> <operand2>`

Returns TRUE if both `<operand1>` and `<operand2>` are unequal to each other. However, if either `<operand1>` or `<operand2>` is NULL, the unequal operator will return NULL.

The Less Than Operator

Syntax: `<operand1> < <operand2>`

Returns TRUE if `<operand1>` is less than `<operand2>`. However, if either `<operand1>` or `<operand2>` is NULL, the less than operator will return NULL.

The Less Than or Equal to Operator

Syntax: `<operand1> <= <operand2>`

Returns TRUE if `<operand1>` is less than or equal to `<operand2>`. However, if either `<operand1>` or `<operand2>` is NULL, the less than or equal to operator will return NULL.

The Greater Than Operator

Syntax: `<operand1> > <operand2>`

Returns TRUE if `<operand1>` is greater than `<operand2>`. However, if either `<operand1>` or `<operand2>` is NULL, the greater than operator will return NULL.

The Greater Than or Equal to Operator

Syntax: `<operand1> >= <operand2>`

Returns TRUE if `<operand1>` is greater than or equal to `<operand2>`. However, if either `<operand1>` or `<operand2>` is NULL, the greater than or equal to operator will return NULL.

VBScript Control Structures

Control structures are an important part of any language. They give a language "life" by allowing programmers to add intelligence to programs with conditional and iterative statements. Various VBScript control structures are listed next, along with how they can be used in VBScript programs.

Call

`Call` is used to transfer program control to another VBScript subroutine. Note that when `Call` is used to transfer control to another subroutine, if that subroutine has any parameters, they should be enclosed in parentheses. However, if `Call` is omitted, subroutine arguments do not need to be enclosed in parentheses. Return values of functions are ignored when they are invoked with the `Call` statement.

Dim

The `Dim` statement is used to declare variables, such as arrays, and assign them storage space. When variables are declared with `Dim`, if they are numeric variables, they are initialized with the value `0`. Otherwise, they are assigned an empty string. The `Dim` statement can be used to declare several types of variables. Various types of variables that can be created with the `Dim` statement are listed next.

Declaring Variant Variables

Syntax: `Dim <VariableName1> , <VariableName2>`

This statement can be used to declare variables of variant type. As shown here, several variables can be defined at the same time by separating them with commas.

Multiple Variables Declarations

Syntax: `Dim <VariableName1> As Integer, <VariableName2>`

One `Dim` statement can be used to declare several variables of more than one type. As in the case of the previous `Dim` command, `<VariableName1>` is declared as an integer variable and `<VariableName2>` is declared as a variant variable.

Declaring Static Arrays

Single Dimension Array Syntax: `Dim <NameOfArray>(50)`

The `Dim` statement can be used to define arrays. In this example, an array of 50 storage locations of type variant is created using the `Dim` statement. If an index range is not specified for an array, VBScript will index the array starting at zero. For example, in this case, `<NameOfArray>` is indexed from `0` to `49`.

Multi Dimension Array Syntax: `Dim <NameOfArray>(5,1 To 5)`

The `Dim` statement can also be used to declare multidimensional arrays. For example, the preceding statement can be used to declare a two-dimensional array by the name of `<NameOfArray>`. As shown in this example, the index range of an array can be customized by using a number range (1 to 5). By adding an `As <VariableType>` command to an array declaration, it is possible to define an array of a certain data type.

Declaring Dynamic Arrays

If you are unsure about the size of an array when it is first declared, VBScript allows the creation of dynamic arrays. Dynamic arrays can be expanded or reduced as needed. Dynamic arrays can be created using the following syntax.

```
Dim <NameOfArray>()
```

Storage space for additional elements can be allocated for a dynamic array using the ReDim statement, as shown next. (Simply indicate, in parentheses, the number of elements the array should have.)

```
ReDim <NameOfArray>(10)
```

As an added incentive, VBScript dynamic arrays can be expanded while preserving existing array values. As shown in the next example, this is done by adding a Preserve statement in between the ReDim statement and the array name.

```
ReDim Preserve <NameOfArray>(20)
```

Note that if a data type is defined for a dynamic array using the As statement, the array's data type cannot be changed using the ReDim statement. Also, if a dynamic array is reduced in size, using the ReDim statement, any data stored in the portion of the array that was deleted is permanently lost.

Do...While...Until...Loop

The Do...Loop control structure can be used to iterate a group of statements until a certain Boolean expression becomes TRUE. The syntax of the Do...Loop control structure is listed next. As shown in the following example, the Boolean expression of a Do...Loop structure can be placed either at the beginning or the end:

```
Do <condition> <BooleanExpression>
… VBScript statements …
Loop
```

As shown next, the Boolean expression of a Do...Loop structure can also be placed at the end of the control structure:

```
Do
… VBScript statements …
Loop <condition> <BooleanExpression>
```

The preceding two examples will repeatedly execute VBScript statements enclosed in the loop structure until <BooleanExpression> becomes TRUE. In the examples, <condition> may be replaced with either While or Until. As the name implies, if While is used, the loop will iterate while <BooleanExpression> is TRUE. In the like manner, if Until is used, the loop will iterate until <BooleanExpression> is TRUE. Note that within a Do...Loop structure, it is possible to transfer control out of the loop using an Exit Do statement.

Erase

Syntax: Erase <NameOfArray>

The Erase statement is used to free memory used by dynamic arrays and reinitialize elements of static arrays. If the array is a dynamic array, all space taken up by the array is freed. Dynamic arrays then need to be reallocated using the `ReDim` statement before they can be used again. If the array is a static array, all array elements are initialized with 0 if its elements are numeric or empty strings otherwise.

Exit

The `Exit` statement causes program control to be transferred out of the control structure it is used in. The control structure can be a loop or a subroutine. Various forms of the `Exit` command are listed next:

> `Exit Do`—Exits a `Do` loop.
> `Exit For`—Exits a `For` loop.
> `Exit Function`—Exits a function.
> `Exit Sub`—Exits a procedure.

For...Next

The `For...Next` control structure can be used to iterate a group of VBScript statements a certain number of times. The syntax of the `For...Next` control structure is listed next:

```
For <LoopCount> = <BeginLoop> To <EndLoop> Step <StepCount>
… VBScript statements …
Next
```

The previous definition can be used to iterate a group of VBScript statements a certain number of times by replacing various labels (enclosed in pointed braces) of the definition, as follows:

> `<LoopCount>`—Name of variable used to keep track of the number of iterations. It's best that your VBScript statements do not alter the value of this variable, because it can easily complicate your code and make it harder to debug.
>
> `<BeginLoop>`—The first value of the iteration sequence.
>
> `<EndLoop>`—The last value of the iteration sequence.
>
> `Step <StepCount>`—Can be replaced with the `<LoopCount>`, which will be incremented after each iteration of the loop. The `Step` statement is optional; by default, `<LoopCount>` will be incremented by one.

Note that the `Exit For` statement can be used to exit a `For` loop.

For Each...Next

The `For Each...Next` control structure is useful for iterating VBScript statements for each object in a collection or each element in an array. The syntax of the `For Each...Next` loop is listed next.

```
For Each <LoopIndex> In <ArrayOrCollection>
… VBScript statements …
Next <LoopIndex>
```

A `For Each…Next` loop can be added to a VBScript program by substituting various labels of the preceding example, as follows:

<LoopIndex>—Name of variable that's used to traverse through the elements of an array or objects in a collection.

<ArrayOrCollection>—Name of an array or collection of objects.

Note that the `Exit For` statement can be used to exit a `For Each` loop. Also note that <LoopIndex> can be omitted in the `Next` <LoopIndex> statement. However, this is not recommended; it can complicate things and cause errors if a `For Each` loop is nested inside another `For Each` loop.

Function

New functions can be defined using the `Function` statement. The syntax of the `Function` statement is as follows:

```
<FunctionType> Function <NameOfFunction> <ArgumentsOfFunction>
… VBScript statements …
<NameOfFunction> = <ReturnValueOfFunction>
End Function
```

A function can be created by replacing various labels of the above definition with the values listed next:

<FunctionType>—Can be left out if it is not needed. By replacing <FunctionType> with `Static`, it is possible to preserve values of local variables in between function calls. Unless you have a reason for doing so, `Static` functions are usually not suitable for recursion (a function calling itself).

<NameOfFunction>—Used to specify the name of the function.

<ArgumentsOfFunction>—Arguments of a function can be specified soon after <NameOfFunction>. By using commas, more than one argument can be specified. An argument can be passed either by value or reference. In order to make an argument pass by value, precede the argument name with `ByVal`; to pass by reference, precede the argument name with `ByRef`. When an argument is passed by value, its original value cannot be changed from within the function. However, when it is passed by reference, the variable used in the function is merely a pointer to the original variable. Therefore, any changes made to the value of a variable passed by reference are actually made to the original variable.

Note that the `Exit Function` statement can be used to exit a function. VBScript procedures created with the `Function` statement are very similar to procedures created with the `SUB` statement. The only difference is that procedures created with the `Function` statement can return values, whereas procedures created with the `Sub` statement cannot.

If...Then...Else

The `If...Then...Else` statement can be used to execute various VBScript statements based on Boolean expressions. The syntax of the `If...Then...Else` control structure is as follows:

```
IF <BooleanExpression> THEN
… VBScript statement …
ELSE IF <BooleanExpression> THEN
… VBScript statement …
ELSE
… VBScript statement …
END IF
```

As shown in the previous example, various VBScript statements can be made to execute using an `If...Then...Else` statement based on various Boolean expressions.

Let

The `Let` command can be used to assign values to variables. The `Let` command is not required to assign a value to a variable. The syntax of the `Let` command is as follows:

```
Let <variableName> = <ValueOfVariable>
```

LSet

`LSet` is used to copy a variable of one user-defined type to a variable of another user-defined type. When a variable is copied with the `LSet` command, it is *left aligned*. The syntax of the `LSet` statement is listed next.

```
LSet <Variable> = <ValueOfVariable>
```

If the length of `<Variable>` is longer than that of `<ValueOfVariable>`, after copying `<ValueOfVariable>` to `<Variable>` the remaining space will be filled in with white spaces. In like manner, if the length of `<Variable>` is less than that of `<ValueOfVariable>`, `<ValueOfVariable>` will be truncated to fit in the space allocated for `<Variable>`. For example, if `<Variable>` can hold only four characters, and `<ValueOfVariable>` contains the string `"ABCDEFG"`, after it is copied to `<Variable>` with the `LSet` command, `<Variable>` will have the value `"ABCD"`.

Mid

`Mid` is a very handy statement for replacing one or more characters of a string with characters from another string. The syntax of the `Mid` statement is listed next.

```
Mid (<Variable>, <Begin>, <NumCharactersToReplace>) = <Replacement>
```

The `Mid` statement can be used by replacing various labels of the preceding example, as follows:

>`<Variable>`—Name of variable containing the string that will be modified.

`<Begin>`—The position to begin replacing text. For example, if `<Variable>` contained the string `"1234"` and you would like `"34"` to be replaced with `"67"`, `<Begin>` will be replaced with `"3"` because the substring `"34"` begins at the third position.

`<NumCharactersToReplace>`—Lists the number of characters that should be replaced by `<Replacement>`. This value can be left out if you wish, in which case the entire `<Replacement>` string will be copied over.

`<Replacement>`—Contains string that will be copied over to `<Variable>`.

On Error

Usually, when a runtime error occurs in a VBScript program, it halts execution of the VBScript program. Using the On Error Resume Next statement, however, it is possible to ignore the error and continue with the program.

Private

By preceding a variable declaration with the Private keyword, it is possible to limit its scope to the script it was declared in.

Public

By preceding a variable declaration with the Public keyword, the scope of a variable can be extended to other scripts.

Randomize

Can be used to initialize the random-number generator. Randomize can be used either with or without a numeric argument. If it is used with a numeric argument, the numeric argument is used to seed the random-number generator. If Randomize is used without an argument, a number from the system clock is used to seed the random-number generator.

Rem

The Rem command is used to document VBScript code. The syntax of the Rem command is listed next:

```
Rem This is a comment
```

Note that the apostrophe (') is equivalent in functionality to the Rem command. The only difference between the Rem statement and the apostrophe is the fact that if Rem is used in the same line with a VBScript statement, it needs to be separated from the VBScript statement with a colon.

RSet

The syntax of the `RSet` command is listed next:

`RSet <Variable> = <StringToCopy>`

The `RSet` command is similar in functionality to the `LSet` command. The only difference is the fact that when a variable is assigned a string using the `RSet` command, it is assigned to the variable *right aligned*.

Set

The `Set` command can be used to assign an object reference to a variable or property. The syntax of the `Set` command is as follows:

`Set <ObjectVariable> = <Object>`

When the keyword `Nothing` is assigned to `<ObjectVariable>`, system resources consumed by the object are freed when no other variables refer to the `<Object>`.

Static

By preceding variable and procedure declarations with the keyword `Static`, it is possible to retain values of variables. When a procedure is declared as a static procedure, all variables in that procedure retain values assigned to them throughout the life of the program. Precede variable declarations of *nonstatic procedures* with the `Static` keyword to preserve their values. (Variable values of static procedures are automatically preserved.)

Sub

The `Sub` statement can be used to create VBScript procedures and is identical to the `Function` statement except for one difference. Procedures created with the `Function` statement can return values; procedures created with the `Sub` statement cannot. The syntax of the `Sub` statement is listed next. Note that the `Exit Sub` statement can be used to transfer control out of a procedure. The syntax of the `Sub` statement is listed next:

```
<ProcedureType> Sub <NameOfProcedure> <ArgumentsOfProcedure>
… VBScript statements …
End Sub
```

A procedure can be created by replacing various labels of the preceding definition with the values listed next:

> `<ProcedureType>`—Can be left out if it is not needed. By replacing `<ProcedureType>` with `Static`, it is possible to preserve values of local variables in between procedure calls. Unless you have a reason for doing so, `Static` functions are usually not suitable for recursion (a function calling itself).

`<NameOfProcedure>`—Used to specify the name of the procedure.

`<ArgumentsOfProcedure>`—Arguments of a procedure can be specified soon after `<NameOfProcedure>`. By using commas, more than one argument can be specified. An argument can be passed either by value or reference. In order to make an argument pass by value, precede the argument name with `ByVal`, and to pass by reference, precede the argument name with `ByRef`. When an argument is passed by value, its original value cannot be changed from within the procedure. However, when it is passed by reference, the variable used in the procedure is merely a pointer to the original variable. Therefore, any changes made to the value of a variable passed by reference is actually made to the original variable.

While...Wend

The `While...Wend` control structure can be used to iterate a group of VBScript statements while a certain Boolean expression is true. The syntax of the `While...Wend` command is listed next:

```
While <BooleanExpression>
… VBScript statements …
Wend
```

VBScript Functions

Various functions supported by VBScript are listed next. The following functions can be used to add a new level of interactivity to a Web site by creating active Web pages. Shortly, you will be shown how these functions can be used to develop various VBScript programs.

Abs

The `Abs` function can be used to obtain the absolute value of a number (for example, `Abs(-30) = 30 = Abs(30)`).

Array

The `Array` function can be used to quickly create an array because it returns a variant containing an array. An example of how the `Array` function can be used is given next. The following two commands create an array with three elements. After the two commands are executed, `Colors(2)` will equal `"Blue"`:

```
Dim Colors As Variant
Colors = Array ( "Red", "Blue", "Green" )
```

Asc

Returns the ASCII character code of a character or the first character of a string. For example, `Asc ("A")` returns 65 and so does `Asc ("America")`.

Atn

Returns the arctangent of a number.

CBool

Returns the Boolean value of an expression passed into the function. For example, `CBool ( A = B )` will return `TRUE` if both A and B contain the same value.

CByte

Converts a number passed into the function into a number of type byte and returns it. For example, if `CByte` is called with the number `123.678`, it will return `123`.

CDate

If a valid date expression is passed into the function, it is converted into date type and returned. Before passing an expression to the `CDate` function, it is possible to determine if it can be converted by `CDate` into date type by using the `IsDate` function.

CDbl

Converts an expression passed into the function into a variant of subtype double.

Chr

Returns the ASCII character of an ASCII code. For example, `Chr(65)` returns the character `A`.

CInt

Converts an expression into a variant of subtype Integer. For example, `CInt (1234.567)` returns `1235`.

CLng

Returns a variant of subtype long after the expression passed into the function is converted into long. For example, `CLng (12345.67)` returns `12346`.

Cos

Returns the cosine of an angle passed into the function.

CSng

Converts a numerical expression passed into the function into a variant of subtype Single. For example, `CSng (12.123456)` returns `12.12346`.

CStr

Converts an expression passed into `CStr` into a string and returns it. For example, `CStr(123.456)` returns the value `"123.456"`.

CVErr

Used to return a user-specified error code. The syntax of `CVErr` is `CVErr(ErrorNumber)`.

Date

Returns the date from the system clock. The value returned by the `Date` command at the time of this writing is `4/1/1996`.

DateSerial

`DateSerial` is a handy function that can be used to calculate various days. By using numerical expressions and using the `DateSerial` function, it is possible to count backward and forward from a date simply by adding and subtracting numbers. The syntax of the `DateSerial` function is as follows:

```
DateSerial (<Year>, <Month>, <Day>)
```

If the current date is 4/1/1996, for example, `DateSerial(1996,4-2,1+28)` returns the value `2/29/1996`. (Of course, if the year were 1997 (not a leap year), the result would have been `3/1/1996`.)

DateValue

Converts an expression passed into the function into a variant of subtype date and returns it. For example, `DateValue("February 29, 1976")` returns `2/29/1976`. If the year is left out, it will be obtained from the system clock.

Day

The `Day` function returns a value between `1` and `31` and can be used to find the day of a date. For example, `Day("4/1/1996")` returns `1`.

Exp

Returns the value of e raised to a power. For example Exp(1) returns 2.71828182845905.

Hex

Returns the hexadecimal (base 16) value of a numerical expression. For example, Hex(10) returns A.

Hour

Returns the number of hours of a time expression. For example, Hour("12:25:34") returns 12.

InputBox

The InputBox function is used to obtain input from the user by presenting a dialog box. The syntax of the InputBox command is as follows:

InputBox(<Prompt>,<Title>,<Default>,<X>,<Y>)

Various arguments of the above command enclosed in pointed brackets can be replaced with the following values:

- <Prompt>—Dialog-box prompt.
- <Title>—Title of dialog box.
- <Default>—Default input value.
- <X>—Horizontal position, in number of twips, from the left side of the screen. A *twip* is 1/20 of a printer's point, which is 1/1,440 of an inch.
- <Y>—Vertical position, in number of twips, from the top of the screen.

InStr

Returns the location of one string in another string. The syntax of InStr is as follows:

InStr (<BeginPosition>, <String1>, <String2>, <ComparisonType>)

- <BeginPosition>—This argument is optional and specifies the starting position of search.
- <String1>—String being searched.
- <String2>—String to locate.
- <ComparisonType>—This argument is optional. Use 0 for a binary search and 1 for a non-case-sensitive search. The default value is 0.

Int, Fix

Both Int and Fix convert numerical expressions into integers. The only difference is the fact that Int converts a negative number with a fraction into a smaller integer, and Fix converts a negative number with a fraction into a larger integer. The following examples illustrate how Int and Fix handle numbers with fractions:

```
Int(11.75) = 11
Fix(11.75) = 11
Int(12.45) = 12
Fix(12.45) = 12
Int(-17.75) = -18
Fix(-17.75) = -17
Int(-7.25) = -8
Fix(-7.25) = -7
```

IsArray

Returns TRUE if a variable is an array and FALSE otherwise.

IsDate

Returns TRUE if an expression can be converted to a valid date and FALSE otherwise.

IsEmpty

Returns TRUE if a variable has been initialized and FALSE otherwise.

IsError

Returns TRUE if an expression is an error code and FALSE otherwise.

IsNull

Returns TRUE if an expression is NULL and FALSE otherwise.

IsNumeric

Returns TRUE if an expression is numeric and FALSE otherwise.

IsObject

Returns TRUE if an expression references an OLE automation object and FALSE otherwise.

LBound

`LBound` can be used to find the minimum index of an array dimension. For example, if `ArrayVariable` is a three-dimensional array declared with the statement `Dim ArrayVariable(5 To 100, 10 To 200, 20 To 300)`, `UBound(ArrayVariable,1)` returns 5, `LBound(ArrayVariable,2)` returns 10, and of course `LBound(ArrayVariable,3)` returns 20.

LCase

Converts a string expression to lowercase and returns it.

Left

Returns a certain number of characters from the left side of a string. For example, `Left("Windows NT", 7)` returns `"Windows"`.

Len

Returns the number of characters of a string expression.

Log

Returns the natural logarithm of a nonnegative numeric expression.

LTrim, RTrim, Trim

Eliminates spaces from a string and returns it. `LTrim` eliminates preceding spaces, `RTrim` eliminates trailing spaces, and `Trim` eliminates both trailing and preceding spaces.

Mid

Returns a certain number of characters from a string. For example `Mid("Windows NT", 0, 7)` returns `"Windows"`.

Minute

Returns the number of minutes when called with the time. For example, `Minute("23:50:45")` returns `50`.

Month

Returns the month when called with a date. For example, `Month("4/1/1996")` returns `4`.

MsgBox

A message box can be displayed using the `MsgBox` command. The syntax of the `MsgBox` command is as follows:

`MsgBox <MessageBoxPrompt>,<ButtonStyle>,<Title>`

By replacing `<ButtonStyle>` with various values shown in Table 17.1, a message box can be customized using the following table. For example, an OK dialog box with a warning message icon can be created by replacing `<ButtonStyle>` with `48`.

Table 17.1. Message box codes.

Button Type	Button Description
0	OK
1	OK and Cancel
2	Abort, Retry, and Ignore
3	Yes, No, and Cancel
4	Yes and No
5	Retry and Cancel
16	Critical Message icon (See Figure 17.8)
32	Warning Query icon (See Figure 17.9)
48	Warning Message icon (See Figure 17.10)
64	Information Message icon (See Figure 17.11)
256	Second button is default
512	Third button is default
4096	All applications are stopped until the user responds to the message box

FIGURE 17.8.
The Critical Message box.

FIGURE 17.9.
The Warning Query box.

FIGURE 17.10.
The Warning Message box.

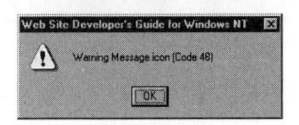

FIGURE 17.11.
The Information Message box.

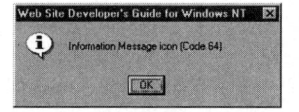

Now

Returns the current date and time from the system clock. The return value is followed by the date and then the time. For example, the Now command returned the string 4/1/1996 23:08:31 at the time of this writing.

Oct

Returns the octal value (base 8) of a numeric expression. For example, Oct(10) returns 12.

Right

Returns a certain number of characters from the right side of a string. For example, Right("Windows NT", 2) returns NT.

Rnd

Returns a random number between 1 and 0. Be sure to seed the random number generator by calling Randomize before using the Rnd function.

Second

Returns the number of seconds of a date expression. For example, Second("18:23:57") returns 57.

Sgn

Returns the sign of a numerical expression. If the expression is 0, 0 is returned. If it is less than 0, -1 is returned. Otherwise, 1 is returned.

Sin

Returns the sine of an angle. For example, Sin (Pi) returns 0.

Sqr

Returns the square root of a nonnegative, numeric expression.

Str

Converts a numeric expression into a string and returns it.

StrComp

The syntax of the `StrComp` function is as follows:

`StrComp (<String1>, <String2>, <ComparisonMethod>)`

After `StrComp` compares both strings, it returns 0 if both strings are identical, -1 if `<String1>` is less than `<STRING2>`, and 1 otherwise. The `<ComparisonMethod>` argument is optional. If it is 0, a binary comparison is performed, and if it is 1, a non-case-insensitive comparison is performed. If `<ComparisonMethod>` is left out, a binary comparison is performed.

String

The `String` function is handy for repeating a character a certain number of times. For example, `String(5,"*")` can be used to create a string of five asterisks.

Tan

The `Tan` function can be used to calculate the tangent of an angle. For example, `Tan (0)` returns 0.

Time

Returns the current time from the system clock. For example, the value 01:23:48 was returned by the `Time` function at the time of this writing.

TimeSerial

This is a very handy function that can be used to perform various time calculations. For example, if the current time is 12:30, `TimeSerial` can be used to calculate the time 25 minutes ago. For example, `TimeSerial(12,30-25, 0)` returns 12:05:00.

TimeValue

Returns an expression passed into the function after converting it into a variant of subtype Date. For example, `TimeValue ("2:35:17pm")` returns 14:35:17.

UBound

`UBound` can be used to determine the maximum size of an array dimension. For example, if `ArrayVariable` is a three-dimensional array defined with the statement `Dim`

ArrayVariable(100,200,300), UBound(ArrayVariable,1) returns 100, UBound(ArrayVariable,2) returns 200, and, of course, UBound(ArrayVariable,3) returns 300.

UCase

Converts strings passed into the function into uppercase and returns them. For example, UCase("Windows NT") returns WINDOWS NT.

Val

The Val function can be used to obtain a number contained in a string. The function scans the string until it encounters a character that is not part of a number. For example, Val("1234 567 in a string") returns the number 1234567.

VarType

The type of a variable can be determined using the VarType function. For example, if IntVariable is an Integer variable, VarType(IntVariable) will return 2. The type of a variable can be determined by examining the return value of VarType according to Table 17.2.

Table 17.2. Variable type codes.

Value Returned	Type of Variable
0	Empty
1	Null
2	Integer
3	Long integer
4	Single-precision, floating-point number
5	Double-precision, floating-point number
6	Currency
7	Date
8	String
9	OLE Automation object
10	Error
11	Boolean
12	Variant
13	Non-OLE Automation object
8192	Array

Weekday

The Weekday function returns a number between 1 and 7. The numbers returned by the Weekday function correspond to the days of the week, as shown in Table 17.3.

Table 17.3. Day codes.

Day Code	Day of Week
1	Sunday
2	Monday
3	Tuesday
4	Wednesday
5	Thursday
6	Friday
7	Saturday

For example, Weekday("April 2, 1996") returns 3—which is, indeed, a Tuesday.

Year

Returns the year of the expression. For example, Year("February 29, 1976") returns 1976.

Applications of VBScript

Various control structures and commands that can be used to create VBScript programs were outlined in preceding sections. The last few sections of the chapter are devoted to applications of these commands and control structures to demonstrate how VBScript can be used to create active Web pages.

Simple Calculator

Using various functions and control structures described earlier, a simple calculator can be created using VBScript. Shortly, you will learn how to create a calculator similar to the one shown in Figure 17.12.

Advanced Web Page Development

Part V

FIGURE 17.12.
The Simple Calculator application.

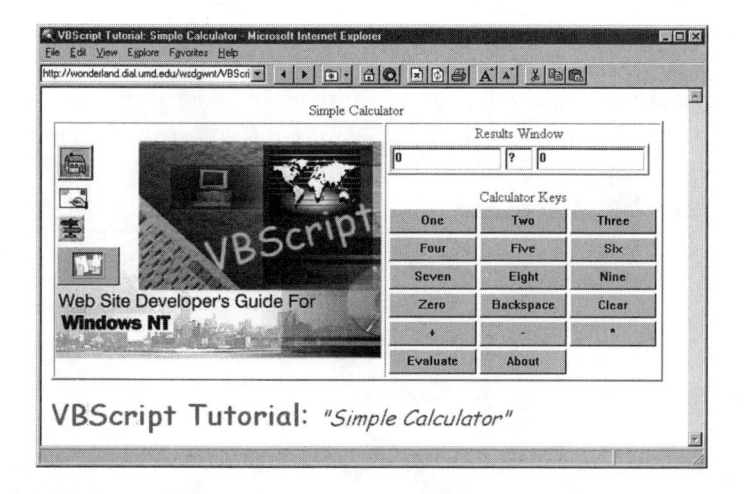

Operators and numbers can be entered into the calculator either by using numeric buttons shown in Figure 17.12 or simply typing them into one of the three text boxes. Before proceeding any further, it is recommended that you experiment with the calculator program and find out how it works. When the Simple Calculator Web page is first invoked and numbers are typed in using various command buttons, they appear in the left-hand text box. After a valid operator is entered into the operator text box, numbers entered next appear in the right-hand text box. At this point, if the Evaluate button is clicked, the VBScript program will evaluate the expression entered and return its value in a dialog box, as shown in Figure 17.13.

FIGURE 17.13.
When the Evaluate button is pressed, the VBScript program calculates the expression entered and returns its value in a dialog box.

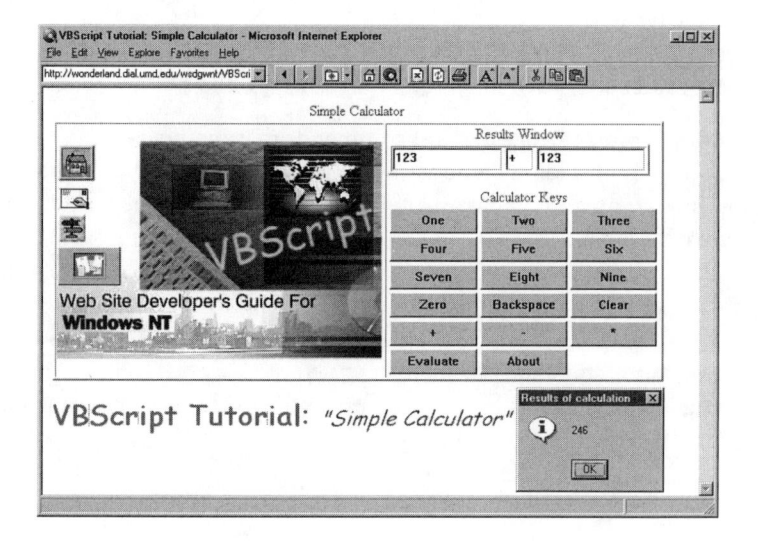

After the OK button in the dialog box shown in Figure 17.13 is pressed, the result of the calculation will be copied to the first text box, as shown in Figure 17.14. The user can then keep on performing calculations using the results of previous calculations.

FIGURE 17.14.
The result of a calculation is copied to the first text box so that it can be used as part of another calculation.

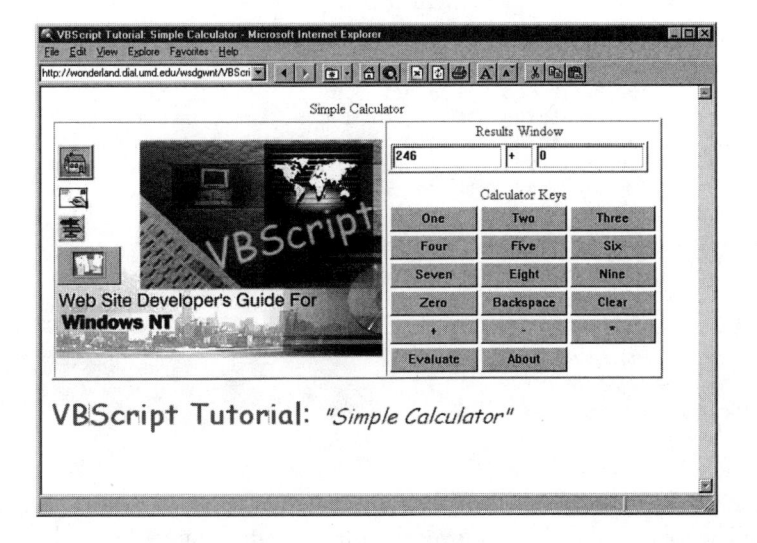

Let's now examine the calculator program in detail and learn how it works. The following VBScript subroutine displays a dialog box similar to the one shown in Figure 17.15 when a user clicks the About button. Note how the string-concatenation operator is used in line 4 to merge two strings:

```
1: Sub BtnAbout_OnClick
2:    titleString = "Web Site Developer's Guide for Windows NT"
3:    helloString = "Simple VBScript calculator by "
4:    helloString = helloString & "Sanjaya Hettihewa."
5:    MsgBox helloString, 64, titleString
6: End Sub
```

FIGURE 17.15.
The About dialog box.

Error checking is an important part of any application. One of VBScript's strengths is its ability to perform various error checks when users enter data into a form. By using the OnChange event, it is possible to check the value of a text box that was recently changed by the user. The subroutine shown next makes sure the user entered a valid number into a text box that is used

Advanced Web Page Development
Part V

to obtain an operand from the user. The error-checking subroutine of the second operand is similar to the one shown next. Note how chr(10) is used to create a multiline string. As you can see in Figure 17.16, when a user enters an invalid number, the following subroutine informs the user and resets the text box:

```
 1: Sub Operand1Box_OnChange
 2:   IF (NOT IsNumeric(Operand1Box.Value)) THEN
 3:     MsgBoxString = "Do not type invalid characters "
 4:     MsgBoxString = MsgBoxString & "into the Results Window! "
 5:     MsgBoxString = MsgBoxString & chr(10)
 6:     MsgBoxString = MsgBoxString & "Results Window will now be reset."
 7:     MsgBox MsgBoxString , 48 , "Invalid input detected!"
 8:     Operand1Box.Value = 0
 9:   END IF
10: End Sub
```

FIGURE 17.16.

Invalid numbers entered by users are detected by the Operand1Box_OnChange *subroutine.*

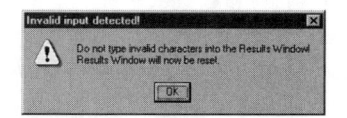

A similar subroutine is used to check that operators entered into the operator text box are valid. The following code listing verifies that operators entered into the operator text box are valid. Note how the underline character (_) is used to join a long expression that spans several lines. If an invalid operator is entered, it is detected by OperatorBox_OnChange subroutine, the text box is reset, and the user is informed of the invalid input, as shown in Figure 17.17:

```
 1: Sub OperatorBox_OnChange
 2:   IF (NOT((OperatorBox.Value = "+" ) OR _
 3:     (OperatorBox.Value = "-" ) OR _
 4:     (OperatorBox.Value = "*" ) OR _
 5:     (OperatorBox.Value = "?" ))) THEN
 6:     MsgString = "Do not type invalid characters "
 7:     MsgString = MsgString & "into the operator text box! "
 8:     MsgString = MsgString & chr(10)
 9:     MsgString = MsgString & "The operator text box will now be reset."
10:     MsgString = MsgString & chr(10) & chr(10)
11:     MsgString = MsgString & "Valid input: +, -, *"
12:     MsgBox MsgString , 48 , "Invalid input detected!"
13:     OperatorBox.Value = "?"
14:   END IF
15: End Sub
```

FIGURE 17.17.

Invalid operators entered into the operator text box are detected by the OperatorBox_OnChange *subroutine.*

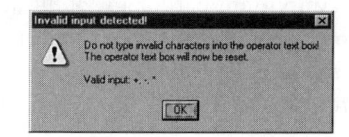

Unleashing the Power of VBScript

Chapter 17

The Delete button is used to delete characters entered into one of the operand text boxes. The subroutine associated with the Delete button, `BtnDelete_OnClick`, is a smart function subroutine. As shown in line 2 of the following code listing, the subroutine first examines the operator text box and determines if a calculation has already been performed. If so, it knows that any numbers added appear on the text box to the right and deletes a digit from that text box. If not, a digit from the left text box is deleted:

```
1:  Sub BtnDelete_OnClick
2:    IF (OperatorBox.Value = "?") THEN
3:      IF ((Len (Operand1Box.Value) > 0) AND (Operand1Box.Value <> 0)) THEN
4:        Operand1Box.Value = Left (Operand1Box.Value, Len (Operand1Box.Value)
          ↪-1)
5:        IF (Len (Operand1Box.Value) = 0) THEN
6:          Operand1Box.Value = 0
7:        END IF
8:      END IF
9:    ELSE
10:     IF ((Len (Operand2Box.Value) > 0) AND (Operand2Box.Value <> 0)) THEN
11:       Operand2Box.Value = Left (Operand2Box.Value, Len (Operand2Box.Value)
          ↪-1)
12:       IF (Len (Operand2Box.Value) = 0) THEN
13:         Operand2Box.Value = 0
14:       END IF
15:     END IF
16:   END IF
17: End Sub
```

The Evaluate button calculates two operands using an operator and returns a value as shown in Figure 17.13. As you can see in line 2 of the following program listing, the `BtnEvaluate_OnClick` subroutine first checks the Operator text box. If a valid operator is found, it performs a calculation and displays it using a dialog box. If not, a dialog box similar to the one shown in Figure 17.18 is displayed. Afterwards, as shown in lines 17 and 18, the operand text boxes are reset so that additional calculations can be performed. Note that the result of the calculation is copied in line 17 to the left operand box so that the result of the calculation can be used as part of another calculation:

```
1:  Sub BtnEvaluate_OnClick
2:    IF (OperatorBox.Value = "?") THEN
3:      MsgBoxString = "A valid operator is required to carry out "
4:      MsgBoxString = MsgBoxString & "an evaluation."
5:      MsgBoxString = MsgBoxString & chr(10)
6:      MsgBoxString = MsgBoxString & "Valid operators are: +, -, *"
7:      MsgBox MsgBoxString , 48 , "Invalid operator!"
8:    ELSE
9:      IF (OperatorBox.Value = "+")  THEN
10:       answer = CDbl(Operand1Box.Value) + CDbl(Operand2Box.Value)
11:     ELSEIF (OperatorBox.Value = "-")  THEN
12:       answer = CDbl(Operand1Box.Value) - CDbl(Operand2Box.Value)
13:     ELSEIF (OperatorBox.Value = "*")  THEN
14:       answer = CDbl(Operand1Box.Value) * CDbl(Operand2Box.Value)
15:     End IF
16:     MsgBox answer , 64 , "Results of calculation"
```

```
17:        Operand1Box.Value = answer
18:        Operand2Box.Value = 0
19:    END IF
20: End Sub
```

FIGURE 17.18.
The operands are evaluated only if a valid operator is found.

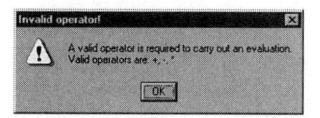

The AddDigit subroutine adds a digit selected via one of the calculator buttons into one of the operand text boxes. As shown in line 4 of the following program listing, if a valid operator is not present, digits are added to the left text box. However, if a valid operator is present, this means that the user has either entered a valid number to the left text box or that it contains the result of a previous calculation (in which case, the digit selected by the user is added to the right text box). When adding digits, there is a possibility that the user will try to add too many digits. This is taken care of in lines 9 and 16, where a separate subroutine is used to inform the reader by displaying a dialog box similar to the one shown in Figure 17.19:

```
1: Sub AddDigit ( digit )
2:    REM Just in case there are any preceding zeros or spaces
3:    Operand1Box.Value = CDbl (Operand1Box.Value)
4:    IF ( OperatorBox.Value = "?") THEN
5:       IF ( Len ( Operand1Box.Value ) < 14 ) THEN
6:          Operand1Box.Value = Operand1Box.Value & digit
7:          Operand1Box.Value = CDbl (Operand1Box.Value)
8:       ELSE
9:          TooManyDigits
10:      END IF
11:   ELSE
12:      IF ( Len ( Operand2Box.Value ) < 14 ) THEN
13:         Operand2Box.Value = Operand2Box.Value & digit
14:         Operand2Box.Value = CDbl (Operand2Box.Value)
15:      ELSE
16:         TooManyDigits
17:      END IF
18:   END IF
19: End Sub
```

FIGURE 17.19.
The AddDigit subroutine prevents users from entering too many digits into a text box.

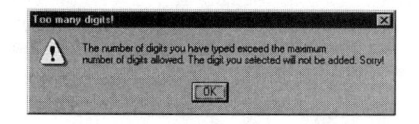

For your reference, the full source code of the Calculator application is given in Listing 17.2.

Listing 17.2. The Calculator Web page.

```
<!--
(C) 1996 Sanjaya Hettihewa (http://wonderland.dial.umd.edu)
All Rights Reserved.
Permission is hereby given to modify and distribute this code
as you wish provided that this block of text remains unchanged.
!-->

<HTML>
<HEAD>
<TITLE>VBScript Tutorial: Simple Calculator</TITLE>
</HEAD>

<TABLE COLSPEC="L20 L20 L20" BORDER=2 WIDTH=10 HEIGHT=10>
<CAPTION ALIGN=top>Simple Calculator</CAPTION>
<TR><TD>
<BODY BGCOLOR="#FFFFFF" TEXT="#0000FF"
      LINK="#B864FF" VLINK="#670000" ALINK="#FF0000">
<IMG ALIGN=TOP SRC="vbscript.jpg">
<TD>

<TABLE BORDER=2 >
<CAPTION ALIGN=top>Results Window</CAPTION>
 <TD>
 <input type=text size=14 maxlength=14 name="Operand1Box" value="0">
 <input type=text size=1 maxlength=1 name="OperatorBox" value="?">
 <input type=text size=14 maxlength=14 name="Operand2Box" value="0">
 </TD>
</TABLE>

<TABLE COLSPEC="L20 L20 L20" >

<CAPTION ALIGN=top>Calculator Keys</CAPTION>
<TR>
 <TD><INPUT TYPE=BUTTON VALUE="One"   NAME="BtnOne"></TD>
 <TD><INPUT TYPE=BUTTON VALUE="Two"   NAME="BtnTwo"></TD>
 <TD><INPUT TYPE=BUTTON VALUE="Three" NAME="BtnThree"></TD>
</TR>
<TR>
 <TD><INPUT TYPE=BUTTON VALUE="Four"  NAME="BtnFour"></TD>
 <TD><INPUT TYPE=BUTTON VALUE="Five"  NAME="BtnFive"></TD>
 <TD><INPUT TYPE=BUTTON VALUE="Six"   NAME="BtnSix"></TD>
</TR>
<TR>
 <TD><INPUT TYPE=BUTTON VALUE="Seven" NAME="BtnSeven"></TD>
 <TD><INPUT TYPE=BUTTON VALUE="Eight" NAME="BtnEight"></TD>
 <TD><INPUT TYPE=BUTTON VALUE="Nine"  NAME="BtnNine"></TD>
</TR>
<TR>
 <TD><INPUT TYPE=BUTTON VALUE="Zero"      NAME="BtnZero"></TD>
 <TD><INPUT TYPE=BUTTON VALUE="Backspace" NAME="BtnDelete"></TD>
 <TD><INPUT TYPE=BUTTON VALUE="Clear"     NAME="BtnClear"></TD>
</TR>
```

continues

Listing 17.2. continued

```
<TR>
 <TD><INPUT TYPE=BUTTON VALUE="+" NAME="BtnPlus"></TD>
 <TD><INPUT TYPE=BUTTON VALUE="-" NAME="BtnMinus"></TD>
 <TD><INPUT TYPE=BUTTON VALUE="*" NAME="BtnMultiply"></TD>
</TR>

<TR>
 <TD><INPUT TYPE=BUTTON VALUE="Evaluate" NAME="BtnEvaluate"></TD>
 <TD><INPUT TYPE=BUTTON VALUE="About" NAME="BtnAbout"></TD>
</TR>

</TABLE>

</TR>
</TABLE>

<P>

<B><FONT FACE="Comic Sans MS" SIZE=6 COLOR=RED>
VBScript Tutorial: <FONT></B>
<I><FONT FACE="Comic Sans MS" SIZE=5 COLOR=BLUE>
 "Simple Calculator" </I><P><FONT>


<SCRIPT LANGUAGE=VBS>
<!-- To hide VBScript code from technologically challenged browsers

Sub BtnAbout_OnClick
 titleString = "Web Site Developer's Guide for Windows NT"
 helloString = "Simple VBScript calculator by "
 helloString = helloString & "Sanjaya Hettihewa."
 MsgBox helloString, 64, titleString
End Sub

Sub Operand1Box_OnChange
 IF (NOT IsNumeric(Operand1Box.Value)) THEN
    MsgBoxString = "Do not type invalid characters "
    MsgBoxString = MsgBoxString & "into the Results Window! "
    MsgBoxString = MsgBoxString & chr(10)
    MsgBoxString = MsgBoxString & "Results Window will now be reset."
    MsgBox MsgBoxString , 48 , "Invalid input detected!"
    Operand1Box.Value = 0
 END IF
End Sub

Sub Operand2Box_OnChange
 IF (NOT IsNumeric(Operand2Box.Value)) THEN
    MsgBoxString = "Do not type invalid characters "
    MsgBoxString = MsgBoxString & "into the Results Window! "
    MsgBoxString = MsgBoxString & chr(10)
    MsgBoxString = MsgBoxString & "Results Window will now be reset."
    MsgBox MsgBoxString , 48 , "Invalid input detected!"
    Operand2Box.Value = 0
 END IF
End Sub
```

```vbscript
Sub OperatorBox_OnChange
 IF (NOT((OperatorBox.Value = "+" ) OR _
    (OperatorBox.Value = "-" ) OR _
    (OperatorBox.Value = "*" ) OR _
    (OperatorBox.Value = "?" ))) THEN
    MsgString = "Do not type invalid characters "
    MsgString = MsgString & "into the operator text box! "
    MsgString = MsgString & chr(10)
    MsgString = MsgString & "The operator text box will now be reset."
    MsgString = MsgString & chr(10) & chr(10)
    MsgString = MsgString & "Valid input: +, -, *"
    MsgBox MsgString , 48 , "Invalid input detected!"
    OperatorBox.Value = "?"
 END IF
End Sub

Sub BtnOne_OnClick
 IF (IsNumeric(Operand1Box.Value)) THEN
    AddDigit ( 1 )
 ELSE
    ResetResultsWindow
 END IF
End Sub
Sub BtnTwo_OnClick
 IF (IsNumeric(Operand1Box.Value)) THEN
    AddDigit ( 2 )
 ELSE
    ResetResultsWindow
 END IF
End Sub
Sub BtnThree_OnClick
 IF (IsNumeric(Operand1Box.Value)) THEN
    AddDigit ( 3 )
 ELSE
    ResetResultsWindow
 END IF
End Sub
Sub BtnFour_OnClick
 IF (IsNumeric(Operand1Box.Value)) THEN
    AddDigit ( 4 )
 ELSE
    ResetResultsWindow
 END IF
End Sub
Sub BtnFive_OnClick
 IF (IsNumeric(Operand1Box.Value)) THEN
    AddDigit ( 5 )
 ELSE
    ResetResultsWindow
 END IF
End Sub
Sub BtnSix_OnClick
 IF (IsNumeric(Operand1Box.Value)) THEN
    AddDigit ( 6 )
 ELSE
    ResetResultsWindow
 END IF
End Sub
```

continues

Listing 17.2. continued

```
Sub BtnSeven_OnClick
 IF (IsNumeric(Operand1Box.Value)) THEN
    AddDigit ( 7 )
 ELSE
    ResetResultsWindow
 END IF
End Sub
Sub BtnEight_OnClick
 IF (IsNumeric(Operand1Box.Value)) THEN
    AddDigit ( 8 )
 ELSE
    ResetResultsWindow
 END IF
End Sub
Sub BtnNine_OnClick
 IF (IsNumeric(Operand1Box.Value)) THEN
    AddDigit ( 9 )
 ELSE
    ResetResultsWindow
 END IF
End Sub
Sub BtnZero_OnClick
 IF (IsNumeric(Operand1Box.Value)) THEN
    AddDigit ( 0 )
 ELSE
    ResetResultsWindow
 END IF
End Sub

Sub BtnDelete_OnClick
 IF (OperatorBox.Value = "?") THEN
    IF ((Len (Operand1Box.Value) > 0) AND (Operand1Box.Value <> 0)) THEN
       Operand1Box.Value = Left (Operand1Box.Value, Len (Operand1Box.Value) - 1)
    IF (Len (Operand1Box.Value) = 0) THEN
       Operand1Box.Value = 0
    END IF
    END IF
 ELSE
    IF ((Len (Operand2Box.Value) > 0) AND (Operand2Box.Value <> 0)) THEN
       Operand2Box.Value = Left (Operand2Box.Value, Len (Operand2Box.Value) - 1)
    IF (Len (Operand2Box.Value) = 0) THEN
       Operand2Box.Value = 0
    END IF
    END IF
 END IF
End Sub

Sub BtnClear_OnClick
 Operand1Box.Value = 0
 Operand2Box.Value = 0
 OperatorBox.Value = "?"
End Sub

Sub BtnPlus_OnClick
 OperatorBox.Value = "+"
End Sub
```

```
Sub BtnMinus_OnClick
 OperatorBox.Value = "-"
End Sub

Sub BtnMultiply_OnClick
 OperatorBox.Value = "*"
End Sub

Sub BtnEvaluate_OnClick
  IF (OperatorBox.Value = "?") THEN
     MsgBoxString = "A valid operator is required to carry out "
     MsgBoxString = MsgBoxString & "an evaluation."
     MsgBoxString = MsgBoxString & chr(10)
     MsgBoxString = MsgBoxString & "Valid operators are: +, -, *"
     MsgBox MsgBoxString , 48 , "Invalid operator!"
  ELSE
     IF (OperatorBox.Value = "+")   THEN
        answer = CDbl(Operand1Box.Value) + CDbl(Operand2Box.Value)
     ELSEIF (OperatorBox.Value = "-") THEN
        answer = CDbl(Operand1Box.Value) - CDbl(Operand2Box.Value)
     ELSEIF (OperatorBox.Value = "*") THEN
        answer = CDbl(Operand1Box.Value) * CDbl(Operand2Box.Value)
     End IF
     MsgBox answer , 64 , "Results of calculation"
     Operand1Box.Value = answer
     Operand2Box.Value = 0
  END IF
End Sub

Sub AddDigit ( digit )
 REM Just in case there are any preceeding zeros or spaces
 Operand1Box.Value = CDbl (Operand1Box.Value)
 IF ( OperatorBox.Value = "?") THEN
    IF ( Len ( Operand1Box.Value ) < 14 ) THEN
       Operand1Box.Value = Operand1Box.Value & digit
       Operand1Box.Value = CDbl (Operand1Box.Value)
    ELSE
       TooManyDigits
    END IF
 ELSE
    IF ( Len ( Operand2Box.Value ) < 14 ) THEN
       Operand2Box.Value = Operand2Box.Value & digit
       Operand2Box.Value = CDbl (Operand2Box.Value)
    ELSE
       TooManyDigits
    END IF
 END IF
End Sub

Sub ResetResultsWindow
 MsgBoxString = "Do not type invalid characters "
 MsgBoxString = MsgBoxString & "into the Results Window! "
 MsgBoxString = MsgBoxString & chr(10)
 MsgBoxString = MsgBoxString & "Use Calculator keys instead. "
 MsgBoxString = MsgBoxString & "Results Window will now be reset."
 MsgBox MsgBoxString , 48 , "Invalid input detected!"
 Operand1Box.Value = 0
```

Listing 17.2. continued

```
 Operand2Box.Value = 0
 OperatorBox.Value = "?"
End Sub

Sub TooManyDigits
 MsgBoxString = "The number of digits you have typed "
 MsgBoxString = MsgBoxString & "exceed the maximum"
 MsgBoxString = MsgBoxString & chr(10)
 MsgBoxString = MsgBoxString & "number of digits allowed. "
 MsgBoxString = MsgBoxString & "The digit you selected will "
 MsgBoxString = MsgBoxString & "not be added. Sorry!"
 MsgBox MsgBoxString , 48 , "Too many digits!"
End Sub

!-->
</SCRIPT>

</BODY>
</HTML>
```

Labeling an Image

VBScript can be used to label a graphic when the mouse is moved over it. The VBScript program listed shortly can be used to label an image. When the Web page containing the VBScript program is first invoked, it looks similar to Figure 17.20. Note the string `Hello! Select a link, please.` is contained in the description text box.

FIGURE 17.20.

Text box contains the string `Hello! Select a link, please.` *when the VBScript Web page is first invoked.*

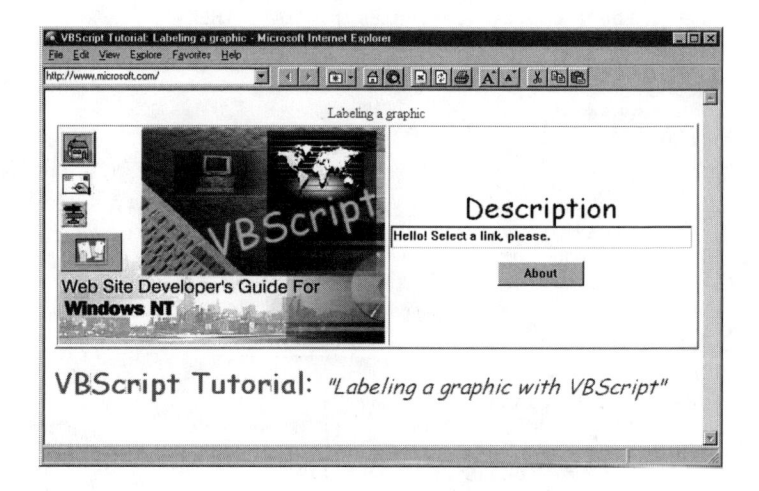

At this point, if the mouse is moved over the graphic in Figure 17.20, the value of the text box changes, as shown in Figure 17.21.

Unleashing the Power of VBScript
Chapter 17

FIGURE 17.21.
When the mouse is moved over the graphic, the value of the text box changes to `No link selected. Please select a link!`*.*

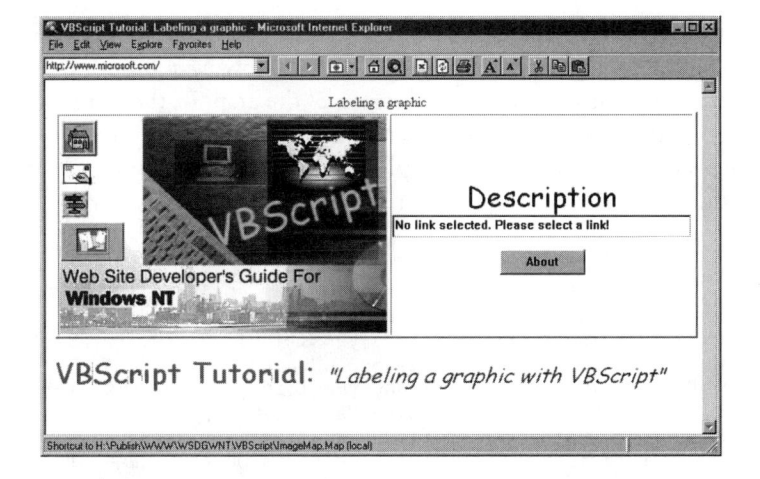

As you can see in Figure 17.22, there are four icons in the graphic to the left of the browser window. When the mouse is moved over any of these icons, the text box will list the description of the text box. For example, when the mouse is over the bulletin-board icon, the value of the text box in Figure 17.21 changes to `Post messages on an online discussion forum`.

FIGURE 17.22.
When the mouse is over one of the icons of the image, the value of the text box changes the icon's description.

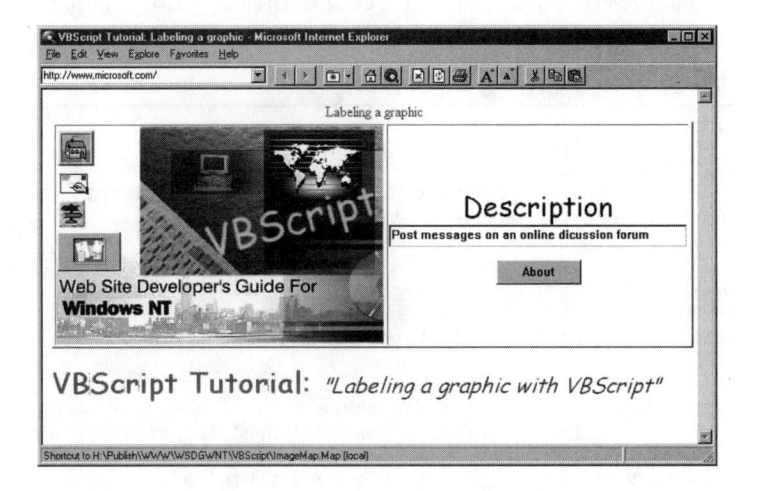

In order to detect mouse movement over the graphic in Figure 17.22, a special identification code needs to be assigned to the graphic. This is done in line 1 of the following code listing:

```
1: <A ID="ImageMapGraphic" HREF="ImageMap.Map">
2: <IMG   ALIGN=TOP SRC="vbscript.jpg" ALT="Sample Graphic" ISMAP BORDER=0>
3: </A>
```

The `ImageMapGraphic_MouseMove` is the heart of the VBScript shown in Figure 17.22. When the mouse is moved over the graphic, the following subroutine is activated. When the mouse pointer falls in a predetermined region of the graphic, the text box is updated with the description of the region the mouse pointer is over, as shown in line 4 of the following program listing. The `HotSpot` subroutine simply returns TRUE if the mouse coordinates passed into the `HotSpot` subroutine fall within a certain region of the graphic:

```
 1: Sub ImageMapGraphic_MouseMove(keyboard,mouse,xPosition,yPosition)
 2:
 3: IF (HotSpot(xPosition, yPosition,  2,  5, 70,  41)) THEN
 4:    Description.Value = "Main Homepage"
 5: ELSE IF (HotSpot(xPosition, yPosition,  2, 49, 70,  82)) THEN
 6:    Description.Value = "Send Feedback"
 7: ELSE IF (HotSpot(xPosition, yPosition,  2, 84, 70, 117)) THEN
 8:    Description.Value = "Site Map"
 9: ELSE IF (HotSpot(xPosition, yPosition,  2, 119, 70, 164)) THEN
10:    Description.Value = "Post messages on an online discussion forum"
11: ELSE
12:    Description.Value = "No link selected. Please select a link!"
13: END IF
14: END IF
15: END IF
16: END IF
```

For your reference, the full source code of the Label Image application is given in Listing 17.3.

Listing 17.3. Labeling a graphic.

```
<!--
(C) 1996 Sanjaya Hettihewa (http://wonderland.dial.umd.edu)
All Rights Reserved.
        Permission is hereby given to modify and distribute this code as you wish
provided that this block of text remains unchanged.
!-->

<HTML>
<HEAD>
<TITLE>VBScript Tutorial: Labeling a graphic</TITLE>
</HEAD>

<BODY BGCOLOR="#FFFFFF" TEXT="#0000FF"
           LINK="#B864FF" VLINK="#670000" ALINK="#FF0000">

<TABLE COLSPEC="L20 L20 L20" BORDER=2 WIDTH=10 HEIGHT=10>
<CAPTION ALIGN=top>Labeling a graphic</CAPTION>
<TR><TD>

<A ID="ImageMapGraphic" HREF="ImageMap.Map">
<IMG  ALIGN=TOP SRC="vbscript.jpg" ALT="Sample Graphic" ISMAP BORDER=0>
</A>

</TD><TD>
```

```
<CENTER><FONT FACE="Comic Sans MS" SIZE=6 COLOR=Black>
Description<FONT></CENTER>
<input type="text" name="Description"
       Value="Hello! Select a link, please." size=45><P>

<CENTER><INPUT TYPE=BUTTON VALUE="About" NAME="BtnAbout"></CENTER>

</TD><TD>

</TR>
</TABLE>

<P>

<B><FONT FACE="Comic Sans MS" SIZE=6 COLOR=RED>
VBScript Tutorial: <FONT></B>
<I><FONT FACE="Comic Sans MS" SIZE=5 COLOR=BLUE>
 "Labeling a graphic with VBScript" </I><P><FONT>
</TD></TR>
</TABLE>

<SCRIPT LANGUAGE="VBS">
<!-- To hide VBScript code from  technologically challenged browsers

Sub BtnAbout_OnClick
   titleString = "Web Site Developer's Guide for Windows NT"
   helloString = "Labeling a graphic with VBScript by "
   helloString = helloString & "Sanjaya Hettihewa."
   MsgBox helloString, 64, titleString
End Sub

Sub ImageMapGraphic_MouseMove(keyboard,mouse,xPosition,yPosition)

IF (HotSpot(xPosition, yPosition,  2, 5, 70, 41)) THEN
  Description.Value = "Main Homepage"
ELSE IF (HotSpot(xPosition, yPosition,  2, 49, 70, 82)) THEN
  Description.Value = "Send Feedback"
ELSE IF (HotSpot(xPosition, yPosition,  2, 84, 70, 117)) THEN
  Description.Value = "Site Map"
ELSE IF (HotSpot(xPosition, yPosition,  2, 119, 70, 164)) THEN
  Description.Value = "Post messages on an online discussion forum"
ELSE
  Description.Value = "No link selected. Please select a link!"
END IF
END IF
END IF
END IF

End Sub

Function HotSpot ( mouseX, mouseY, TopX , TopY, BottomX, BottomY)
 HotSpot = (mouseX >= TopX) AND _
           (mouseX <= BottomX) AND _
           (mouseY >= topY) AND _
           (mouseY<=bottomY)
End Function
```

continues

Listing 17.3. continued

```
!-->
</SCRIPT>

</BODY>
</HTML>
```

Summary

VBScript, a subset of Visual Basic, is an easy-to-use scripting language that can be used to create active Web pages. It enables Web-site developers to create various client-side solutions and make a Web site easier and more interesting to navigate.

Introduction to Windows NT CGI Programming

18

IN THIS CHAPTER

- Introduction to CGI **490**
- Applications of CGI **492**
- CGI Basics **493**
- CGI Issues **496**
- CGI Environment Variables **499**
- CGI Perl Scripts **503**
- CGI C Scripts **505**
- A Few Things to Note About Developing CGI Applications **506**
- Accessing Environment Variables Available to CGI Scripts **511**
- Using CGI to Provide Customized Content **514**
- Setting Up a Feedback Form **519**

One of the best things about the World Wide Web is that you can use it to interact with millions of users to obtain and provide different information. Due to the dynamic nature of this information, static HTML pages alone are not enough. There has to be a way to display dynamic information to those surfing your Web site based on what they need. CGI is a mechanism that enables you to do just that. *CGI* stands for *Common Gateway Interface*. After you have your Web site all set up and have created some Web pages, it's time to think about making your Web site dynamic by setting up CGI scripts on your Web server. By utilizing CGI, you can exploit the World Wide Web to its fullest potential because it allows you to interact with browsers of your Web site.

Feedback forms, e-mail forms, database query interfaces, database update mechanisms, Web page counters, and search engines are all applications of CGI. Thanks to the user-friendly development environment of Windows NT, by the end of this chapter you will be able to develop CGI scripts, experiment with them, and harness the power of interactive Web interfaces. This chapter first provides you with an introduction to CGI and explains how CGI works. Then you are shown practical applications of CGI and how CGI scripts can be utilized to enhance your Web site. Next, you are shown how to develop CGI programs. C and Perl are used to illustrate how CGI programs can be created to perform various tasks. At the end of this chapter, you will be able to utilize CGI to interact with your Web site browsers.

Introduction to CGI

Before going any further, an introduction to CGI is in order. CGI is a standard for various programs at your Web site that you can use to interact with users surfing your site. Because CGI is a standard, it is not browser- or server-dependent and can be moved from one Web server to another while still retaining its full functionality.

Just like application programs, CGI programs can be written in almost any programming language that will let you either create an executable program or let you interpret it in real time with another program (as in the case of awk and Perl). The following lists a few languages that you can utilize to create CGI applications under Windows NT:

- awk
- C/C++
- FORTRAN
- Pascal
- Perl
- Visual Basic
- NT Batch scripts

Depending on your expertise, what's available, and the nature of your CGI projects, you will have to choose the best language to suit your needs. Customarily, CGI scripts are stored in the CGI-BIN directory of the Web server's document root directory. All files and pathnames of a Web site are relative to this directory.

Benefits of an Interactive Web Site

Plain text HTML files retrieved by Web clients are static. The information contained in these files never changes unless you manually edit them to make changes. However, by utilizing CGI scripts, your Web pages can be created dynamically each time a client accesses them. To the client, it will look as if the page has been specially created for him or her based on the information needed. Obviously, this is a very powerful tool for interacting with Web surfers. You should utilize CGI to make your Web site interactive so that you can provide customized content and enable those browsing your Web site to interact with the information you provide.

Benefits of CGI are invaluable to any Web site. These benefits range from having a customized input form for feedback to allowing someone browsing your Web site to update and retrieve information from a database on your server. By setting up a customized e-mail feedback form, you can make sure you are provided with all the information you need. Furthermore, you can be sure that your e-mail feedback form will always work because it does not depend on how the e-mail capability of your client's Web browser is set up (in case it is not set up correctly for e-mail). In the "Setting Up a Feedback Form" section, you will be shown how to utilize CGI to set up an e-mail feedback page. Furthermore, if you want to set up a database that collects data from users browsing your Web site, you can use a CGI script to update information provided by these users to a database. With the aid of CGI, it is possible to update a database on your server without your direct human intervention. As you can see, the possibilities and applications of CGI are endless.

One of CGI's best features is its capability to let Web surfers interact with databases on your server. For example, you might have a Microsoft Access database on your server that needs to be updated with information provided by users surfing your Web site. You might also need to make parts of this database available to authenticated users for querying. Although you can use plain old e-mail to correspond with people, and manually perform database queries and updates, this is not very practical after you start getting more and more visitors. Eventually, you will end up spending the whole day answering and responding to e-mail. (Maybe you do this already, but just imagine how much worse it will be!) By setting up a simple form, you can perform updates to your database by utilizing a CGI script. Keep on reading, and soon you will find out how easy it is to use CGI to interact with people browsing your Web site.

Dynamic content that is output by CGI programs can be made portable across other Web servers. For example, if in the output of a CGI script, a hypertext link has to be created to the main home page of a Web server, you can use the CGI environment variable SERVER_NAME. By using this CGI variable as opposed to hard coding the home page in the CGI program, the CGI script will be portable across various Web servers.

> **TIP**
>
> Whenever possible, you should make use of such CGI variables to make moving scripts from one Web server to another as effortless as possible.

By utilizing CGI to make your Web site interactive, users visiting your Web site will be able to easily find the information they need. Because your Web site is easy to navigate, these users will visit it again and again for more information. CGI also enables you to customize what people see when browsing your Web site by providing dynamic content. Furthermore, you can use a CGI script to provide content that's customized for the Web browser being used to access the information.

Applications of CGI

Many organizations and individuals are using CGI for a variety of tasks, from having a simple counter on a Web page to counting the number of accesses to a CGI script managing an entire store front-end. This CGI script can allow users visiting a Web site to look at various merchandise being sold and even place orders. In addition to this, various Web sites offer search capabilities of the site to make finding information easier.

You can use CGI whenever you want to interact with those browsing your Web site, to get feedback from those browsing your Web site, or to provide dynamic content. The following lists a few applications of CGI that you can use to enhance the capabilities of your Web site:

- Setting up a guest book
- Setting up a feedback form
- Adding a counter to a Web page
- Designing a database front-end for the Web
- Allowing Web surfers to visit various Web pages via a pull-down list
- Enabling those browsing your Web site to e-mail comments
- Providing customized Web pages based on Web browsers being used by a client
- Enabling those browsing your Web site to search your Web site

This chapter demonstrates how to add most of these capabilities to your Web site. Before moving on to more advanced topics, it's time to cover the basics of CGI.

CGI Basics

A CGI script is typically used to provide dynamic content to the client that called the CGI script. CGI scripts communicate with Web browsers, as shown in Figure 18.1. If the CGI script is an interactive script, typically a form with various input controls is sent to the Web client. After filling in the form, the user submits it to the Web server. The Web server then uses CGI to call the CGI script with data from the Web client. The CGI script processes the data, possibly accessing a database on the server, and sends a message to the client that made the request. If the CGI script is a noninteractive CGI script, the output of the script is sent directly to the client that called the CGI script with its URL.

FIGURE 18.1.
Architecture of a typical Web server with CGI scripts.

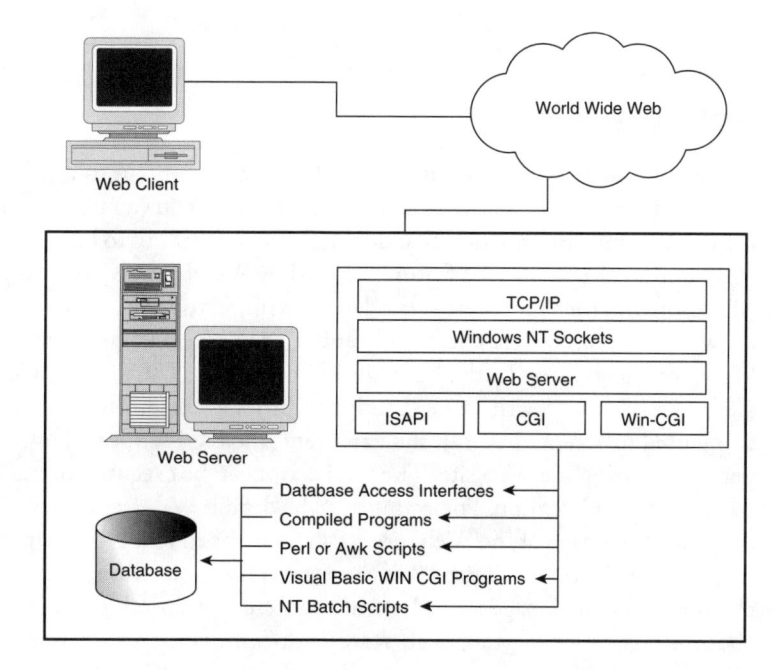

When a CGI script is called, the Web server first examines the REQUEST_METHOD used to call the CGI script to determine how the Web client is sending data to the CGI script. This process is shown in Figure 18.2. If the REQUEST_METHOD used to call the CGI script is GET, any data supplied by the Web client for the CGI script is found immediately following the URL name of the CGI script. Therefore, this information will be stored in the environment variable QUERY_STRING. On the other hand, if the REQUEST_METHOD used was POST or PUT, the size of input for the CGI script is stored in CONTENT_LENGTH. CONTENT_LENGTH contains the size of data supplied to the CGI script in bytes. The CGI script can then read from standard input the number of bytes returned by `CONTENT_LENGTH` to find out data given to the CGI script. If you are confused about all these strange environmental variables, don't worry—they are all discussed in the "CGI Environment Variables" section.

FIGURE 18.2.
How Web servers determine and handle the `REQUEST_METHOD`, *which calls the CGI scripts.*

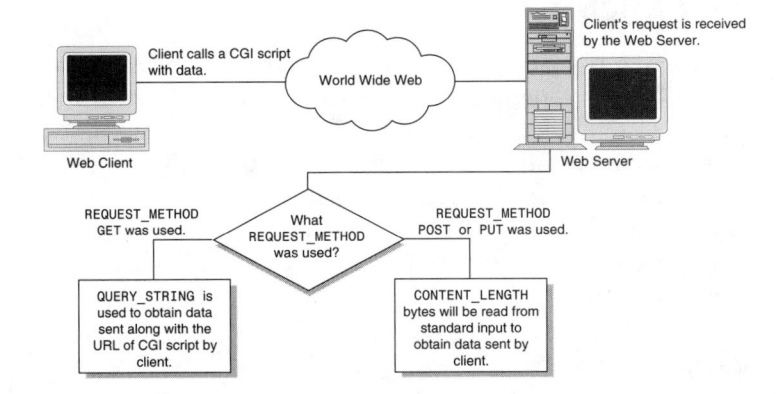

How CGI Works

Although a major use of CGI is to provide dynamic content to those browsing your Web site, CGI programs do not always need to be interactive. You can use noninteractive CGI scripts to provide dynamic information that does not need user input to be created. For example, in order to take advantage of various features offered by Web browsers such as Netscape Navigator and Microsoft Internet Explorer, it is relatively simple to write a CGI program to determine the browser being used by a client and send a page specially designed to take advantage of that browser's capabilities. In the "Using CGI to Provide Customized Content" section, you will see how easy it is to write a CGI script to provide customized content based on the browser being used to access a page. In such an event, the CGI script will not need to interact with the person browsing the Web site. The CGI script can be executed transparently to the user without any user intervention. For example, if the default Web page of a Web server is `welcome.html`, the main Web page of the Web server can be mapped to a CGI script by creating a URL-CGI mapping, as shown in Figure 18.3. Such a script can determine the browser being used by the client and display a page with dynamic content optimized for the browser being used by the client. Please refer to your Web server's documentation for more information on creating URL-CGI mappings.

If a CGI script—such as the one described previously—does not make use of user input, what happens when a client accesses the page is very simple. First, the client connects to the Web server and requests a Web page. Because the document requested is linked to a CGI script, the Web server executes the CGI program that the page is linked to. Output of the CGI program is then sent to the client that requested the page. Afterward, the connection between the Web server and the Web client is closed. This interaction is shown in Figure 18.4.

FIGURE 18.3.
You can map a Web page URL to a CGI script to provide dynamic content.

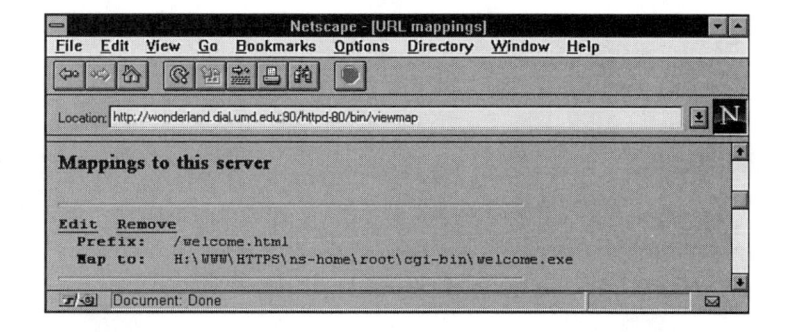

FIGURE 18.4.
You can use a noninteractive CGI script to provide dynamic content.

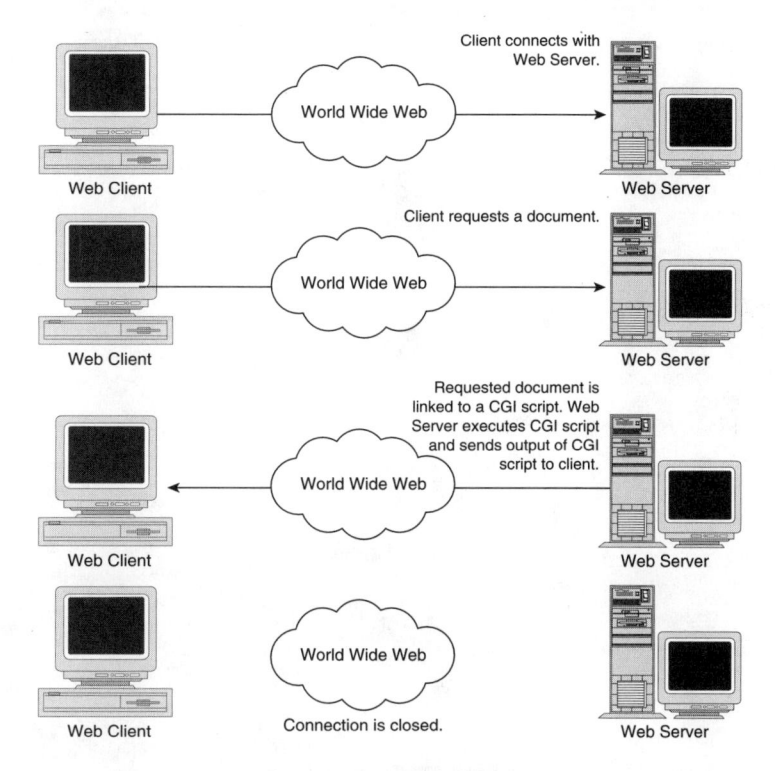

One of the greatest aspects of CGI is its capability to interact with those browsing your Web site. You can ask a user to fill out a form and then submit the form. The CGI script can then validate the user's input, ask the user to complete any incomplete information, and process the user's input, as shown in Figure 18.5.

In the case of a CGI script interacting with a Web client to display dynamic content, first a Web page with various controls is sent to the Web browser. After the user fills in the form, the form is submitted to the Web server to be processed. Depending on the REQUEST_METHOD used to communicate with the CGI script, the CGI script obtains data sent from the client, processes the data, and displays its output to *standard output*. Everything written to standard output by the CGI script will be visible to the client that called the CGI script.

FIGURE 18.5.
You can use an interactive CGI script to provide dynamic content.

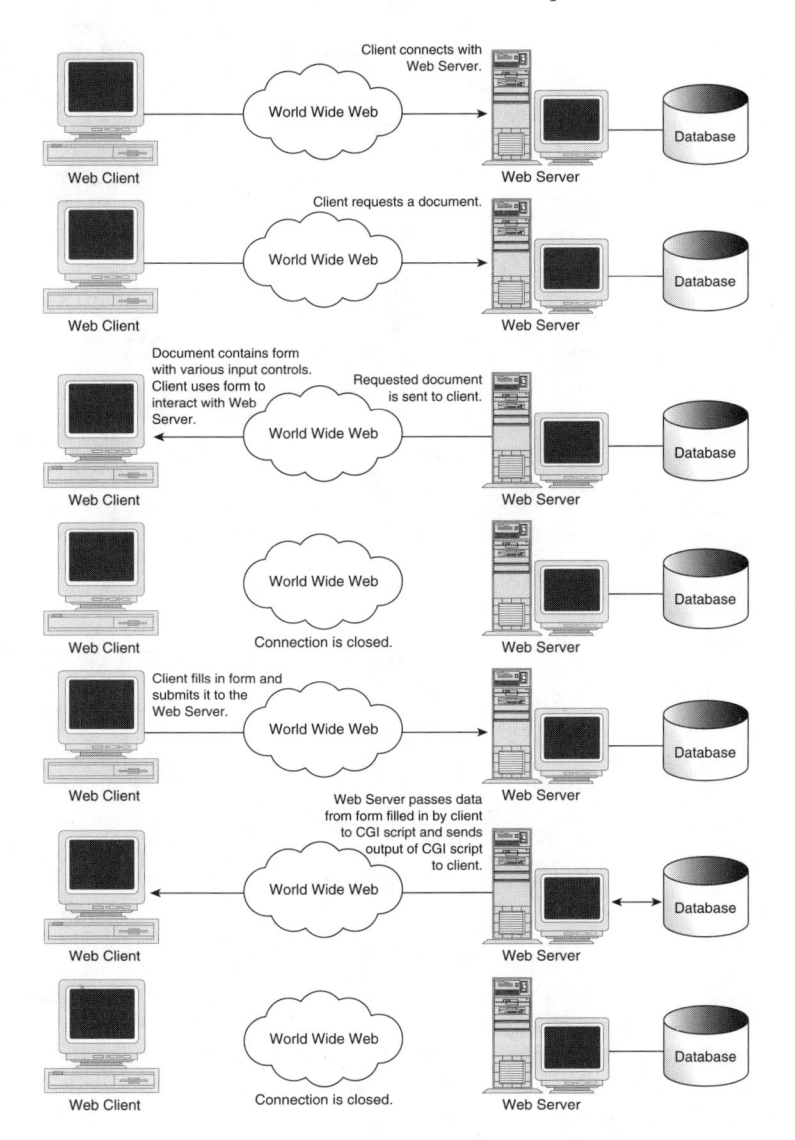

CGI Issues

When setting up CGI scripts, there are a few things you should be concerned with. Each time you allow a CGI script to be executed by someone surfing your Web site, you are allowing someone to execute a program on your server. This can potentially lead to security breaches. Although this might sound a little perilous, it's not as bad as it sounds, provided that you follow a few guidelines. As long as it is utilized properly, CGI is very safe.

Processing Time

Another issue is the time it takes for a CGI script to fulfill a client's request. If you will be providing the data to those browsing your Web site in real time, you should ensure that, at most, no one has to wait longer than about 5 to 10 seconds. If it's going to take longer to process a request, you should obtain the e-mail address of the person requesting the information and simply e-mail the information when the data is processed. If it takes longer than about 10 seconds to process a request, a person waiting at the other end might think there is something wrong and simply stop waiting.

> **NOTE**
>
> If you need to provide data in real time and CGI scripts take longer than about 10 seconds to execute, it's a very good indication that you are outgrowing your server and need more processing power and/or RAM. This might also be an indication of a bottleneck, such as an inefficient database access driver or a poorly written CGI script.

Multiple Instances of the Same Script

Due to the nature of HTTP, it's possible that two or more clients will call the same CGI script at the same time. If the CGI script locks various files or databases when it is processing data, this can cause problems, potentially causing loss of data. CGI scripts should be capable of handling such a situation without any problem. This can be done by making sure the CGI application does not lock databases or files that might potentially be accessed by another instance of the same application.

Security

Although CGI is a very powerful tool for making information available to those browsing your Web site, you need to be aware of certain things. The first thing you should be concerned about is security. You should be particularly careful about CGI scripts that take input from a Web client and use that data (without checking) as a command-line argument. An example of this would be using an e-mail address supplied by a Web client to call Blat, a command line e-mail program. When using such an e-mail address, make sure there is no possibility of it being interpreted as a command-line command. Your CGI scripts should always check for special control characters to avoid potential security breaches. If you have various sections of your Web site protected with a password, you might want to disable directory browsing of your Web server.

By disabling directory browsing, you're preventing someone from "snooping around" your Web site by browsing various directories and their contents, unless that person knows the URL of a certain page or is transferred to a page from one of your own pages.

Controlling Access to CGI Directory

You should be cautious about who has access to your Web server's CGI directory. It's very dangerous to allow users who upload files to your Web site via FTP to have access to your CGI directory. It doesn't take much knowledge in programming to write a potentially malicious program, upload it to the CGI directory, and execute it with a Web browser. Therefore, you should control who has access to your CGI directory via FTP or any other method.

Transmitting Sensitive Data

You should never set up CGI applications to distribute potentially harmful personal information unless the Web server is configured to encrypt the data before it is transmitted over the Internet. If you will be distributing financial information or credit card numbers, you should not use CGI unless you have configured your Web server to encrypt data before it is transmitted over the Internet. If you need to transmit sensitive data and your Web server does not encrypt data before transmitting, you should consider a medium such as PGP (Pretty Good Privacy) protected e-mail to transmit such data.

Validating Users

If you validate users who access parts of your Web site, you should never use the IP address returned by the Web server as the real IP address of the Web client. It's possible to trick the Web server into believing the client making the HTTP request is requesting the data from a site other than the site the Web client is connecting from. Even if you protect a certain area of your Web server with a password and a user ID, this data might be intercepted by a third party. Someone might be able to intercept a valid user ID and password when a legitimate user uses it to access your Web site. If the Web server being used supports data encryption, this won't be a problem; however, it will be a problem if you are not using any Web server–based encryption. In such a case, you should use an OTP (One-Time Password) mechanism to validate users. An OTP authorizing mechanism works by making sure a password used once cannot be used again. Such a mechanism typically sends a challenge string to the client who wants to gain access. The client then uses a special program to find out the correct response string for the challenge string supplied by the server. This is done by typing the user's secret password and the challenge string and obtaining a response string generated by this special program. The response string is then sent to the server. The server validates the user and remembers the response string so that it can't be used again. The next time the user wants to gain access, the server will send a different challenge string to the client that can be decoded only with the user's secret password. Because the user's secret password never travels across the Internet, this is a safe way of authorizing users. However, unless an encryption technology is used, the content being accessed by a client might still be intercepted by a clever person with too much free time. For more information on such an OTP mechanism, you might want to visit

http://www.yahoo.com/Computers_and_Internet/Security_and_Encryption/S_KEY/

CGI Environment Variables

Each time the Web server executes a CGI script, it creates a number of environment variables to pass information to the CGI script. These variables inform the CGI script how the script is being invoked as well as provide information about the server and the Web browser being used by the client. Depending on how the CGI script is invoked, some environment variables may not be available in some cases.

Environment variables supplied to CGI scripts are always all uppercase. When they are being accessed by a C program or Perl script, or whichever language you are using, be sure to use all uppercase letters.

This section discusses the environment variables available to CGI scripts. By accessing these variables, CGI scripts can obtain certain information, such as the browser used to invoke the script. After the following discussion about environment variables, you learn how to access these variables from a Perl script, as well as a C program via CGI.

AUTH_TYPE

Some Web servers can be configured to authenticate users. If the server has authenticated a user, the authentication type used to validate the user is stored in the AUTH_TYPE variable. The authentication type is determined by examining the Authorization Header the Web server might receive with an HTTP request.

CONTENT_LENGTH

Sometimes CGI scripts are invoked with additional information. This information is typically input for the CGI program. The length of this additional information is specified by the number of bytes taken up by the additional information in this variable. If a CGI script is called with the PUT or POST method, CONTENT_LENGTH is used to determine the length of the input.

CONTENT_TYPE

MIME content types are used to label various types of objects (HTML files, Microsoft Word files, GIF files, and so on). The MIME content type for data being submitted to a CGI script is stored in CONTENT_TYPE. For example, if data is submitted to a CGI script using the GET method, this variable will contain the value application/x-www-form-urlencoded. This is because responses to the form are encoded according to URL specifications.

GATEWAY_INTERFACE

The CGI specification revision number is stored in the GATEWAY_INTERFACE environment variable. The format of this variable is CGI/revision. By examining this variable, a CGI script can determine the version of CGI that the Web server is using.

HTTP_ACCEPT

Various Web clients can handle different MIME types. These MIME types are described in the HTTP_ACCEPT variable. MIME types accepted by the Web client calling the CGI script will be a list separated by commas. This list takes the format type/subtype, type/subtype. For example, if the Web client supports the two image formats GIF and JPEG, the HTTP_ACCEPT list will contain the two items image/gif, image/jpeg.

HTTP_USER_AGENT

By looking at this value, the Web browser used by the client can be determined. For example, if Netscape 2.0 beta 4 is being used by the client, the HTTP_USER_AGENT variable will contain the value Mozilla/2.0b4 (WinNT; I). The general format of this variable is software/version library/version.

PATH_INFO

The PATH_INFO variable is usually used to pass various options to a CGI program. These options follow the script's URL. Clients may access CGI scripts with additional information after the URL of the CGI script. PATH_INFO will always contain the string that was used to call the CGI script after the name of the CGI script. For example, PATH_INFO will have the value /These/Are/The/Arguments if the CGI script FunWithNT.EXE is called with the following URL:

http://your_server.your_domain/cgi-bin/FunWithNT.EXE/These/Are/The/Arguments

PATH_TRANSLATED

In the event the CGI script needs to know the absolute pathname of itself, the CGI script can obtain this information from PATH_TRANSLATED. For example, if the CGI script being invoked is HelloNTWorld.EXE, all CGI scripts are stored in H:\www\http\ns-home\root\cgi-bin, and the CGI script is accessed with the URL http://your_server.your_domain/root/cgi-bin/HelloNTWorld.EXE, PATH_TRANSLATED will contain the value H:\www\http\ns-home\root\cgi-bin\HelloNTWorld.EXE. If the CGI program needs to save or access any temporary files in its home directory, it can use PATH_TRANSLATED to determine its absolute location by examining this CGI variable.

QUERY_STRING

You may have noticed that when you submit some forms, there is a string of characters after a question mark, followed by the URL name of the script being called. This string of characters is referred to as the *query string* and contains everything after the question mark. When a CGI script is called with the GET method, QUERY_STRING typically contains variables and their values as entered by the person who filled out the form. QUERY_STRING is sometimes used by various search engines to examine the input when a form is submitted for a keyword search. For example, if a CGI application is executed using the URL http://www.server.com/cgi-bin/application.exe?WindowsNT=Fun, QUERY_STRING will contain the string WindowsNT=Fun.

REMOTE_ADDR

The IP address of the client that called the CGI program is stored in the REMOTE_ADDR environment variable. Due to security reasons, the value of this variable should never be used for user authentication purposes. It's not very hard to trick your Web server into believing a client is connecting to your Web server from a different IP address.

REMOTE_HOST

If the Web server can do a DNS lookup of the client's IP address and finds the alias of the IP address, the REMOTE_HOST variable will contain the alias name of the client's IP address. Some Web servers allow DNS lookups to be turned on or off. If you will be using this variable to find the IP address alias of clients, be sure the DNS lookup option is turned on. The Web server can find the IP address aliases of most clients, but it might not be capable of getting the aliases of some clients. In such an event, the REMOTE_HOST variable will not be assigned the client's DNS alias value; it will just contain the client's IP address. This value should never be used for user authentication purposes.

REMOTE_IDENT

If the Web server being used supports RFC 931 identification, this variable will contain the user name retrieved from the server. Unfortunately, this value cannot be trusted when transmitting sensitive data. Typically, a Web server obtains this value by contacting the client that initiated the HTTP request and speaking with the client's authentication server. Visit http://www.pmg.lcs.mit.edu/cgi-bin/rfc/view?number=931 for additional information about RFC 931 and the Authentication Server Protocol.

REMOTE_USER

Some Web servers support user authentication. If a user is authenticated, the CGI script can find out the user name of the person browsing the Web site by looking at the value of the

REMOTE_USER environment variable. The REMOTE_USER CGI variable is available only if the user has been authenticated using an authentication mechanism.

REQUEST_METHOD

A client can call a CGI script in a number of ways. The method used by the client to call the CGI script is in the REQUEST_METHOD variable. This variable can have a value like HEAD, POST, GET, or PUT. CGI scripts use the value of this variable to find where to obtain data passed to the CGI script.

SCRIPT_NAME

All files on a Web server are usually referenced relative to its document root directory. SCRIPT_NAME contains the virtual pathname of the script called relative to the document root directory. For example, if the document root directory is c:\www\http\ns-home\root, all CGI scripts are stored in c:\www\http\ns-home\root\cgi-bin\ and the CGI script HelloNTWorld.EXE is called, the SCRIPT_NAME variable will contain the value \cgi-bin\HelloWorld.EXE. The advantage of this variable is that it allows the CGI script to refer to itself. This is handy if, somewhere in the output, the script's URL needs to be made into a hypertext link.

SERVER_NAME

The domain name of the Web server that invoked the CGI script is stored in this variable. This domain name can either be an IP address or DNS alias.

SERVER_PORT

Typically, Web servers listen to HTTP requests on port 80. However, a Web server can listen to any port that's not in use by another application. A CGI program can find out the port from which the Web server is serving HTTP requests by looking at the value of the SERVER_PORT environment variable. When displaying self-referencing hypertext links at runtime by examining the contents of SERVER_NAME, be sure to append the port number of the Web server (typically port 80) by concatenating it with the value of SERVER_PORT.

SERVER_PROTOCOL

Web servers speak the *Hypertext Transport Protocol (HTTP)*. The version of HTTP the Web server is using can be determined by examining the SERVER_PROTOCOL environment variable. The SERVER_PROTOCOL variable contains the name and revision data of the protocol being used. This information is in the format protocol/revision. For example, if the server speaks HTTP 1.0, this variable will have the value HTTP/1.0.

SERVER_SOFTWARE

The name of the Web server that invoked the CGI script is stored in the SERVER_SOFTWARE environment variable. This environment variable is in the format name/version. If a CGI script is designed to make use of various special capabilities of a Web server, the CGI script can determine the Web server being used by examining this variable before those special capabilities are used.

CGI Perl Scripts

This section introduces you to Perl and how you can set up CGI Perl scripts on Windows NT Web servers. The Internet contains many CGI Perl scripts written by various people. By using these scripts and customizing them to suit your needs, you can easily improve a Web site. A comprehensive tutorial of Perl is beyond the scope of this book, so this chapter discusses only the basics of writing CGI Perl scripts.

Perl stands for *Practical Extraction and Report Language*. With the growth of the World Wide Web, Perl is being used increasingly to write CGI programs. Most of the best features of C, sed, awk, and sh are incorporated in Perl. This allows Perl scripts to be developed in the least amount of time possible by avoiding reinventing the wheel for fundamental tasks such as string manipulation. The expression syntax of Perl corresponds quite closely to the expression syntax of C programs. This makes Perl an easy language to learn for those who are already familiar with C. One of the best things about Perl is its portability. Perl is an interpreted language that is available for a number of hardware platforms including PCs, Macs, and various flavors of UNIX. Unlike most languages, and utilities, Perl does not impose limits on the size of data. As long as you have enough system resources, Perl will happily read the contents of an entire file into a string. Thanks to various optimizing algorithms built into Perl, scripts written in Perl are robust and fast.

Before proceeding any further, you need to obtain Perl for Windows NT and install Perl on your Web server. Perl for Windows NT is provided free of charge on the Internet. You can obtain it from http://info.hip.com/ntperl/. After obtaining Perl for NT, create a directory for Perl and copy the Perl distribution file to this directory. Then decompress the distribution file. When uncompressing the distribution file, be sure to use the option to use stored directory names in the archive. If this option is not used, all files will be extracted to the Perl directory you created, and you'll find yourself in a mess! After the archive is decompressed, run install.bat to install Perl on your server. Then you need to copy Perl.EXE to the root CGI directory of your Web server, which enables your Web server to execute Perl CGI scripts.

> **NOTE**
>
> When decompressing the ZIP file, be sure to use a 32-bit unzipping program that supports long filenames. Otherwise, the distribution files may not be properly installed. WinZip is a fine file decompressing program that supports long filenames and a variety of file compression formats. You can obtain WinZip from
>
> `http://www.winzip.com/WinZip/download.html`

After installing Perl, you need to reboot your server for the installation directory paths to become effective. Failure to do this will cause Perl to greet you with an `Unable to locate DLL` message. (Yes, I was naíve and tried it!) If you don't feel like rebooting your server, there is an alternative. You can simply copy all files in the `Perl\bin` directory to the CGI directory of your Web server. However, this is *not* recommended in a production Web server. Doing this opens several security holes.

Before creating CGI applications, it is recommended that you check your Web server settings and find out the name of its CGI directory. The remainder of this chapter assumes this directory to be `CGI-BIN`.

Perl Resources on the Internet

After you're comfortable with CGI and using CGI Perl scripts, for more information about Perl and sample CGI Perl scripts, you might want to give the following URLs a click:

> **Yahoo!—Computers and Internet:Internet:World Wide Web:Programming:Perl Scripts**
>
> `http://www.yahoo.com/Computers_and_Internet/Internet/World_Wide_Web/Programming/Perl_Scripts/`
>
> **Yahoo!—Computers and Internet:Languages:Perl**
>
> `http://www.yahoo.com/Computers_and_Internet/Languages/Perl/`

To keep up-to-date with the latest news on Perl for Windows NT, you might also want to consider joining the following mailing lists:

> **Perl-Win32—Perl discussion list**
>
> To subscribe, send e-mail to:
>
> `majordomo@mail.hip.com`
>
> Include the following in the message body:
>
> `subscribe Perl-Win32`
>
> **Perl-Win32_announce—Perl announcements**
>
> To subscribe, send e-mail to:
>
> `majordomo@mail.hip.com`

Include the following in the message body:

```
subscribe Perl-Win32_announce
```

The Perl discussion list is a relatively high-volume mailing list. However, this list is read by many Windows NT Perl programmers and will answer any questions you might have when starting out with Perl.

CGI C Scripts

Because you're reading this book, chances are that you have at least heard of C and possibly know how to program in C. Therefore, an introduction to the C programming language will not be provided. For more information, please refer to one of the many fine books that have been written about programming in C.

C is a general-purpose language with very few restrictions imposed on the programmer. It is also a portable language that can be moved from one computer to another as long as only standard POSIX/ANSI C function calls are used. There are many CGI programs written in C on the Internet that you can use to enhance the capabilities of your Web site. For more information on C CGI programs, please look up

http://www.yahoo.com/Computers_and_Internet/Internet/World_Wide_Web/Programming/

By using various Windows API calls from C programs, you can further exploit the capabilities of C and Windows NT. Although a command-line C compiler for Windows NT can be obtained from `ftp://ftp.cygnus.com/pub/sac/gnu-win32/`, it is recommended that you invest in a C compiler with a GUI development environment such as Microsoft Visual C++ or Borland C++.

"Content Type" Returned by CGI Applications

All CGI scripts have one thing in common: the first two lines displayed by all CGI programs that display text output are the same. The first line displayed by all CGI programs that display text is `Content-type: text/html`. This line of text is always followed by two blank lines. Typically, ASCII character 10 is used twice immediately after this line of text to create the blank lines.

For example, the first line of output for all CGI C programs with text output is

```
printf("Content-type: text/html%c%c",10,10) ;
```

The first line of output for all CGI Perl scripts with text output is

```
print "Content-type: text/html\n\n";
```

A Few Things to Note About Developing CGI Applications

A small note about programming in CGI is in order before moving into writing CGI programs. Sooner or later, when you write your own programs or try out examples, you'll get error messages generated by your Web server when you call the CGI script. Although things might get somewhat frustrating for you, don't give up! Most likely, the error message you receive from your Web server is due to a small oversight on your behalf. After a while, if you're still not getting anywhere with debugging your CGI script, it's time for you to start printing everything you can think of to standard output. Perhaps a variable you thought contained a value contains nothing but a NULL string. Perhaps an environmental variable you thought would be available to your script is not available. It's also possible that you left out the most important thing of all: the first line of all CGI scripts, as mentioned in the preceding section.

Rather than try to debug CGI scripts by executing them on your Web server, you can execute them from the command prompt as well. It is possible to execute CGI programs by running them from the command prompt to find out what really happens. In order to do this, you need to manually set various CGI environment variables to make the CGI program believe that it's really being invoked by a Web server. Environmental variables can be defined by using the SET command, with the following syntax:

```
SET VARIABLE_NAME=VARIABLE_VALUE
```

For example, you can create a batch file with the following variable declarations to test CGI programs when running them from the command prompt. Please note that you may need to change the value of QUERY_STRING if your CGI script makes use of arguments:

```
SET SERVER_SOFTWARE=Netscape-Communications/1.12
SET SERVER_NAME=your.host.name
SET GATEWAY_INTERFACE=CGI/1.1
SET SERVER_PROTOCOL=HTTP/1.0
SET SERVER_PORT=80
SET REQUEST_METHOD=GET
SET SCRIPT_NAME =/cgi-bin/ScriptName.exe
SET QUERY_STRING=ArgumentsToCGIScript
SET REMOTE_HOST =000.000.000.000
SET REMOTE_ADDR =000.000.000.000
SET CONTENT_TYPE=application/x-www-form-urlencoded
SET HTTP_ACCEPT=image/gif, image/x-xbitmap, image/jpeg, image/pjpeg, */*
SET HTTP_USER_AGENT=Mozilla/2.0b4 (WinNT; I)
```

Hello World!, CGI

It's customary for the first program written in a new language or programming interface to display the string Hello World!. Although this is a very simple application of CGI, it will teach you the basics of CGI scripts as well as how CGI scripts are called by Web browsers. The Hello

World! script is demonstrated in Perl as well as C to make you more familiar with both languages and syntaxes of calling Perl and CGI scripts.

The Hello World! CGI script will simply display the current day, time, arguments passed in, and the browser being used by the client to access the CGI script. And of course, the string Hello World!. will also be displayed!

Hello World! CGI Script in Perl

The script that displays Hello World! and the additional information is very simple to write in Perl. The code for this Perl script is in Listing 18.1; the output of the Perl script appears in Figure 18.6.

> **SECURITY NOTE**
>
> Do not place PERL.EXE in your CGI directory. A user with malicious intent can potentially use PERL.EXE to execute commands on your NT Server. Rather than place PERL.EXE in your CGI directory, create a CGI extension mapping and place PERL.EXE in a directory that's not accessible via your Web server. Refer to your Web server documentation for information about creating CGI extension mappings.

Listing 18.1. Hello World!—Perl.

```perl
# Sanjaya Hettihewa, http://wonderland.dial.umd.edu/
# December 31, 1995
# "Hello World" CGI Script in Perl
# Display content type being outputted by CGI script
print "Content-type: text/html\n\n";

# Label title of contents being outputted
print "<TITLE>Perl CGI Script Demonstration</TITLE>\n";

# Display text
print "<H1>Hello World!</H1>\n";
print "<H3>Welcome to the fun filled world of<BR>\n";
print "Windows NT CGI programming with Perl!</H3><BR><BR>\n";
print "The Web browser you are using is:";

# Display value of the environmental variable HTTP_USER_AGENT
print $ENV{"HTTP_USER_AGENT"} , "<BR>\n" ;
print "Arguments passed in: ";

# Display value of the environmental variable QUERY_STRING
print $ENV{"QUERY_STRING"} , "<BR>\n" ;

# Obtain date and time from the system
($sec, $min, $hour, $mday, $mon, $year, $wday, $yday, $isdst) = localtime(time);
```

continues

Listing 18.1. continued

```
# display time
print "\nThe current time is: ";
print  $hour, ":", $min, ":", $sec , "<BR>\n";

# display date
print "\nThe current date is: ";
print $mon + 1 , "/", $mday , "/", $year, "<BR>\n";
```

FIGURE 18.6.
Output of the Hello World! CGI Perl script.

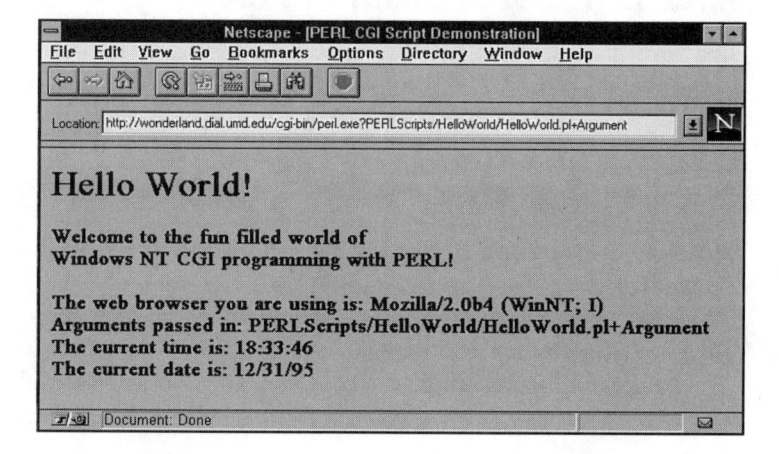

Pay particular attention to how the Perl CGI script is invoked. In the case of this example, the URL used to invoke the CGI script is

```
http://wonderland.dial.umd.edu/cgi-bin/perl.exe?PERLScripts/HelloWorld/
HelloWorld.pl+Argument
```

When calling a Perl script on a Windows NT Web server, the general syntax of the URL is

```
http://A/B?C+D
```

where

- A is the host name of the Web server; in this example, it is wonderland.dial.umd.edu.
- B is the relative path to PERL.EXE; in this example, it is cgi-bin/perl.exe.
- C is the location of the Perl script. This path is relative to the location of PERL.EXE.
- D contains any arguments passed into the Perl script. These arguments can be obtained by examining the contents of the CGI environment variable QUERY_STRING.

As you can see from the preceding example, when Perl scripts are called with arguments, the URLs can become quite long. You can avoid this by creating aliases for Perl scripts on your

Web server. (Please consult your Web server's documentation for more information on creating aliases for URLs.) For example, if an alias called `Hello` was created for

`http://wonderland.dial.umd.edu/cgi-bin/perl.exe?PERLScripts/HelloWorld/HelloWorld.pl`

the URL to call the preceding Perl CGI script will be reduced to

`http://wonderland.dial.umd.edu/Hello+Argument`

Whenever you have complex URLs for CGI scripts, create an alias for the CGI script. By hiding gory details such as long and complicated URL paths, your Web site will actually look friendlier to someone browsing your Web site. It will also save you time whenever you refer to such CGI scripts from one of your Web pages because you will have to do less typing. If you're still not convinced, it's much easier to remember

`http://wonderland.dial.umd.edu/Hello+Argument`

as opposed to

`http://wonderland.dial.umd.edu/cgi-bin/perl.exe?PERLScripts/HelloWorld/HelloWorld.pl+Argument`

Hello World! CGI Script in C

Listing 18.2 shows the C program that displays the same information as the preceding Perl example; the output of the C script appears in Figure 18.7.

Listing 18.2. Hello World!—C.

```c
/* Sanjaya Hettihewa, http://wonderland.dial.umd.edu/
 * December 31, 1995
 * "Hello World" CGI Script in C
 */

/* Libraries containing special functions used in program */
#include <stdio.h>
#include <stdlib.h>
#include <time.h>

main ( )
{
/* Obtain current time */
   time_t          currentTime ;
   struct tm       *timeObject ;
   char            stringTime[128] ;
   currentTime = time ((time_t *) NULL ) ;
   timeObject  = localtime (&currentTime) ;

/* Display content type being outputted by CGI script */
   printf ("Content-type: text/html\n\n");
```

continues

Listing 18.2. continued

```c
/* Displaying simple text output */
  printf ("<TITLE>C CGI Script Demonstration</TITLE>\n");
  printf ("<H1>Hello World!</H1>\n");
  printf ("<H3>Welcome to the fun filled world of<BR>\n");
  printf ("Windows NT CGI programming with C!</H3><BR><BR>\n");

/* Display value of the environmental variable HTTP_USER_AGENT */
  printf ("The Web browser you are using is: ");
  if ( getenv ( "HTTP_USER_AGENT" ) != NULL )
    printf ( "%s%s" , getenv ( "HTTP_USER_AGENT" ) ,"<BR>\n") ;

/* Display value of the environmental variable QUERY_STRING */
  printf ("Arguments passed in: ");
  if ( getenv ( "QUERY_STRING" ) != NULL )
    printf ( "%s%s", getenv ( "QUERY_STRING" ) ,"<BR>\n") ;

/* Display date and time using strftime() to format the date */
  strftime ( stringTime, 128, "%H:%M:%S", timeObject ) ;
  printf   ("\nThe current time is: %s<BR>\n", stringTime );
  strftime ( stringTime, 128, "%m/%d/%y", timeObject ) ;
  printf   ("\nThe current date is: %s\n", stringTime );

  return   ( 0 ) ;
}
```

FIGURE 18.7.
Output of the Hello World! CGI C script.

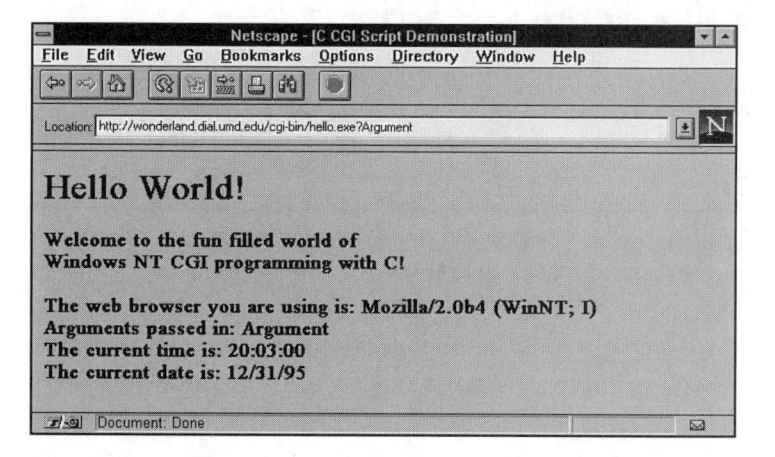

CGI C programs are accessed differently than Perl CGI scripts. C programs can be directly executed by the Web server. However, Perl scripts have to be interpreted using the Perl interpreter. After compiling the C program into an executable program, it should be placed either in the CGI directory of your Web server or in a directory that's a child of the CGI directory. In this example, the executable program was placed in the cgi-bin directory, and the URL used to invoke the CGI script is

http://wonderland.dial.umd.edu/cgi-bin/hello.exe?Argument

When a CGI program on a Windows NT Web server is called, the general syntax of the URL is

http://A/B?C

where

> A is the host name of the Web server. In this example, it is wonderland.dial.umd.edu.
>
> B is the relative path to the executable program from the Web server's document root directory. In this example, it is cgi-bin/hello.exe.
>
> C contains any arguments passed into the C program. You can obtain these arguments by examining the contents of the CGI environment variable QUERY_STRING.

Accessing Environment Variables Available to CGI Scripts

A thorough introduction to various programming languages and how you can utilize them to develop CGI applications is beyond the scope of this book. Therefore, most CGI applications developed in this chapter are developed using the C programming language. However, to give you a feel for how various programming languages can be used to write CGI applications, you are shown how various environmental variables can be accessed by using Perl and C.

Accessing CGI Environment Variables from a C Program

The following C program displays all CGI variables that have been set by the Web server. Note that all environmental variables may not be defined depending on how the script is called. The following CGI program will display all CGI variables that have been defined by the Web server before invoking the CGI script shown in Listing 18.3.

Listing 18.3. CGI variables from C.

```
/* C Program to display CGI environment variable values defined by the Web server
before the CGI program is invoked */

#include <stdio.h>
#include <stdlib.h>
#define   NUM_ENVIRONMENT_VARIABLES 19

main ( )
{
/* Define the data structure that stores all the CGI variable
   names */
```

continues

Listing 18.3. continued

```c
    char* environmentVariables[] =
        { "SERVER_SOFTWARE",    "SERVER_NAME",
          "GATEWAY_INTERFACE",  "SERVER_PROTOCOL",
          "SERVER_PORT",        "REQUEST_METHOD",
          "PATH_INFO",          "PATH_TRANSLATED",
          "SCRIPT_NAME",        "QUERY_STRING",
          "REMOTE_HOST",        "REMOTE_ADDR",
          "AUTH_TYPE",          "REMOTE_USER",
          "REMOTE_IDENT",       "CONTENT_TYPE",
          "CONTENT_LENGTH",     "HTTP_ACCEPT",
          "HTTP_USER_AGENT" } ;
    int   count ;

    printf("Content-type: text/html%c%c",10,10) ;
    printf("%s%s" ,
           "<PRE>\n",
           "<TITLE>CGI Environmental Variables Demonstration</TITLE>\n") ;

/* Loop through all CGI variables that were defined earlier */
    for (count = 0; count < NUM_ENVIRONMENT_VARIABLES; count++)
/* Check if a certain CGI variable has been defined by the Web server
   and print its value if the CGI variable has been defined */
    if ( getenv ( environmentVariables[count] ) != NULL )
        printf     ( "%17s = %s\n" , environmentVariables[count] ,
                     getenv ( environmentVariables[count] ) ) ;

    printf("</PRE>\n") ;
    return   ( 0 ) ;
}
```

The output of the preceding CGI script appears in Figure 18.8. As you can see from the URL, the URL of the CGI script is followed by additional arguments to the CGI script. Notice how the Web server has passed the arguments following the URL to the CGI script by using an environment variable.

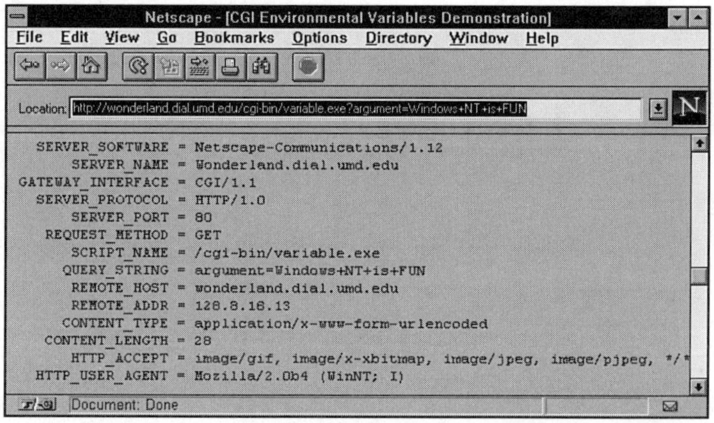

FIGURE 18.8.
Output of a CGI program written in C when called with an argument after the URL of the CGI program.

Accessing CGI Environment Variables from a Perl Script

Similarly, CGI scripts can be accessed very easily from a Perl script. The CGI Perl script that displays values of various CGI variables is in Listing 18.4.

Listing 18.4. CGI variables from Perl.

```
# Print the first line of all CGI scripts
print "Content-type: text/html\n\n";
print "<TITLE>PERL CGI Variable Demonstration</TITLE>\n";

printf( "<PRE>\n" );

foreach $EnvVar ( SERVER_SOFTWARE, SERVER_NAME, GATEWAY_INTERFACE,
                  SERVER_PROTOCOL, SERVER_PORT, REQUEST_METHOD,
                  PATH_INFO, PATH_TRANSLATED, SCRIPT_NAME, QUERY_STRING,
                  REMOTE_HOST, REMOTE_ADDR, AUTH_TYPE, REMOTE_USER,
                  REMOTE_IDENT, CONTENT_TYPE, CONTENT_LENGTH, HTTP_ACCEPT,
                  HTTP_USER_AGENT )

# Loop through all environment variables and display the values of all
  CGI variables that have been defined by the Web server.

{
  if ( $ENV{"$EnvVar"} ) {
    printf( "%17s = %s\n",  $EnvVar, $ENV{"$EnvVar"} );
  }
}

printf( "</PRE>\n" );
exit( 0 );
```

The output of the preceding Perl script appears in Figure 18.9. Note again how the Perl script is being called. The URL of the Perl script is made up of the URL of PERL.EXE and the location of the Perl script with respect to the location of PERL.EXE.

FIGURE 18.9.

Output of a CGI script written in Perl to display CGI variables.

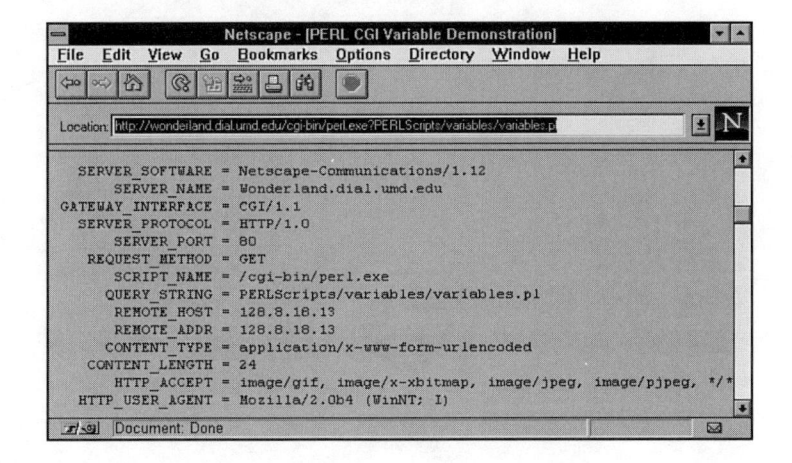

Using CGI to Provide Customized Content

With the expansion of the World Wide Web, more and more Web browsers are being invented. Although there are many Web browsers available for Windows NT, their capabilities differ greatly. At the time this book was written, Netscape accounted for about 70 percent of all Web browsers being used. In all likelihood, with the release of Internet Explorer 3.0, this will change when Microsoft's Internet Explorer becomes more widely used. If the appearance of your Web site is very important to you, you might want to consider setting up a CGI script to provide a customized Web page, depending on the browser being used. Clearly, this is not practical for a very large Web site. However, by setting up a very simple CGI script as shown next, you can find out which Web browser is being used by the user browsing your Web site. If the browser being used is Netscape Navigator or Microsoft's Internet Explorer, you can provide a richly formatted Web page with various HTML enhancements, or otherwise provide a basic page with the same content.

Most Web pages that make use of special HTML tags (such as Netscape enhancements to HTML) look very attractive when viewed with a browser that supports the special HTML tags used. However, these pages tend to look less attractive when viewed with browsers that do not support the enhancements. The percentage of people with Web browsers that do not support various enhancements to HTML can be as high as 40 percent. For these Web browsers, it's possible to set up a CGI script that will display the same content that's formatted by using standard HTML. Such a CGI script can display customized content, as shown in Figure 18.10, based on the CGI variable HTTP_USER_AGENT.

FIGURE 18.10.
Using a CGI program to provide customized content based on the Web browser being used.

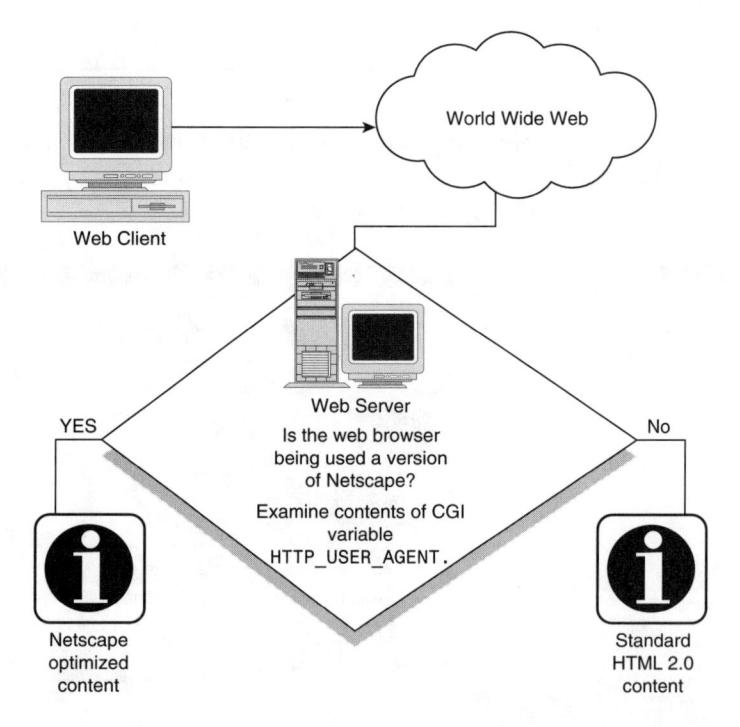

The CGI script in the following code listing is very simple. It first determines the Web server being used by looking at the environment variable HTTP_USER_AGENT. Depending on the value of this variable, a page with Netscape enhancements to HTML can be displayed if the browser being used is Netscape. On the other hand, a page that contains only standard HTML 2.0 can be displayed if the browser used by a Web surfer is not Netscape. By modifying the script, you can always add more customized pages for other browsers. Such a script can be used for important pages like the main home page of your organization. By utilizing CGI to provide dynamic content, you will give a good impression to someone browsing the contents of your Web site. You can ensure that a user with an advanced Web browser will see richly formatted Web pages. It is not feasible to support more than two custom Web pages. Both Internet Explorer and Netscape Navigator interpret HTML tags more or less the same way. You might want to create one page with Netscape and Internet Explorer extensions and another that uses only standard HTML 2.0.

> **NOTE**
>
> Listing 18.5. is not optimized for speed of processing but for ease of reading. Because it is written to demonstrate how a CGI program can be written to provide customized content, it focuses on teaching CGI fundamentals and not on optimizing the code. You can make it more efficient by reading chunks of the file at a time rather than reading and outputting the file character by character.

Listing 18.5. Customized Web pages on-the-fly.

```
/* (C) 1995 Sanjaya Hettihewa http://wonderland.dial.umd.edu/
 * January 1, 1996
 * Program to output a customized Web page based on
   Web browser being used.
 */

/* Special function libraries being used by this program */
#include <stdio.h>
#include <stdlib.h>
#include <string.h>

/* Please note the use of double quotes. This is because a single quote is
   used to quote the next character */

/* If you provide content specialy formatted for a different browser, please
   change the following */
#define   SPECIAL_BROWSER_SUB_STRING "Mozilla"

/* Please change the following to the full path name of the HTML file that's
    specially formatted */
#define   SPECIAL_BROWSER_PAGE "H:\\www\\https\\ns-home\\root\\documents\\WSDGNT\\special.htm"
```

continues

Listing 18.5. continued

```c
/* Please change the following to the full path name of the HTML file that's
    formatted using standard HTML */
#define  OTHER_BROWSER_PAGE     "H:\\www\\https\\ns-
home\\root\\documents\\WSDGNT\\regular.htm"

/* Please change the following to the e-mail address of your Web site
    administrator */
#define  WEBMASTER              "mailto:Webmaster@wonderland.dial.umd.edu"

static int DisplayPage ( char *pageName ) ;

main ( )
{

/* The "First Line" of all CGI scripts... */
   printf("Content-type: text/html%c%c",10,10) ;

/* Find out what Web browser is being used */
   if ( getenv ( "HTTP_USER_AGENT" ) == NULL ) {
     printf("FATAL ERROR: HTTP_USER_AGENT CGI variable undefined!\n") ;
     return  ( 0 ) ;
   }

/* Display appropriate page based on browser being used by client */
   if (strstr (getenv ("HTTP_USER_AGENT" ), SPECIAL_BROWSER_SUB_STRING)!=NULL)
     DisplayPage ( SPECIAL_BROWSER_PAGE ) ;
   else
     DisplayPage ( OTHER_BROWSER_PAGE ) ;
   return  ( 0 ) ;

}

/* Contents of file passed into this function will be displayed to standard
    output. The Web server will transmit what's displayed to standard output
    by this CGI script to the client that called the CGI script */
int DisplayPage ( char *pageName )
{

   FILE *inFile    ;
   char character  ;

/* Check to ensure a valid file name is given */
   if ((inFile = fopen(pageName, "r")) == NULL) {
       printf ( "FATAL ERROR: Content file can't be opened! %s<BR>", pageName);
       printf ( "Please contact the   <A HREF=%s>Webmaster.</A><BR>",
              WEBMASTER );
      return ( 0 ) ;
   }

/* Displaying contents of file to standard output
    Please note that this can be done more efficiently by reading chunks of the
    file at a time */
   fscanf  ( inFile  , "%c" , &character ) ;
   while ( !feof(inFile) ) {
      printf ( "%c" , character ) ;
     fscanf   ( inFile  , "%c" , &character ) ;
```

```
    }
    fclose(inFile);
    return ( 1 ) ;

}
```

Because the purpose of this program is to provide customized content based on the browser being used to browse your Web site, you need to create two separate Web pages. The first Web page is sent to any non-Netscape browser, assuming it does not parse various HTML-enhanced tags as does Netscape. This Web page can be very simple. For the purpose of this demonstration, assume that you need to display a number of options inside a table. Because browsers that do not support the <TABLE> tag might interpret this tag differently, you will have no control over what your Web site will look like when viewed with a different browser. To remedy this situation, you can use the preceding CGI program. For Web browsers that do not support enhanced HTML tags, you can create a non-table version of the same page using only standard HTML. By doing this, the appearance of your Web site can be controlled no matter what browser is being used to access your Web pages.

The following is the standard HTML Web page designed for non-Netscape browsers. In case you're interested in knowing where this Web page is referenced in the CGI program, this file will be saved at

H:\\www\\https\\ns-home\\root\\documents\\WSDGNT\\regular.htm

The location of the preceding file is defined in the C program so that its contents can be displayed for non-Netscape browsers. In the C program, the location of the preceding file is defined in OTHER_BROWSER_PAGE:

```
<TITLE>Standard HTML page</TITLE>
<BODY>
Welcome to the standard HTML page for technically challenged Web browsers.
<P>
Option One<BR>
Option Two<BR>
Option Three<BR>
</BODY>
```

The following is the Netscape-enhanced HTML Web page that is specially designed for those browsing your Web site with Netscape. The following HTML code displays the same three options that are displayed by the standard HTML page. However, the options are displayed inside a table with some additional Netscape enhancements. Because the C program needs to know the location of this file for the purpose of this example, the following page is located at

H:\\www\\https\\ns-home\\root\\documents\\WSDGNT\\special.htm

In the C program, the full pathname of the preceding file is stored in SPECIAL_BROWSER_PAGE. The contents of this file are displayed by the CGI program whenever Netscape Navigator is used. You will need to change this variable depending on where you store the Netscape-enhanced Web page:

```
<TITLE>Netscape Enhanced page</TITLE>
<BODY>
<CENTER>
<TABLE BORDER=15 CELLPADDING=10 CELLSPACING=10 >
<TR>
<TD >
Welcome to the
<FONT SIZE=4>Ne</FONT><FONT SIZE=5>ts</FONT><FONT SIZE=6>ca</FONT><FONT SIZE=7>pe</FONT>
<FONT SIZE=6>En</FONT><FONT SIZE=5>ha</FONT><FONT SIZE=4>nc</FONT><FONT SIZE=3>ed
</FONT>
 Web page!
</TD>
<TD >Option One<BR></TD >
<TD >Option Two<BR></TD >
<TD >Option Three<BR></TD >
</TR>
</TABLE>
</CENTER>
</BODY>
```

After compiling the preceding program and placing it in your Web server's CGI directory, depending on the browser being used to call the CGI script, the appropriate page will be displayed. When compiling the C program, please be sure to change SPECIAL_BROWSER_PAGE, OTHER_BROWSER_PAGE, and WEBMASTER. The output of the CGI program to provide customized content appears in Figures 18.11 and 18.12. For the purpose of this example, the two Web browsers Netscape and Mosaic were used. Note how the enhanced HTML page is displayed when accessing the script with Netscape, and the standard HTML page is displayed when accessing the script with Mosaic.

FIGURE 18.11.
Output of a CGI program when it is invoked by using Netscape.

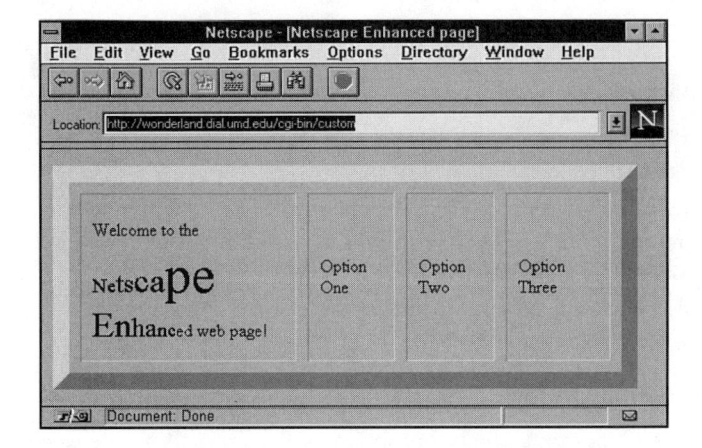

FIGURE 18.12.
Output of a CGI program when invoked with a non-Netscape browser such as Mosaic.

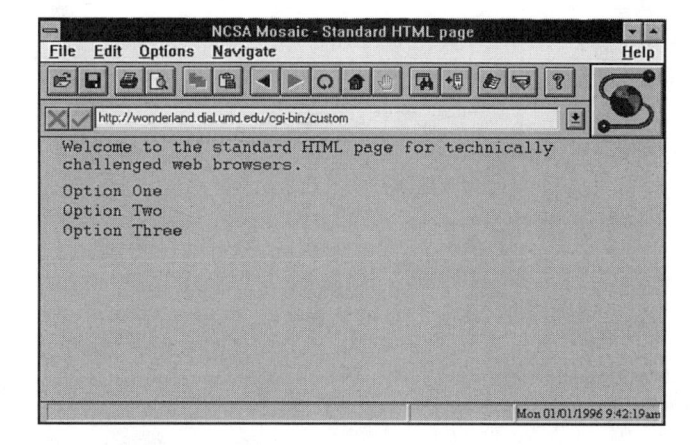

Setting Up a Feedback Form

One of the best things about CGI is that it lets you interact with people browsing your Web site. What better way is there to interact with them than ask for their feedback? By using a Windows NT command-line mail utility called Blat and another CGI program that can be used to e-mail the contents of a form, you can set up a feedback form at your Web site in just a few minutes.

After setting up Blat, you need to create a feedback form. This feedback form will be used by users who want to e-mail their feedback to you. Before setting up the form, you need to download the program that will process the contents of the form after it's submitted. The program you need to download is wwwmail.exe, and you can download it from

http://www.esf.c-strasbourg.fr/misc/amsoft.exe?www

After downloading wwwmail.exe, you need to copy it to the CGI directory of your Web server. Then you need to create a page that displays after the user submits his or her feedback. This page can then thank the user for the feedback and allow the user to choose another link to follow.

Now all that's left to do is to create a feedback form and a response page that will display after the form is submitted. See Listing 18.6 for a simple feedback page. You can utilize a similar page to set up a feedback form at your Web site. There are a few values that you need to change to customize the feedback form, depending on how your Web site is organized. These values are

```
name="mailto"           value="user_ID@your.site"
name="WWWMail-Page"     value=<"Full Path of page to display after submitting the
form">
action=<"your CGI Directory>/wwwmail.exe/cgi-bin/feedback.hfo">
```

Listing 18.6. Feedback form.

```
<HTML>
<HEAD>
<title>Feedback Form Demonstration</title>
</HEAD>

<BODY>
<FORM   method=POST
        action="/cgi-bin/wwwmail.exe/cgi-bin/feedback.hfo">
<INPUT TYPE=hidden name="mailto"
        value="Webmaster@wonderland.dial.umd.edu">
<INPUT TYPE=hidden name="WWWMail-Page" value="H:\www\netscape_commerce\ns-home\root\documents\feedback\ThanksForFeedback.html">

<PRE>
<b>Subject:</b> <SELECT name="subject">
  <OPTION> I have some Feedback
  <OPTION> I have a comment...
  <OPTION> I have a suggestion...
  <OPTION> I need assistance with...
  <OPTION> Other
</SELECT>
<B>Your E-mail address please:</B>     <INPUT name="sender" SIZE=30>
<b>Your name Please:</b>               <INPUT name="name" SIZE=30 >
<b>Your phone # (If you wish)</b>      <INPUT name="phoneno" SIZE=20 >
<b>Would you like a reply from me?</b> <SELECT name="Reply">
  <OPTION> If you wish
  <OPTION> Yes, please
  <OPTION> No thanks
</SELECT>
<b>Is this message urgent?</b>         <SELECT name="Urgency">
  <OPTION> Not particularly
  <OPTION> Yes, very urgent
  <OPTION> Not at all
</SELECT>

<b>Please type your message and press the submit button:</b>
<TEXTAREA name="comments" cols=65 rows=3> </TEXTAREA>
<input type=submit value="Please click here to send message">
</FORM>
</PRE>
</BODY>
</HTML>
```

> **TIP**
>
> In order to provide the user with a set of predefined selections, you can have a pull-down list using the <SELECT/OPTION> tag.

After setting up a form similar to the one in the preceding listing, you will have a feedback form that looks like the form shown in Figure 18.13.

FIGURE 18.13.
A generic feedback form.

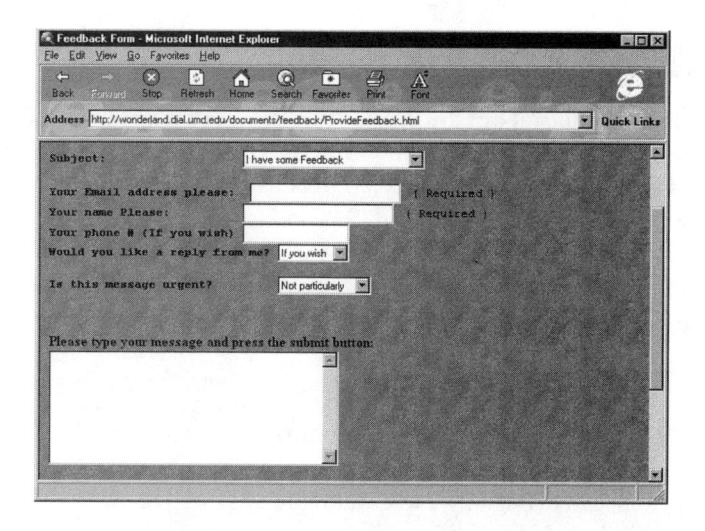

Now you need to create a page like the one shown in Figure 18.14. After the feedback form is submitted, this page will be displayed by the CGI script to thank the user for the feedback. The location of this page is defined in the variable WWWMail-Page of the HTML form. After the form is filled in and submitted, the page defined in WWWMail-Page should let the user know that you received the feedback and will get in touch with the user soon. It will also be helpful if you can let users know how soon you will be able to get in touch with them. Also, this page should provide a hypertext link to another page at your Web site so the user can continue to browse your Web site with ease.

FIGURE 18.14.
After the feedback form is submitted, the user will see a "thank you" page defined in hidden CGI variable WWWMail-Page.

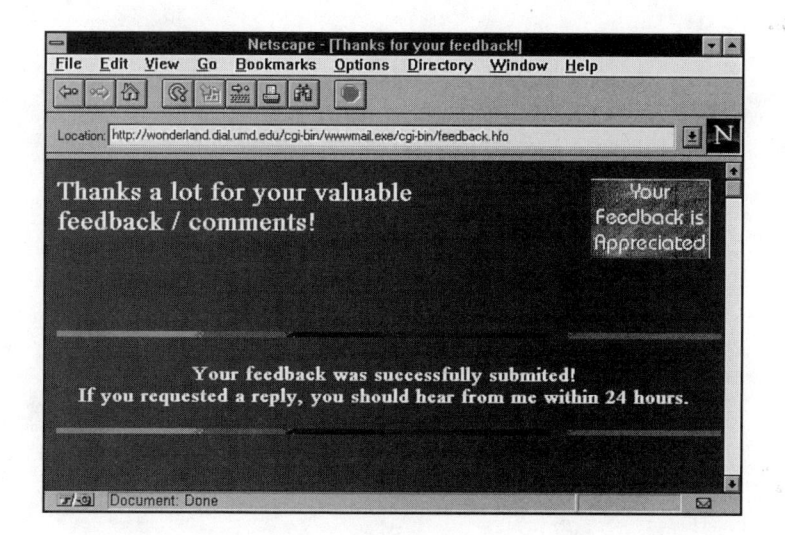

Summary

One of the best things about the World Wide Web is how you can use it to distribute information to millions of people. CGI allows you to interact with this large audience of people. This chapter is an introduction to using CGI to enhance the capabilities of your Web site as well as how to write CGI scripts in Perl and C. Various aspects of setting up CGI scripts, such as security, are also covered in this chapter so that the CGI scripts you develop and set up will not be a threat to the security of your Web server. Various practical applications of CGI are illustrated along with the source code so that you can modify examples presented to enhance your Web site.

In order to become more familiar with the topics covered in this chapter, you need to spend some time with either C or Perl. After writing some CGI programs and experimenting with the effects of making changes to them, you will discover how CGI scripts work as well as gain more experience in debugging and developing CGI scripts. Afterward, you will be able to create various CGI applets to perform many specialized tasks. As you gain more experience, CGI programs you once thought to be very complicated will be easy for you. By utilizing CGI and unleashing its potential to make the contents of your Web site easier to navigate, you will have an outstanding Web site with many repeat visitors.

Writing Java Applets

19

IN THIS CHAPTER

- Java Break   524
- Understanding Java   525
- Creating a Java Applet   528
- Compiling Java Applets   544
- Embedding Java Applets in HTML   545

As exciting as the World Wide Web is, its frequent users are always expecting more from it. Simple presentation of information and form processing capabilities for a Web site are acceptable and the norm, but the Web lacks true interactive communication with a user. As a result, most Web sites are quite dull. A site may have spiffy graphics and loads of good information, but no sites are interactive in real time.

The reasons for this situation are numerous. First, the Web is painfully slow for most users. People accessing the Web at modem speeds have built up a tolerance for slowly painting graphics. When they submit forms for further information, they are accustomed to the time necessary to route this information to a site, have the server perform work based on the information, and return the results. This slowness truly inhibits the idea of real-time interactive communication with the user.

A second reason for the lack of interactive sites is that most Web pages are treated as client/server applications in the very lightest of definitions. Most site developers view client/server technology simply as a client accessing data on the server. In a true client/server relationship, data should be passed back and forth between the client and server machines, but neither machine should do all the work itself. Data-intensive, time-consuming functions should be performed on the server, which is typically a robust machine that has vast access to databases. A local PC can handle the simpler functions. Having the client do some of the processing minimizes the amount of traffic between the user's computer and servers on the Internet, resulting in quicker access. In addition, because the many functions are being performed on a local computer, the speed of the overall Web site appears to be much faster.

Finally, and most importantly, the ability to write interactive applications that run on a user's computer was not widely available until now. But thanks to the work of developers at Sun Microsystems (www.sun.com), there is a new technology that is becoming wildly popular.

Java Break

Sun's Java is the answer to the dilemma regarding how to run truly complex Internet applications on your computer. It solves the mystery of writing a single application that can work on any machine. Because Java applications run on your computer, they are fast and highly interactive. Because the resulting applications are small, they come across the Internet as fast as most graphic files. Because Java was written especially for the Internet and is based on C++, it is extremely powerful and robust.

This chapter takes an introductory look at how to create Java applications. It does not cover every feature of Java or Java programming. It is meant to serve as an introduction for those who want to begin writing their own Internet applications. You learn how to write a basic Java application and some of the necessary, related functions. Coverage of each method and function of the entire Java programming language clearly extends beyond the scope of this book, but there are a couple of good Java books already on the market, such as *Presenting Java* and *Teach Yourself Java in 21 Days*, both from Sams.net Publishing. This chapter examines a simple

Java application and disseminates each function of it and every line of significant code. Through this process, you will acquire appropriate knowledge for writing your own Java applications.

In order to write Java applications, you should have an adequate understanding of C/C++ and the concepts of object-oriented development. Of course, experience with Windows development or a similar graphical user interface helps. This chapter works off this base of knowledge to present Java application development. For more information on C/C++ and object-oriented programming, check out *Teach Yourself C++ in 21 Days* from Sams Publishing.

Understanding Java

If you searched for *Java* on the Internet with a search engine, chances are you would find two types of results. The first would be links to gourmet coffee stands and the second would be links to a new language for the Web. This chapter deals with the latter.

Java has grown from its roots at Sun Microsystems and was developed primarily as a language for creating software for electronic consumer products. Normally, C++ was the language of choice for creating embedded software in such systems, but as the developers worked, they discovered numerous disadvantages with C++. Therefore, they decided to create a language that was extremely similar to C++, but that removed some of the complexity of C++ that often caused more havoc than good for the developer. The result is a language that enables application developers to easily create object-oriented programs that are very secure, portable across different machine and operating system platforms, and dynamic enough to allow for easy expandability. Because C++ is a common development language, there is little need for vast amounts of training like an entirely new language would require; therefore, Java can be more easily adopted.

Applets Work on Any Computer

But what *exactly* is Java? The Java language is a compiler-based language. That is, once a developer has written the Java code, that code must be passed through another program called a *compiler*. The compiler translates the textual code a programmer writes into something the machine understands. In the world of C++ and similar languages, the compiler creates an executable program that can run on a computer. However, that executable program has been compiled for a particular machine and cannot also be run on a different machine. Computers may look similar on the outside or even in the way they work, but the very core of the machine can be drastically different. This difference is why an application written and compiled on a Macintosh cannot run on a Windows PC or a UNIX machine.

Although Java is a compiler-based language like C++, it has been modified so that a single compiled application may work on any type of computer. How is this possible? Java code is compiled into a compact and optimized program called an *applet*. The applet consists of instructions called *bytecodes* that are then fed to a program called a *runtime module*. The runtime module translates the bytecodes into machine instructions for a particular computer.

Sun Microsystems has created a Web browser for Java applications called HotJava. This browser works like typical Web browsers, but it includes the runtime program that reads Java instructions and translates them into machine instructions. Other browsers such as Netscape Navigator 2.0 also offer a Java runtime module in its browser so that Netscape users can view Java applets as well. The runtime program is the only Java-related program written specifically for each type of computer.

To illustrate how Java works, assume that there is a Java application on a Web page that you want to view with Windows 95 and Netscape. When you view that page with Netscape, Netscape retrieves the Java applet and passes that applet to a Java runtime program that is bundled with Netscape. That runtime program, in this case written specifically for Windows 95, reads the Java applet's instructions and translates them to function appropriately with Windows 95. It's similar to being able to put any brand coffee into any brand coffeemaker.

Object-Oriented Programming

Java, because of its roots with C++, is even more tightly integrated with object-oriented concepts. Object-oriented languages enable developers to create Windows-type applications with less effort than with traditional techniques. Object-oriented languages rely on the concepts of objects, properties, and methods. These concepts can be related to a coffeemaker and the process of making coffee.

Clearly, in this case the coffeemaker is the object you are working with to perform a task. Properties of the coffeemaker might include the color of the plastic and where it is located in your kitchen, things that are attributes of the coffeemaker. Methods are actions that an object can perform. For instance, the Make Coffee button triggers the process of making coffee. There also may be events associated with this coffeemaker. *Events* are the triggers that cause an object do something. For example, if the coffeemaker has a timer built into it and the capability to start coffee at a particular time, the clock triggers the brewing process when the correct time occurs.

With object-oriented technology, a Java applet can react differently according to different types of input. Also, because pieces of the object are treated as components, you can replace components easily. This component approach of object-oriented programming also enables Java to handle multiple things at once, independently of each other. A Java applet can have multiple components working on continuously updating live information from a variety of sources while another component is available to handle user interaction. Each independently running task is referred to as a *thread* in Java. You can think of the thread as a series of events that occur in a line. The lines run parallel to each other, but the threads do not necessarily affect each other.

Secure and Robust

You cannot listen to a coffee commercial without hearing about its robustness, and you should expect no less from computerized Java. When Java applications are compiled, they are heavily scrutinized to avoid possible problems. The language itself removes many of the error-prone functions associated with C++, and Java even does dynamic checking for errors while the applet is running. This checking helps protect the developers from creating errors and forces them to not use ambiguous declarations that a language like C++ would allow. As an example, programs written in languages such as C++ historically had to remember to free resources that they had allocated during execution. A Java application does not need to explicitly release memory; the Java interpreter automatically handles this function for you.

The way Java implements this robustness also indirectly heightens security on the applet. Because Java forces developers to be more structured, there are fewer chances for information to be illegally altered in the applet. Security is also heightened with the use of encryption and compression. Java can squeeze and scramble the contents of its applets to limit the threat of tampering.

What Can You Do with Java?

The capabilities of Java outlined in the preceding sections allow for more dynamic, animated, and interactive Web pages in the future. To make you fully appreciate what these features can offer to the Web and you, the section examines an example of a Java application.

> **TIP**
>
> Earlier, alpha versions of Java applets may not run on newer Web browsers that support Java. To determine whether a Web page is using an older version of Java, examine the HTML source for the Web page. Newer versions of Java use the <APPLET> tag to indicate a Java application; older versions use the <APP> tag.

Netscape offers a daily crossword puzzle at its site. You can access this page by jumping to Netscape (http://www.netscape.com). Then choose to view Java information on Navigator 2.0. A list appears with a few sample Java applications.

One nice feature of Java is that you do not have to explicitly invoke a Java application. Most Web browsers will automatically display the application—in this case, a screen similar to that in Figure 19.1. This crossword puzzle applet is an excellent example of a Java application that is very graphic in nature and requires user interaction. It also stresses the importance of adding instructions or creating clearly intuitive interfaces for Java applets. Each Java applet may behave entirely differently from other Java applets, and the user requires instruction for the first time an applet is used.

FIGURE 19.1.
This crossword puzzle application demonstrates how Java applets allow for enhanced interaction between a user and a Web page.

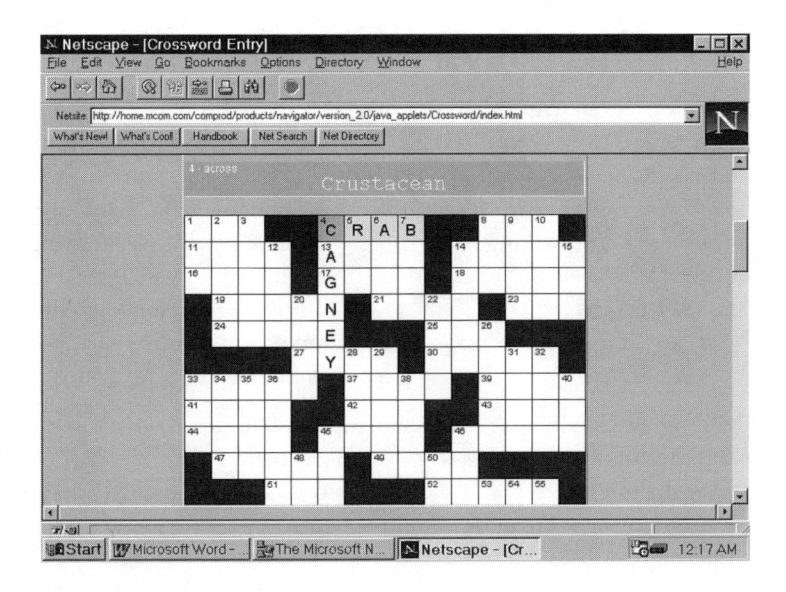

Notice that when you view the crossword puzzle page, the crossword puzzle itself is embedded in the Web page, just like an inline GIF image. From the HTML source code, you can control where the Java application appears, just as you would images.

To work on the crossword puzzle, click any row or column in the puzzle to highlight that row or column. The hint for that row or column is then displayed at the top of the puzzle. To toggle between horizontal row selections and vertical column selections, press the spacebar. When you're ready, you can enter the word you think is the answer into the currently highlighted area. Incorrect letters are then highlighted in red.

As you can see, this Java application is accepting many different types of events from the user: the keyboard for text entry, the space bar for row/column selection, and the mouse for selecting rows or columns in the puzzle. This application also demonstrates how Java can produce very graphical results by drawing the board, highlighting appropriate sections, and adding multicolor text.

Creating a Java Applet

So, now that you have an idea of what a Java applet is and what it can do, how do you write your own specific Java applet? This chapter examines the coding and creation of a single Java applet, which will help you further understand the technology so that you can create your own custom applets. The applet that this chapter examines is the Marquee applet. At times, you may want scrolling text to appear on your Web page. For instance, if you were designing a Web site that tracked stock prices, you might want to implement the familiar ticker symbol line. The ticker line consists of a solid rectangle in which text and numbers are scrolled. The information in the ticker scrolls off the left side of the ticker line and returns on the right side of the ticker area. This applet is also very similar to the Windows Marquee screen saver, which has been aptly renamed in Windows 95 as Scrolling Marquee. The idea is the same; text you enter is scrolled across the screen until it disappears, and it then scrolls back onto the screen from the opposite side.

Writing this effect in Java ensures that the applet can run on a plethora of operating systems and hardware platforms. The computer that the application is running on must simply have the Java interpreter software installed on it. If the computer is using Netscape Navigator 2.0, HotJava, or a similar Web browser to view Java applications, then this interpreter is included.

Choosing Java as the development tool also enables you to use graphics for smoother scrolling and have greater font and color control. You can also set the applet to run continuously in the background, which is essential for the effect as well. The text should continuously loop around the marquee area instead of just scrolling once. Java offers support for these requirements.

Parameters for the Marquee Applet

The Marquee applet exists as a Java applet embedded in a Web page. Because it is embedded, it takes on all of the typical attributes of Java applets. It exists within a window as defined by the HTML code and is loaded/unloaded appropriately as the Web page is loaded and unloaded from the Web browser. The applet will also accept additional parameters from the Web page, defining the nature of the applet.

For this applet, the HTML document for a Web page can set several options:

- text—This text is scrolled within the applet's window. The default is Scrolling Marquee.
- direction—The marquee's text may scroll either to the left or to the right. This parameter may be set to right to indicate that direction; otherwise, the default is left.
- speed—The scrolling text may be sped up or slowed down by modifying this value. Speed is measured in milliseconds; therefore, a value of 1000 is equivalent to a one-second delay. The default is one tenth of a second (100 milliseconds).
- bgcolor—This parameter indicates what the background color of the applet's window should be. The value must consist of a nine-digit number. The number represents three separate three-digit numbers. These individual numbers represent values between 000 and 255. Each three-digit number represents the amounts of red, blue, and green color, respectively. This parameter is similar to the #00 to #FF values typically found in the HTML <BODY> tag for setting colors. Instead of using hexadecimal values, however, this Java applet is expecting decimal numbers. The default is white (255255255).
- fgcolor—Just as the background color for the marquee may be determined through HTML, so can the text color. This value expects the same nine-digit color format as explained in the bgcolor value. The default is dark blue (000000128).

Advanced Web Page Development

Part V

Assuming that this Java applet is correctly embedded within your Web page, the result may be a screen similar to the one in Figure 19.2.

FIGURE 19.2.
A sample of the Marquee Java applet within the Netscape browser window.

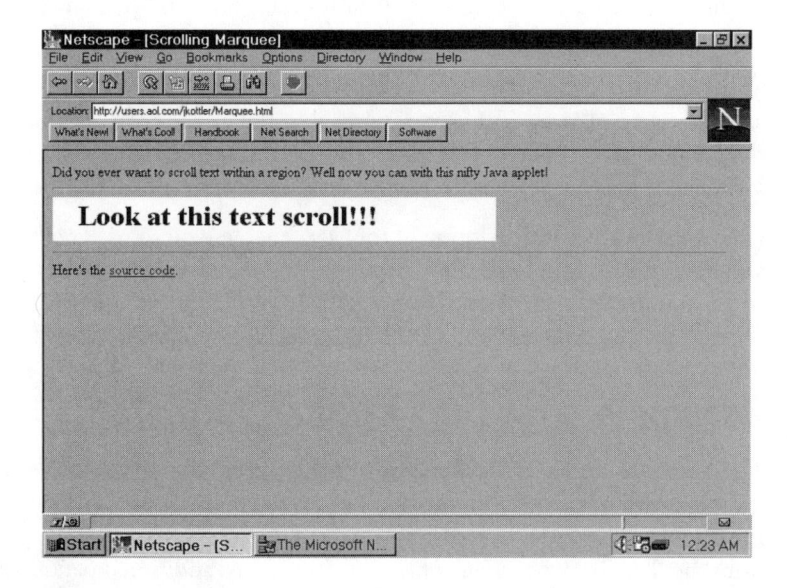

The Marquee Applet's Code

Listing 19.1 shows the complete code listing for the Marquee Java applet.

Listing 19.1. The code for `Marquee.java`.

```
// *******************************
//    Application: MARQUEE.JAVA
// *******************************

import java.awt.*;

public class Marquee extends java.applet.Applet implements Runnable {
  Thread   appThread;
  Font     fFont;
  String   sMsg;
  int      speed=100;
  int      direction=-1;
  int      x=0;
  int      bg_red=255,bg_green=255,bg_blue=255;
  int      fg_red=0,fg_green=0,fg_blue=128;

  // Bunch of setup stuff, read in values from HTML
  public void init() {
    String sParam;

    // Use the Times Roman font, BOLD 32pt.
```

```java
      fFont = new java.awt.Font("TimesRoman",Font.BOLD,32);

      // Get the text to scroll from HTML
      sParam = getParameter("text");
      if (sParam==null)
        sMsg="Scrolling Marquee";
      else
        sMsg=sParam;

      // Default is to scroll left, can specify right
      // Set from HTML
      sParam = getParameter("direction");
      if (sParam!=null){
        if (sParam.equalsIgnoreCase("right"))
          direction=1;
      }

      // How fast to scroll
      sParam = getParameter("delay");
      if (sParam!=null)
        speed=Integer.valueOf(sParam).intValue();

      // Find background color for Marquee window
      // Like <BODY> tag's #FFFFFF format, but uses
      // Decimal:
      //     255255255 is white
      //     000000000 is black
      sParam = getParameter("bgcolor");
      if (sParam!=null){
        // Check that the string looks long enough
        if (sParam.length()==9){
          // Get the Red value (0-255)
          bg_red=Integer.valueOf(sParam.substring(0,3)).intValue();
          // Get the Green value (0-255)
          bg_green=Integer.valueOf(sParam.substring(3,6)).intValue();
          // Get the Blue value (0-255)
          bg_blue=Integer.valueOf(sParam.substring(6,9)).intValue();
        }
      }

      // Find foreground color for Marquee text
      // Works same as background above
      sParam = getParameter("fgcolor");
      if (sParam!=null){
        if (sParam.length()==9){
          fg_red=Integer.valueOf(sParam.substring(0,3)).intValue();
          fg_green=Integer.valueOf(sParam.substring(3,6)).intValue();
          fg_blue=Integer.valueOf(sParam.substring(6,9)).intValue();
        }
      }
    }   // End of INIT


// Paint to the applet's Window within Web browser
// "g" represents that window's canvas
public void paint(Graphics g) {
   Dimension      d = size();
   FontMetrics    fm;
```

continues

Listing 19.1. continued

```java
    // We have a pointer to the font we want to use from above,
    // now we have to set it.
    g.setFont(fFont);
    fm=g.getFontMetrics();

    // Use rectangle to paint background color
    // drawRect is the border, fillRect is interior
    g.setColor(new java.awt.Color(bg_red,bg_green,bg_blue));
    g.drawRect(0,0,d.width,d.height);
    g.fillRect(0,0,d.width,d.height);

    // Set text color and draw it
    g.setColor(new java.awt.Color(fg_red,fg_green,fg_blue));
    g.drawString(sMsg,x,fFont.getSize());

    // Update text position
    x+=(10*direction);
    // If we're scrolling right and outside window, then wrap
    if (x>d.width-1 && direction==1)
      x=-fm.stringWidth(sMsg);
    // If we're scrolling left and outside window, then wrap
    if (x<-fm.stringWidth(sMsg) && direction==-1)
      x=d.width-1;
  }  // End of PAINT

  public void start() {
    // Create a thread to run in background
    appThread = new Thread(this);
    appThread.start();
  }

  public void stop() {
    appThread.stop();
  }

  public void run() {
    while (true){   // While applet is running on page...
      repaint();    // update graphics
      try {
        // Pause the thread, which pauses the animation
        Thread.currentThread().sleep(speed);
      }

      // Exception handling for interrupted thread
      catch (InterruptedException e) {
      }
    }
  }  // End of RUN
}  // End of MARQUEE Class
```

At first glance, the code certainly appears daunting. However, it is really not as confusing as it may seem. The following sections explain each line of this applet.

> **NOTE**
>
> A single comment line for a Java code listing begins with the double forward slash (//). Comments may span multiple lines by beginning the comment block with /* and ending it with */.

Imported Java

If you are familiar with other languages such as C and C++, you may quickly realize that the first line of the Java code, `import java.awt.*`, resembles the familiar `#include` statement in C. Like the `#include` statement, Java's `import` statement allows the application you are writing to import code from other sources. In this case, Java can retrieve code from other Java classes.

One of the nice features of the `import` statement is that it can import multiple classes using the wildcard (*) notation. Because this applet draws results to the applet window, it requires several classes from the AWT (Abstract Window Toolkit). This toolkit serves as the mediator between the Java applet and the operating system. Because every computer system uses different operating systems and supports different hardware, translating GUI functions appropriately is necessary in order for Java to maintain its cross-platform advantage. The AWT takes requests for drawing information to the screen or managing windows and associated controls. The Java interpreter translates these requests to draw information correctly onto your computer's screen, whatever type of computer it may be.

You probably will include the AWT in one way or another in most of your Java applets. The `import` statement in Listing 19.1 imports all of the AWT classes. Some of these classes include support for drawing windows, buttons, graphics such as rectangles and polygons, fonts, and colors, for instance.

When importing classes, all those related to Java specifically begin with `java`. If you have your own custom classes, you may reference them as well. A Java applet is built on dozens of classes that you invoke within your own program. It is important that you include all of the Java methods that your program will require.

Because the Java language is built on classes, there is a class hierarchy. (For a complete description of these classes, their properties and methods, and their relationships, see Sun's Java site at www.javasoft.com.) Therefore, you can specify a particular class to use in your applet instead of using them all through the * notation. You must separate the levels along the hierarchy with a period (.). The period is essential to identifying objects and methods and specifying relations within the Java language. Suppose that you were going to place a button somewhere within your Java applet. To use the appropriate class to handle the buttons, you would use the following line:

```
import java.awt.button;
```

Because you usually import many classes into your final Java applet, it is sometimes more convenient to use the wildcard notation (*) to import all classes within the group of classes.

Head of the Class

Whether or not you realize it, you are creating a class when you create an applet. The Java language uses a truly object-oriented approach, and your applet is treated as a leaf on the end of the object-oriented tree. So it should be no surprise that the first thing you must do when creating a Java applet is create its class. The Marquee applet declares itself using the following syntax:

```
public class Marquee extends java.applet.Applet implements Runnable
```

This line creates a Java applet or class with a particular name and options. This example creates the class Marquee, which will become a Java *interface*. An interface is similar to subclassing or inheriting another class with one important difference: interfaces do not inherit all the excess baggage from the superclass. An interface only implements the methods of the class that are specific for the applet.

The extends java.applet.Applet code instructs this class to inherit the capabilities of the main Java applet class, which allows this Marquee class to be used as an applet by the Java interpreter. The actual definition of the applet is defined by the methods that you implement within your applet, as you will see in a moment. The implements Runnable portion of this line instructs Java to use threads to control this applet.

As mentioned earlier in the chapter, threads are processes that run independently of other processes. They can be thought of as a series of instructions that execute without interfering with each other. This concept is similar to multitasking, which is found in many operating systems. In fact, operating systems use threads for tasks in one fashion or another.

Because you want the text within the marquee window to scroll continuously in the background, you need to implement a thread for this Java applet. You may argue that you do not have to implement a thread to scroll the text. This is true, but if you did not use a thread, the Java interpreter would end up spending all its time processing this single application. This is not effective when more than one Java applet exists on a page.

Now that the class is defined, any code that exists between the starting brace ({) and the ending brace (}) is implemented in that class. On the first line past the first starting brace, notice that a number of variables are declared. If you have experience with C or C++, you should recognize some familiar data types. Some of the types, such as Font or Thread, are specific Java data types. Also, notice that these variables are defined before any additional methods are introduced to the class. This order causes the variables to have a wider scope. Each of these variables are available to any method within the Marquee class.

The `init` Method

Every Java applet must be initialized. Because Java is an object-oriented language, it is important to remember that there may be multiple instances of a class that you design. For example, you may use this Marquee applet on the main page of your Web site as well as in an additional page deeper in the site. Therefore, you must initialize each instance of this applet if each instance is to contain different data and display different results. The Java interpreter triggers the `init` method automatically. Typically this triggering occurs after the Java applet is first retrieved from the network. Once the applet is created on the client computer, the applet is started and this is the first function that is executed.

You can use the `init` method for many different purposes. Often it is used to allocate resource memory, retrieve additional resources from the Internet, retrieve the parameters sent to the applet from the Web page, and set properties of the applet, such as color or position. In the Marquee applet, the `init` method is used to set the font to be used in the applet and retrieve the parameters passed into the applet from the HTML document for a Web page. The `init` method is actually a function within the `Marquee` class and is defined appropriately. It is a simple method that accepts no arguments and returns no value. It is also made public so that other applets or the interpreter may invoke the method.

Getting the Right Font

The first line after the string declaration within the `init` method uses the `Font` class from the Java AWT:

```
fFont = new java.awt.Font("TimesRoman",Font.BOLD,32);
```

Because fonts are drawn to the computer screen, each system may handle this function differently. In addition, each system may have different names that identify a Times Roman font. Therefore, it is up to the AWT to process this request and set up a pointer to the correct font type to use when drawing the text later in the applet. As you can see from the line of code, the `new` instruction allocates memory for the new font object that is created from the `Font` class. That memory is assigned to the `fFont` variable for future reference within the applet.

Parameters

The next four sections of the `init` method retrieve variables passed in from the HTML document of a Web page. This capability allows Java applets to be more generic. Suppose you want to scroll text to the right on one Web page and to the left on another. You could write two separate applets—one that scrolls text to the left and another that scrolls text to the right—but that would be foolish. Instead, you could pass a parameter from the HTML document for a Web page that determines the direction: left or right. That parameter would then be read by a single Java applet, which would take the appropriate action. This capability to pass information between the Web page and an applet allows for even greater dynamic Web pages when coupled with the JavaScript language. JavaScript can control what parameters to pass to the Java applet based on criteria that you specify. Later in this chapter you learn how to embed Java applets and pass parameters to those applets.

Each parameter that is passed into a Java applet is named, which makes it much easier to parse through the arguments and retrieve the correct ones. The sParam is a temporary string used to hold the results of an argument. The getParameter method retrieves the argument that is specified within the method's parentheses:

```
sParam = getParameter("text");
```

In the preceding line, the "text" parameter is passed in from the HTML for the page. For example, the HTML source for a Web page could include the following tag for a Java applet:

```
<param name=text value="Look at this text scroll!!!">
```

This tag indicates to the Java applet that the "text" parameter is to be set to "Look at this text scroll!!!". Therefore, the getParameter would set the string sParam to "Look at this text scroll!!!".

Testing the Strings

After reading in a parameter, you may want to perform some tests on the data returned. Most Java applets accommodate Web page developers who may neglect to include all of the parameters for the applet. When a parameter is not yet specified in HTML retrieved in the Java applet through the getParameter method, the result of the getParameter method is null.

On the surface, this result appears to be harmless. However, it can prove to be quite disastrous. What if an applet is reading a parameter to be converted to a number to be used in an equation and that parameter is not specified? The applet may encounter an error. Although error handling is built into Java, it is good practice to catch errors before they occur. In the Marquee applet, each parameter is tested to determine whether it was set to null. If so, a default value is substituted.

The second parameter read by the applet specifies the direction in which text is to scroll within the Marquee applet. After the parameter is read and guaranteed not to be set to null, the applet checks the value of the parameter. The default direction for scrolling is to the left; therefore only the "right" condition needs to be considered:

```
if (sParam.equalsIgnoreCase("right"))
```

Your first inclination may be to test the string returned by getParameter using the == notation. Experienced C developers quickly realize that this notation is not suitable for strings. The equivalence test (==) is only appropriate for testing logical equivalence between numbers or Boolean values. Strings must be compared using a dedicated method that is a member of the string class.

Strings defined within Java inherit the string class, which contains many methods. Examples of just a few of these methods are: length, substring, and append. The method for comparing strings is inherited as well. The equalsIgnoreCase method tests whether two strings are equivalent. The string sParam in the preceding line of code is tested via its equalsIgnoreCase method with the data passed into that method ("right"). If the result is true, appropriate action is taken to change the direction of the scrolling text. As the method clearly indicates, the strings are compared, but the case of individual letters in those strings is ignored.

Converting Strings to Numbers

One of the requirements for this applet is to be able to specify parameters other than text from within a Web page. These parameters include background and foreground colors to use for the marquee, as well as the speed at which the text scrolls. The actual parameters that are read from the HTML document for a Web page are treated as strings. In the applet, however, these values must be treated as numbers.

Java offers numerous class conversion methods for converting between strings and numbers and vice-versa. In the case of the Marquee applet, several values are to be read in from the Web page and processed as integer values, or more specifically, int values:

```
speed=Integer.valueOf(sParam).intValue();
```

You must use the Integer class to process a string and convert it appropriately. This class contains the valueOf method that converts the string (which sParam holds the value for from the Web page) to an Integer object format. However, because the Java application requires int values and not objects, you must also invoke the intValue method. The intValue method is invoked for the integer object that is a product of the valueOf method. The result is an int value that is returned to the speed variable.

Substrings and Lengths of Strings

Values are passed from the Web page to the Marquee applet that indicate the colors to use for the background of the window, as well as the text that scrolls within that window. For simplicity, the requirements defined these color numbers to be nine digits in length. Each number actually consists of three separate numbers, each three digits in length, which are concatenated together. These three numbers represent the amount of red, green, and blue to mix respectively to form a color. These individual components may range in value between 000 and 255. This format is similar to the one that the HTML <BODY> tag uses to indicate colors; however, the numbers are represented in decimal as opposed to hexadecimal. Table 19.1 shows examples of valid colors for the Marquee applet.

Table 19.1. Sample color values for the Marquee Java applet.

Value	Color
000000000	Black
255000000	Red
000255000	Green
000000255	Blue
255255000	Yellow
255128000	Orange
255000255	Purple
255255255	White
128128128	Medium Gray

Because a color number is passed as a nine-character string, this string must be separated into three components, each three characters in length. The easiest approach to this process is to use the substring method. This method retrieves only a particular number of characters from a main string. As with the equalsIgnoreCase method, the substring method comes with any string you create in Java.

The substring method accepts two parameters. The first specifies the starting position within the string from which you would like to begin reading. The second parameter indicates the position immediately after the last character in the string that you would like to read.

```
sParam.substring(0,3)
sParam.substring(3,6)
```

The preceding two lines return two separate pieces of the string sParam. Assume that sParam holds the value 255196000. In this case, sParam.substring(0,3) would return the value 255, and sParam.substring(3,6) returns 196. You may notice that the substring method retrieves the characters starting at and including the first parameter of the method and ending at the character just before the second parameter of the method.

> **NOTE**
>
> You can identify each character of a string by a number in Java methods such as substring or charAt. The numbering of these characters begins at zero and ends at one less than the length of the string.

The substring method returns a particular range of characters from the string between zero and one less than the length of the string. But how do you determine the length of a string? Java strings also inherit another method: length. This method determines the number of characters that a string consists of and returns that number for you to use.

Painting Applets

Any Java applet that draws to the applet window or uses buttons, windows, or other objects that the AWT offers, requires the `paint` method. This method may be triggered either through your own code or automatically by the Java interpreter. For instance, the interpreter may trigger the method when the Web browser window is resized.

If you are familiar with GUI development, you already know the unparalleled importance of the `paint` method. This method is triggered any time a window is to be repainted. This method has the appropriate source code for drawing graphics or controlling the placement of GUI objects. In the Marquee applet, this method is the appropriate place for painting the background color of the applet's window and for drawing the text within that window at a particular location.

The `paint` method, like the `init` method, is a public method, which means that other applets or the Java runtime module, not just other methods within the `Marquee` class, can call this method. The `paint` method does not return a value, but it does accept one argument, the `Graphics` class. You can think of this class as the canvas that is linked to the Java applet. The Java applet may then paint on this canvas by using methods associated with this class.

In the Marquee applet, this canvas is painted with the appropriate background color, and new text is drawn on the canvas in the correct color at a particular location. On subsequent `paint` events, which are triggered later in the applet by a thread, the location of this text is updated to give the illusion that it is scrolling. To prevent text streaks, the background must first be painted each time the text is drawn. Painting the background clears the window, which removes the text that was already drawn at the old position, before the text is drawn at the new position.

Setting the Current Font

The applet sets the font to use when drawing the text. Earlier in the `init` method, the font object was prepared and stored as `fFont`. The `setFont` method uses that `font` class and sets the current font for drawing text on the canvas using that class. At the same time the font metrics—information such as the width and height of the font—are retrieved for use later in the method:

```
g.setFont(fFont);
fm=g.getFontMetrics();
```

> **NOTE**
>
> Remember to use the `setFont` method to set the current font to draw with on the canvas. A common mistake is to expect that when an instance of the `font` class is created that it also sets the font for drawing.

After the font object has been initialized, the background of the window is painted to the appropriate colors found earlier by the `init` method. This process involves drawing an opaque rectangle that occupies the entire width and height of the Java applet window. In order to know how big a rectangle to paint, the applet must be able to determine the size of its own window. Fortunately, Java offers a `Dimension` object that holds information regarding the dimensions of the applet's window after its `size` method is invoked.

Three steps are used to draw the rectangle. First, the current drawing color must be set to the background color specified by the Web page and read by the `init` method. Because this is a custom color, you must create a new object to hold it. The color of the object is determined by using the `Color` method in the AWT class. This method accepts three integer values that represent the amount of red, green, and blue to mix together to create the final color. Only after the new color object has been created may the current drawing color for the canvas be set by the `setColor` method:

```
g.setColor(new java.awt.Color(bg_red,bg_green,bg_blue));
```

The rectangle is then drawn to fill the window, effectively painting the applet's window. AWT supports two methods for drawing rectangles: `drawRect` and `fillRect`. The difference is that `drawRect` draws a transparent rectangle, and `fillRect` draws an opaque rectangle. The border of the rectangle is drawn in the current color when `drawRect` is used, and the solid rectangle is painted with the current color when `fillRect` is used. The Marquee applet uses both methods to explicitly draw the opaque rectangle with a border of the same color. This approach was used so that both the `fillRect` and `drawRect` methods would be demonstrated. It is more efficient to use the `fillRect` by itself and to stretch its coordinates wide enough to compensate for the border typically drawn with `drawRect`. The following is the code for these methods:

```
g.drawRect(0,0,d.width,d.height);
g.fillRect(0,0,d.width,d.height);
```

As you can see, both `drawRect` and `fillRect` expect four parameters. Each parameter specifies the coordinates to use when drawing the rectangle. These coordinates designate the left position, top position, width, and height of the rectangle, respectively.

Writing Text

After the background of the applet window has been painted, the Marquee application is ready to draw text on top of it. As with most drawing methods of the `Graphics` class, text is drawn using the current color. If the current color is not appropriate, a new color object must be chosen. If the current color was used for drawing text in the Marquee applet, the color would be the same as the background color, effectively not painting text at all. The applet must therefore create a new color to use:

```
g.setColor(new java.awt.Color(fg_red,fg_green,fg_blue));
g.drawString(sMsg,x,fFont.getSize());
```

The current color to use for drawing text is set in the same fashion as the rectangle's drawing color. A new color object is created using the parameters passed in from the Web page to the applet and is assigned as the current color. The `drawString` method then draws a line of text using the current color. This method expects three parameters: the text to display, the horizontal position of the text, and the vertical position of the text. The positions describe where the text is to be drawn, starting at the first character in the text.

Reading Font Information

After the text is drawn to the canvas, the variable representing the horizontal position of the text is updated appropriately for the direction in which it is to scroll. Immediately following this update, two conditionals check to see whether the text has scrolled completely outside of the applet's window. The first condition determines whether the text has scrolled past the right side of the window if it is scrolling to the right. The second condition determines whether the text has scrolled past the left side of the window when it is scrolling left. In both instances, the space that the text occupies when drawn is required. This size is necessary to ensure that the entire length of the text has scrolled beyond the bounds of the window, not just the starting point of the text:

```
if (x>d.width-1 && direction==1) x=-fm.stringWidth(sMsg);
if (x<-fm.stringWidth(sMsg) && direction==-1) x=d.width-1;
```

If the current horizontal position of the text (x) is greater than the width of the window and the text is scrolling to the right, the text should reappear on the left. However, if the horizontal position (x) was merely reset to zero, the effect would not appear correctly. The text would scroll beyond the right side of the window and then reappear in full on the left side of the window. Instead, the text should scroll on from the left, starting with its last character. To accomplish this effect, the horizontal position of the text must be as far to the left as the amount of space that the entire text string occupies. This same theory works for text that scrolls to the left, only the parameters are different.

So how is the amount of space required by the drawn text calculated? Java provides this feature for the applet developer. Earlier in the `paint` event, the `FontMetrics` object was introduced. This object allows the applet to query particular information regarding the font being used. In the Marquee example, the applet must determine how much space text in a particular font requires. The `FontMetrics` class features a method `stringWidth` that performs this calculation. Most fonts consist of individual characters that require different widths, depending on the character. For example, the *W* character may be four times wider than the *I* character. Therefore, for the `stringWidth` to return an accurate measurement for the width of the text, you must pass the text to be measured into the method.

Threads

Earlier in this chapter you were introduced to threads. Threads are vital in operating systems for processing multiple tasks at once. Threads are equally as important in order for the Java interpreter to work with several applets at once. A *thread* is basically a series of instructions that define the nature of the applet. Typically, threads have a start point and an end point, but these points are not required. For instance, in the Marquee applet, a single thread is used to instruct the application to continuously scroll text. This task is accomplished by constantly forcing the applet window to be repainted. The thread instruction to repaint the window is continuously looped and is started or stopped as determined by the interpreter.

The Java runtime program starts the applet when the Web page that the applet exists on is loaded and stops the applet when the page is unloaded. It is important to notice that the applets are either started or stopped; they are not unloaded from memory. Therefore, they are still available. If an applet uses threads, those threads are still running. For performance, it is important to prepare appropriate `start` and `stop` methods within your Java applet that control the threads within your applet.

The `start` Method

Each time the Marquee applet is started, the `start` method is triggered, which in turn starts a thread that scrolls the text:

```
public void start() {
    appThread = new Thread(this);
    appThread.start();
}
```

These lines of code in the `start` event create the thread object and start it. You may notice the keyword `this` in the line that creates the thread object. Often you may want to refer to the current object within your Java applet, which is accomplished through the use of the `this` keyword. In the case of the preceding `start` method, `this` refers to the current applet.

The `stop` Method

Just as there is a method that your applet may use to control what happens when the applet is started, there is an equivalent method that is triggered when the applet is stopped. As mentioned earlier, it is important to stop running threads when the applet is stopped for performance reasons:

```
public void stop() {
    appThread.stop();
}
```

The `stop` method for the Marquee applet is fairly basic. It is triggered when the applet is stopped and its sole responsibility is to stop execution of the application's thread.

The run Method

Because the Marquee applet has `implements Runnable` in its class definition, a run method is available that may be used for thread execution. The run method constructs the instructions that a thread is to follow. The requirements of the Marquee example indicate that the text should be continuously flowing. Therefore, the first thing that is implemented in the run method is an infinite loop. Now you are probably wondering why you would ever want to implement an infinite loop. The fact of the matter is that threads may be interrupted by other threads or by the Java interpreter. When the applet is stopped or closed, this loop is stopped because the thread is halted.

The loop implements two simple tasks: repainting the window to update the scrolling text and causing the thread to pause momentarily for effect. The repaint method forces the window of the applet to be redrawn, triggering the paint event discussed earlier. The sleep method for the current thread delays the thread for a predetermined number of milliseconds. As you can see from Listing 19.2, the sleep method belongs to the object Thread. To clarify which thread should be stopped (particularly useful with multithreaded applets that use several threads at once), the currentThread method is used.

Listing 19.2. The run method implements the instructions for a thread in a Java applet.

```
public void run() {
    while (true){
        repaint();
        try {
            Thread.currentThread().sleep(speed);
        }
        catch (InterruptedException e) {
        }
    }
}
```

Exception Handling

Although you should always try to avoid errors, some errors cannot be detected through your code. These types of errors are often referred to as *exceptions*. Java handles these exceptions more elegantly than most languages and allows your code to perform based on the occurrence of an exception. Java cannot do it all for you, however. It will handle exceptions gracefully for you, but in order for your program to do something about an exception, you must specify the portion of code where the error may occur. You must also create code that handles what happens when the exception occurs.

Java uses the keywords `try` and `catch` in this process. Each of these keywords is followed by a set of opening and closing braces (`{}`) that indicate the block of code to be applied to each keyword. In Listing 19.2, the Marquee applet instructs Java to be wary of exceptions that may occur while the thread is paused. A typical exception that may be raised while a thread is paused is `InterruptedException`. The fact that a thread was sleeping when another thread interrupted it may cause an error.

The `catch` keyword indicates the block of code to execute when a particular exception is raised. In the Marquee application, an `InterruptedException` error may occur. When it does, the `catch` keyword will trap that error and safely prevent the applet from crashing. Although the applet could have performed some action based on this event, it is not necessary in this case, and therefore no code exists in the `catch` section of the Marquee applet.

Because you are specifying to the Java interpreter what section of code may raise exceptions, you must also indicate which type of exception to expect. The `catch` keyword accepts one argument, the type of exception to catch. If you specify a different type of exception than the one actually raised, the block of code following the `catch` statement may not be executed.

The block of code following the `catch` statement that handles exceptions is aptly called an *exception handler*. This is one method by which exceptions may be trapped. As with most any language, there is more than one way to accomplish the same thing. Another approach is to use the `throws` statement, which triggers a specific Java class when an exception is raised.

Compiling Java Applets

Sun Microsystems offers the Java Developer's Kit (JDK) at its Web site. The JDK includes several binary programs for compiling, disassembling, and debugging Java applets. To compile an applet like the Marquee applet shown in Listing 19.1, you first need to create a new file called `Marquee.java` and key in the code. I recommend that you create a special subdirectory for your Java applet. In this case, a Marquee subdirectory would suffice. The `Marquee.java` file that you create should be in this subdirectory as well.

Once you are ready to compile the applet, you must use the `javac` program that is included with the JDK. Run the `javac` compiler program from the directory that holds the applet you want to compile.

The result of this compilation is a `.class` file that you may embed into your HTML documents for Web pages. When you compile the Marquee applet, a `Marquee.class` file is generated in the current working directory.

Most developers who write applications experience errors. Some experience more errors than others. Because the `javac` program is a console-based application, the results are pumped to the screen. And if you have more errors than there are lines of text, those error messages will zip by. I recommend that you make a quick batch file to help you compile your Java project. For the Marquee applet, I wrote the simple batch file shown in Listing 19.3 on a Windows 95 PC. It served two purposes: it paused the output of errors so that I could actually read them, and it made invoking the compiler easier because I named it JC.BAT. One word of caution, though; remember to change the name of the applet you are compiling if you plan on using this batch file for additional applets in the future.

Listing 19.3. A DOS batch file for compiling Java applets.

```
@echo off
c:\java\bin\javac Marquee.java > results
type results | more
```

Embedding Java Applets in HTML

Now that you know how to create an applet, how do you use it with your Web page? Java-enabled browsers support the embedding of applets with the <APPLET> tag. One of the greatest advantages to Java applets is that you may place them anywhere on a page, just as you would inline graphics. The <APPLET> tag has a corresponding ending tag, </APPLET>. Between these two tags, you may use additional <PARAM> tags to specify parameters for the Java applet. Listing 19.4 shows a simple HTML document for embedding the Marquee applet.

Listing 19.4. Embedding the Marquee applet.

```
<HTML>
<HEAD>
<TITLE>
Scrolling Marquee
</TITLE>
</HEAD>

<BODY>
Did you ever want to scroll text within a region?
Well now you can with this nifty Java applet!
<HR>

<APPLET CODE="Marquee.class" WIDTH=500 HEIGHT=50>
<param name=text value="Look at this text scroll!!!">
<param name=direction value="left">
<param name=delay value="250">
<param name=bgcolor value="255255255">
<param name=fgcolor value="000000128">
</APPLET>

<HR>
Here's the <A HREF="Marquee.java">source code</A>.
</BODY>

</HTML>
```

The <APPLET> Tag

As you can see from Listing 19.4, the Java applet and pertinent information is embedded in the HTML document within the <APPLET> and </APPLET> tags. The <APPLET> tag requires three parameters: CODE, WIDTH, and HEIGHT:

```
<APPLET   CODE = "classname.class"
        WIDTH = width in pixels
       HEIGHT = height in pixels>
```

CODE—This parameter specifies the applet to be embedded on the Web page. In the case of the Marquee example, the code would be "Marquee.class".

WIDTH—This parameter specifies the width of the applet's window in pixels. The Marquee applet reads this information using the size method discussed in the "Painting Applets" section of this chapter.

HEIGHT—Just as WIDTH determines the width of an applet's window, HEIGHT determines its height in pixels.

The <PARAM> Tag

By now you are well aware that Java applets accept parameters from the Web page into which they are embedded. Parameters are optional, and default values should always be used for Java applets. However, when parameters are specified by the Web page, they are identified by single <PARAM> tags. Each parameter passed to the Java applet must have its own <PARAM> tag. The <PARAM> tag accepts two parameters of its own—NAME and VALUE:

```
<PARAM  NAME = Java parameter to change
       VALUE = "Java parameter's value">
```

NAME—A Java applet may accept multiple parameters. To indicate which parameter the Web page is changing, the Web page must specify the parameter's name within the <PARAM> tag.

VALUE—Once the parameter to be changed has been identified, the actual value it is to be changed to must be passed from the Web page. The value must be enclosed by quotation marks because it is treated as a string by Java.

Summary

In this chapter, you began your first steps toward learning Java. It may not seem like much, but you have seen skills that will be used repeatedly when coding Java. With the advent of new powerful scripting languages, such as JavaScript and VBScript, these skills are more important than ever.

IN THIS PART

- Interfacing Internet Information Server with ODBC Databases **549**
- Building Dynamic Web Pages with SQL Server **595**

PART VI

Using Internet Information Server with Databases

Interfacing Internet Information Server with ODBC Databases

20

IN THIS CHAPTER

- Installing Microsoft dbWeb **550**
- Using the Miscrosoft dbWeb Administrator **555**
- Creating a Custom Guest Book Using Microsoft dbWeb **589**

At one time or another, everyone wants to provide a means to either capture data from Internet clients that access their Web sites or display information in databases to Internet clients that access their Web sites. With the Internet Information Server, you can accomplish this using one of three methods:

- Using the Internet Database Connector (an ISAPI dynamic link library), included with the Internet Information Server, to create custom HTML documents.
- Writing a custom CGI application and creating custom HTML documents.
- Using Microsoft dbWeb to provide a point-and-click interface to your ODBC databases.

Of these three options, I think you'll find that dbWeb is the easiest because both the Internet Database Connector and CGI applications require much more technical experience and custom development of C (or C++) applications. Microsoft dbWeb version 1.1 executes as a Windows NT service. It is a multithreaded ISAPI dynamic link library that has been written to provide customizable access to any Open Database Connectivity (ODBC) database for which you have a 32-bit ODBC driver. Microsoft dbWeb takes advantage of the multithreaded capabilities of Windows NT to provide superior performance and usability. It includes another program, called the dbWeb Administrator, that you use to define a database schema. (A *schema* is nothing more than the interface between your ODBC database and dbWeb, and is maintained in an Access database.) The schema defines the ODBC database system name (DSN) and the fields to display for query by example (QBE), tabular (multiple rows of records), freeform (a single record), or insert/update/delete database forms. You can even create customizable forms using handwritten HTML documents to provide a different look and feel.

You can currently obtain Microsoft dbWeb from the Microsoft WWW site at http://www.microsoft.com/intdev/dbweb/. You will also be able to obtain the final release on the Windows NT Resource Kit later in 1996. In this chapter, you will learn how to install Microsoft dbWeb and how to use the Microsoft dbWeb Administrator. You will then learn how to interface Microsoft dbWeb to an ODBC database by creating HTML forms to allow Internet clients that visit your site to leave contact-related information (a guest book, in other words).

Installing Microsoft dbWeb

You can use Microsoft dbWeb 1.1 with Internet Information Server version 1.0 or later. To use dbWeb with Windows NT Server 3.51 and IIS 1.0, however, you must meet a few additional requirements. First, you must update your Windows NT Server installation to Service Pack 4. Second, you must have ODBC 2.5 or later installed on your server. As part of the dbWeb installation, the setup program will offer to copy the ODBC 2.5 setup files to your computer. After installing dbWeb, you can install the ODBC 2.5 drivers. Just make sure you install the ODBC

Interfacing Internet Information Server with ODBC Databases

Chapter 20 551

drivers, as described in the following steps, or dbWeb will fail to function. Microsoft dbWeb works best with Windows NT Server 4.0 and the Internet Information Server 2.0. The rest of this discussion assumes that you are using NT Server 4.0 and IIS 2.0.

To install Microsoft dbWeb, follow these steps:

1. Copy dbweb11.exe to an empty directory on the computer where you want to install Microsoft dbWeb. I commonly use the temporary directory C:\TEMP for my installations, and recommend that you do the same.

2. Execute the self-extracting archive dbweb11.exe. You will then be prompted by the Installshield Self-extracting EXE message box to install dbWeb (press the Yes button) or to Exit (press the No button). Click the Yes button.

3. Next, a message box is displayed informing you that the files will be extracted from the archive. Another message box is displayed, informing you of the delay while the Installshield wizard is being set up to guide you through the rest of the installation. At this point, the dialog box shown in Figure 20.1 is displayed.

FIGURE 20.1.
The first screen of the Microsoft dbWeb *Setup wizard.*

4. Click the Next button to display the Microsoft dbWeb License Agreement dialog box. After reading the agreement, click the Accept button to continue. If you do not agree to the license terms, click the Exit button to exit the Setup program.

5. The Choose Destination Location dialog box is displayed after you click the Accept button.

The default directory is `C:\DBWEB`, but I prefer to install all of my IIS-related files in the IIS root directory (the default is `%SystemRoot%\System32\InetSrv`). So, to change the location where the dbWeb source files are installed, click the Browse button. This will display the Change Directory dialog box, where you can specify an alternate location. After you have specified the new location, click the OK button. If the directory does not exist, you will be prompted to create it; after you do that you are returned to the Choose Destination Location dialog box.

6. Click the Next button to display the dialog box shown in Figure 20.2. You should leave the dbWeb Server and dbWeb Administrator checked, but the Microsoft ODBC 2.5 and Examples are optional components. Because you are a new user of dbWeb, I recommend that you install the examples because they are the only tutorial files available. If you are using Windows NT Server 3.51, you should install the ODBC 2.5 files so you can install them later, as described at the end of this step-by-step list.

FIGURE 20.2.
Selecting the Microsoft dbWeb *components to install.*

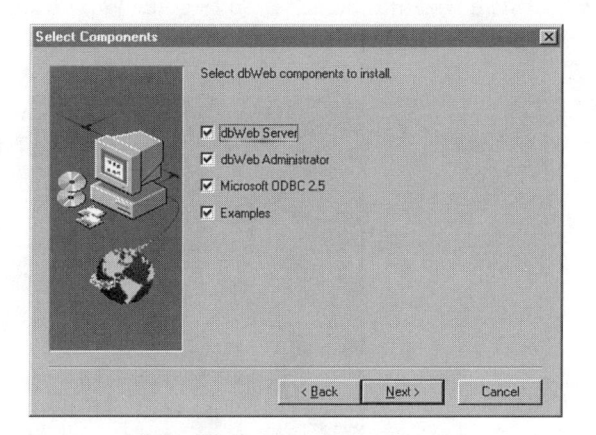

7. Click the Next button; the dialog box shown in Figure 20.3 appears. If the directories displayed do not correctly identify the IIS wwwroot directory or the IIS script directory, you should change them to list the correct directories. Otherwise, leave them as they appear. The IIS script directory is a virtual directory in which all of your executable files reside. These executable files can include ISAPI DLLs, Internet Database Connector .IDC and .HTX files, CGI scripts, or other executable code. The final choice is the subdirectory name for the dbWeb script path (where the dbWeb ISAPI DLL will reside). It will be created under the IIS script directory. It is not necessary to change this directory unless your IIS installation uses nonstandard directory names.

Interfacing Internet Information Server with ODBC Databases

Chapter 20 553

> **TIP**
>
> When you install the Internet Information Server, I recommend that you choose an alternate installation directory (like D:\InetSrv) on a physically separate drive from where you installed Windows NT Server for enhanced performance and data integrity. Furthermore, this new drive should be an NTFS partition so you can make use of the capability to assign permissions and audit access to these directories. For more information, refer to Chapter 5, "IIS Preparation and Installation."

FIGURE 20.3.
Specifying the Microsoft dbWeb *component directories.*

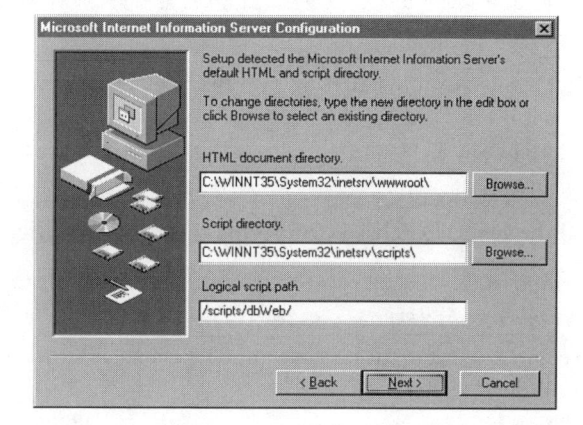

8. Click the Next button. The Microsoft dbWeb source files, the example files, and the ODBC files will be copied to the destination directories you specified in step 7.

9. The Information message box is displayed, informing you of the successful installation of Microsoft dbWeb. Click the OK button to close this message box.

10. If you choose to copy the ODBC setup files, another Information message box is displayed. Click the OK button to close the message box.

11. The registry will then be updated, and a new item will be added to your program group for the dbWeb Administrator. Following this, another message box is displayed asking if you would like to review the readme file. Click the Yes button (a good idea) to read the file, or the No button to exit the Setup program.

12. At this point you might think you are ready to roll, but you are not finished yet. Instead, you must configure the dbWeb service to start at system bootup. This is similar to the modifications you made for the TCP/IP Printing service, described in Chapter 5 in step 5 of the section titled "Installing the Microsoft TCP/IP Printing Service." The only difference is that the name of the service changes to dbWeb Service.

13. If you want to get to work with dbWeb now, click the Start button to start the dbWeb Service. Otherwise, the service will start automatically the next time you reboot.

14. Click the OK button to close the Services applet. Then close the Control Panel dialog box, and you are ready to get to work as described in the next section, "Using the Microsoft dbWeb Administrator."

> **NOTE**
>
> If you are using a version of ODBC older than version 2.5, remember that you must install the new version as described below before you can use Microsoft dbWeb.

15. After a successful installation you may delete the dbweb11.exe file located in your temporary installation directory, although you should keep a copy of this file available on a network drive or a tape backup in case you need to reinstall dbWeb sometime in the future.

To install the Open Database Connectivity version 2.5 drivers, follow these steps:

1. Change to the ODBC32 subdirectory of your dbWeb installation. By default, this is %SystemRoot%\System32\InetSrv\dbWeb\ODBC32.

2. Execute the installation program, setup.exe. This displays the ODBC Driver Pack 3.0 Setup dialog box.

3. Click the Continue button. A search will occur for previously installed components. Another ODBC Driver Pack 3.0 dialog box is displayed that contains three buttons: Complete, Custom, and Change Folder.

4. The default installation directory for all files is the %SystemRoot%\System32. This should not be changed unless you have previously installed ODBC files in another directory. To change the installation directory, click the Change Folder button. This displays the Change Folder dialog box, where you may specify an alternate installation directory. When this has been completed, click the OK button to return to the ODBC Driver Pack 3.0 dialog box.

5. Choose the Complete (recommended) button to install all components, or the Custom button to specify which components to install. If you choose the Custom button, the ODBC Driver Pack 3.0–Custom dialog box is displayed. You can choose which desktop ODBC drivers to install (MS Access, FoxPro and dBASE, Paradox, Text, or Excel), which server ODBC drivers to install (either SQL Server or Oracle), and various other components. When you have completed your modifications, choose the Continue button.

6. The ODBC Driver Pack 3.0—Choose Program Group dialog box is displayed. Choose an existing Program Manager group in the Existing Groups listbox or enter a name for a new group in the Program Group field. Then click the Continue button.

7. A check is made to ensure that you have enough free space, that the files will be copied to your installation directories, and that the new icons and/or program group will be created.

8. The Data Sources dialog box is displayed so that you can immediately add a new ODBC data source for use by any ODBC-compliant application. This is discussed later in this chapter in the section titled "Creating the ODBC Data Source"; for now, just click the Close button.

9. Finally, you are greeted with a successful setup confirmation message box. Just click the OK button to close the message box and exit the Setup program.

> **TIP**
>
> If you will be developing ODBC-compliant applications (Visual C++, Visual Basic, and so on), be sure to read the various readme files (located in the ODBC program group) for changes in using the ODBC 2.5 drivers.

Using the Microsoft dbWeb Administrator

Before you can actually create HTML documents to take advantage of Microsoft dbWeb, you must use the dbWeb Administrator to create your dbWeb schema. This means you must become familiar with the dbWeb Administrator, which is located in the Programs group. This is not really very difficult. In this section you will learn how to configure the dbWeb Administrator to tailor it for your use, how to create a dbWeb data source, and how to create a dbWeb schema so that you can access your ODBC database.

You might want to consider this as a discussion of the basic functions of the dbWeb Administrator, because you will not actually create a product you can use. Rather, this section is devoted to describing the various dialog boxes, data types, and dbWeb methods to give you an understanding of how to use dbWeb with your custom ODBC databases. In the section "Creating a Custom Guest Book Using Microsoft dbWeb," you learn, by example, how to use dbWeb to create a form-driven guest book that uses a SQL Server database.

Configuring dbWeb Preferences

There are a couple basic configuration options that you should set before using the dbWeb Administrator to actually create your ODBC data source and database schema. By setting these properties beforehand, you will not need to change the individual properties for your dbWeb data sources and database schemas later. These properties are divided into two sections. First, you can specify the basic properties for the dbWeb Administrator. Second, you can specify the properties that define how the dbWeb server (the actual service that performs the real work) will operate.

Specifying the dbWeb Administrator Properties

To set the dbWeb Administrator options, choose Preferences from the Edit menu to display the Administrator Preferences dialog box. (See Figure 20.4.) Then follow these steps:

FIGURE 20.4.
Specifying the Microsoft dbWeb preferences.

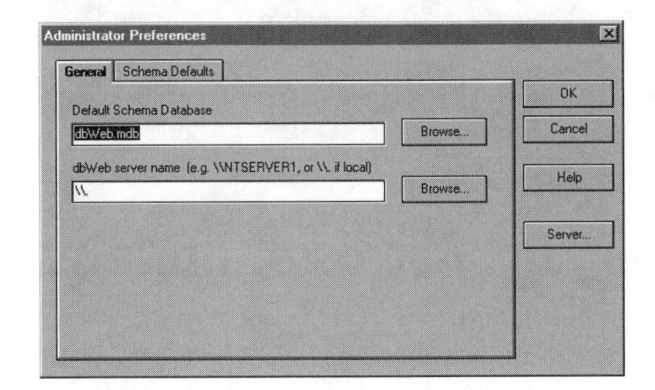

1. If the default Access database (dbWeb.MDB) is not suitable to hold your dbWeb schemas, you can change the name in the Default Schema Database field. The only real reason to change this entry, however, is if you will be sharing a schema database. You might have multiple IIS servers on your network and want to share a single schema database, for example.

> **NOTE**
>
> If you share a single schema database, you must also make sure that all ODBC data source names match on each computer. Otherwise, dbWeb will be unable to access the ODBC database and will generate error messages instead of the expected HTML code.

2. If you will be using dbWeb with a remote IIS server, you should also change the name in the dbWeb server name field to correspond to the computer name of the IIS server (\\SRV, for example).
3. Click on the Schema Defaults tab to display the properties sheet shown in Figure 20.5.

FIGURE 20.5.
Specifying the default schema properties.

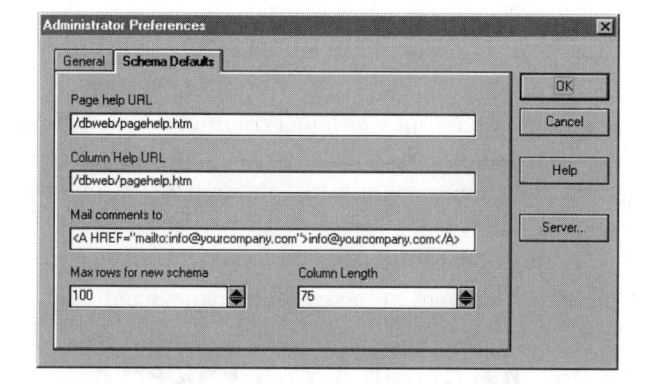

4. Each dbWeb HTML page may have an HTML Web page associated with it to display information concerning how to use the displayed page. This is basically a help file for the page. To assign a default help page, you can specify a relative path and filename in the Page help URL field. This page is accessed from the Help button inserted onto the page by dbWeb.
5. Each column of information displayed on a dbWeb HTML page may also have an HTML Web page associated with it to display information describing the columns of data on the displayed page. This is another help file for the page, but is accessed any time a column header is selected on a page created by dbWeb. In essence, each column will have a hypertext link associated with it to access a specific HTML help document. If there is no specific document, the default document will be displayed. To assign a default column help page, you can specify a relative path and filename in the Column Help URL field.

> **TIP**
>
> Because the information displayed by the default page and column is used for any dbWeb page where you have not given specific instructions, you should create a generic page, and a generic column, HTML help file. You might, for example, want to create HTML pages that will inform the user that the help pages have been inadvertently omitted. This help page could include a bit of text with a hypertext link to e-mail the Web administrator. After the Web administrator receives the message he can create the custom page and column help files.

6. To provide users who access your Web pages the ability to send you e-mail, change the references in the Mail comments to field to your e-mail address. For users to send e-mail to me, for example, I have changed the tag

   `<A HREF="info@yourcompany.com"> info@yourcompany.com</A>`

   to the tag

   `<A HREF="mailto:webmaster@nt-guru.com">webmaster@nt-guru.com</A>`

7. To specify the default maximum number of rows to be displayed by a query, just change the number in the Max rows for new schema field.

8. To specify the default width of a column, which will also determine the size of the edit box displayed on a form, enter a new value in the Column Length field. This field can be overridden on a column-by-column basis as you create your forms, but you should choose a value that represents the most commonly used field size in your databases to save a little time editing the various properties sheets.

9. Click the Close button to save your changes and return to the dbWeb Administrator.

Specifying the dbWeb Server Properties

After you have specified the default configuration options for the dbWeb Administrator, turn your attention to the default behavior of the dbWeb Service. To specify these properties, choose Preferences from the Edit menu to display the Administrator Preferences dialog box. Click the Server button to display the Server Preferences dialog box. (See Figure 20.6.) Then follow these steps:

FIGURE 20.6.
Specifying the dbWeb *server properties.*

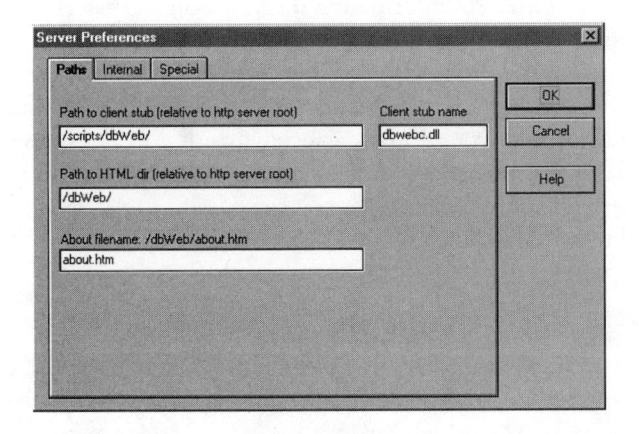

1. The Paths properties includes the following options that you may configure. (You should not have to change any of these options unless you experience problems with the dbWeb service finding its files or finding your HTML files, or if you have created a custom dynamic link library to replace the default client stub.)

Interfacing Internet Information Server with ODBC Databases
Chapter 20 559

- Path to client stub—Specifies the relative (to the IIS WWWRoot directory) path of the dbWeb client stub.

- Client stub name—Specifies the name of the dbWeb client stub. The client stub is an ISAPI DLL (dbwebc.dll). This DLL is responsible for connecting to the ODBC database, for processing the ODBC query, and for building the HTML pages that are eventually displayed on your client's Web browser.

- Path to HTML dir—Specifies the relative (to the IIS WWWRoot directory) path for your HTML files.

- About filename—Specifies the name of the HTML file used to describe dbWeb.

2. Click on the Internal tab to display the Internal properties sheet, shown in Figure 20.7, where you can configure the following options:

FIGURE 20.7.
Specifying the dbWeb server internal properties.

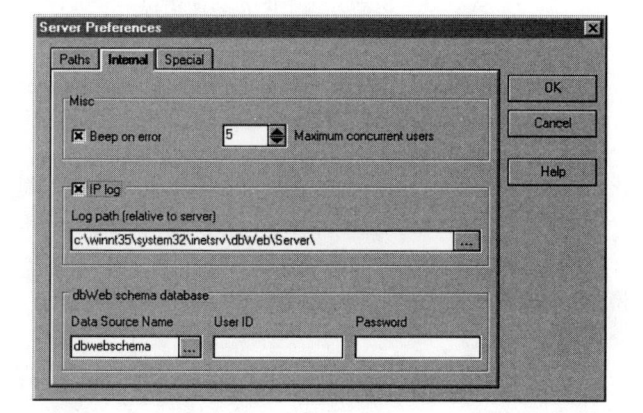

- Beep on error—Specifies that when a dbWeb error occurs, a beep sound should be played. This can be used to notify a site administrator (at the computer where dbWeb is installed) that errors are occurring in real time. The site administrator can then look at the application event log to determine the cause.

- Maximum concurrent users—Specifies the maximum number of users who can access dbWeb at one time. Unless you expect to support only a maximum of 5 users at a time, you should change this value. This setting really requires a bit of trial and error to set properly. A starting value of 10 is sufficient for most sites. If you have a very active site, however, you will want to increase this value to support anywhere from 25 to 100 concurrent users.

- IP log—Check this box, and the Log path field will become active. The file specified in the log path will be used to capture information from your connected clients, such as their TCP/IP addresses, and store it as a text file.

> **TIP**
>
> If you manage a high-volume site, you can gain an additional performance benefit by disabling the IP log check box. However, by disabling IP logging, you will lose the ability to track your database activity based on an IP address.

- dbWeb schema database—This group field includes the following fields that can be used to define the characteristics of the ODBC data source used by dbWeb:
    - Data Source Name—Specifies the data source name used by dbWeb to access the schema database. By default, this is dbwebschema.
    - User ID—Specifies the user name to be used to access the schema database.
    - Password—Specifies the password to be used in conjunction with the user name to access the schema database.

3. Clicking on the Special tab displays the properties sheet, shown in Figure 20.8, where you can specify the following options:

FIGURE 20.8.
Specifying the dbWeb server special properties.

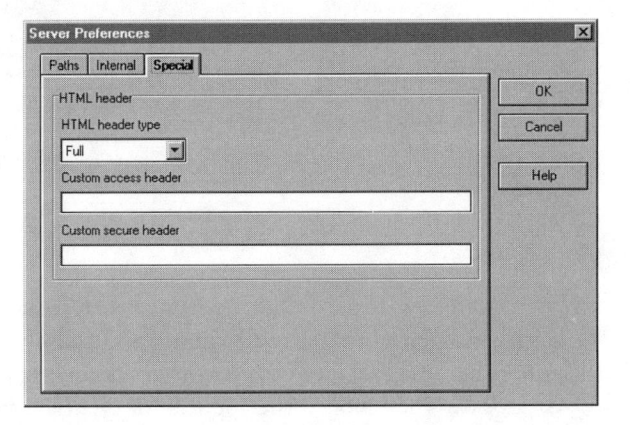

- HTML header type—This drop-down listbox includes two choices: Full and Custom. The default is Full, and when selected, dbWeb will display its own default HTML headers. If this is not acceptable, you can choose Custom. If you choose the Custom setting, the information you enter in the following fields will be used:
    - Custom access header—Specifies custom HTML code to be displayed as the document header whenever a client accesses an ODBC database using dbWeb.
    - Custom secure header—Specifies custom HTML code to be displayed as the document header whenever a client accesses an ODBC database that requires a user account and password as defined by the custom properties for the ODBC database using dbWeb.

> **TIP**
>
> One of the many reasons to use a custom access header or a custom secure access header is to display a user-customized greeting message. When a user connects to an ODBC database that requires user authentication (meaning a valid user account and password), your HTML-secure custom header could display his name as part of the document header. You could display similar greetings, warnings, or other textual content with the custom access header.

4. After all modifications have been completed, click the OK button to return to the Administrator Properties dialog box. Then click the OK button to return to the dbWeb Administrator.

Creating the ODBC Data Source

The first step in the chain to getting the dbWeb server to actually create Web pages for you is to define the ODBC data source. The ODBC data source specifies information to access the actual database and displays information about the database as well. For an Access database, for example, this could include the actual path and filename of the database and of the system database (used for record locking), and other options. Each ODBC data source may have unique properties associated with it, so you'll have to play it by ear when configuring the data source and fill out the information requested by the dialog boxes for each type of ODBC driver you choose.

Defining the ODBC System Data Source

A SQL Server database is the most likely type of database to be used. This is because SQL Server includes much more functionality and increased performance in a multiuser environment. So this is the ODBC driver you will learn how to configure here. First, to create the ODBC data source, you must have created an ODBC-compliant database. For this discussion, I'll assume you have already created the database. The next step is to create the link between the dbWeb Administrator and your ODBC database. This can be accomplished by performing the following steps:

1. Select the Data Sources and Schemas entry in the Data Sources window of the dbWeb Administrator.
2. The buttons on the top of the window now include a New Datasource button. Click this button to display the Data Source dialog box.
3. Click the Manage button to display the Data Sources dialog box.
4. Click the System DSN button to display the System Data Sources dialog box.

5. Click the Add button to display the Add Data Source dialog box.
6. Select the SQL Server entry in the Installed ODBC Drivers listbox. Then click the OK button.
7. The ODBC SQL Server Setup dialog box appears. Click the Expand button to expand the dialog box. (See Figure 20.9.)

FIGURE 20.9.
Specifying the dbWeb *system data source name.*

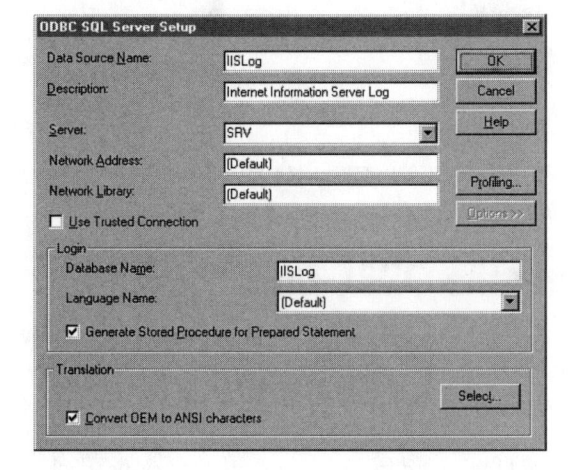

8. In the Data Source Name field, enter a unique name (such as IISLogs).
9. In the Description field, enter a comment to describe the DSN.
10. Specify the SQL Server to connect to in the Server field.
11. Normally, the default Network Address (for Microsoft SQL Server this is a named pipe that, by default, uses the form of \\ServerName\pipe\sql\query, where ServerName is the computer name of the SQL Server installation) and Network Library (for Microsoft SQL Server, this is DBNMPTW.DLL, which will use named pipes) fields should be left as they appear. If you will be using more than one type of connection to SQL Server databases, you may need to change these values. To determine the correct entries, you should consult with the SQL Server administrator of the SQL Server installation to which you want to connect.
12. To ensure the integrity of your connection to SQL Server, you can enable the Use Trusted Connection check box. This check box is applicable only to Microsoft SQL Server 6.0 or higher. A trusted connection is a means of authenticating the connection between dbWeb and your SQL Server database based on the supplied user name and password. This option is applicable only when you utilize named pipes, or the multi-protocol, SQL Server network libraries.

> **NOTE**
>
> The Generate Stored Procedure for Prepared Statement check box is an ODBC performance enhancement and should be left enabled. This option will create and precompile any SQL Server procedures that may be used. If this option is disabled, the procedure will be created and complied on demand. The Convert OEM to ANSI characters check box provides translations of the IBM-PC OEM character set to the Windows ANSI character set and should be enabled unless your database makes use of high-order (above character 128) graphics characters in the PC OEM character set.

13. In the Database Name field, enter the name of the SQL Server database you created (such as IISLogs).
14. Click the OK button to return to the System Data Source dialog box.
15. Click the Close button to return to the System Data Source dialog box.
16. Click the Close button to return to the Data Source dialog box.

And that's all there is to creating an ODBC data source name. If you will be using a different ODBC database, just choose the ODBC driver in step 4 to match your ODBC-compliant database.

Specifying the Data Source Profile Properties

After you have created the ODBC data source, you need to configure the dbWeb Administrator to use the data source. This consists of three configuration steps and one informational step. They are as follows:

1. Select the Data Sources and Schemas entry in the Data Sources window of the dbWeb Administrator.
2. The buttons on the top of the window now include a New Datasource button. Click this button to display the Data Source dialog box, as shown in Figure 20.10.

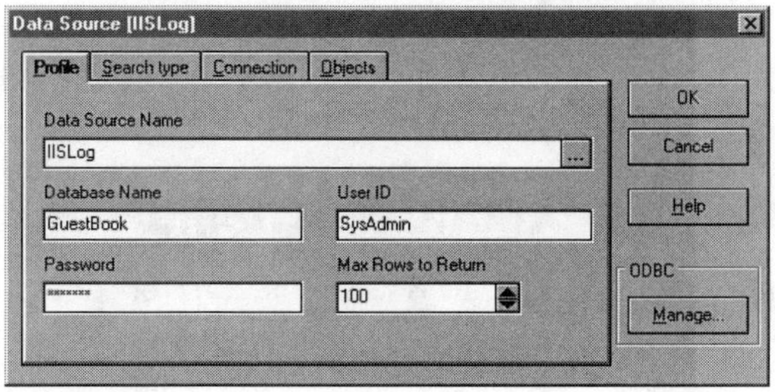

FIGURE 20.10.
Creating a dbWeb *system data source.*

3. In the Profile properties sheet, fill out the following fields:
   - Data Source Name—Specifies the name of the ODBC data source to use. This should be the same name as the database you specified in step 8 of the section titled "Creating the ODBC System Data Source."

> **TIP**
>
> If you click the ... button, the ODBC Data Sources dialog box will appear. You can select an ODBC data source from the list, and when you click the OK button the data source name will be automatically entered in the Data Source Name field.

   - Database Name—Depending on the type of ODBC database used, this field may not be relevant. For a SQL Server database, however, this should be the name of the table contained within the SQL Server database to be accessed.
   - User ID—Specifies the user account to be used to access the specified database.
   - Password—Specifies the password to be supplied with the user account to authorize access to the database.
   - Max Rows to Return—Specifies the maximum number of rows to be returned in a single query.

4. Click the Search type tab to display the Search type properties sheet, where you can choose between using the default search order as defined by your database or to always perform case-insensitive searches.

5. Click the Connection tab to display the Connection properties sheet, where you can specify a timeout value between concurrent connections, to always disconnect between concurrent queries, and to use a secure connection. A secure connection specifies that the Web browser display a login screen on which you can specify a user name and password. This user name and password will be used to access the ODBC database.

6. Click the Objects tab to display the Objects properties sheet, where the objects in your database (tables, views, and procedures) will be displayed. This is an informative display only.

7. Click the OK button to create your data source and return to the dbWeb Data Source window.

Creating the Database Schema

Creating your database schema is where the real work of using the dbWeb Administrator occurs. But it is not going to be as bad as you think, because Microsoft has utilized the Wizard technology introduced with Windows 95 to make creating a database schema easier. After you

Interfacing Internet Information Server with ODBC Databases

Chapter 20

create the schema, however, you will need to fine-tune it to meet your specifications. The basic process to create your database schema is as follows:

1. Select your data source in the Data Sources window. Then click the New Schema button.

2. The New Schema dialog box appears, as shown in Figure 20.11. Click the Schema Wizard button.

FIGURE 20.11.
Creating a new schema.

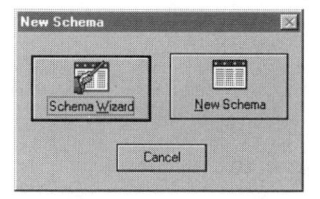

3. The Choose a table dialog box appears, as shown in Figure 20.12. Select the desired table in the Tables field and click the Next button.

FIGURE 20.12.
Choosing tables for the new schema.

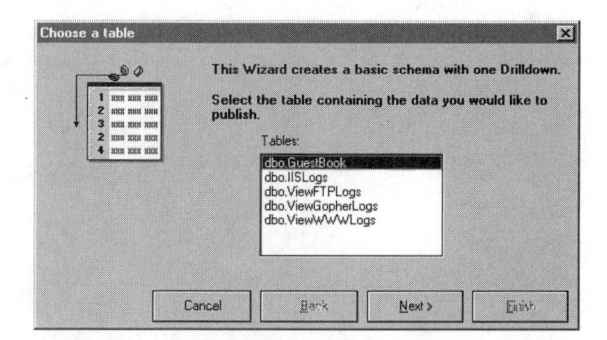

4. The Choose the data columns to query dialog box appears, as shown in Figure 20.13. Select the column you want to use in your query by example form in the Available fields list.

FIGURE 20.13.
Choosing columns to use in the query by example form.

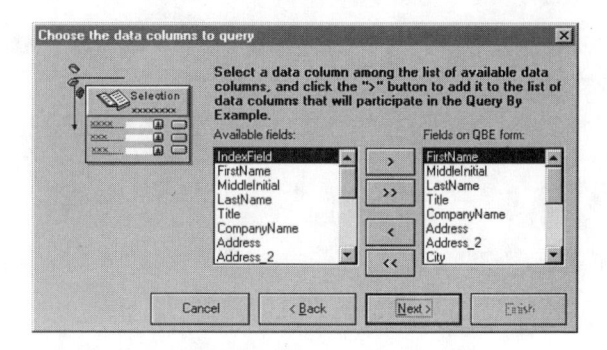

Part VI — Using Internet Information Server with Databases

5. Click the > button to move the selected field to the Fields on QBE form list.
6. Repeat steps 4 and 5 for each field in the table you want to use. Then click the Next button.

> **TIP**
>
> Click the >> button to move all of the columns listed in the Available fields list to the Fields on QBE form list.

7. The Choose tabular form data columns dialog box appears. Select the column you want to use in your query by example form in the Available fields list.
8. Click the > button to move the selected field to the Fields on Tabular form list.
9. Repeat steps 7 and 8 for each field in the table you want to use. Then click the Next button.
10. The Specify a Drilldown Automatic Link dialog box appears, shown in Figure 20.14.

FIGURE 20.14.
Specifying the drilldown link.

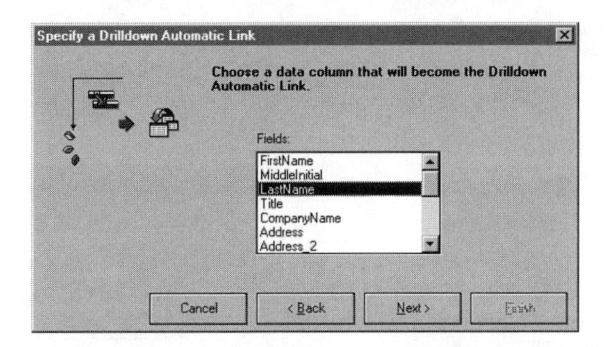

11. Choose a column in the Fields list to use as the link to jump to the next item (drilldown) in the hierarchical level of your table. Then choose the Next button. By default, this drilldown link will be specified as a zoom to the same schema, meaning that it will display multiple records with the same field.

> **NOTE**
>
> You can change this property to specify no drill down, a static link to a URL, a dynamic link specified in the table column, a zoom to the same schema, or a jump to another schema by specifying the property for the field in the Tabular properties sheet.

12. The Enter schema name dialog box appears, as shown in Figure 20.15. Enter a unique (within the schema) name and click the Finish button to return to the Data Sources window of the dbWeb Administrator.

FIGURE 20.15.
The final touch to building the schema.

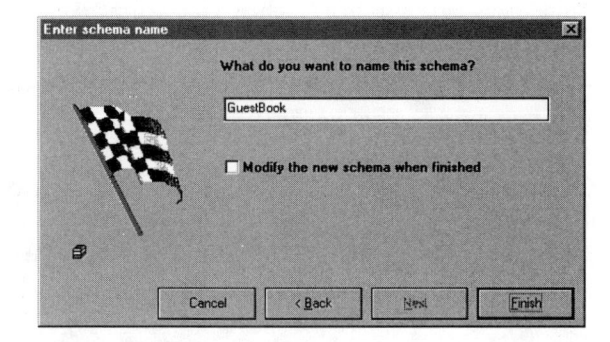

Repeat steps 1 through 12 for each table within the database for which you want to create a schema. After you create all of your schemas, you can move on to fine-tuning the individual properties. These properties are explained in the following sections and include:

- Specifying the Database Schema Properties
- Specifying the Schema Tables
- Specifying the Schema Joins and Constraints
- Specifying the Schema Query By Example Properties
- Specifying the Schema Tabular Form Properties
- Specifying the Schema Freeform Properties
- Specifying the Schema Insert/Update/Delete Form Properties
- Specifying the Schema Custom HTML Form Properties

Specifying the Database Schema Properties

The default properties you specified when you configured the dbWeb Administrator are used to set some of the default properties for your schemas. These defaults are useful because, if you forget to define a specific Web help page for your page (or column) help pages, the defaults will be used instead. This way, your Internet clients will not see an error message. Instead, they'll be greeted by your custom help file that verifies the omission of a specific help page and requests the client to e-mail the Web administrator to correct the omission. There are other useful tidbits of information you may want to define for each schema as well. To do so, follow these steps:

1. Double-click a data source (such as IISLogs) to expand it and display the schemas below the data source name.
2. Select the schema (such as GuestBook) and click the Modify Schema button. The dialog box shown in Figure 20.16 then appears.

FIGURE 20.16.

Configuring the database schema properties.

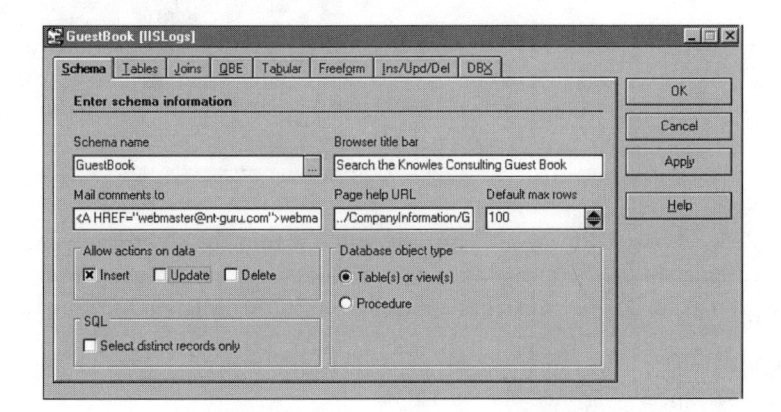

3. The name of the schema is displayed in the Schema name field. If you decide that your original schema name is unsatisfactory, you can change it by clicking the un-named button to the right of the Schema name field. This displays the Schema Name dialog box. Enter the new name in the Schema name field and click the OK button to return to the Schema properties sheet.
4. To specify a title to be displayed in the caption bar of the client Web browser, enter a value in the Browser title bar field.
5. To specify an e-mail address to be displayed on the bottom of the Web page created by dbWeb, change the HTML tag in the Mail comments to field. The default tag may not be applicable for all schemas, and you may need to change it based on the page content. You might have a Web page to sell products and want any e-mail to be sent to sales@yourcompany.com, for example.
6. To specify a custom help file to be accessed from the Help button created by dbWeb, enter a relative URL in the Page help URL field. A relative URL is based on the

default directory of WWWRoot\DbWeb, so if you place your help file in a different subdirectory, such as WWWRoot\CompanyInformation, your entry should look something like

../CompanyInformation/GuestBookQBEPageHelp.htm

You can also use an absolute URL, such as

http://www.nt-guru.com/CompanyInformation/GuestBookQBEPageHelp.htm

7. To specify the maximum number of rows to be returned in a single query, enter the value in the Default max rows field.

8. To specify the types of actions an Internet client can perform on your database, enable the appropriate check box in the Allow actions on data group. This can be Insert to add records to the database, Update to modify records in the database, or Delete to remove records from the database.

> **CAUTION**
>
> Allowing someone to update or delete records in your database could be asking for trouble. A malicious user could stop by and have a bit of fun if you allow just anyone to update or delete information. If you do support these options, you should also use the Secure Connection option (accessible from the Data Source Connection tab) to validate the user.

9. To limit the returned rows to single instances of a record, enable the Select distinct records only option in the SQL group.

10. To specify the type of database objects the schema will define, enable the appropriate radio button in the Database object type group. This can be Table(s) or view(s) to define access to tables, views, or querydefs contained within the database. It can also be Procedure if you want to define access to executable functions contained within the database.

11. When you have completed your definitions, click the OK button to accept your modifications and return to the Data Sources window, or click the Apply button to immediately update the schema with your changes. This is useful when you are making continuous modifications and testing each action.

Specifying the Schema Tables

Most databases include more than one table, and many of these tables are related to one another. In order to define how the schema will display data in such a situation, you might need to configure it to include multiple tables. This can be accomplished by following these steps:

1. Double-click a data source (such as dbpubs) to expand it and display the schemas below the data source name.
2. Select the schema (such as Author_Titles) and click the Modify Schema button. Click the Tables tab to display the properties sheet shown in Figure 20.17.

FIGURE 20.17.
Specifying the tables for the database schema.

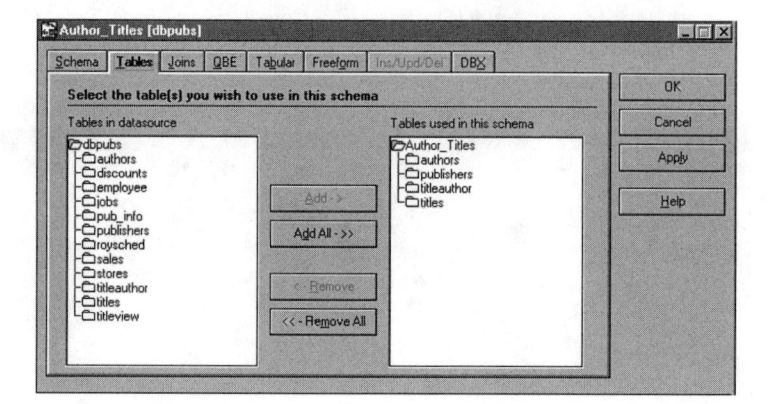

3. The tables contained within the database will be displayed in the Tables in datasource listbox. To specify an individual table to use with your schema, select it and click the Add button to copy the table definition to the Tables used in this schema listbox.
4. Repeat step 3 for each table to add to the schema. To add all of the tables, click the Add All button. To remove a table definition, select the table in the Tables used in this schema listbox and click the Remove button.
5. When you have completed your definitions, click the OK button to accept your modifications and return to the Data Sources window, or click the Apply button to immediately update the schema with your changes. This is useful when you are making continuous modifications and testing each action.

Specifying the Schema Joins and Constraints

If you have multiple tables that you want to combine into a single table, you must define a join. A *join* is where two or more tables have records with a common field. This common field is used to link these records. The dbWeb sample pubs database, for example, uses the author_id field to define a relationship between the author table and the titles table. The pubs database

Interfacing Internet Information Server with ODBC Databases

Chapter 20

also uses the `pub_id` field to define a relationship between the `titles` table and the `publishers` table. This relationship is used to combine the three tables to display the author, title, publisher, and other relevant information. If these tables were accessed separately, the information would not be nearly as useful to the reader. To create a join, you must first have defined multiple tables for the schema, as described in the preceding section titled "Specifying the Schema Tables." When that has been accomplished you can define your joins by following these steps:

1. Double-click a data source (such as `dbpubs`) to expand it and display the schemas below the data source name.
2. Select the schema (such as `Author_Titles`) and click the Modify Schema button. Click the Joins tab to display the properties sheet shown in Figure 20.18.

FIGURE 20.18.
Specifying the table joins for the database schema.

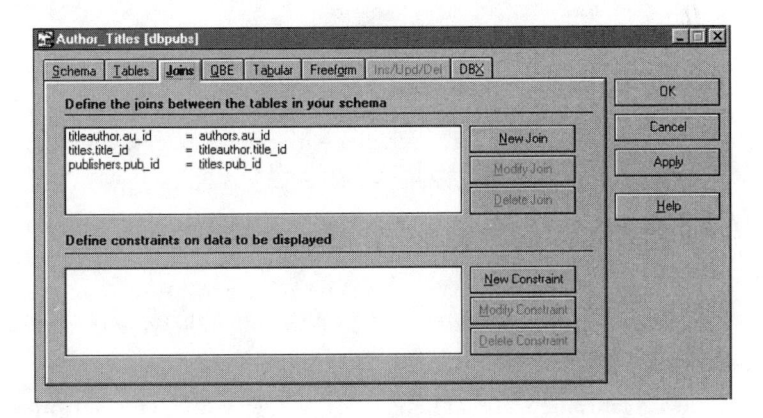

3. To define a new join, click the New Join button and the Joins dialog box will be displayed. (See Figure 20.19.)

FIGURE 20.19.
Creating a new join.

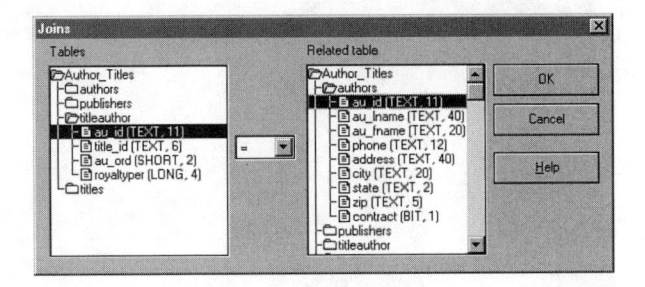

4. Select a table in the Tables list. Double-click the table to expand it and display the individual table columns. Select the appropriate column (such as `au_id`).
5. Select a table in the Related table listbox. Double-click the table to expand it and display the individual table columns. Select the appropriate column (such as `au_id`).

6. Specify the join type using the drop-down listbox.
7. Click the OK button to create the join and return to the Joins properties sheet. To modify an existing join, select the join and click the Modify Join button. To delete an existing join, select the join and click the Delete Join button.

> **NOTE**
>
> Modifying or deleting a join will affect the query by example, tabular, freeform, insert/update/delete, and custom forms you create. So, use care when designing and creating your joins. Otherwise you may spend more time rebuilding your forms than you do accomplishing any useful work.

8. When you have completed your definitions, click the OK button to accept your modifications and return to the Data Sources window or click the Apply button to immediately update the schema with your changes. This is useful when you are making continuous modifications and testing each action.

You can also specify a constraint on the returned records. A *constraint* is a set of rules that defines a set of values that the record must follow in order to be included in the result set returned by the query. You may want to make sure that no author records with a null (or empty) au_id field be returned. This is accomplished by following these steps:

1. Follow steps 1 and 2 in the section about specifying the schema joins and constraints to create a new join. Then click the New Constraint button to display the Constraints dialog box. (See Figure 20.20.)

FIGURE 20.20.

Creating a table constraint.

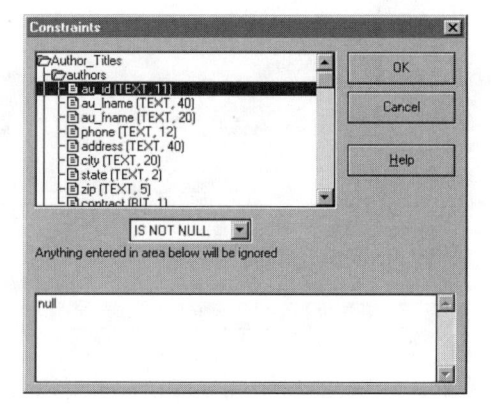

2. Select a table and double-click the table to expand it and display the individual table columns. Select the appropriate column (such as au_id).
3. Specify the constraint type using the drop-down listbox.
4. A default specification will be entered in the lower listbox, with a brief description of the requirements below the drop-down listbox. Change the default specification to meet your constraint requirements.

> **NOTE**
>
> Even if your constraint does not require a specification, such as in this example, you must enter a value in the lower listbox. Otherwise the OK button will remain disabled, and you will be unable to create the constraint.

5. Click the OK button to create the constraint and return to the Joins properties sheet. To modify an existing constraint, select the constraint and click the Modify Constraint button. To delete an existing constraint, select the constraint and click the Delete Constraint button.
6. After you have completed your definitions, click the OK button to accept your modifications and return to the Data Sources window or click the Apply button to immediately update the schema with your changes. This is useful when you are making continuous modifications and testing each action.

Specifying the Schema Query By Example Properties

The *query by example* (QBE) form is the most useful form provided by dbWeb. It is used to search your database based on user-supplied search criteria. You can define the search fields, the types of searches the user may perform, column heads, and other relevant information. Before you do so, however, you must first have defined the tables, joins, and constraints as described in the previous sections. Otherwise, you will not obtain the desired results. To define your QBE form, follow these steps:

1. Double-click a data source (such as IISLogs) to expand it and display the schemas below the data source name.
2. Select the schema (such as GuestBook) and click the Modify Schema button. Click the QBE tab to display the properties sheet shown in Figure 20.21.

Part VI *Using Internet Information Server with Databases*

FIGURE 20.21.
Specifying the columns to be used in the query by example form.

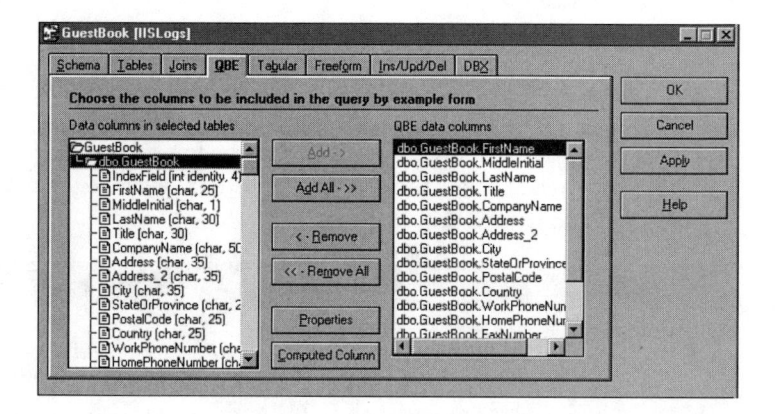

3. Select a table in the Data columns in selected tables listbox. Double-click the table to expand it and display the individual table columns. Select the appropriate column (such as dbo.GuestBook.FirstName).
4. Click the Add button to add the column to the QBE data columns listbox.
5. Repeat step 3 for each column in the table you want to display in your QBE form.
6. Repeat steps 3 and 4 for each table. If you will use all the columns in all of the tables, click the Add All button to copy all of the table and column definitions to the QBE data columns listbox.

TIP

The order in which tables and columns are added to the QBE data columns listbox also defines the order in which they will be displayed on the QBE form. If you need to modify the order later, you can change the sequence by setting the Col sequence and Row sequence properties.

7. To create a column to be displayed on the QBE form based on a computed value, click the Computed Column button to display the Computed Column Expression Builder dialog box. This will let you select the columns to use as the base, the expression that will create the computed column, and the resulting data type.
8. To modify the column properties, select the column in the QBE data columns listbox and click the Properties button.
9. A Properties dialog box, as shown in Figure 20.22, is displayed.

FIGURE 20.22.
Specifying the column properties.

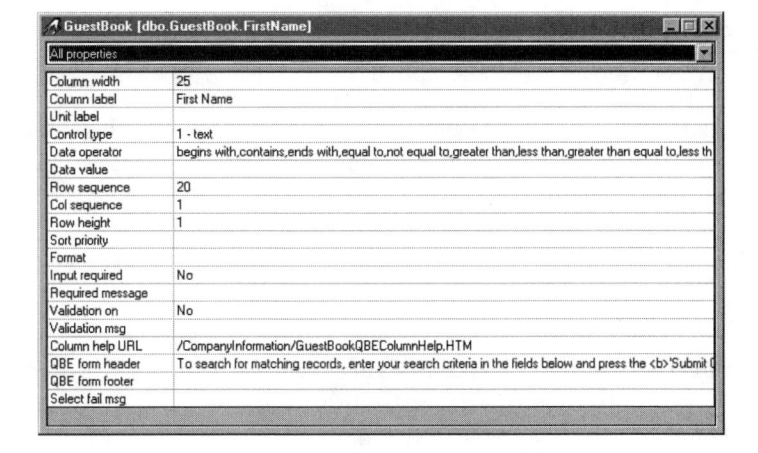

Column width	25
Column label	First Name
Unit label	
Control type	1 - text
Data operator	begins with,contains,ends with,equal to,not equal to,greater than,less than,greater than equal to,less th
Data value	
Row sequence	20
Col sequence	1
Row height	1
Sort priority	
Format	
Input required	No
Required message	
Validation on	No
Validation msg	
Column help URL	/CompanyInformation/GuestBookQBEColumnHelp.HTM
QBE form header	To search for matching records, enter your search criteria in the fields below and press the \<b>'Submit (
QBE form footer	
Select fail msg	

10. At the top of the dialog box is a drop-down listbox that determines which properties for the columns and QBE form will be displayed. This can be `All properties` to include both column and form properties, `Column Properties` to display just column properties, or QBE Form Properties to display just the form-related properties. These properties are summarized in Table 20.1.

Table 20.1. The QBE properties.

Name	Description	Note
`Column width`	Specifies the maximum width for data entry.	
`Column label`	Specifies a label, to the left of the form input field, to be displayed for the column.	By default, this value is the actual name of your column. To provide a more intuitive look to your form, you should change this value.
`Unit label`	Specifies a label to be displayed to the right of the form input field.	
`Control type`	Specifies the type of data.	This value can be 1 for text, 2 for a radio button, 3 for a listbox, 4 for a combo box, or 5 for a check box.

continues

Table 20.1. continued

Name	Description	Note
Data operator	Specifies the search methods to be employed.	This can be `begins with`, `contains`, `ends with`, `equal to`, `not equal to`, `greater than`, `less than`, `greater than or equal to`, `less than or equal to`, `>`, `>=`, `<`, `<=`, `=`, `<>`.
Data value	Specifies a default value to be displayed for the column.	
Row sequence	Specifies the row order of the column.	
Col sequence	Specifies the column sequence to be displayed on the form.	By default, this value is always `1`.
Row height	Specifies the height of the input form to be displayed on the form.	By default, this value is always `1`.
Sort priority	Specifies a sort order.	
Format	Specifies a format mask for the data.	
Input required	Specifies that the field must have a value to be accepted.	Values can be `No` or `Yes`. The default is `No`.
Required message	Specifies the message to be displayed if the field is a required field and the user does not enter a value.	
Validation on	Specifies that the data must match the format specified in the `Format` property to be accepted.	Values can be `Yes` or `No`. The default is `No`.

Name	Description	Note
Validation msg	Specifies a message to be displayed if the column does not match the valid format.	
Column help URL	Specifies a relative URL, or an absolute URL if desired, to be displayed when the column hot link is activated.	
QBE form header	Specifies a custom header to be displayed on the top of the Web page instead of the default dbWeb header.	
QBE form trailer	Specifies a custom message to be displayed on the bottom of the Web page in addition to the default dbWeb trailer.	
Select fail msg	Specifies a custom message to be displayed if the query fails.	

11. After modifying the properties for the column, click the Close button in the Properties dialog box to return to the QBE properties sheet.
12. Repeat steps 8 through 11 for each column.
13. When you have completed your definitions and modified the column properties, click the OK button to accept your modifications and return to the Data Sources window or click the Apply button to immediately update the schema with your changes. This is useful when you are making continuous modifications and testing each action.

Specifying the Schema Tabular Form Properties

The tabular form is used to display the database result set returned by the query as a series of records. Before you can create a tabular form, however, you must have defined the tables, joins,

Using Internet Information Server with Databases

Part VI

and constraints as described in the previous sections. To define your tabular form, follow these steps:

1. Double-click a data source (such as IISLogs) to expand it and display the schemas below the data source name.
2. Select the schema (such as GuestBook) and click the Modify Schema button. Click the Tabular tab to display the properties sheet shown in Figure 20.23.

FIGURE 20.23.
Specifying the columns to be used in the tabular form.

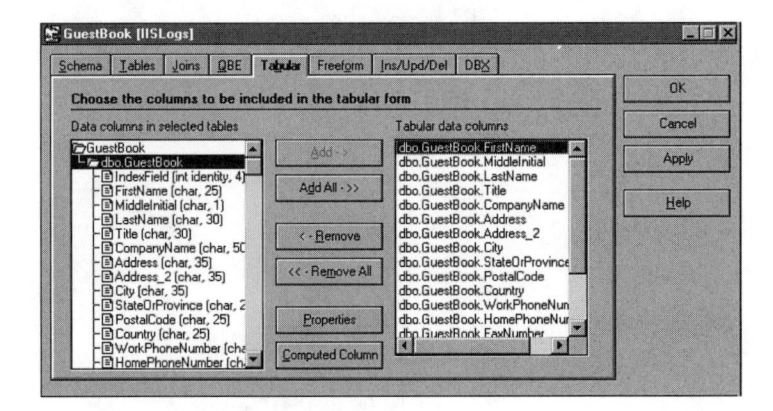

3. Select a table in the Data columns in selected tables listbox. Double-click the table to expand it and display the individual table columns. Select the appropriate column (such as dbo.GuestBook.FirstName).
4. Click the Add button to add the column to the Tabular data columns listbox.
5. Repeat step 3 for each column in the table you want to display in your tabular form.
6. Repeat steps 3 and 4 for each table. If you will use all the columns in all of the tables, just click the Add All button to copy all of the table and column definitions to the Tabular data columns listbox.

TIP

The order in which tables and columns are added to the Tabular data columns listbox also defines the order in which they will be displayed on the tabular form. If you need to modify the order later, you can change the sequence by setting the Col sequence property.

7. To create a column to be displayed on the Tabular form based on a computed value, click the Computed Column button to display the Computed Column Expression Builder dialog box. This will let you select the columns to use as the base, the expression to create the computed column, and the resulting data type.

8. To modify the column properties, select the column in the Tabular data columns listbox and click the Properties button.
9. A Properties dialog box, similar to that shown in Figure 20.22, will be displayed.
10. At the top of the dialog box is a drop-down listbox that determines which properties for the columns and tabular form will be displayed. This can be All properties to include both column and form properties, Column Properties to display just column properties, or Tabular Form Properties to display just the form-related properties. These properties are summarized in Table 20.2.

Table 20.2. The Tabular properties.

Name	Description	Note
Display when	Specifies when to display the column.	Value can be Always, Default on, or Default off.
Column width	Specifies the maximum width for data entry.	
Column label	Specifies a label, to the left of the form input field, to be displayed for the column.	By default, this value is the actual name of your column. To provide a more intuitive look to your form you should change this value.
Col sequence	Specifies the column sequence to be displayed on the form.	By default, this value is always 1.
Row height	Specifies the height of the input form to be displayed on the form.	By default, this value is always 1.
Sort priority	Specifies a sort order.	
Format	Specifies a format mask for the data.	
Column help URL	Specifies a relative URL, or an absolute URL if desired, to be displayed when the column hot link is activated.	

continues

Table 20.2. continued

Name	Description	Note
`Automatic Link URL`	Specifies the type of link to execute when the column is selected.	Choosing this property will display the Automatic Link From dialog box where you may specify the type of link (None, Static, Dynamic, Drill down, or Schema link) and the link properties.
`Tabular page header`	Specifies a custom header to be displayed on the top of the Web page instead of the default `dbWeb` header.	
`Tabular page trailer`	Specifies a custom message to be displayed on the bottom of the Web page in addition to the default `dbWeb` trailer.	

11. After modifying the properties for the column, click the Close button on the Properties dialog box to return to the Tabular properties sheet.
12. Repeat steps 8 through 11 for each column.
13. When you have completed your definitions and modified the column properties, click the OK button to accept your modifications and return to the Data Sources window or click the Apply button to immediately update the schema with your changes. This is useful when you are making continuous modifications and testing each action.

Specifying the Schema Freeform Properties

The *freeform* form is used to display the database result set returned by the query in series of records displayed in a column-, rather than row-, oriented fashion. It is usually invoked when the user enables the Use full-screen output even if more than one row is returned check box on the QBE form. Before you can create a freeform form, however, you must first have defined the tables, joins, and constraints as described in the previous sections. To define your freeform form, follow these steps:

1. Double-click a data source (such as IISLogs) to expand it and display the schemas below the data source name.
2. Select the schema (such as GuestBook) and click the Modify Schema button. Click the Freeform tab to display the properties sheet shown in Figure 20.24.

FIGURE 20.24.
Specifying the columns to be used in a freeform form.

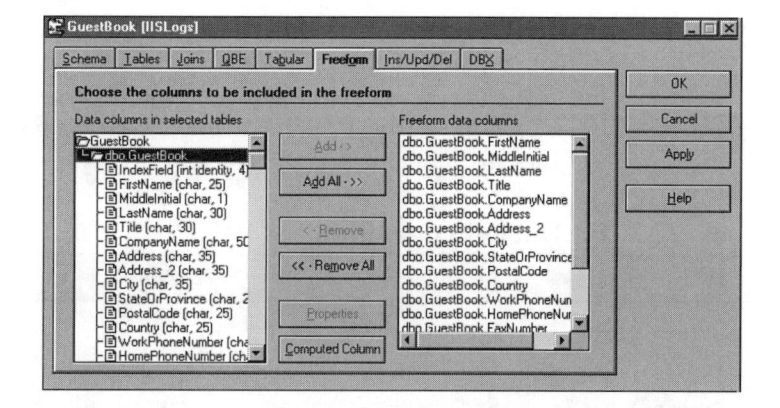

3. Select a table in the Data columns in selected tables listbox. Double-click the table to expand it and display the individual table columns. Select the appropriate column (such as dbo.GuestBook.FirstName).
4. Click the Add button to add the column to the Freeform data columns listbox.
5. Repeat step 3 for each column in the table you want to display in your freeform form.
6. Repeat steps 3 and 4 for each table. If you will use all the columns in all of the tables, click the Add All button to copy all of the table and column definitions to the Freeform data columns listbox.

TIP

The order in which tables and columns are added to the Freeform data columns listbox also defines the order in which they will be displayed on the freeform form. If you need to modify the order later, you can change the sequence by setting the Row sequence and Col sequence properties.

7. To create a column to be displayed on the freeform form based on a computed value, click the Computed Column button to display the Computed Column Expression Builder dialog box. This will let you select the columns to use as the base, the expression to create the computed column, and the resulting data type.
8. To modify the column properties, select the column in the Freeform data columns listbox and click the Properties button.
9. A Properties dialog box, similar to that shown in Figure 20.22, will be displayed.
10. At the top of the dialog box is a drop-down listbox that determines which properties for the columns and freeform form will be displayed. This can be All properties to include both column and form properties, Column Properties to display just column properties, or Freeform Form Properties to display just the form-related properties. These properties are summarized in Table 20.3.

Table 20.3. The Freeform properties.

Name	Description	Note
Column width	Specifies the maximum width for data entry.	
Column label	Specifies a label, to the left of the form input field, to be displayed for the column.	By default, this value is the actual name of your column. To provide a more intuitive look to your form you should change this value.
Row sequence	Specifies the row order of the column.	
Col sequence	Specifies the column sequence to be displayed on the form.	By default, this value is always 1.
Row height	Specifies the height of the input form to be displayed on the form.	By default, this value is always 1.
Sort priority	Specifies a sort order.	
Format	Specifies a format mask for the data.	

Name	Description	Note
Column help URL	Specifies a relative URL, or an absolute URL if desired, to be displayed when the column hot link is activated.	
Automatic Link URL	Specifies the type of link to execute when the column is selected.	Choosing this property will display the Automatic Link From dialog box where you may specify the type of link (None, Static, Dynamic, Drill down, or Schema) and the link properties.
Freeform page header	Specifies a custom header to be displayed on the top of the Web page instead of the default dbWeb header.	
Freeform page trailer	Specifies a custom message to be displayed on the bottom of the Web page in addition to the default dbWeb trailer.	
Freeform record header	Specifies a custom header to be displayed at the top of each record.	

11. After modifying the properties for the column, click the Close button on the Properties dialog box to return to the Tabular properties sheet.
12. Repeat steps 8 through 11 for each column.
13. When you have completed your definitions and modified the column properties, click the OK button to accept your modifications and return to the Data Sources window or click the Apply button to immediately update the schema with your changes. This is useful when you are making continuous modifications and testing each action.

Specifying the Schema Insert/Update/Delete Form Properties

The Ins/Upd/Del (Insert/Update/Delete) form is used to insert, update, or delete records in your database. This form is accessed by choosing a radio button (Insert, Update, or Delete) next to the Submit or Reset form buttons displayed at the bottom of the Web page for a tabular result set or a Web page with a freeform record layout. After the radio button has been selected and the user clicks the form Submit button, the Ins/Upd/Del form is displayed. Before you can create an Ins/Upd/Del form, however, you must first have defined the tables, joins, and constraints as described in the previous sections. To define your Ins/Upd/Del form, follow these steps:

1. Double-click a data source (such as IISLogs) to expand it and display the schemas below the data source name.
2. Select the schema (such as GuestBook) and click the Modify Schema button. Click the Ins/Upd/Del tab to display the properties sheet shown in Figure 20.25.

FIGURE 20.25.
Specifying the columns to be used in the Insert/Update/Delete form.

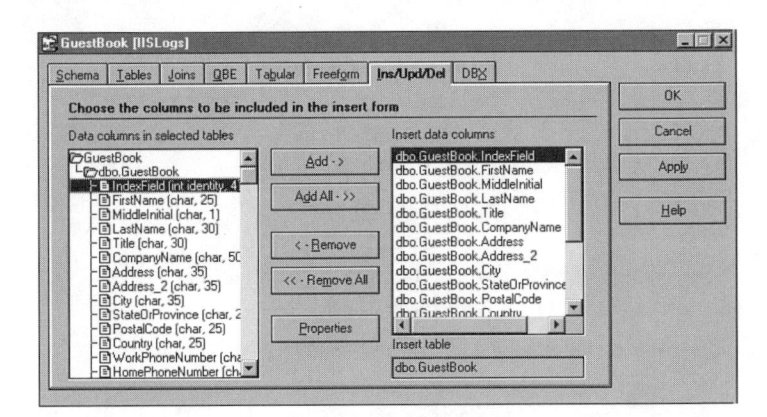

3. Select a table in the Data columns in selected tables listbox. Double-click the table to expand it and display the individual table columns. Select the appropriate column (such as dbo.GuestBook.FirstName).
4. Click the Add button to add the column to the Insert data columns listbox.
5. Repeat step 3 for each column in the table you want to display in your Ins/Upd/Del form.
6. Repeat steps 3 and 4 for each table. If you will use all the columns in all of the tables, click the Add All button to copy all of the table and column definitions to the Insert data columns listbox.

Interfacing Internet Information Server with ODBC Databases

Chapter 20

> **TIP**
>
> The order in which tables and columns are added to the Insert data columns listbox also defines the order in which they will be displayed on the Ins/Upd/Del form. If you need to modify the order later, you can change the sequence by setting the `Row sequence` and `Col sequence` properties.

7. To modify the column properties, select the column in the Insert data columns listbox and click the Properties button.
8. A Properties dialog box, similar to that shown in Figure 20.22, will be displayed.
9. At the top of the dialog box is a drop-down listbox that determines which properties for the columns and Ins/Upd/Del form will be displayed. This can be All properties to include both column and form properties, Column Properties to display just column properties, or Ins/Upd/Del Form Properties to display just the form-related properties. These properties are summarized in Table 20.4.

Table 20.4. The Ins/Upd/Del properties.

Name	*Description*	*Note*
`Key`	Specifies whether the field is an index field.	There must be at least one unique index field in order to update or delete a record. The key property can be set to `none`, `non-updatable`, `updatable`, or `counter`.
`Column width`	Specifies the maximum width for data entry.	
`Column label`	Specifies a label, to the left of the form input field, to be displayed for the column.	By default, this value is the actual name of your column. To provide a more intuitive look to your form you should change this value.
`Unit label`	Specifies a label to be displayed to the right of the form input field.	

continues

Table 20.4. continued

Name	Description	Note
Control type	Specifies the type of data.	This will be 1 for text, 2 for a radio button, 3 for a listbox, 4 for a combo box, or 5 for a check box. It cannot be changed on this form.
Data value	Specifies a default value to be displayed for the column.	
Row sequence	Specifies the row order of the column.	
Col sequence	Specifies the column sequence to be displayed on the form.	By default, this value is always 1.
Row height	Specifies the height of the input form to be displayed on the form.	By default, this value is always 1.
Sort priority	Specifies a sort order.	
Format	Specifies a format mask for the data.	
Input required	Specifies that the field must have a value to be accepted.	Values can be No or Yes. The default is No.
Required message	Specifies the message to be displayed if the field is a required field, and the user does not enter a value.	
Validation on	Specifies that the data must match the format specified in the Format property to be accepted.	Values can be Yes or No. The default is No.
Validation msg	Specifies a message to be displayed if the column does not match the valid format.	

Interfacing Internet Information Server with ODBC Databases
Chapter 20

Name	Description	Note
Column help URL	Specifies a relative URL, or an absolute URL if desired, to be displayed when the column hot link is activated.	
Insert form header	Specifies a custom header to be displayed on the top of the Web page instead of the default dbWeb header.	
Insert form trailer	Specifies a custom message to be displayed on the bottom of the Web page in addition to the default dbWeb trailer.	
Insert success msg	Specifies a custom message to be displayed if the insert succeeds.	
Insert fail msg	Specifies a custom message to be displayed if the insert fails.	

10. After modifying the properties for the column, click the Close button on the Properties dialog box to return to the Ins/Upd/Del properties sheet.
11. Repeat steps 8 through 11 for each column.
12. When you have completed your definitions and modified the column properties, click the OK button to accept your modifications and return to the Data Sources window or click the Apply button to immediately update the schema with your changes. This is useful when you are making continuous modifications and testing each action.

Specifying the Schema Custom HTML Form Properties

If the default tabular or freeform forms are not to your liking, you can create custom forms and invoke them from your HTML pages. The best example on how to do this is the North Wind Traders sample database installed by the dbWeb Setup program. I'm not really very impressed with the custom forms option because it requires that you build a custom HTML document, which is a lot of work. Another reason you may decide to use custom forms, however, is to insert graphics on your Web page. But you should know that to do this, the graphics files cannot be part of your ODBC database; they must reside as separate images on your WWWRoot path. I decided, and I think you will too, that if you are going to go to this much trouble you'll want to use the Internet Database Connector (IDC) that ships with the Internet Information Server. But for a small database that you want to customize, it may be worth the trouble. So just to give you an idea on how to interface your custom forms with dbWeb, follow these steps:

1. Double-click a data source (such as IISLogs) to expand it and display the schemas below the data source name.
2. Select the schema (such as GuestBook) and click the Modify Schema button. Click the DBX tab to display the properties sheet shown in Figure 20.26.

FIGURE 20.26.
Specifying a custom form to be used with dbWeb.

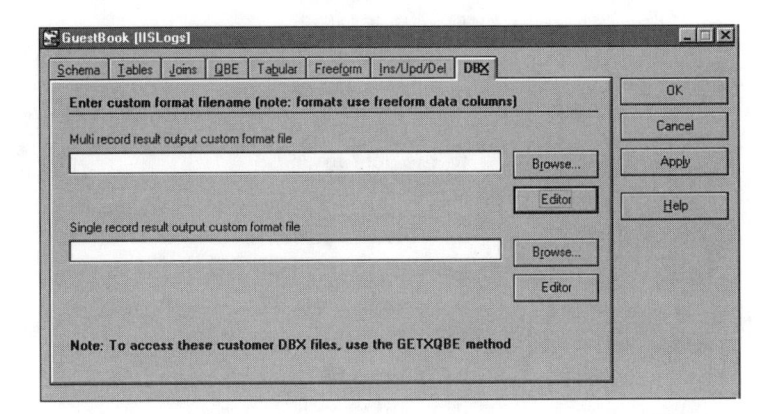

3. Enter the relative or absolute URL for the form to be used in place of the default tabular form in the Multi record result output custom format file field.
4. Enter the relative or absolute URL for the form to be used in place of the default freeform form in the Single record result output custom format file field.

NOTE

Clicking the Editor button will display the DBX Editor dialog box. You can use this dialog box to select the columns you want to add to your form. After you have done so, save the file by selecting File|Save from the menu. Then you will have to edit the file to create a real HTML document that you can use. To invoke these forms from a HTML file, you need to create a link with the following syntax:

`/scripts/dbweb/dbwebc.dll/SchemaName?getxqbe`

where *SchemaName* is the name of your schema with the custom forms.

5. When you have completed your definitions and modified the column properties, click the OK button to accept your modifications and return to the Data Sources window or click the Apply button to immediately update the schema with your changes. This is useful when you are making continuous modifications and testing each action.

Creating a Custom Guest Book Using Microsoft dbWeb

Now that you have learned the basic operations of dbWeb, you probably want to get to work and actually use it. This section walks you through the basic process of creating a guest book that you can use on your Internet Information Server site. The first step in this process is to create a database; then you create the guest book table. The following SQL Server script is what I used to create the sample guest book:

```
CREATE TABLE dbo.GuestBook (
    IndexField int IDENTITY (1, 1) NOT NULL ,
    FirstName char (25) NULL ,
    MiddleInitial char (1) NULL ,
    LastName char (30) NULL ,
    Title char (30) NULL ,
    CompanyName char (50) NULL ,
    Address char (35) NULL ,
    Address_2 char (35) NULL ,
    City char (35) NULL ,
    StateOrProvince char (25) NULL ,
    PostalCode char (25) NULL ,
    Country char (25) NULL ,
    WorkPhoneNumber char (14) NULL ,
    HomePhoneNumber char (14) NULL ,
    FaxNumber char (14) NULL ,
    E_Mail char (25) NULL ,
    URL char (255) NULL ,
    Note text NULL ,
    Contact char (1) NULL
)
GO
```

Although you can use another ODBC-compliant database, such as Microsoft Access, I used SQL Server. I chose this route because SQL Server can execute procedures automatically. These procedures will be used to check the contact field and send me e-mail whenever new users request that I contact them. As part of the procedure, the contact field will be reset so that I will not receive duplicate e-mail messages. Another reason I chose SQL Server is because it was easy to assign a key field. (This is the IndexField specified in the second line of the script.) This field uses the identity property to automatically insert a unique counter whenever a user inserts a record into the database. This field is not displayed on my dbWeb pages, but dbWeb uses this field as the unique key for updates or deletes. If you do not specify a unique key, it is possible that dbWeb will update or delete multiple rows of data in your table.

After you create the database, you need to create the ODBC data source as described in the section of this chapter titled "Creating the ODBC Data Source." After that, it is a simple matter of creating the dbWeb data source and the schema, and setting the various column properties, as described in the preceding sections. Although these operations do take a bit of time, they are not complex tasks. The fun part really comes into play when you have to create your custom forms. Fun, you say? Am I joking, you ask?

Well, the truth is, I am joking. As part of this experiment I decided to use Microsoft FrontPage 1.1 to create my forms. But I found out the hard way that FrontPage does not support the dbWeb interface. FrontPage assumes that a form name must start with a character, and dbWeb requires a name using the syntax of *ControlType,SchemaName,ColumnName* (such as 1,GuestBook,FirstName), although you can also use the format *ControlType, TableName,ColumnName* (such as 1,dbo.GuestBook,FirstName). But FrontPage has such a nice user interface for form creation that I decided I would use it anyway. This meant, however, that I had to create the form with bogus names for each form control and then edit them manually using a text editor. The result was well worth it, though, and can be seen in Figure 20.27.

FIGURE 20.27.
A guest book form inserting data into a SQL Server database using dbWeb.

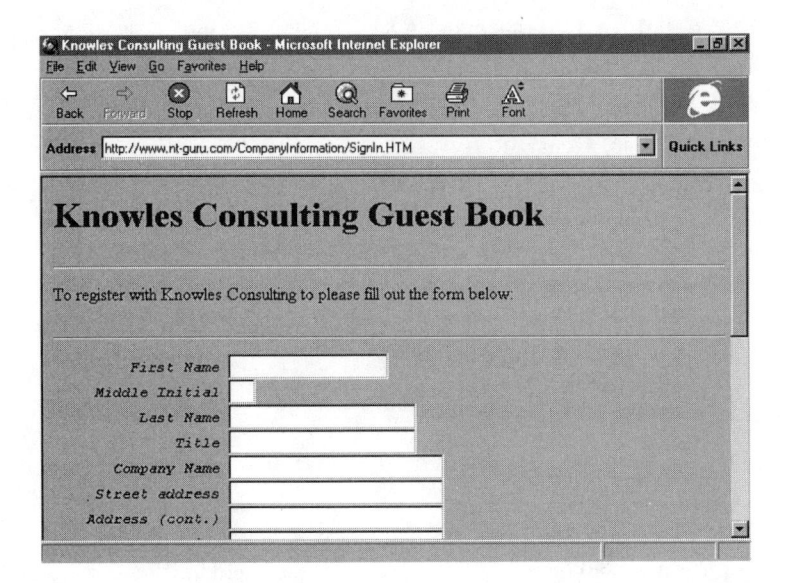

The HTML code used to create this form follows:

```
<html>
<head>
<title>Knowles Consulting Guest Book</title>
</head>
<body>
<h1>Knowles Consulting Guest Book</h1>
<hr>
```

Interfacing Internet Information Server with ODBC Databases

Chapter 20   591

```html
<p>To register with Knowles Consulting to please fill out the form below:</p>
<hr>
<form action="/scripts/dbweb/dbwebc.dll/GuestBook?insert" method="POST">
<blockquote>
<pre><em>        First Name </em><input type=text size=25 maxlength=25 name="1,dbo.GuestBook,FirstName">
  <em>Middle</em> <em>Initial</em> <input type=text size=1 maxlength=1 name="1,dbo.GuestBook,MiddleInitial">
       <em>Last</em> <em>Name</em> <input type=text size=30 maxlength=30 name="1,dbo.GuestBook,LastName">
<em>            Title </em><input type=text size=30 maxlength=30 name="1,dbo.GuestBook,Title">
<em>    Company Name </em><input type=text size=35 maxlength=50 name="1,dbo.GuestBook,CompanyName">
<em>  Street address </em><input type=text size=35 maxlength=35 name="1,dbo.GuestBook,Address">
<em> Address (cont.) </em><input type=text size=35 maxlength=35 name="1,dbo.GuestBook,Address_2">
<em>             City </em><input type=text size=35 maxlength=35
➥ name="1,dbo.GuestBook,City">
<em>  State/Province </em><input type=text size=25 maxlength=25 name="1,dbo.GuestBook,StateOrProvince">
<em> Zip/Postal code </em><input type=text size=25 maxlength=25 name="1,dbo.GuestBook,PostalCode">
<em>         Country </em><input type=text size=25 maxlength=25 name="1,dbo.GuestBook,Country">
<em>      Work Phone </em><input type=text size=14 maxlength=14 name="1,dbo.GuestBook,WorkPhoneNumber">
<em>      Home Phone </em><input type=text size=14 maxlength=14 name="1,dbo.GuestBook,HomePhoneNumber">
<em>             FAX </em><input type=text size=14 maxlength=14 name="1,dbo.GuestBook,FaxNumber">
<em>          E-mail </em><input type=text size=25 maxlength=255 name="1,dbo.GuestBook,E_Mail">
<em>    Home Page URL </em><input type=text size=25 maxlength=255
➥name="1,dbo.GuestBook,URL">
         <em>Note</em> <textarea name="1,dbo.GuestBook,Note" rows=2 cols=44></textarea></pre>
<pre><input type=checkbox name="5,dbo.GuestBook,Contact" value="Y">
➥ Please contact me as soon as possible regarding this matter.
</pre>
</blockquote>
<p><input type=submit value="Submit Form"> <input type=reset
➥ value="Reset Form"> <a href="/CompanyInformation/GuestBookPageHelp.HTM">
➥<img src="/Graphics/Buttons/help.gif" align=absmiddle border=0></a> <a href="http://www.nt-guru.com"><img src="/Graphics/Buttons/home.gif" align=absmiddle border=0></a></p>
</form>
<hr>
<table width=100%>
<tr><td width=50%><address><font size=2><em>Copyright &#169; 1996 Knowles
➥ Consulting. All rights reserved</em></font> </address>
</td><td align=right width=50%><div align=right>
<address><font size=2><em>Last Updated: June 21, 1996</em></font> </address>
</div>
</td></tr>
```

```
</table>
</body>
</html>
```

I've highlighted a few of the nonstandard areas of this text in bold to point out these areas of particular interest. The first item is the form action. Rather than call a custom FrontPage CGI script, I've converted this form to use dbWeb. It was rather easy, too. All that was needed was to change the URL to

```
/scripts/dbweb/dbwebc.dll/GuestBook?insert
```

When the Submit button is invoked, the Insert method is activated and the data contained in the form is inserted into the database defined by the GuestBook schema. There are other dbWeb methods you can use as well; they are described in the dbWeb help file under the Developer Reference topic. A few that I would like to point out as particularly useful when creating custom forms to use with dbWeb are as follows:

- getqbe—Displays the dbWeb query by example form on the Web browser.
- getresults—Obtains the results set and displays the data using the tabular form if more than one record is returned, or the freeform form if only one record is returned.
- getinsert—Obtains the insert form and displays it on the Web browser.
- getupdate—Obtains the update form and displays it on the Web browser.
- insert—Inserts the data specified by the column tags into the database.
- update—Updates the data specified by the column tags in the database.
- delete—Deletes the data specified by the column tags from the database.

You can use these dbWeb methods with your custom Web pages to access and control the behavior of dbWeb. On my home page, for example, I've created a link to the dbWeb QBE form using the syntax

```
http://www.nt-guru.com/scripts/dbweb/dbWebc.dll/GuestBook?getqbe
```

This invokes the query by example form, shown in Figure 20.28, that I use to search my guest book. To make my custom guest book form a little more consistent with the Web pages produced by dbWeb, I inserted the same help and home buttons that will invoke a custom help page and jump to my home page, respectively.

FIGURE 20.28.
The dbWeb *query by example form for the guest book.*

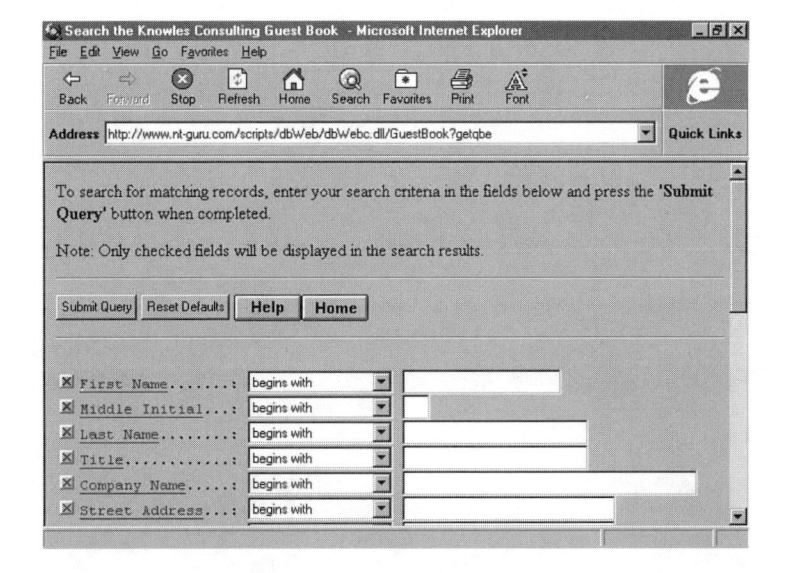

Summary

This chapter explores some of the features of dbWeb. It explains how to install dbWeb and how to configure the dbWeb Administrator and the dbWeb Server. You have learned how to create an ODBC data source and a dbWeb schema. You have also learned how to configure the various properties for your QBE, tabular, freeform, and insert/update/delete forms. Finally, you have seen how it all comes together with dbWeb by taking a look at the HTML source code for a sample guest book. In Chapter 21, "Building Dynamic Web Pages with SQL Server," you'll learn how to build dynamic Web pages using the Internet Database Connector (IDC) and how to build semi-static Web pages with Microsoft SQL Server 6.5. Before moving on to the next chapter, consider the following:

- dbWeb has a built-in graphical user interface to its core functionality. This means you can use a point-and-click methodology to design your schema.
- dbWeb provides the ability to design table joins, or set table constraints, to modify the query dbWeb sends on your behalf dynamically.
- dbWeb can be used to build quick and easy-to-use forms to search your database with built-in links to help files.
- dbWeb does not assume you know much about HTML, but does provide customization for HTML-proficient users.

dbWeb is a tool designed for rapid development of interactive HTML documents. If you need more control, the Internet Database Connector may be your ticket.

Building Dynamic Web Pages with SQL Server

IN THIS CHAPTER

- Using the Internet Database Connector **596**
- Using the SQL Server Web Assistant **614**

There are several ways to build dynamic Web pages using the Internet Information Server. A *dynamic* Web page is one that interacts with the user or changes periodically. Most people think of ActiveX technologies and Internet Explorer 3.0 when the word *interactive* is mentioned, but this chapter will focus on interacting with ODBC-compliant databases. In Chapter 20, "Interfacing Internet Information Server with ODBC Databases," you learned how to build interactive Web pages using an add-on tool called Microsoft dbWeb. In this chapter, you will explore some of the other options that are provided with the Internet Information Server base product and with Microsoft SQL Server 6.5 for making dynamic Web pages.

Some of the reasons to use the Internet Database Connector instead of dbWeb include

- Query control—If you are an experienced database developer with knowledge of your database's query language, the IDC offers finer levels of control. The IDC requires you to specify a query rather than supplying one for you. This requirement should be considered a blessing rather than a burden because it provides fine-tuned control of what will be returned by your query.
- Layout control—If you are an experienced HTML developer, the IDC offers finer control over how the user will interact with your Web page. Since you create the input forms used to obtain the query and the Web pages to display the query result, you also get to determine exactly how the Web page will look.
- Reusability—You can copy the basic components of an IDC skeleton (the source code consisting of the Web pages, .HTX, and .IDC files) to quickly build a variant input form or query result page. Microsoft dbWeb requires that you build an entirely new data source and schema. There is no code reusability.

Using the Internet Database Connector

The Internet Information Server has the built-in capability to interface with any ODBC-compliant database for which you have a 32-bit ODBC driver. There is more work involved in developing an interactive Web page using the Internet Database Connector (IDC) than there is using Microsoft dbWeb, but the IDC provides more fine-tuned control. Another good thing about the IDC is that unlike dbWeb, the IDC does not require form names to start with a number. This means that you can use Microsoft FrontPage to develop your forms from start to finish.

In this section, you will learn how to use the IDC to create an interactive guest book, which looks a lot like the guest book created with dbWeb in Chapter 20. There are three steps for the creation of this or any other interactive IDC Web page. First, you must create the Web page form. Next, you must create an IDC interface file. Finally, you must create another HTML file to use as a template for the resulting output created by your query.

> **NOTE**
>
> You also need to create the ODBC database and the system data source name (DSN) to create an interactive Web page using the Internet Database Connector. For more information on how to create the system DSN, refer in Chapter 20 to the section titled "Creating the ODBC System Data Source."

Creating the Web Page Forms

You can use any text editor to create your forms, but I prefer a What-You-See-Is-What-You-Get (WYSIWYG) editor such as Microsoft FrontPage (see Figure 21.1). Microsoft FrontPage makes it easy to build your form using the familiar Windows GUI. It is not imperative that you know how to write HTML documents, although knowing syntax for HTML helps considerably if you have to edit a document manually or if a problem crops up during the development stage.

FIGURE 21.1.
Creating your form with Microsoft FrontPage.

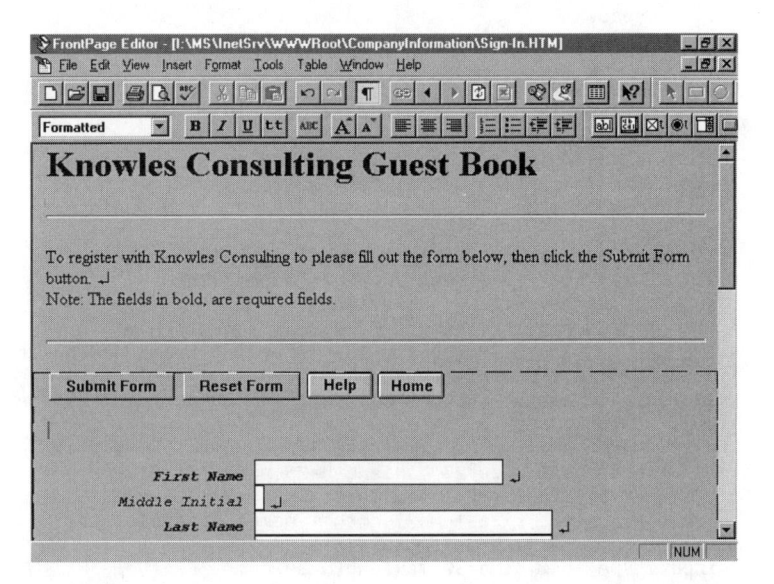

There are two forms you must create to build a working guest book. First, you'll need to create a form to insert information into your ODBC database. Second, you'll need to create a form to query your database. This form is optional because you may not want to allow your Internet clients to browse your database. However, I am including it here because it does illustrate the basic techniques that are required to query your database and display the resulting data on a Web page. The ability to query and to display the data is what really makes a form interactive.

TIP

If you look closely at the HTML source code in the next few sections, you will see a reference to a database column called Hide. This variable is used to prevent the display of a client's information on the WWW. While you may still view the data by using another ODBC front-end, such as Access, the queries used to find and display the guest book specifically exclude any information that's Hide column is set to Y. The client sets this variable by checking the Do not post this information on the Web for others to see check box at the end of the form.

Creating the Input Form

The basic form I created to enter information into my guest book was built using the following HTML code:

```
1.      <html>
2.      <head>
3.      <title>Knowles Consulting Guest Book</title>
4.      </head>
5.      <body>
6.      <h1>Knowles Consulting Guest Book</h1>
7.      <hr>
8.      <p>To register with Knowles Consulting to please fill out the form below, then click the Submit Form button.</p>
9.      <p>Note: The fields in bold, are required fields. </p>
10.     <hr>
11.     <form action="/Scripts/Sign-In-IDC.IDC" method="get">
12.     <p><input type=submit value="Submit Form">
<input type=reset value="Reset Form">
<a href="/CompanyInformation/GuestBookPageHelp.HTM">
<img src="/Graphics/Buttons/help.gif" align=absmiddle border=0></a>
<a href="http://www.nt-guru.com">
<img src="/Graphics/Buttons/home.gif" align=absmiddle border=0></a></p>
13.     <blockquote>
14.     <pre><em>           </em><em><b>First Name</b></em><em>   </em>
<input type=text size=25 maxlength=25 name="FirstName">
15.         <em>Middle</em> <em>Initial</em>
<input type=text size=1 maxlength=1 name="MiddleInitial">
16.            <em><b>Last Name</b></em>
<input type=text size=30 maxlength=30 name="LastName">
17.     <em>          Title  </em>
<input type=text size=30 maxlength=30 name="Title">
18.     <em>    Company Name  </em>
<input type=text size=35 maxlength=50 name="CompanyName">
19.     <em>   Street address  </em>
<input type=text size=35 maxlength=35 name="Address">
```

Building Dynamic Web Pages with SQL Server
Chapter 21

```
20.     <em> Address (cont.) </em>
<input type=text size=35 maxlength=35 name="Address_2">
21.     <em>           City </em>
<input type=text size=35 maxlength=35 name="City">
22.     <em>    State/Province </em>
<input type=text size=25 maxlength=25 name="StateOrProvince">
23.     <em> Zip/Postal code </em>
<input type=text size=25 maxlength=25 name="PostalCode">
24.     <em>          Country </em>
<input type=text size=25 maxlength=25 name="Country" value="US">
25.     <em>       Work Phone </em>
<input type=text size=14 maxlength=14 name="WorkPhoneNumber">
26.     <em>       Home Phone </em>
<input type=text size=14 maxlength=14 name="HomePhoneNumber">
27.     <em>            FAX </em>
<input type=text size=14 maxlength=14 name="FaxNumber">
28.     <em>           E-mail </em>
<input type=text size=25 maxlength=255 name="E_Mail">
29.     <em>    Home Page URL </em>
<input type=text size=25 maxlength=255 name="URL">
30.             <em>Note</em>
<textarea name="Note" rows=2 cols=44></textarea></pre>
31.<pre><input type=checkbox name="Contact" value="Y">
Please contact me as soon as possible regarding this matter.
32.     </pre>
33.     <pre><input type=checkbox name="Hide" value="Y">
Do not post this information on the web for others to see.</pre>
34.     </blockquote>
35.     <p><input type=submit value="Submit Form">
<input type=reset value="Reset Form">
<a href="/CompanyInformation/GuestBookPageHelp.HTM">
<img src="/Graphics/Buttons/help.gif" align=absmiddle border=0></a>
<a href="http://www.nt-guru.com">
<img src="/Graphics/Buttons/home.gif" align=absmiddle border=0></a></p>
36.     </form>
37.     <table width=100%>
38.<tr><td width=50%><address><font size=2>
<em>Copyright &#169; 1996 Knowles Consulting. All rights reserved</em>
</font> </address>
39.</td><td align=right width=50%><div align=right><address>
<font size=2><em>Last Updated: June 21, 1996</em></font>
</address></div></td></tr>
40.     </table>
41. </body>
42.     </html>
```

NOTE

The preceding HTML code should not include the line numbers. These numbers are only included in the text to make the discussion easier to follow.

The first and last two lines of the text are required for any HTML document. Line 3 specifies the title of the document, which will be displayed on the caption bar of the Web browser. Line 5 specifies the beginning of the document body. Line 6 is the document header. Lines 7 and 10 insert a horizontal rule (line break) into the document to divide the instructions on how to use the form (lines 8 and 9) from the header and the form. Line 11 is the beginning of the form, and includes the Internet Database Connector definition as well as the type of action to be performed (a GET rather than the more commonly used POST).

This definition (/Scripts/Sign-In-IDC.IDC) file is associated with the Internet Database Connector ISAPI dynamic-link library HTTPODBC.DLL, which can be found in your InetSrv\Server subdirectory. You'll learn more about the IDC definition files in the next section, "Creating the Internet Database Connector Interface File." For now, just mark this spot in your HTML file as the executable file to which your form's output will be passed.

Moving on, lines 12 and 35 are the form's Submit, Reset, Help, and Home buttons. These buttons are used to submit the information entered into the form by the user, to clear the form, to display a help file, and to return to the home page, respectively. You should notice that both the Help button and the Home button are image files. When the user selects one of these buttons, the page associated with the hypertext link will be displayed. This is a different action than that performed by the Submit and Reset buttons, which are really form controls. This is because there are only two basic form buttons supported in the HTML definition. One button submits the form, and one button clears the form.

Line 13 (the <blockquote> tag) is used to indent the form's Input fields (lines 14 through 33). Line 36 is the end of the form. Lines 37 through 40 include a table definition, the copyright information, and a form last-update notification.

That's about all it takes to create the form that sends an entry to your database. To create a form that allows a user to query your guest book and view the resulting data, use the following:

```
 1: <html>
 2: <title>Search the Knowles Consulting Guest Book</title>
 3: <BODY>
 4: <hr>
 5: <h1>Search the Knowles Consulting Guest Book</h1>
 6: To search for matching records, enter your search criteria in the fields
➥ below and press the 'Submit Query' button
when completed.
 7: <p>Type in any of these boxes to match against people in the guestbook.
➥Use the '%' symbol as a wildcard. A blank field here will match any entry.<br>
 8: <form action="/Scripts/SearchGuestBook.IDC" method=get>
 9: <p><input type=submit value="Submit Form">
➥<input type=reset value="Reset Form"> <a href="/CompanyInformation
/GuestBookPageHelp.HTM">
➥<img src="/Graphics/Buttons/help.gif" align=absmiddle border=0></a>
<a href="http://www.nt-guru.com">
➥<img src="/Graphics/Buttons/home.gif" align=absmiddle border=0></a></p>
10: <blockquote>
11: <pre><em>        First Name </em>
```

```
➥<input type=text size=25 maxlength=25 name="FirstName">
12:     <em>Middle</em>  <em>Initial</em>
➥<input type=text size=1 maxlength=1 name="MiddleInitial">
13:         <em>Last</em>  <em>Name</em>
➥<input type=text size=30 maxlength=30 name="LastName">
14: <em>           Title    </em>
➥<input type=text size=30 maxlength=30 name="Title">
15: <em>     Company Name   </em>
➥<input type=text size=35 maxlength=50 name="CompanyName">
16: <em>   Street address  </em>
➥<input type=text size=35 maxlength=35 name="Address">
17: <em>  Address (cont.)  </em>
➥<input type=text size=35 maxlength=35 name="Address_2">
18: <em>              City </em><input type=text size=35 maxlength=35 name="City">
19: <em>   State/Province  </em>
➥<input type=text size=25 maxlength=25 name="StateOrProvince">
20: <em>  Zip/Postal code  </em>
➥<input type=text size=25 maxlength=25 name="PostalCode">
21: <em>          Country  </em>
➥<input type=text size=25 maxlength=25 name="Country">
22: <em>       Work Phone  </em>
➥<input type=text size=14 maxlength=14 name="WorkPhoneNumber">
23: <em>       Home Phone  </em>
➥<input type=text size=14 maxlength=14 name="HomePhoneNumber">
24: <em>              FAX  </em>
➥<input type=text size=14 maxlength=14 name="FaxNumber">
25: <em>           E-mail  </em>
➥<input type=text size=25 maxlength=255 name="E_Mail">
26: <em>    Home Page URL  </em><input type=text size=25 maxlength=255 name="URL">
27:             <em>Note</em>  <textarea name="Note" rows=2 cols=44></textarea>
➥</pre>
28: <p><input type=submit value="Submit Form">
➥<input type=reset value="Reset Form"> <a href="/CompanyInformation/GuestBookPageHelp.HTM">
➥<img src="/Graphics/Buttons/help.gif" align=absmiddle border=0></a>
<a href="http://www.nt-guru.com">
➥<img src="/Graphics/Buttons/home.gif" align=absmiddle border=0></a></p>
29: </form>
30: <hr>
31: <table width=100%>
32: <tr><td width=50%><address><font size=2>
➥<em>Copyright &#169; 1996 Knowles Consulting. All rights reserved</em>
➥</font> </address>
33: </td><td align=right width=50%><div align=right><address><font size=2>
➥<em>Last Updated: June 21, 1996</em></font>
</address>
34: </div></td></tr>
35: </table>
36: </body>
37: </html>
```

Although this form looks similar to the form used to enter information into the ODBC database, there are a few differences. First, the form title (Line 2), header (Line 5), and instructions (Line 7) are different. This is not too surprising since this Web page's purpose is to provide a mechanism for the user to query or search your guest book. The previous HTML document's purpose is to request that the user fill out a form so he can enter the information into your guest book. Second, the form calls the /Scripts/SearchGuestBook.IDC IDC interface file (Line 8) rather than the Scripts/Sign-In-IDC.IDC IDC interface file used with the input form. This is because I wanted to perform a different action—a database query instead of a database insert. Lines 10–29 define the actual form that will be displayed on the Web browser. The rest looks almost the same except for the Contact and Hide database columns, which are not included on the query form. This is because a user has no need to search your guest book using these fields as search criteria. After all, while you may want to provide a listing of people who have visited your Web site as a service, you do not want users to know who you may have contacted or who does not want their information made public.

As you can see, creating the forms to insert data into your database or to query and display the results seems quite easy. Unfortunately, there is more to it than this. You also need to create the IDC interface and HTML template files before you can actually use the forms to enter information into your database or to query and display the result set on the Web.

Creating the Internet Database Connector Interface File

The next step in building your guest book using the Internet Database Connector is to build the IDC definition files. These files contain information about the ODBC data source, the template file used to display the result set, and most importantly, the database query to execute. You will need to create three IDC files.

The first file will be called Sign-In-IDC.IDC. It is used by the Sign-In.HTM form you created earlier. The source code follows:

```
1.      Datasource: IISLogs
2.      Username: sa
3.      Template: Sign-In-IDC.HTX
4.      RequiredParameters: FirstName, LastName
5.      SQLStatement:
6.      + if exists (
7.      +    select * from GuestBook
8.      +    where FirstName='%FirstName%' and MiddleInitial = '%MiddleInitial%' and
9.      +    LastName='%LastName%' and Address = '%Address%' and Address_2 = '%Address_2%' and
10.     +    City = '%City%' and StateOrProvince = '%StateOrProvince%' and
11.     +    PostalCode = '%PostalCode%' and Hide = '%Hide%'
12.     +    )
13.     +       select result='duplicate'
14.     +else
15.     +    INSERT INTO GuestBook
16.     +    (FirstName, MiddleInitial, LastName, Title, CompanyName, Address,
17.     +    Address_2, City, StateOrProvince, PostalCode, Country, WorkPhoneNumber, HomePhoneNumber,
18.     +    FaxNumber, E_Mail, URL, Note, Contact, Hide)
19.     +    VALUES('%FirstName%', '%MiddleInitial%', '%LastName%', '%Title%',
```

```
20.     + '%CompanyName%', '%Address%', '%Address_2%', '%City%',
'%StateOrProvince%',
21.     + '%PostalCode%', '%Country%', '%WorkPhoneNumber%', '%HomePhoneNumber%',
22.     + '%FaxNumber%', '%E_Mail%', '%URL%', '%Note%', '%Contact%', '%Hide%');
```

Line 1 specifies the ODBC system DSN used to access the ODBC database. Line 2 specifies the user name. If you are using SQL Server with the mixed (or integrated) security model, as I am, this option is ignored. Instead, the user-account is validated using the IUSR_*ServerName* account (where *ServerName* is the name of the server on which IIS is installed), which is created by the IIS setup program. However, depending on your ODBC database, you may need to supply the Password option and specify a valid password to access your ODBC database. Line 3 specifies the HTML template file, which either informs the user that the data was entered into the database successfully or that a duplicate entry has been found. Line 4 specifies that the First Name (FName) and Last Name (LName) fields must be entered on the form; otherwise, the record will not be entered into the database.

> **NOTE**
>
> There are other defined parameters that you can use in an IDC file. These are summarized in Table 21.1.

Lines 5 through 12 are a series of SQL select statements that, when executed, will return a result set containing the first name, middle initial, last name, address lines, city, state, postal code and Hide flag. If all of these fields match the data that is entered by the user, line 13 is executed and the result is determined to be a duplicate entry. A duplicate entry will not be accepted, and the user will be informed of this fact via the message defined in the HTML template (more on this in the next section). If the record is not a duplicate, the insert statement after line 14 (the else clause) is executed and the record is inserted into the database. The user will see a success message, as defined by the HTML template.

The query for the guest book requires two IDC definition files. The first one, called SearchGuestBook.IDC, is used to define the search parameters. The source code is

```
Datasource: IISLogs
Username: sa
Template: SearchGuestBook.HTX
SQLStatement:
+SELECT FirstName, LastName,
+FROM GuestBook
+WHERE FirstName like '%FirstName%'
+and LastName like '%LastName%'
+and Hide <> 'Y'
DefaultParameters:FirstName=%,LastName=%
```

This source code looks very similar to the Sign-In-IDC.IDC file. Indeed, the only real difference is that SearchGuestBook.IDC does not search for duplicate records. Instead, it executes a query to find records based only on the first and last names specified by the user. If the user does not specify one, or both, of these fields, a wildcard (% character) will be substituted in the empty field (as specified by the `DefaultParameters` entry). The `DefaultParameters` entry is used to create a substitution mechanism to supply default values for a field in the query if the user does not explicitly enter a value. When this query is executed, the template file `SearchGuestBook.HTX` will be used to display the result set, which consists of first and last names. At this point, the user can click one of these entries to expand it and display more detail. This will execute the final IDC file called `GuestBookDetails.IDC`. The source code for this file is

```
Datasource: IISLogs
Username: sa
Template: GuestBookDetails.HTX
SQLStatement:
+SELECT FirstName, MiddleInitial, LastName, Title, CompanyName, Address, Address_2,
+City, StateOrProvince, PostalCode, Country, WorkPhoneNumber, HomePhoneNumber,
 FaxNumber,
+E_Mail, URL, Note
+FROM GuestBook
+WHERE FirstName = '%FName%' and LastName = '%LName%' and Hide <> 'Y'
```

> **NOTE**
>
> Notice in both of these queries that the Hide column is used to make sure that only records that do not contain a Y will be displayed. This is to prevent you from displaying information that a user requests remain confidential on the Web.

This IDC definition file uses the `GuestBookDetails.HTX` template file to display the result set on the Web browser. The IDC definition file will display the matching records using the detail form in the template file. The query that is executed will select all of the fields that match the user-specified `FName` and `LName` fields. These fields are actually specified in the `SearchGuestBook.HTX` template file, which you will examine in the next section.

Table 21.1. The IDC parameters.

Parameter	Description	Note
Datasource	Specifies the data source name (DSN) used to connect to the ODBC-compliant database.	This is a required field.

Parameter	Description	Note
DefaultParameters	Specifies a default value to be used in the query if the user does not explicitly supply a value for a field.	
Expires	Specifies a time, in seconds, to wait before refreshing a cached page.	By default, an output page is not cached by httpodbc.dll. It will only be cached if the Expires parameter is used.
MaxFieldSize	Specifies the maximum buffer size to be allocated per field by httpodbc.dll.	
MaxRecords	Specifies the maximum number of records to be returned by httpodbc.dll.	
Password	Specifies a password to be used with the associated user name to access an ODBC database.	
RequiredParameters	Specifies the parameters that must be supplied by the user.	
SQLStatement	Specifies the SQL select statement (or query) to be executed.	This is a required field.
Template	Specifies the HTML template file that will be used to display the result set.	This is a required field.
UserName	Specifies a user name that will be used to access the ODBC database.	
Content-Type	Specifies a valid MIME type describing the returned result set.	

Creating the Internet Database Connector HTML Template

Well, you made it to the last step of the process: the creation of the HTML template files. It's important to understand how these files work, because these files determine just what the user will see on his Web browser. Before you look at the files, however, it may pay off to learn a bit about what an HTML template (or .HTX) file contains. Basically, an HTX file contains extensions to the HTML language. These extensions will be enclosed in a <%' '%> tag pair. The returned result set will be merged with the HTML document between the <%begindetail%> and <%enddetail&> tag pairs. There are also several HTX variables, summarized in Table 21.2, which, when combined with the if-else-endif flow control statement, determine how your output will appear.

Table 21.2. The HTX extensions.

Extension	Description	Note
ALL_HTTP	All HTTP headers that are not parsed into one of the other listed variables in this table.	
AUTH_TYPE	Specifies the authorization type in use.	If the user has been authenticated by the server, the return value will be Basic. Otherwise, the entry will not be present.
BeginDetail	Specifies the beginning of a detail record block.	
CONTAINS	String includes the specified character.	Can only be used in an if-else-endif statement.
CONTENT_LENGTH	Specifies the number of bytes the script can expect to receive from the client.	
CONTENT_TYPE	The content type of the information supplied in the POST request.	
CurrentRecord	Specifies the current record number.	Can only be used in an if-else-endif statement.

Extension	Description	Note
`else`	Else.	The `else` clause of an `if-else-endif` statement block.
`endif`	Endif.	The end of `if-else-endif` statement block.
`<%EndDetail%>`	Specifies the end of the detail record block.	
`EQ`	Equal to.	Can only be used in an `if-else-endif` statement.
`LT`	Less than.	Can only be used in an `if-else-endif` statement.
`GATEWAY_INTERFACE`	Specifies the revision level of the CGI specification.	
`GT`	Greater Than	Can only be used in an `if-else-endif` statement.
`HTTP_ACCEPT`	Returns special case HTTP header information.	
`if`	If.	The `if` clause of an `if-else-endif` statement block.
`MaxRecords`	Specifies the maximum number of records that can be returned.	Can only be used in an `if-else-endif` statement.
`PATH_INFO`	Additional path information as given by the client.	This value will contain the trailing part of the URL after the script name but before the query string (if any query string was supplied).
`PATH_TRANSLATED`	The same as `PATH_INFO`, but without any virtual path name translation.	
`QUERY_STRING`	Specifies the information after the ? in a script query.	
`REMOTE_ADDR`	Specifies the IP address of the client.	

continues

Table 21.2. continued

Extension	Description	Note
REMOTE_HOST	Specifies the host name of the client.	
REMOTE_USER	Specifies the user name supplied by the client and authorized by the server.	
REQUEST_METHOD	Specifies the HTTP request method.	
SCRIPT_NAME	Specifies the name of the script being executed.	
SERVER_NAME	Specifies the name of the server (or IP address) as it should appear in self-referencing URLs.	
SERVER_PORT	Specifies the TCP/IP port on which the request was received.	
SERVER_PORT_SECURE	Specifies a 0 or 1, where 1 is an encrypted (such as a secure) port.	
SERVER_PROTOCOL	Specifies the name and version of the request.	Usually HTTP/1.0.
SERVER_SOFTWARE	Specifies the name and version number of the Web server under which the IIS extension is executing.	
UNMAPPED_REMOTE USER	Specifies the user name before an authentication filter mapped the user name to a Windows NT user name.	
URL	Specifies the URL of the request.	

Building Dynamic Web Pages with SQL Server

Chapter 21

The first file is called `Sign-In-IDC.HTX`, and contains the following code:

```
1.   <html>
2.   <title>Knowles Consulting Guest Book</title>
3.   <BODY>
4.   <hr>
5.   <h1>Knowles Consulting Guest Book</h1>
6.   <hr>
7.   <%begindetail%>
8.   <%enddetail%>
9.   <%if CurrentRecord EQ 0 %>
10.    <h2>Information registered. Thanks!</h2>
11.    <p>
12.    <table border="1" width="100%">
13.    <caption align="top">Details for <%idc.FirstName%> <%idc.LastName%></caption>
14.    <tr>
15.    <td><%if idc.FirstName EQ ""%>
16.    <%else%>
17.    First Name:</td><td><%idc.FirstName%><td><tr>
18.    <%endif%>
19.    <tr>
20.    <td><%if idc.MiddleInitial EQ ""%>
21.    <%else%>
22.    Middle Initial:</td><td><%idc.MiddleInitial%><td><tr>
23.    <%endif%>
24.    <tr>
25.    <td><%if idc.LastName EQ ""%>
26.    <%else%>
27.    Last Name:</td><td><%idc.LastName%><td><tr>
28.    <%endif%>
29.    <tr>
30.    <td><%if idc.Title EQ ""%>
31.    <%else%>
32.    Title:</td><td><%idc.Title%><td><tr>
33.    <%endif%>
34.    <tr>
35.    <td><%if idc.CompanyName EQ ""%>
36.    <%else%>
37.    Company Name:</td><td><%idc.CompanyName%><td><tr>
38.    <%endif%>
39.    <tr>
40.    <td><%if idc.Address EQ ""%>
41.    <%else%>
42.    Street Address:</td><td><%idc.Address%><td><tr>
43.    <%endif%>
44.    <tr>
45.    <td><%if idc.Address_2 EQ ""%>
46.    <%else%>
47.    Address (cont):</td><td><%idc.Address_2%><td><tr>
48.    <%endif%>
49.    <tr>
50.    <td><%if idc.City EQ ""%>
51.    <%else%>
52.    City:</td><td><%idc.City%><td><tr>
53.    <%endif%>
54.    <tr>
55.    <td><%if idc.StateOrProvince EQ ""%>
```

```
56.     <%else%>
57.     State/Province:</td><td><%idc.StateOrProvince%><td><tr>
58.     <%endif%>
59.     <tr>
60.     <td><%if idc.PostalCode EQ ""%>
61.     <%else%>
62.     Postal Code:</td><td><%idc.PostalCode%><td><tr>
63.     dif%>
64.     <tr>
65.     <td><%if idc.Country EQ ""%>
66.     <%else%>
67.     Country:</td><td><%idc.Country%><td><tr>
68.     <%endif%>
69.     <tr>
70.     <td><%if idc.WorkPhoneNumber EQ ""%>
71.     <%else%>
72.     Work Phone Number:</td><td><%idc.WorkPhoneNumber%><td><tr>
73.     <%endif%>
74.     <tr>
75.     <td><%if idc.HomePhoneNumber EQ ""%>
76.     <%else%>
77.     Home Phone Number:</td><td><%idc.HomePhoneNumber%><td><tr>
78.     <%endif%>
79.     <tr>
80.     <td><%if idc.FaxNumber EQ ""%>
81.     <%else%>
82.     Fax Phone Number:</td><td><%idc.FaxNumber%><td><tr>
83.     <%endif%>
84.     <tr>
85.     <td><%if idc.E_Mail EQ ""%>
86.     <%else%>
87.      E-Mail Address:</td><td><%idc.E_Mail%><td><tr>
88.     <%endif%>
89.     <tr>
90.     <td><%if idc.URL EQ ""%>
91.     <%else%>
92.     Home Page URL:</td><td><%idc.URL%><td><tr>
93.     <%endif%>
94.     <tr>
95.     <td><%if idc.Note EQ ""%>
96.     <%else%>
97.     Note:</td><td><%Note%><td><tr>
98.     <%endif%>
99.     </table>
100.    <p>
101.    <%else%>
102.    <h2><I><%idc.FirstName%> <%idc.LastName%></I> is already registered.</h2>
103.    <%endif%>
104.    <hr>
105.    <table width=100%>
106.    <tr><td width=50%><address><font size=2>
<em>Copyright &#169; 1996 Knowles Consulting. All rights reserved</em>
</font> </address>
107.    </td><td align=right width=50%><div align=right>
108.    <address><font size=2><em>Last Updated: June 21, 1996</em></font> </address>
109.    </div>
110.    </td></tr>
```

```
111.    </table>
112.    </body>
113. r</html>
```

Although this code is longer than you might expect, it is not really as complex at it seems. This is because when the page displays the confirmation message that the client data was accepted, it also creates a table containing the submitted data. If the data was not accepted, an error message stating that the user is already registered is displayed. The important parts of this record are contained between lines 9 and 101. Line 9 is the start of the major IF-ELSE-ENDIF statement block. If the CurrentRecord parameter is equal to 0, which will be true if the IDC returns a record in the result set, then the record was accepted. If a result set consists of multiple rows, then the CurrentRecord parameter will be 0 the first time the <%begindetail%> <%enddetail%> block is executed. Each subsequent time the <%begindetail%> <%enddetail%> block is executed the CurrentRecord counter will be incremented by one. Each row statement includes an IF-ELSE-ENDIF statement block to check if the column is a non-null value. If it is, the else statement is executed, which builds the row. Each row contains a tag and the value of the column. The rest of the document just includes the standard copyright and update information that you've already seen.

The next HTX file is the SearchGuestBook.HTX file. The source code is

```
<html>
<title>Guest Book Query Results</title>
<BODY>
<h1>Selected Guest Book Contents</h1>
<%begindetail%>
<%if CurrentRecord EQ 0 %>
<h2>Here are the selected contents of the guest book.
Click a name to get details:</h2>
<p>
<%endif%>
Name: <a href="/Scripts/
GuestBookDetails.IDC?FName=<%FirstName%>&LName=<%LastName%>">
<b><%FirstName%>
<%LastName%></b></a>
<p>
<%enddetail%>
<%if CurrentRecord EQ 0 %>
<h2>Sorry, no entries in the guest book match those criteria.</h2>
<%endif%>
<p>
<hr>
<table width=100%>
<tr><td width=50%><address><font size=2>
<em>Copyright &#169; 1996 Knowles Consulting. All rights reserved</em></font>
</address>
</td><td align=right width=50%><div align=right>
<address><font size=2><em>Last Updated: June 21, 1996</em></font> </address>
</div>
</td></tr>
</table>
</body>
</html>
```

Using Internet Information Server with Databases

This is a very simple HTX file. Between the `<%begindetail%>` and `<%enddetail%>` tags, you'll find the statement

```
Name: <a href="/Scripts/GuestBookDetails.IDC?FName=<%FirstName%>&
LName=<%LastName%>"><b><%FirstName%>
<%LastName%></b></a>
```

This is how the hypertext link is created between the search results page and the `GuestBookDetail.HTX` file. I mentioned in the previous section that the `GuestBookDetails.IDC` file uses the parameters passed to it in the `FName` and `LName` parameters to search the database for matching records to display. Well, this is where they are set and converted to a hypertext link all in one step. What's interesting about this line of code is that a form is not used; instead, the `GuestBookDetails.IDC` script is executed by the IDC directly, which then passes the `FName` and `LName` parameters to the `GuestBookDetails.IDC` script. Kind of nifty isn't it? The final file is the detail form used by the `GuestBookDetails.IDC` file to display the result set. It is called `GuestBookDetails.HTX`, and is quite similar to the `Sign-In-IDC.HTX` file. In fact, they share the same table definition code:

```
<html>
<title>Guest Book Entry Details</title>
<BODY>
<h1>Guest Book Entry Details</h1>
<hr>
<%begindetail%>
<p>
<table border="1" width="100%">
<caption align="top">Details for <%FirstName%> <%LastName%></caption>
<tr>
<td><%if FirstName EQ ""%>
<%else%>
First Name:</td><td><%FirstName%><td><tr>
<%endif%>
<tr>
<td><%if MiddleInitial EQ ""%>
<%else%>
Middle Initial:</td><td><%MiddleInitial%><td><tr>
<%endif%>
<tr>
<td><%if LastName EQ ""%>
<%else%>
Last Name:</td><td><%LastName%><td><tr>
<%endif%>
<tr>
<td><%if Title EQ ""%>
<%else%>
Title:</td><td><%Title%><td><tr>
<%endif%>
<tr>
<td><%if CompanyName EQ ""%>
<%else%>
Company Name:</td><td><%CompanyName%><td><tr>
<%endif%>
<tr>
<td><%if Address EQ ""%>
<%else%>
```

Chapter 21

```
Street Address:</td><td><%Address%><td><tr>
<%endif%>
<tr>
<td><%if Address_2 EQ ""%>
<%else%>
Address (cont):</td><td><%Address_2%><td><tr>
<%endif%>
<tr>
<td><%if City EQ ""%>
<%else%>
City:</td><td><%City%><td><tr>
<%endif%>
<tr>
<td><%if StateOrProvince EQ ""%>
<%else%>
State/Province:</td><td><%StateOrProvince%><td><tr>
<%endif%>
<tr>
<td><%if PostalCode EQ ""%>
<%else%>
Postal Code:</td><td><%PostalCode%><td><tr>
<%endif%>
<tr>
<td><%if Country EQ ""%>
<%else%>
Country:</td><td><%Country%><td><tr>
<%endif%>
<tr>
<td><%if WorkPhoneNumber EQ ""%>
<%else%>
Work Phone Number:</td><td><%WorkPhoneNumber%><td><tr>
<%endif%>
<tr>
<td><%if HomePhoneNumber EQ ""%>
<%else%>
Home Phone Number:</td><td><%HomePhoneNumber%><td><tr>
<%endif%>
<tr>
<td><%if FaxNumber EQ ""%>
<%else%>
Fax Phone Number:</td><td><%FaxNumber%><td><tr>
<%endif%>
<tr>
<td><%if E_Mail EQ ""%>
<%else%>
E-Mail Address:</td><td><%E_Mail%><td><tr>
<%endif%>
<tr>
<td><%if URL EQ ""%>
<%else%>
Home Page URL:</td><td><%URL%><td><tr>
<%endif%>
<tr>
<td><%if Note EQ ""%>
<%else%>
Note:</td><td><%Note%><td><tr>
<%endif%>
</table>
```

```
<p>
<%enddetail%>
<p>
<hr>
<table width=100%>
<tr><td width=50%><address><font size=2>
<em>Copyright &#169; 1996 Knowles Consulting. All
rights reserved</em></font> </address>
</td><td align=right width=50%><div align=right>
<address><font size=2><em>Last Updated: June 21, 1996</em></font> </address>
</div>
</td></tr>
</table>
</body>
</html>
```

Notice that the table definition is between the `<%begindetail%>` and `<%enddetail%>` tags. This will display one or more records on the page, depending on the number of records returned in the result set. The only real difference between this page and the others you have examined is that no check occurs to verify that at least one record was found. However, this check is not needed. After all, to get to this page in the first place, you must have clicked on a hypertext link created in the previous page (`SearchGuestBook.HTX`), which would only have been created if a record was found. There are other tags, like the `<%begindetail%>` and `<%enddetail%>` tags, which you can use in your HTX files. These additional tags are summarized in Table 21.2.

Using the SQL Server Web Assistant

While you can use the Internet Database Connector to build dynamic Web pages that interact with the user, you can also use the Web Assistant. The main difference between the IDC and the Web Assistant is that the Web Assistant is not designed to interact with the user. Instead, it is designed to publish a database online. It does this by creating static Web pages; but perhaps *static* is the wrong word. Most people consider a static page to be a Web page that does not change its contents. However, with the Web Assistant, these Web pages can be automatically refreshed when a new record is inserted into the database, or when a specific time interval is reached. This means the Web page contents could change. In essence, once more you have the ability to create a dynamic Web page. If you combine the IDC with the Web Administrator, you can build a fully interactive online order system, for example.

Creating an interactive online order system would require an event-driven processing methodology, where you would respond to actions that occur, rather than a hierarchical methodology, where you would control the data flow in a step-by-step process. Let me show you how this could work. First, lets lay a few rules for the groundwork:

- You have an ODBC database containing your product inventory. This inventory database contains the quantity, price, and a description of the items.
- You want to publish an online catalog using this information.
- You want to accept client orders from the online catalog.

To bring these three basic ideas together and build an interactive order-entry database, you'd have to build the following constructs:

- Online catalog—You could use the Web Administrator to build this Web page using a query designed to select all items from your product inventory database whenever the item quantity is greater than one. Anytime the database changes, you could have the Web Administrator rebuild the page. The Web page could include a hypertext link to another Web page containing the order form.

- Order form—The order form will use the Internet Database Connector to insert an order record into the Order databases.

- Order database—This database would contain information about the client and product ordered. It might contain order number, date, name, address, payment, product, and so on, fields. For optimum results, this would be a client/server database (such as SQL Server) rather than an application database (such as Access) so that you could benefit from the ability to execute code automatically (like triggers or scheduled procedures). In this fashion, whenever an order record is entered into the database your code could automatically decrement the quantity for the item contained in your product inventory database. This same code could automatically notify a sales or shipping representative. This code could update other databases. These databases could be used by applications within your company to automate the shipping and billing processes.

The basic work flow, then, to obtain an order would follow these basic steps:

1. The client connects to your Web site.
2. The client selects your catalog to browse through it.

> **TIP**
>
> You could create a custom query form using the IDC to search for specific items in your catalog. The description field could be used as a searchable text field, for example, so the client could specify the type of items of interest. The returned result set, based on his query, could be displayed on another custom IDC HTML page. The user could then follow the same order process once he selects the item to order.

3. The client selects an item and clicks a link to order the item.
4. An order form appears. The user fills out the relevant data fields and submits the form. This submission inserts a record into the Order database.
5. The Order database insert trigger is activated. This could send an e-mail message requesting manual intervention to continue the order and shipping process. Or, the trigger could cause a cascade of events to occur in which one or more databases are

updated (like the quantity field for the item in the product inventory database), applications are executed, and finally the product is shipped to the user.

6. When the product inventory database is updated to reflect that there is one fewer of the ordered item, the Web Administrator could update the online catalog page so the next user will see an accurate count for the item. If the current user purchases the item, then attempts to reorder the item based on his cached online version of the catalog, your IDC order form would report an error since the query executed by the IDC would return real-time results (the query would return no records as the quantity field in the product inventory database would be 0).

To use the Web Assistant to build your Web pages, follow these steps:

1. Launch the SQL Server Web Assistant, located in the SQL Server 6.5 program group, to display the SQL Server Web Assistant - Login dialog box (see Figure 21.2).

FIGURE 21.2.

Specifying the SQL Server parameters for the Web Assistant.

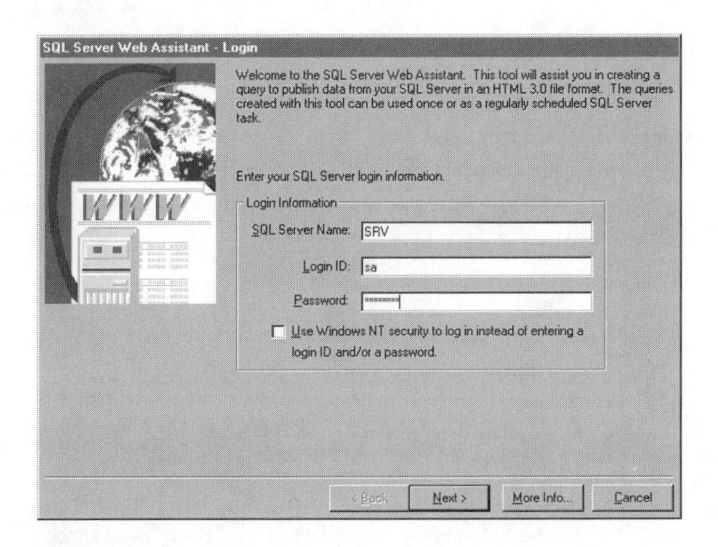

2. Enter the name of your SQL Server installation in the SQL Server Name field.
3. Enter a user name in the Logon ID field.
4. Enter a password for the user name in the Password field.

> **NOTE**
>
> If you are using the mixed, or integrated, security models, you can enable the Use Windows NT security to log in instead of entering a login ID and/or a password check box. This way, your current credentials will be used.

5. Click the Next button to display the dialog shown in Figure 21.3.

FIGURE 21.3.
Specifying the SQL Server database for the Web Assistant.

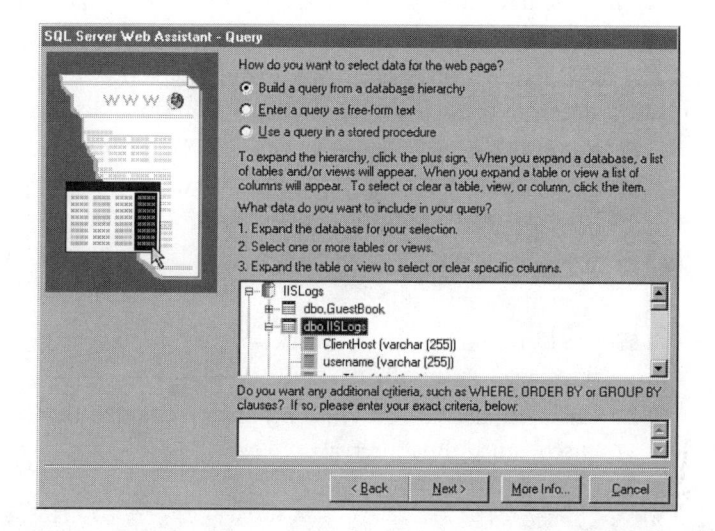

6. In the How do you want to select data for the Web page? group, specify one of the following:

  - Build a query from a database hierarchy—This option specifies that the database table you select will be posted on the Web in its entirety, unless you specify additional restrictions in the query window at the bottom of the dialog.

  - Enter a query as free-form text—When selected, the dialog box will change to let you choose a database and enter a free-form query. This free-form query will be used to return a result set. This result set will be displayed on the Web page created by the Web Assistant.

  - Use a query in a stored procedure—When selected, the dialog box will change to allow you to choose a database, choose a stored procedure in the database, and enter any command-line arguments for the stored procedure.

> **TIP**
>
> You can publish multiple tables simply by selecting the listbox. If you only want to publish part of a table, you can expand the table item and select the specific fields you want to publish.

7. When you have made your selection, click the Next button. For this discussion, I will assume you have chosen the Build a query from a database hierarchy option and selected a single table.

8. The SQL Server Web Assistant - Scheduling dialog will appear. Choose one of the following from the Scheduling Options drop-down listbox:

   - Now—This option specifies that the Web page will be created immediately.
   - Later—This option specifies that the Web page will be created one time at a user-specified date and time.
   - When Data Changes—This option specifies that the Web page will be re-created automatically whenever the database changes.
   - On Certain Days of the Week—This option specifies that the Web page will be re-created on specific days at specific times.
   - On a Regular Basis—This option specifies that the Web page will be re-created at scheduled time intervals.

> **TIP**
>
> For high-traffic sites, the On Certain Days of the Week or On a Regular Basis options can be particularly useful. While the data would not be updated in real-time, it could be updated frequently enough to promote a sense of continuity (for example, new products would constantly be added to the database) to the client. This could benefit you by lowering the system resource demands on your server during peak activity periods. This lowering of resource requirements means your server could support more simultaneous user connections.

9. Click the Next button, and the SQL Server Web Assistant - File Options dialog box will appear (see Figure 21.4).

10. Specify a path and filename for the Web page in the Type the file name of the web page field.

FIGURE 21.4.
Specifying the Web Assistant Web page parameters.

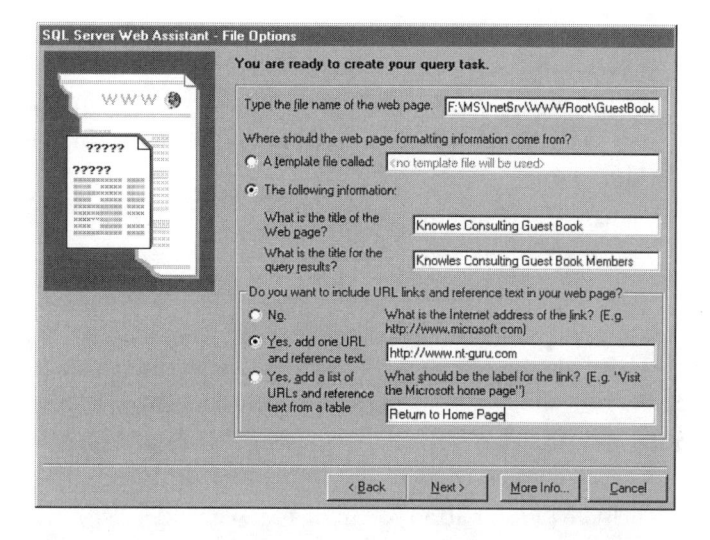

11. Choose the A template file called radio button and enter the name of the HTML template file to be used to format your output. Or, choose The following information radio button and specify the Web page title in the What is the title of the web page? field, then enter a subtitle in the What is the title for the query results? field.

12. If you want to add an HTML hypertext link, enable the Yes, add one URL and reference text radio button and supply a single URL and description. Or, enable the Yes, add a list of URLs and reference text from a table radio button and specify the table name containing this information.

13. Click the Next button to display the SQL Server Web Assistant - Formatting dialog box, shown in Figure 21.5.

FIGURE 21.5.
Specifying the Web Assistant Web page formatting parameters.

14. Specify the size of the HTML header to be used for the result columns in the How do you want the results title to look? field.
15. Specify how the result rows will be displayed by enabling the Fixed font radio button to use a fixed-width font, or the Proportional font radio button to use a proportional-width font.
16. To make the results rows more visible, enable the Bold check box. To emphasize the result rows, enable the Italic check box.
17. To insert a time/date timestamp at the beginning of the page, enable the Insert an update date/time stamp at the top of the page check box.
18. To include column name headers on the output, enable the Include column or view column names with the query results check box.
19. To limit the number of rows on a single Web page, enable the Limit the query results to check box and enter a value in the rows field.
20. Click the Finish button to build your Web page.

Summary

In this chapter you have learned by example how to build a guest book using the Internet Database Connector. You have learned how to build the HTML forms, how to build the IDC definition files, and how to build the HTML template files. You have also learned how to use the SQL Server Web Assistant to build Web pages to display data from your database in a semi-static form. While not interactive, this method does provide the ability to publish extremely large amounts of data on the Web. If combined with the interactive capabilities provided by the IDC, an interactive online system can be built.

The primary reason to use the Internet Database Connector over a corresponding Microsoft dbWeb implementation is for enhanced control over the behavior (including the look and feel) of the Web page and the query used to return the resulting data. Since the IDC is a predefined interface that uses HTML documents, .HTX, and .IDC files to interface with a database, it is easier than developing a custom CGI application, which requires development with a compiler. Since the IDC is an ISAPI application, it runs in the context of the Internet Information Server. This is a more efficient method than a corresponding custom CGI application, which runs in a separate process address space, meaning you have less overhead and improved user response time.

In the next chapter you will learn how to use the Windows NT Performance Monitor to build charts, logs, reports, and alerts. This will give you a good foundation to begin to tune your server and unleash the full potential of your Internet Information Server.

IN THIS PART

- The Performance Monitor **623**
- Tuning the Server **641**

Performance Tuning and Optimization Techniques

PART VII

The Performance Monitor

22

IN THIS CHAPTER

- Using The Performance Monitor **624**

The Performance Monitor can monitor almost everything that is happening on your system, so gaining a basic understanding of its usage is quite important. In the next chapter you will learn about specific performance counters you can use to tune various system components. In this chapter you will learn the basic functions of the Performance Monitor, including how to create and configure charts, logs, reports, and alerts. Keep in mind that performance tuning can be very complex, and entire books are devoted to just this particular program and its usage, so it may take some time for you to get the hang of using the Performance Monitor and the associated performance counters.

Using the Performance Monitor

The Performance Monitor is used to monitor a system in real-time. That is, the event objects you monitor are occurring right now, and the value you see for the event object reflects the actual value of the event object with a minimal time lag. You can use the Performance Monitor on the computer you want to monitor, which will affect the performance on that computer slightly, or you can use it remotely from another computer, which will impact your network bandwidth more than it will the performance of the computer you are monitoring. The amount of performance degradation will vary from unnoticeable to appreciable, depending on the number and frequency of monitored events.

The Performance Monitor defines events, as I put it, as *objects*. An object is an item such as a system, a processor, a process, a thread, or a similar item. Objects are further divided into *counters*. For example, the system object includes counters for % Total Processor Time (the total amount of processor usage on the system), % Total Interrupt Time (the total number of interrupts generated on the system), and % Total Privileged Time (the total amount of processor time spent in the kernel on the system), among others. Within a counter, you may also have one or more *instances*. For example, if you have more than one processor on your system and view the Processor Counter % Processor Time (the total amount of processor utilization for a particular processor), then you will find multiple entries in the Instance field. Instance counts start with 0 and increase by one for each additional item. If you have two processors, then your Instance field will include 0 for the first processor and 1 for the second processor. You could also have multiple named instances, rather than numbers. If you monitor the RAS Port object counter, for example, the Instance field could include COM1, COM2, and COM3, up to as many RAS connections as you have installed.

The Performance Monitor supports four types of views, each of which displays the performance object counters in a different format to provide you with unique capabilities. These include the following:

- Chart—This view can display values for performance counters in either a line (Graph) or bar (Histogram) chart. The most useful view to quickly display performance data over a period of time is the line chart and for performance peaks is the histogram chart. It can become cluttered and difficult to read if you attempt to view more than 10 active performance counters.

- Log—This view is used to capture all the performance counters for a particular object to a file. This captured file may be read in to the Performance Monitor at a later date for in-depth analysis. You can load in a log file and then chart it, for example.

> **TIP**
>
> When using this option, you should remember that you can only view object counters that you have previously captured. However, you do not have to view all the object counters that you captured. You may select a subset of these counters to view. This is one way to start with the big picture and then narrow it down to a specific incident. It is always better to capture any performance counters that you think you may need, rather than limit the capture to a few specific performance counters that you know you will need.

- Report—This view can display a large series of performance object counter values in real-time. It is an instantaneous view of the performance counters, so you may only view the current value. This value will change at the next update interval, which means the value you are monitoring may be reset to 0 before you can evaluate it.
- Alert—This view is used to set conditions based on performance object counters and is used to alert you when this condition is met. For example, you may want to be informed when your server's paging file grows beyond its current minimum allocation, so that you can increase the minimum allocation size and increase overall system performance. Anytime a paging file grows beyond the minimum, there is a significant amount of overhead involved in expanding the page file. Additionally, any page file expansion may be fragmented, which will slow down retrieval of paged data.

The Performance Monitor Toolbar

The Performance Monitor toolbar, as shown in Figure 22.1, provides quick access to the Performance Monitor feature set. From left to right, the toolbar buttons perform the following functions:

- View a chart—Changes the default view to the chart view.
- View the alerts—Changes the default view to the alert view.
- View output log file status—Changes the default view to the log view.
- View report data—Changes the default view to the report view.

FIGURE 22.1.
The Performance Monitor toolbar.

- Add counter—Displays the Add To *Item* dialog where *Item* can be either a chart, an alert, a log, or a report. Use this as a quick mechanism to add performance object counters.
- Modify selected counter—When you select an object counter in the legend and press this button, the Edit *Item* Entry dialog displays; in it you may change the item's color, scale, line width, and line style if viewing a chart, or other attributes for alerts, logs, and reports.
- Delete selected counter—This button deletes the object counter selected in the legend from a chart, alert, log, or report.
- Update counter data—Use this button to update the display when you have set the Update Time to Manual Update.
- Place a commented bookmark into the output log—Bookmarks insert a comment into a log file to refresh your memory of the usage of captured object counters.
- Options—This button displays the Options dialog for the selected view.

Creating Charts

Creating a chart consists of selecting the performance objects, configuring the view, and then saving the chart for future use. You can follow these steps to create a chart:

1. Make sure the default view, as shown in Figure 22.2, is for a chart. If a different view is displayed, you can click the View a chart button on the toolbar, choose View | Chart, or press Ctrl+C.

FIGURE 22.2.
The Performance Monitor chart view.

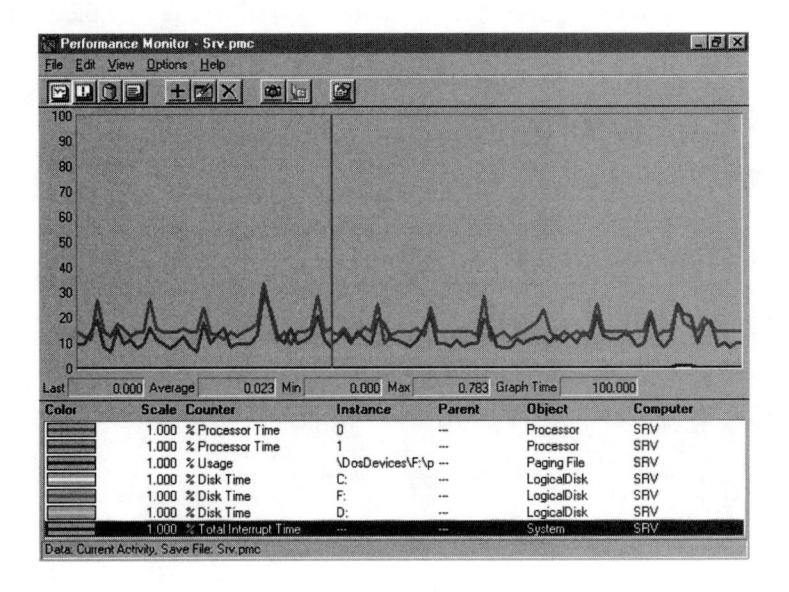

2. Choose Edit | Add to Chart, press the Add counter button on the toolbar, or press Ctrl+I. All these will display the Add to Chart dialog, as shown in Figure 22.3. This dialog is used to select the performance object counters to monitor.

FIGURE 22.3.
The Add to Chart dialog.

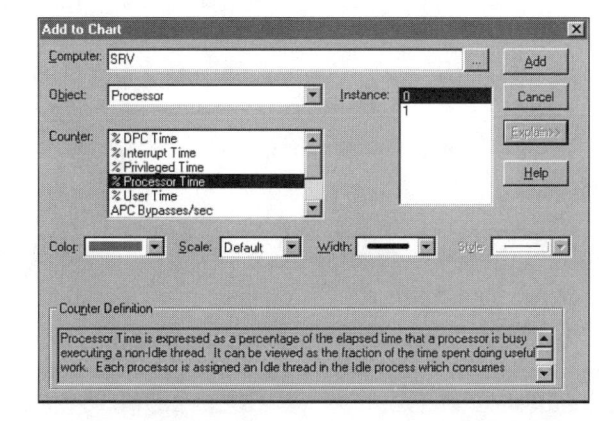

3. First, choose the event type (performance object) to monitor in the Object: field.
4. Choose the event subtype (object counter) to monitor in the Counter: field.

> **TIP**
>
> If you are unsure of the object counter's properties, click the Explain button. This expands the dialog and displays a short description of the counter.

5. Finally, choose an instance of the object counter, if applicable. An *instance* differentiates between one or more occurrences of an object counter. Not all object counters include an instance number.

> **TIP**
>
> You can select a different source to monitor by specifying the name of a remote computer in the Computer: field, or you can click the button at the end of the field to display the Select Computer dialog where you can browse the network for the computer you wish to monitor. Once you have selected the computer you wish to monitor, repeat steps 3 through 5. This can be particularly useful if you want to monitor multiple servers simultaneously for comparison.

6. To specify a different color for the performance object counter to use for its display, select a color from the Color: field.

7. To change the default scale for the object counter, select a multiplier or divisor from the Scale: field. This can be a very useful option. By choosing a smaller divisor you can force all of the chart to be visible when a performance counter's maximum value is at the top of the chart. By choosing a higher multiplier you can force the counter to be visible when the counter is too low to be readily visible.

8. To change the line thickness displayed in the chart, choose a different selection from the Width: field.

9. To change the line from a solid line to a series of dashes or dots to differentiate chart lines of the same color, select a pattern from the Style: field.

10. Once you have made all your choices, press the Add button to add the object counter to the Performance Monitor's display list.

11. Repeat steps 2 through 10 for each object counter you want to monitor. When you have finished, press the Done button to return to the Performance Monitor Chart view.

> **TIP**
>
> To select a range of object counters, select the first counter in the range; then while holding the Shift key, select the last counter in the range. To select noncontiguous items, select the first counter, and then while holding the Ctrl key, select the next counter. Repeat this for each counter. Repeat these same steps for the Instance field if you want to monitor multiple object counters for multiple instances. The Performance Monitor automatically selects a color and line width for each item.

To modify the chart configuration, choose Options|Chart to display the Chart Options dialog, as shown in Figure 22.4. Now you can select the following items:

FIGURE 22.4.
The Chart Options dialog.

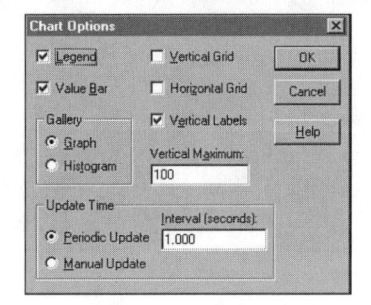

- Legend—This item displays a map legend at the bottom of the chart, which contains each monitored item. This includes the color of the item, the item name, the instance, parent, object, and computer.
- Value Bar—This item is displayed just above the legend and contains the last value, average value, minimum value, maximum value, and graph time of a selected legend item. The graph time is the time it takes in seconds for a performance counter to completely fill the display area.
- Vertical Grid—Use this item to subdivide the vertical chart axis. When selected, vertical reference lines are drawn on the displayed window.
- Horizontal Grid—Use this item to subdivide the horizontal chart axis. When selected, horizontal reference lines are drawn on the displayed window.
- Vertical Labels—This item enables or disables the vertical scale numbers displayed to the left of the chart window.
- Gallery—This item selects the chart type. It can display either a line chart by selecting the Graph option or a bar chart by selecting the Histogram option.
- Vertical Maximum—Use this item to specify a different maximum scale for the vertical axis. The default is 100.
- Update Time—Use this item to specify the time when the chart should be updated. You can specify to automatically update the chart by specifying a value (in seconds) for the Periodic Update option or specify a manual chart update by choosing the Manual Update option. If you select the Manual Update option, the chart will only be updated when you choose Options | Update Now, the Update counter now toolbar button, or Ctrl+U.

After all this work, you should save the chart in case you want to use it again. Do this by choosing the File | Save Chart Settings from the File menu. This displays the familiar File Save As dialog the first time you save the chart where you may specify the filename and directory to store the file, and updates the file thereafter. To load a previously saved chart, choose File | Open.

TIP

To save all Performance Monitor views (Chart, Log, Report, and Alert), choose File | Save Workspace. This saves all chart views and the selected performance counter objects along with the window placement to a file.

Creating Logs

Creating a log consists of selecting the performance objects, configuring the log options, and then starting the log capture. Once performance data has been captured to a log, you may then load this data back into the Performance Monitor for analysis. You can follow these steps to create the log:

1. Make sure the default view, as shown in Figure 22.5, is for a log. If a different view is displayed, you can click the View output Log file status button on the toolbar, choose View | Log, or press Ctrl+L.

FIGURE 22.5.
The Performance Monitor log view.

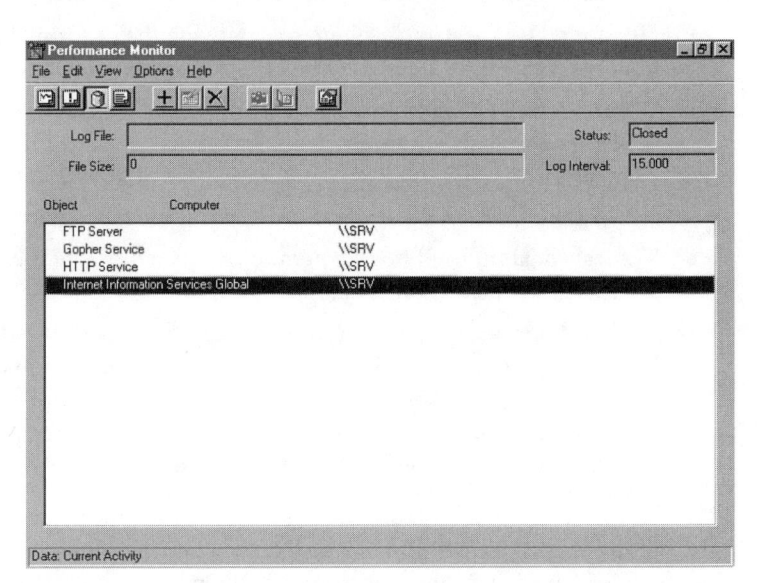

2. Choose Edit | Add to Log, press the Add counter button on the toolbar, or press Ctrl+I. Any of these commands will display the Add To Log dialog, as shown in Figure 22.6.

FIGURE 22.6.
The Add To Log dialog.

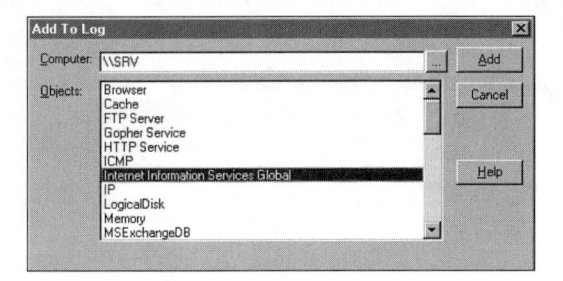

3. This dialog is used to select the performance object to monitor. To select an object, highlight the object in the Objects: field, then press the Add button. To select a range of object counters, select the first counter in the range, then while holding the Shift key select the last counter in the range. To select noncontiguous items, select the first counter and then, while holding the Ctrl key, select the next counter.

> **TIP**
>
> If you are unsure of the events to monitor for your first-time use, select them all, but only capture these events for a maximum of five minutes because the log file can become quite large. The log file then can be used with the chart, or report, view to look at specific object counters. As you view these different object counters and become familiar with their use, you can then limit your logs to just those counters of interest.

4. After you have made your choices, the Cancel button will change to the Done button. Press this button to return to the Performance Monitor's main window.
5. At this point, all the performance objects will be listed in the Log window. However, you are not ready to capture data yet. First, you have to modify the log options to specify a file to place the captured data in and specify an update interval. These features are accessible from the Log Options dialog. To display this dialog, choose Options|Chart, press the Options button on the toolbar, or press Ctrl+O.

> **NOTE**
>
> To automatically update the log, specify a value (in seconds) for the Periodic Update option. To manually update the log, select the Manual Update option. If you select the Manual Update option, the chart will only be updated when you choose Options | Update Now, the Update counter now button on the toolbar, or press Ctrl+U.

6. To start your data capture, press the Start Log button in the Log Options dialog. Once this option is enabled, the Status: field changes from Closed to Open, and the File Size: field displays the size of the data-capture file. The longer you capture data, the larger this file will be, so you should not capture data on a drive containing your network client files because this could prevent a client from being able to save his data files. Of course, this assumes that you are capturing a large amount of data over a significant amount of time.

Once you have captured all the data you want for analysis, open the Log Options dialog and click the Stop Log button. This closes the log file. To use this captured data, choose Options | Data From to display the Data From dialog where you may load a log file. Once you load a log file, you may then chart it (to create a new chart, just choose New Chart from the File menu) or use it to generate alerts or reports. You can also change the object to log by redisplaying the Add To Log dialog and adding objects. However, before you can append these new objects, be sure to select the Options | Data From menu option and change the setting from Log File to Current Activity. You may then use the Start button in the Log Options dialog to append your data to the capture file.

> **TIP**
>
> Don't forget to save your log options by choosing the File | Save Log Setting As menu option.

Creating Reports

The report view is useful for viewing large amounts of performance object counters simultaneously. The only hitch is that the counter value displayed is always the last known value of the counter. You cannot view a series of values over a period of time. Only a chart view in linegraph mode can display a series of counter data over a period of time. You will find the report view most useful for monitoring complex items, such as your entire network.

For example, network-related counters include objects such as AppleTalk, Browser, FTP Server, ICMP, IP, Gateway Services for NetWare, MacFile Server, NBT Connections, NetBEUI, NetBEUI Resource, Network Interface, Network Segment, NWLink IPX, NWLink SPX, NWLink NetBIOS, RAS Port, RAS Total, Redirector, Server, Server Work Queues, TCP, UDP, and WINS Server. That's a lot of object counters to monitor, and if you have installed other network components or third-party products, you may have even more object counters.

To create a report, follow these steps:

1. Make sure the default view, as shown in Figure 22.7, is for a report. If a different view is displayed, you can click the View Report data button on the toolbar, choose View | Report, or press Ctrl+R.

FIGURE 22.7.
The Performance Monitor report view.

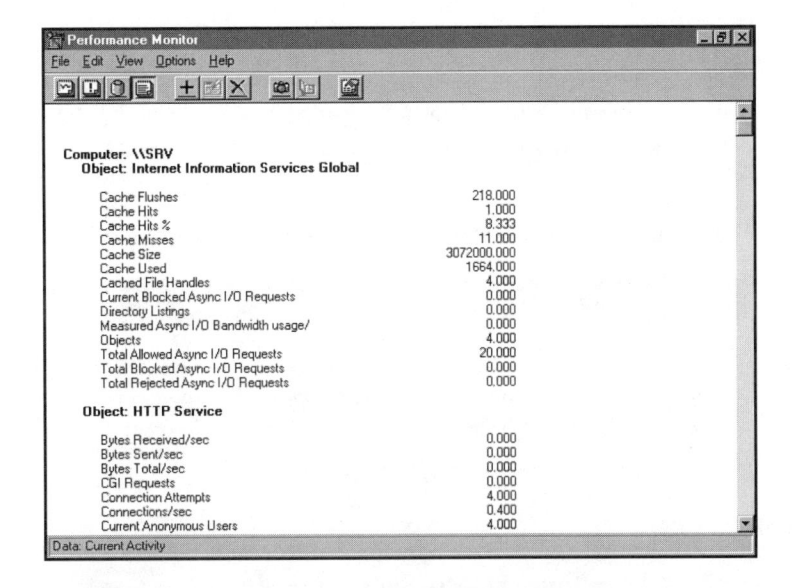

2. Choose Edit | Add to Report, press the Add counter button on the toolbar, or press Ctrl+I. All these selections will display the Add to Report dialog, as shown in Figure 22.8. This dialog is similar to the Add to Chart dialog and is used to select the performance object counters to monitor.

FIGURE 22.8.
The Add to Report dialog.

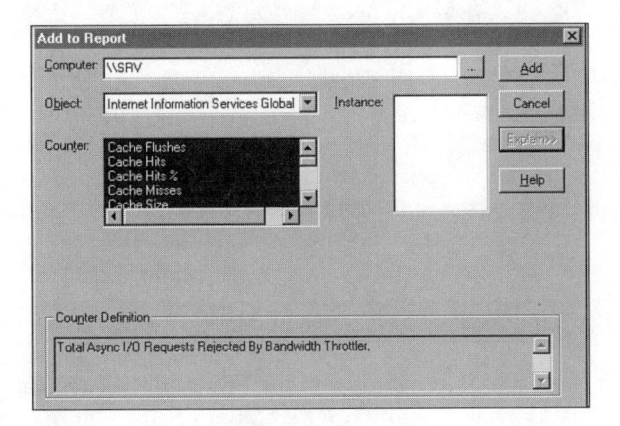

3. First, choose the event type (performance object) to monitor in the Object: field.
4. Then choose the event subtype (object counter) to monitor in the Counter: field.

> **TIP**
>
> If you are unsure of the counter's properties, click the Explain button. This will expand the dialog and display a short description of the counter.

5. Choose an instance of the object counter, if applicable.

> **TIP**
>
> You can select a different computer to monitor by specifying the name of a remote computer in the Computer: field. Once you have selected the computer, repeat steps 3 through 5. This is useful for monitoring multiple servers simultaneously to quickly check the load of a particular server.

6. When you have made all your choices, press the Add button to add the object counter to the Performance Monitor's display list.
7. Repeat steps 2 through 6 for each object counter you want to monitor. When you have finished, press the Done button to return to the Performance Monitor Report view.

> **NOTE**
>
> To change the update interval for an automatic update, specify a value (in seconds) for the Periodic Update option. To change from automatic to manual updates, select the Manual Update option. Just remember, if you choose the Manual Update option, the chart will only be updated when you select Options | Update Now, the Update counter now button on the toolbar, or press Ctrl+U.

> **TIP**
>
> Don't forget to save your report configuration by choosing the File | Save Report Settings As menu option. You never know when you may want to use this configuration again.

Creating Alerts

The alert view is the best way to automatically inform you of a problem with your server. It can inform you of low disk space, high processor utilization, network errors, or other items that might concern you. Keep in mind that an alert can only be sent if the Performance Monitor is running. If you want to automate specific alerts, then you should obtain the Windows NT Resource Kit or check the Microsoft FTP site (`ftp.microsoft.com`) for a downloadable copy. This includes the DATALOG.EXE program that can perform the same alerting and logging features of Performance Monitor, but runs as a service. The MONITOR.EXE program installs the service and stops and starts the alert or logging features.

> **NOTE**
>
> In order to use the alert service, you must first create a Performance Monitor workspace file that contains your alert and log settings. If you will be monitoring any activity on a remote computer, be sure to create a user account with sufficient network privileges. When configuring the service startup values, configure the service to use the This Account option in the Log On As group.

To create an alert, follow these steps:

1. Make sure the default view, as shown in Figure 22.9, is for an alert. If a different view is displayed, you can click the View the Alerts button on the toolbar, choose View | Alerts, or press Ctrl+A.

FIGURE 22.9.
The Performance Monitor alert view.

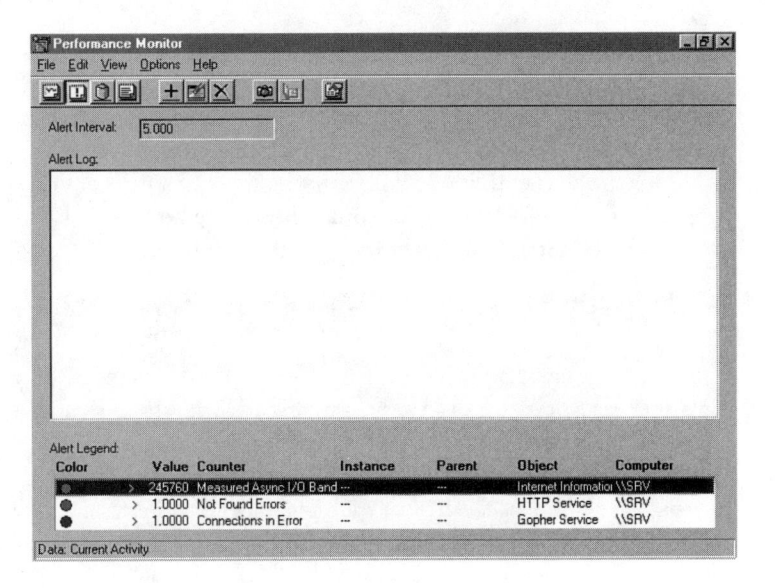

2. Next, choose Edit | Add to Report, press the Add counter button on the toolbar, or press Ctrl+I. This will display the Add to Alert dialog, as shown in Figure 22.10, which you can use to select the performance object counters to monitor.

FIGURE 22.10.
The Add to Alert dialog.

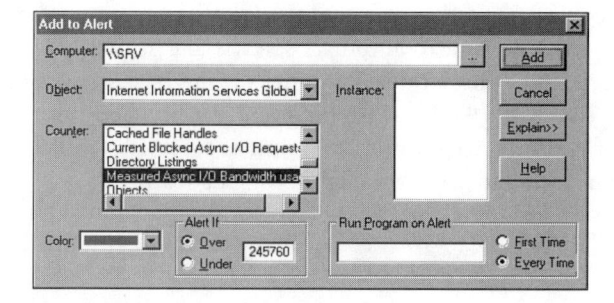

3. First, choose the event type (performance object) to monitor in the Object: field.
4. Next, choose the event subtype (object counter) to monitor in the Counter: field.

> **TIP**
>
> If you are not sure what the object counter is used for, click the Explain button. This will expand the dialog and display a short description of the counter.

5. Choose an instance of the object counter, if applicable. An instance differentiates between one or more occurrences of an object counter, and not all object counters include an instance number.
6. To specify a different color for the performance object counter to use for its display, select a color from the Color: field.
7. In the Alert If field, choose either Over or Under and specify a value in the data field for the alert condition. For example, if you want an alert sent when your disk drive has less than 10MB free, you would choose the LogicalDisk object and the Free Megabytes counter, then select the Under radio button, and specify the value as 10.

> **TIP**
>
> To specify the same alert condition for multiple instances (like two or more logical disks), select a range of instances by highlighting the first instance in the range, then while holding the Shift key, select the last instance in the range. To select a noncontiguous range, select the first instance, and then while holding the Ctrl key, select the next instance. Repeat this for each instance. The Performance Monitor will automatically select a color for each instance.

8. In the Run Program on Alert field, you can specify a command line to be executed either every time the alert condition is met or only the first time the alert condition is met by enabling either the Every Time or First Time radio button.

> **TIP**
>
> The preceding option is particularly useful if you have a pager and a command line program, which can be used to dial your pager and send you a notification message.

9. Once you have made all your choices, press the Add button to add the object counter to the Performance Monitor's display list.
10. Repeat steps 2 through 9 for each object counter you would like to monitor. When you have finished, press the Done button to return to the Performance Monitor alert view.

To modify the alert configuration, choose Options|Alert, which will display the Alert Options dialog, shown in Figure 22.11. This is where you may select the following items:

FIGURE 22.11.
The Alert Options dialog.

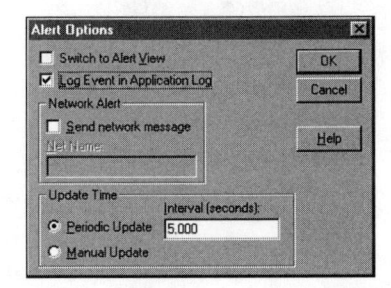

- Switch to Alert View—This option automatically switches the Performance Monitor to the alert view when an alert condition is met.
- Log Event in Application Log—Use this option to log the alert condition in the computer's application log.
- Network Alert—This option broadcasts a message to the domain users, specifying the alert condition. To send a message to a specific user, enter a user name in the Net Name: field. This name can specify a name from a different domain by prefacing the user name with the domain name like *DomainName\UserName* where *DomainName* is the name of the external domain, and *UserName* is the name of the user in the external domain (SRV\Administrator, for example).

- Update Time—Use this item to specify the alert update interval. You can specify an automatic update interval by specifying a value (in seconds) for the Periodic Update option or a manual alert update interval by choosing the Manual Update option. If you select the Manual Update option, then the alert conditions will only be checked when you choose Options | Update Now, the Update counter now toolbar button, or Ctrl+U.

> **TIP**
>
> It is a good idea to save the alert settings by choosing File | Save Alert Settings As and specifying a file to save your settings.

Not all performance object counters are useful for specifying alert conditions. The object counters I find most useful, and which you may find useful as well, are summarized in Table 22.1.

Table 22.1. Performance object counters for alerts.

Counter	Instance	Condition	Description
LogicalDisk Object			
% Free Space	Per Drive	Under	Useful for notification in a low free-space situation. Specify the minimum percentage of free space per drive in the Alert If value field. Set this value to 10 or higher for useful warnings. Any value below this may notify you too late for your users' comfort.
Free Megabytes	Per Drive	Under	Useful for notification in a low disk-space situation. Specify the minimum free space in MB per drive in the Alert If value field. On a large drive (over 1GB) set this value to 100 or less if you want to run on the ragged edge.
Memory Object			
Pages/sec.	5 to 10	Over	Set this to 5 for a notification that the system is paging too often and as an indication that a memory upgrade may improve performance if consistent alerts are sent. Set this value to 10 to be notified that a memory upgrade is required as the system is definitely paging too much.

Counter	Instance	Condition	Description
Network Interface Object			
Current Bandwidth	Per Network Transport Protocol	Over	Set this value to 50000000bps for a notification that your network transport protocol has reached 50 percent capacity.
Network Segment Object			
%Network Utilization	Per Network Adapter	Over	Set this value to 50 for a notification that your network segment has reached 50 percent of its carrying capacity.
Redirector Object			
Network Errors/sec	N/A	Over	If you have any errors, you should spend more time isolating them. This value should be set to 1.
Server Object			
Error System	N/A	Over	Any value over 1 indicates a problem with the server. If detected, you should examine the system log for the cause of the error or spend some time with the Performance Monitor, as specified in the Finding Network Bottlenecks section, to help isolate the error.
Errors Logon	N/A	Over	This item notifies you that someone is attempting to hack into your system. A good threshold value is from 3 to 10.
Errors Access Permissions	N/A	Over	This item informs you of potential users trying to access files they should not be, in order to gain access to privileged data. A good threshold value is from 3 to 10.
Pool Nonpaged Failures	N/A	Over	This item should be set to 1, as this indicates a lack of nonpageable memory for the server service. An error indicates that the server is unable to process a client request for lack of resources. This value also indicates a physical memory shortage.

continues

Table 22.1. continued

Counter	Instance	Condition	Description
Server Object			
Pool Paged Bytes		Over	This item should be set to 1, as this indicates a lack of pageable memory for the server service. An error indicates that the server is unable to process a client request for a lack of resources. This value also indicates a physical memory shortage or that the pagefile setting is too low.
Server Work Queues Object			
Work Item Shortages	Per Network Adapter	Over	This value should be set to 0, as any indication represents a problem with the server service. If errors are encountered, the MaxWorkItems value should be increased.

Summary

This chapter discusses the basics of using the Performance Monitor to create charts, logs, alerts, and reports to give you an idea of how to use these features. The goal in this chapter is not to explain every detail of the Performance Monitor, but instead to give you a good understanding of the features and provide you the ability to use the Performance Monitor in your day-to-day activities. In the next chapter, you will look at using the Performance Monitor to tune your server, the Internet Information Server, and SQL Server.

Tuning the Server

23

IN THIS CHAPTER

- Performance Tuning with the Performance Monitor **642**
- Configuring SQL Server **668**

Whether you are using the Internet Information Server for Internet or intranet publishing, your goal is to obtain the maximum performance from it. Tuning the base platform (Windows NT Server) is an excellent starting point. However, depending on your IIS implementation, you may need to tune other components as well. For example, if you are using SQL Server to store your IIS logs or for dynamic WWW pages, then you will need to tune SQL Server. In this chapter, you will learn how to tune Windows NT Server, Internet Information Server, and SQL Server using some Performance Monitor examples. Along the way, you will work with a few programs I wrote to illustrate the type of bottlenecks you may encounter. If you need additional information on how to use the Performance Monitor, you may want to refer back to Chapter 22, "The Performance Monitor."

Keep in mind that the Internet Information Server basically provides the same services as a file server. It consumes processor cycles, as an application server does, and it provides shared resources (files, WWW pages, and so on) to network clients. You can think of the Internet as a large WAN connected to your internal network. The methods you use to tune for optimum IIS performance are the same methods you would apply to any application or file server.

Performance Tuning with the Performance Monitor

Performance tuning is based on finding your bottleneck (the item causing a performance limitation) and doing something to correct it. The primary goal with performance tuning is to provide adequate system performance. This basically falls into four categories: processor, memory, disk subsystem, and network. If these components are performing well, users will not complain about system performance. This section looks at each component and provides sample Performance Monitor workspaces to illustrate the process of finding bottlenecks in these areas.

> **NOTE**
>
> The sample Performance Monitor charts, alerts, reports, logs, and workspace files can be found in the \SOURCE\CHAP22 subdirectory on the CD-ROM.

It's unavoidable. After you find and eliminate one bottleneck, another will always be exposed. Let's look at an example to illustrate this point.

Say you have a server with a 100MHz Pentium processor, 32MB of main memory, a lightning-fast pair of EIDE disk drives, an EIDE disk controller, and a 16-bit network adapter, and your primary concern is providing a fast user response time for shared files and SQL Server access. Where do you think the performance bottleneck would be? in the processor? the memory? the disk subsystem? the network adapter? Based on my experience, it would probably turn out to be the disk subsystem. This would be caused by the EIDE, which would use the standard ATDISK driver provided with Windows NT Server; this driver can only support one pending I/O request at a time. It's not really the fault of the driver, but the hardware the driver supports. Almost all IDE (and EIDE) disk controllers use programmed I/O (or PIO). A PIO controller uses the processor to move data from the disk, through the disk controller, to system memory. This requires a high percentage of processor time and limits the device to one I/O request at a time.

The solution would be to replace the EIDE disks and controller with SCSI disk drives and a SCSI controller that supports direct memory access (DMA). A controller that supports DMA will move data from the disk to system memory without processor intervention.

But even here you need to exercise good judgment. Don't choose an 8-bit or a 16-bit SCSI controller if you have a 32-bit expansion bus; instead choose a 32-bit SCSI controller. The basic idea is to choose a disk controller with the largest I/O bus that your expansion bus supports for the fastest data transfer rate. Otherwise, the process requires copying data from the disk drive to memory below 1MB for an 8-bit controller and below 16MB for a 16-bit controller. The data will then have to be copied to the application or system buffer above 16MB if you have more than 16MB installed in your system. This copying of data is referred to as *double buffering* and can severely hamper system performance.

Now that you have increased the performance of your I/O subsystem compared to the base system, another performance bottleneck may be exposed. Most likely, this is the processor because SQL Server can be very processor intensive. Adding an additional Pentium processor and dedicating this processor to SQL Server will increase SQL Server performance. Once this has occurred, you'll probably find that replacing your current network adapter with a 32-bit network adapter and adding additional memory can increase performance even more. This can go on and on. Eventually, you will have to draw the line based on your budget and your acceptable performance requirements.

Finding Processor Bottlenecks

Finding processor bottlenecks on your server is not an easy task, but it is possible. To start, use the performance counters I have included in Processor.PMW. This workspace file includes processor chart, alert, and report view settings. These object counters are listed in Table 23.1, which includes a description of each object counter.

Table 23.1. Processor performance object counters.

Counter	Instance	Parent	Description
System Object			
% total processor time	N/A	N/A	This is the percentage of processor time that is currently in use on your system. The basic formula for calculation is ((% CPU in Use on CPU 0) + (% CPU in Use on CPU 1) ... + (% CPU in Use on CPU x)) / Total number of CPUs.
System calls/sec	N/A	N/A	The number of system service calls that are executed per second. If this value is lower than the number of interrupts/sec, a hardware adapter is generating excessive interrupts.
Context switches/sec	N/A	N/A	The frequency of switches between executing threads. A high value indicates that a program's use of critical sections or semaphores should have a higher priority to achieve a higher throughput and less task switching.
Processor queue length	N/A	N/A	The number of threads waiting in the processor queue for processor cycles. A consistent value of 2 or higher indicates a processor bottleneck. This value will always be 0 unless at least one thread is being monitored.
Interrupts/sec	Per processor	N/A	The number of interrupts the system is servicing.
Thread Object			
% processor time	Per processor	Idle	The percentage of processor time the thread is using.

Using a baseline chart, as shown in Figure 23.1, will help you become familiar with your system in an idle state. You should then use the same counters to obtain a baseline in a normal working state, which will help locate the processor bottleneck.

FIGURE 23.1.

Using Performance Monitor to isolate processor bottlenecks.

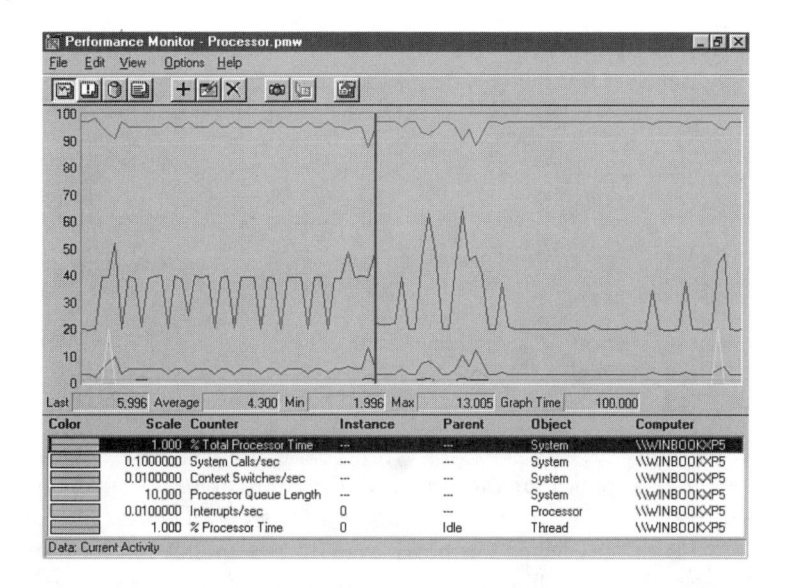

Next, use these counters on an active system. Examine the % Total Processor Time. If this value is consistently above 90 percent, you have a processor bottleneck. It is then time to examine each process in the system to see which one is using more of the processor than it should. If you have too many processes to view in a chart, you can use the report view. To select these processes, choose Edit|Add to Chart and select Process as the object type. Then select the % Processor Time for the Counter. Next, select each application listed in the Instance field. The process that has the highest peak is generally your performance bottleneck. Let's take a look at this process in a little more detail, with an example performance hog.

In a multithreaded environment, such as Windows NT Server, a processor shares CPU cycles among multiple threads. Each of these threads can be running or waiting for execution. For example, while an application is waiting for user input or is waiting for a disk I/O request, it is not scheduled for execution. That means other threads that can perform work will execute instead. However, this is based on the application design, and in this regard not all applications are created equal. Many applications have been ported from a different application environment and may not make efficient use of the Win32 APIs. If you had ported an MS-DOS application to a Win32 console application, for example, you may have left programming constructs that consumed processor cycles indiscriminately. These constructs may have constantly polled for user input, incremented a counter, or something similar. Here's an example of such a programming construct:

```c
#include <stdio.h>
#include <stdlib.h>

int main (void)
{
unsigned long uMaxNumber,x;
char chUserInput;

for(x=0;x=4294967295;x++)
{
uMaxNumber=x;
}
printf("Counter = %d", uMaxNumber);
chUserInput=getchar();

return (0);
}
```

When this application executes, it utilizes from 80 to 98 percent of the processor, as shown in Figure 23.2. This is the definition of a *processor-intensive application*. Notice that I have the process object selected for the BadExample.EXE application (or instance). This is the same object counter you will use (but of course you will use different process instances) to determine what percentage of the processor your applications are using and to determine which process is the bottleneck.

FIGURE 23.2.

An example of a processor-intensive application displayed with Performance Monitor.

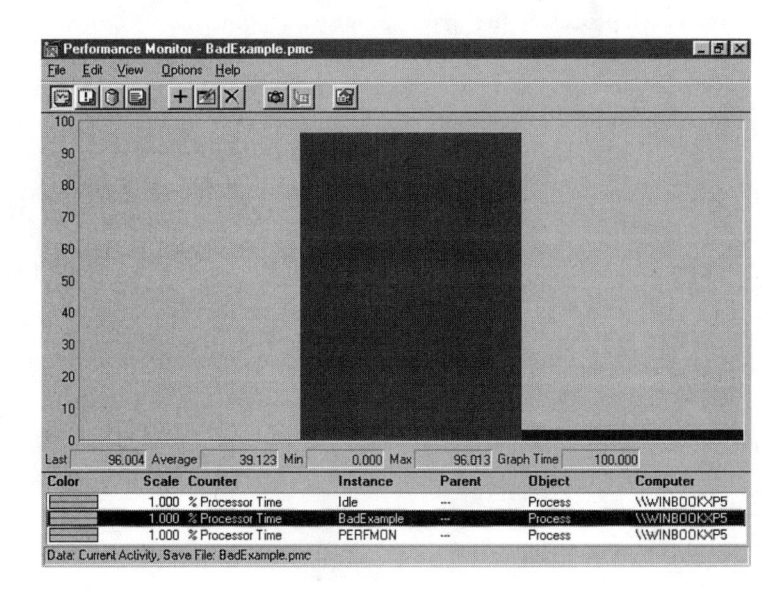

Tuning the Server

Chapter 23

The Visual C++ project file, source code, and executable for this application are included in the \SOURCE\CHAP23\BADEXP subdirectory on the CD-ROM and are called BadExp.mak, BadExp.C, and BadExp.EXE, respectively. On a uniprocessor system, this code snippet will use most of your available processor cycles. However, on a multiprocessor system, the other processors will remain available to process other application requests. If you have a multiprocessor system, try the BadExample.EXE application and add the Processor %Total Processor Time for each processor to your chart. One of these processors will show 80 to 98 percent utilization, while the other processors will continue to function normally.

To see how a multithreaded processor-intensive application affects performance on a multiprocessor system, take a look at BadExp3.mak, BadExp3.C, and BadExp3.EXE. These are multithreaded versions of the application. Each will spawn three threads and will equally distribute the load among them. This is demonstrated in Figure 23.3. My system is only a uniprocessor machine, so the load per thread is between 30 and 33 percent. But if you have three or more processors, then three of these processors should show 80 to 90 percent processor utilization. Notice in this example that the thread object has been selected. This is the object counter you will use to determine which thread of a process is the bottleneck in your processor.

FIGURE 23.3.
A multithreaded example of a processor-intensive application displayed with Performance Monitor.

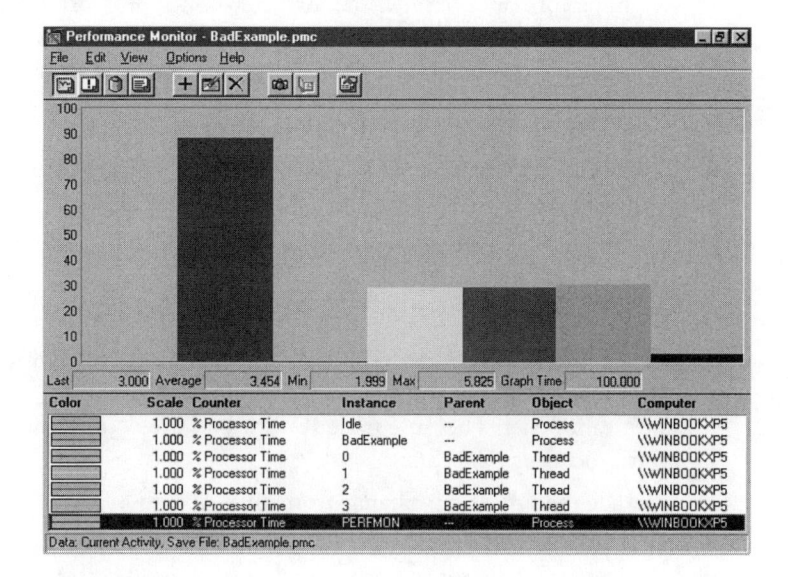

When you have isolated a processor-intensive application, what can you do about it? Well, there are several things you can do depending on your resources and the application.

If you have access to the source code, you can

- Use a profiler to modify the application to be less processor intensive. This could include making more efficient use of critical sections or semaphores. For example, if your application spawns multiple threads, you should set the thread priorities to make more efficient use of these control mechanisms. That way, the threads are not constantly being switched in and out of the processor queue and performing less work than the overhead involved in switching them in and out of the processor queue. The processor cycles consumed by switching the thread in and out of the processor queue (which would occur whenever the thread cannot access a data construct protected by a critical section) can be used by the thread to perform real work instead.
- Rewrite the application to spread the load by distributing it among several computers.
- Rewrite the application to use thread affinities so that the application would use a specific processor (or processors) in a multiprocessor system. This allows for higher system performance because the threads will not be constantly switched to different processors. As a thread is switched, it often requires that the processor cache be flushed to maintain data coherency. That slows down the overall system performance.

If you do not have access to the source code, you can try the following:

- Inform the manufacturer of the problem and try to get them to fix it.
- Run the application at off-peak times by using the Scheduler service.
- Start the application from the command line with the start command at a lower priority. For example, start *AppName* /low, where *AppName* is the name of the application to execute.
- Add additional processors. This will only benefit the system if you have multiple threads/processes to execute. For the Microsoft BackOffice products, this can provide significant benefits because these applications are designed with multithreading/ multiprocessing concepts.
- Upgrade the processor. Change from an 80486 to a Pentium, a Pentium to a Pentium Pro, or from an Intel processor to a RISC processor.
- Upgrade the processor to one with a larger internal cache. For example, the 486/DX4 (75MHz and 100MHz) models include a 16KB cache over the default 8KB cache of the other 486 models.
- Upgrade the secondary system cache. This item is quite important when adding additional memory to the system. As you increase system memory, the cache has to map a larger address space into the same size cache. This can increase the cache miss ratio and degrade performance.

Finding Memory Bottlenecks

If you do nothing else to your system, adding additional memory will almost always increase system performance. This is because Windows NT Server will use this memory instead of virtual memory and thus decrease paging. It will also be used by the cache manager to cache all data accesses. This includes remote (that is, network) or local resource access. The other Microsoft BackOffice components can also benefit from this increased memory. For example, SQL Server can use some of this memory for its data cache, its procedure cache, and for the temporary database.

Start with the big picture and then narrow down the search to a specific application to find the memory resource hog. A good starting point is to use the performance counters listed in Table 23.2 to see if you have a problem. If a problem is found, then you can use the process object's memory-related counters to see which application is the resource hog.

Table 23.2. Memory performance object counters.

Counter	Instance	Description
Memory Object		
Pages/sec	N/A	This item is the number of pages read from or written to disk to resolve memory references to pages that were not in physical memory at the time.
Available bytes	N/A	The amount of free virtual memory.
Committed bytes	N/A	The amount of memory that has been committed to use by the operating system as opposed to memory that has been merely reserved for use by the operating system.
Page faults/sec	N/A	The number of virtual memory page faults that occurred on the system because the physical page was not in the process's working set or main memory. A page may not need to be read from disk if the page is available on the standby list or is in use by another process that shares the page and has it in its working set.
Cache faults/sec	N/A	The number of page faults that occur in the cache manager in reference to a memory page that is not in the cache.
Paging File Object		
% usage	Per page file	The amount of use of a specific page file.
% usage peak	Per page file	The maximum use of a specific page file.

Part VII — Performance Tuning and Optimization Techniques

> **TIP**
>
> You can use the Windows NT Task Manager, accessible by right-clicking the taskbar and selecting Task Manager, to get a quick indication of your memory usage. Just click the Performance tab to display the Memory dialog. Check the Available value in the Physical Memory group to see if it is higher than 1MB for a Windows NT Server computer or 4MB for a Windows NT Workstation. If you don't have this much memory, you will have a performance degradation due to excessive paging.

The first step in isolating the memory bottleneck is to load the Memory.PMW workspace file into the Performance Monitor. This workspace includes basic counters for the chart, alert, and report views. Again, you want to obtain one baseline for an inactive system, and one for your normally active system. If you have a memory-intensive process, then your chart will look similar to the one shown in Figure 23.4. This particular chart is based on a log file (Memory.LOG) I captured while running the MemHog.EXE program. However, the same basic object counter activity will be displayed in real time for a memory-intensive application as well.

FIGURE 23.4.
An example of a systemwide memory shortage displayed with the Performance Monitor.

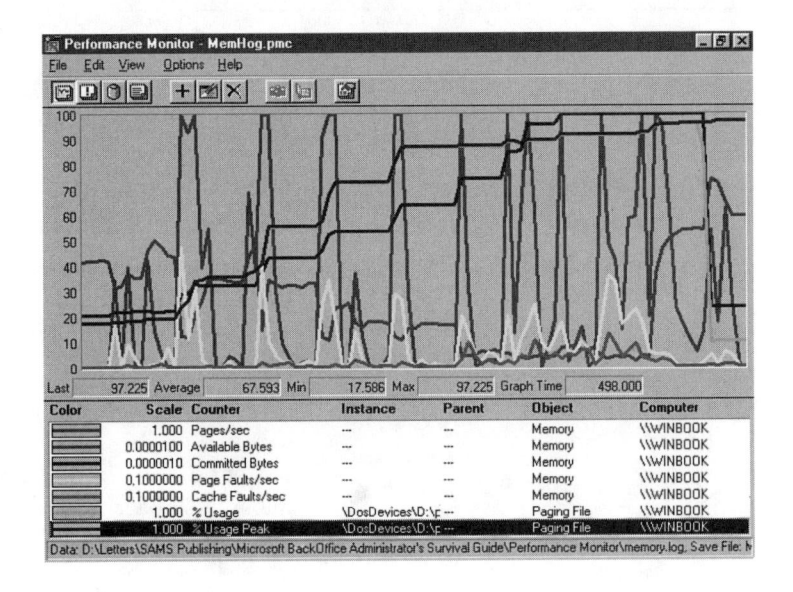

You should watch the behavior of these counters. The behavior displayed in the chart shown in Figure 23.4 is an indication of memory-related problems. Specifically, you should note the following behaviors:

- Pages/sec—Notice the high peaks for this counter. This indicates a great deal of paging activity, generally because your system does not contain enough physical memory to handle the demands placed on it by the application. If you see such activity on your system, you should look closer to see which application is placing such a load on the system. It may be normal behavior for the application, in which case you should add more physical memory to increase system performance.

- Page Faults/sec—Notice that the peaks here follow the peaks for the Pages/sec counter. That, too, is an indication that your system is paging heavily. A consistent value over 5 indicates that your system is paging more than it should; a consistent value of 10 or higher is a desperate cry for help. Adding physical memory is the only cure. In my example, these counters only peak to a high value and then drop back to a normal level. But on an active file or application server, the activity should be more linear.

- Available Bytes—This counter indicates the amount of virtual address space available to your system. As applications utilize memory and page to disk, this value will decrease. When it drops below 10MB, you will most likely see a message warning you that virtual memory is running low and urging you to close some applications or increase your virtual memory settings. If this counter is consistently low after running an application, it generally indicates a system memory leak.

- Committed Bytes—As the Available Bytes counter decreases, the Committed Bytes counter increases. This demonstrates that the process is allocating memory from the virtual address space, but is not necessarily using it. Still, your virtual address space is a limited resource, and you should watch this counter to check for applications which allocate memory, but do not use it. This behavior should be noted, and you should discuss it with the manufacturer. Notice in my example that this counter steps up as the paging file activity steps up. This is an indication that the application is making use of the memory it is allocating. Consistently high values are an indication that adding physical memory will increase system performance. You should also note the counter value when an application ends. If this counter does not return to the original value, the application has a memory leak or a hidden process that is not terminating properly.

- Cache Faults/sec—This counter should be compared with Page Faults/sec to determine whether you actually are paging too much in a normal system. If this counter reads less than the Page Faults/sec counter, you are definitely paging too much and should add physical memory.
- Usage—This counter indicates your current paging file activity. If this value is consistently larger than your minimum paging file size, you should increase your minimum paging file size. A significant amount of system overhead is involved in growing the page file, and any page file growth is not *contiguous*, which means that more overhead is involved in accessing pages stored in this section of the page file. Notice here that the paging file use is incremental in steps of 10MB, and when the application terminates, the usage counter drops back to the original (or slightly smaller) value. If your usage counter does not return to the original value after running an application, then it has either a memory leak or a hidden process that is not terminating.
- Usage Peak—This counter indicates the maximum use of your page file. If this value consistently reaches 90 percent, your virtual address space is too small and the size of your paging file should be increased. When the counter hits above 75 percent, you will generally notice a significant system performance degradation.

> **NOTE**
>
> The MemHog.EXE program and make file can be found in the SOURCE\CHAP23\MEMHOG subdirectory. This program allocates up to 100MB of memory, in 1MB allotments. For every 10MB of memory allocated, the program sleeps for 30 seconds. I have the program suspend execution for 30 seconds per 10MB so that the system will use quite a bit of the processor to grow the pagefile and allocate the memory during heavy use of the paging file. This high-volume processor utilization will mask the memory utilization curve of the application.
>
> The purpose of this program is to simulate an application that is making heavy use of your system memory. You will not find many commercial programs that actually allocate 100MB in less than 10 seconds. Also, the program uses the memset command to populate each 1MB memory block with a series of asterisks. This is so the memory is actually accessed. If you do not perform this step, the memory will be merely allocated, but not used. The Committed Bytes object counter will then max out momentarily as the virtual memory address space is increased, but no paging activity will take place because no memory was physically used.

The previous example, shown in Figure 23.4, illustrates a general systemwide memory-related problem. But in the real world, you need to find the specific cause of the problem. This, too, can be achieved with the Performance Monitor. Instead of looking at systemwide object counters, you want to narrow the search to the process object counters to find the process that is using your system memory.

Note that this looks quite similar to the display shown in Figure 23.4. You should see the same basic peaks for Memory Page Faults/sec as for Process Page Faults/sec, although if you directly overlay the Memory Page Faults/sec with the Process Page Faults/sec, you will notice that the Memory counter is a bit higher than the Process counter. This is because the Memory counter is a systemwide counter and includes other paging activity from other processes. The corresponding system to process counters are displayed in Table 23.3 to aid you in your analysis.

Table 23.3. Corresponding system to process object counters.

Counter	*Process Counter*
Memory Object	
Page Faults/sec	Page Faults/sec
Available Bytes	Virtual Bytes
Committed Bytes	Private Bytes
Paging File Object	
Usage	Page File Bytes
Usage Peak	Page File Bytes Peak

Because I knew which process was the problem, my chart only includes the MemHog application. In order to find a real-world application problem, you should select all the process instances except for the system processes unless you are looking for a system process memory leak. A couple other process object counters you may find useful in your diagnosis of a memory intensive application are

- Pool Nonpaged Bytes—The nonpaged pool is a system resource area devoted to system components. Allocations from this area cannot be paged out to disk. This is a finite resource; if you run out of nonpaged pool bytes, some system services may fail.

- Pool Paged Bytes—The paged pool is also a system resource area devoted to system components, but allocations from this area may be paged to disk. However, it is also a finite resource, so if you run out of paged pool bytes a system service may fail.

> **NOTE**
>
> Both the Pool Paged Bytes and Pool Nonpaged Bytes counters are very useful in tracking down a process that is incorrectly making system calls and using all the available pool bytes.

- Virtual Bytes Peak—This counter is the maximum size of the virtual memory address space used by the process.
- Working Set—This counter indicates the size of the application's working set (the amount of memory assigned by the operating system for use by the application) in bytes. The working set includes pages that have been used by the process's threads. When memory is low, pages will be trimmed from the working set to provide additional memory for other processes. As the pages are needed, they will be pulled from main memory if the page has not already been removed or read from the paging file.
- Working Set Peak—This counter indicates the maximum working-set size in bytes.

> **TIP**
>
> By monitoring the working set for a particular process and comparing it to the Working Set Peak, you can determine whether adding memory will increase the performance of the process. The idea here is to add memory until the working set and Working Set Peak values are equal. This will provide the maximum benefit to the process. You should consider that this may prove to be an unrealistic goal if your budget is limited.

Finding Disk Bottlenecks

Finding disk bottlenecks is easier than finding processor or memory bottlenecks because disk bottleneck performance degradations are readily apparent. There are only four performance counters to monitor for bottlenecks:

- % Disk Time—This counter is the percentage of elapsed time that the disk is servicing read or write requests. It also includes the time the disk driver is waiting in the disk queue.

- Disk Queue Length—This counter indicates the number of pending I/O service requests. A value greater than 2 indicates a disk bottleneck. On a multidisk subsystem, such as a striped set or striped set with parity, a little calculating is needed to determine the presence of a disk bottleneck. The basic formula is

    Disk Queue Length - Number of Physical Disk drives in the multidisk configuration

    If this value is greater than 2, it indicates a disk bottleneck. For example, if you have a striped set with 3 disk drives, and a queue length of 5, you get an acceptable value of 2 (5 = 3 = 2).

- Avg. Disk Transfer/sec—This counter is the time in seconds of the average disk transfer. However, it is not used just to gain this information; rather, it is used in connection with the Memory Pages/sec counter.

- Memory Pages/sec—Use this counter with the Avg. Disk Transfer/sec counter in the following formula to determine how much of your disk bandwidth is used for paging:

    Percent Disk Time Used for Paging = (Memory Pages/sec × Avg. Disk Transfer/sec) × 100.

When I perform disk diagnostics, I break my Performance Monitor charts into two different settings. I use the % Disk Time, Disk Queue Length, and Avg. Disk Transfer/sec counters previously mentioned, plus the Memory Pages/sec from the logical disk object, to determine the performance of the disk on a drive-letter basis. I then use the same counters from the physical disk object to determine my hardware disk performance. If you look in the SOURCE\CHAP23 subdirectory on the CD-ROM, you will find the LogicalDisk.PMW and PhysicalDisk.PMW Performance Monitor workspace files. These files include basic chart, alert, and report examples for you to use as a starting point.

To see these examples in action, run two copies of the Performance Monitor, loading LogicalDisk.PMW into one copy and PhysicalDisk.PMW into the other. Then run the DiskHog.EXE program. This program takes one command-line argument—the drive letter to write its data file to (for example, DiskHog H:). The default, if no drive letter is specified, is drive C:. This program will write up to 1,000 1MB blocks of data to the file DumpFile.DAT, which can total almost 1GB.

The purpose of this program is twofold. First, it can be used to demonstrate disk activity on logical drives (as shown in Figure 23.5) and disk activity on physical drives (as shown in Figure 23.6). Second, the program can be used to test your alert conditions for low disk space. When the program finishes writing the data file, it informs you of how much data was written and prompts you to press a key to continue. At this point, it will delete the data file it created.

> **NOTE**
>
> Remember that `DiskHog.EXE` is a simulation designed to overload your disk I/O subsystem. It cannot be used to demonstrate a normal usage pattern for a file server. It is designed to illustrate detection of performance bottlenecks with the Performance Monitor.

> **CAUTION**
>
> If you run this program and place the data file on a compressed drive, it will most likely run to completion and write almost a gigabyte of data, even if you have fewer than a couple of hundred megabytes free on the drive. This is because the data block it writes is composed of 1MB blocks of asterisks (*) and is easily compressible.

FIGURE 23.5.
An example of a disk-intensive application displayed with Performance Monitor on logical drives.

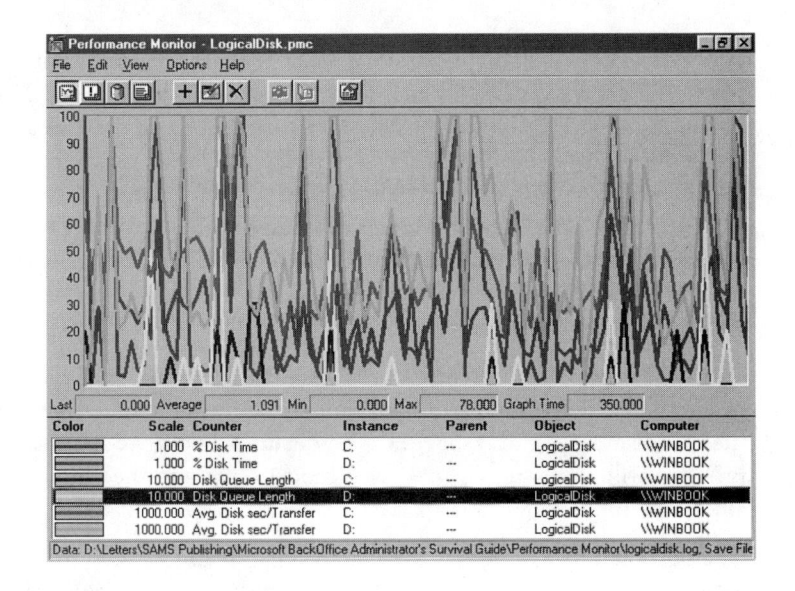

FIGURE 23.6.
An example of a disk-intensive application displayed with Performance Monitor on physical drives.

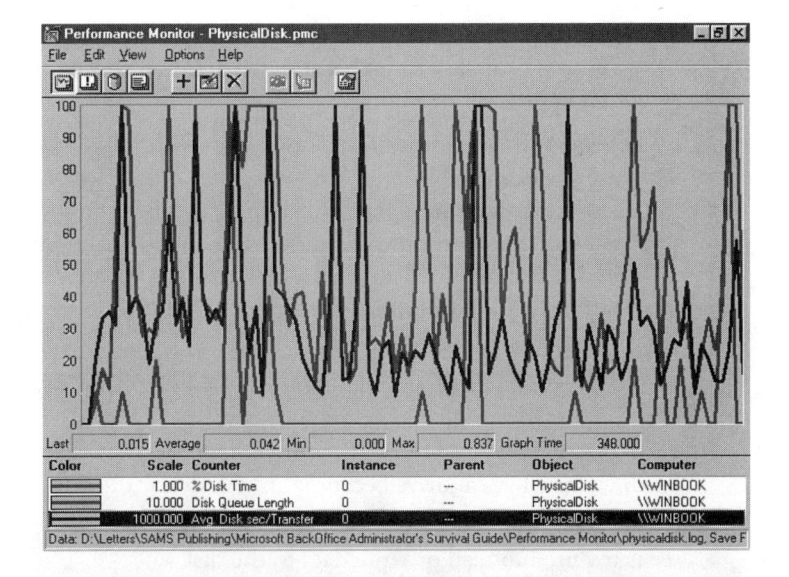

> **TIP**
>
> When using Performance Monitor to determine disk activities, you may want to change the default capture rate. I break mine down into intervals of 5 seconds, 1 second, 1/10 second, and 1/100 second, depending on the amount of data I want to capture and the server activity.

If you find a bottleneck, there are several options for you to implement aside from those mentioned in the beginning of this section:

- Create a mirror set. This can double your read performance if your disk driver can support multiple asynchronous I/O requests. This rules out most IDE and EIDE controllers, which use the default ATDISK driver.

- Create a striped set with or without parity. This can increase both read and write performance if your disk driver can support multiple asynchronous I/O requests. Your best bet is to use a 32-bit SCSI bus master controller.

- If your budget is limited, spend your money on a fast SCSI controller and average disk drives (in terms of seek time) because the SCSI controller has more of an impact on a two-drive system.
- If you have sufficient funds, purchase drives with the lowest possible seek time to optimize your disk subsystem. This is because the time spent seeking tracks (to find the data) versus the time spent transferring the data is on the order of 10 to 1 or higher. That simply means your disk drives spend more time searching for data than they do transferring the data. Faster seek times mean there will be less time wasted looking for the data and more time spent transferring the data.
- Distribute the work load (one reason to use the LogicalDisk.PMW example) to place highly accessed data files on different drives. For example, you can place the application files for Microsoft Office on your first physical drive and your SQL Server databases on your second physical drive. Do not place them on different logical drives on the same physical drive because this will defeat the purpose of distributing the load.
- If you use a FAT file system, defragment it occasionally. This will prevent the multiple seeks required to read or write data to the disk.
- If you have volume over 400MB, you should choose the NTFS file system. NTFS partitions make more efficient use of the disk to provide better performance. For example, a FAT partition can support a maximum of 65,536 clusters. On a large partition, the cluster size may be as large as 64KB. A cluster is the minimum allocation unit, so if you store a 512-byte file, you have wasted 63.5KB. NTFS partitions can have up to 2^{64} clusters to access the partition, so the cluster size can be much smaller and therefore waste less space.

> **NOTE**
>
> Executive Software has a disk defragmenter called DiskKeeper that runs as a Windows NT service. It can defragment both your NTFS and FAT partitions.

Finding Network Bottlenecks

Chapter 4, "Choosing a Platform for Windows NT Server," discusses most of the network performance tuning options provided by the graphical interface tools such as the Control Panel applets and the hardware alternatives. However, you may want to look in Appendix C, "The Registry Editor and Registry Keys," which includes some other mechanisms for configuring the Windows NT services. Keep in mind that altering any of the registry keys may prevent a Windows NT service from automatically tuning itself for maximum performance. I have included another sample Performance Monitor workspace file, displayed in Figure 23.7, called Network.PMW. This includes a chart, alert, and report view to aid you in your network diagnostics.

FIGURE 23.7.
Using Performance Monitor to isolate network bottlenecks.

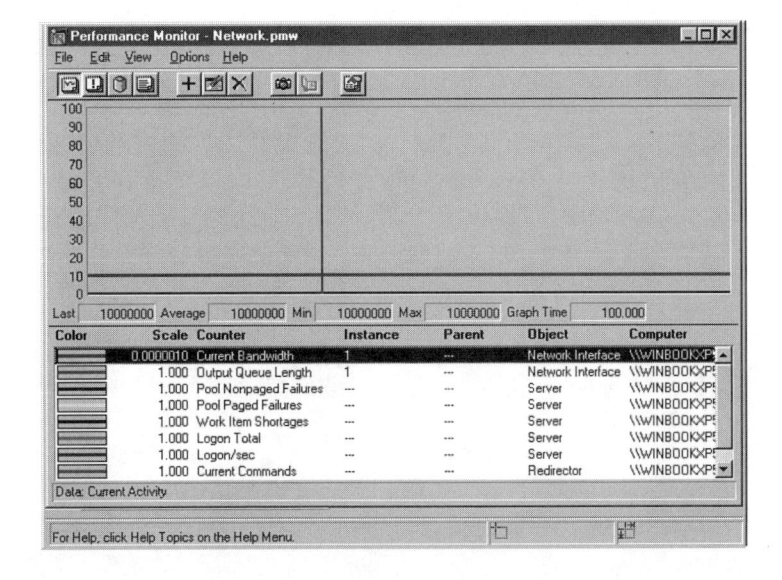

The performance object counters included in the chart and alert views are provided to give you a means to monitor how busy your server is and to determine basic network utilization. The object counters I consider important for these determinations are summarized in Table 23.4.

Table 23.4. Summary of network performance counters.

Counter	Instance	Description
	Network Interface Object	
Current Bandwidth	Per interface	An estimated value of the current network utilization in bits per second.
	Network Segment Object	
Network Utilization	Per adapter	An estimated value of the percentage of the network bandwidth currently in use on the network segment.
	Server Object	
Pool Nonpaged Failures	N/A	The number of times allocations from the nonpaged memory pool have failed.
Pool Paged Failures	N/A	The number of times allocations from the paged memory pool have failed.

continues

Table 23.4. continued

Counter	Instance	Description
Server Object		
Work Item Shortages	N/A	The number of times a work item could not be allocated. This counter can indicate that the `InitWorkItems` and `MaxWorkItems` parameters for the LanMan Server service need to be increased.
Logons Total	N/A	This number is a total count, since the computer was last rebooted, of all interactive logons, remote logons, service logons, and failed logons.
Logons/sec	N/A	The rate at which all interactive logons, remote logons, service logons, and failed logons are occurring.
Server Work Queues Object		
Work Item Shortages	Per processor	The number of failed work-item allocations. A number greater than 1 indicates that the `MaxWorkItem` parameter should be increased.
Queue Length	Per processor	This counter indicates the current number of requests currently waiting in the server queue. A number consistently higher than 4 indicates that a faster processor could improve performance.
Redirector Object		
Current Commands	N/A	Indicates the number of outstanding network requests waiting to be serviced. If this number is greater than the number of network adapters installed in the computer, a network bottleneck is present. Adding an additional network adapter may increase performance.

Counter	Instance	Description
Network Errors/sec	N/A	Indicates that serious network errors have occurred. These errors are generally logged in the system event log, so you should look there for further information. If an error occurs, you should take immediate notice and attempt to resolve the situation.

> **NOTE**
>
> The Network Interface Current Bandwidth counter will only be available if you install the Network Monitor Agent. It can be used to determine whether your network is overloaded. A value of 50000000.0000 is the 50-percent mark, which indicates that you should consider segmenting your network. Some network administrators prefer to plan for additional growth and will split the network segment at the 30-percent to 40-percent mark. The Network Segment Network Utilization counter only applies if you have the TCP/IP protocol installed. This counter is in fractional percentages, and at an indication of 50 percent or higher, the network segment should be split as well.

Finding IIS Bottlenecks

Depending on the size and activity of your Internet Information Server installation, you may run into a few performance-related problems. But before you try to configure the IIS services for better performance, you should try using the Performance Monitor to look at processor, memory, disk, or network bottlenecks, as described in the previous sections. Only after you have done your best to solve those problems should you move on to optimizing your IIS services. The good news is that there are several IIS counters you can use to determine just how heavy a load your IIS server is carrying, as well as counters to scrutinize each service.

You should start your performance tuning with the general IIS counters, described in Table 23.5, to get a basic look at how well your IIS server is performing. To determine how well a specific service is performing, you can use the counters in Table 23.6 for your WWW Publishing service, Table 23.7 for your FTP Publishing service, and Table 23.8 for your Gopher Publishing service. You should pay particular attention to the global cache counters mentioned in Table 23.5 because you may modify the size of this cache by modifying the registry key

`HKEY_LOCAL_MACHINE\System\CurrentControlSet\Services\InetInfo\Parameters\MemoryCacheSize`. The default is to allocate 3MB (3072000 bytes), and the legal values range from 0 (which disables caching entirely) to FFFFFFF (or 4GB). If you are encountering large numbers of cache flushes or misses or if you have a poor hit ratio, increasing this value may improve performance. You should be careful, however, to make sure that you only use physical memory that is not required by the base operating system or SQL Server; otherwise, you may affect these systems and cause poor IIS performance.

Table 23.5. Summary of global IIS performance counters.

Counter	Description
Cache Flushes	Specifies how often a cached memory region expired due to changes in IIS files or the directory tree.
Cache Hits	Specifies how often a reference to a file, a directory tree, or an IIS-specific object was found in the cache.
Cache Hits %	Specifies the hit ratio of all cache requests.
Cache Misses	Specifies how often a reference to a file, a directory tree, or an IIS-specific object was not found in the cache.
Cache Size	Specifies the size of the shared memory cache.
Cache Used	Specifies the total number of bytes in use (file handles, IIS-specific objects, and so on) in the cache.
Cached File Handles	The total number of file handles contained in the cache.
Current Blocked Async I/O Requests	The total number of current asynchronous I/O requests blocked by the bandwidth throttle.
Directory Listings	Specifies the total number of directory listings contained in the cache.
Measured Asnyc I/O Bandwidth Usage	Specifies the total amount of asynchronous I/O bandwidth average over a minute.
Objects	Specifies the total number of objects (file handle objects, directory listing objects, and so on) contained in the cache.

Counter	Description
Total Allowed Async I/O Requests	The total number of asynchronous I/O requests permitted by the bandwidth throttle.
Total Blocked Async I/O Requests	The total number of asynchronous I/O requests blocked by the bandwidth throttle.
Total Rejected Async I/O Requests	The total number of asynchronous I/O requests rejected by the bandwidth throttle.

Table 23.6. Summary of HTTP service performance counters.

Counter	Description
Bytes Received/sec	Specifies the rate (in bytes per second) at which the HTTP server is receiving data.
Bytes Sent/sec	Specifies the rate (in bytes per second) at which the HTTP server is transmitting data.
Bytes Total/sec	Specifies the total amount of data that is being transmitted, or received, by the HTTP server in bytes/second.
CGI Requests	Specifies the number of Common Gateway Interface (CGI) requests received by the HTTP server.
Connection Attempts	Specifies the total number of attempts made to connect to the HTTP server.
Connections/sec	Specifies the number of connections to the HTTP server per second.
Current Anonymous Users	Specifies how many anonymous users are currently connected to the HTTP server.
Connection Attempts	Specifies the number of times a connection to the server was attempted.
Current CGI Requests	Specifies how many CGI requests are currently being processed by the HTTP server.
Current Connections	Specifies the current number of connections to the HTTP server.

continues

Table 23.6. continued

Counter	Description
Current ISAPI Extension Requests	Specifies the current number of ISAPI requests being processed by the server.
Current NonAnonymous Users	Specifies the total number of users currently connected to the HTTP server using a domain user account.
File Received	Specifies the total number of files received by the HTTP server.
File Sent	Specifies the total number of files transmitted by the HTTP server.
File Total	Specifies the sum of the total number of files transmitted and received.
Get Requests	Specifies the total number of HTTP requests using the GET method.
Head Requests	Specifies the total number of HTTP requests using the HEAD method.
ISAPI Extension Requests	Specifies the total number of ISAPI requests being processed by the server.
Logon Requests	Specifies the total number of logon attempts that have been made by the HTTP server.
Maximum Number of Anonymous Users	Specifies the maximum number of simultaneously connected anonymous users.
Maximum CGI Requests	Specifies the maximum number of simultaneous CGI requests processed by the HTTP server.
Maximum Connection	Specifies the maximum number of simultaneous connections to the HTTP server.
Maximum ISAPI Extension Requests	Specifies the maximum number of simultaneous ISAPI requests processed by the HTTP server.
Maximum NonAnonymous Users	Specifies the maximum number of simultaneously connected users using a domain user account.
Not Found Errors	Specifies the total number of requests that failed because of a missing document.

Counter	Description
Other Requested Methods	Specifies the total number of HTTP requests that do not use the GET, HEAD, or POST methods. This can include PUT, DELETE, LINK, or other methods.
Post Requests	Specifies the total number of HTTP requests using the POST method.
Total Anonymous Users	Specifies the total number of anonymous users that have ever connected to the HTTP server.
Total NonAnonymous Users	Specifies the total number of users that have ever connected to the HTTP server using a domain user account.

Table 23.7. Summary of the FTP server performance counters.

Counter	Description
Bytes Received/sec	Specifies the rate (in bytes per second) at which the FTP server is receiving data.
Bytes Sent/sec	Specifies the rate (in bytes per second) at which the FTP server is transmitting data.
Bytes Total/sec	Specifies the total amount of data that is being transmitted, or received, by the FTP server in bytes per second.
Current Anonymous Users	Specifies how many anonymous users are currently connected to the FTP server.
Current Connections	Specifies the current number of connections to the FTP server.
Current NonAnonymous Users	Specifies the total number of users currently connected to the FTP server using a domain user account.
File Received	Specifies the total number of files received by the FTP server.
File Sent	Specifies the total number of files transmitted by the FTP server.

continues

Table 23.7. continued

Counter	Description
Logon Attempts	Specifies the total number of logon attempts that have been made by the FTP server.
Maximum Anonymous Users	Specifies the maximum number of simultaneously connected anonymous users.
Maximum Connections	Specifies the maximum number of simultaneous connections to the FTP server.
Maximum NonAnonymous Users	Specifies the maximum number of simultaneous connected users using a domain user account.
Total Anonymous Users	Specifies the total number of anonymous users that have ever connected to the FTP server.
Total NonAnonymous Users	Specifies the total number of users that have ever connected to the FTP server using a domain user account.

Table 23.8. Summary of Gopher service performance counters.

Counter	Description
Aborted Connections	Specifies the total number of connections that failed due to errors or over-limit requests made to the Gopher server.
Bytes Received/sec	Specifies the rate (in bytes per second) at which the Gopher server is receiving data.
Bytes Sent/sec	Specifies the rate (in bytes per second) at which the Gopher server is transmitting data.
Bytes Total/sec	Specifies the total amount of data that is being transmitted, or received, by the Gopher server in bytes per second.
Connection Attempts	Specifies the total number of attempts made to connect to the Gopher server.
Connections in Error	Specifies the number of errors that occurred while being processed by the Gopher server.

Counter	Description
Current Anonymous Users	Specifies how many anonymous users are currently connected to the Gopher server.
Current Connections	Specifies the current number of connections to the Gopher server.
Current NonAnonymous Users	Specifies the total number of users currently connected to the Gopher server using a domain user account.
Directory Listing Sent	Specifies the total number of directory listings transmitted by the Gopher server.
File Sent	Specifies the total number of files transmitted by the Gopher server.
File Total	Specifies the sum of the total number of files transmitted and received.
Gopher Plus Requests	Specifies the total number of Gopher Plus requests received by the Gopher server.
Logon Requests	Specifies the total number of logon attempts that have been made by the Gopher server.
Maximum Anonymous Users	Specifies the maximum number of simultaneously connected anonymous users.
Maximum NonAnonymous Users	Specifies the maximum number of simultaneously connected users using a domain user account.
Maximum Connections	Specifies the maximum number of simultaneously connected users to the Gopher server.
Searches Sent	Specifies the total number of searches performed by the Gopher server.
Total Anonymous Users	Specifies the total number of anonymous users which have ever connected to the Gopher server.
Total NonAnonymous Users	Specifies the total number of users that have ever connected to the Gopher server using a domain user account.

Configuring SQL Server

After you optimize Windows NT Server to provide the best possible performance, you can turn your attention to configuring SQL Server. After you make your SQL Server configuration changes, you might need to make changes to your Windows NT Server configuration to fine-tune its performance. The easiest way to modify SQL Server's configuration is with the SQL Enterprise Manager; however, you can use an ISQL command-line prompt if you prefer. This section looks at the various options and describes both the good and bad sides of these options. In the next section, you will look at using the Performance Monitor to help you determine whether your configuration choices are working as well as expected.

The first step is to load the SQL Enterprise Manager. Next, click a registered server to connect to the SQL Server installation you want to configure. Then right-click the server name and choose Configure from the pop-up menu. The Server/Configuration dialog box will appear. Choose the Configuration tab to display the available options on the properties sheet. To change the current value, enter a new value in the Current column for the specific option. Repeat this step for each option you want to change. After you make all your modifications, click the OK button to return to the SQL Enterprise Manager main window. Table 23.9 lists the options you can change.

> **TIP**
>
> To set any of these options from an ISQL command prompt, you can use the stored procedure `sp_configure`. The basic syntax follows:
>
> `sp_configure 'option', 'value'`
>
> where `option` and `value` are specified in Table 23.9.

Table 23.9. The SQL Server configuration options.

Option	Minimum Value	Maximum Value	Default Value	Requires Restart to be Placed in Effect	Description
allow updates	0	1	0	No	Specifies that users with appropriate permissions will be able to modify system tables directly. Use this option with care because it is possible to damage system tables

Option	Minimum Value	Maximum Value	Default Value	Requires Restart to be Placed in Effect	Description
					and corrupt a database quite easily.
backup buffer size	1	10	1	No	Specifies the size (in 32-page increments) of the dump and load buffers used to increase the backup performance.
backup threads	0	32	5	Yes	Specifies the number of threads to be reserved for striped operations (such as a dump or load).
database size	2	10,000	2	Yes	Specifies the default size, in megabytes, for newly created databases. This minimum size is based on the model database. If you make a change to the model database, it determines the minimum size of all databases created after the change.
Default language	0	9,999	0	Yes	Specifies the default language to use with SQL Server. It is best (and easiest) to set this value using the SQL Server Setup utility.
fill factor	0	100	0	Yes	Specifies how full (a percentage from 0 to 100, where 0 specifies the SQL Server default) the data page will be whenever SQL Server creates a new index. You can override this value by

continues

Table 23.9. continued

Option	Minimum Value	Maximum Value	Default Value	Requires Restart to be Placed in Effect	Description
					using the CREATE INDEX command.
language in cache	3	100	3	No	Specifies the maximum number of languages that can be held simultaneously in the system cache.
LE threshold maximum	2	500,000	200	N/A	Specifies the maximum number of page locks that can be held before escalating to a table lock.
LE threshold percent	0	100	0	N/A	Specifies the percentage of page locks that can be held on a table before escalating to a table lock.
locks	5000	2,147,483,647	5000	Yes	Specifies how many locks are available for use by SQL Server. Each lock requires about 32 bytes of memory. If you run out of locks, a process fails or it is suspended until a lock is available. I recommend that you specify a minimum of 50,000 locks. You may need more if you have complex stored procedures or queries, or a large number of users accessing SQL Server.
logwrite sleep	1	500	0	N/A	Specifies the time, in milliseconds, before a write to the log that a delay will occur if the buffer is not full.

Option	Minimum Value	Maximum Value	Default Value	Requires Restart to be Placed in Effect	Description
max async IO	1	50	8	Yes	Specifies the maximum number of asynchronous I/O requests that can be issued by SQL Server. Increase this value if you have a stripe set, a stripe set with parity, or a RAID 5 hardware array. I recommend that you increase this value by half the number of spindles in the system. If you have five disk drives, for example, the entry should be 20 ($(5 \times 8) / 2 = 20$). You can increase this value if you have an exceptionally fast I/O subsystem.
max text repl size	0	2,147,483,647	65,536	N/A	Specifies the maximum size, in bytes, of text or image data that can be added to a replicated column in a single `insert`, `update`, `writetext`, or `updatetext` statement.
max worker threads	10	1,024	255	Yes	Specifies the maximum number of threads SQL Server can use to support client connections and perform internal maintenance. Increasing this value if you have more than one processor installed on the system can improve performance.

continues

Table 23.9. continued

Option	Minimum Value	Maximum Value	Default Value	Requires Restart to be Placed in Effect	Description
media retention	0	365	0	Yes	Specifies the time you plan to keep each disk used for a database or transaction log.
memory	1000	1,048,576	Based on amount of memory installed	Yes	Specifies the number of 2KB units to be used by SQL Server. This is the number one item to change for maximum performance. I recommend that you allocate as much memory as possible for SQL Server's usage. You should leave a minimum of 16MB for Windows NT Server, however. If you have additional services, such as Services for Macintosh, Gateway Services for Novell, DHCP, WINS, and so on, plan on allocating an additional 2MB per service. You can allocate any leftover memory to SQL Server. In a 64MB system, for example, I generally allocate between 32MB and 48MB to SQL Server.
nested triggers	0	1	1	Yes	Specifies whether nested triggers are enabled (1) or disabled (0).

Option	Minimum Value	Maximum Value	Default Value	Requires Restart to be Placed in Effect	Description
network packet size	512	32,767	4096	No	Specifies the size, in bytes, of the network packet size to use. This value can be overridden by the client application.
open databases	5	32,767	20	Yes	Specifies the maximum number of databases that can be opened simultaneously. Each database allocation consumes about 1KB of system memory.
open objects	100	2,147,483,647	500	Yes	Specifies the maximum number of database objects that can be opened simultaneously. Each object allocation consumes about 70 bytes.
procedure cache	1	99	30	Yes	Specifies the amount of memory (a percentage from 0 to 100 percent) to allocate to the procedure cache after the SQL Server allocation demands have been satisfied. If you modify the default settings for memory allocations as recommended, you also may want to change this value. In a high-memory system (64MB or more), I recommend a value between 30 and 40

continues

Table 23.9. continued

Option	Minimum Value	Maximum Value	Default Value	Requires Restart to be Placed in Effect	Description
					percent, depending on the number of users and active stored procedures.
RA worker threads	0	255	3	N/A	Specifies the number of read-ahead worker threads to allocate.
recovery flags	0	1	0	Yes	Specifies what information SQL Server displays during the recovery process. If you are having problems, setting this value to 1 enables additional diagnostic messages that may help to isolate the problem.
recovery interval	1	32,767	5	No	Specifies the maximum number of minutes SQL Server can use to recover a database. Increase this value if you have very complex or large databases.
remote access	0	1	0	Yes	Specifies that remote SQL Servers can access this server (1) or cannot access this server (0).
remote conn timeout	-1	32,767	10	N/A	Specifies the maximum number of minutes to wait before closing inactive server-to-server connections.

Option	Minimum Value	Maximum Value	Default Value	Requires Restart to be Placed in Effect	Description
tempdb	0	2044	0	Yes	Specifies the size (in MB) of RAM to allocate for temporary databases. This is the second most important performance option that you can use because the temporary database is constantly in use for temporary objects (tables, procedures, sorts, and so on). Use this option with care, however, because it directly affects the amount of available RAM that can be used by other system processes. If you have more than 64MB of RAM, it certainly will benefit you to use an additional 16MB to 64MB of RAM for the temporary database, depending on the type of queries you will be executing.
user connections	5	32,767	10	Yes	Specifies the maximum number of simultaneous user connections that can be established with this server. Each connection consumes about 37KB of system memory. This value should be based on the number

continues

Table 23.9. continued

Option	Minimum Value	Maximum Value	Default Value	Requires Restart to be Placed in Effect	Description
					of legal license agreements you have purchased, and, for what it's worth, it is better to have a few too many connections than to run out of available connections. At the very least, you should use the SQL Administrator to check for connections that have been terminated but not removed from SQL Server's connection list and manually terminate them to free up available connections.
user options	0	4,096	0	N/A	Specifies a bit mask to be used to set various user options which may be overridden on a per-user basis using the SET command.

> **NOTE**
>
> Many of the changes you make will be put into effect only after you shut down and restart SQL Server.

SQL Server for Windows NT includes performance counters you can use to monitor the activity of your server for informational purposes and to fine-tune the performance of your SQL

Server installation. If you look in the SQL Server for Windows NT Program Manager group, you will find a predefined set of performance counters you can use to check the basic activity of your server. It's not always enough to use just these settings, however, which is why I have included Table 23.10. You can use this table to determine which counters may be of interest to you.

> **NOTE**
>
> Depending on which version of SQL Server you are using, the counters may be different.

Table 23.10. The SQL Server Performance Monitor counters.

Object	Counter	Description
SQLServer	I/O Log Writes/sec	Specifies the number of log pages written to disk per second. Because almost all database activity is transaction based, which means that changes must be written to the log before they can be applied to the database, this is a good counter to watch to determine whether your disk is a bottleneck for SQL Server performance.
SQLServer	I/O Batch Writes/sec	Specifies the number of asynchronous writes in a single batch (generally as part of the checkpoint process). The higher the value, the better the SQL Server performance. Monitor this value as you make changes to segment and device allocations to see whether your changes are increasing or decreasing performance.
SQLServer	I/O Batch Average Size	Specifies the average number of pages (2KB) written to disk during a batch operation. The higher the value, the better. You can use this counter to determine whether your changes to the `max async i/o` parameter are effective. If you increase the `max async i/o` value too much, this counter decreases.

continues

Table 23.10. continued

Object	Counter	Description
SQLServer	I/O Batch Max Size	Specifies the maximum number of pages (2KB) that have been written to disk. The higher the value, the better the overall performance. This counter also can be used to determine whether the max asyon i/o parameter setting is effective. If this counter lowers after your changes, decrease the value for the max async i/o parameter.
SQLServer	I/O Page Reads/sec	Specifies the number of physical disk reads per second. The lower the number, the better. If this value is too high, you can change the procedure cache percentage to increase the amount of memory allocated to the data cache. A larger data cache lowers the number of physical disk reads.
SQLServer	I/O Single page Writes/sec	Specifies the number of physical disk writes per second. Like the I/O Page Reads/sec counter, a lower number is better. If a high value is encountered, it might be beneficial to increase the size of the data cache.
SQLServer	I/O Outstanding Reads	Specifies the number of pending physical disk reads. You can use this value to determine how well your I/O subsystem is performing. A high value over an extended period of time is an indication that the I/O subsystem is a bottleneck in SQL Server performance.
SQLServer	I/O Outstanding Writes	Specifies the number of pending physical disk writes. Like the I/O Outstanding Reads counter, a high value over an extended period of time is an indication that the I/O subsystem is a bottleneck.
SQLServer	I/O Transactions/sec	Specifies the number of Transact SQL batches per second. A higher value is better.
SQLServer	I/O - Trans. Per Log Record	Specifies the number of transactions that were packed into a single log record before being written to disk. A higher value is better.

Object	Counter	Description
SQLServer	Cache Hit Ratio	Specifies the percentage of time in which requested data was found in the data cache. The higher the value, the better. If your hit rate routinely drops below 60 to 70 percent, increasing the size of the data cache might improve SQL Server performance.
SQLServer	Cache Flushes	Specifies the number of cache buffers that need to be flushed to disk in order to free a buffer for use by the next read. When cache flushes occur, you should increase the size of your data cache or increase the checkpoint frequency to provide additional buffers and increase performance.
SQLServer	Cache - Avg. Free Page Scan	Specifies the average number of buffers that needed to be scanned in order to find a free buffer. When this value increases above 10, increase the size of the data cache or the frequency of the checkpoint process to free additional buffers and increase performance.
SQLServer	Cache - Max Free Page Scan	Specifies the maximum number of buffers that had to be scanned in order to find a free buffer. When this value increases above 10, increase the size of the data cache or the frequency of the checkpoint process to free additional buffers and increase performance.
SQLServer	Cache - Scan Limit Reached	Specifies the number of times the scan limit was reached while searching for free buffers. If this value is consistently high, increase the size of the data cache or the checkpoint frequency to free up additional buffers.
SQLServer	Network Reads/sec	Specifies the number of tabular data stream packets read from the network. A higher value indicates higher network activity.
SQLServer	Network Writes/sec	Specifies the number of tabular data streams written to the network. A higher value is an indication of higher network activity.

continues

Table 23.10. continued

Object	Counter	Description
SQLServer	Network Command Queue Length	Specifies the number of outstanding client requests waiting to be serviced by the SQL Server worker threads. A higher value is an indication that increasing the number of worker threads may improve performance. If performance does not increase, it may be an indication that the processor is a bottleneck, and adding an additional processor may increase overall throughput.
SQLServer	User Connections	Specifies the number of current users connected to SQL Server.
SQLServer-Locks	Total Locks	Specifies the total number of locks currently in use by SQL Server.
SQLServer-Locks	Total Exclusive Locks	Specifies the total number of exclusive (meaning no other process can access the locked area) locks in use by SQL Server.
SQLServer-Locks	Total Shared Locks	Specifies the total number of shared (meaning the lock will not prevent other users from reading the locked data) locks in use by SQL Server.
SQLServer-Locks	Total Blocking Locks	Specifies the number of locks blocking other processes from continuing. (A blocked process is one that requires a lock on the same area.)
SQLServer-Locks	Total Demand Locks	Specifies the number of locks blocking other processes that need to obtain a shared lock on the same data area.
SQLServer-Locks	Table Locks - Exclusive	Specifies the number of exclusive locks on tables in use by SQL Server.
SQLServer-Locks	Table Locks - Shared	Specifies the number of shared locks on tables currently in use by SQL Server.
SQLServer-Locks	Table Locks - Total	Specifies the total number of table locks in use by SQL Server.
SQLServer-Locks	Extent Locks - Exclusive	Specifies the number of exclusive extent locks in use on databases (eight pages at a time) that are being allocated or freed.

Object	Counter	Description
SQLServer-Locks	Extent Locks - Shared	Specifies the number of shared extent locks in use on databases (eight pages at a time) that are being allocated or freed.
SQLServer-Locks	Extent Locks - Total	Specifies the total number of extent locks in use. An extent lock prevents an exclusive lock from being set.
SQLServer-Locks	Intent Locks - Exclusive	Specifies the total number of exclusive intent locks in use. An intent lock indicates the intention of obtaining the requested type of lock; it does not indicate that the lock has currently been granted. An intent lock prevents an exclusive lock from being granted to another process that needs to lock the same data area.
SQLServer-Locks	Intent Locks - Shared	Specifies the total number of shared intent locks in use.
SQLServer-Locks	Intent Locks - Total	Specifies the total number of intent locks in use by SQL Server.
SQLServer-Locks	Page Locks - Exclusive	Specifies the number of exclusive locks on pages.
SQLServer-Locks	Page Locks - Shared	Specifies the number of shared locks on pages.
SQLServer-Locks	Page Locks - Update	Specifies the number of update locks on pages.
SQLServer-Locks	Page Locks - Total	Specifies the total number of locks on pages.
SQLServer-User	Memory	Specifies the amount of memory (in 2KB units) allocated to a user connection.
SQLServer-User	CPU Time	Specifies the cumulative amount of time allocated to a user connection.
SQLServer-User	Physical I/O	Specifies the number of disk reads/writes for the currently executing Transact SQL statement.
SQLServer-User	Locks Held	Specifies the number of locks currently held by the user connection.

continues

Table 23.10. continued

Object	Counter	Description
SQLServer-Log	%Full	Specifies the amount (in a percentage) of the transaction log that is currently in use. Setting an alert for each transaction log on each database of importance can be a great help because it can provide you with an early warning.
SQLServer-Log	Size	Specifies the current allocation (in MB) of the transaction log.

Summary

In this chapter, you have looked at how to optimize your server using sample Performance Monitor charts, alerts, reports, and workspace files. These files, used in conjunction with sample programs, illustrate how to find processor, memory, disk, and network bottlenecks. You have also looked at the performance counters you can use to determine how well your IIS server and SQL Server installations are performing.

Appendixes

IN THIS PART

- Glossary **685**
- HTML Reference **713**
- The Registry Editor and Registry Keys **761**

PART VIII

Glossary

A

access control entry (ACE)   An entry in an access control list. Each access control entry defines the protection or auditing to be applied to a file or other object for a specific user or group of users.

access control list (ACL)   The part of a security descriptor that enumerates both the protections for accessing and the auditing of that accessing applied to an object. The owner of an object has discretionary access control of the object and can change the object's ACL to allow or disallow others' access to the object. Access control lists are ordered lists of access control entries.

access right   A permission granted to a process to manipulate a particular object in a particular way (by calling a service, for example). Different object types support different access rights. These access rights are stored in an object's access control list.

access token or **security token**   An object that uniquely identifies a user who has logged on. An access token is attached to all of the user's processes and contains the user's security identifier (SID), the SIDs of any groups to which the user belongs, any privileges that the user owns, the default owner of any objects that the user's processes create, and the default access control list to be applied to any objects that the user's processes create. See also *privilege*.

access violation   An attempt to carry out a memory operation that is not allowed by Windows NT memory management. An access violation has nothing to do with the Security Manager's checking of user-mode access rights to objects.

Four basic kinds of actions can cause access violations:

- Attempting an invalid operation, such as writing to a read-only buffer.
- Attempting to access memory beyond the limit of the current program's address space (also known as a *length violation*).
- Attempting to access a page to which the system forbids access. (For example, code is not allowed to run in the low-order 64KB of the Windows NT user-mode address.)
- Attempting to access a page that is currently resident but is dedicated to the use of an executive component. (For example, user-mode code is not allowed access to a page that the kernel is using.)

address class   In a TCP/IP world, the address class definition describes the type of network subnet. These are divided into three classes: class A address (such as 206.0.0.0), class B address (such as 206.170.0.0) and class C address (such as 206.170.127.0). Each higher class (from A–C) designates a lower granularity of IP addresses. A class C address can only contain 256 IP addresses (from .0 to .255), while a class B address can contain 65536 IP addresses (0.0 to 255.255) and a class A address can contain 16,777,216 (from 0.0.0 to 255.255.255) IP addresses.

Glossary

Appendix A

address space or **virtual address space**   The set of addresses available for a process's threads to use. In Windows NT, every process has a unique address space of 4GB; 2GB of this address space is reserved for the operating system and 2GB of the address space is available for the process.

administrative alert   A message sent to a computer or user by the Alerter Service to announce a critical problem or low resource supply on a computer, such as a low-disk-space warning.

Alerter Service   A Windows NT service designed to send alert messages. This service requires that the Windows NT Messenger service also be running in order to actually send an alert to a computer or user.

algorithm   In its most general sense, an algorithm is any set of instructions that can be followed to carry out a particular task. In computer usage, an algorithm is a set of instructions within a program. If you choose the Network option in the Control Panel, for example, you see the message `A binding algorithm failed`. This means that the program was unable to execute a set of instructions designed to bind together elements necessary for a functional network configuration.

allocation units   See *clusters or allocation units*.

anonymous-level security token   The type of security token used when a server impersonates a client. When the client calls the server, if the client specifies an anonymous impersonation mode, the server cannot access any of the client's identification information, such as its security identifier or privileges. The server will have to use an anonymous-level security token when representing the client in successive operations. See also *access token or security token*.

application programming interface (API)   A set of routines an application program uses to request and carry out lower-level services performed by the operating system.

Programming code is built using a series of function calls, or *routines*, that perform certain actions. For example, suppose that every workday you got up at 7 a.m., showered, dressed, fixed and ate breakfast, brushed your teeth, and then drove to work. If you were really a computer and never deviated from this pattern, a programmer could write a program for you called `DAILY_ROUTINE` that would perform these actions automatically. So, instead of having to specify each action, the programmer could just write `DAILY_ROUTINE` in the code, and the actions would be carried out. Thus, in this example, `DAILY_ROUTINE` would constitute an API.

archive bit   An attribute stored on the disk to indicate that a directory or file has changed. Backup programs use this bit to determine whether to copy a file to a backup medium (such as a tape). After a file is copied, this bit is reset. See also *hidden bit, read-only bit,* and *system bit*.

asymmetric multiprocessing (AMP)   A multiprocessing methodology that uses one processor to execute the operating system and another processor to execute applications. See also *symmetric multiprocessing*.

audit   The ability to record information about object access. An object could be a file, a directory, a process, or another auditable object. This auditing information is stored in the Security event log and may be viewed by an administrator using the Event Viewer.

audit policy   A set of rules that specifies the type of information to be audited. Many audit policies include user authentication (to know who has logged on to your system), and object access (to determine who is using what resources on your computer).

> **NOTE**
>
> To enable systemwide auditing, use the Audit option from the Policy menu on User Manager for domains. To enable directory or file auditing, use File Manager or the Windows Explorer. To enable printer auditing, use Print Manager.

authentication package   A subsystem that verifies that the logon information a user supplies matches the information stored in a security database.

AUTOEXEC.NT and CONFIG.NT files   Windows NT configures the MS-DOS environment by reading the AUTOEXEC.BAT file when you log on, and by reading the AUTOEXEC.NT and CONFIG.NT files when you start an application in a new command window. The AUTOEXEC.NT and CONFIG.NT files are the Windows NT versions of AUTOEXEC.BAT and CONFIG.SYS.

When you log on to Windows NT, the path and environment variables stored in the AUTOEXEC.BAT file are appended to the Windows NT path and environment settings. Because this portion of the operating environment is established at logon, the values set for the path and environment variables are available to each application you use. If you change these values, you must log off from and then log on to Windows NT again so that the changes take effect.

When you start an MS-DOS–based or a 16-bit Windows-based application in a new command window, Windows NT reads the CONFIG.NT and AUTOEXEC.NT files to configure the environment for the application. If you change an application's driver in the CONFIG.NT file, for example, restarting the application puts the change into effect. You can edit these files just as you would CONFIG.SYS and AUTOEXEC.BAT. The files are located in the *SystemRoot*\SYSTEM32 directory, where *SystemRoot* is the root directory of your Windows NT installation (generally, C:\WINNT35).

backup domain controller (BDC)   For a Windows NT Server domain, this refers to a server that contains a copy of the security policy and the master database for a domain and, along with the primary domain controller, authenticates domain logons. See also *primary domain controller*.

bad-sector mapping A technique used by the Windows NT file system to handle write errors. When an error is detected, the file system takes a free block, writes the data to that block instead of to the bad block, and updates a bad-block map. A copy of this map is written to disk.

basic input/output system (BIOS) A system component, generally a ROM or flash memory chip, used to contain processor instructions to operate a system peripheral, such as a disk controller, keyboard, or video controller. The BIOS is used as an intermediary device to provide device independence. An operating system can call a BIOS function instead of controlling the device directly. Windows NT, however, generally uses the BIOS only to boot the computer and instead requires a specific device driver to control the peripheral. See also *flash memory* and *read-only memory*.

batch file A text file containing commands to be noninteractively processed in a logical order. The AUTOEXEC.NT file is an example of a batch file.

batch process A process (application) that executes in the background without user intervention. The Windows NT Scheduler service can be used to initiate a batch process, such as a backup program, at a specific time.

bayonet nut connector A T-shaped connector used in a thin Ethernet-based network to connect the network adapter to the network segment. The base of the connector attaches to the network adapter, and the input and output network cable attaches to the top of the connector.

binding A series of bound paths from the upper-layer network services and protocols to the lowest layer of adapter card device drivers. Each network component can be bound to one or more network components above it or below it to make the component's services available to any component that can benefit from them.

boot partition The boot partition for Windows NT is a volume, formatted for a Windows NT file system or file allocation table file system, that has the Windows NT operating system and its support files. The boot partition can be (but does not have to be) the same as the system partition. It cannot be part of a stripe set or volume set, but it can be part of a mirror set. See also *system partition*.

browse A process of enumerating network resources—for example, a list of shared directories or printers. See also *enumeration operation*.

browser See *Web browser*.

C2-level security A standard implemented by the U.S. Government's National Computer Security Council that requires discretionary access to computer resources and auditing.

circular dependency A dependency in which an action that appears later in a chain is contingent on an earlier action. Suppose that three services (A, B, and C) are linked. A is dependent on B to start. B is dependent on C to start. A circular dependency results when C is dependent on A to start. See also *dependency*.

client/server application   An application divided into two or more components at the API level. The application commonly is divided into a client application that executes on a network client computer and a server application that executes on a different computer. This distributes the load and can improve performance by using a fast computer to run the server, which processes the data, and a client computer to display the data.

clusters or **allocation units**   In data storage, a *cluster* is a disk-storage unit consisting of a fixed number of sectors (storage segments on the disk) that the operating system uses to read or write information; typically, a cluster consists of between two and eight sectors, each of which holds a certain number of bytes (characters).

A formatted disk is divided into sectors, and a cluster is a set of contiguous sectors allocated to files as a single unit. This clustering of sectors reduces disk fragmentation but may result in wasted space within the cluster.

Under both the Windows NT file system (NTFS) and file allocation table (FAT) system, the size of a cluster is based on the size of the partition. With NTFS, however, you can override this with a switch, which forces a smaller (or larger) cluster size. For example, the command `FORMAT D: /fs:NTFS /v:D_Drive /a:512` formats the `D:` drive as NTFS with a sector size of 512 bytes and labels the drive as `D_Drive`. With a FAT partition, the size of a cluster cannot be changed; the larger the partition, the more sectors you have per cluster. Therefore, with a FAT partition you can have 1, 2, 4, 8, 16, 32, and 64 sectors per cluster.

Common Gateway Interface (CGI)   An application interface used to customize the behavior of a Web page. A CGI application executes as a separate process. It is commonly used with Web-based forms to capture client information.

`CONFIG.NT` **files**   See `AUTOEXEC.NT` *and* `CONFIG.NT` *files.*

control set   All Windows NT startup-related data not computed during startup is saved in one of the registry hives. This startup data is organized into control sets, each of which contains a complete set of parameters for starting up devices and services. The registry always contains at least two control sets, each of which contains information about all the configurable options for the computer: the current control set and the `LastKnownGood` control set. See also `LastKnownGood` *control set.*

cooperative multitasking   A multitasking methodology that can halt the execution of one process and start the execution of another process only at the discretion of the currently executing application. See also *preemptive multitasking.*

corrupted data   Data in memory or on disk that has been unintentionally changed, thereby altering or obliterating its meaning.

current control set   The control set used most recently to start the computer, which contains any changes made to the startup information during the current session. See also `LastKnownGood` *control set.*

cyclic redundancy check (CRC)   A procedure used on disk drives to ensure that the data written to a sector is read correctly later.

This procedure also is used when checking for errors in data transmission. The procedure is known as a *redundancy check* because each data transmission includes not only data but extra (redundant) error-checking values. The sending device generates a number based on the data to be transmitted and sends its result along with the data to the receiving device. The receiving device repeats the same calculation after transmission. If both devices obtain the same result, it is assumed that the transmission is error free.

Data Source Name   Specifies a name to an ODBC data source. The data source defines the connection characteristics between the application using the data source and the ODBC database. These characteristics might include the filename of an Access database, a user name to log on to the database, timeout values, buffer sizes, or other information relevant to accessing the database.

deadlock condition   A runtime-error condition that occurs when two threads of execution are blocked, each waiting to acquire a resource that the other holds, and both are unable to continue running.

debugger breakpoints   Set by the user of the Kernel Debugger (KD) before running the Windows NT Executive, a breakpoint is put into the Executive code at an instruction. Then, when the Executive is run, if and when that instruction is executed, execution is stopped, and the current values of registers and flags are displayed. KD breakpoints are sticky in the sense that they remain in the program until explicitly removed. It is possible for code to have breakpoints in it that are never explicitly removed. See also *Kernel Debugger*.

default gateway   Specifies a host (a router or another computer) to forward TCP/IP packets outside the local subnet. A *gateway* is generally a point where two networks interface. You may, for example, have two subnets (called A and B). For these subnets to be accessible from each other, they would be joined together using a router. The IP address of this router would be used as the default gateway by network clients in subnets A and B.

dependency   A situation in which one action must take place before another can happen. If action A does not occur, for example, action D cannot occur. Some Windows NT drivers have dependencies on other drivers or groups of drivers. Driver A will not load unless some driver from the G group loads first, for example. See also *circular dependency*.

device driver   A low-level (usually kernel mode) operating system component that is used as the interface to accessing physical hardware. A device driver is an individual file that provides easy replacement. Some device drivers (such as the 4mm DAT driver) may be loaded dynamically anytime by the operating system, while other device drivers may only be loaded at boot time (such as a disk controller driver). The `AHA174X.SYS` device driver, for example, provides the software (operating system) interface to the hardware (I/O ports, registers, and so on) for my Adaptec 1742/a SCSI controller.

dial-up networking The client side of a client/server service to provide network access to physically remote network clients using modems, ISDN, and X.25 adapters. Generally the dial-up networking client will use a modem and standard phone line to connect to his network. The modem will be used as a network adapter to transmit and receive network packets from the attached network (or Internet). The dial-up networking client supports the PPP and SLIP interfaces and the TCP/IP, IPX/SPX, and NetBEUI network transport protocols.

Directory Replicator Service A Windows NT service used to export or import a directory tree. Only a Windows NT Server computer can act as a directory export server, although any Windows NT computer can act as a directory import partner. The most common use of this service is to replicate the logon scripts from one domain controller (not necessarily the primary domain controller) to all the other domain controllers in the domain. See also *export path* and *import path*.

disk duplexing A fault-tolerant capability provided with Windows NT Server that uses a second disk or partition on a physically separate disk controller to create a redundant copy of a disk or partition. If the primary disk controller or disk drive fails, the second copy can be used to keep the system up and running.

disk mirroring A fault-tolerant capability provided with Windows NT Server that uses a second disk or partition to make a redundant copy of a disk or partition in case of a failure of the primary disk or partition.

disk striping See *striped set* and *striped set with parity*.

domain For Windows NT Server, a collection of computers that share a common-accounts database and security policy. Each domain has a unique name. A domain is a set of servers and workstations grouped together for efficiency and security, and is the basic administrative unit in Windows NT Server. A network can be divided, for example, into domains by department, workgroup, or building floor.

Domains keep large networks manageable. Users displaying a list of servers see only the servers for their domain, for example. But they still can access resources on servers in any domain if they have been granted the necessary rights.

domain controller See *primary domain controller*.

domain name A UNIX-based operating system defines a common name for a group of computers, very similar in concept to a Windows NT domain. A domain name is a mechanism used for address resolution. You Web server may be known as www.yourdomainname.com, or your e-mail address may be YourName@YourDomain.com. In both cases, the hostname will be converted to a specific IP address to establish a connection.

domain name service (DNS) An RFC-defined service under TCP/IP-based service for resolving NetBIOS computer names to TCP/IP IP addresses. A DNS server uses several host files, such as LMHOST, which is an ASCII file that contains computer names and IP addresses. See also *Dynamic Host Configuration Protocol, Windows Internet Naming Service,* and *WINS proxy agent*.

domain synchronization A process for keeping a consistent copy of the account database on all domain controllers. The primary domain controller contains the original copy of the account database and is responsible for copying these changes to the backup domain controllers. After a change is made, the domain controller informs the backup domain controllers that an update has been made. Then the backup domain controllers request the updates to maintain a consistent copy of the account database. This prevents a user from gaining access to the network based on stale data.

dongle An adapter that connects to the parallel port and contains a software key. Protected software often uses this type of mechanism to prevent software piracy.

down level An earlier operating system, such as Windows for Workgroups or LAN Manager, that still can interoperate with Windows NT Workstation or Windows NT Server.

Dynamic Host Configuration Protocol (DHCP) A client/server mechanism for automatically configuring TCP/IP IP addresses on networked client computers using the TCP/IP protocol. Windows NT Server includes the DHCP service, which is used to supply a TCP/IP address to a network client that includes a DHCP client, such as Windows NT Workstation, Windows NT Server, Windows 95, Windows for Workgroups, and MS-DOS clients using the MS-DOS Connection. See also *Windows Internet Naming Service*.

dynamic link library (DLL) A library of routines that user-mode applications access through ordinary procedure calls. The operating system automatically modifies the user's executable image to point to DLL procedures at runtime. That way, the code for the procedures does not have to be included in the user's executable image and may be shared with other executable images.

enumeration operation The counting, accessing, or listing of an entire set of similar objects. When the last object in the set is counted, accessed, or listed, the enumeration operation is complete.

error logging The process by which errors that cannot readily be corrected by the majority of end users are written to a file instead of being displayed onscreen. System administrators, support technicians, and users can use this log file to monitor the condition of the hardware in a Windows NT computer, to tune the configuration of the computer for better performance, and to debug problems as they occur.

exception A synchronous error condition resulting from the execution of a particular computer instruction. Exceptions can be hardware-detected errors, such as division by zero, or software-detected errors, such as a guard-page violation. See also *guard-page protection*.

Executive The part of the Windows NT operating system that runs in kernel mode. *Kernel mode* is a privileged processor mode in which a thread has access to system memory and to hardware. (In contrast, user mode is a nonprivileged processor mode in which a thread can access system resources only by calling system services.) The Windows NT Executive provides process structure, thread scheduling, interprocess communication, memory management, object management, object security, interrupt processing, I/O capabilities, and networking.

The Windows NT kernel is the part of the Windows NT Executive that manages the processor. It performs thread scheduling and dispatching, interrupt and exception handling, and multiprocessor synchronization. It also provides primitive objects to the Windows NT Executive, which uses them to create user-mode objects.

executive messages   Two types of character-mode messages occur when the Windows NT kernel detects an inconsistent condition from which it cannot recover: stop messages and hardware-malfunction messages.

Character-mode stop messages always are displayed on a full character-mode screen rather than in a Windows-mode message box. They also are uniquely identified by a hexadecimal number and a symbolic string, as in the following example:

```
*** STOP: 0x00000001
APC_INDEX_MISMATCH
```

The content of the symbolic string may suggest, to a trained technician, the part of the kernel that detected the condition from which there was no recourse but to stop. However, keep in mind that the cause actually may be in another part of the system.

Character-mode hardware-malfunction messages are caused by a hardware condition detected by the processor. The first one or two lines of a hardware-malfunction message may differ, depending on which company manufactured the computer. These lines always convey the same idea, however, as shown in the following example for an x86-based computer:

```
Hardware malfunction Call your hardware vendor for support.
```

The additional lines in each manufacturer's message screen also differ in format and content.

The Executive displays a Windows-mode status message box when it detects conditions within a process (generally, an application) that you should know about. Status messages can be divided into three types:

- System-information messages. All you need to do is read the information in the message box and click the OK button. The kernel continues running the process or thread.

- Warning messages. Some advise you to take an action that will enable the kernel to keep running the process or thread. Others warn you that although the process or thread will continue running, the results may not be correct.

- Application-termination messages. These warn you that the kernel is about to terminate a process or a thread.

export path The local path on a Windows NT Server computer that contains the directories and files to copy to import partners. An *import partner* is a Windows NT computer that has an executing Directory Replicator Service and specifically has been configured to copy the directories and files in the export path. See also *Directory Replicator Service* and *import path*.

extended attribute Windows NT file allocation table files have four basic parts: the data, the file system attributes (such as creation time and date, and file allocation table attributes), the security descriptors, and the extended attributes (EAs). EAs make up the set of extended information about a file and are structured as name/value pairs. Typical Windows NT system uses of EAs are actions, such as storing the icon of an executable image or indicating that the file is a symbolic link.

extended partition This is created from free space on a hard disk and can be subpartitioned into zero or more logical drives. The free space in an extended partition also can be used to create volume sets or other kinds of volumes for fault-tolerance purposes. Only one of the four partitions allowed per physical disk can be an extended partition, and no primary partition must be present in order to create an extended partition.

family set A group of tapes containing the same tape name and one or more backup sets created by NTBACKUP. A family set can be thought of as a single logical tape, even though it consists of more than one physical tape.

file control block (FCB) In MS-DOS, a 36-byte block of memory that contains all the information MS-DOS needs to know about an open file, such as the filename, what drive it is on, current file size, and date and time of creation.

File Transfer Protocol (FTP) A language used to send or receive files over the Internet using a client/server architecture.

flash memory A set of memory chips installed on the computer and used to store instructions for a computer to execute, or data to be read by the processor. Flash memory is similar to ROM in that its purpose is to support read-only operations. It can be written to, however, by using a special program to change its contents. Flash memory generally is used to contain your system BIOS and is a better choice than ROM because it enables the user to upgrade the system BIOS. See also *basic input output system, random access memory,* and *read-only memory*.

Fully Qualified Domain Name (FQDN) A host name with the domain name appended. If your computer name is roadtrip and your domain name is nt-guru.com, for example, then your FQDN would be roadtrip.nt-guru.com.

gateway See *default gateway*.

global group A series of one or more user accounts logically grouped into a single unit and available domainwide. Global groups are available only on a Windows NT domain. See also *local group*.

globally unique identifier (GUID) See *universally unique identifier*.

guard-page protection The Windows NT Virtual Memory Manager can put a guard page at the end of a data structure, such as a dynamic array, and generate a warning message when a user-mode thread accesses the guard-page memory. The user-mode process can respond appropriately, for example, by extending the array.

handle In general, a unique identifier (often an integer) by which a client refers to an object in the Windows NT operating system. Clients call servers to get the handle of the object on which the client wants to operate. Then the client sends requests for operations to the object, referring to the object by its handle. The server actually does the operation. This ensures that the client does not operate on the object directly.

In the registry, each of the first-level key names begins with HKEY to indicate to software developers that this is a handle that can be read by a program. A *handle* is a value used to provide a unique identifier for a resource so that a program can access it.

hardware abstraction layer (HAL) The lowest layer of the Windows NT operating system and part of the Executive. The HAL is used to provide platform independence. It communicates directly with the expansion bus, motherboard cache, programmable interrupt controller, and other system-specific components. All that is needed to convert Windows NT from a uniprocessor (single CPU) to a multiprocessor version of Windows NT is to use a supported motherboard with two or more CPUs and a multiprocessor HAL. The rest of the operating system components remain the same.

hexadecimal A base-16 number system that consists of the digits 0 through 9 and the uppercase and lowercase letters A (equivalent to decimal 10) through F (equivalent to decimal 15).

hidden bit An attribute stored on the disk to indicate that a directory or file should not be displayed. File Manager, for example, does not display hidden files unless the View Hidden|System Files option is enabled. System files required for the operation of your computer often are hidden. The BOOT.INI file, for example, which is required by Windows NT to determine the location of the operating system to boot, is normally hidden. See also *archive bit, read-only bit,* and *system bit.*

high memory area (HMA) A 64KB memory block located just above the 1MB address in a Virtual DOS Machine (VDM). This memory becomes visible when the A20 address line is turned on, enabling 21-bit addressing in the VDM.

hive The registry is divided into parts called hives, which are analogous to the cellular structure of a beehive. A hive is a part of the registry that maps to a file on your hard disk. Each user profile is a separate hive, which means that it is also a separate file. Therefore, an administrator can copy a user profile as a file, and view, repair, or copy entries using the Registry Editor on another computer.

home directory A local or shared directory specified as the user's default directory with User Manager.

hotkey   In a user interface, hotkeys provide an alternative to the mouse for manipulating interface objects. Instead of using the mouse, for example, you can press the key combination Alt+F to open the File menu on the menu bar. Alt+F is a hotkey.

Hypertext Markup Language (HTML)   A set of rules that utilize ASCII-based tags to format text, display objects, and create links within a document or Web page.

Hypertext Transfer Protocol (HTTP)   The common protocol, or language, used by World Wide Web (WWW) servers and Web browsers as the communication link between client and server.

Hypertext Transfer Protocol Secure (HTTPS)   The protocol, or language, used by World Wide Web (WWW) servers and Web browsers as a secure communication link between client and server. This secure link is obtained through the use of data encryption.

I/O bus   A hardware path inside a computer used for transferring information to and from the processor and various input and output devices.

impersonation   The capability of a thread in one process to take on the security identity of a thread in another process and to perform operations on the other thread's behalf. Impersonation is used by the Windows NT environment subsystems and network services to access remote resources on behalf of client applications.

import path   The local path on a Windows NT Server computer that has an executing Directory Replicator Service. The directories and files of the export partner are copied to this relative path. See also *Directory Replicator Service* and *export path*.

INF file   One of a set of files used by the setup program during Windows NT installation, maintenance setup, or both. An INF file generally contains a script for the setup program to follow, along with configuration data that ends up in the registry.

input/output address   All peripherals connected to your expansion bus use one or more I/O ports to communicate with a device driver to control the physical device, to transfer data to/from the system and the device, or both. A communication port (COM1), for example, has a base I/O address of 03F8h and eight I/O ports for communicating with the device and to transfer data.

input/output control (IOCTL)   An IOCTL command enables a program to communicate directly with a device driver. This is done, for example, by sending a string of control information recognized by the driver. None of the information passed from the program to the device driver is sent to the device itself (in other words, the control string sent to a printer driver is not displayed by the printer).

installable file system (IFS)   A file system that can be loaded into the operating system dynamically. Windows NT can support multiple installable file systems at one time, including the file allocation table file system, the high-performance file system, the Windows NT file system, and the CD-ROM file system. Windows NT automatically determines the format of a storage medium and reads and writes files in the correct format.

Internet access provider (IAP) A company that provides you with a raw Internet connection. There are no associated services, such as those which could be provided by an ISP (see *Internet Service Provider*).

Internet Database Connector An Internet Information Service extension. The extension is an ISA application that provides a customizable interface to an ODBC database from an HTML document.

Internet Protocol (IP) A low-level network protocol designed to provide a means of identifying a particular host. Every host on the Internet requires a unique IP address.

Internet Server Application Programming Interface (ISAPI) A set of APIs used by developers to customize the behavior of the IIS WWW server. It is similar to the common gateway interface in purpose, with the exception that ISAPI applications execute within the same process as the Web server rather than as a separate process. This can provide a substantial performance increase over CGI applications.

Internet service provider (ISP) A company that provides you with your Internet connection and services. These services can include domain name registration, IP address allocation, WWW site hosting, and so on.

interrupt An asynchronous operating system condition that disrupts normal execution and transfers control to an interrupt handler. Interrupts can be issued by both software and hardware devices requiring service from the processor. When software issues an interrupt, it calls an interrupt service routine. When hardware issues an interrupt, it signals an interrupt request line.

interrupt request level (IRQL) A ranking of interrupts by priority. A processor has an interrupt request level setting that threads can raise or lower. Interrupts that occur at or below the processor's IRQL setting are masked, whereas interrupts that occur above the processor's IRQL setting are not. Software interrupts are almost always lower priority than hardware interrupts.

IP address A 32-bit number represented as a series of numbers between 0 and 255 separated by periods. For example, the IP address for my server is `206.170.127.65`.

ISA Usually used to describe the Industry Standard Architecture I/O bus, however, it is also used to describe an Internet Server Application. An Internet Server Application is an ISAPI application that extends the functionality of the HTTP server.

JavaScript A programming language designed as part of the Microsoft ActiveX development efforts. JavaScript applications are executable code embedded as objects within HTML documents. These applications can be used to provide interactive Web pages. JavaScript is based on the Java language by Sun Microsystems, which in turn is based on the C++ object model.

kernel The Windows NT kernel is the part of the Windows NT Executive that manages the processor. It performs thread scheduling and dispatching, interrupt and exception handling, and multiprocessor synchronization. It also provides primitive objects to the Windows NT Executive, which uses them to create user-mode objects.

Kernel Debugger (KD)   The Windows NT Kernel Debugger is a 32-bit application used to debug the kernel and device drivers, and to log the events leading up to a Windows NT Executive stop, status, or hardware-malfunction message.

The Kernel Debugger runs on another Windows NT host computer connected to your Windows NT target computer. The two computers send debugging (troubleshooting) information back and forth through a communications port that must be running at the same baud rate on each computer. See also *debugger breakpoints, system debugger,* and `WINDBG.EXE`.

kernel mode   See *Executive*.

keyword   A special type of command parameter that includes a value. The syntax of the `width` keyword illustrates this (for example, `width = 40`).

LastKnownGood (LKG) control set   The most recent control set that correctly started the system and resulted in a successful startup. The control set is saved as the `LKG` control set when you have a successful logon.

A copy of the control set used to start the system also is stored as the `Clone` subkey in the registry. At startup time, the Service Control Manager copies the `Clone` subkey to the `LastKnownGood` control set before any new changes are made to the control set. This helps to ensure that the computer always contains a working control set. See also *current control set*.

local area network (LAN)   A group of computers physically located in a single area and connected to each other over a high-speed medium to shared resources. See also *wide area network*.

local group   A series of one or more user accounts logically grouped into a single unit and available domainwide on a domain, or available only on the local Windows NT Workstation. See also *global group*.

local procedure call (LPC)   A local procedure call performs exactly like a remote procedure call except that it is used only on a single computer. It provides a means of building distributed applications but testing them on a single computer. To initiate an LPC call for a distributed application, change the computer name to a single period for the connection string. For example, use

`\\.\pipe\sql\query`

instead of

`\\`*computername*`\pipe\sql\query`

to connect a SQL client application to the SQL Server that is on the same computer as the SQL Server application.

local security authority (LSA)   A component of the Windows NT security system that maintains all aspects of local security on a system. This collection of information is known as the *local security policy*. The local security policy identifies, among other things, the following: domains trusted to authenticate logon attempts, who may access the system, how they may access it (locally, from the network, or as a service), who is assigned privileges, and what security auditing is to be performed.

mandatory user profile   A user profile that cannot be changed by the user and, because of this, may be shared by multiple users. See also *user profile*.

mapped I/O or **mapped file I/O**   File I/O performed by reading and writing to virtual memory backed by a file.

memory control block (MCB)   MS-DOS organizes available memory as a pool of blocks maintained as a chain (or linked list). The MCB occupies the bottom 16 bytes of each memory block and, among other things, points to the next memory block in the chain. If an MCB is corrupted, MS-DOS cannot find the next block in the chain and does not know which memory blocks have been allocated and which have not.

mounting a volume   Finding a file system that recognizes the format of a volume and associating the file system with the volume. Windows NT does this automatically the first time a program accesses a volume (or, for other forms of removable media such as floppy disks or CD-ROMs, each time the user reinserts the floppy disk or CD into a drive and performs I/O on it). A volume must be mounted before I/O operations can be performed on it.

multihomed   A computer with more than one TCP/IP IP address assigned to it. A multihomed computer has more than one network adapter, with each network adapter assigned a unique IP address. A multihomed computer is often used to combine separate physical network segments into a single logical network by forwarding IP packets between the two segments.

multiprocessing   The capability to execute more than one program at a time by dividing the processor cycles among several applications.

multithreading   The capability to subdivide a process into one or more executable components. See also *thread*.

named pipe   An interprocess communication mechanism that enables one process to send data to another local or remote process. See also *pipe*.

NetBIOS Extended User Interface (NetBEUI)   A network transport protocol supported by all Microsoft network operating systems and some IBM network operating systems. It has a maximum number of 255 simultaneous computer connections, and has been superseded by the NetBEUI Frame (NBF) Protocol, which does not have the 255-computer connection limit.

Network Basic Input/Output System (NetBIOS)   A network API set, rather than a network transport protocol, and is defined for use by applications for utilization of network resources.

network control block (NCB)   A block of sequential data of fixed length. This data includes an operation code that indicates the operation to be performed and elements that indicate the status of the operation. See also *opcode*.

network news transfer protocol (NNTP)   Specifies a network protocol used to support the online bulletin board system (BBS) functionality of Internet newsgroups.

network transport   This can be a particular layer of the Open System Interconnect (OSI) reference model between the network layer and the session layer, or a communications protocol between two different computers on a network.

object   A single runtime instance of a Windows NT–defined object type. It contains data that can be manipulated only by using a set of services provided for objects of its type.

In Windows NT Performance Monitor, an object is a standard mechanism for identifying and using a system resource. Objects are created to represent individual processes, sections of shared memory, and physical devices. Performance Monitor groups counters by object type. Each object type also can have several instances. The Processor object type, for example, has multiple instances if a system has multiple processors. The Physical Disk object type has two instances if a system has two disks. Some object types (such as Memory and Server) do not have instances.

opcode   Operation code is usually a number that specifies an operation to be performed. An opcode is often the first component in a contiguous block of data; it indicates how other data in the block should be interpreted. See also *network control block*.

Open Database Connectivity (ODBC)   ODBC provides a logical mechanism to access an ODBC-aware database. An ODBC-aware database is any database (such as Microsoft SQL Server or Microsoft Access) that you create that has an ODBC driver. The ODBC driver is used as a layer between your application and the database. This layer provides a uniform mechanism to access any ODBC database. This provides a means to build a database using Microsoft Access today, and switch it to a Microsoft SQL Server database, just by building the SQL Server database and supplying a new definition for the Data Source Name (DSN). Your application would remain the same. See also *Data Source Name*.

paging file or **swap file**   A system file containing the contents of virtual pages that have been temporarily removed from physical memory by the Virtual Memory Manager.

With virtual memory under Windows NT, some of the program code and other information is kept in RAM, whereas other information is temporarily swapped to a virtual-memory paging file. When that information is required again, Windows NT pulls it back into RAM and, if necessary, swaps other information to virtual memory. This activity is invisible, although you might notice that your hard disk is working. The resulting benefit is that you can run more programs at one time than your system's RAM usually would allow. See also *virtual memory*.

parameter   Parameters are used in commands entered at the Windows NT command prompt to customize that particular use of the command. The MS-DOS COPY command, for example, has two parameters: the path to the file to copy and the path to where the copy will be placed. These two parameter values can be any valid path; by changing these each time you use the COPY command, you are customizing the command.

parity   A mechanism used to ensure data integrity. The basic methodology combines (using an XOR algorithm) the binary values in an element and then sets a parity bit based on the result. This result bit is a 1 if the XOR result was 1, or a 0 if the XOR result was 0. The parity bit can be used to determine data changes.

partition   A portion of a physical disk that functions as though it were a physically separate unit. You can use a partitioning program, such as FDISK for the MS-DOS and OS/2 operating systems and Disk Administrator for Windows NT, to create these unformatted units. You then must use the FORMAT command (from the command prompt or from within Disk Administrator) to format the disk for use with a specific file system. A partition usually is referred to as a *primary* or an *extended partition*. See also *volume*.

partition table   A structure on a disk that the operating system uses to divide a disk into logical divisions called *partitions*, which then can be formatted to a specific file system. Primary partitions are defined by a data entry in the main partition table of a hard disk. Extended partitions are defined by a non-data entry in the main partition table.

permission   A rule associated with an object (usually a directory, file, or printer) in the form of a discretionary access control list (DACL) used to regulate which users or groups can have access to the object and in what manner. You can set file and directory permissions only on drives formatted to use the Windows NT File System. See also *right*.

pipe   An interprocess communication (IPC) mechanism. Writing to and reading from a pipe is much like writing to and reading from a file, except that the two processes actually are using a shared memory segment to communicate data. An unnamed pipe is a local IPC methodology and can be used only among processes running on the same computer. See also *named pipe*.

Point-to-Point Protocol (PPP)   A protocol definition used to link two networks (or individual computers) together. The Microsoft implementation supports PPP connections using TCP/IP, IPX/SPX, or NetBEUI network transport protocols.

preemptive multitasking   A multitasking methodology that can halt the execution of a process and start the execution of another process at the discretion of the operating system. Generally, a preemptive multitasking operating system, such as Windows NT, is based on a timeslice in which each process executes for a specific number of CPU cycles. See also *cooperative multitasking* and *timeslice*.

primary domain controller (PDC)   For a Windows NT Server domain, the server that maintains the original copy of the security policy and master database for a domain and, along with backup domain controllers, authenticates domain logons. Any changes made to the account policies and account database have to occur on the primary domain controller. These changes then are replicated to the backup domain controllers. See also *backup domain controller* and *replication*.

primary partition   A portion of a physical disk that can be marked as active for use by an operating system. *Active* means that the power-on self-test routine can locate a boot sector on the partition. There can be up to four primary partitions (or up to three if there is already an extended partition) per physical disk. A primary partition cannot be subpartitioned.

privilege   The representation of most user rights in access tokens. An example of one is the backup privilege. Holders of that privilege are allowed to bypass file system security to back up and restore data on a disk. In a secure system, not all users have that privilege. See also *access token or security token*.

privileged instruction   Instructions that have access to system memory and the hardware.

process   A logical division of labor in an operating system. A Windows NT process is created when a program runs. A process can be an application (such as Microsoft Word or CorelDRAW!), a service (such as Event Log or Computer Browser), or a subsystem (such as POSIX). In Windows NT, it comprises a virtual address space, an executable program, one or more threads of execution, some portion of the user's resource quotas, and the system resources that the operating system has allocated to the process's threads. A process is implemented as an object. See also *object*.

random access memory (RAM)   A set of memory chips installed in the computer and used to store computer instructions to be loaded and executed by the processor, or used to store data. RAM can be read from or written to an unlimited number of times. See also *flash memory* and *read-only memory*.

read-only bit   An attribute stored on the disk to indicate that a directory or file cannot be modified (written to). System files required for the operation of your computer often are marked as read-only. The NTLDR file required by Windows NT to load the operating system to boot, for example, normally is marked as read-only. See also *archive bit, hidden bit,* and *system bit*.

read-only memory (ROM)   A set of memory chips installed on the computer and used to store instructions for a computer to execute, or data to be read by the processor. ROM cannot be written to—hence the name *read-only*—and generally is used to contain boot instructions used by the processor to initialize and access a physical device. Your system ROM is used to boot the computer, for example, but your video ROM is used to draw data on the computer screen. See also *flash memory* and *random access memory*.

registry   A secure, unified database that stores application-configuration data, hardware-configuration data (such as device-driver configuration data, network protocol, and adapter card settings), and user data in a hierarchical form for a Windows NT Workstation or Windows NT Server computer.

registry key   The configuration data in the registry is stored in a hierarchical form, and keys are the building blocks of this hierarchy. In the registry, there are four top-level keys that contain per-computer and per-user databases. Each key can contain data items, called *value entries*, and also can contain additional subkeys. In the registry structure, keys are analogous to directories, and the value entries are analogous to files. See also *value entries*.

Remote Access Software (RAS)   The server side of a client/server service to provide network access to physically remote network clients using modems, ISDN, and X.25 adapters. The client side of the service is referred to as Dial-Up Networking. See also *dial-up networking*.

remote procedure call (RPC)   A message-passing facility that enables a distributed application to call services available on various computers in a network without regard to their locations. Remote network operations are handled automatically. RPC provides a procedural, rather than a transport-centered, view of networked operations. See also *local procedure call*.

remote procedure call (RPC) binding   A logical connection between the client and server, or the process by which the client establishes a logical connection to the server.

remote procedure call (RPC) connection   A transport-level virtual circuit between the client and server. The RPC runtime establishes the circuit when the client binds to the server interface instance. Connections are not visible to the client. A client may have more than one connection to the server.

remote procedure call (RPC) endpoint   An endpoint identifies a specific server instance (or address space) on a host. The format of the endpoint depends on the transport protocol used. There are well-known endpoints and dynamic endpoints. *Well-known endpoints* are registered in the name service database. *Dynamic endpoints* are assigned to server instances at runtime.

remote procedure call (RPC) protocol sequence   A character string that identifies the network protocols used to establish a relationship between a client and a server. The protocol sequence contains a set of options that the RPC runtime must know about to establish a binding. These options include the RPC protocol, the format of the network address, and the transport protocol. For example, a sample protocol sequence string might be as follows:

```
ncacn_ip_tcp
```

remote procedure call (RPC) server   The program or computer that processes remote procedure calls from a client.

replication   The process of copying the original account policies, account database, and logon scripts from the primary domain controller to the backup domain controllers in a Windows NT domain. See also *backup domain controller, Directory Replicator Service,* and *primary domain controller*.

request for comment (RFC)   A document that defines a specification for interaction, or functionality, of a TCP/IP component.

revision level A revision level is built into many Windows NT data structures, such as security descriptors and access control lists. This enables the structure to be passed between systems or stored on disk, even though it is expected to change in the future.

right Authorizes a user to perform certain actions on the system. In most situations, rights should be provided to a user by adding that user's account to one of the built-in groups that already possesses the needed rights, instead of by administering the user-rights policy. Rights apply to the system as a whole and are different from permissions, which apply to specific objects. See also *permission*.

root directory In a file system structured as a hierarchy of directories on a partition or volume, the root directory is the parent of all the other directories. The root directory name in the File Allocation Table (FAT), High Performance File System (HPFS), and New Technology File System (NTFS) is a backslash (\).

route When discussed in the presence of a network protocol, a route is the path that was used by the source computer to transmit information to the destination computer.

router A hardware device used to combine two different network segments. Data addressed to a host outside the local segment will be passed to the intended recipient by the router. It is also possible to use software in combination with your server's hardware to emulate a router. However, a dedicated router can support more users than a software emulation.

Routing for the Internet Protocol (RIP) A Windows NT service that provides dynamic update capabilities to the TCP/IP routing table. See also *route*.

secrets Encrypted pieces of information.

Secure Socket Layer (SSL) A network protocol enhancement used to provide a secure method to transfer data between a Web browser and Web server. A Web server that accepts credit card numbers, for example, would do so using SSL.

security accounts manager (SAM) A Windows NT–protected subsystem that maintains the security-accounts database.

security descriptor A data structure that houses all the security information related to an object. It contains a discretionary access control list, a system access control list that controls auditing on the object, an owner, and a primary group of the object.

security identifier (SID) A number that identifies a user, a global group of users, a local group of users, or a domain within Windows NT.

security token See *access token or security token*.

semaphore Generally, semaphores are signaling devices or mechanisms. However, in Windows NT, system semaphores are objects used to synchronize activities on an interprocess level. When two or more processes share a common resource such as a printer, video screen, or memory segment, for example, semaphores are used to control access to those resources so that only one process can alter them at any particular time.

serial line Internet protocol (SLIP)   An older protocol definition used to link two networks (or individual computers) together using the TCP/IP network transport protocol.

server message block (SMB)   A block of data containing a work request from a workstation to a server, or containing the response from the server to the workstation. SMBs are used for all communications that go through the server or workstation service, such as file I/O, creating and removing remote connections, or performing any other network function that the redirector needs to carry out.

Microsoft network redirectors use this structure to send remote requests or information over the network to a remote computer, which can be a Windows NT Workstation, Windows NT Server, or other Microsoft Network–compatible computer.

sharepoint   A shared directory or printer on a Windows NT computer that network clients can connect to in order to access the resource.

Simple Mail Transfer Protocol (SMTP)   Defines a protocol used to send or receive e-mail messages to or from other SMTP mail servers. The SMTP protocol is used almost exclusively for providing Internet mail capabilities.

Simple Network Management protocol (SNMP)   Defines a protocol for reporting statistical information, configuring software components, or configuring hardware components, from an SNMP management console (like HP OpenView).

single system image (SSI)   A domain that has the logon service running and that propagates its user-accounts database throughout the domain.

standalone   A workstation or server that is not currently a member of a domain. Or, a workstation or server at which logon requests are not validated by a logon server.

striped set   A unit created by combining multiple physical disk drives into a single logical unit. This logical unit is divided into blocks that are split among the disk drives to increase disk throughput by reading or writing multiple blocks in a single operation.

striped set with parity   A fault-tolerant implementation of a striped set that uses a single-parity block for each stripe to increase disk throughput and provide a means of protection from a single disk failure. If a single disk drive fails, the parity block can be exclusively combined (XOR) with the remaining data blocks to re-create the missing data block and provide access to the data with only a slight performance penalty.

Structured Query Language (SQL)   A standardized programming language used to access data stored in an application database. Generally, SQL is used to access SQL Server databases, but also may be used by an application to access data stored in a proprietary database, such as a Microsoft Access database.

subnet   A subcomponent of a larger network component. In a TCP/IP-based network, a subnet is part of a larger subnet based on its class definition. For example, my class C address 206.170.127.64 is a subnet of another class C address 206.170.127.25. See also *address class*.

swap file   See *paging file or swap file.*

switch   A special type of command parameter denoted by a leading slash (/) or leading dash (-). Switches normally are used for parameters that are simple toggles (on/off switches). In the CHKDSK command, for example, an optional parameter is the /f switch. If it is used, CHKDSK attempts to fix any problems it finds on a disk. If it is not used, CHKDSK only reports the problems and does not attempt to fix them.

symmetric multiprocessing (SMP)   A multiprocessing methodology that uses all processors installed on the computer to execute the operating system and all applications. See also *asymmetric multiprocessing.*

syntax   The rules governing the structure and content of commands entered into the computer. When you enter commands at the Windows NT command prompt, for example, if the structure and content of a command violate the syntax rules, the Windows NT command processor cannot interpret the command and generates a syntax error message.

system bit   An attribute stored on the disk to indicate that a directory or file is reserved for use by the operating system. The NTDETECT.COM file, for example, which is required by Windows NT to detect the hardware on your system as part of the operating system boot procedure, normally is marked as a system file. See also *archive bit, hidden bit,* and *read-only bit.*

system debugger   The Windows NT system debugger (NTSD) is a 32-bit application that supports the debugging of user-mode applications and dynamic link libraries. NTSD also can read and write paged and nonpaged memory, and supports multiple-thread debugging and multiprocess debugging.

NTSD enables you to display and execute program code, set breakpoints that stop the execution of your program, and examine and change values in memory. NTSD also enables you to refer to data and instructions by name rather than by address. It can access program locations through addresses, global symbols, or line-number references, making it easy to locate and debug specific sections of code. You can debug C programs at the source-file level as well as at the machine-code level. You also can display the source statements of a program, the disassembled machine code of the program, or a combination of source statements and disassembled machine code.

In contrast to NTSD, the Windows NT Kernel Debugger (KD) supports the debugging of kernel-mode code. It cannot be used to set breakpoints in user-mode or to read or write paged-out memory. KD also does not provide support for threads. However, it does support multiprocess debugging.

You therefore would use NTSD for debugging user-mode programs and KD for debugging the Kernel and device drivers. See also *Kernel Debugger* and WINDBG.EXE.

system files   Files used by the operating system or the file system to store special system data. NTFS uses them to store special data on the file system.

Operating systems use these files to store information and programs used to start the computer and load the operating system. MS-DOS system files include IO.SYS, MSDOS.SYS, and COMMAND.COM. Windows NT system files include NTLDR, NTDETECT.COM, BOOT.INI, and several of the files in the SystemRoot\SYSTEM32 directory.

system partition The system partition for Windows NT is the volume that has the hardware-specific files needed to load Windows NT. On x86-based computers, it must be a primary partition that has been marked as active for startup purposes and must be located on the disk that the computer accesses when starting up the system. There can be only one active system partition at a time, which is denoted onscreen by an asterisk. If you want to use another operating system, you first must mark its system partition as active before restarting the computer.

Partitions on a RISC-based computer are not marked active. Instead, they are configured by a hardware-configuration program supplied by the manufacturer. On RISC-based computers, the system partition must be formatted for the file allocation table file system. On either type of computer, the system partition can never be part of a stripe set or volume set, but it can be part of a mirrored set. See also *boot partition*.

T connector In network terminology this type of connector reflects a physical attribute. The top of the T is considered the network segment, while the base of the T is the connection between the network segment and the network adapter. When this connection is physically viewed it looks like the letter T.

TCP/IP The combination of the Transmission Control Protocol with the Internet Protocol. In essence, TCP is concerned with the data, while IP is concerned with the delivery of the data from the source to destination computers. This is the most widely used combination of network protocols for connecting large networks, or for connecting any network to the Internet.

terminated process In Windows NT, a *process object* is a program invocation, including the address space and resources required to run the program. When the Windows NT Executive terminates a process, it quits running the program and returns the address space and resources to the system. From the user's point of view, the application is no longer running.

thread An executable entity that belongs to one (and only one) process. It comprises a program counter, a user-mode stack, a kernel-mode stack, and a set of register values. All threads in a process have equal access to the process's address space, object handles, and other resources.

In Windows NT Performance Monitor, threads are objects within processes that execute program instructions. They allow concurrent operations within a process and enable one process to execute different parts of its program on different processors simultaneously. Each thread running on a system shows up as an instance for the Thread object type and is identified by association with its parent process. If Print Manager has two active threads, for example, Performance Monitor identifies them as Thread object instances `Printman ==> 0` and `Printman ==> 1`.

timeslice   An operating system algorithm used in process management. The basic mechanism assigns each process a time (usually in nanoseconds) limit. When the time limit is reached, the active process is suspended, and an inactive process is resumed. When the time limit is up for this resumed process, it too will be suspended to allow the next inactive process to execute. When the last process executes and uses its timeslice, the first process will then be executed and the loop restarted.

Transmission Control Protocol (TCP)   A high-level network protocol that is designed to provide a reliable transmission pathway between hosts.

transport driver interface (TDI)   A Windows NT interface for network redirectors and servers for use in sending network-bound requests to network transport drivers. This interface provides transport independence by abstracting transport-specific information.

trap   A processor's mechanism for capturing an executing thread when an unusual event (such as an exception or interrupt) occurs, and then transferring control to a fixed location in memory where the handler code resides. The trap handler determines the type of condition and transfers control to an appropriate handling routine.

trust relationship   A link between domains that enables passthrough authentication, in which a user has only one user account in one domain, yet can access the entire network. User accounts and global groups defined in a trusted domain can be given rights and resource permissions in a trusting domain, even though those accounts don't exist in the trusting domain's database. A trusting domain honors the logon authentications of a trusted domain.

universal naming convention (UNC) name   A name given to a device, computer, or resource to enable other users and applications to establish an explicit connection and access the resources over the network. Also known as the *uniform naming convention*. The following example shows the syntax of a UNC name:

`\\<computername>\<sharename>\<filename>`

universal resource identifier (URI)   A unique identifier to indicate the type of resource to be acquired and the protocol to be used to acquire the resource. A Web page URL (like `http://www.nt-guru.com`) uses the `http` URI, which specifies that the hypertext transfer protocol be used to retrieve the resource (the default HTML document for the `www.nt-guru.com` site). URIs come in many flavors, such as `https` (for hypertext transfer protocol secure resources), `file` (for locally defined resources), `mailto` (for electronic mail), and so on.

universal resource locator (URL)   A unique identifier to locate a resource on the Internet. The following example shows the syntax for the WWW server, FTP server, and Gopher server that are maintained on my server:

```
http://www.nt-guru.com
```

```
ftp://ftp.nt-guru.com
```

```
gopher://gopher-nt-guru.com
```

universally unique identifier (UUID)   A unique identification string associated with the remote procedure call interface. Also known as a *globally unique identifier*.

These identifiers consist of 8 hexadecimal digits followed first by a hyphen, then by three groups of 4 hexadecimal digits with each group followed by a hyphen, and finally by 12 hexadecimal digits. For example, this is a syntactically correct identifier:

```
12345678-1234-1234-1234-123456789ABC
```

The identifiers on the client and server must match in order for the client and server to bind.

User Datagram Protocol (UDP)   A high-level network protocol that is designed to provide an unreliable transmission pathway between hosts. This method is faster, but should only be used in low-error networks or when data coherency is not required.

user mode   See *Executive*.

user profile   A copy of the user environment (Program Manager groups, desktop settings, and application-configuration information) stored both locally on the user's computer and on a server in the domain if so configured in User Manager. A profile initially is created with the User Profile Editor and saved as a file on a server. See also *mandatory user profile*.

value entries   The value for a specific entry under a key or subkey in the registry. Value entries appear as a string with three components: a name, a type, and the value. See also *registry key*.

VBScript   A programming language designed as part of the Microsoft ActiveX development efforts. VBScript applications are executable code embedded as objects within an HTML document. These applications can be used to provide interactive Web pages. VBScript is based on the Microsoft Visual Basic language.

virtual address space   See *address space or virtual address space*.

virtual device driver   An emulation of a physical device. While a device driver provides an interface to control a real physical device, a virtual device driver provides an interface to a logical (not physically present) device. You use a virtual device driver every time you run a console application, for example. While each application thinks it has an 80×24 character physical display screen assigned for its exclusive use, in reality the application is writing to a virtual screen. This screen is wrapped up in a window frame provided by the operating system. See also *device driver*.

virtual DOS machine (VDM) Provides a complete MS-DOS environment and a character-based window in which to run an MS-DOS–based application. Any number of VDMs can run simultaneously.

virtual memory A logical view of memory that does not necessarily correspond to the memory's physical structure.

Normally, virtual memory is the space on your hard disk that Windows NT uses as if it were actually memory. Windows NT does this through the use of the paging file. Virtual memory also can be unused address space that is allocated to a process but not yet in use. In this case, the memory will not physically exist anywhere until it is actually used (that is, until data or code is loaded into it).

The benefit of using virtual memory is that you can run more applications at one time than your system's physical memory would otherwise allow. The drawbacks are the disk space required for the virtual-memory paging file and the decreased execution speed when swapping is required. See also *paging file or swap file*.

volume A file-based medium that has been initialized with a file system structure (for example, a floppy disk, a hard disk, a tape reel, or a particular partition on a hard disk). A disk partition or collection of partitions that have been formatted for use by a file system and that also can be used as volume sets, stripe sets, and mirrored sets. See also *partition*.

Web browser The client component of a client/server application that utilizes the HTTP protocol to communicate with the Web server. A Web browser is often a GUI application that provides an interface to Internet services, which can include the WWW, FTP, and Gopher services.

Web server The server component of a client/server application used to display content on a Web browser using HTTP as the linkage between client and server. A Web server's capabilities may be customized using application programming interfaces such as ISAPI, CGI, and ActiveX, and languages such as C/C++, Visual Basic, and Perl.

wide area network (WAN) A group of computers or a group of LANs physically located in separate areas and connected to each other over a low-speed medium to share resources. WANs generally use low-speed phone lines or leased lines to connect, although higher-speed lines are available. See also *local area network*.

WINDBG.EXE The Windows NT debugger, which is a 32-bit application that, along with a collection of DLLs, is used for debugging the kernel, device drivers, and applications. The same application also can be used on all hardware platforms, although there is a different build of it for each platform. It can be used for remote or local debugging and also with the System Recovery option in the Control Panel.

Windows Internet Naming Service (WINS) A client/server mechanism for resolving NetBIOS computer names for network clients using the TCP/IP protocol. WINS performs a similar service as domain name service for UNIX-based systems, except that you do not have to manually modify a host file because WINS automatically updates its internal database of computer names to IP addresses. Windows NT Server includes the WINS service, which is the server side of the application and is used to supply a TCP/IP IP address to a network client that includes a WINS client when a request is made to access to a computer by name rather than an IP address. Current WINS clients include Windows NT Workstation, Windows NT Server, Windows 95, Windows for Workgroups, and MS-DOS clients using the MS-DOS Connection. See also *domain name service, Dynamic Host Configuration Protocol,* and *WINS proxy agent.*

WINS proxy agent   Acts as an interpreter for computers that use the TCP/IP protocol, but that do not support the WINS protocol. When a computer makes a request by computer name, the proxy agent queries the WINS server to obtain the TCP/IP IP address. This IP address then is forwarded to the requesting computer. A WINS proxy agent can be a Windows NT Server, Windows NT Workstation, or Windows for Workgroups 3.11 computer.

working set   The set of virtual pages in physical memory at any moment for a particular process. In a virtual memory system such as Windows NT, a memory management system provides a large address space to each process by mapping the process's virtual addresses into physical addresses as the processes' threads use them. When physical memory becomes full, the memory management system swaps selected memory contents to disk, reloading them from disk on demand.

World Wide Web (WWW)   An Internet-derived service. The service consists of two components: a WWW server and a WWW client (or Web browser). A Web server transmits the requested document, or Web page, when requested by a Web browser. The document may contain text, graphics, audio-video clips, or links to additional documents. See also *File Transfer Protocol, Gopher, Hypertext Markup Language,* and *Hypertext Transfer Protocol.*

HTML Reference

IN THIS APPENDIX

- How This Reference Is Structured **714**
- HTML Element List **715**
- Defining Special Characters on Your Web Page **749**
- HTML Summary for the Internet Information Server and the Internet Assistant for Word for Windows **754**

The Hypertext Markup Language (HTML) is in constant flux. This appendix focuses on the HTML elements that are currently in use. This includes the HTML 2.0 tags, which are specified in RFC 1866, as well as some of the proposed tags for HTML 3.2. It also includes some HTML tag extensions supported by the Microsoft Internet Explorer version 2.0.

This appendix is meant to be an easy-to-use reference for the major HTML tags. It is by no means a definitive HTML reference; an entire book would be needed for that. Of course, any book devoted to HTML will probably be out-of-date by the time you read it.

> **TIP**
>
> For the latest information on HTML specification, check out `http://www.w3.org`. For the latest HTML extensions supported by the Microsoft Internet Explorer, use `http://www.microsoft.com/ie`. For the latest on Netscape Navigator HTML extensions, take a look at `http://home.netscape.com`.

This reference is divided into two basic sections. The first section is an HTML reference that includes HTML tags and extensions currently supported by the Microsoft Internet Explorer and Netscape Navigator. Following this are two tables that list the HTML tags supported by the Internet Information Server and Internet Assistant for Microsoft Word, respectively. This should make life a little easier when you are creating WWW pages that may be used by multiple Web browsers.

How This Reference Is Structured

Each element (or *tag*, if you prefer) is listed in alphabetical order to make searching for the tag a little easier. Within each element definition, the minimum attributes for the element are described, as are all possible attributes. If an element allows other elements to be embedded within it, or if an element is restricted to the context of a set of elements, this, too, is mentioned. To make this list a little shorter and more descriptive (it is possible for groups to contain other groups that more fully display the nesting and recursion that can occur within a group), this reference uses the group definitions defined in RFC 1866. These groups include the following:

- BLOCK—Includes the groups BLOCK.FORM, LIST, PREFORMATTED, and TABLE, and the entities DL and P.
- BLOCK.FORMS—Contains the BLOCKQUOTE, FORM, and ISINDEX entities.
- BODY.CONTEXT—Can contain the groups BLOCK, HEADING, and TEXT, and the HR and ADDRESS entities. It is recommended that this group only contain the BLOCK, HEADING, TEXT, HR, ADDRESS, and IMG entities.

This recommendation means that all text within a body should be enclosed in a block. Instead of this format:

```
<H1>HEADING</H1>
Textual Information
```

it is recommended that the following format be used:

```
<H1>Heading</H1>
<P>Textual information</P>
```

- FONT—Contains the TT, B, and I entities.
- HEADING—Contains the H1, H2, H3, H4, H5, and H6 entities.
- LIST—Contains the DIR, MENU, OL, and UL entities.
- PHRASE—Contains the EM, CITE, CODE, KBD, SAMP, STRONG, and VAR entities.
- PREFORMATTED—Contains the LISTING, PRE, and XMP entities.
- TEXT—Contains the PHRASE and FONT groups, the A, IMG, and BR entities, and parsed character data. Parsed character data is any valid character data after the data has been parsed and all special character entities have been replaced.

> **NOTE**
>
> The internationalization proposal also includes the BDO, Q, SPAN, SUB, and SUP entities in the TEXT group.

HTML Element List

<A>

Description: Anchors a piece of text and/or image that is identified as a hypertext link. This element must have either an HREF or a NAME attribute. The HREF attribute defines a URL as the destination target. A NAME attribute defines a destination target within the current document. To associate a target in an external document, an HREF attribute may be used with the #name suffix on the URL. This will load the associated document and position the display at the selected location of the NAME tag. It is also possible to use an HREF attribute with a URL consisting solely of #name to jump to a location within the current document. If the REL attribute is present in a document/object (A) that has an HREF to a document/object (B), the REL attribute identifies a relationship that B has to A that A recognizes/verifies/authorizes. If the REV attribute is present in document/object B with an HREF to document/object A, the REV attribute identifies a relationship that B has to A, but which must be verified by checking with A.

Minimum Attributes: `<A HREF="...">CharacterData...</A>`

All Attributes: `<A NAME="...">CharacterData...</A>`

Elements Allowed Within: `<A HREF="..." NAME="..." REL="..." REV="..." URN="..." TITLE="..." METHODS="..." LANG="..." DIR=LTR|RTL CHARSET="..." ID="..." CLASS="..." MD="..." TARGET=..." SHAPE="...">CharacterData...</A>`

Allowed in Context of: Members of groups HEADING and TEXT, but not element `<A>`.

Notes: Any element that permits group TEXT.

The internationalization proposal introduced the LANG, DIR, and CHARSET attributes. The CHARSET attribute is a hint as to which character set should be used by the hyperlink. Prior proposals suggested changing the NAME attribute to the ID attribute, thus declaring the NAME attribute as obsolete. The ID attribute would then be added to various elements that previously used the NAME attribute. However, with the current style sheet proposal (which includes the ID, MD, and CLASS attributes), this is very likely to change. The REL and REV attributes are rarely used or supported. These relationships are more commonly identified in the document HEAD using the LINK element. The URN attribute is for a Universal Resource Number, and is currently not used or supported. TITLE and METHODS are also rarely used or supported. TARGET is a Netscape 2.0 extension. The SHAPE attribute is proposed to provide a mechanism to define multiple `<A>` elements, with corresponding hotzones in the proposed FIG element. This would perform the same basic function as the ISMAP element without developing a `cgi-bin` application. An alternate proposal is defined by the MAP element.

`<ABBREV>`

Description: Changes the character rendering of the contents to logically represent abbreviations.

Minimum Attributes: `<ABBREV>CharacterData...</ABBREV>`

All Attributes: `<ABBREV LANG="..." DIR=LTR|RTR ID="..." CLASS="...">CharacterData...</ABBREV>`

Elements Allowed Within: TBD.

Allowed in Context of: TBD.

`<ACRONYM>`

Description: Changes the character rendering of the contents to logically represent acronyms.

Minimum Attributes: `<ACRONYM>CharacterData...</ACRONYM>`

All Attributes: `<ACRONYM LANG="..." DIR=LTR|RTR ID="..." CLASS="...">CharacterData...</ACRONYM>`

Elements Allowed Within: TBD.

Allowed in Context of: TBD.

<ADDRESS>

Description: Defines a separated multiline set of text to be rendered for address/contact information.

Minimum Attributes: <ADDRESS>*CharacterData*...</ADDRESS>

All Attributes: <ADDRESS LANG="..." DIR=LTR¦RTR ALIGN=LEFT¦RIGHT¦CENTER¦JUSTIFY ID="..." CLASS="..." CLEAR=LEFT¦RIGHT¦ALL¦"..." NOWRAP>*CharacterData*...</ADDRESS>

Elements Allowed Within: Members of group TEXT or element <P>.

Allowed in Context of: Any element that permits members of the group BODY.CONTENT.

Notes: Text within an address is generally rendered in italics. The internationalization proposal introduced the LANG, DIR, and ALIGN attributes.

<APPLET>

Description: This element replaces the APP element, which is used to invoke a JAVA application. Web browsers that support the APP element will ignore all APPLET attributes except for the PARAM attribute. Those Web browsers that do not support the APPLET element should ignore both it and the PARAM element, and should instead process the element content. So in essence, the alternative HTML is the content of the APPLET element. The file that contains the compiled applet subclass is named CODE. This name is relative to the base URL of the applet and cannot be an absolute URL. The WIDTH and HEIGHT elements provide the initial width and height, in pixels, of the applet's display area. CODEBASE specifies the base URL for the applet; ALT specifies the parsed character data to be displayed if the Web browser supports the APPLET element but cannot or will not run the applet; NAME specifies an applet instance; ALIGN specifies the display alignment; and VSPACE and HSPACE specify the reserved space around the applet in pixels.

Minimum Attributes: <APPLET CODE="..." WIDTH="..." HEIGHT="...">*CharacterData*...</APPLET>

All Attributes: <APPLET CODE="..." WIDTH="..." HEIGHT="..." CODEBASE="..." ALT="..." NAME="..." ALIGN=LEFT¦RIGHT¦TOP¦TEXTTOP¦MIDDLE¦ABSMIDDLE¦BASELINE¦BOTTOM¦ABSBOTTOM VSPACE="..." HSPACE="...">*CharacterData*...</APPLET>

Elements Allowed Within: <PARAM> element and any other elements that would have been allowed in the document at this point.

Allowed in Context of: TBD.

Notes: The APPLET element is a Netscape Navigator 2.0 extension.

<APPLICATION>

See <APPLET>

<AREA>

Description: Specifies a single area of an image that, if selected, will jump to the hypertext link identified by the HREF attribute. COORDS specifies the position of an area, in pixels, of the image in comma-separated x,y coordinates (the upper-left corner is defined as 0,0). For the SHAPE attribute, RECT (the default) is left, top, right, bottom; a CIRCLE is center x, center y, radius; a POLYGON is successive x and y vertices. The NOHREF attribute specifies that the region should not generate a link. The ALT attribute defines optional parsed character data to describe the area that can be displayed by Web browsers that do support images.

Minimum Attributes: <AREA COORDS="...">

All Attributes: <AREA COORDS="..." SHAPE=RECT¦CIRCLE¦POLYGON HREF="..." NOHREF ALT="...">

Elements Allowed Within: None.

Allowed in Context of: <MAP>.

Notes: There is no corresponding end tag. The AREA element is a proposed enhancement to support client-side image maps. This element is a Netscape 2.0 extension that currently only supports the SHAPE=RECT attribute, and ALT is not defined.

<AU>

Description: Changes the character rendering of the contents to logically represent an author's name.

Minimum Attributes: <AU>CharacterData...</AU>

All Attributes: <AU LANG="..." DIR=LTR¦RTR ID="..." CLASS="...">CharacterData...</AU>

Elements Allowed Within: TBD.

Allowed in Context of: TBD.

<B>

Description: Displays rendered text in a bold font.

Minimum Attributes: <B>CharacterData...</B>

All Attributes: `<B LANG="..." DIR=LTR¦RTL ID="..." CLASS="...">CharacterData...</B>`

Elements Allowed Within: Members of group `TEXT`.

Allowed in Context of: Any element that permits group `FONT`.

Notes: A Web browser that does not support the `BOLD` element may render the text in another fashion. This rendering, however, must be distinct from the rendering produced by the `<I>` element.

<BANNER>

Description: A proposal for corporate logos, navigational aids, disclaimers, or other informational material that should not be scrolled with the rest of the document.

Minimum Attributes: `<BANNER>CharacterData...</BANNER>`

All Attributes: `<BANNER LANG="..." DIR=LTR¦RTR ID="..." CLASS="...">CharacterData...</BANNER>`

Elements Allowed Within: TBD.

Allowed in Context of: `<BODY>`.

<BASE>

Description: Specifies an absolute URL to be used by relative URLs within the document. It must be a complete filename, and it is normally the original URL of the document.

Minimum Attributes: `<BASE HREF="...">`

All Attributes: `<BASE HREF="..." TARGET="...">`

Elements Allowed Within: N/A.

Allowed in Context of: `<HEAD>`.

<BASEFONT>

Description: Specifies a base-font size to be used within the document instead of the default of 3.

Minimum Attributes: `<BASEFONT SIZE=1¦2¦3¦4¦5¦6¦7>`

All Attributes: `<BASEFONT SIZE=1¦2¦3¦4¦5¦6¦7>`

Elements Allowed Within: TBD.

Allowed in Context of: TBD.

Notes: The `BASEFONT` element is a Netscape Navigator extension.

<BDO>

Description: Used as a directional override to deal with unusual pieces of text where the directionality cannot be specifically determined. The DIR attribute is required, but is different in context than when used for inline text markup. For BDO, the DIR attribute specifies the directionality of all characters, including those with strong directional context.

Minimum Attributes: `<BDO DIR=LTR¦RTR>CharacterData...</BDO>`

All Attributes: `<BDO LANG="..." DIR=LTR¦RTR>CharacterData...</BDO>`

Elements Allowed Within: Members of group TEXT.

Allowed in Context of: Any element that permits members of group TEXT.

Notes: This is a proposed element of the internationalization of HTML.

<BGSOUND>

Description: Plays an audio file as a background sound. SRC specifies the location of the file to be played, and LOOP specifies the number of iterations.

Minimum Attributes: `<BACKGROUND SRC="...">`

All Attributes: `<BACKGROUND SRC="..." LOOP="...">`

Elements Allowed Within: None.

Allowed in Context of: TBD.

Notes: Microsoft Internet Explorer 2.0 extension.

<BIG>

Description: Specifies that the physical rendering of the font be increased if practical.

Minimum Attributes: `<BIG>CharacterData...</BIG>`

All Attributes: `<BIG LANG="..." DIR=LTR¦RTR ID="..." CLASS="...">CharacterData...</BIG>`

Elements Allowed Within: TBD.

Allowed in Context of: TBD.

Notes: A Netscape Navigator 2.0 extension.

<BLINK>

Description: Specifies that the physical rendering of the enclosed text be a blinking font.

Minimum Attributes: `<BLINK>CharacterData...</BLINK>`

All Attributes: `<BLINK>CharacterData...</BLINK>`

Elements Allowed Within: TBD.

Allowed in Context of: TBD.

Notes: A Netscape 1.1 extension. Most Web browsers ignore this element.

<BLOCKQUOTE>

Description: Specifies that a multiline set of text be rendered as quoted text.

Minimum Attributes: `<BLOCKQUOTE>CharacterData...</BLOCKQUOTE>`

All Attributes: `<BLOCKQUOTE LANG="..." DIR=LTR|RTR ALIGN=LEFT|RIGHT|CENTER|JUSTIFY>CharacterData...</BLOCKQUOTE>`

Elements Allowed Within: Members of BODY.CONTENT.

Allowed in Context of: Any element that permits members of group BODY.FORMS.

Notes: Typically rendered in enclosed quotes or as an indented paragraph in an italic font.

<BODY>

Description: Specifies the actual content of the document, as opposed to HEAD, which contains information about the document itself. All displayable elements should be within the body of the document. BACKGROUND specifies a path/filename to an image to be used as a tiled background bitmap. BGCOLOR specifies a background color.

Minimum Attributes: `<BODY>CharacterData...</BODY>`

All Attributes: `<BODY LANG="..." DIR=LTR|RTR ID="..." CLASS="..." BACKGROUND="..." BGCOLOR="..." BGPROPERTIES=FIXED TEXT="RRGGBB" LINK="RRGGBB" VLINK="RRGGBB" ALINK="RRGGBB">CharacterData...</BODY>`

Elements Allowed Within: Members of BODY.CONTENT.

Allowed in Context of: HTML.

Notes: Netscape Navigator requires a RRGGBB (red green blue) format for the color elements, while Microsoft Internet Explorer 2.0 can accept BLACK, MAROON, GREEN, OLIVE, NAVY, PURPLE, TEAL, GRAY, SILVER, RED, LIME, YELLOW, BLUE, FUCHSIA, AQUA, and WHITE instead of an RBG value. The TEXT, LINK, ALINK, and VLINK attributes are Netscape Navigator extensions that also work with IE 2.0. In addition, the IE 2.0 supports the BGPROPERTIES (only with the FIXED attribute) to specify a nonscrolling background image.

<BQ>

Description: Specifies a multiline set of text to be rendered as quoted text.

Minimum Attributes: `<BQ>CharacterData...</BQ>`

All Attributes: `<BQ LANG="..." DIR=LTR|RTR ID="..." CLASS="..." CLEAR=LEFT|RIGHT|ALL|"..." NOWRAP>CharacterData...</BQ>`

Elements Allowed Within: `<CREDIT>`. Others TBD.

Allowed in Context of: `<BQ>`. Others TBD.

Description: Specifies a new line without separating the text with additional vertical space.

Minimum Attributes: `<BR>`

All Attributes: `<BR CLEAR=LEFT|RIGHT|ALL|"..." ID="..." CLASS="...">`

Elements Allowed Within: None.

Allowed in Context of: Any element that permits group TEXT.

Notes: A Netscape Navigator 1.1 extension.

<CAPTION>

Description: Specifies a label for a table or figure. The ALIGN attribute specifies where the caption should be placed.

Minimum Attributes: `<CAPTION>CharacterData...</CAPTION>`

All Attributes: `<CAPTION ALIGN=TOP|BOTTOM|LEFT|RIGHT LANG="..." DIR=LTR|RTR ID="..." CLASS="...">CharacterData...</CAPTION>`

Elements Allowed Within: TBD.

Allowed in Context of: `<FIG> <TABLE>`.

Notes: Netscape Navigator 1.1 extension.

<CENTER>

Description: CENTER encloses text between the left and right margins.

Minimum Attributes: `<CENTER>CharacterData...</CENTER>`

All Attributes: `<CENTER>CharacterData...</CENTER>`

Elements Allowed Within: TBD.

Allowed in Context of: `<A>`. Others TBD.

Notes: A Netscape Navigator 1.1 extension. This element has been replaced by the ALIGN=CENTER attribute in Netscape Navigator 2.0.

<CITE>

Description: Changes the character rendering of the text to logically display a citation.

Minimum Attributes: `<CITE>CharacterData...</CITE>`

All Attributes: `<CITE DIR=LTR|RTR ID="..." CLASS="...">CharacterData...</CITE>`

Elements Allowed Within: Members of group TEXT.

Allowed in Context of: Any element that permits elements of group PHRASE.

Notes: Typically rendered in an italic font.

<CODE>

Description: Changes the character rendering of the text to logically display computer code. Intended for short words or phrases. The PRE element is recommended for multiline listings.

Minimum Attributes: `<CODE>CharacterData...</CODE>`

All Attributes: `<CODE DIR=LTR|RTR ID="..." CLASS="...">CharacterData...</CODE>`

Elements Allowed Within: Members of group TEXT.

Allowed in Context of: Any element that permits elements of group PHRASE.

Notes: Typically displayed in a fixed-width font.

<COL>

Description: Specifies column-based defaults for a table. SPAN specifies how many columns are contained within the table with a default of 1. WIDTH specifies the width of the column in pixels (although this may be overridden by appending a two-character code to the unit pt = points, pi = picas, in = inches, cm = centimeters, mm = millimeters, em = em units, and px = pixels) in the span. ALIGN and VALIGN specify the horizontal and vertical alignment of text within a cell. If ALIGN=CHAR, the CHAR specifies a character to be used for alignment. The default is a decimal point. CHAROFF specifies an offset from the alignment character.

Minimum Attributes: <COL>

All Attributes: <COL LANG="..." DIR=LTR¦RTR ID="..." CLASS="..." SPAN=nn WIDTH="..." ALIGN=LEFT ¦RIGHT¦CENTER¦JUSTIFY¦CHAR CHAR="." CHAROFF+"..." VALIGN=TOP¦BOTTOM¦MIDDLE¦BASELINE>

Elements Allowed Within: None.

Allowed in Context of: <COLGROUP> and <TABLE>.

Notes: This element is part of the new specification and is not currently widely implemented.

<COLGROUP>

Description: Specifies a group of one or more columns and assigns defaults for all the columns in the group. CHAROFF specifies an offset from the alignment character, in pixels (although this may be overridden by appending a two-character code to the unit pt = points, pi = picas, in = inches, cm = centimeters, mm = millimeters, em = em units, and px = pixels) in the span. ALIGN and VALIGN specify the horizontal and vertical alignment of text within a cell. If ALIGN=CHAR, then CHAR specifies a character to be used for alignment. The default is a decimal point.

Minimum Attributes: <COLGROUP>*CharacterData*...</COLGROUP>

All Attributes: <COLGROUP LANG="..." DIR=LTR¦RTR ID="..." CLASS="..." ALIGN=LEFT¦RIGHT¦ CENTER¦JUSTIFY¦CHAR CHAR="." CHAROFF+"..." VALIGN=TOP¦BOTTOM¦MIDDLE¦BASELINE> *CharacterData*...</COLGROUP>

Elements Allowed Within: <COL>.

Allowed in Context of: <TABLE>.

Notes: This element is part of the new specification and is not currently widely implemented.

<CREDIT>

Description: Specifies the name of a source of a block quotation or figure.

Minimum Attributes: <CREDIT>*CharacterData*...</CREDIT>

All Attributes: <CREDIT LANG="..." DIR=LTR¦RTR ID="..." CLASS="...">*CharacterData*... </CREDIT>

Elements Allowed Within: TBD.

Allowed in Context of: <BQ> <FIG>.

<DD>

Description: Specifies the separate multiline definition of a definition list (<DL>).

Minimum Attributes: `<DD>CharacterData...</DD>`

All Attributes: `<DD LANG="..." DIR=LTR|RTR ID="..." CLASS="...">CharacterData...</DD>`

Elements Allowed Within: Members of groups BLOCK and TEXT.

Allowed in Context of: <DL>.

Notes: Generally rendered as indented text in a normal font.

<DEL>

Description: Specifies that text be physically rendered to logically represent deleted text.

Minimum Attributes: `<DEL>CharacterData...</DEL>`

All Attributes: `<DEL LANG="..." DIR=LTR|RTR ID="..." CLASS="...">CharacterData...</DEL>`

Elements Allowed Within: TBD.

Allowed in Context of: TBD.

Notes: This element is proposed as a replacement to the <S> and <STRIKE> elements.

<DFN>

Description: Specifies a logical rendering of the text to represent a definition in a term/definition pair.

Minimum Attributes: `<DFN>CharacterData...</DFN>`

All Attributes: `<DFN LANG="..." DIR=LTR|RTR ID="..." CLASS="...">CharacterData...</DFN>`

Elements Allowed Within: TBD.

Allowed in Context of: TBD.

Notes: Usually rendered in bold text.

<DIR>

Description: Specifies an unordered list of single-line <LI> items.

Minimum Attributes: `<DIR></DIR>`

All Attributes: `<DIR COMPACT LANG="..." DIR=LTR|RTR ALIGN=LEFT|RIGHT|CENTER|JUSTIFY></DIR>`

Elements Allowed Within: `<LI>`, but not any elements of group `BLOCK`.

Allowed in Context of: Any element of group `LIST`.

`<DIV>`

Description: A proposed element, to be used with the `CLASS` attribute, for specifying different types of containers (chapters, sections, abstracts, or appendixes).

Minimum Attributes: `<DIV>CharacterData...</DIV>`

All Attributes: `<DIV LANG="..." DIR=LTR|RTR ALIGN=LEFT|RIGHT|CENTER|JUSTIFY ID="..." CLASS="..." NOWRAP CLEAR=LEFT|RIGHT|ALL|"...">CharacterData...</DIV>`

Elements Allowed Within: TBD.

Allowed in Context of: `<BODY>`.

`<DL>`

Description: Specifies a definition list. Each item in the list is expected to have two components, which are identified by the `<DT>` and `<DD>` elements.

Minimum Attributes: `<DL></DL>`

All Attributes: `<DL COMPACT LANG="..." DIR=LTR|RTR ALIGN=LEFT|RIGHT|CENTER|JUSTIFY></DL>`

Elements Allowed Within: `<LH>`, `<DT>`, and `<DD>`.

Allowed in Context of: Any element that permits group `BLOCK`.

`<DT>`

Description: Specifies the term in a definition list.

Minimum Attributes: `<DT>CharacterData...</DT>`

All Attributes: `<DT LANG="..." DIR=LTR|RTR>CharacterData...</DT>`

Elements Allowed Within: Members of group `TEXT`.

Allowed in Context of: `<DL>`.

Notes: Typically rendered in a bold font.

<EM>

Description: Changes the character rendering to assume an emphasized attribute.

Minimum Attributes: `<EM>CharacterData...</EM>`

All Attributes: `<EM LANG="..." DIR=LTR|RTR ID="..." CLASS="...">CharacterData...</EM>`

Elements Allowed Within: Members of group TEXT.

Allowed in Context of: Any element that permits group PHRASE.

Notes: Typically rendered in an italic font.

<EMBED>

Description: Specifies a container for inserting objects directly into an HTML page. Embedded objects are supported by application-specific plug-ins.

Minimum Attributes: `<EMBED SRC="...">`

All Attributes: `<EMBED SRC="..." HEIGHT="..." WIDTH="..." attribute_1="..." attribute_2="..." ...>CharacterData...</EMBED>`

Elements Allowed Within: `<NOEMBED>`.

Allowed in Context of: TBD.

Notes: A Netscape Navigator 2.0 extension.

<FIG>

Description: An advanced form of the IMG element that specifies an image with optional overlays, text, and hotzones.

Minimum Attributes: `<FIG SRC="...">`

All Attributes: `<FIG SRC="..." LANG="..." DIR=LTR|RTR ID="..." CLASS="..." CLEAR=LEFT|RIGHT|ALL|"..." NOFLOW MD="..." ALIGN=LEFT|RIGHT|CENTER|JUSTIFY|BLEEDLEFT WIDTH=Value HEIGHT=Value UNITS="..." IMAGEMAP="..."></FIG>`

Elements Allowed Within: `<OVERLAY>`, `<CAPTION>`, and `<CREDIT>`. All others TBD.

Allowed in Context of: TBD.

<FN>

Description: Specifies the rendering of text as a logical footnote. The reference location for a footnote is expected to be an A element with an HREF attribute that references the ID of the FN element.

Minimum Attributes: `<FN ID="...">CharacterData...</FN>`

All Attributes: `<FN LANG="..." DIR=LTR¦RTR ID="..." CLASS="...">CharacterData...</FN>`

Elements Allowed Within: TBD.

Allowed in Context of: TBD.

<FONT>

Description: Specifies the size of the font used for the following text in one of the seven defined sizes or as a plus/minus of the BASEFONT.

Minimum Attributes: `<FONT SIZE=1¦2¦3¦4¦5¦6¦7>`

All Attributes: `<FONT SIZE=1¦2¦3¦4¦5¦6¦7 COLOR="..." FACE="...">`

Elements Allowed Within: TBD.

Allowed in Context of: TBD.

Notes: Netscape Navigator requires a RRGGBB (red green blue) format for the color elements, while Microsoft Internet Explorer 2.0 can accept BLACK, MAROON, GREEN, OLIVE, NAVY, PURPLE, TEAL, GRAY, SILVER, RED, LIME, YELLOW, BLUE, FUCHSIA, AQUA, and WHITE instead of an RBG value. FACE is an IE 2.0 extension that is currently not defined.

<FORM>

Description: Creates a fill-out form that is displayed on the Web browser. The browser then sends the information to an application on the server, which is identified as a URL by the ACTION attribute. If METHOD=GET (the default), the information is appended to the ACTION URL, which on most systems becomes the environment value QUERY_STRING. If METHOD=POST (the preferred method), the input is sent in a data body, available as stdin, with the data length set in the environment variable CONTENT_LENGTH. Form data is a stream of NAME/VALUE pairs separated by the & character. Each NAME/VALUE pair is a URL encoded in hexadecimal form. At least one of the following is expected in the FORM contents: INPUT, SELECT, or TEXTAREA.

Minimum Attributes: `<FORM></FORM>`

All Attributes: `<FORM ACTION="..." METHOD=GET¦POST ENCTYPE="..." LANG="..." DIR=LTR¦RTR ACCEPT-CHARSET="..." SCRIPT="..."></FORM>`

Elements Allowed Within: Members of group BODY.CONTENT and any of the elements <INPUT>, <SELECT>, and <TEXTAREA>, but not element <FORM>.

Allowed in Context of: Any element that permits members of group BLOCK.FORM.

<FRAME>

Description: Specifies a single frame in a frameset. The SRC value is a URL of the document to be displayed within the frame. The NAME element assigns a name to the frame that will be used as the target of a hypertext link. The SCROLLING attribute defines whether the frame should have a scrollbar, and defaults to the value AUTO. If the NORESIZE attribute is present, the frame cannot be resized by the user.

Minimum Attributes: <FRAME>

All Attributes: <FRAME SRC="..." NAME="..." MARGINWIDTH="..." MARGINHEIGHT="..." SCROLLING=YES¦NO¦AUTO NORESIZE>

Elements Allowed Within: None.

Allowed in Context of: <FRAMESET>.

Notes: A Netscape Navigator 2.0 extension that defines multiple windows for viewing a document. The following entries are reserved for the NAME attribute: _BLANK, _SELF, _PARENT, and _TOP. These entries have the following definitions: new unnamed window, load in the same window, load in the parent window, and load in the top window, respectively. The units defined for MARGINWIDTH and MARGINHEIGHT are in pixels.

<FRAMESET>

Description: Used instead of the BODY element in an HTML document to define the layout of sub-HTML documents, or frames, that make up the page. The ROWS and COLUMNS values are comma-separated lists defining the row height and column width of the frames.

Minimum Attributes: <FRAMESET>CharacterData...</FRAMESET>

All Attributes: <FRAMESET ROWS="..." COLS="...">CharacterData</FRAMESET>

Elements Allowed Within: <FRAME>, <FRAMESET>, and <NOFRAMES>.

Allowed in Context of: <HTML>.

Notes: A Netscape Navigator 2.0 extension. The ROWS and COLS values are restricted to integer values with an optional suffix to define the unit of measure.

`<H1>`

Description: A level-1 heading.

Minimum Attributes: `<H1>`*CharacterData*`...</H1>`

All Attributes: `<H1 LANG="..." DIR=LTR¦RTR ALIGN=LEFT¦RIGHT¦CENTER¦JUSTIFY ID="..." CLASS="..." CLEAR=LEFT¦RIGHT¦ALL¦"..." SEQNUM=nnn SKIP=nnn DINGBAT=entity-name SRC="..." MD="..." NOWRAP>`*CharacterData*`...</H1>`

Elements Allowed Within: Members of group TEXT.

Allowed in Context of: Any element that permits members of group HEADING.

`<H2>`

Description: A level-2 heading.

Minimum Attributes: `<H2>`*CharacterData*`...</H2>`

All Attributes: `<H2 LANG="..." DIR=LTR¦RTR ALIGN=LEFT¦RIGHT¦CENTER¦JUSTIFY ID="..." CLASS="..." CLEAR=LEFT¦RIGHT¦ALL¦"..." SEQNUM=nnn SKIP=nnn DINGBAT=entity-name SRC="..." MD="..." NOWRAP>`*CharacterData*`...</H2>`

Elements Allowed Within: Members of group TEXT.

Allowed in Context of: Any element that permits members of group HEADING.

`<H3>`

Description: A level-3 heading.

Minimum Attributes: `<H3>`*CharacterData*`...</H3>`

All Attributes: `<H3 LANG="..." DIR=LTR¦RTR ALIGN=LEFT¦RIGHT¦CENTER¦JUSTIFY ID="..." CLASS="..." CLEAR=LEFT¦RIGHT¦ALL¦"..." SEQNUM=nnn SKIP=nnn DINGBAT=entity-name SRC="..." MD="..." NOWRAP>`*CharacterData*`...</H3>`

Elements Allowed Within: Members of group TEXT.

Allowed in Context of: Any element that permits members of group HEADING.

`<H4>`

Description: A level-4 heading.

Minimum Attributes: `<H4>`*CharacterData*`...</H4>`

All Attributes: `<H4 LANG="..." DIR=LTR|RTR ALIGN=LEFT|RIGHT|CENTER|JUSTIFY ID="..." CLASS="..." CLEAR=LEFT|RIGHT|ALL|"..." SEQNUM=nnn SKIP=nnn DINGBAT=entity-name SRC="..." MD="..." NOWRAP>CharacterData...</H4>`

Elements Allowed Within: Members of group TEXT.

Allowed in Context of: Any element that permits members of group HEADING.

`<H5>`

Description: A level-5 heading.

Minimum Attributes: `<H5>CharacterData...</H5>`

All Attributes: `<H5 LANG="..." DIR=LTR|RTR ALIGN=LEFT|RIGHT|CENTER|JUSTIFY ID="..." CLASS="..." CLEAR=LEFT|RIGHT|ALL|"..." SEQNUM=nnn SKIP=nnn DINGBAT=entity-name SRC="..." MD="..." NOWRAP>CharacterData...</H5>`

Elements Allowed Within: Members of group TEXT.

Allowed in Context of: Any element that permits members of group HEADING.

`<H6>`

Description: A level-6 heading.

Minimum Attributes: `<H6>CharacterData...</H6>`

All Attributes: `<H6 LANG="..." DIR=LTR|RTR ALIGN=LEFT|RIGHT|CENTER|JUSTIFY ID="..." CLASS="..." CLEAR=LEFT|RIGHT|ALL|"..." SEQNUM=nnn SKIP=nnn DINGBAT=entity-name SRC="..." MD="..." NOWRAP>CharacterData...</H6>`

Elements Allowed Within: Members of group TEXT.

Allowed in Context of: Any element that permits members of group HEADING.

`<HEAD>`

Description: Defines general information about the document. None of the elements are displayed.

Minimum Attributes: N/A

All Attributes: `<HEAD LANG="..." DIR=LTR|RTR></HEAD>`

Elements Allowed Within: `<TITLE>`, `<ISINDEX>`, `<BASE>`, `<META>`, `<LINK>`, and `<NEXTID>`.

Allowed in Context of: `<HTML>`.

<HPn>

Description: Specifies a set of HPn elements, where n = 1, 2, 3, 4, 5, or 6, and corresponds to the heading levels H1–H6. This tag will specify the font size of the text and highlight the text as well.

Minimum Attributes: `<HPn>CharacterData...</HPn>`

All Attributes: `<HPn>CharacterData...</HPn>`

Elements Allowed Within: N/A.

Allowed in Context of: N/A.

Notes: This element is rarely used and should be considered obsolete.

<HR>

Description: Defines a horizontal divider (or rule), which is a line between sections of text. The SRC attribute can be used to specify a custom image for the rule.

Minimum Attributes: `<HR>`

All Attributes: `<HR DIR=LTR¦RTR ALIGN=LEFT¦RIGHT¦CENTER¦JUSTIFY ID="..." CLASS="..." CLEAR=LEFT¦RIGHT¦ALL¦"..." SRC="..." MD="..." SIZE=Number WIDTH=Number¦Percent NISHADE>`

Elements Allowed Within: None.

Allowed in Context of: Any element that permits members of group BODY.CONTENT.

Notes: Netscape Navigator 2.0 extensions include the SIZE, WIDTH, ALIGN, and NOSHADE attributes, although only the ALIGN=LEFT¦RIGHT¦CENTER options are implemented.

<HTML>

Description: Defines the HTML document. All elements must be bracketed within the `<HTML>` `</HTML>` tags.

Minimum Attributes: `<HTML></HTML>`

All Attributes: `<HTML VERSION="..." LANG="..." DIR=LTR¦RTR></HTML>`

Elements Allowed Within: `<HEAD>`, `<BODY>`, and `<PLAINTEXT>`.

<I>

Description: Specifies that rendered text be displayed in an italic font.

Minimum Attributes: `<I>CharacterData...</I>`

All Attributes: `<I LANG="..." DIR=LTR¦RTR ID="..." CLASS="...">CharacterData...</I>`

Elements Allowed Within: Members of group TEXT.

Allowed in Context of: Any element that permits members of group FONT.

<IMG>

Description: Defines an image file to be inserted into the current document with associated text. The ALT attribute defines the parsed character data to be displayed in place of the image for Web browsers that do not support image insertion. The ISMAP attribute is only meaningful if the IMG element is within the contents of an A element. A corresponding cgi-bin application will receive the HREF input values, when a selectable portion of the image is clicked by the client.

Minimum Attributes: <IMG SRC="...">

All Attributes: <IMG SRC="..." ALT="..." ISMAP LANG="..." DIR=LTR¦RTR ID="..." CLASS="..." MD="..." ALIGN=LEFT¦RIGHT¦TOP¦MIDDLE¦BOTTOM¦TEXTTOP¦ABSMIDDLE¦BASELINE¦ABSBOTTOM HEIGHT=Value WIDTH=Value UNITS="..." BORDER=Value LOWSRC="..." HSPACE=Value Vspace=Value USEMAP="..." DYNSRC="..." START=FILEOPEN¦MOUSEOVER CONTROLS LOOP=Number¦INFINITE¦-1 LOOPDELAY=Number>

Elements Allowed Within: None.

Allowed in Context of: Any element that permits group TEXT.

Notes: The BORDER, HEIGHT, WIDTH, HSPACE, VSPACE, and LOWSRC attributes are Netscape Navigator 1.1 extensions. The DYNSRC, START, CONTROLS, LOOP, and LOOPDELAY attributes are IE 2.0 extensions. DYNSRC identifies a video clip or VRML world to be displayed. If START=MOUSEOVER, the image is displayed until the mouse is over the image. CONTROLS will display a set of controls under the animation image. LOOP is defined as the number of times the image will be replayed when activated. If LOOP is set to INFINITE or 1, the video clip will play indefinitely. LOOPDELAY determines the time, in milliseconds, between replays of the video clip.

<INPUT>

Description: Specifies a input field as part of the contents in a form. TYPE=TEXT is the default. NAME defines the symbolic name of the returned field to the server upon submission. This attribute must be present, except when TYPE=SUBMIT¦RESET. For TYPE=CHECKBOX¦RADIO, the name may be the same for multiple INPUT elements. TYPE=RADIO ensures that only one name is selected. For TYPE=PASSWORD, the value should be obscured, generally by an asterisk (*), so that the actual password is not readable onscreen when entered. VALUE defines the label for a push button. CHECKED specifies that the push button, or radio INPUT, to be preconfigured to a selected state. TYPE=IMAGE defines an image specified in the URL and defined in the SRC attribute, which, when clicked, submits the form and sends the x,y coordinates to the receiving URL. The SIZE and MAXLENGTH attributes are only used with a TYPE=TEXT or TYPE=PASSWORD attribute, where SIZE is the physical size of the displayed input field expressed in characters and rows, and MAXLENGTH is the maximum number of characters that will be accepted as input.

Minimum Attributes: `<INPUT>`

All Attributes: `<INPUT TYPE="TEXT¦PASSWORD¦CHECKBOX¦RADIO¦SUBMIT¦RESET¦HIDDEN¦IMAGE¦FILE¦RANGE¦SCRIBBLE¦JOT" LANG="..." DIR=LTR¦RTR ID="..." CLASS="..." NAME="..." VALUE="..." SRC="..." CHECKED SIZE="..." MAXLENGTH=Number ALIGN=LEFT¦RIGHT¦TOP¦MIDDLE¦BOTTOM ACCEPT="..." DISABLED ERROR="..." MIN=Number MAX=Number MD="...">`

Elements Allowed Within: None.

Allowed in Context of: `<FORM>`.

`<INS>`

Description: Specifies that rendered text be displayed as logically inserted text.

Minimum Attributes: `<INS>CharacterData...</INS>`

All Attributes: `<INS LANG="..." DIR=LTR¦RTR ID="..." CLASS="...">CharacterData...</INS>`

Elements Allowed Within: TBD.

Allowed in Context of: TBD.

`<ISINDEX>`

Description: This is a precursor to the `<FORM>` element, and is usually created by a server-side script. When placed in the BODY of a document, the ISINDEX requires that the ACTION attribute points to a `cgi-bin` application to handle a query. A simple INPUT field with the prompt `This is a searchable index. Enter search keywords:` is produced. When placed in the HEAD of a document, the ISINDEX informs the Web browser that the document is an index document that can be examined using a keyword search.

Minimum Attributes: `<ISINDEX>`

All Attributes: `<ISINDEX LANG="..." DIR=LTR¦RTR ACTION="..." PROMPT="...">`

Elements Allowed Within: None.

Allowed in Context of: The element `<HEAD>` and any element that permits members of group BLOCK.FORMS.

`<KBD>`

Description: Specifies that rendered text be displayed as keyboard input.

Minimum Attributes: `<KBD>CharacterData...</KBD>`

All Attributes: `<KBD LANG="..." DIR=LTR|RTR ID="..." CLASS="...">`*CharacterData*`...</KBD>`

Elements Allowed Within: Members of group TEXT.

Allowed in Context of: Any element that permits members of group PHRASE.

Notes: Typically displayed with a fixed-width font.

<LANG>

Description: Changes the default language context for subsequent elements. A LANG attribute on an element will override the default language context for the particular element.

Minimum Attributes: `<LANG>`*CharacterData*`...</LANG>`

All Attributes: `<LANG ID="..." CLASS="...">`*CharacterData*`...</LANG>`

Elements Allowed Within: TBD.

Allowed in Context of: TBD.

<LH>

Description: Defines a list header to be used as a title for a list.

Minimum Attributes: `<LH>`*CharacterData*`...</LH>`

All Attributes: `<LH LANG="..." DIR=LTR|RTR ID="..." CLASS="...">`Character Data`...</LH>`

Elements Allowed Within: TBD.

Allowed in Context of: `<DL>`, `<OL>`, and `<UL>`.

<LI>

Description: Defines a list item.

Minimum Attributes: `<LI>`*CharacterData*`...</LI>`

All Attributes: `<LI LANG="..." DIR=LTR|RTR ALIGN=LEFT|RIGHT|CENTER|JUSTIFY within UL TYPE=DISK|CIRCLE|SQUARE within OL TYPE=A|I within OL VALUE=n>`*CharacterData*`...</LI>`

Elements Allowed Within: Members of group TEXT and BLOCK.

Allowed in Context of: `<DIR>`, `<MENU>`, `<OL>`, and `<UL>`.

Notes: The TYPE and VALUE attributes are Netscape Navigator extensions.

<LINK>

Description: Specifies that a relationship between this document and another document exists. Multiple LINK elements may exist within a document. If the REL attribute is present in document/object (A) with an HREF to a document/object (B), LINK identifies a relationship that B has to A that A recognizes/verifies/authorizes. If the REV attribute is present in document/object (B) with an HREF to a document/object (A), LINK identifies a relationship that B has to A, but that must be verified by checking with A.

Minimum Attributes: <LINK HREF="...">

All Attributes: <LINK HREF="..." REL="..." REV="..." LANG="..." DIR=LTR¦RTR CHARSET="..." URN="..." TITLE="..." METHODS="...">

Elements Allowed Within: None.

Allowed in Context of: <HEAD>.

<LISTING>

Description: Specifies that separated multiline text be rendered as it exists, with all line breaks intact.

Minimum Attributes: <LISTING>CharacterData...</LISTING>

All Attributes: <LISTING WIDTH="...">CharacterData...</LISTING>

Elements Allowed Within: None.

Allowed in Context of: Any element that permits members of group BLOCK.

Notes: The assumed width is 132 characters. Some Web browsers no longer support this attribute.

<MAP>

Description: Specifies a name and description for a client-side image map. An *image map* is a set of areas on the image that may be used to select specific hypertext links. NAME defines the map name to be used with the USEMAP attribute on an IMG element.

Minimum Attributes: <MAP NAME="..."></MAP>

All Attributes: <MAP NAME="..."></MAP>

Elements Allowed Within: <AREA>.

Allowed in Context of: TBD.

<MARQUEE>

Description: Defines an area in which visual scrolling will be used to display the content of the element.

Minimum Attributes: `<MARQUEE>CharacterData...</MARQUEE>`

All Attributes: `<MARQUEE ALIGN=LEFT¦RIGHT¦TOP¦MIDDLE¦BOTTOM BEHAVIOR=SCROLL¦SLIDE¦ALTERNATE BGCOLOR="RRBBGG"¦COLORNAME DIRECTION=LEFT¦RIGHT HEIGHT=Number¦NumberPercent HSPACE=Number LOOP=Number¦INFINITE¦-1 SCROLLAMOUNT=Number SCROLLDELAY=Number VSPACE=Number>CharacterData...</MARQUEE>`

Elements Allowed Within: TBD.

Allowed in Context of: TBD.

Notes: This element is an Microsoft Internet Explorer 2.0 extension. The `BGCOLOR` attribute can accept `BLACK`, `MAROON`, `GREEN`, `OLIVE`, `NAVY`, `PURPLE`, `TEAL`, `GRAY`, `SILVER`, `RED`, `LIME`, `YELLOW`, `BLUE`, `FUCHSIA`, `AQUA`, and `WHITE`. The `BEHAVIOR` attribute specifies how the text will scroll (`SCROLL`): completely in and out, slide (`SLIDE`) in and stay, or bounce (`ALTERNATE`) between the sides of the marquee. The `DIRECTION` attribute specifies in which direction the text will flow; the `HEIGHT` attribute specifies how high the marquee should be; `HSPACE` and `VSPACE` determine, in pixels, the amount of surrounding whitespace; and the `LOOP` attribute specifies how many iterations of the marquee are to be played. `SCROLLAMOUNT` specifies the number of pixels in the marquee text, and `SCROLLDELAY` specifies the number of milliseconds between repeated redraws of the marquee text.

<MENU>

Description: Defines an unordered list consisting of separate multiline `<LI>` (list item) elements.

Minimum Attributes: `<MENU></MENU>`

All Attributes: `<MENU COMPACT LANG="..." DIR=LTR¦RTR ALIGN=LEFT¦RIGHT¦CENTER¦JUSTIFY></MENU>`

Elements Allowed Within: Element `<LI>`, but not members of group `BLOCK`.

Allowed in Context of: Any element that permits members of group `LIST`.

<META>

Description: Used within the `HEAD` element to embed document-meta information not defined by any HTML element. The `HTTP-EQUIV` element binds the element to an `HTTP` response header. If present, the `NAME` attribute is used to identify this meta information, and should not be used within the `HTTP` response header. If the `NAME` attribute is not present, it can be assumed that the name is the same as the value of HTTP-EQUIV. The CONTENT attribute defines the meta-information content to be associated with the given name of the HTTP response header.

Minimum Attributes: `<META CONTENT="...">`

All Attributes: `<META HTTP-EQUIV="..." NAME="..." CONTENT="..." URL="...">`

Elements Allowed Within: None.

Allowed in Context of: `<HEAD>`.

Notes: The URL attribute is a Netscape Navigator extension. Netscape Navigator 1.1 has added an automatic refresh capability by assigning the HTTP-EQUIV attribute to REFRESH, the CONTENT attribute to a number of seconds, and the URL attribute to a file to load.

<NEXTID>

Description: Specifies the only attribute (N) as the number to be used by automatic-hypertext editors.

Minimum Attributes: `<NEXTID N="...">`

All Attributes: `<NEXTID N="...">`

Elements Allowed Within: None.

Allowed in Context of: `<HEAD>`.

Notes: RFC 1866 recommends that this element not be used.

<NOBR>

Description: Specifies that all text within the enclosed tags cannot have line breaks inserted between them.

Minimum Attributes: `<NOBR>CharacterData...</NOBR>`

All Attributes: `<NOBR>CharacterData...</NOBR>`

Elements Allowed Within: TBD.

Allowed in Context of: TBD.

Notes: This element is a Netscape Navigator 1.1 extension.

<NOEMBED>

Description: Defines content within an EMBED context that is to be ignored by those Web browsers that support embedded plug-in applications. However, if the Web browser does not support embedded plug-ins, the content specified in the NOEMBED element will be displayed.

Minimum Attributes: `<NOEMBED>CharacterData...</NOEMBED>`

All Attributes: `<NOEMBED>CharacterData...</NOEMBED>`

Elements Allowed Within: TBD.

Allowed in Context of: `<EMBED>`.

Notes: A Netscape Navigator 2.0 extension to supported specific application plug-ins.

<NOFRAMES>

Description: Specifies content to be displayed by Web browsers that do not support frames.

Minimum Attributes: `<NOFRAMES>CharacterData...</NOFRAMES>`

All Attributes: `<NOFRAMES>CharacterData...</NOFRAMES>`

Elements Allowed Within: TBD.

Allowed in Context of: `<FRAMESET>`.

Notes: A Netscape Navigator 2.0 extension.

<NOTE>

Description: Specifies that rendered text be displayed as a logical note. The `SRC` attribute specifies an image to be displayed before the note.

Minimum Attributes: `<NOTE>CharacterData...</NOTE>`

All Attributes: `<NOTE LANG="..." DIR=LTR¦RTR ID="..." CLASS="..." CLEAR=LEFT¦RIGHT¦CENTER¦ALL¦"..." SRC="..." MD="..."></NOTE>`

Elements Allowed Within: TBD.

Allowed in Context of: TBD.

<OL>

Description: Defines an ordered (such as a numbered) list.

Minimum Attributes: `<OL></OL>`

All Attributes: `<OL COMPACT LANG="..." DIR=LTR¦RTR ALIGN=LEFT¦RIGHT¦CENTER¦JUSTIFY ID="..." CLASS="..." CLEAR=LEFT¦RIGHT¦CENTER¦ALL¦"..." CONTINUE SEQNUM=Value START=Value TYPE=A¦I¦1></OL>`

Elements Allowed Within: `<LH>` and `<LI>`.

Allowed in Context of: Any element of group LIST.

Notes: Both TYPE and START are Netscape Navigator extensions.

<OPTION>

Description: Specifies a choice in a SELECT element. SELECTED specifies that the option is selected by default.

Minimum Attributes: `<OPTION>CharacterData...`

All Attributes: `<OPTION SELECTED VALUE="..." LANG="..." DIR=LTR|RTR ID="..." CLASS="..." DISABLED ERROR="..." SHAPE="...">CharacterData...</OPTION>`

Elements Allowed Within: May only contain parsed character data.

Allowed in Context of: `<SELECT>`.

<OVERLAY>

Description: Specifies one or more images to be overlayed on a FIG element.

Minimum Attributes: `<OVERLAY SRC="...">`

All Attributes: `<OVERLAY SRC="..." MD="..." UNITS=PIXELS|EN X=Value Y=Value WIDTH=Value HEIGHT=Value IMAGEMAP="...">`

Elements Allowed Within: None.

Allowed in Context of: `<FIG>`.

<P>

Description: Specifies a paragraph break and separates two blocks of text with vertical whitespace.

Minimum Attributes: `<P>`

All Attributes: `<P ALIGN=LEFT|RIGHT|CENTER|JUSTIFY|INDENT WRAP=ON|OFF NOWRAP CLEAR=LEFT|RIGHT|ALL|"..." LANG="..." DIR=LTR|RTR ID="..." CLASS="...">CharacterData...</P>`

Elements Allowed Within: Members of group TEXT.

Allowed in Context of: Any element that permits members of group BLOCK.

`<PARAM>`

Description: Defines a general-purpose mechanism to pass parameters to an APPLET application, where NAME is the name of the parameter and VALUE is the data to be obtained by the APPLET application using the getParameter() method.

Minimum Attributes: `<PARAM NAME="..." VALUE="...">`

All Attributes: `<PARAM NAME="..." VALUE="...">`

Elements Allowed Within: None.

Allowed in Context of: `<APPLET>`.

`<PERSON>`

Description: Specifies the rendering of text on the display to logically represent the names of personnel, thus allowing automatic extraction by indexing programs.

Minimum Attributes: `<PERSON>`*CharacterData...*`</PERSON>`

All Attributes: `<PERSON LANG="..." DIR=LTR¦RTR ID="..." CLASS="...">`*CharacterData...*`</PERSON>`

Elements Allowed Within: TBD.

Allowed in Context of: TBD.

`<PLAINTEXT>`

Description: Specifies that separated multiline text be rendered as it exists, with all line breaks intact, and that all HTML tags within the enclosed elements be ignored.

Minimum Attributes: `<PLAINTEXT>`*CharacterData...*`</PLAINTEXT>`

All Attributes: `<PALINTEXT WIDTH="..." LANG="..." DIR=LTR¦RTR>`*CharacterData...*`</PLAINTEXT>`

Elements Allowed Within: None.

Allowed in Context of: `<HTML>`.

Notes: Typically displayed in a fixed-width font. Some Web browsers no longer support this attribute.

`<PRE>`

Description: Specifies that separated multiline text be rendered as it exists, with all line breaks intact.

Minimum Attributes: `<PRE>CharacterData...</PRE>`

All Attributes: `<PRE WIDTH=Number LANG="..." DIR=LTR|RTR ID="..." CLASS="..." CLEAR=LEFT|RIGHT|ALL|"...">CharacterData...</PRE>`

Elements Allowed Within: Elements `<A>`, `<HR>`, `<BR>`, and parsed character data.

Allowed in Context of: Any element that permits members of group BLOCK.

Notes: Typically displayed in a fixed-width font.

`<Q>`

Description: Specifies that rendered text be displayed as a logical short quotation.

Minimum Attributes: `<Q>CharacterData...</Q>`

All Attributes: `<Q LANG="..." DIR=LTR|RTR ID="..." CLASS="...">CharacterData...</Q>`

Elements Allowed Within: Members of group TEXT.

Allowed in Context of: Any element that permits members of group TEXT.

Notes: A proposed element that is to be displayed in those quotation marks appropriate to the specified language.

`<S>`

Description: Specifies that rendered text be displayed with a strikeout character.

Minimum Attributes: `<S>CharacterData...</S>`

All Attributes: `<S LANG="..." DIR=LTR|RTR ID="..." CLASS="...">CharacterData...</S>`

Elements Allowed Within: TBD.

Allowed in Context of: TBD.

Notes: A proposed element to replace the STRIKE element.

`<SAMP>`

Description: Specifies that rendered text be displayed as a logical sequence of literal characters.

Minimum Attributes: `<SAMP>CharacterData...</SAMP>`

All Attributes: `<SAMP LANG="..." DIR=LTR|RTR ID="..." CLASS="...">CharacterData...</SAMP>`

Elements Allowed Within: Members of group TEXT.

Allowed in Context of: Any element that permits members of group PHRASE.

Notes: Typically rendered with a fixed-width font.

`<SELECT>`

Description: Defines a menu of a series of inputs in a FORM, each identified with the OPTION element. At least one OPTION element is expected within the SELECT contents. The NAME is a symbolic name returned to the server. The SIZE determines the number of OPTION statements physically visible when the form is displayed by the Web browser.

Minimum Attributes: `<SELECT NAME="...">CharacterData...</SELECT>`

All Attributes: `<SELECT NAME="..." SIZE=Value MULTIPLE LANG="..." DIR=LTR|RTR ID="..." CLASS="..." ALIGN=TOP|MIDDLE|BOTTOM|LEFT|RIGHT DISABLED ERROR="..." SRC="..." MD="..." WIDTH=Value HEIGHT=Value UNITS=PIXELS|EM>CharacterData...</SELECT>`

Elements Allowed Within: `<OPTION>`.

Allowed in Context of: `<FORM>`.

`<SMALL>`

Description: Specifies that rendered text be displayed with a smaller font, if practical.

Minimum Attributes: `<SMALL>CharacterData...</SMALL>`

All Attributes: `<S LANG="..." DIR=LTR|RTR ID="..." CLASS="...">CharacterData...</S>`

Elements Allowed Within: TBD.

Allowed in Context of: TBD.

Notes: A Netscape Navigator 2.0 extension.

`<SPAN>`

Description: Specifies a generic container to set language characteristics for container content.

Minimum Attributes: `<SPAN>CharacterData...</SPAN>`

All Attributes: `<SPAN LANG="..." DIR=LTR|RTR>CharacterData...</SPAN>`

Elements Allowed Within: Members of group TEXT.

Allowed in Context of: Any element that permits members of group TEXT.

Notes: Another internationalization proposal.

<STRIKE>

Description: Specifies that rendered text be displayed with a strikeout character.

Minimum Attributes: <STRIKE>CharacterData...</STRIKE>

All Attributes: <STRIKE >CharacterData...</STRIKE>

Elements Allowed Within: TBD.

Allowed in Context of: TBD.

<STRONG>

Description: Specifies that rendered text be displayed with stronger emphasis.

Minimum Attributes: <STRONG>CharacterData...</STRONG>

All Attributes: <STRONG LANG="..." DIR=LTR|RTR ID="..." CLASS="...">CharacterData...</STRONG>

Elements Allowed Within: Members of group TEXT.

Allowed in Context of: Any element that permits members of group PHRASE.

Notes: Typically rendered as bold text.

<SUB>

Description: Specifies that rendered text be displayed as a subscript.

Minimum Attributes: _{CharacterData...}

All Attributes: _{CharacterData...}

Elements Allowed Within: Parsed character data.

Allowed in Context of: Any element that permits members of group TEXT.

<SUP>

Description: Specifies that rendered text be displayed as a superscript.

Minimum Attributes: ^{CharacterData...}

All Attributes: ^{CharacterData...}

Elements Allowed Within: Parsed character data.

Allowed in Context of: Any element that permits members of group TEXT.

HTML Reference
Appendix B

<TAB>

Description: Aligns text according to a defined horizontal position. Text is positioned by using the TO and/or ALIGN attributes, or by using the INDENT attribute.

Minimum Attributes: <TAB>CharacterData...

All Attributes: <TAB ID="..." INDENT=ens TO="..." ALIGN=LEFT¦RIGHT¦CENTER¦DECIMAL DP="...">CharacterData...

Elements Allowed Within: TBD.

Allowed in Context of: TBD.

<TABLE>

Description: Defines a series of rows of table cells. The order in the sequence is important and consists of at least one TR element, possibly some COL or COLGROUP elements, at most one THEAD, at most one TFOOT, at most one TBODY, and at most one CAPTION element.

Minimum Attributes: <TABLE></TABLE>

All Attributes: <TABLE LANG="..." DIR=LTR¦RTR ID="..." CLASS="..." ALIGN=LEFT¦RIGHT¦CENTER¦JUSTIFY¦BLEEDLEFT¦BLEEDRIGHT WIDTH="..." COLS=Number BORDER="..." FRAME=VOID¦ABOVE¦BELOW¦HSIDES¦LHS¦RHS¦VSIDES¦BOX¦BORDER RULES=NONE¦BASIC¦ROWS¦COLS¦ALL CELLSPACING="..." CELLPADDING="..." CLEAR=LEFT¦RIGHT¦ALL¦"..." NOFLOW UNITS=EN¦RELATIVE¦PIXELS COLSPEC="..." DP="..." NOERAP></TABLE>

Elements Allowed Within: <CAPTION>, <COL>, <COLGROUP>, <THEAD>, <TFOOT>, <TBODY>, and <TR>.

Allowed in Context of: Any element that permits members of group BLOCK.

<TBODY>

Description: Defines a series of table-row definitions, and specifies the defaults for all rows in the group. Table rows within a TABLE content are grouped into at most one THEAD, at most one TFOOT, and at least one TBODY (in that order).

Minimum Attributes: <TBODY>

All Attributes: <TBODY LANG="..." DIR=LTR¦RTR ID="..." CLASS="..." ALIGN=LEFT¦RIGHT¦CENTER¦JUSTIFY¦CHAR CHAR="..." CHAROFF="..." VALIGN=TOP¦BOTTOM¦MIDDLE¦BASELINE>CharacterData...</TBODY>

Elements Allowed Within: <TR>.

Allowed in Context of: <TABLE>.

<TD>

Description: Defines a data cell as part of a TABLE. The AXIS and AXES attributes define concise labels for cells. The ROWSPAN and COLSPAN attributes define the number of rows and columns spanned by a cell.

Minimum Attributes: <TD>

All Attributes: <TD LANG="..." DIR=LTR|RTR ID="..." CLASS="..." AXIS="..." AXES="..." NOWRAP ROWSPAN=Value COLSPAN=Value ALIGN=LEFT|RIGHT|CENTER|JUSTIFY|CHAR|DECIMAL CHAR="..." CHAROFF="..." DP="..." VALIGN=TOP|MIDDLE|BOTTOM|BASELINE WIDTH=Value BGCOLOR="...">CharacterData...</TD>

Elements Allowed Within: Members of group BODY.CONTENT.

Allowed in Context of: <TR>.

Notes: This element is an extension in both Netscape Navigator and the Microsoft Internet Explorer 2.0. The values JUSTIFY|CHAR are new and not widely implemented. The BGCOLOR attribute can accept BLACK, MAROON, GREEN, OLIVE, NAVY, PURPLE, TEAL, GRAY, SILVER, RED, LIME, YELLOW, BLUE, FUCHSIA, AQUA, and WHITE.

<TEXTAREA>

Description: Specifies a multiline input field as part of a FORM element, where NAME defines a symbolic name to be returned to the server upon submission of the form.

Minimum Attributes: <TEXTAREA NAME="..." ROWS="..." COLS="..."></TEXTAREA>

All Attributes: <TEXTAREA NAME="..." ROWS="..." COLS="..." LANG="..." ID="..." CLASS="..." WRAP=OFF|VIRTUAL|PHYSICAL ALIGN=LEFT|RIGHT|TOP|MIDDLE|BOTTOM DISABLED ERROR="...">CharacterData...</TEXTAREA>

Elements Allowed Within: Only parsed data.

Allowed in Context of: <FORM>.

<TFOOT>

Description: This element encloses a series of table-row definitions, and specifies defaults for all rows in the group. Table rows grouped within this TABLE element have at most one THEAD, at most one TFOOT, and at least one TBODY.

Minimum Attributes: <TFOOT>

All Attributes: <TFOOT LANG="..." DIR=LTR|RTR ID="..." CLASS="..." ALIGN=LEFT|RIGHT|CENTER|JUSTIFY|CHAR CHAR="..." CHAROFF="..." VALIGN=TOP|MIDDLE|BOTTOM|BASELINE>CharacterData...</TFOOT>

Elements Allowed Within: `<TR>`.

Allowed in Context of: `<TABLE>`.

`<TH>`

Description: Defines a header cell as part of the `TABLE` construct.

Minimum Attributes: `<TH>`

All Attributes: `<TH LANG="..." DIR=LTR|RTR ID="..." CLASS="..." AXIS="..." AXES="..." NOWRAP ROWSPAN=Value COLSPAN=Value ALIGN=LEFT|RIGHT|CENTER|JUSTIFY|CHAR|DECIMAL CHAR="..." CHAROFF="..." DP="..." VALIGN=TOP|MIDDLE|BOTTOM|BASELINE WIDTH=Value BGCOLOR="...">CharacterData...</TD>`

Elements Allowed Within: Members of group `BODY.CONTENT`.

Allowed in Context of: `<TR>`.

Notes: This element is an extension both in Netscape Navigator and the Microsoft Internet Explorer 2.0. The values `JUSTIFY|CHAR` are new and not widely implemented. The `BGCOLOR` attribute can accept `BLACK`, `MAROON`, `GREEN`, `OLIVE`, `NAVY`, `PURPLE`, `TEAL`, `GRAY`, `SILVER`, `RED`, `LIME`, `YELLOW`, `BLUE`, `FUCHSIA`, `AQUA`, and `WHITE`.

`<THEAD>`

Description: This element encloses a series of table-row definitions, and specifies defaults for all rows in the group. Table rows grouped within this `TABLE` element have at most one `THEAD`, at most one `TFOOT`, and at least one `TBODY`.

Minimum Attributes: `<THEAD>`

All Attributes: `<THEAD LANG="..." DIR=LTR|RTR ID="..." CLASS="..." ALIGN=LEFT|RIGHT|CENTER|JUSTIFY|CHAR CHAR="..." CHAROFF="..." VALIGN=TOP|MIDDLE|BOTTOM|BASELINE>CharacterData...</THEAD>`

Elements Allowed Within: `<TR>`.

Allowed in Context of: `<TABLE>`.

`<TITLE>`

Description: Defines a label commonly used by Web browsers to display a document tile on the caption.

Minimum Attributes: `<TITLE>CharacterData...</TITLE>`

All Attributes: `<TITLE LANG="..." DIR=LTR|RTR>CharacterData...</TITLE>`

Elements Allowed Within: Only parsed data.

Allowed in Context of: <HEAD>.

<TR>

Description: This element defines a table row.

Minimum Attributes: <TR>

All Attributes: <TR LANG="..." DIR=LTR¦RTR ID="..." CLASS="..." ALIGN=LEFT¦RIGHT¦CENTER¦JUSTIFY¦CHAR¦DECIMAL CHAR="..." CHAROFF="..." VALIGN=TOP¦MIDDLE¦BOTTOM¦BASELINE DP="...">CharacterData...</TR>

Elements Allowed Within: <TD> and <TH>.

Allowed in Context of: <TBODY>, <TFOOT>, and <THEAD>.

<TT>

Description: Specifies that rendered text be displayed as a fixed-width teletype font.

Minimum Attributes: <TT>CharacterData...</TT>

All Attributes: <TT LANG="..." DIR=LTR¦RTR ID="..." CLASS="...">CharacterData...</TT>

Elements Allowed Within: Members of group TEXT.

Allowed in Context of: Any element that permits members of group FONT.

<U>

Description: Specifies that rendered text be displayed in an underlined font.

Minimum Attributes: <U>CharacterData...</U>

All Attributes: <U LANG="..." DIR=LTR¦RTR ID="..." CLASS="...">CharacterData...</U>

Elements Allowed Within: TBD.

Allowed in Context of: TBD.

Notes: Generally rendered as an underlined font; however, some Web browsers will display this as an italic font.

<UL>

Description: Defines an unordered (such as a bulleted) list.

Minimum Attributes: <UL></UL>

All Attributes: `<UL COMPACT LANG="..." DIR=LTR¦RTR ALIGN=LEFT¦RIGHT¦CENTER¦JUSTIFY ID="..." CLASS="..." CLEAR=LEFT¦RIGHT¦CENTER¦ALL¦"..." PLAIN SRC="..." MD="..." DINGBAT="..." WRAP=VERT¦HORIZ TYPE=DISK¦CIRCLE¦SQUARE></UL>`

Elements Allowed Within: `<LH>` and `<LI>`.

Allowed in Context of: Any element of group LIST.

<VAR>

Description: Specifies that rendered text be displayed as a logical variable name.

Minimum Attributes: `<VAR>CharacterData...</VAR>`

All Attributes: `<VAR LANG="..." DIR=LTR¦RTR ID="..." CLASS="...">CharacterData...</VAR>`

Elements Allowed Within: Members of group TEXT.

Allowed in Context of: Any element that permits members of group PHRASE.

Notes: Typically rendered in an italic font.

<WBR>

Description: Used to specify a line break in a no-break zone.

Minimum Attributes: `<WBR>`

All Attributes: `<WBR>`

Elements Allowed Within: None.

Allowed in Context of: `<NOBR>`.

Notes: A Netscape Navigator 2.0 extension.

<XMP>

Description: Specifies that a separated multiline text be rendered as it exists, with the same line breaks as in the source document.

Minimum Attributes: `<XMP>CharacterData...</XMP>`

All Attributes: `<XMP WIDTH="..." LANG="..." DIR=LTR¦RTR ID="..." >CharacterData...</XMP>`

Elements Allowed Within: None.

Allowed in Context of: Any element that permits members of group BLOCK.

Notes: Typically rendered in a fixed-width font with an assumed width of 80 characters. Some Web browsers no longer support this element.

Defining Special Characters on Your Web Page

When you develop your Web page, you may run into the occasional problem where you need to define a special character. The format to do so is to concatenate an &, a #, a two-digit number, and a ;, as specified in Table B.1. There are also a few additional special-character sequences you may use, including &copy for the copyright symbol, &reg for the trademark symbol, &shy for a soft hyphen,   for a non-breaking space, &quot for a quotation mark, &lt for a less-than symbol, &gt for a greater-than symbol, and &amp for an ampersand symbol.

Table B.1. The HTML coded character set.

Key Value	Description
&#00;-&#08;	Unused
&#09;	Horizontal tab
&#10;	Line feed
&#11;-	Unused
&#13;	Carriage return
&#14;-&#31;	Unused
&#32;	Space
&#33;	Exclamation point
&#34;	Quotation mark
&#35;	Number sign
&#36;	Dollar sign
&#37;	Percent sign
&#38;	Ampersand
&#39;	Apostrophe
&#40;	Left parenthesis
&#41;	Right parenthesis
&#42;	Asterisk
&#43;	Plus sign
&#44;	Comma
&#45;	Hyphen
&#46;	Period (fullstop)
&#47;	Solidus (slash)

HTML Reference
Appendix B

Key Value	Description
0-9	Digits 0–9
&#58;	Colon
&#59;	Semicolon
&#60;	Less than
&#61;	Equal sign
&#62;	Greater than
&#63;	Question mark
&#64;	Commercial at
A-Z	Letters A–Z
&#91;	Left square bracket
&#92;	Reverse solidus (backslash)
&#93;	Right square bracket
&#94;	Caret
&#95;	Horizontal bar (underscore)
&#96;	Acute accent
a-z	Letters a–z
&#123;	Left curly brace
|	Vertical bar
&#125;	Right curly brace
&#126;	Tilde
&#127;-Ÿ	Unused
	Nonbreaking space
&#161;	Inverted exclamation
&#162;	Cent sign
&#163;	Pound sterling
&#164;	General currency sign
&#165;	Yen sign
&#166;	Broken vertical bar
&#167;	Section sign
&#168;	Umlaut (dieresis)
&#169;	Copyright
&#170;	Feminine ordinal

continues

Table B.1. continued

Key Value	Description
&#171;	Left angle quote, guillemotleft
&#172;	Not sign
&#173;	Soft hyphen
&#174;	Registered trademark
&#175;	Macron accent
&#176;	Degree sign
&#177;	Plus or minus
&#178;	Superscript two
&#179;	Superscript three
&#180;	Acute accent
&#181;	Micro sign
&#182;	Paragraph sign
&#183;	Middle dot
&#184;	Cedilla
&#185;	Superscript one
&#186;	Masculine ordinal
&#187;	Right angle quote, guillemotright
&#188;	Fraction one-fourth
&#189;	Fraction one-half
&#190;	Fraction three-fourths
&#191;	Inverted question mark
&#192;	Capital A, grave accent
&#193;	Capital A, acute accent
&#194;	Capital A, circumflex accent
&#195;	Capital A, tilde
&#196;	Capital A, dieresis or umlaut mark
&#197;	Capital A, ring
&#198;	Capital AE dipthong (ligature)
&#199;	Capital C, cedilla
&#200;	Capital E, grave accent
&#201;	Capital E, acute accent
&#202;	Capital E, circumflex accent

Key Value	Description
&#203;	Capital E, dieresis or umlaut mark
&#204;	Capital I, grave accent
&#205;	Capital I, acute accent
&#206;	Capital I, circumflex accent
&#207;	Capital I, dieresis or umlaut mark
&#208;	Capital Eth, Icelandic
&#209;	Capital N, tilde
&#210;	Capital O, grave accent
&#211;	Capital O, acute accent
&#212;	Capital O, circumflex accent
&#213;	Capital O, tilde
&#214;	Capital O, dieresis or umlaut mark
&#215;	Multiply sign
&#216;	Capital O, slash
&#217;	Capital U, grave accent
&#218;	Capital U, acute accent
&#219;	Capital U, circumflex accent
&#220;	Capital U, dieresis or umlaut mark
&#221;	Capital Y, acute accent
&#222;	Capital THORN, Icelandic
&#223;	Small sharp s, German (sz ligature)
&#224;	Small a, grave accent
&#225;	Small a, acute accent
&#226;	Small a, circumflex accent
&#227;	Small a, tilde
&#228;	Small a, dieresis or umlaut mark
&#229;	Small a, ring
&#230;	Small ae dipthong (ligature)
&#231;	Small c, cedilla
&#232;	Small e, grave accent
&#233;	Small e, acute accent
&#234;	Small e, circumflex accent

continues

Table B.1. continued

Key Value	Description
&#235;	Small e, dieresis or umlaut mark
&#236;	Small i, grave accent
&#237;	Small i, acute accent
&#238;	Small i, circumflex accent
&#239;	Small i, dieresis or umlaut mark
&#240;	Small eth, Icelandic
&#241;	Small n, tilde
&#242;	Small o, grave accent
&#243;	Small o, acute accent
&#244;	Small o, circumflex accent
&#245;	Small o, tilde
&#246;	Small o, dieresis or umlaut mark
&#247;	Division sign
&#248;	Small o, slash
&#249;	Small u, grave accent
&#250;	Small u, acute accent
&#251;	Small u, circumflex accent
&#252;	Small u, dieresis or umlaut mark
&#253;	Small y, acute accent
&#254;	Small thorn, Icelandic
&#255;	Small y, dieresis or umlaut mark

HTML Summary for the Internet Information Server and the Internet Assistant for Word for Windows

Not all tags described in the preceding section are supported by the Internet Information Server or the Internet Assistant for Word for Windows. So to make life just that much easier for you, I have listed the supported tags for these in Tables B.2 and B.3, respectively.

Table B.2. HTML tags supported by the Internet Explorer 2.0.

Begin Tag	End Tag	Description
`<A HREF=#X>`	`</A>`	Creates a hypertext link where X is a reference to a bookmark.
`<A HREF=X>`	`</A>`	Creates a hypertext link where X is a URL pointing to another document, file, or bookmark.
`<A NAME>`	`</A>`	Creates a bookmark anchor, a reference for other hypertext links to jump to.
`<ADDRESS>`	`</ADDRESS>`	Creates an address. This usually contains the author's name, street address, and e-mail address.
`<AREA>`	`</AREA>`	Defines an area on the screen to be used as a hotspot.
`<B>`	`</B>`	Displays the enclosed text in bold.
`<BASE>`	`</BASE>`	Defines the document's URL.
`<BASEFONT>`	N/A	Sets the default font.
`<BGSOUND>`	N/A	Specifies a default sound track for the document.
`<BLOCKQUOTE>`	`</BLOCKQUOTE>`	Delineates a block of text quoted from another source.
`<BODY>`	`</BODY>`	Marks the beginning and ending of the document content and specifies document attributes.
` `	N/A	Creates a line break. Note that there is no corresponding end tag.
`<CAPTION>`	N/A	Specifies a table caption, or header. Must be used within a table tag.
`<CENTER>`	`</CENTER>`	Centers enclosed text.
`<CITE>`	`</CITE>`	Defines a citation, which is generally displayed as italic text.
`<CODE>`	`</CODE>`	Defines a line of source code. Note that this is usually displayed as monospaced text.
`<COMMENT>`	N/A	Specifies a comment within the document. Note that this is not displayed on the client's screen.
`<DFN>`	`</DFN>`	Creates a definition for an item that you are describing for the first time. Note that this is usually displayed as bold text.
`<DIR>`	`</DIR>`	Creates a directory list.

continues

Table B.2. continued

Begin Tag	End Tag	Description
`<DL COMPACT>`	N/A	Creates a compact definition list, which means there will be no vertical space between the term and the term description. Note that the `<DL>`...`</DL>` tags are automatically applied.
`<DL>`	`</DL>`	Creates a definition list consisting of two columns. The term is on the left, and the term description is on the right.
`<EM>`	`</EM>`	Displays text with extra emphasis. Note that this is usually displayed in italic or bold type.
`<FONT>`	`</FONT>`	Changes the displayed font.
`<FORM>`	`</FORM>`	Creates a form field used to capture information entered by the client.
`<H1>`	`</H1>`	Creates a document header level 1.
`<H2>`	`</H2>`	Creates a document header level 2.
`<H3>`	`</H3>`	Creates a document header level 3.
`<H4>`	`</H4>`	Creates a document header level 4.
`<H5>`	`</H5>`	Creates a document header level 5.
`<H6>`	`</H6>`	Creates a document header level 6.
`<HEAD>`	`</HEAD>`	Marks the beginning and ending of the document header.
`<HR>`	N/A	Inserts a line on the page. Usually used to provide a visual break between information on the screen. Note that there is no corresponding end tag.
`<HTML>`	`</HTML>`	Marks the beginning and ending of an HTML document.
`<I>`	`</I>`	Displays the enclosed text in italics.
`<IMG>`	N/A	Inserts an in-line graphic image in either a GIF or JPG format. Note that there is no corresponding end tag.
`<INPUT>`	N/A	Specifies a form control. There is no corresponding end tag.
`<ISINDEX>`	N/A	Indicates a searchable index is present. There is no corresponding end tag.
`<KBD>`	`</KBD>`	Displays text you want the user to type on the screen. Usually displayed as a monospaced font.

Begin Tag	End Tag	Description
<LI>	</LI>	Indicates a single item in a list. Used within a <OL></OL> or <UL></UL> tag pair.
<LISTING>	</LISTING>	Displays text in a fixed-width typeface.
<MENU>	</MENU>	Creates a list of items to display.
<MAP>	</MAP>	Specifies a series of hotspots.
<META>	N/A	Defines non-HTML-related information. There is no corresponding end tag.
<NOBR>	</NOBR>	Disables automatic line breaks.
<OL>	</OL>	Creates an ordered (such as a numbered) list.
<OPTION>	</OPTION>	Defines a choice in a listbox.
<P>	N/A	Marks the end of a paragraph. There is no corresponding end tag.
<PLAINTEXT>	</PLAINTEXT>	Displays text onscreen in a fixed-width font without processing the text for embedded HTML tags.
<PRE WIDTH=X>	</PRE>	Displays preformatted text, but overrides the default width (80 characters).
<PRE>	</PRE>	Displays preformatted text.
<S>	</S>	Identifies text that has been struck out. Note that this usually appears with a line through the middle of the text.
<SAMP>	</SAMP>	Displays a sample item. Note that this is usually displayed in a monospaced font enclosed with single quote marks.
<SELECT>	</SELECT>	Specifies a listbox or a drop-down list.
<STRIKE>	</STRIKE>	Identifies text that has been struck out. Note that this usually appears with a line through the middle of the text.
<STRONG>	</STRONG>	Displays text with extra emphasis (more emphasis than the <EM> tag displays). Note that this is usually displayed in bold type.
<TABLE>	</TABLE>	Specifies the beginning and ending of a table. Note that the supported tags and structure are based on the HTML 3.2 draft standard. They may change in the future.

continues

Table B.2. continued

Begin Tag	End Tag	Description
<TITLE>	</TITLE>	Marks the beginning and ending of the document title. Note that the title is displayed on the Web browser's caption bar.
<TT>	</TT>	Displays text in a fixed-width typeface.
<U>	</U>	Displays the enclosed text with an underline.
<UL>	</UL>	Creates a bulleted list.
<VAR>	</VAR>	Displays a variable name, usually entered by the user. Note that this is generally displayed in italics.
<WBR>	N/A	Enables automatic line breaks within a nobreak <NOBR></NOBR> section. Note that there is no corresponding end tag.
<XMP>	</XMP>	Displays text in a fixed-width font.

Table B.3. HTML tags supported by the Word Internet Assistant.

Begin Tag	End Tag	Description
<A HREF=#X>	</A>	Creates a hypertext link where X is a reference to a bookmark.
<A HREF=X>	</A>	Creates a hypertext link where X is a URL pointing to another document, file, or bookmark.
<A NAME>	</A>	Creates a bookmark anchor, a reference for other hypertext links to jump to.
<ADDRESS>	</ADDRESS>	Creates an address. This usually contains the author's name, address, and e-mail address.
<B>	</B>	Displays the enclosed text in bold.
<BLOCKQUOTE>	</BLOCKQUOTE>	Delineates a block of text quoted from another source.
<BODY>	</BODY>	Marks the beginning and ending of the document content and specifies document attributes.
 	N/A	Creates a line break. Note that there is no corresponding end tag.
<CENTER>	</CENTER>	Centers enclosed text.

HTML Reference
Appendix B

Begin Tag	End Tag	Description
`<CITE>`	`</CITE>`	Defines a citation, which is generally displayed as italic text.
`<CODE>`	`</CODE>`	Defines a line of source code. Note that this is usually displayed as monospaced text.
`<DFN>`	`</DFN>`	Creates a definition for an item that you are describing for the first time. Note that this is usually displayed as bold text.
`<DIR>`	`</DIR>`	Creates a directory list.
`<DL COMPACT>`	N/A	Creates a compact definition list, which means there will be no vertical space between the term and term description. Note that the `<DL>`...`</DL>` tags are automatically applied.
`<DL>`	`</DL>`	Creates a definition list consisting of two columns. The term is on the left, the term description on the right.
`<EM>`	`</EM>`	Displays text with extra emphasis. Note that this is usually displayed in italic or bold type.
`<FORM>`	`</FORM>`	Creates a form field used to capture information entered by the client.
`<H1>`	`</H1>`	Creates a document header level 1.
`<H2>`	`</H2>`	Creates a document header level 2.
`<H3>`	`</H3>`	Creates a document header level 3.
`<H4>`	`</H4>`	Creates a document header level 4.
`<H5>`	`</H5>`	Creates a document header level 5.
`<H6>`	`</H6>`	Creates a document header level 6.
`<HEAD>`	`</HEAD>`	Marks the beginning and ending of the document header.
`<HR>`	N/A	Inserts a line on the page. Usually used to provide a visual break between information on the screen. Note that there is no corresponding end tag.
`<HTML>`	`</HTML>`	Marks the beginning and ending of an HTML document.
`<I>`	`</I>`	Displays the enclosed text in italics.

continues

Table B.3. continued

Begin Tag	End Tag	Description
<IMG>	N/A	Inserts an in-line graphic image. The image must be in either a GIF or JPG format. Note that there is no corresponding end tag.
<KBD>	</KBD>	Displays text you want the user to type on the screen. Note that this is usually displayed as a monospaced font.
<MENU>	</MENU>	Creates a list of items to display.
<META>	N/A	Defines non-HTML-related information. Note that this is usually inserted automatically by the Word Internet Assistant.
<OL>	</OL>	Creates an ordered (such as a numbered) list.
<P>	N/A	Marks the end of a paragraph. Note that there is no corresponding end tag.
<PRE WIDTH=x>	</PRE>	Displays preformatted text, but overrides the default width (80 characters).
<PRE>	</PRE>	Displays preformatted text.
<SAMP>	</SAMP>	Displays a sample item. Note that this is usually displayed in a monospaced font enclosed with single quote marks.
<STRIKE>	</STRIKE>	Identifies text that has been struckout. Note that this usually appears with a line through the middle of the text.
<STRONG>	</STRONG>	Displays text with extra emphasis (more emphasis than the <EM> tag). Note that this is usually displayed in bold type.
<TITLE>	</TITLE>	Marks the beginning and ending of the document title. Note that the title is displayed on the Web browser's caption bar.
<TT>	</TT>	Displays text in a fixed-width typeface.
<U>	</U>	Displays the enclosed text with an underline.
<UL>	</UL>	Creates a bulleted list.
<VAR>	</VAR>	Displays a variable name, usually entered by the user. This is generally displayed in italics.

The Registry Editor and Registry Keys

IN THIS APPENDIX

- The Registry **762**
- The Registry Editor **764**
- Useful Registry Keys **767**

Although Microsoft has made the Registry Editor available as a tool to help you when you call for technical support, it is not an officially supported application. This is why you will not see the Registry Editor in any of your program groups. However, I find this tool so useful that the first thing I do after I have installed Windows NT Server is add this tool to my Administrative Tools group. You, too, can do this by creating a new program item for the Administrative Tools group and specifying `Registry Editor` for the Description and `REGEDT32.EXE` for the command line. Windows NT 4.0 will also install the Windows 95 version of the Registry Editor (`regedit.exe`) if it does not detect a shared Windows 3.*x* and Windows NT installation. I prefer to use `regedt32.exe` because it provides more exact control, but it lacks the capability to search the registry by value. So when I'm looking for a specific key, I use `regedit.exe`. The rest of this discussion will focus on using `regedt32.exe`.

> **WARNING**
>
> The Registry Editor is a powerful tool that you should use with extreme care. All the configuration information for Windows NT is stored in the registry (in binary format). If you inadvertently delete a registry key or value that is required, it is possible that Windows NT will refuse to load. Your only recourse at that point is to restore the original registry from a recent tape backup or to use the repair process.

Before you start hacking away with the Registry Editor, an explanation of the registry is in order. Once that is out of the way, you'll take a look at how to use the Registry Editor. After that, you will examine the available registry keys, which you can use to modify the configuration of the various services. Finally, you will learn other little tidbits that can be handy from time to time.

The Registry

The registry is the central storehouse for all configuration information for Windows NT Server. The registry replaces the Windows 3.*x* `.ini` files, although applications can still use `.ini` files if desired. The registry contains information about the hardware platform, performance data, the installed software, all configuration settings for the services and device drivers, and all OLE, DDE, and file associations. Some of this information is backed up by files stored on your hard disk in your `SystemRoot\System32\Config` subdirectory, while the rest of the keys are created and stored only in memory. Table C.1 summarizes the relationship between the primary registry keys and the files that are used to store these keys. The registry, like the NTFS file system or a SQL Server database, uses a transaction log (the `.LOG` version of the file) to make sure any change to the registry either succeeds or fails entirely. This ensures the integrity of the registry. Another interesting registry file is the `SYSTEM.ALT` file, which contains a copy of the previous system registry hive since the last time a user logged on to the system. This file is used by the `LastKnownGood` operation to replace a failed or corrupted system registry hive.

Table C.1. The registry keys and associated files.

Registry Key	Filename
SOFTWARE	SOFTWARE, SOFTWARE.LOG
SYSTEM	SYSTEM, SYSTEM.LOG, SYSTEM.ALT
SAM	SAM, SAM.LOG
SECURITY	SECURITY, SECURITY.LOG
USER	AAAAA###, AAAAA###.LOG *
DEFAULT	DEFAULT, DEFAULT.LOG

*User profiles are stored in the following form: the first five characters of the user name, plus three digits (starting with 000) to create a unique filename. For example, my user name is Arthur and my local user profile is stored in the files `ARTHU000` and `ARTHU000.LOG`, while my domain user profile is stored in the files `ARTHU001` and `ARTHU001.LOG`. I use the same user name for both my local and domain user accounts. Only users who have logged on to the computer locally, or who are configured to use a roaming profile, will have these registry files. The registry is basically composed of seven hives. A *registry hive* is a collection of registry keys, subkeys, values, and data. `HKEY_LOCAL_MACHINE` is the root key for the configuration information of a computer, and has several important subkeys:

- **HARDWARE**—This key contains information about the detected hardware on your system, including your processor, disk controller, video adapter, and serial and parallel ports.
- **SAM**—This key, an acronym for Security Account Manager, contains all the user and group data.
- **SECURITY**—This key contains system security-related data.
- **SOFTWARE**—This key contains all systemwide configuration data for the software installed on a computer.
- **SYSTEM**—This key contains all system-specific configuration data for system services and device drivers installed on a computer.
- **HKEY_CLASSES_ROOT**—This is a subkey of `HKEY_LOCAL_MACHINE\SOFTWARE` and contains all the OLE, DDE, and file-association information.
- **HKEY_CURRENT_CONFIG**—This is a copy of the `HKEY_LOCAL_MACHINE\CurrentControlSet\Hardware Profiles\Current` registry key. It includes information (such as your video driver state) about the currently loaded profile.
- **HKEY_USERS**—This key is the root key for all user-specific configuration data for a computer. It contains the user profiles of all users who have logged in locally to the computer. `HKEY_CURRENT_USER` is a subkey of `HKEY_USERS` and contains a profile of any currently logged on user.

> **CAUTION**
>
> The SAM and SECURITY keys are protected keys, which is why they are displayed as gray, rather than yellow, folders in the Registry Editor. As such, they are inaccessible. The only way to see the data in these keys is to take ownership of these keys. However, if you do that, the operating system will be unable to access those keys, essentially making your computer unusable. You can restore the protected keys from a repair disk or a previous tape backup (where you also backed up the registry).

The Registry Editor

The Registry Editor is a useful tool for administrators. It is used to tune the performance of your server, to configure your installation, and to solve client-related problems. As mentioned in the previous section, the registry is composed of keys, subkeys, values, and data. Each data element is one of the following types:

- REG_SZ—A regular string.
- REG_MULTI_SZ—A multiple string value where each string is separated by a carriage return.
- REG_EXPAND_SZ—An expanded string. This type of string will expand an embedded environment string into its actual value. For example, if you include the value %SystemRoot% in your string, the value of %SystemRoot% (normally C:\WINNT35) will be inserted into the string at the specified location.
- REG_BINARY—A binary data element.
- REG_DWORD—A 32-bit data value.

The first time you use the Registry Editor, four tiled windows are displayed. Each window is a shortcut to a specific registry key. For convenience, I have tiled my view in Figure C.1. Notice that this view appears quite similar to the view in the File Manager. You have expandable folders, which are like directories, in the left window; a split bar in the middle; and a right window that displays the subkeys, which are like subdirectories. Values are displayed in the right window with their associated data, which are like files. If you want to expand or compress a folder, simply double-click it. Similarly, double-click a value (in the right window only) to edit its data.

Appendix C

> **TIP**
>
> The first time you use the Registry Editor, you should set it on read-only mode via the Options | Read Only Mode menu option. This will prevent you from accidentally deleting any keys or other elements while you browse through the registry.

FIGURE C.1.
The Registry Editor in tiled-display mode.

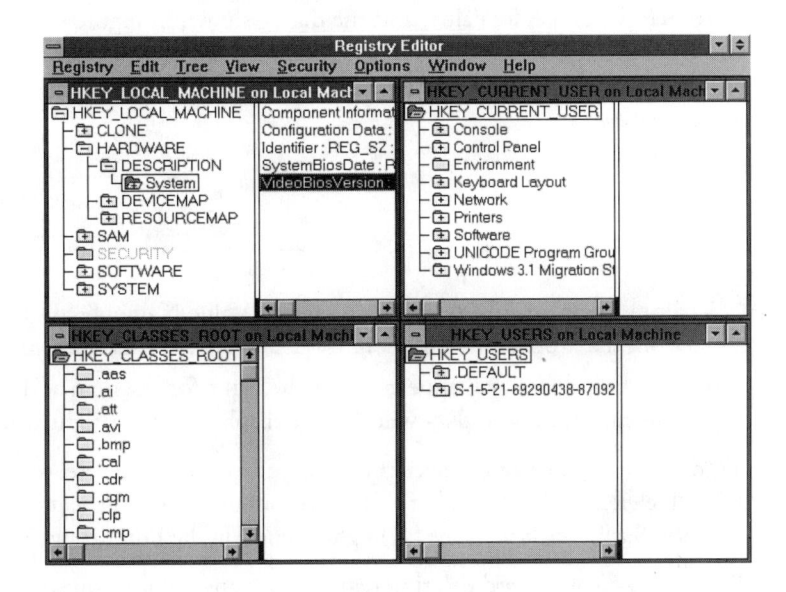

The primary purpose of the Registry Editor is to manipulate registry keys and values. If you want to create a new key or add a new subkey to a existing key, follow these steps:

1. Select and highlight the key in the left window under which you want the subkey to be created.
2. Select Edit | Add Key, and the dialog shown in Figure C.2 will appear.

FIGURE C.2.
The Add Key dialog.

3. Enter the name of the new key in the Key Name: field. Then enter a class type (REG_SZ, REG_MULTI_SZ, REG_EXPAND_SZ, REG_BINARY, or REG_DWORD) in the Class: field. Click the OK button.

If you want to add a new value to a key, follow these steps:

1. Select and highlight the desired key in the left window.
2. Select Edit | Add Value, and the dialog shown in Figure C.3 will appear.

FIGURE C.3.
The Add Value dialog.

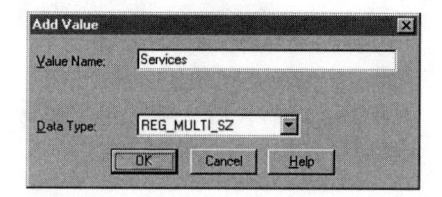

3. Enter the name of the new value in the Value Name: field, then select the data type from the drop-down listbox in the Data Type: field. Click the OK button.
4. The Edit dialog will appear. Enter the value for the item and press the OK button. The new value and data will then be displayed in the right window.

To delete a key or value, select the item and press the Delete key, or use the menu option Edit | Delete. To delete a value's data item, double-click the value (in the right window) and press the Backspace key for the highlighted entry in the Edit dialog. Then click the OK button.

Before you go overboard deleting registry keys and values, you should save them. You can do so by selecting the key in the left window, then using the menu option Registry | Save Key. If you make a mistake while editing the key or value, you can use the Registry | Restore menu option to restore the key you just saved. You can use the Registry | Load Hive menu option to load a complete registry hive file under a new key. You will specify the name of the registry key in the Key Name: field of the Load Hive dialog. A couple other menu options that can come in handy include the following:

- Registry | Select Computer—Use this option to open and manipulate a remote computer's registry, just as you would your own local registry.
- Registry | Close—Use this option to close a remote or local registry.
- Registry | Open Local—Use this option to reopen your registry if you had previously closed it.
- Registry | Print Subtree—Use this option to print a copy of the selected registry key.
- Registry | Save Subtree As—Use this option to save a copy of the selected subtree in text format.

- View | Display Binary Data—When this option is checked, you will be able to view selected binary data in a split-hex dump format rather than in the raw format.
- View | Find Key—Use this menu option to search the registry for a specific key.
- Security | Permissions—Use this option to view or specify security settings for a selected key.
- Security | Auditing—When selected, this option will display the dialog shown in Figure C.4. You can use this dialog to enable auditing of the selected registry key. If you want to enable auditing of all keys, select HKEY_LOCAL_MACHINE and the Security | Auditing option.
- Security | Owner—Use this option to take ownership of a registry key.

FIGURE C.4.
The Registry Key Auditing dialog.

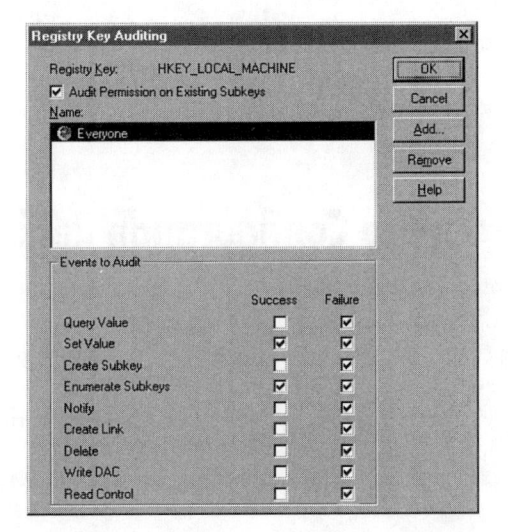

Useful Registry Keys

This section is divided into four basic subsections. Each of these areas contains tables of registry keys that you can use to manually configure various aspects of a service, including the Internet Information Server services. The first section discusses basic network services, the second section discusses NBF transport protocol settings, the third section discusses some of the memory-related registry keys, and the final section includes miscellaneous registry keys that may prove useful.

> **TIP**
>
> You can use the Repair Disk utility (`RDISK.EXE`) to create a backup of your existing registry before you make any system modifications. This way, you can restore your entire configuration and re-enable the self-tuning capabilities.

> **NOTE**
>
> I have not included all the keys that are available. For those of you who want more information, I suggest purchasing the *Windows NT Resource Kit* (Microsoft Press) because it includes a help file that provides additional information about some of the keys in the following table as well as about some keys that I have chosen not to include here. However, I have included some extra information, based on my experience working with Windows NT Server, that may not be documented in the Resource Kit.

System Service Configuration Registry Keys

This section covers registry keys for system services that are not configurable from a Control Panel applet. There are settings in the registry that are configurable from Control Panel applets, and whenever possible you should use that interface to modify a setting. However, before you modify any system-service settings in the following tables, you should be aware that modifying a system-service entry may make you responsible for the tuning of your server. Normally, Windows NT Server is self-tuning, but adding a key may disable the self-tuning capability. Modifying an existing key, however, generally will not disable Windows NT Server's self-tuning capability.

The Internet Information Server registry entries are divided into four types. There are the general keys, as summarized in Table C.2. The server-specific keys are summarized in Tables C.3 through C.5. The keys listed in Tables C.2 through C.5 are not all the registry keys; rather, these are the keys that I think are important and that cannot be set though any other interface (such as the Internet Service Manager). For more information on the IIS service registry keys, take a look at 10_IIS.HTM, which is located in your `IISRoot\Admin\htmladoc` directory. The Server service is responsible for sharing resources on the network, and Table C.6 includes a listing of registry keys that you can use to change the default behavior of the Server service. The Workstation service is used to access shared resources on the network, and Table C.7 includes a listing of registry keys you can use to modify the default behavior of the Workstation service. The

NetLogon service is used to replicate the user/group account information from the primary domain controller (PDC) to the backup domain controllers (BDCs) on the network, and Table C.8 includes a listing of the registry keys and descriptions that you can modify to change behavior of the NetLogon service. Table C.9 includes miscellaneous registry keys and descriptions that you can modify to change other system service configurations.

Table C.2. Internet Information Server service registry keys.

Default	Minimum	Maximum	Description
HKEY_LOCAL_MACHINE\SYSTEM\CurrentControlSet\Services\InetInfo\Parameters\ListenBackLog Key			
15	1	Unlimited	Specifies the number of active connections to remain in a queue waiting to be serviced. A highly visited site might improve its site performance by changing this value to 50.
HKEY_LOCAL_MACHINE\SYSTEM\CurrentControlSet\Services\InetInfo\Parameters\LogFileBatchSize Key			
65536	0	0xFFFFFFFF	Specifies the size of the log file cache. Log file writes are cached at the server until the number of log records to be written exceeds this size. A highly active site may obtain a performance benefit by increasing this value.
HKEY_LOCAL_MACHINE\SYSTEM\CurrentControlSet\Services\InetInfo\Parameters\MemoryCacheSize Key			
3145728	0	0xFFFFFFFF	Specifies the size of the Internet Information Server cache. The Internet Information Server caches file handles, directory listings, and other objects. A highly active site with sufficient physical RAM may obtain a performance benefit by increasing this value.

continues

Table C.2. continued

Default	Minimum	Maximum	Description

HKEY_LOCAL_MACHINE\SYSTEM\CurrentControlSet\Services\InetInfo\Parameters\ObjectCacheTTL Key

| 30 | 0 | 0xFFFFFFFF | Specifies the time, in seconds, that objects in the Internet Information Server cache will be retained. A highly active site may obtain a performance benefit by increasing this value. To obtain the maximum performance benefit, you should increase the size of your cache by changing the MemoryCacheSize key as well. |

Table C.3. World Wide Web Publishing Service registry keys.

Default	Minimum	Maximum	Description

HKEY_LOCAL_MACHINE\SYSTEM\CurrentControlSet\Services\W3CSVC\Parameters\AllowGuestAccess Key

| 1 | 0 | 1 | Specifies that guest logons are accepted (the default), or rejected (0) for the HTTP server. Whenever a user logs on to the system, the HTTP server will either accept or reject a user authentication for non-domain members based on the setting of this flag. Under Windows NT, the guest account's default configuration may have too many permissions available to the account. This could cause site administration problems and security breaches. For added security, it is best to set the AllowGuestAccess key to 0 to prevent abuse. |

Appendix C

Default	Minimum	Maximum	Description
HKEY_LOCAL_MACHINE\SYSTEM\CurrentControlSet\Services\W3CSVC\Parameters\AllowSpecialCharInShell Key			
0	0	1	Specifies that clients may use special characters (such as the & character, which is used to separate multiple batch commands) in batch files. Using these types of special characters, it is possible to execute random commands on the server. This could cause a security breach. Unless you really must provide this type of access to your server, I recommend you leave this option disabled (the default).
HKEY_LOCAL_MACHINE\SYSTEM\CurrentControlSet\Services\W3CSVC\Parameters\CacheExtensions Key			
1	0	1	Specifies that IIS extensions (dynamic link libraries such as the dbWeb extension dbwebc.dll) be cached (1) or not cached (0) by the HTTP server. Since caching offers a performance improvement at the cost of physical memory, one of the few reasons to disable caching is because you need to free up some memory to be used by other applications.
HKEY_LOCAL_MACHINE\SYSTEM\CurrentControlSet\Services\W3CSVC\Parameters\CheckForWAISDB Key			
0	1	1	Specifies that the HTTP server will support the Wide Area Information Server (WAIS) Toolkit searches. The WAIS Toolkit is included with the Windows NT Resource Kit, and is not normally supported by IIS. The HTTP server bases the decision to support WAIS Toolkit

continues

Table C.3. continued

Default	Minimum	Maximum	Description
			searches by setting this flag to 1, then checking whether `waislook.exe` was found on the system path. The default is 0, no WAIS Toolkit searches supported.

HKEY_LOCAL_MACHINE\SYSTEM\CurrentControlSet\Services\W3CSVC\Parameters\CreateProcessAsUser Key

Default	Minimum	Maximum	Description
0	1	1	Specifies that the HTTP server will execute CGI processes using the system context rather than the user context when enabled (1). The default is 0, and should not be changed arbitrarily. Allowing CGI applications to execute using the more powerful privileges assigned to the system increases the potential for a serious security breach.

HKEY_LOCAL_MACHINE\SYSTEM\CurrentControlSet\Services\W3CSVC\Parameters\CreateProcessWithNewConsole Key

Default	Minimum	Maximum	Description
0	1	1	Specifies that the HTTP server will execute CGI in process with a new console. This is particularly useful when your CGI scripts include I/O redirection (such as that used with the | symbol). However, the default is 0 because this option also degrades overall system performance.

Default	Minimum	Maximum	Description
HKEY_LOCAL_MACHINE\SYSTEM\CurrentControlSet\Services\W3CSVC\Parameters\ReturnURLUsingHostName Key			
0	1	1	When enabled (1), this option specifies that the HTTP server will supply a hostname, rather than an IP address, whenever the server is requested to supply a hostname. This is only valid if a hostname has been entered in the DNS properties sheet of the Microsoft TCP/IP Properties dialog.

Table C.4. FTP Publishing service registry keys.

Default	Minimum	Maximum	Description
HKEY_LOCAL_MACHINE\SYSTEM\CurrentControlSet\Services\MSFTPSVC\Parameters\EnablePortAttack Key			
0	1	1	When enabled (1), this option specifies that the FTP server support access to FTP ports (as defined in the FTP RFC) other than the default of 20 (the FTP Data Port). The reason this option is disabled (0) by default is because allowing clients to connect to other FTP ports (less than 20, or between 21 and 1024) creates higher security risks.
HKEY_LOCAL_MACHINE\SYSTEM\CurrentControlSet\Services\MSFTPSVC\Parameters\AnnotateDirectories Key			
0	1	1	When enabled (1), this option specifies that the FTP server supply additional information to describe the current directories. This information is contained in a hidden file in each root directory called ~ftpsvc~.ckm.

Table C.5. Gopher Publishing service registry keys.

Default	Minimum	Maximum	Description
HKEY_LOCAL_MACHINE\SYSTEM\CurrentControlSet\Services\GopherSVC\Parameters\CheckForWAISDB Key			
0	1	1	Specifies that the Gopher server will support Gopher-based searches. The WAIS Toolkit, included with the Windows NT Resource Kit, can be used to supply the search capabilities. The Gopher server bases the decision to support WAIS Toolkit searches by setting this flag to 1, then looking to see if waislook.exe was found on the system path. The default is 0, no WAIS Toolkit searches supported.

Table C.6. Server service registry keys.

Default	Minimum	Maximum	Description
HKEY_LOCAL_MACHINE\SYSTEM\CurrentControlSet\Services\LanmanServer\Parameters\InitConnTable Key			
8	1	128	This value's data is used to set the initial number of tree connections to be allocated in the connection table. The Server service automatically increases this value as needed. However, it is best to increase this value for better performance initially, because the overhead involved in increasing this value as part of the self-tuning characteristics is higher in terms of resource usage.

Default	Minimum	Maximum	Description

HKEY_LOCAL_MACHINE\SYSTEM\CurrentControlSet\Services\LanmanServer\Parameters\InitFileTable Key

16	1	256	This value's data entry specifies the initial number of file entries to be pre-allocated in the file table of each server connection. Set this to a higher value if your users use a higher number of files on a frequent basis. The Server service will automatically adjust the number of file-table entries upward if needed; however, pre-allocating them can improve performance.

HKEY_LOCAL_MACHINE\SYSTEM\CurrentControlSet\Services\LanmanServer\Parameters\InitSessTable Key

4	1	64	This value is used to specify the initial allocation of session entries in the session table for each server connection.

HKEY_LOCAL_MACHINE\SYSTEM\CurrentControlSet\Services\LanmanServer\Parameters\InitWorkItems Key

Depends on system configuration	1	512	This value is used to specify an initial allocation of work items to be used by the Server service. This value will increase as needed, but pre-allocating a higher value can increase performance. A work item is a receive buffer used to contain a user data request.

HKEY_LOCAL_MACHINE\SYSTEM\CurrentControlSet\Services\LanmanServer\Parameters\MaxMpxCbt Key

50	1	100	This value specifies a suggested maximum number of outstanding simultaneous requests to the server. Increasing this value can improve performance, but this occurs at the expense of work-item usage.

continues

Table C.6. continued

Default	Minimum	Maximum	Description

HKEY_LOCAL_MACHINE\SYSTEM\CurrentControlSet\Services\LanmanServer\Parameters\MaxWorkItems Key

| Depends on system configuration | 1 | 512 | This value is used to specify the maximum number of work items to be used by the Server service. If this number is reached, the server will initiate a flow-control algorithm and a noticeable performance decrease. |

HKEY_LOCAL_MACHINE\SYSTEM\CurrentControlSet\Services\LanmanServer\Parameters\MaxWorkItemIdleTime Key

| 300 | 10 | 1800 | This value specifies the maximum time, in seconds, that a work item has to be idle before it is freed for reuse. Decreasing this value can improve performance on systems that have reached their maximum allocation of work items, and that have a significant amount of idle network requests. |

HKEY_LOCAL_MACHINE\SYSTEM\CurrentControlSet\Services\LanmanServer\Parameters\RawWorkItems Key

| Depends on system configuration | 1 | 512 | This value is used to specify the number of work items to be allocated by the Server service. A higher value can improve performance, but at the expense of system memory. |

HKEY_LOCAL_MACHINE\SYSTEM\CurrentControlSet\Services\LanmanServer\Parameters\MaxRawWorkItems Key

| Depends on system configuration | 1 | 512 | This value is used to specify the maximum number of work items to be used by the Server service to service raw I/O requests. Raw I/O has less overhead than standard I/O, and offers the potential for increased performance. If the maximum number of raw work items is reached, then raw I/O requests will be rejected. |

Appendix C — The Registry Editor and Registry Keys

Default	Minimum	Maximum	Description
HKEY_LOCAL_MACHINE\SYSTEM\CurrentControlSet\Services\LanmanServer\Parameters\MinFreeWorkItems Key			
2	0	10	This value specifies the minimum number of available work items that must be available before a potentially blocking SMB (server message block) is processed. A higher value can be used to ensure that more work items are available for nonblocking requests, but this may cause a blocking request to fail.
HKEY_LOCAL_MACHINE\SYSTEM\CurrentControlSet\Services\LanmanServer\Parameters\MinRcvQueue Key			
2	0	10	This value is used to specify the minimum number of available work items necessary before the server will begin allocating additional work items. A higher value can ensure the availability of work items for processing client requests, but a value too high will not make efficient utilization of your system's resources.
HKEY_LOCAL_MACHINE\SYSTEM\CurrentControlSet\Services\LanmanServer\Parameters\ScavTimeOut Key			
30	1	300	This value specifies the time, in seconds, that it takes for the scavenger to wake up for service requests. A smaller value can increase performance, but at the expense of processor usage.
HKEY_LOCAL_MACHINE\SYSTEM\CurrentControlSet\Services\LanmanServer\Parameters\ThreadCountAdd Key			
Depends on the system configuration (generally 1)	0	10	This value's data specifies how many threads per processor the Server service should use. Increasing this value can increase performance but will require additional memory.

continues

Table C.6. continued

Default	Minimum	Maximum	Description

HKEY_LOCAL_MACHINE\SYSTEM\CurrentControlSet\Services\LanmanServer\Parameters\ThreadPriority Key

1	0	15	Specifies the server thread priorities in relation to the base priority of the server process. Increasing this value can improve server performance at the cost of interactive responsiveness. Values can be 0 (normal), 2 (background), 1 (foreground), and 15 (real-time). Setting your server thread priority to the real-time setting is not really a good idea because it will consume the majority of the CPU cycles, and may prevent other threads from executing in an acceptable fashion.

HKEY_LOCAL_MACHINE\SYSTEM\CurrentControlSet\Services\LanmanServer\Parameters\BlockingThreads Key

Depends on system configuration	1	9999	This value is used to specify the number of threads that are reserved to service a potentially blocking request. A higher value can increase performance, but at the expense of system memory. Too many allocated threads can impede performance due to excessive task switching.

HKEY_LOCAL_MACHINE\SYSTEM\CurrentControlSet\Services\LanmanServer\Parameters\NonBlockingThreads Key

Depends on system configuration	1	9999	This value is used to specify the number of threads that are reserved for service requests that will not block the service thread for a significant period of time. A higher value can increase performance, but at the expense of system memory. Too many allocated threads can impede performance due to excessive task switching.

Default	Minimum	Maximum	Description
HKEY_LOCAL_MACHINE\SYSTEM\CurrentControlSet\Services\LanmanServer\Parameters\Hidden Key			
0	0	1	Set this value's data entry to 1 to hide a server from client browse requests on the network. Users will not see this as an available resource, but they can still connect to it if they know the server name and resource name. Set it to 0 (default) to allow the server to be visible in browse requests.
HKEY_LOCAL_MACHINE\SYSTEM\CurrentControlSet\Services\LanmanServer\Parameters\SizReqBuf Key			
4356	512	65536	This value specifies the size of the Server service request buffers. A higher value may increase performance, but at the cost of system memory.

Table C.7. Workstation service registry keys.

Default	Minimum	Maximum	Description
HKEY_LOCAL_MACHINE\SYSTEM\CurrentControlSet\Services\LanmanWorkstation\Parameters\MaxCmds Key			
15	0	255	This value's data specifies the number of work buffers that the redirector will reserve to service network requests. Increasing this value may increase performance, but at the expense of nonpaged memory pool usage. Each additional command allocates about 1KB, but this memory will not be consumed unless the client actually makes use of the additional buffers.

continues

Table C.7. continued

Default	Minimum	Maximum	Description
\multicolumn{4}{l}{HKEY_LOCAL_MACHINE\SYSTEM\CurrentControlSet\Services\LanmanWorkstation\Parameters\MaxCollectionCount Key}
16	0	65535	Writes to character-mode named pipes less than this value will be buffered. Increasing this value above the default of 16 may improve performance for network applications that utilize character-mode named pipes. Changing this value will not affect SQL Server performance.
\multicolumn{4}{l}{HKEY_LOCAL_MACHINE\SYSTEM\CurrentControlSet\Services\LanmanWorkstation\Parameters\CharWait Key}
3600	0	65535	This value specifies the time, in milliseconds, for an instance of a named pipe to become available when a client open request is issued. If your named pipe application server is very busy, increasing this value can improve the likelihood that your client application will connect. However, increasing this value also may increase the time a client spends waiting for the application to error out if no named pipes are available.
\multicolumn{4}{l}{HKEY_LOCAL_MACHINE\SYSTEM\CurrentControlSet\Services\LanmanWorkstation\Parameters\CollectionTime Key}
250	0	65535000	This value specifies the time, in milliseconds, that character-mode named pipes with write-behind caching will allow the data to remain in the pipe. Increasing this value above the default may increase performance of the application. Changing this value will not affect SQL Server performance.

The Registry Editor and Registry Keys

Appendix C

Default	Minimum	Maximum	Description
HKEY_LOCAL_MACHINE\SYSTEM\CurrentControlSet\Services\LanmanWorkstation\Parameters\SizCharBuf Key			
512	64	4096	This value's data entry specifies the maximum number of bytes that will be written into a character-mode named-pipe buffer. Increasing this value may improve performance of named pipe applications, and will not affect SQL Server performance.
HKEY_LOCAL_MACHINE\SYSTEM\CurrentControlSet\Services\LanmanWorkstation\Parameters\CacheFileTimeout Key			
10	0	N/A	This value specifies the maximum number of time, in seconds, for data to remain in the file cache. If your clients repeatedly reuse (close, then reopen) data files beyond the 10-second default, then increasing this value may improve client performance.
HKEY_LOCAL_MACHINE\SYSTEM\CurrentControlSet\Services\LanmanWorkstation\Parameters\ServerAnnounceBuffers Key			
20	0	N/A	This value specifies the number of buffers to be used for server announcements. If you have many servers and are losing announcement messages (check your event log), increasing this value can improve the ability to receive and process server announcements.
HKEY_LOCAL_MACHINE\SYSTEM\CurrentControlSet\Services\LanmanWorkstation\Parameters\MailslotBuffer Key			
5	0	Limited by available memory	If your application is losing mail slot messages, increase this value above the default of 5 buffers.

Table C.8. Netlogon service registry keys.

Default	Minimum	Maximum	Description

HKEY_LOCAL_MACHINE\SYSTEM\CurrentControlSet\Services\NetLogon\Parameters\MaximumMailslotMessages Key

Default	Minimum	Maximum	Description
500	0	4294967295	This value specifies the maximum number of mail-slot messages that the NetLogon service can queue for processing. If you have a heavily congested network, increasing this value can improve your network's capability to receive and process mail-slot messages sent to the NetLogon service. Each mail-slot message consumes about 1500 bytes of nonpaged memory until it is processed by the NetLogon service.

HKEY_LOCAL_MACHINE\SYSTEM\CurrentControlSet\Services\NetLogon\Parameters\MaximumMailslotTimeout Key

Default	Minimum	Maximum	Description
10	5	4294967295	This value specifies the maximum time, in seconds, a mail-slot message is held. Messages older than this time will be ignored. This parameter should only be changed on a heavily congested network, because each mail-slot is generally processed in a fraction of a second. However, if the server is severely overloaded, it may discard mail-slot messages that are older than 10 seconds (default) because it cannot process them quickly enough.

HKEY_LOCAL_MACHINE\SYSTEM\CurrentControlSet\Services\NetLogon\Parameters\MailslotDuplicateTimeout Key

Default	Minimum	Maximum	Description
2	0	5	This value specifies the time, in seconds, that the NetLogon service will use to compare received mail-slot messages and discard duplicates. If your server can receive but not respond to mail-slot messages, set this value to 0 to disable the

Default	Minimum	Maximum	Description
			discard function. Such a situation could occur if there is a bridge or router that is filtering outgoing network packets. In such a situation, the server can receive the messages, but cannot respond to them.

HKEY_LOCAL_MACHINE\SYSTEM\CurrentControlSet\Services\NetLogon\Parameters\Pulse Key

Default	Minimum	Maximum	Description
300	60	3600	This value specifies the time, in seconds, for the NetLogon service to group changes to the domain controller's account database. Only after this time has expired will the changes be sent to the backup domain controllers.

HKEY_LOCAL_MACHINE\SYSTEM\CurrentControlSet\Services\NetLogon\Parameters\PulseConcurrency Key

Default	Minimum	Maximum	Description
20	1	500	This value specifies the maximum number of pulses the domain controller will send to backup domain controllers. Increasing this value can decrease the time it takes to replicate the domain controller's account changes to the BDCs, but can place a significant load on the server. Decreasing this value will lower the load on the server, but increase the time it takes to replicate the account modifications.

HKEY_LOCAL_MACHINE\SYSTEM\CurrentControlSet\Services\NetLogon\Parameters\PulseMaximum Key

Default	Minimum	Maximum	Description
7200	60	86400	This value specifies the time, in seconds, to wait before sending a pulse to a BDC. Each BDC will be sent a pulse at this frequency whether or not its account database is up-to-date. Increasing this value

continues

Table C.8. continued

Default	Minimum	Maximum	Description
			can be useful for networks that have little or no user account modifications, or for heavily congested networks, to delay the user account replication process.

HKEY_LOCAL_MACHINE\SYSTEM\CurrentControlSet\Services\NetLogon\Parameters\PulseTimeout1 Key

Default	Minimum	Maximum	Description
5	1	120	This value specifies the maximum time, in seconds, a BDC should take to respond to a pulse from the PDC. If a BDC fails to respond in this time frame, it is considered unresponsive. An unresponsive BDC is not considered (doesn't increment the pulse counter) in the maximum number of pulses limited by the `PulseConcurrency` settings. If the BDC is unresponsive, another pulse will be sent to a different BDC. If and when the first BDC responds, it will partially replicate the account changes and add to the load on the PDC. So if you have several slow BDCs, or a congested network, increasing this time setting can improve overall PDC response by limiting the number of simultaneous pulses the PDC must respond to.

HKEY_LOCAL_MACHINE\SYSTEM\CurrentControlSet\Services\NetLogon\Parameters\PulseTimeout2 Key

Default	Minimum	Maximum	Description
300	60	3600	This value specifies the maximum time, in seconds, in which a BDC should complete a partial replication of the account database. Even though a BDC has responded in the time frame specified by the `PulseTimeout2` setting, it must

Default	Minimum	Maximum	Description
			continue to respond at the interval specified in this setting or be considered unresponsive. This setting is only valid when many changes have occurred on the primary domain controller and more than one RPC call is required from the BDC to obtain all of the changes.

HKEY_LOCAL_MACHINE\SYSTEM\CurrentControlSet\Services\NetLogon\Parameters\Randomize Key

Default	Minimum	Maximum	Description
2	1	120	This value specifies the maximum time, in seconds, that a BDC will delay before requesting the account changes from the PDC. The BDC will wait between 0 seconds and the `Randomized` value before responding to the PDC. This value must be less than `PulseTimeout1`.

HKEY_LOCAL_MACHINE\SYSTEM\CurrentControlSet\Services\NetLogon\Parameters\ReplicationGoverner Key

Default	Minimum	Maximum	Description
100	0	100	This value (a percentage) specifies the size of the data, and the frequency of the calls to the BDC for replication to occur. For example, a value of `25` will utilize a buffer 32KB in size instead of the default of 128KB, and will only have an outstanding replication call 25 percent of the time. Setting this value too low may prevent replication from completing. Setting this value to `0` will prevent replication from occurring at all.

HKEY_LOCAL_MACHINE\SYSTEM\CurrentControlSet\Services\NetLogon\Parameters\Update Key

Default	Minimum	Maximum	Description
Yes	Yes	No	This value specifies that the NetLogon service should replicate the entire database each time it is started.

Table C.9. Miscellaneous service registry keys

Default	Minimum	Maximum	Description
colspan="4"	`HKEY_LOCAL_MACHINE\SYSTEM\CurrentControlSet\Services\Browser\Parameters\MaintainServerList` **Key**
Auto	Yes	No	This value is used to determine the possibility of a server or workstation becoming a browse master. A *browse master* is a computer that caches computer and shared-resource names that other computers can access to view resources (that is, *browse*) on the network. If this value is set to Auto, then the Master Browse Server determines whether a requesting computer will become a backup browse master. If set to Yes, the computer is always a backup browse master. If set to No, the computer will never be a backup browse master.
colspan="4"	`HKEY_LOCAL_MACHINE\SYSTEM\CurrentControlSet\Services\Rdr\Parameters\Connect` **Key**
300	0	N/A	This value specifies the maximum number of seconds to wait for a network connect or disconnect operation to complete.
colspan="4"	`HKEY_LOCAL_MACHINE\SYSTEM\Print\Printers\Printer Name\SpoolDirectory` **Key**
N/A	N/A	N/A	Set this value to the directory you wish to use for all of your printer spooling for a specific printer. The `Printer Name` entry above is a place holder for the name of the printer you installed (for example, HP DeskJet 310).

NetBEUI Frame Protocol Configuration Registry Keys

For the most part, Windows NT is completely self-tuning in its management of network transport protocols, and for the average network, you should never have to change any of the following settings. However, for those of you who are experiencing problems or have WAN connections, I have included some of the configurable registry settings for the NetBEUI Frame (NBF) in Table C.10.

Table C.10. NBF protocol configuration registry keys.

Default	Minimum	Maximum	Description
HKEY_LOCAL_MACHINE\SYSTEM\Services\NBF\Parameters\DefaultT1Timeout **Key**			
6000000	0	N/A	This value specifies the initial time, in 100-nanosecond units, to use for T1 timeouts. The T1 time specifies the time that NBF waits for a response after sending a logical link control (LLC) poll packet before resending it. While NBF will adapt over time, it may be useful to increase this value if NBF will be connecting over a congested network or low network bandwidth (such as a WAN link), or to slow computers.
HKEY_LOCAL_MACHINE\SYSTEM\Services\NBF\Parameters\DefaultT2Timeout **Key**			
1500000	0	N/A	This value specifies the initial time, in 100-nanosecond units, to use for T2 timeouts. A T2 timeout is the maximum amount of time to wait after receiving an LLC poll packet before responding. It must be significantly less than DefaultT1Timeout; one half or less is a good rule of thumb. Increasing this value may prove useful if NBF will be connecting over a congested network or low network bandwidth (such as a WAN link), or to slow computers.

continues

Table C.10. continued

Default	Minimum	Maximum	Description
HKEY_LOCAL_MACHINE\SYSTEM\Services\NBF\Parameters\DefaultTiTimeout Key			
300000000	0	N/A	This value specifies the initial time, in 100-nanosecond units, to use for Ti timeouts. A Ti timeout is the maximum time for NBF to wait before sending an LLC poll packet to ensure that the link is still active. Increasing this value may prove useful if NBF will be connecting over a congested network or low network bandwidth (such as a WAN link), or to slow computers.
HKEY_LOCAL_MACHINE\SYSTEM\Services\NBF\Parameters\LLCMaxWindowSize Key			
10	0	Number of frames	This value specifies the number of LLC I frames that NBF can send before polling and waiting for a response. Adjusting this value can be useful for network connections that have variable reliability problems.
HKEY_LOCAL_MACHINE\SYSTEM\Services\NBF\Parameters\LLCRetries Key			
8	1	N/A	This value specifies the number or retry attempts that NBF will make after a T1 timeout before closing the connection. Setting this value to 0 will force a continuous retry operation. Adjusting this value can be useful for network connections that have high reliability problems.
HKEY_LOCAL_MACHINE\SYSTEM\Services\NBF\Parameters\AddNameQueryRetries Key			
3	0	Number of frames	This value is used to specify the number of retry attempts for NBF when sending ADD_NAME_QUERY and ADD_GROUP_NAME_QUERY frames. If your network drops many packets, increasing this value can improve address registration.

Default	Minimum	Maximum	Description
HKEY_LOCAL_MACHINE\SYSTEM\Services\NBF\Parameters\AddNameQueryTimeout Key			
5000000	0	Number of frames	This value specifies the timeout, in 100-nanosecond units, that NBF will wait before sending successive ADD_NAME_QUERY and ADD_GROUP_NAME_QUERY frames. If your network drops many packets, increasing this value can improve address registration.
HKEY_LOCAL_MACHINE\SYSTEM\Services\NBF\Parameters\GeneralRetries Key			
3	0	Number of frames	This value specifies the number of retry operations that NBF will use when sending STATUS_QUERY and FIND_NAME frames. If your network drops many packets, increasing this value can improve network operations.
HKEY_LOCAL_MACHINE\SYSTEM\Services\NBF\Parameters\GeneralTimeout Key			
5000000	0	Number of frames	This value specifies the timeout, in 100-nanosecond units, that NBF will use in retry operations when sending successive STATUS_QUERY and FIND_NAME frames. If your network drops many packets, increasing this value can improve network operations.
HKEY_LOCAL_MACHINE\SYSTEM\Services\NBF\Parameters\NameQueryRetries Key			
3	0	Number of frames	This value specifies the number of retry operations that NBF will use when sending NAME_QUERY frames. If your network drops many packets, increasing this value can improve network operations.

continues

Table C.10. continued

Default	Minimum	Maximum	Description
HKEY_LOCAL_MACHINE\SYSTEM\Services\NBF\Parameters\NameQueryTimeout Key			
	5000000	Number of frames	This value specifies the timeout, in 100-nanosecond units, that NBF will use in retry operations when sending successive NAME_QUERY frames. If your network drops many packets, increasing this value can improve network operations.
HKEY_LOCAL_MACHINE\SYSTEM\Services\NBF\Parameters\QueryWithoutSourceRouting Key			
0	0	1	Setting this value to 1 will specify that half of the packets sent over the network will not include source-routing information. This is useful for bridges that cannot forward frames containing source routing information.
HKEY_LOCAL_MACHINE\SYSTEM\Services\NBF\Parameters\WanNameQueryRetries Key			
5	0	Number of frames	This value specifies the number of retry operations that NBF will use when sending NAME_QUERY frames when connected to a server using a Remote Access Software (RAS) link. If your connection drops many packets, increasing this value can improve network operations.

Memory-Related Registry Keys

One of the biggest performance benefits for your server can be gained by manually tuning the various memory settings to increase the performance of a particular service. The settings listed in Table C.11 can aid you in tuning your server. However, these settings will generally override the self-tuning characteristics of Windows NT Server, so they should be used with care. You should also be prepared for failure messages from other services that use the paged and nonpaged memory pools. These error messages will generally show up in the system log, but third-party applications may also use these memory pools. If a third-party application generates an error, it will most likely be in the application log.

> **TIP**
>
> If you start your memory-tuning efforts with a single service and test this setting for at least a week before modifying any other service, you can achieve better results. Start with your most essential service, then move to your least essential service. This way, when an error message does occur, you can just reset the service to its previous configuration.

Pay close attention to your logs, and use the Performance Monitor (I suggest setting alerts) to track the various services, including paged-pool and nonpaged-pool memory-related failures settings, such as the Server object `Pool Paged Failures` and `Pool Nonpaged Failures` counters. These features can tell you when you have gone too far with a particular service. If these errors start to occur, you should lower the memory settings you have changed or increase the overall system-pool settings. Keep in mind that your system only has so much physical RAM it can allocate to the system-nonpaged-memory pool, so you cannot increase the nonpaged-memory-pool settings indefinitely.

Table C.11. Memory-related registry keys.

Default	*Minimum*	*Maximum*	*Description*
HKEY_LOCAL_MACHINE\SYSTEM\CurrentControlSet\Control\Session Manager\Memory Management\IoPageLockLimit Key			
512KB	0	Physical Memory– Padding	This value is used to specify the amount of memory, in bytes, that can be locked for I/O operations. Increasing this value can increase I/O performance on an I/O-bound server. The maximum value is determined by the physical memory minus a padding factor. This padding is about 7MB for small systems, and increases as the physical memory increases. For a 64MB system, the padding is about 16MB; for a 512MB system, the padding is about 64MB.

continues

Table C.11. continued

Default	Minimum	Maximum	Description
	HKEY_LOCAL_MACHINE\SYSTEM\CurrentControlSet\Control\Session Manager\Memory Management\NonPagedPoolSize **Key**
0	0	80 percent of physical memory	This value determines the amount of physical memory that is allocated to the nonpaged memory pool. The nonpaged memory pool is used by system services and various API calls to allocate memory that is not paged to disk. The default setting of 0 specifies that the system use a pool size based on the amount of physical memory installed on the computer.
	HKEY_LOCAL_MACHINE\SYSTEM\CurrentControlSet\Control\Session Manager\Memory Management\PagedPoolSize **Key**
0	0	128MB	This value specifies the size of the paged memory pool. The paged memory pool is used by system services and various API calls to allocate memory that can be paged to disk. A default setting of 0 will allocate 32MB for the paged memory pool.
	HKEY_LOCAL_MACHINE\SYSTEM\CurrentControlSet\Services\LanmanServer\Parameters\MaxNonpagedMemoryUsage **Key**
Depends on system and server configuration	1MB	Variable depending on size of system physical memory	This value is used to specify the Server service's usage of the nonpaged memory pool. Increasing this can increase performance at the expense of physical memory used, and may cause another system to fail for lack of nonpageable memory.

Default	Minimum	Maximum	Description

HKEY_LOCAL_MACHINE\SYSTEM\CurrentControlSet\Services\LanmanServer\Parameters\MaxPagedMemoryUsage Key

Depends on system and server configuration	1MB	Variable depending on size of system page files	This value is used to specify the Server service's usage of the paged memory pool. Increasing this value can increase performance at the expense of pageable memory used, and may cause another system to fail for lack of pageable memory. If you specify a value for MaxNonPagedUsage, you should specify a value here as well.

HKEY_LOCAL_MACHINE\SYSTEM\CurrentControlSet\Services\MacFile\Parameters\PagedMemLimit Key

0×4e20 (20000KB)	0×3e8 (1000KB)	0×3e800 (256000KB)	This value specifies the amount of paged pool memory that the Services for Macintosh will use. Performance will increase as this value increases, but the paged pool memory is a limited resource, and increasing this value may cause a failure in another service. This value should not be set lower than 1000KB.

HKEY_LOCAL_MACHINE\SYSTEM\CurrentControlSet\Services\MacFile\Parameters\NonPagedMemLimit Key

0×fa0 (4000KB)	0×ff (256KB)	0×3e80 (16000KB)	This value specifies the amount of nonpaged pool memory (physical RAM) that the Services for Macintosh will use. Performance will increase as this value increases, but the nonpaged memory pool is a limited resource and increasing this value may cause a failure in another service.

Miscellaneous Registry Keys

Table C.12 describes registry keys you can modify to configure items such as the Windows NT source installation path, the ability to log on automatically, the ability to display a user splash screen at logon, and other miscellaneous settings.

Table C.12. Miscellaneous registry keys.

Default	Minimum	Maximum	Description
HKEY_LOCAL_MACHINE\SOFTWARE\Windows NT\Current Version\Winlogon\ShutdownWithoutLogon Key			
0	0	1	Set this value to 1 to add the Shutdown button to the Logon dialog so that anyone can shut down the server without logging on to the system. Set this value to 0 (default) to require a logon to the system in order to shut down the system.
HKEY_LOCAL_MACHINE\SOFTWARE\Windows NT\Current Version\Winlogon LegalNoticeCaption Key			
N/A	N/A	N/A	Set this value's data string to the text you want displayed in a message box whenever a user logs on to the system. Use this as a disclaimer to protect yourself from unauthorized users. In order to make this message box visible, you must also set LegalNoticeText to a non-null value.
HKEY_LOCAL_MACHINE\SOFTWARE\Windows NT\Current Version\Winlogon LegalNoticeText Key			
N/A	N/A	N/A	Set this value's data string to the text you want displayed in the caption bar of the message box whenever a user logs on to the system. In order to make this message box visible, you must also set LegalNoticeCaption to a non-null value.

The Registry Editor and Registry Keys

Appendix C

795

Default	*Minimum*	*Maximum*	*Description*
HKEY_LOCAL_MACHINE\SOFTWARE\Windows NT\Current Version\Winlogon\AutoAdminLogon Key			
0	0	1	Set this value's data to 1 to automatically log on to the system and bypass the logon dialog. Set it to 0 to restore the original settings and require a user logon via the logon dialog box. In order to perform this action, you will need to create the AutoAdminLogon key with the Registry Editor with a data type of REG_SZ. This value must be used in conjunction with the DefaultUserName and DefaultPassword values.
HKEY_LOCAL_MACHINE\SOFTWARE\Windows NT\Current Version\Winlogon\DefaultPassword Key			
N/A	N/A	N/A	Set this value's data to the password for the user name you want to use to automatically log on to the system. This will bypass the logon dialog. In order to perform this action, you will need to create the DefaultPassword key with the Registry Editor. Set the type to REG_SZ. This data value is unprotected and is thereby visible to all users who log on to the system. That means that any user can thereby obtain the user name and password. This value must be used in conjunction with the DefaultUserName and AutoAdminLogon values.
HKEY_LOCAL_MACHINE\SOFTWARE\Windows NT\Current Version\Winlogon\DefaultUserName Key			
N/A	N/A	N/A	Set this value's data to the default user name you want to use in the automatic logon process. This value must be used in conjunction with the AutoAdminLogon and DefaultPassword values.

continues

Table C.12. continued

Default	Minimum	Maximum	Description
colspan=4	**HKEY_LOCAL_MACHINE\SOFTWARE\Windows NT\Current Version\IniFileMapping Key**		
N/A	N/A	N/A	This key contains information related to the mapping of configuration data entries. You will find references to `USR:`, which specifies that the configuration information is contained in `HKEY_CURRENT_USER`, or `SYS:`, which is a reference to the `HKEY_LOCAL_MACHINE\SOFTWARE` key. For example, the `MSMAIL32.INI` entry is `USR:Software\Microsoft\Mail`, which means that when Microsoft Mail starts, it will look in `HKEY_CURRENT_USER\Software\Mail` for configuration data.
colspan=4	**HKEY_LOCAL_MACHINE\SOFTWARE\Windows NT\Current Version\SourcePath Key**		
N/A	N/A	N/A	Change this value's data if you want to change the source media path, which is used to copy the device drivers whenever you add new hardware or software to your system. The preferred method is to use a UNC filename (such as `\\SRV\CD-ROM\I386`) instead of a mapped drive letter (such as `E:\I386`).
colspan=4	**HKEY_LOCAL_MACHINE\SYSTEM\CurrentControlSet\Control\SessionManager\RegisterProcessors Key**		
4	1	Number of CPUs supported by OEM kernel	If you have a multiprocessor kernel installed on your system, you can change this value's data to support more than the maximum (default) of 4 processors for Windows NT Server.

Appendix C

Default	Minimum	Maximum	Description
HKEY_LOCAL_MACHINE\SYSTEM\CurrentControlSet\Control\WOW\LPT_timeout Key			
15	0	None	Change this value's data from 15 (default) to increase the number of seconds that a 16-bit Windows application will wait before timing out. If your 16-bit Windows application experiences printer timeout problems, increasing this value in 5-second increments might solve the problem.
HKEY_LOCAL_MACHINE\SYSTEM\CurrentControlSet\Control\WOW\DefaultSeparateVDM Key			
0	0	1	Set this value to 1 to have 16-bit Windows applications run in separate address spaces by default. Set it to 0 (default) to use a shared address space.

INDEX

SYMBOLS

% disk time counter, 654
% full counter, 682
% processor time counter, 644
% total processor time counter, 644
% usage counter, 649
% usage peak counter, 649
* wildcard notation, 533
+ addition operator (VBScript), 451
- subtraction operator (VBScript), 451
{} (ending braces), 544
3D objects
   CorelWEB.GALLERY, 389-390
   CorelWEB.Transit, 391-392
   home pages, creating with Web 3D, 383-387
   renderings, 381
   Web 3D, 380-383
   Web.Designer, 387-389
56KB leased line, 14

A

<A HREF> HTML tag (Internet Explorer), 754
<A NAME> HTML tag
   Internet Explorer, 754
   Word Internet Assistant, 758
<A> HTML tag, 333, 715-716

<ABBREV> HTML tag

UNLEASHED

<ABBREV> HTML tag, 716
Aborted Connections counter, 666
About dialog box subroutine (VBScript), 475
About filename property (dbWeb), 559
Abs function (VBScript), 463
Abstract Window Toolkit (AWT), 533
Access (Web publishing), 375-378
    databases, 376-378
    Internet Assistant for Access (installing), 376
Access Control Entries (ACEs), 57, 686
Access Control Lists (ACLs), 57, 686
Access Internet tools (Web sites), 376
access rights, 686, 705
    assigning permissions to databases, 161
    Internet, restricting, 201-202
    privileges, 703
    user accounts (security), 275-276
    Web sites, 149-150
access tokens, 686
access violations, 686
accessing
    network firewalls, 271-273
    objects (enumeration operations), 693
    systems, 297
Accessories command (Start menu), 289

Accessories dialog box, 167
Account command (Policies menu), 277
Account Lockout option (Account Policy dialog box), 278
Account Policy dialog box, 277
accounts
    domains, 66
    Guest, 276
    passwords, 140, 152, 157
    users
        configuring policies, 277-278
        displaying, 284
        protecting, 276
        security, 275-277
ACEs (access control entries), 57, 686
ACLs (access control lists), 57, 686
<ACRONYM> HTML tag, 716
Activate command (Scope menu), 225
active content home pages (security), 267-268
Active Leases command (Scope menu), 230, 232
Active Leases dialog box, 230, 232
active links (HTML documents), 414
ActiveX, 34-35, 181, 268
adapters
    buses, 80
    dongles, 693
    networks
        adding, 92-97
        adding IP addresses, 147
        adding subnet masks, 147

bayonet nut connectors, 689
security, 96
segments, 96
RAS, 121
Add To Item dialog box, 626
Add and Read option (permissions), 281
Add command (Server menu), 222
Add Data Source dialog box, 162, 562
Add DHCP Server on the Server List dialog box, 222
Add Key command (Edit menu), 765
Add Key dialog box, 765
Add option (permissions), 281
Add Reservations command (Scope menu), 231
Add Reserved Clients dialog box, 231
Add Static Mappings dialog box, 248
Add to Alert dialog box, 636
Add to Chart command (Edit menu), 627, 645
Add to Chart dialog box, 627, 633
Add to Log command (Edit menu), 630
Add to Log dialog box, 630
Add to Report command (Edit menu), 633, 636
Add to Report dialog box, 633
Add Users and Groups dialog box, 284, 301
Add Value dialog box, 766

Index

Add WINS Server command (Server menu), 241
Add WINS Server dialog box, 241
AddDigit subroutine (VBScript), 478
adding
  buttons, 400
  CD-ROMs, 84
  counters, 626
  DHCP servers, 222
  IP addresses to network adapters, 147
  network adapters, 92-97
  processors, 97, 648
  RAS adapters, 121
  registry keys, 765
  scopes
    configurations, 228
    DHCP client reservations, 231
  servers (WINS), 241, 246
  subnet masks to network adapters, 147
  virtual servers, 145-146
addition operator (VBScript), 451
address class, 686
<ADDRESS> HTML tag, 329, 717
  Internet Explorer, 754
  Word Internet Assistant, 758
addresses
  e-mail, troubleshooting, 196
  input/output, 697
  IP, 10, 13, 207, 698
    adding to network adapters, 147
    DHCP, 211, 214
    Exchange Server, 199
    firewalls, 272
    networks, 256
    RIP for Internet Protocol, 107
    routable, 39
    scopes, 207
    static, 212
    subnets, 223
  SMTP, 197
  space, 687
  TCP/IP, 207
  URLs, 412
  WINS, mapping, 235
administrative alerts, 687
Administrative Tools group, 762
Administrator (dbWeb), 555
  properties, 556-558
Administrator Preferences dialog box, 556, 558
Administrator Properties dialog box, 561
administrators, 61
  FrontPage Server Administrator, 341-345
    installing extensions, 342-343
    managing server extensions, 343-345
Advanced IP Addressing dialog box, 110, 147, 292
Advanced Research Projects Agency (ARPA), 5
advertising
  Web site newsgroups, 42
  WWW sites, 18, 40
agents (proxy), 712
  WINS, 236-239
<AHREF> HTML tag (Word Internet Assistant), 758
Alert command (Options menu), 637
Alert Options dialog box, 637
Alert view, 635
  Performance Monitor, 625
Alerter Service, 687
alerts
  administrative, 687
  creating, 635-638, 640
  NTFS, 279
  object counters, 638-640
  selecting, 636
  viewing, 625
Alerts command (View menu), 635
algorithms, 687
  timeslices, 709
ALIGN keyword, 331
aligning paragraphs, 319
All Events command (View menu), 306
ALL HTTP extension, 606
allocation units, 687, 690
Allow Anonymous Connections option (FTP Publishing Service properties sheet), 151
Allow Anonymous option (WWW Publishing Service properties sheet), 141
Always option (Internet Explorer properties sheets), 183
AMP (asymmetric multiprocessing), 50, 60, 687
anchors, 333
AND operator (VBScript), 452
Anonymous Logon option
  Gopher Publishing Service properties sheet, 157
  WWW Publishing Service properties sheet, 140

anonymous-level security tokens, 687
antiquated systems, 82
APIs (Application Programming Interfaces), 687
   ISAPI, 430, 698
<APPLET> HTML tag, 527, 546, 717-718
applets
   Java
      compiling, 544-545
      embedding in HTML, 545-546
   Marquee
      embedding, 545
      stop method, 542
applets (Java), 525-526
   alpha versions, 527
   creating, 528-544
   initializing, 535-538
   Marquee
      code for, 530-533
      color values, 537-538
      parameters, 529-530
      run method, 543
      start method, 542
   painting, 539-541
   threads, 542-544
application programming interfaces (APIs), 687
<APPLICATION> HTML tag, 527, 546, 717-718
application-termination messages, 694
ApplicationName switch, 49
applications
   Calculator, 473
   CGIs, 429, 492-493
      developing, 505-506
   client/server, 206, 690

disk-intensive
   logical drives, 656
   physical drives, 657
HotDog Pro,
   customizing, 402-410
infected systems,
   recovering, 268-270
Internet security,
   264-267
ISAPI, 33-34, 429-430
   defined, 428-429
   testing, 430
   third-party, 430
ISAs, 431, 439-440, 442
JAVAC, 544
label image, 485
logs, 302
multiprocessing, 700
processor intensive, 646, 648
   starting, 648
RAS, 126
shortcut keys,
   customizing HotDog Pro, 400-402
TAPI, 50
trojan horses, 267
VBScript
   function and control structure examples, 473-488
   Hello World!, 447-450
viruses, removing, 269
Windows NT Server (robust), 48
archive bits, 687
archiving events, 306-307
<AREA> HTML tag, 718
   Internet Explorer, 755
ARPA (Advanced Research Projects Agency), 5
   DARPA, 6

ARPA-###.REV configuration file, 256, 260
ARPAnet, 6-7
Array function (VBScript), 463
arrays
   dynamic, declaring with Dim statement, 456
   encapsulated, 228
   multidimensional, declaring with Dim statement, 456
   static, declaring with Dim statement, 456
Asc function (VBScript), 463
assigning database permissions, 161
associating file types, 168-172
associations, editing file types, 170
Asymetrix Web 3D, *see* **Web 3D**
asymmetric multiprocessing (AMP), 50, 60, 687
ATM (asynchronous transfer mode), 15, 105
Atn function (VBScript), 463
attributes
   extended, 695
   HTML documents
      paragraphs, 318-320
      text, 320, 322
   HTML tags
      <A>, 715
      <ABBREV>, 716
      <ACRONYM>, 716
      <ADDRESS>, 717

Index

<APPLET>, 717
<AREA>, 718
<AU>, 718
<B>, 718
<BACKGROUND>, 720
<BANNER>, 719
<BASE>, 719
<BASEFONT>, 719
<BDO>, 720
<BIG>, 720
<BLINK>, 721
<BLOCKQUOTE>, 721
<BODY>, 721

, 722
<CAPTION>, 722
<CENTER>, 722
<CITE>, 723
<CODE>, 723
<COL>, 723
<COLGROUP>, 724
<CREDIT>, 724
<DD>, 724
<DEL>, 725
<DFN>, 725
<DIR>, 725
<DIV>, 726
<DL>, 726
<DT>, 726
<EM>, 726
<EMBED>, 727
<FIG>, 727
<FN>, 727
<FONT, 728
<FORM>, 728
<FRAME>, 729
<FRAMESET>, 729
<H1>, 729
<H2>, 730
<H3>, 730
<H4>, 730
<H5>, 730
<H6>, 731

<HEAD, 731
<HPn>, 731
<HR>, 732
<HTML>, 732
<I>, 732
<IMG>, 733
<INPUT>, 733
<INS>, 734
<ISINDEX>, 734
<KBD>, 734
<LANG>, 734
<LH>, 735
<LI>, 735
<LINK>, 735
<LISTING>, 736
<MAP>, 736
<MARQUEE>, 736
<MENU>, 737
<META>, 737
<NEXTID>, 738
<NOBR>, 738
<NOEMBED>, 738
<NOFRAMES>, 738
<NOTE>, 739
<OL>, 739
<OPTION>, 739
<OVERLAY>, 740
<P>, 740
<PARAM>, 740
<PERSON>, 740
<PLAINTEXT>, 741
<PRE>, 741
<Q>, 741
<S>, 742
<SAMP>, 742
<SELECT>, 742
<SMALL>, 743
<SPAN>, 743
<STRIKE>, 743
<STRONG>, 743
<SUB>, 744
<SUP>, 744
<TAB>, 744
<TABLE>, 744

<TBODY>, 745
<TD>, 745
<TEXTAREA>, 746
<TFOOT>, 746
<TH>, 746
<THEAD>, 747
<TITLE>, 747
<TR>, 747
<TT>, 747
<U>, 748
<UL>, 748
<VAR>, 748
<WBR>, 749
<XMP>, 749
pages, 325-326
permissions
   directories, 283-284
   files, 283-284
<AU> HTML tag, 718
Audit command (Policies menu), 298, 688
Audit Policy dialog box, 298
auditing, 688
   directories, 299-302
   enabling configuration
      systems, 297-299
   events, 298
   files, 298-302
   groups, 298
   logoffs, 298
   logons, 298
   objects, 298
   permissions, 300
   policies, 688
   printers, 688
   processes, tracking, 299
   restarting, 299
   security policies, 299
   shutdowns, 299
   systems, 299
   user rights, 298
   users, 298

Auditing command
   (Policies menu), 300
Auditing command
   (Security menu), 298,
   767
AUTH TYPE extension,
   606
AUTH_TYPE CGI
   environment variable,
   499
authenticating domains, 98
authentication packages,
   688
Authentication Server
   protocol Web site, 501
authentications,
   encrypting, 288, 290
auto-dialing, 176
auto-replies on the
   Internet, preventing, 202
AUTOEXEC.NT files, 688,
   690
automatically open new log
   option (Log to File radio
   button), 148
autorun scripts, 396
Available Bytes counter,
   649, 651
Avg. Disk Transfer/sec
   counter, 655
AVI (Audio-Video Inter-
   leave) files, 175, 380
AWT (Abstract Window
   Toolkit), 533

B

B-nodes (DHCP), 210-211
<B> HTML tag, 718
   Internet Explorer, 755
   Word Internet Assistant,
      758
Backbone Network Service
   (vBNS), 7

background sounds (Web
   sites), 175
backgrounds, 381
   bitmaps, 325
   graphics, 413
   HTML documents, 413
   tiled, 325
backup domain
   controller (BDC), 67, 98,
   688
BackupDirPath (Registry
   keys), 253
backups
   archive bits, 687
   DHCP servers, 212
bad-sector mappings, 689
Balance option (Server
   dialog box), 100
bandwidths, 15-16
   graphics, 381
<BANNER> HTML tag,
   719
banners (HTML
   documents), 412
<BASE> HTML tag, 719
   Internet Explorer, 755
<BASEFONT> HTML tag,
   719
   Internet Explorer, 755
Basic Input/Output
   System, see BIOS
Basic option (WWW
   Publishing Service
   properties sheet), 141
Basic Rate Interfaces
   (BRIs), 16
batch files, 689
batch processes, 689
bayonet nut connectors,
   689
BBSs (bulletin board
   systems), 33
   newsgroups, 42

BDC (backup domain
   controller), 67, 98, 688
<BDO> HTML tag, 720
<BDSOUND> HTML tag,
   720
Beep on error property
   (dbWeb), 559
BeginDetail extension, 606
bgcolor option, 529
<BGSOUND> HTML tag,
   326
   Internet Explorer, 755
<BIG> HTML tag, 720
binary data type, 228
binary subtraction
   operator (VBScript), 451
bindings, 93, 689
   RPCs, 704
Bindings properties sheet,
   94-95
Bindings Review and
   Configuration dialog box,
   109
BIOS (basic input/output
   system), 689
   Intel, 79, 90
   Windows NT, 49
bitmap backgrounds, 325
bits
   archive, 687
   hidden, 696
   read-only, 703
   system, 707
   see also archive bits;
      hidden bits; read-only
      bits; system bits
<BLINK> HTML tag, 720
<BLOCKQUOTE> HTML
   tag, 329, 721
   Internet Explorer, 755
   Word Internet Assistant,
      758

Index

blocks
  ECB formats, 433-434
  NCB, 701
  SMBs, 706
  see also ECBs
<BODY> HTML tag, 326, 721-722
  Internet Explorer, 755
  Word Internet Assistant, 758
<BOLD> HTML tag, 314
books, *see* **guest books**
Boolean operators (VBScript), 452
BOOT configuration file, 256-257
boot partitions, 689
boot sector viruses, 265
bottlenecks
  disks
    budgets, 658
    finding, 654-658
    mirror sets, 657
    striped sets, 657
    troubleshooting, 656
  IIS, finding, 661-667
  memory, finding, 649-654
  networks
    finding, 658-661
    Performance Monitor, 659
  processors
    finding, 643-648
    Performance Monitor, 645
**
 HTML tag, 722**
  Internet Explorer, 755
  Word Internet Assistant, 758
breakpoints (debugger), 691
BRIs (Basic Rate Interfaces), 16
  installing IIS, 105

broadcasts, 210
  WINS, 236
browse, 689
browsers, 711
  ActiveX, 268
  backgrounds, 381
  HTML
    documents, 315
    tags, 322
  Internet Explorer, 166, 187-188
    AVI files, 175
    cache settings, 179-181
    character sets, 184-185
    colors, 175
    configuring, 168
    configuring appearances, 173-175
    connections, 175-179
    displaying Web pages, 174
    installing, 167-168
    URLs, 175
  OLE, 268
  scripting, 268
  security, 267-268
  Web browsers (HotJava), 526
  WWW, 32
  see also Internet Explorer
browsing, 155
  domains, 236
BtnDelete_OnClick subroutine (VBScript), 477
BtnEvaluate_OnClick subroutine, 477
BtnHello subroutine, 448
BtnHello_OnClick subroutine, 448
BtnTime_OnClick subroutine, 449
buffering (double), 79
buffers (FIFO), 120

Build External Hypertext Link dialog box, 417
building
  databases, logging Web site activity, 159-161
  ODBC data sources, 161-162
  queries, 617
bulleted lists, creating, 326-327, 332
bulletin board systems (BBSs), 33
buses
  adapters, 80
  DMA, 80
  double buffering, 79
  EISA, 80, 90
  I/O, 78-82, 697
    expansions, 78
  ISA, 79
    expansions, 79
  MCA, 80
  PCI, 81
  PCMCIA, 81
  speed, 79
  troubleshooting, 79, 82
  VLBs, 80
  Windows NT Server, 82
businesses
  ISPs, 19-20
    references, 20
  ordering, 37
  publishing, 36
button bars (HotDog Pro, customizing), 399-401
buttons
  adding, 400
  Calculator program
    Delete, 477
    Evaluate, 474, 477
  deleting, 400
  moving, 400
bytes (data types), 228
Bytes Received/sec counter, 663, 665-666

Bytes Sent/sec counter, 663, 665-666
Bytes Total/sec counter, 663, 665-666

C

C (programming language)
    CGI scripts, 505
    Hello World! CGI scripts, 509-510
C CGI programs Web site, 505
C2-level security, 689
Cache - Avg. Free Page Scan counter, 679
Cache - Max Free Page Scan counter, 679
Cache - Scan Limit Reached counter, 679
Cache configuration file, 256-258
Cache Faults/sec counter, 649, 652
Cache Flushes counter, 662, 679
Cache Hit Ratio counter, 679
Cache Hits % counter, 662
Cache Hits counter, 662
Cache Manager, 90
Cache Misses counter, 662
Cache Size counter, 662
Cache Used counter, 662
Cached File Handles counter, 662
caches
    deleting, 181
    settings (Internet Explorer), 179-181
    upgrading, 648
    validating, 245
Calculator program, 473
Call statement (VBScript), 455
calls
    function routines, 687
    LPCs, 699
    RPCs, 53, 704
        bindings, 704
        connections, 704
        endpoints, 704
        Exchange Server, 200
        protocol sequences, 704
        servers, 704
<CAPTION> HTML tag, 722
    Internet Explorer, 755
catalogs, 615
    publishing, 23-24
CBool function (VBScript), 464
CByte function (VBScript), 464
CD-ROM
    adding, 84
    HotDog Pro, 396
CDate function (VBScript), 464
CDbl function (VBScript), 464
<CENTER> HTML tag, 320, 722
    Internet Explorer, 755
    Word Internet Assistant, 758
centralized administration, 61
CGIs, 490-492
    applications, 492-493
    basic functions, 493-496
    C scripts, 505
    developing applications, 505-506
    environment variables, 499-503
        accessing variables, 511-522
        AUTH_TYPE, 499
        CONTENT_LENGTH, 499
        CONTENT_TYPE, 499
        GATEWAY_INTERFACE, 500
        HTTP_ACCEPT, 500
        HTTP_USER_AGENT, 500
        PATH_INFO, 500
        PATH_TRANSLATED, 500
        QUERY_STRING, 501
        REMOTE_ADDR, 501
        REMOTE_HOST, 501
        REMOTE_IDENT, 501
        REMOTE_USER, 501
        REQUEST_METHOD, 502
        SCRIPT_NAME, 502
        SERVER_NAME, 502
        SERVER_PORT, 502
        SERVER_PROTOCOL, 502
        SERVER_SOFTWARE, 502
    interactive Web sites, 491-494
    issues, 496-499
        controlling access to CGI directories, 498
        duplicating scripts, 497
        processing time, 497
        security, 497-504
        transmitting sensitive data, 498
        validating users, 498-499
    Perl scripts, 503-504
        Internet resources, 504-506

Index

providing customized content, 513-518
scripts
Hello World!, 506-510
Hello World! in C, 509-510
Hello World! in Perl, 507-509
setting up feedback forms, 518-521
CGI Perl scripts Web sites, 504
CGI Requests counter, 663
CGI (Common Gateway Interface), 35, 690
applications versus ISAPI applications, 428-429
challenge-response authentication mechanisms, 276
Change Folder dialog box, 554
Change Icon dialog box, 170
Change option (permissions), 281
Change Option Type dialog box, 228
Channel Service Unit/Data Service Unit (CSU/DSU), 14
character sets, configuring Internet Explorer, 184-185
character modes (executive messages), 694
Chart command (Options menu), 631
Chart command (View menu), 626
Chart Option dialog box, 628

Chart view (Performance Monitor), 624, 626
charts
creating, 626-629
viewing, 625
Chat command (Options menu), 628
Check Security Certificates Before option (Internet Explorer properties sheet), 183
Choose a Table dialog box, 565
Choose Destination Location dialog box, 551
Choose Permissions commands (Security menu), 283
Choose Program Group dialog box, 555
Chr function (VBScript), 464
CInt function (VBScript), 464
circuit-switched networks on the Internet, 5
circular dependency, 689
<CITE> HTML tag, 321, 723
Internet Explorer, 755
Word Internet Assistant, 758
classes (address class), 686
classes (Java)
defining, 534
importing, 533-534
Client Properties dialog box, 230-231
Client stub name property (dbWeb), 559
clients, 31
applications, 206, 690
connecting, 126
database models, 31

DHCP, 213, 228-230
configurations, 213-215, 229
IDs, 215
leases, 230
overlays, 215
reservations, 231
Dial-Up Networking, 692
non-WINS clients (subnet networks), 238
RAS, 120
servers, 109
supporting with Internet service, 12
viruses, 203-204
WINS, 238, 248-249
registrations, 235
CLng function (VBScript), 464
Clone subkey, 699
Close command (Registry menu), 766
clusters, 687, 690
code
HTML input forms, 598-599
Java comments, 533
Marquee applet, 530-533
opcodes, 701
VBScript, hiding, 447
<CODE> HTML tag, 321, 723
Internet Explorer, 755
Word Internet Assistant, 758
<COL> HTML tag, 723
<COLGROUP> HTML tag, 724
Color dialog box, 414
colors
HTML documents, 412
links, 414

object counters, 628
special text colors, creating HTML documents with Microsoft Word, 364-365
Colors dialog box, 175
columns
   dbWeb queries, 566
   QBE, 574
   table headers, 333
   tabular forms, 578
command-line programs (IPCONFIG syntax), 228
commands
   Computer menu (Services), 137
   DHCP Options menu
      Defaults, 227
      Scope, 226
   Edit menu
      Add Key, 765
      Add to Chart, 627, 645
      Add to Log, 630
      Add to Report, 633, 636
      Add Value, 766
      Delete, 766
      Preferences, 556, 558
      Tag Information, 416
   File menu
      New, 383
      New Chart, 632
      New Other, 200
      Open, 383, 629
      Open Project, 422
      Project Manager, 422
      Properties, 194
      Publish Document, 422
      Save, 588
      Save Chart Settings, 629

Save Log Setting As, 632
Save Report Settings As, 634
Save Workspace, 629
Format menu
   Document, 411
Help menu (Contents), 398
Insert menu
   Hypertext Target, 416
   Image, 418
   Image Advanced, 418
   Jump to Document on Another System, 417
   Jump Within this Document, 416
   Launch an Internet Service, 420
   Table, 419
Internet Service Manager, 136
keywords, 699
Log menu
   Log Type, 307
   Save As, 307
Mappings menu
   Initiate Scavenging, 250
   Static Mappings, 248
Models menu
   Create Simple Model, 385
   Create Text Models, 385
Object menu (Permissions), 161
Options menu
   Alert, 637
   Chart, 628, 631
   Data From, 632
   Global, 226

   Preferences, 244
   Read Only Mode, 765
   Update Now, 629, 631, 634
   parameters, 701
   switches, 707
Permissions menu (Security), 283
Policies menu
   Account, 277
   Audit, 298, 300, 688
   User Rights, 276
Properties menu, 137
   Pause Service, 137
   Service Properties, 139, 150, 156
Registry menu
   Close, 766
   Load Hive, 766
   Open Local, 766
   Print Subtree, 766
   Restore, 766
   Save Key, 766
   Save Subtree, 766
   Select Computer, 766
Scene menu (Generate Snapshot), 385
Scope menu
   Activate, 225
   Active Leases, 230, 232
   Add Reservations, 231
   Create, 223
   Deactivate, 225
   Delete, 225
Scope Properties menu (DHCP Options), 213
Security menu
   Auditing, 298, 767
   Choose Permissions, 283
   Owner, 286, 767
   Permissions, 767

configuring
Index

Server menu
  Add, 222
  Add WINS Server, 241
  Communications Ports, 127
  Configuration, 242, 253
  Delete WINS Server, 241
  Replication Partners, 246
Start menu (Accessories), 289
syntax, 707
Tools menu
  Customize Button Bar, 400
  Options, 203, 402
  Shortcut Keys, 401
  Template from Document, 421
Users menu (Permissions), 126
View menu
  Alerts, 635
  All Events, 306
  Chart, 626
  Database, 244
  Display Binary Data, 767
  Filter Events, 305
  Find Key, 767
  FTP, 139
  Gopher, 139
  Log, 630
  Options, 169, 174
  Report, 632
  Sort by Comment, 138
  Sort by Server, 138
  Sort by Service, 138
  Sort by State, 138
  Special Characters, 415
  Tags, 415
  WWW, 139

Comment option
  FTP Publishing Service properties sheet, 152
  Gopher Publishing Service properties sheet, 157
  WWW Publishing Service properties sheet, 141
<COMMENT> HTML tag (Internet Explorer), 755
comments
  Java code, 533
  RFCs, 704
Committed Bytes counter, 649, 651
Common Gateway Interface, *see* **CGI**
Communications Ports command (Server menu), 127
compacting
  DHCP databases, 232
  WINS databases, 249
companies
  ISPs, 19-20
    references, 20
  ordering, 37
  publishing, 36
comparison operators (VBScript), 454
compatibility
  HotDog Pro, 395
  Windows NT Server, 50
compilers, 525
compiling Java applets, 544-545
component events, 304
compressing folders, 764
compression support, 57
Computed Column Expression Builder dialog box, 574, 578, 582

Computer menu commands (Services), 137
concatenating strings (VBScript), 449
conditions (deadlock), 691
CONFIG.NT files, 688, 690
Configuration command (Server menu), 242, 253
configuration files
  BOOT, 256-257
  CACHE, 256-258
  DNS, 255
    ARPA-###.REV, 256, 260
  PLACE.DOM, 256, 258-260
Configuration Manager, 53
configurations
  DHCP clients, 213-215
  scopes, adding, 228
  software, 98-101
  system services registry keys, 768-769
  TCP/IP (DNS), 110
  WINS (TCP/IP), 111
Configure Port Usage dialog box, 124
configuring
  dbWeb, 556
  DHCP clients, 229
  frame protocols, 787
  FTP
    directories, 153-155
    messages, 152-153
    publishing services, 150-152
  Gopher
    directories, 158-159
    properties sheets, 156-157
    publishing services, 156-157

IMC, 192-201
  startup values, 199
Internet Explorer, 168
  appearances, 173-175
  cache settings, 179-181
  character sets, 184-185
  *configuring proxy
    servers, 178*
  connections, 175-179
  rating systems, 185-186
  search pages, 172-173
  security, 181-183
  start pages, 172-173
modems, 124
NBF protocol
  configurations
  registry keys, 787-790
RAS, 126
registry keys (WINS
  servers), 253-254
scopes, 225-227
  *creating new options,
    227-228*
servers (PPTP packets),
  291
SNMP (traps properties),
  117
SQL Server, 668,
  670-676
systems, enabling audits,
  297-299
TCP/IP, 207
  printing services, 119
user account policies,
  276-278
Windows NT Server
  firewalls, 290-297
WINS, 210
  SNMP, 114
  *WINS Manager,
    241-247*

WWW publishing
  services, 139-141, 148
  *configuring properties,
    149-150*
  directories, 142
**Confirmation dialog box,
  171**
**Connect to Server option
  (Internet Service
  Manager), 137**
connecting
  clients, 126
  Exchange Server sites,
    199-200
  IIS (Windows NT
    Server), 11-12
  Internet, 9, 13
    56KB leased lines, 14
    bandwidths, 15-16
    dial-up, 14
    frame relay, 14-15
    FTP Server, 12
    Gopher Server, 12
    hardware, 13
    IAPs, 17
    ISPs, 17-20
    setting up networks, 10
    WWW Server, 11
  RAS, monitoring,
    127-128
  servers, 137
**connecting to Internet
  ISDNs, 16-17**
**Connection Attempts
  counter, 663, 666**
Connection Timeout
  FTP Publishing Service
    properties sheet, 151
  Gopher Publishing
    Service properties
    sheet, 156
  WWW Publishing
    Service properties
    sheet, 140

connections
  Internet Explorer,
    175-179
  RPCs, 704
**Connections in Error
  counter, 666**
**Connections/sec counter,
  663**
connectors
  bayonet nut, 689
  IMC, 190
  Internet Database
    Connector, 698
  T, 708
  see also IDC
constraints, 570-573
**Constraints dialog box,
  572**
**CONTAINS extension,
  606**
**CONTENT LENGTH
  extension, 606**
**CONTENT TYPE
  extension, 606**
**Content-Type parameter
  (IDC), 605**
**CONTENT_LENGTH
  CGI environment
  variable, 499**
**CONTENT_TYPE CGI
  environment variable,
  499**
**Contents command (Help
  menu), 398**
**Context switches/sec
  counter, 644**
**Control Panel dialog box,
  554**
**Control Panel System
  Properties dialog box, 99**
control sets, 690
  current, 690
  LastKnownGood, 699

control structures (VBScript), 455
   For Each...Next, 458
   For...Next, 458
   While...Wend, 463
controllers, 66-67
   disk subsystems (single), 85-87
   DMA, 80
   domains, 692
     backup, 67
     creating, 67
     primary, 67
     synchronizing, 693
   PDCs, 702-703
   replications, 704
converting
   e-mail messages, troubleshooting, 196
   RPCs, 53
   strings to numbers in Java applets, 537
cooperative multitasking, 690, 702
coorporations
   ISPs, 19-20
     references, 20
   ordering, 37
   publishing, 36
Copying File dialog box, 168
Corel, 387-389
CorelWEB.GALLERY, 389-390
CorelWEB.Transit, 391-392
   HTML Transit, 392
CorelWEB.Transit dialog box, 391
corporate directories, 36
corrupted data, 690
Cos function (VBScript), 464

counters
   adding, 626
   alerts, 638-640
   colors, 628
   deleting, 626
   FTP, 665-666
   Gopher, 666-667
   HTTP, 663-665
   IIS, 662-663
   instances, 634
   memory, 649
   Network Interface Current Bandwidth, 661
   networks, 659
   objects (Performance Monitor), 250
   Performance Monitor, 624
   processors, 644-645
   ranges, 628
   scales, 628
   SQL Server (Performance Monitor), 677-682
   systems, 653
   updating, 626
counting objects (enumeration operations), 693
CPU Time counter, 681
CRC (cyclic redundancy check), 691
Create command (Scope menu), 223
Create HotDog Program Group dialog box, 397
Create Hypertext Link dialog box, 420
Create Scope dialog box, 223
Create Simple Model command (Models menu), 385

Create Supervisor Password dialog box, 185
Create Table dialog box, 419-420
Create Template dialog box, 421
Create Text Models command (Models menu), 385
<CREDIT> HTML tag, 724
CSnet, 6
CSng function (VBScript), 464
CStr function (VBScript), 465
CSU/DSU (Channel Service Unit/Data Service Unit), 14
Current Anonymous Users counter, 663, 667
Current Bandwidth counter, 659
Current Blocked Async I/O Requests counter, 662
Current Commands counter, 660
Current Connections counter, 663, 665, 667
current control sets, 690
Current ISAPI Extension Requests counter, 664
Current NonAnonymous Users counter, 664-665, 667
Current Sessions option (FTP Publishing Service properties sheet), 152
CurrentRecord extension, 606
Custom access header property (dbWeb), 560
Custom secure header property (dbWeb), 560

Customize Button Bar command (Tools menu), 400
Customize Button Bar dialog box, 400
Customize Shortcut Keys dialog box, 401
customizing
  content with CGIs, 513-518
  HotDog Pro, 395, 399
    application shortcut keys, 401-402
    applications, 402-410
    button bars, 399-401
  message boxes, 469
CVErr function (VBScript), 465
cyclic redundancy check (CRC), 691

D

DARPA (Defense Advanced Research Projects Agency), 6
Data From command (Options menu), 632
Data From dialog box, 632
data, *see* **publishing**
data snooping, 181
Data Source dialog box, 561
Data Source Name, 691
data source name ODBC (dbWeb), 560
data sources
  dbWeb systems, creating, 563
  ODBC, 563-564
    building, 161-162
    creating, 162, 561-563
    defining, 561-563

Data Sources dialog box, 161
data types, 228, 764
Database command (View menu), 244
database schema, creating dbWeb, 564-567
databases
  assigning permissions, 161
  backups (DHCP servers), 212
  building, 159-161
  DHCP, compacting, 232
  integrating, 37
  Internet Database Connector, 698
  ODBC, 701
    dbWeb, 550, 554
    logging Web site activity, 149
  ordering, 615
  registry, 703
  replications (DHCP servers), 212
  schema
    constraints, 570-573
    joins, 570-573
    properties, 567-569
    troubleshooting, 569
  Web publishing with Microsoft Access, 376-378
  WINS, compacting, 249
Datasource parameter (IDC), 604
Date dialog box (VBScript), 449
Date function (VBScript), 465
DateSerial function (VBScript), 465
DateValue function (VBScript), 465

Day function (VBScript), 465
DbFileNm (registry keys), 252
dbWeb, 550
  Administrator, 555
    properties, 556-558
  column queries, 566
  configuring, 556
  data sources, 563
  database schemas
    creating, 564-567
    tables, 565
  directories, 553
  drilldown links, 566
  guest books, creating, 589-590, 592
  help files, 557, 592
  installing, 550-555
  IP logging, 560
  ODBC
    data source name, 560
    data source profiles, 563-564
    data sources, creating, 561-563
    installing, 554
  passwords, 560
  QBE properties, 573-575, 577
  schemas
    constraints, 570-573
    database properties, 567-569
    delete forms, 584-587
    freeform form properties, 580-583
    HTML form properties, 587-589
    insert forms, 584-585, 587
    joins, 570-573
    properties, 557
    tables, 570

tabular form properties, 577-580
update forms, 584-585, 587
servers
  internal properties, 559
  properties, 558-561
setup wizard, 551
TCP/IP printing services, 553
user IDs, 560
Web site, 550
dbWeb License Agreement dialog box, 551
DBX Editor dialog box, 588
<DD> HTML tag, 328, 724
DDLs (dynamic link libraries), 33-34
Deactivate command (Scope menu), 225
deadlock conditions, 691
debugger
  breakpoints, 691
  Kernel Debugger, 691, 699
  NTSD, 707
declarations (DTDs), 314
declaring
  dynamic arrays with Dim statement, 456
  multidimensional arrays with Dim statement, 456
  multiple variables with Dim statement, 456
  static arrays with Dim statement, 456
  variant variables, 456
default gateways, 691
Default Parameters parameter (IDC), 605
Defaults command (DHCP Options menu), 227

Defense Advanced Research Projects Agency (DARPA), 6
defining
  joins, 571
  ODBC data sources, 561-563
  properties (HTML documents), 411-414
  special characters, 749, 754
definition files (IDC), 604
<DEL> HTML tag, 725
Delete button (Calculator program), 477
Delete command (Edit menu), 766
Delete command (Scope menu), 225
delete forms
  properties, 584-585, 587
  properties sheets, 585-587
Delete WINS Server command (Server menu), 241
deleting
  buttons, 400
  caches, 181
  counters, 626
  joins, 572
  objects, 385
  permissions, 286
  scopes, 223, 225
  WINS servers, 239
delivering e-mail messages, 198
denial of service (Exchange Server), 201
Denied Access On dialog box, 150
dependency, 689, 691
design models for Windows NT Server, 51-54

designing
  DHCP protocols, 207-212
  DNS, 254-255
  Web sites, 380
    CorelWEB.GALLERY, 389-390
    Web 3D, 380-381
    Web.Designer, 387-389
  WINS, 235-236
destination hosts (e-mail), 196
destination IP address (firewalls), 272
destination IP ports (firewalls), 272
determining variable types with VarType function, 472
device drivers (virtual), 710
<DFN> HTML tag, 725
  Internet Explorer, 755
  Word Internet Assistant, 758
DHCP (Dynamic Host Configuration Protocol), 106, 109, 206, 693
  B-nodes, 210-211
  client reservations, adding, 231
  clients, 213, 228-230
    configurations, 213-215
    configuring, 229
    IDs, 215
    leases, 230
    overlays, 215
    reservations, 231
  databases, compacting, 232
  DNS, 254-255
    servers, 214

H-nodes, 211
implementing, 207
installing, 112-114, 209-220
IP addresses, 211, 214
lease expirations, 213
M-nodes, 211
NetBIOS, 214
overlays, 215
P-nodes, 211
protocols, designing, 207-212
rebinding, 208, 215
renewals, 215
RFCs (routers), 210
routers, 210, 213
scopes, 207, 221-222
  configuring, 225-227
  creating, 222-225
  deleting, 223, 225
  options, creating, 227-228
  properties, 226-227
servers, 212, 215
  adding, 222
  backups, 212
  database replications, 212
  DHCP Manager, 221-222
  registry keys, 233-234
  replications, 212
  static IP addresses, 212
subnets, 223
  masks, 213
WINS, 214, 254-255
  configuring, 210
  see also subnets
DHCP Manager, 63
  servers, 221-222
DHCP Manager Active Leases dialog box, 230
DHCP Options command (Scope Properties menu), 213

DHCP Options: Default Values, 227
DHCP Options dialog box, 226
DHCP Options menu commands
  Defaults, 227
  Scope, 226
dial-in clients, connecting, 126
dial-up connections, 14
Dial-Up Networking, 177, 692
  auto-dialing, 176
  security, 287-290
Dial-Up Networking dialog box, 289-290
dialing, *see* **modems**
dialog boxes
  Accessories, 167
  Account Policy, 277
  Active Leases, 230, 232
  Add Data Source, 162, 562
  Add DHCP Server on the Server List, 222
  Add Key, 765
  Add Reserved Clients, 231
  Add Static Mappings, 248
  Add to Alert, 636
  Add to Chart, 627, 633
  Add To Item, 626
  Add to Log, 630
  Add to Report, 633
  Add Users and Groups, 284, 301
  Add Value, 766
  Add WINS Server, 241
  Administrator Preferences, 556, 558
  Administrator Properties, 561

Advanced Addressing, 147
Advanced IP Addressing, 110, 292
Alert Options, 637
Audit Policy, 298
Bindings Review and Configuration, 109
Build External Hypertext Links, 417
Change Folder, 554
Change Icon, 170
Change Option Type, 228
Chart Option, 628
Choose a Table, 565
Choose Destination Location, 551
Choose Program Group, 555
Client Properties, 230-231
Colors, 175, 414
Computed Column Expression Builder, 574, 578, 582
Configure Port Usage, 124
Confirmation, 171
Constraints, 572
Control Panel, 554
Control Panel System Properties, 99
Copying Files, 168
CorelWEB.Transit, 391
Create HotDog Program Group, 397
Create Hypertext Link, 420
Create Scope, 223
Create Supervisor Password, 185
Create Table, 419-420
Create Template, 421

dialog boxes
Index

Customize Button Bar, 400
Customize Shortcut Keys, 401
Data From, 632
Data Sources, 161, 561
Date (VBScript), 449
DBX Editor, 588
Denied Access On, 150
DHCP Manager Active Leases, 230
DHCP Options, 226
DHCP Options: Default Values, 227
Dial-Up Networking, 289-290
Directory, 144
Directory Auditing, 300
Directory Permissions, 283, 285
Directory Properties, 144, 154, 158
Drilldown Automatic Link, 566
Edit, 766
Edit File Type, 170
Edit Item Entry, 626
Edit Phonebook Entry, 128
Edit Tag Information, 416
Editing Action For Type, 171
Enter schema name, 567
Enter Target ID, 417
Event Detail, 304
Event Viewer Filter, 305
Exchange Server Setup, 191
File Option, 618
File Permissions, 286
File Save As, 629
Files Needed, 167
Filter, 305

Format Document, 411
Formatting, 619
FrontPage Server Administrator, 341
FTP Service Properties, 153
FTP Service Properties for *ComputerName*, 150
Generate Snapshot, 385, 386
Global Group Membership, 284
Gopher Service Properties, 158
Gopher Service Properties for *ComputerName*, 156
Grant Access On, 150
Hello World! (VBScript), 448
HotDog Pro Welcome, 399
HotDog Select Picture, 400
Insert Image, 418
Insert Picture, 365
Install New Modem, 122
Installation Complete, 397
Internet Connector Properties, 201
Internet Explorer License Agreement, 168
Internet Mail Connector Properties, 194, 198
Internet Ratings, 185
Joins, 571
Local Group Membership, 284
Log Options, 631
Log Settings, 307
Microsoft Internet Explorer V3.0 Install Kit dialog box, 168

Microsoft SNMP Properties, 118
Microsoft TCP/IP Properties, 109, 147, 292
Modify Surface and Color, 385
Network, 93, 108, 112, 114, 288, 291
Network Configuration, 287-288
Network Settings Change, 147, 288
New Database, 160
New Phonebook Entry, 289
New Schema, 565
Notifications, 196
ODBC Data Sources, 564
ODBC Driver Pack 3.0 Custom, 554
ODBC Driver Pack 3.0 Setup, 554
ODBC SQL Server Setup, 162, 562
Open Web dialog box, 346
Operability, 196
Options, 179, 402
Policy, 276
Preferences, 242
Project Manager, 422
Project Manager Links, 422
Properties, 185, 574
Proxy Settings, 178
Publishing Directories, 131
Pull Properties, 247
Push Properties, 247
RAS Server Protocol Configuration, 287
Registration Details, 396

dialog boxes

Registry Key Auditing, 767
Remote Access Setup, 124, 287, 288
Replication Partners, 246
Save As, 307
Scheduling, 618
Schema Name, 568
Security Add, 293
Select Components to Install, 397
Select Destination Directory, 397
Select Directory, 144, 146, 155
Select Folder, 397
Select Hypertext Target, 416
Select Network Adapter, 121
Select Network Protocol, 109
Select Network Service, 114
Server, 100
Server/Configuration, 668
Service, 199
Set Up Files, 391
Site Services Account, 192
SMTP Properties, 197
Snapshot and Animation Settings, 386
Special Access, 287
Special Directory Access, 285
Special File Access, 286
Static Mappings, 248
System Data Sources, 561
Systems Settings Change, 167
Tags, 416

TCP/IP Security, 293
Time (VBScript), 449
Virtual Memory, 99-100
Welcome to HotDog!, 398
Windows NT Setup, 109
WINS Server Configuration, 242, 253
WWW Service Properties, 142, 148-149
WWW Service Properties for *ComputerName*, 139
WWW Site Properties, 149

Digital Alta Vista Web site, 41
Dim statement (VBScript), 455
declaring
multidimensional arrays, 456
multiple variables, 456
static arrays, 456
dynamic arrays, 456
<DIR> HTML tag, 327, 725
Internet Explorer, 755
Word Internet Assistant, 758
direct memory access (DMA), 80
direction option, 529
directories, 36, 41-42
auditing, 299-302
backups (archive bits), 687
CGIs, controlling access, 498
creating with HTML tags, 327
dbWeb, 553

export paths, 695
FTP publishing services, configuring, 153-155
Gopher publishing services, configuring, 158-159
home, 155, 696
logging site activity, 148
permissions, 282
attributes, 283-284
setting, 280-287
root, 705
sharepoints, 706
virtual, 142
creating, 144-145, 154, 158-159
WWW publishing services, 142
properties, 142-143
Directory Auditing dialog box, 300
Directory dialog box, 144
Directory Listing Sent counter, 667
Directory Listings counter, 662
Directory Permissions dialog box, 283, 285
Directory Properties dialog box, 144, 154, 158
Directory Replicator Service, 692
export paths, 695
import paths, 697
directory trees, 142
Directory Replicator Service, 692
disabling
caches, 181
WINS protocols, 96
disconnecting users, 127
disk duplexing, 58, 60
disk mirroring, 58-59

Disk Queue Length counter, 655
disk striping with parity, 58, 60
   drives, 87
   troubleshooting, 87
disk subsystems, 82-84
   antiquated systems, 82
   EIDE, 83
   hardware (RAID), 91-92
   IDE, 83
   multiple, 87-88
   network adapters, adding, 92-97
   SCSI, 88-89
   single, 85-87
DiskKeeper, 658
disks
   bottlenecks
      budgets, 658
      finding, 654-658
      mirror sets, 657
      striped sets, 657
      troubleshooting, 656
   duplexing, 692
   mirroring, 692
   partitioning, 59, 702
   striped sets, 706
   striping, 692
Display Binary Data command (View menu), 767
displaying
   images (Web pages), 331
   links (colors), 414
   message boxes, 468
   Select Network dialog box, 114
   tabbed tables, 317-318
   user accounts, 284
<DIV> HTML tag, 726
division operator (VBScript), 451

<DL COMPACT> HTML tag
   Internet Explorer, 755
   Word Internet Assistant, 759
<DL> HTML tag, 328, 726
   Internet Explorer, 755
   Word Internet Assistant, 759
DLLs (dynamic link libraries), 693
   ActiveX, 268
   ISAPI applications, 428
   loading/unloading, 429
DMA (direct memory access), 80, 643
DNS (Domain Name Server), 83, 107, 206, 254, 295, 692
   configuration files, 255
      ARPA-###.REV, 260
      BOOT, 256-257
      CACHE, 256-258
      PLACE.DOM, 256, 258-260
   designing, 254-255
   DHCP, 254-255
   domain lookup file, 258
   Exchange Server, 198
   FQDN, 259
   installing, 115-116, 255
   ODBC, logging Web site activity, 149
   records (SOA), 259
   servers, 214
   subnet lookup files, 259
   TCP/IP, 110
   Windows Resolution, enabling, 111
Do…Loop control structure, 457
DoBackupOnTerm (registry keys), 253

document attributes (FrontPage editor Web page design), 350-351
Document command (Format menu), 411
document type declarations (DTDs), 314
documents
   entering text, 414-415
   external, inserting links, 417
   HotDog Pro, 410
   HTML, 312-313, 315
      bulleted lists, 326-327
      colors, 412
      colors of links, 414
      creating (Microsoft Word), 364-369
      creating templates, 422
      creating with HotDog Pro, 410-411
      creating with IIS SDK, 428
      defined, 313-314
      defining properties, 411-414
      displaying text with fixed-width fonts, 323-324
      headers, creating, 324-325
      HotDog Pro, 394
      hypertext link, creating, 333-335
      inserting graphics, 329-332
      links, 413
      lists, 327
      page attributes, 325-326
      paragraph attributes, 318-320
      proportional fonts, 317

searchable indexes, 412
styles, 316-318
text, 413
text attributes, 320, 322
titles, 316
troublehsooting, 329
HTML tags, inserting, 415-417
infected systems, recovering, 268-269, 270
inserting graphics, 418
inserting hypertext links, 416-417
Internet command, inserting, 420-421
Internet security, 264-267
projects, 422
publishing, 422
SGML, 313
tables, inserting, 418-420
titles, 413
Domain Name Server, *see* **DNS**
domains, 66, 692
accounts, 66
Guest, 276
authenticating, 98
BOOT configuration file, 256
controllers, 692
backup, 67
primary, 67
creating, 67
DNS records, 259
FQDN, 695
groups, 140, 152
lookup file, 258
master models, 69-72
models, 68

names, 13, 39, 214, 692
ISPs, 18
registering, 17
PDCs, 702-703
Server Manager, 62
servers (single models), 68
single, 68
synchronizing, 693
trust relationships, 66, 72, 709
User Manager, 63
virtual, 18
Windows NT, 65
WINS, 236
see also DNS
dongles, 693
DoStaticDataInit (registry keys), 252
double buffering, 79
downloading
files (security), 265
graphics, 331
HotDog Pro, 394
Internet Assistant for Access, 376
Internet Assistant for Excel, 369
Internet Assistant for Microsoft PowerPoint, 373
Internet Assistant for Word, 363
Internet Explorer, 166
DRAM (Dynamic Random Access Memory), 89
drawing rectangles, 540
drawRect method, 540
drawString method, 541
Drilldown Automatic Link dialog box, 566
drilldown links, 566

drivers
devices, 691
fault-tolerant, 59
virtual device drivers, 710
drives
disk subsystems (single), 85-87
IIS installation data, 106
RAID, selecting, 91
striping with parity, 87
drop boxes (FTP), 18
DSN interactive Web pages, 597
<DT> HTML tag, 328, 726
DTD (Document Type Declaration), 314
duplexing, *see* **disks, duplexing**
duplicating CGI scripts, 497
dynamic arrays
declaring with Dim statement, 456
ReDim statement, 456
dynamic endpoints, 704
Dynamic Host Configuration Protocol, *see* **DHCP**
dynamic link libraries, *see* **DLLs**
dynamic random access memory, *see* **DRAM**
dynamic Web pages, 24, 596

E

e-mail, 13
addresses, troubleshooting, 196
destination hosts, 196
IMC, 190
ISPs, 18

messages
 conversions, 196
 delivering, 198
 flames, 201
 protecting, 202-203
 protocol errors, 196
 relay hosts, 193, 198
 sending, 190
 timeout errors, 197
E-mail option (Gopher Publishing Service properties sheet), 157
EAs (Extended Attributes), 695
ECBs (Extension Control Blocks), 431
 formats, 433-434
Edit dialog box, 766
Edit File Type dialog box, 170
Edit Item Entry dialog box, 626
Edit menu commands
 Add Key, 765
 Add to Chart, 627, 645
 Add to Log, 630
 Add to Report, 633, 636
 Add Value, 766
 Delete, 766
 Preferences, 556, 558
 Tag Information, 416
Edit Phonebook Entry dialog box, 128
Edit Tag Information dialog box, 416
editing file type associations, 170
Editing Action For Type dialog box, 171
editors
 FrontPage, 350-358
  document attributes, 350-351
  frames, 351-353
  FrontPage scripts, 356-357
  tables, 354-355
  templates, 358-359
 Registry Editor, 233
  troubleshooting, 252
 WYSIWYG, 597
EIDE (Enhanced Integrated Drive Electronics), 83
EISA (Enhanced Industry Standard Architecture), 77, 80, 90
electronic mail, *see* **e-mail**
else extension, 607
<EM> HTML tag, 320, 726
 Internet Explorer, 755
 Word Internet Assistant, 759
<EMBED> HTML tag, 727
embedding
 Java applets in HTML, 545-546
 Marquee applet, 545
enabling
 audits, configuring systems, 297-299
 DNS for Windows Resolution, 111
 IP packets, 112
 LMHOSTS Lookup, 111
 printers (audits), 688
encapsulated arrays, 228
encrypting, 276
 authentications, 288-290
 ISPs, 289-290
 plain text, 288
 secrets, 705
endif extension, 607
ending braces ({}), 544
endpoints (RPCs), 704

Enhanced Industry Standard Architecture (EISA), 77, 80, 90
Enhanced Integrated Drive Electronics (EIDE), 83
Enhanced Run Length Limited (ERLL), 82
Enhanced Small Device Interface (ESDI), 82
Enter schema name dialog box, 567
Enter Target ID dialog box, 416
entering text documents, 414
enumeration operations, 693
environment variables (CGI), 499-503
 accessing variables
  C program, 511-512
  Perl script, 512-522
 AUTH_TYPE, 499
 CONTENT_LENGTH, 499
 CONTENT_TYPE, 499
 GATEWAY_INTERFACE, 500
 HTTP_ACCEPT, 500
 HTTP_USER_AGENT, 500
 PATH_INFO, 500
 PATH_TRANSLATED, 500
 QUERY_STRING, 501
 REMOTE_ADDR, 501
 REMOTE_HOST, 501
 REMOTE_IDENT, 501
 REMOTE_USER, 501
 REQUEST_METHOD, 502
 SCRIPT_NAME, 502
 SERVER_NAME, 502
 SERVER_PORT, 502

SERVER_PROTOCOL, 502
SERVER_SOFTWARE, 502
environmental subsystems (Windows NT), 54-56
EQ extension, 607
equivalence operator (VBScript), 454
Erase statement (VBScript), 457
ERLL (Enhanced Run Length Limited), 82
error checking (VBScript), 475
errors
  bad-sector mapping, 689
  CRC, 691
  exceptions, 693
  logging, 693
  protocols, 196
  SGML, 314
  timeout, 197
ESDI (Enhanced Small Device Interface), 82
Ethernet, 14
Evaluate button (Calculator program), 474, 477
Event Detail dialog box, 304
Event Viewer, 61
  Windows NT, 302-303
Event Viewer Filter dialog box, 305
events
  archiving, 306-307
  auditing, 298
  components, 304
  filtering, 305-306
  OnChange, 475
  Performance Monitor, 624, 631
  viewing, 304-305

Excel (Web publishing), 368-372
  Internet Assistant for Excel, installing, 369-370
  spreadsheets, 370-373
exception handling Java applets, 543-544
exceptions, 693
Exchange Server, 190
  DNS, 198
  e-mail messages, protecting, 202-203
  IMC, 191
    configuring, 192-199
    installing, 191-192
  Internet, 190-191, 196
    connecting sites, 199-200
  IP addresses, 199
  MIME, 193
  protocols, troubleshooting, 196
  RPCs, 200
  security, 200-204
    denial of service, 201
    viruses, 203-204
  servers, 190
  SMTP, 190
  timeout errors, 197
Exchange Server Setup dialog box, 191
Excite Web site, 41
Executive, 693-694
  HAL, 696
  kernel modes, 698-699
executive messages, 694
Executive Software (DiskKeeper), 658
Exit For statement (VBScript), 458
Exit Function statement (VBScript), 459

Exit statement (VBScript), 457
Exp function (VBScript), 465
expanding folders, 764
expansions
  I/O buses, 78
  ISA, 79
Expert option (Internet Explorer properties sheets), 183
expiration leases (DHCP), 213
Expires parameter (IDC), 605
exponential operator (VBScript), 451
export paths, 695
exporting
  directory trees (Directory Replicator Service), 692
  extensions, 431
  snapshots, 381
extended attributes (EAs), 695
extended partitions, 695
extensible platforms, 33-34
Extension Control Blocks, *see* **ECBs**
extensions
  exporting, 431
  HTML Web site, 714
  HTX, 606
  installing FrontPage server administrator, 342-343
  managing FrontPage server administrator, 343-345
Extent Locks - Exclusive counter, 680
Extent Locks - Shared counter, 681

Index

Extent Locks - Total counter, **681**
external documents, inserting links, **417**
external tools (HotDog Pro), **396**

F

Failed Queries/sec object counter, **250**
Failed Releases/sec object counter, **250**
family sets, **695**
FAT clusters, **690**
FAT files (disk bottlenecks), **658**
fault-tolerant
   drivers, 59
      disk duplexing, 60
      disk mirroring, 59
      disk striping with parity, 60
      network adapters, 60
   drivers (uninterruptible power supply), 60
   Windows NT, 49
FCB (file control block), **695**
fgcolor option, **529**
FIFO (first in first out), **120**
<FIG> HTML tag, **727**
File Manager, **62**
File menu commands
   New, 383
   New Chart, 632
   New Other, 200
   Open, 383, 629
   Open Project, 422
   Project Manager, 422
   Properties, 194

   Publish Document, 422
   Save, 588
   Save Chart Settings, 629
   Save Log Setting As, 632
   Save Report Settings As, 634
   Save Workspace, 629
File Option dialog box, **618**
File Permissions dialog box, **286**
File Received counter, **664-665**
File Save As dialog box, **629**
File Sent counter, **664-665, 667**
File Total counter, **664, 667**
File Transfer Protocol, *see* FTP
filenames
   HotDog Pro, 397
   NTFS, 57
files
   associations, editing, 170
   auditing, 298-302
   AUTOEXEC.NT, 688
   AVI, 175, 380
   backups (archive bits), 687
   batch, 689
   bits (read-only), 703
   CONFIG.NT, 688
   configuration DNS, 255-260
   downloading security, 265
   export paths, 695
   help (dbWeb), 557, 592
   HTML, 335
   I/O mappings, 700

   IDC (Sign-In-IDC.HTX), 609, 611
   IFS, 697
   INF, 697
   INI, 762
   interfaces, creating, 602-605
   logging site activity, 148
   paging, 701
   partitioning (boot), 689
   permissions, 282
      attributes, 283-284
      setting, 280-287
   registry keys, 763
   SearchGuestBook.HTX, 611
   Sign-In-IDC.IDC, 602-603
   snapshots, exporting, 381
   swap, 701
   SYSTEM.MDB, 232-233
   systems, 707
   WINDBG.EXE, 711
Files Needed dialog box, **167**
fillRect method, **540**
Filter dialog box, **305**
Filter Events command (View menu), **305**
filtering events, **305-306**
filters (ISAPI), **34**
financing IIS, **105-106**
Find All Servers option (Internet Service Manager), **137**
Find Key command (View menu), **767**
finding bottlenecks
   disks, 654-658
   IIS, 661-667
   memory, 649-654
   networks, 658-661
   processors, 643-648

fingering, 295
firewalls, 270-273
  configuring Windows NT Server, 290-297
  destination IP addresses, 272
  destination IP ports, 272
  protocols, 272
  source IP addresses, 272
  source IP ports, 272
first in first out (FIFO), 120
Fix function (VBScript), 466
fixed-width fonts, displaying HTML documents, 323-324
flames, 201
flash memory, 695
floating-point division operator, 451
<FN> HTML tag, 727
folders (Registry Editor), 764
<FONT> HTML tag, 322, 728
  Internet Explorer, 756
fonts
  HTML documents, 412
    fixed-width, 323-324
  proportional, 317
  reading Java applets, 541
  selecting for Java applets, 535
  setting current Java applets, 539-540
  sizes, 322
  TrueType, creating HTML documents with Microsoft Word, 365
For Each...Next control structure (VBScript), 458

For...Next control structure (VBScript), 458
<FORM> HTML tag, 728
  Internet Explorer, 756
  Word Internet Assistant, 759
Format Document dialog box, 411
Format menu command (Document), 411
formats (ECBs), 433-434
formatting
  document text, 414
  table cells, creating HTML documents with Microsoft Word, 367
Formatting dialog box, 619
forms
  creating for Web pages, 597-598
  delete properties, 584-587
  freeforms
    properties, 580-583
    properties sheets, 582-583
  HTML properties, 587-589
  inputs, creating, 598-602
  insert properties, 584-587
  orders, 615
  tabular properties, 577-580
  update properties, 584-587
FQDN (fully qualified domain name), 259, 695
frame relay, 14-15
  bandwidths, 15-16
<FRAME> HTML tag, 728
frames (FrontPage Editor Web page design), 351-353

frames protocol configuration (registry keys), 787
<FRAMESET> HTML tag, 729
freeform forms
  properties, 580-583
  properties sheets, 582-583
  queries, 617
FrontPage Editor, 350-358, 597
  installing, 338-339
  server administrator, 341-345
  To Do List, 348
  verifying links, 349
  Web page design, 350-359
    document attributes, 350-351
    frames, 351-353
    FrontPage scripts, 356-357
    tables, 354-355
    templates, 358-359
FrontPage Explorer, 345-347
FrontPage Server, 340
  Administrator
    installing extensions, 342-343
    managing extensions, 343-345
  changing the default port, 341
FrontPage Server Administrator dialog box, 341
FTP (File Transfer Protocol), 294, 695
  drop box, 18
  HTML, 335

Index

performance counters, 665-666
publishing services
   configuring, 150-152
   configuring directories, 153-155
   configuring messages, 152-153
   creating virtual directories, 154
   home directories, 155
   properties sheet, 151-152
   troubleshooting, 152
registry keys, 773
sites (security), 264
troubleshooting, 106
FTP command (View menu), 139
FTP Server, 31
   Internet, connecting to, 12
   publishing services, 33
FTP Service Properties dialog box, 153
FTP Service Properties for *ComputerName* dialog box, 150
Full Control option (permissions), 281
fully qualified domain name (FQDN), 259, 695
Function statement (VBScript), 459
functions
   GetExtensionVersion, 431-433
   GetServerVariable, 432, 435-437
   HttpExtensionProc, 431-435
   ReadClient, 432, 437
   routines, 687

   ServerSupportFunction, 432, 438-439
   VBScript, 463-473
      Abs, 463
      Array, 463
      Asc, 463
      Atn, 463
      CBool, 464
      CByte, 464
      CDate, 464
      CDbl, 464
      Chr, 464
      CInt, 464
      CLng, 464
      Cos, 464
      CSng, 464
      CStr, 465
      CVErr, 465
      Date, 465
      DateSerial, 465
      DateValue, 465
      Day, 465
      Exp, 465
      Fix, 466
      Hex, 466
      Hour, 466
      InputBox, 466
      Instr, 466
      Int, 466
      IsArray, 467
      IsDate, 464, 467
      IsEmpty, 467
      IsError, 467
      IsNull, 467
      IsNumeric, 467
      IsObject, 467
      LBound, 467
      LCase, 468
      Left, 468
      Len, 468
      Log, 468
      LTrim, 468
      Mid, 468

      Minute, 468
      Month, 468
      MsgBox, 468
      Now, 470
      Oct, 470
      Right, 470
      Rnd, 470
      RTrim, 468
      Second, 470
      Sgn, 470
      Sin, 470
      Sqr, 470
      Str, 470
      StrComp, 471
      String, 471
      Tan, 471
      Time, 471
      TimeSerial, 471
      TimeValue, 471
      Trim, 468
      UBound, 471
      UCase, 472
      Val, 472
      VarType, 472
      Weekday, 473
      Year, 473
   WriteClient, 432, 437-438

G

Gallery option (Chart Options dialog box), 629
GATEWAY INTERFACE extension, 607
GATEWAY_INTERFACE CGI environment variable, 500
gateways (defaults), 691
Generate Snapshot command (Scene menu), 385
Generate Snapshot dialog box, 385-386

Get Requests counter, 664
GetExtensionVersion function (ISAs), 431-433
GetServerVariable function (ISAs), 432, 435-437
GIFs (Graphical Interchange Formats), 325
    files, exporting snapshots, 381
Global command (Options menu), 226
Global Group Membership dialog box, 284
global groups, 695
Gopher, 295, 335
    performance counters, 666-667
    publishing services
        configuring, 156-157
        configuring directories, 158-159
        configuring properties sheets, 156-157
        creating virtual directories, 158-159
    publishing text, 25
    registry keys, 774
Gopher command (View menu), 139
Gopher Plus Requests counter, 667
Gopher Server, 12, 31
    publishing services, 33
Gopher Service Properties dialog box, 158
Gopher Service Properties for *ComputerName* dialog box, 156
Grant Access On dialog box, 150

granting
    access rights, 150
    permissions, 127
    access rights, 686
Graphical Interchange Formats (GIFs), 325, 381
graphics
    3D, designing, 384
    backgrounds, 413
    bandwidths, 381
    CorelWEB.GALLERY, 389-390
    CorelWEB.Transit, 391-392
    downloading, 331
    inserting, 329-332
    inserting into documents, 418
    labeling in VBScript, 484
    objects, inserting into home pages, 385
    ray traced, 386
    realistic with shadows, 386
    rendering, 385
    solid models, 386
    troubleshooting, 329
    Web 3D, 381-383
    Web.Designer, 387-389
    wireframes, 386
greater than operator (VBScript), 455
greater than or equal to operator (VBScript), 455
Group Conflicts/sec object counter, 250
Group Registrations/sec object counter, 250
Group Renewals/sec object counter, 251
groups
    auditing, 298
    domains, 140, 152
    local, 699
        Guests, 276

GT extension, 607
guard-page protection, 696
Guest domain accounts, 276
guest books, creating with dbWeb, 589-590, 592
Guests local groups, 152, 276

H

H-nodes, 211
<H1> HTML tag, 324, 729
    Internet Explorer, 756
    Word Internet Assistant, 759
<H2> HTML tag, 730
    Internet Explorer, 756
    Word Internet Assistant, 759
<H3> HTML tag, 730
    Internet Explorer, 756
    Word Internet Assistant, 759
<H4> HTML tag, 730
    Internet Explorer, 756
    Word Internet Assistant, 759
<H5> HTML tag, 730
    Internet Explorer, 756
    Word Internet Assistant, 759
<H6> HTML tag, 731
    Word Internet Assistant, 759
<H7> HTML tag, 324
HAL (hardware abstraction layer), 54, 97, 696
handles, 696
hard drives (disk subsystems), 85-87

Index

hardware, 13, 18
   RAID, 91-92
   upgrades, 89
   Windows NT Server, 77
HARDWARE registry key, 763
Haynes & Company Web site, 40
Head Requests counter, 664
<HEAD> HTML tag, 731
   Internet Explorer, 756
   Word Internet Assistant, 759
headers
   HTML documents
      creating, 324-325
      troubleshooting, 325
   table columns, 333
Hello World! application with VBScript, 447-450
Hello World! CGI script, 506-510
   C, 509-510
   Perl, 507-509
Hello World! dialog box (VBScript), 448
Hello World! Web page VBScript example, 449
help desks, 37
help files (dbWeb), 557, 592
Help menu commands (Contents), 398
Hex function (VBScript), 466
hexadecimals, 696
hidden bits, 696
Hide, 598, 604
hiding VBScript code, 447
hives, 696
HKEY CLASSES ROOT registry key, 764

HKEY CURRENT CONFIG registry key, 764
HKEY USERS registry key, 764
HMA (high memory area), 696
home directories, 155, 696
home pages
   creating with Web 3D, 383-387
   Microsoft Excel, 369
   Microsoft VBScript, 446
   objects, inserting, 385
   see also sites, Web sites; WWW, sites
Horizontal Grid option (Chart Options dialog box), 629
hosting servers, 17
hostname networks, 256
hosts
   Internet, 8-9
   IP addresses, 13
hot swapping, 91
HotDog Pro, 394-396
   compatibility, 395
   customizing, 395, 399
      application shortcut keys, 401-402
      applications, 402-410
      button bars, 399-401
   documents, 410
      defining properties, 411-414
      entering text, 414-415
      HTML, creating, 410-411
      inserting HTML tags, 415-417
      inserting hypertext links, 416-417
      inserting into Internet command, 420

      inserting tables, 418-420
   external tools, 396
   filenames, 397
   graphics, inserting into documents, 418
   HTML, 395
   HTML documents, 394
      creating templates, 421
      publishing, 422
   installing, 396-398
   projects, 395, 422
   spell checker, 395
   templates, 410
   tutorial, 397-398
HotDog Pro Select Picture dialog box, 400
HotDog Pro Welcome dialog box, 399
HotJava, 526
hotkeys, 697
HotSpot subroutine (VBScript), 486
Hour function (VBScript), 466
<HPn> HTML tag, 731
<HR> HTML tag, 329, 732
   Internet Explorer, 756
   Word Internet Assistant, 759
HSE STATUS ERROR status code, 435
HSE STATUS PENDING status code, 435
HSE STATUS SUCCESS AND KEEP CONN status code, 435
HSE STATUS SUCCESS status code, 435
HSE VERSION INFO structure, 432

HTML (Hypertext Markup Language) UNLEASHED

HTML (Hypertext Markup Language), 312-314, 697, 714
- codes (input forms), 598-599
- defined, 313-314
- documents, 313-315
  - *bulleted lists, 326-327*
  - *colors, 412*
  - *colors of links, 414*
  - *creating (Microsoft Word), 364-369*
  - *creating templates, 421*
  - *creating with HotDog Pro, 410-411*
  - *creating with IIS SDK, 428*
  - *defining properties, 411-414*
  - *displaying text with fixed-width fonts, 323-324*
  - *headers, creating, 324-325*
  - *HotDog Pro, 394*
  - *hypertext link, creating, 333-335*
  - *inserting graphics, 329-332*
  - *inserting hypertext links, 416-417*
  - *links, 413*
  - *lists, 327*
  - *numbered lists, 326-327*
  - *paragraph attributes, 318-320*
  - *projects, 422*
  - *proportional fonts, 317*
  - *publishing, 422*
  - *searchable indexes, 412*
  - *text, 413*
  - *text attributes, 320, 322*
  - *titles, 316*
  - *troubleshooting, 329*
- DTD, 314
- embedding Java applets, 545-546
- extensions Web site, 714
- form properties, 587-589
- HotDog Pro, 395
- IE, 312
- parsers, 315
- special characters, defining, 749, 754
- styles, 316-318
- tags, 313, 329, 714
  - <A>, 333, 715-716
  - <ABBREV>, 716
  - <ACRONYM>, 716
  - <ADDRESS>, 329, 717
  - <APPLET>, 527, 546, 717-718
  - <AREA>, 718
  - <AU>, 718
  - <B>, 718
  - <BANNER>, 719
  - <BASE>, 719
  - <BASEFONT>, 719
  - <BDO>, 720
  - <BGSOUND>, 326, 720
  - <BIG>, 720
  - <BLINK>, 720
  - <BLOCKQUOTE>, 329, 721
  - <BODY>, 326, 721-722
  - <BOLD>, 314
  -
, 722
  - browsers, 322
  - <CAPTION>, 722
  - <CENTER>, 320, 722
  - <CITE>, 321, 723
  - <CODE>, 321, 723
  - <COL>, 723
  - <COLGROUP>, 724
  - creating tables, 332-333
  - <CREDIT>, 724
  - <DD>, 328, 724
  - <DEL>, 725
  - <DFN>, 725
  - <DIR>, 327, 725
  - <DIV>, 726
  - <DL>, 328, 726
  - <DT>, 328, 726
  - <EM>, 320, 726
  - <EMBED>, 727
  - <FIG>, 727
  - <FN>, 727
  - <FONT>, 322, 728
  - <FORM>, 728
  - <FRAME>, 728
  - <FRAMESET>, 729
  - <H1>, 324, 729
  - <H2>, 730
  - <H3>, 730
  - <H4>, 730
  - <H5>, 730
  - <H6>, 731
  - <H7>, 324
  - <HEAD>, 731
  - <HPn>, 731
  - <HR>, 329, 732
  - <HTML>, 732
  - <I>, 320, 732
  - <IMG>, 330, 732-733
  - <INPUT>, 733
  - <INS>, 734
  - inserting into documents, 415-417
  - *Internet Explorer, 754-758*
  - <ISINDEX>, 734
  - <KBD>, 321, 734
  - <LANG>, 734
  - <LH>, 735
  - <LI>, 735
  - <LINK>, 735
  - <LISTING>, 323, 736
  - <MAP>, 736

\<MARQUEE\>, 736-737
\<MENU\>, 327, 737
\<META\>, 737
\<NEXTID\>, 737
\<NOBR\>, 738
\<NOEMBED\>, 738
\<NOFRAMES\>, 738
\<NOTE\>, 739
\<OL\>, 739
\<OPTION\>, 739
\<OVERLAY\>, 740
\<P\>, 317, 740
\<PARAM\>, 546, 740
\<PERSON\>, 740
\<PLAINTEXT\>, 323, 741
\<PRE\>, 323, 741
\<Q\>, 741
\<S\>, 321, 742
\<SAMP\>, 742
\<SELECT\>, 742
\<SMALL\>, 743
\<SPAN\>, 743
\<STRIKE\>, 321, 743
\<STRONG\>, 320, 743
\<SUB\>, 744
\<SUP\>, 744
\<TAB\>, 744
\<TABLE\>, 332, 744
Tags dialog box, 415-416
\<TBODY\>, 745
\<TD\>, 332, 745
\<TEXTAREA\>, 746
\<TFOOT\>, 746
\<TH\>, 332, 746
\<THEAD\>, 747
\<TITLE\>, 747
\<TR\>, 332, 747
\<TT\>, 321, 747
\<U\>, 748
\<UL\>, 748

\<VAR\>, 748
\<WBR\>, 749
Word Internet Assistant, 758-760
\<XMP\>, 749
templates, creating, 606-614
tutorial, 398
HTML Header Type property (dbWeb), 560
HTML tags (VBScript program definitions), 446
HTML Transit, 392
\<HTML\> HTML tag, 732
Internet Explorer, 756
Word Internet Assistant, 759
HTTP (Hypertext Transfer Protocol), 32, 335, 697
performance counters, 663-665
servers (ISAs), 431
HTTP ACCEPT extension, 607
HTTP_ACCEPT CGI environment variable, 500
HTTP_USER_AGENT CGI environment variable, 500
HttpExtensionProc function (ISAs), 431-435
HTTPS (Hypertext Transfer Protocol Secure), 335, 697
HTX extensions, 606
hypertext links
creating, 333-335
documents, inserting into, 416-417
Hypertext Markup Language, *see* **HTML**
Hypertext Target command (Insert menu), 416

I

I/O
buses, 78-82, 697
adapters, 80
DMA, 80
double buffering, 79
EISA, 80
expansions, 78
ISA, 79
MCA, 80
PCI, 81
PCMCIA, 81
servers, 81
troubleshooting, 79, 82
VLBs, 80
Windows NT Server, 82
mappings, 700
I/O - Trans. Per Log Record counter, 678
I/O Batch Average Size counter, 677
I/O Batch Max Size counter, 678
I/O Batch Writes/sec counter, 677
I/O Log Writes/sec counter, 677
I/O Manager, 54
I/O Outstanding Reads counter, 678
I/O Outstanding Writes counter, 678
I/O Page Reads/sec counters, 678
I/O Single page Writes/sec counter, 678
I/O Transactions/sec counter, 678
\<I\> HTML tag, 320, 732
Internet Explorer, 756
Word Internet Assistant, 759

IAPs (Internet access providers), 17-18, 698
ICMP, 294
IDC (Internet database connector), 588, 596
  files
    definitions, 604
    SearchGuestBook.HTX, 611
    Sign-In-IDC.HTX, 609, 611
  HTML templates, creating, 606-614
  interface files, creating, 602-605
  layout, 596
  parameters, 603-604
  SQL Server (Web Assistant), 614-620
  Web pages, creating forms, 597-598
IDE (integrated drive electronics), 83
identifiers
  handles, 696
  SIDs, 705
  URIs, 709
  UUID, 710
IDs
  DHCP clients, 215
  scopes, 112
  users (dbWeb), 560
IE (Internet Explorer), 24
  HTML, 312
if extension, 607
If...Then...Else statement (VBScript), 459
IFS (Installable File System), 697
IIS (Internet Information Server), 30, 35
  bottlenecks, finding, 661-667
  defined, 30

  extensible platforms, 33-34
  financing, 105-106
  FTP Server, 12
  Gopher Server, 12
  hosts (IP addresses), 13
  installing, 129-132, 553
    location, 104-106
    networks, 113
    placing data on drives, 106
    RAS, 105
    servers, 105
    troubleshooting, 106
  logs, 307-308
  performance counters, 662-663
  performance levels, 39-40
  preinstallation requirements, 106-112
  registry keys, 769-770
  security, 104
    user accounts, 276-277
  servers, 31
  sites
    managing, 138
    managing with views, 138-139
  TCP/IP, 30
  virtual domains, 18
  Windows NT Server, 11-12, 76
    robust, 48
    security, 275
  WWW Server, 11
IIS SDK, 428
  ISAPI applications, 428-429
Image Advanced command (Insert menu), 418
Image command (Insert menu), 418
ImageMapGraphic_ MouseMove subroutine, 486

images
  backgrounds, creating HTML documents with Microsoft Word, 364-365
  CorelWEB.GALLERY, 389-390
  CorelWEB.Transit, 391-392
  displaying Web pages, 331
  inserting inline images, creating HTML documents with Microsoft Word, 366
  inserting into documents, 418
  labeling in VBScript, 484
  objects, inserting into home pages, 385
  ray-traced, 386
  realistic with shadows, 386
  renderings, 385
  solid models, 386
  SSIs, 706
  three-dimensional, designing, 384
  Web 3D, 381-383
  Web.Designer, 387-389
  wireframes, 381-382, 386
IMC (Internet Mail Connector), 190
  configuring, 192-201
    startup values, 199
  Exchange Server, 191
  installing, 191-192
  message notifications, 197
  MIME, 193
  protocols, troubleshooting, 196
  SMTP, 200
  timeout errors, 197

Index

<IMG> HTML tag, 330, 732-733
   Internet Explorer, 756
   Word Internet Assistant, 759
impersonations, 697
implementing DHCP, 207
import partners (export paths), 695
import paths, 697
import statements, importing Java classes, 533-534
importing
   directory trees (Directory Replicator Service), 692
   Java classes, 533-534
indexes (HTML documents), 412
Industry Standard Architecture (ISA), 79
INF files, 697
infected systems, recovering, 268-270
infinite loops, 543
INI files, 762
init method
   font selection, 535
   initializing Java applets, 535-538
   parameters, 535-536
   testing strings, 536-537
initializing Java applets, 535-538
   converting strings to numbers, 537
   length of strings, 537-538
   parameters, 535-536
   selecting fonts, 535
   substrings, 537-538
   testing strings, 536-537
Initiate Scavenging command (Mappings menu), 250

InitTimePause (registry keys), 252
inline images, 366
input
   addresses, 697
   BIOS, 689
   I/O buses, 697
   see also I/O
input forms, creating, 598-602
input/output control (IOCTL), 697
<INPUT> HTML tag, 733
   Internet Explorer, 756
InputBox function (VBScript), 466
<INS> HTML tag, 734
insert forms
   properties, 584-587
   properties sheets, 585-587
Insert Image dialog box, 418
Insert menu commands
   Hypertext Target, 416
   Image, 418
   Image Advanced, 418
   Jump to Document on Another System, 417
   Jump Within this Document, 416
   Launch an Internet Service, 420
   Table, 419
Insert Picture dialog box, 365
inserting
   graphics, 329-332
      documents, 418
   HTML tags (Tags dialog box), 415-417
   Internet command into documents, 420-421
   links into external documents, 417

   objects into home pages, 385
   special characters, 415
   tables into documents, 418-420
Install New Modem dialog box, 122
Install New Modem wizard, 122
installable file system (IFS), 697
Installation Complete dialog box, 397
installing
   dbWeb, 550-555
   DHCP, 112-114, 209-220
   DNS, 115-116
   extensions (FrontPage Server Administrator), 342-343
   FrontPage, 338-339
   HotDog Pro, 396-398
   IIS, 129-132, 553
      location, 104-106
      networks, 113
      placing data on drives, 106
      preinstallation requirements, 106-112
      RAS, 105
      servers, 105
   IMC, 191-192
   Internet Assistant for Access, 376
   Internet Assistant for Excel, 369-370
   Internet Assistant for PowerPoint, 373
   Internet Assistant for Word, 363
   Internet Explorer, 167-168
   ODBC, 554

RAS, 120
  adapters, 121
  modems, 123-125
  properties, 123
  servers, 122, 125
RIP, 115
SNMP, 116-118
TCP/IP
  printing, 118-119
  protocols, 108-112
  simple, 118
  troubleshooting, 106
  Windows Internet, 114
  WINS, 236-241
instances
  object counters, 634
  Performance Monitor, 624
Instr function (VBScript), 466
integer-division operator (VBScript), 452
Integrated Drive Electronics (IDE), 83
Integrated Services Digital Networks (ISDNs), 16-17, 105
integrating databases, 37
Intel
  BIOS, 90
  I/O buses, 79
Intent Locks - Exclusive counter, 681
Intent Locks - Shared counter, 681
Intent Locks - Total counter, 681
interactive CGI Web sites, 491-494
interfaces
  APIs, 687
  BRIs, 16
  CGI, 35
  default gateways, 691
  ESDI, 82

files, creating, 602-605
ISAPI, 33-34, 430-432, 698
NetBEUI, 700
ODBC databses, 550
PRIs, 16
SCSI, 83
TAPI, 50
TDI, 709
see also CGI
internal properties (dbWeb servers), 559
Interner Explorer (AVI files), 175
Internet, 20
  access rights, restricting, 201-202
  applications (security), 264-265
  ARPA, 5
  ARPAnet, 6
  auto-replies, preventing, 202
  circuit-switched networks, 5
  collecting data, 25-26
  commands, inserting into documents, 420-421
  connecting, 9, 13
    56KB leased lines, 14
    bandwidths, 15-16
    dial-ups, 14
    frame relay, 14-15
    FTP Server, 12
    Gopher Server, 12
    IAPs, 17-18
    ISDNs, 16-17
    ISPs, 17-20
    setting up networks, 10
    WWW Server, 11
  CSnet, 6
  document security, 264-265
  domain names, 13
  e-mail, 13

events, archiving, 306-307
Exchange Server, 190-191, 196
  connecting sites, 199-200
  hardware, 13
  history of, 5-7
  hosts, 8-9
  IP addresses, 13
  IIS, 30
  messages, troubleshooting, 201
  networks
    protocols, 274-275
    switches, 5
    wrappers, 5
  newsgroups, 18
  NSFnet, 7
  packet-switched network protocol, 5
  packets, routing, 6
  publishing, 36-39
    catalogs, 23-24
    text, 24-25
  publishing data, 21-25
  RAS, 105, 128-129
  resources
    CGI Perl scripts, 504-506
    Perl, 504-506
  routers, 12
  security, 39, 104, 181, 264
    browsers, 267-268
    challenge-response authentication mechanisms, 276
    configuring user accounts, 276-277
    Dial-Up Networking, 287-290
    enabling audits, 297-299
    encrypting, 276

Index

firewalls, 270-273
NTFS, 279-280
passwords, 276
proxy agents, 270-274
recovering infected systems, 268-270
trojan horses, 265-267
user accounts, 275-276
viruses, 203-204, 265-267
selling products, 26-27
service providers, 4
requirements, 12-13
TCP/IP, 6
technical support, 21-23
transmissions, 8
URLs, 4
vBNS, 7
Windows NT Server security, 275
WINS server, 249
see also WWW
Internet access providers (IAPs), 17-18, 698
Internet Assistant
Access, 376
Excel, 369-370
PowerPoint Web site, 373
PowerPoint, installing, 373
Word, 363
Internet Connector Properties dialog box, 201
Internet Database Connector (IDC), 34, 588, 698
Internet Explorer, 166, 187-188
cache settings, 179-181
colors, 175
configuring, 168
appearances, 173-175
character sets, 184-185
search pages, 172-173
start pages, 172-173
connections, configuring, 175-179
file types, associating, 168-172
HTML tags, 754-758
installing, 167-168
properties sheets, 174
proxy servers, 177-178
rating systems, 185-186
security, 181-183
signing, 166
URLs, 175
Web pages, displaying, 174
Internet Explorer (IE), 24
Internet Explorer License Agreement dialog box, 168
Internet Explorer V3.0 Install Kit dialog box, 168
Internet Mail Connector Properties dialog box, 194, 198
Internet Mail Connector (IMC), 190
Internet Protocol, *see* **IP**
Internet Ratings dialog box, 185
Internet Server Application Programming Interface, *see* **ISAPI**
Internet Server Applications (ISAs), 79, 698
Internet Service Manager, 136
commands, 136
Server Manager, 137
sites, managing, 137-138
Internet service providers, *see* **ISPs**
InterNIC (IP addresses), 10
interoperating with non-WINS clients, 236
Interrupt ReQuest Level (IRQL), 698
interrupts, 698
Interrupts/sec counter, 644
intranets
publishing, 36-39
security, 39
invalid operations (access violations), 686
inventory, 37
IOCTL (input/output control), 697
IP (Internet Protocol), 6, 698
addresses, 10, 13, 207, 698
adding to network adapters, 147
DHCP, 211, 214
Exchange Server, 199
firewalls, 272
networks, 256
RIP for Internet Protocol, 107
routable, 39
scopes, 207
static, 212
subnets, 223
logging dbWeb, 560
packets, enabling, 112
ports, 294
firewalls, 272
RIP, 107
IP Address Only option (Preferences dialog box), 244
IP log property (dbWeb), 559

IPCONFIG command-line program syntax, 228
IRC (Internet Relay Chat), 297
IRQL (Interrupt ReQuest Level), 698
ISA (Industry Standard Architecture), 79, 698
ISAPI (Internet Information Server Application Programming Interface), 33-34, 698
  applications, 429-430
    CGIs, 429
    defined, 428-429
    testing, 430
  CGIs, 35
  creating with IIS SDK, 428
  DLLs, 33-34
  filters, 34
  interfaces, 430-432
  Internet Database Connector, 34
  third-party applications, 430
ISAPI Extension Requests counter, 664
IsArray function (VBScript), 467
ISAs (Internet Server Applications), 431, 439-440, 442
  ECB formats, 433-434
  functions
    GetExtensionVersion, 432-433
    GetServerVariable, 432, 435-437
    HttpExtensionProc, 432-435
    ReadClient, 432, 437
    ServerSupportFunction, 432, 438-439
    WriteClient, 432, 437-438
  HTTP servers, 431
IsDate function (VBScript), 464, 467
ISDNs (Integrated Services Digital Networks), 16-17
  BRIs, installing IIS, 105
IsEmpty function (VBScript), 467
IsError function (VBScript), 467
<ISINDEX> HTML tag, 734
  Internet Explorer, 756
IsNull function (VBScript), 467
IsNumeric function (VBScript), 467
IsObject function (VBScript), 467
ISPs (Internet service providers), 17-19, 107, 255, 698
  businesses, 19-20
  domain names, 18
    name registrations, 17
  e-mail, 18
  encrypting, 289-290
  FTP drop box, 18
  hardware, 18
  Internet, connecting to, 20
  newsgroups, 18
  references, 20
  security, encrypting, 276
  servers, 17
  technical support, 19

J

Java, 524-528
  applets, 525-526
    alpha versions, 527
    code for Marquee applet, 530-533
    color values of Marquee, 537-538
    compiling, 544-545
    creating, 528-544
    embedding in HTML, 545-546
    initializing, 535-538
    painting, 539-541
    parameters for Marquee applet, 529-530
    threads, 542-544
  classes, importing, 533-534
  compilers, 525
  defining classes, 534
  HotJava, 526
  initializing
    converting strings to numbers, 537
    length of strings, 537-538
    parameters, 535-536
    substrings, 537-538
    testing strings, 536-537
  object-oriented programming, 526
  robustness, 527
  security, 527
Javac program, 544
JavaScript, 698
joins, 570-573
Joins dialog box, 571
JPEG (Joint Picture Experts Group), 325
  files, exporting snapshots, 381

Jump to Document on Another System command (Insert menu), 417
Jump Within this Document command (Insert menu), 416

K

<KBD> HTML tag, 321, 734
   Internet Explorer, 756
   Word Internet Assistant, 759
KD (Kernel Debugger), 691, 699
kernel modes, 694, 698
kernels, 54
Key Manager, 203
keys, creating, 765
keywords, 699
   ALIGN, 331
   users, 412
   VBScript
      Nothing, 462
      Private, 461
      Public, 461
      Static, 462

L

Label Image program, 485
   (listing 21.3), 486-488
labeling images in VBScript, 484
<LANG> HTML tag, 734
Language option (Internet Explorer properties sheets), 186
languages
   Java, 524-528
      applets, 525-526
      defining classes, 534
      importing classes, 533-534
      initializing, 535-538
      object-oriented programming, 526
      robustness, 527
      security, 527
   JavaScript, 698
   VBScript, 710
LANs (local area networks), 699
LastKnownGood control set, 690, 699
Launch an Internet Service command (Insert menu), 420
launching Web Assistant, 616
layout (IDC), 596
LBound function (VBScript), 467
LCase function (VBScript), 468
lease expirations (DHCP), 213
leased lines (56KB), 14
leases (DHCP clients), 230
Left function (VBScript), 468
Legend option (Chart Options dialog box), 629
Len function (VBScript), 468
length violations, 686
less than operator (VBScript), 454
less than or equal to operator (VBScript), 455
Let statement (VBScript), 460
<LH> HTML tag, 735
<LI> HTML tag, 735
   Internet Explorer, 756
libraries (DLLs), 33-34, 693

linear chain replications (WINS servers), 240
<LINK> HTML tag, 735
linking DLLs, 693
links
   colors, 414
   drilldown, 566
   HTML documents, 413
   hypertext
      creating, 333-335
      inserting into documents, 416-417
   inserting into external documents, 417
   verifying FrontPage, 349
<LISTING> HTML tag, 323, 736
   Internet Explorer, 756
listings
   Calculator Web page, 479-484
   CGI variables from C, 511-512
   CGI variables from Perl, 513
   Code for Marquee.java, 530-533
   Customized Web pages on the fly, 515-517
   directories, 41-42
   DOS batch file for compiling Java applets, 545
   Embedding the Marquee applet, 545
   Feedback form, 520
   Hello World!—C, 509-510
   Hello World!—Perl, 507-508
   Hello World! Web page VBScript example, 449
   Label Image program, 486-488

listings

UNLEASHED

Run method implements the instructions for a thread in a Java applet, 543
Skeleton.C source code, 440
Skeleton.DEF source code, 442
Skeleton.H source code, 440
lists, 327
  ACEs, 686
  ACLs, 686
  bulleted, creating, 326-327, 332
  numbered, creating, 326-327
LKG control set, 699
LMHOSTS Lookup, enabling, 111
Load Hive command (Registry menu), 766
loading DLLs, 429
local area networks (LANs), 699
Local Group Membership dialog box, 284
local groups, 699
  Guests, 152, 276
Local IPC Manager, 53
local procedure calls (LPCs), 699
local security authority (LSA), 700
location properties, installing RAS, 123
Locks Held counter, 681
Log command (View menu), 630
Log Event in Application option (Alert Options dialog box), 637

log file directory option (Log to File radio button), 148
Log function (VBScript), 468
Log menu commands, 307
Log Options dialog box, 631
Log Settings command (Log menu), 307
Log Settings dialog box, 307
Log Type command (Log menu), 307
Log view (Performance Monitor), 625, 630
LogDetailedEvents (registry keys), 253
LogFilePath (registry keys), 252
logging
  errors, 693
  IP (dbWeb), 560
logging on, auditing, 298
logging site activity, 147-149
  automatically open new log option, 148
  building databases, 159-161
  SQL Server, 159-161
LoggingOn (registry keys), 253
logical drives (Performance Monitor), 656
logoffs, auditing, 298
Logon Attempts counter, 666
Logon Requests counter, 664, 667
Logon Script, 64
Logons Total counter, 660
Logons/sec counter, 660

logs
  administrators, 61
  applications, 302
  creating, 630
  IIS, 307-308
  saving, 632
  security, 302
  systems, 302
  updating, 631, 634
long filenames
  HotDog Pro, 397
  NTFS, 57
long integer data type, 228
lookup files (subnets), 258
loop statement (VBScript), 457
loops (infinite), 543
LPCs (local procedure calls), 53, 699
LSA (local security authority), 700
LSet statement (VBScript), 460
LT extension, 607
LTrim function (VBScript), 468

M

M-nodes (DHCP), 211
MAC (Media Access Control), 230
macro viruses, 266
mail, *see* e-mail
mailing lists (Perl listing), 504
mailto, 335
managers, *see* individual manager names
mandatory user profiles, 700
<MAP> HTML tag, 736
  Internet Explorer, 756

mappings
  bad-sector, 689
  I/O, 700
  WINS addresses, 235
Mappings menu commands
  Initiate Scavenging, 250
  Static Mappings, 248
Marquee applet
  color values, 537-538
  embedding, 545
  run method, 543
  start method, 542
  stop method, 542
<MARQUEE> HTML tag, 736-737
masks (subnets), 213
  adding to network adapters, 147
Master Boot Record (MBR), 265
master domains, 69-72
MaxFieldSize parameter (IDC), 605
Maximize Throughput for File Sharing option (Server dialog box), 100
Maximize Throughput for Network Application option (Server dialog box), 101
Maximum Anonymous Users counter, 666-667
Maximum CGI Requests counter, 664
Maximum concurrent users property (dbWeb), 559
Maximum Connection counter, 664
Maximum Connections counter, 666

Maximum Connections option
  FTP Publishing Service properties sheet, 151
  Gopher Publishing Service properties sheet, 156
  WWW Publishing Service properties sheet, 140
Maximum ISAPI Extension Requests counter, 664
Maximum NonAnonymous Users counter, 664, 667
Maximum Number of Anonymous Users counter, 664
Maximum Password Age option (Account Policy dialog box), 277
MaxRecords extension, 607
MaxRecords parameter (IDC), 605
MBONE protocol, 294
MBR (Master Boot Record), 265
MCA (Microchannel Architecture), 80
McastIntvl (registry keys), 252
McastTtl (registry keys), 252
MCB (memory control block), 700
Media Access Control (MAC), 230
MemHog.EXE program, 652
memory
  access violations, 686
  bottlenecks, finding, 649-654
  Cache Manager, 90

  DMA, 643
  DRAM, 89
  FCB, 695
  flash, 695
  HMA, 696
  object counters, 649
  paging files, 701
  RAM, 703
  registry keys, 790-793
  ROM, 703
  SRAM, 89
  swap files, 701
  troubleshooting, 653
  upgrades, 89-91
  virtual, 710
  Virtual Memory Manager, 54
memory control block (MCB), 700
Memory counter, 681
Memory Pages/sec counter, 655
<MENU> HTML tag, 327, 737
  Internet Explorer, 756
  Word Internet Assistant, 759
Merit Network Inc. Web site, 9
message boxes
  customizing, 469
  displaying, 468
messages
  administrative alerts, 687
  application-termination, 694
  e-mail
    conversions, 196
    delivering, 198
    protecting, 202-203
  executive, 694
  flames, 201
  FTP, configuring, 152-153
  IMC notifications, 197

Internet, troubleshooting, 201
sending, 127
SMBs, 706
system-information, 694
warning, 694

<META> HTML tag, 737
Internet Explorer, 756
Word Internet Assistant, 759

methods
drawRect, 540
drawString, 541
fillRect, 540
init
font selection, 535
initializing Java applets, 535-538
parameters, 535-536
testing strings, 536-537
paint, 539
repaint, 543
run Java applet threads, 543
setFont, 539-540
start Java applet threads, 542
stop Java applet threads, 542
substring, 538

MFM (Modified Frequency Modulation), 82

Microchannel Architecture (MCA), 80

Microsoft Access Internet tools Web sites, 376

Microsoft Access Web publishing, 375-378
databases, 376-378
Internet Assistant for Access (installing), 376

Microsoft dbWeb, *see* **dbWeb**

Microsoft dbWeb License Agreement dialog box, 551

Microsoft Excel
Web publishing, 368-372
Internet Assistant for Excel, installing, 369-370
spreadsheets, 370-373
Web site, 369

Microsoft Exchange Server, *see* **Exchange Server**

Microsoft Exchange Server Setup dialog box, 191

Microsoft FrontPage Web site, 338

Microsoft Internet Explorer V3.0 Install Kit dialog box, 168

Microsoft Office
Web publishing, 362-378
Web site, 362

Microsoft Office Internet tools Web site, 362

Microsoft PowerPoint
slide shows, converting into HTML, 374-376
Web publishing, 372-375
converting a PowerPoint slide show into HTML, 374-376
Internet Assistant for PowerPoint, installing, 373
Web site, 373

Microsoft SNMP Properties dialog box, 118

Microsoft TCP/IP Properties dialog box, 109, 147, 292

Microsoft VBScript, 446

Microsoft VBScript home page, 446

Microsoft VBScript information Web site, 446

Microsoft Word
creating HTML documents, 364-369
background images, 364-365
formatting table cells, 367
inserting inline images, 366
inserting tables, 366
inserting video, 366
special text colors, 364-365
TrueType fonts, 365
Web publishing, 362-368
Internet Assistant for Word, installing, 363

Mid function (VBScript), 468

Mid statement (VBScript), 460

MigrateOn (registry keys), 253

MIME, 171, 193

Minimize Memory User option (Server dialog box), 100

Minimum Password Age option (Account Policy dialog box), 277

Minimum Password Length option (Account Policy dialog box), 277

Minute function (VBScript), 468

mirror sets (disk bottlenecks), 657

mirroring disks, 692

networks

Index

MOD operator (VBScript), 452
Models menu commands, 385
modems
 configuring, 124
 RAS, installing, 123-125
 selecting, 122
Modified Frequency Modulation (MFM), 82
Modify Surface and Color dialog box, 385
monolithic database model, 31
Month function (VBScript), 468
mounting volumes, 700
moving buttons, 401
MsgBox function (VBScript), 468
multidimensional arrays, declaring with Dim statement, 456
multihomed servers, 249, 291, 700
Multimedia Marketing Group Web site, 42
multiple variables, declaring with Dim statement, 456
multiplication operator (VBScript), 451
multiprocessing, 700
 AMP, 687
 symmetric, 707
multitasking
 cooperative, 690
 preemptive, 702
multithreading, 700
 Windows NT Server, 50

N

named pipes, 700
names
 domains, 13, 39, 214, 692
 ISPs, 18
 registering, 17
 WINS, resolving, 234
NBF protocol configuration (registry keys), 787-790
NCB (network control block), 701
NetBEUI (NetBIOS Extended User Interface), 700
 frame protocol configuration (registry keys), 787
NetBIOS (Network Basic Input/Output System), 214, 234, 700
Netlogon registry keys, 782-785
Network Alert option (Alert Options dialog box), 637
Network Command Queue Length counter, 680
Network Configuration dialog box, 287-288
Network dialog box, 93, 108, 112, 114, 288, 291
Network Errors/sec counter, 661
Network Interface Current Bandwidth counter, 661
Network News Transfer Protocol (NNTP), 701
Network Reads/sec counter, 679
Network Settings Change dialog box, 147, 288

Network Utilization counter, 659
Network Writes/sec counter, 679
networking dial-ups, 177, 691
 security, 287-290
networks
 adapters
  adding, 60, 92-97
  adding IP addresses, 147
  adding subnet masks, 147
  security, 96
 auto-dialing, 176
 bindings, 689
 bottlenecks
  finding, 658-661
  Performance Monitor, 659
 CACHE configuration file, 256-257
 circuit-switched, 5
 connectors (bayonet nut), 689
 CSnet, 6
 DARPA, 6
 default gateways, 691
 DNS, 255
 domains, 692
  names, 13
  single models, 68
 Ethernet, 14
 firewalls, 271-273
 FTP Server, 12
 hostnames, 256
 hosts (IP addresses), 13
 installing IIS, 113
 Internet (history of), 6-7
 IP addresses, 256
 ISPs support services, 19
 LANs, 699
 NetBIOS, 700

NNTP, 701
NSFnet, 7
packet-switched, 5
packets, routing, 5
performance counters, 659
processors, adding, 97
protocols, 274-275
   TCP, 709
   TCP/IP, 708
proxy servers, 177-178
RAS, 120
routers, 112, 705
routes, 705
security proxy agents, 273-274
segments, 96
servers, selecting, 98
setting up connections, 10
sites, 137
SNMP, 107
subnets, 706
   address class, 686
switches, 5
transporting, 701
vBNS, 7
WANs, 32, 711
wrappers, 5
WWW Server, 11
New Chart command (File menu), 632
New command (File menu), 383
New Database dialog box, 160
New Other command (File menu), 200
New Phonebook Entry dialog box, 289
New Push Partner Default Configuration option (Preferences dialog box), 246

New Schema dialog box, 565
New Technology File System, *see* NTFS
news, 335
newsgroups, 18
   publicizing Web sites, 42
Next statement (VBScript), 458
<NEXTID> HTML tag, 737
NFS protocol, 297
NFSnet, 7
NNTP (Network News Transfer Protocol), 296, 701
No Access option (permissions), 280
<NOBR> HTML tag, 738
   Internet Explorer, 756
nodes, 210-211
<NOEMBED> HTML tag, 738
<NOFRAMES> HTML tag, 738
None option (Internet Explorer properties sheets), 184
NoOfWrkThds (registry keys), 252
Normal option (Internet Explorer properties sheets), 183
NOT operator (VBScript), 453
<NOTE> HTML tag, 739
Nothing keyword (VBScript), 462
notifications (IMC), 197
Notifications dialog box, 196
Now function (VBScript), 470

NTFS (New Technology File System), 57
   clusters, 690
   compression support, 57
   filenames, 57
   partitions, installing IIS, 143
   security, 57, 279-280
NTP protocol, 296
NTSD (Windows NT System Debugger), 707
Nudity option (Internet Explorer properties sheets), 186
numbered lists, creating, 326-327
numbers, converting strings to, 537

O

object counters
   systems, 653
   WINS (Performance Monitor), 250
Object Manager, 52
Object menu commands (Permissions), 161
object-oriented programming, 526
object-reference operator (VBScript), 454
objects, 701
   3D
      creating home pages with Web 3D, 383-387
      Web 3D, 380-383
   auditing, 298, 688
   CorelWEB.GALLERY, 389-390
   CorelWEB.Transit, 391-392

Index

counters
  adding, 626
  alerts, 638-640
  colors, 628
  deleting, 626
  instances, 634
  memory, 649
  processors, 644-645
  ranges, 628
  scales, 628
  updating, 626
deleting, 385
enumeration operations, 693
graphical Web sites, 381
inserting, 385
Performance Monitor, 624
processes, 703, 708
ray traced, 386
realistic with shadows, 386
semaphores, 705
solid models, 386
Web.Designer, 387-389
wireframes, 386
Oct function (VBScript), 470
ODBC (Open DataBase Connectivity), 701
  building data sources, 161-162
  Data Source Name, 693
  data sources
    creating, 162, 561-563
    defining, 561-563
    profile properties, 563-564
  databases, 550
    logging Web site activity, 149
  dbWeb, 554
    configuring, 556
    data source name, 560
    installing, 550-555
    passwords, 560
  DNS, logging Web site activity, 149
  installing, 554
  interactive Web pages, 597
ODBC Data Sources dialog box, 564
ODBC Driver Pack 3.0 Custom dialog box, 554
ODBC Driver Pack 3.0 Setup dialog box, 554
ODBC SQL Server Setup dialog box, 162, 562
OK dialog boxes, 469
<OL> HTML tag, 739
  Internet Explorer, 757
  Word Internet Assistant, 760
OLE browsers, 268
On Error Resume Next statement (VBScript), 461
OnChange event, 475
one-time passwords (OTPs) Web site, 499
online catalogs, 615
Only If Sending More Than One Line Of Text option (Internet Explorer properties sheet), 183
opcodes, 701
Open command (File menu), 383, 629
Open DataBase Connectivity, *see* **ODBC**
Open Local command (Registry menu), 766
Open Market Commercial Sites Index Web site, 41
Open Project command (File menu), 422
Open Web dialog box, 346
Operability dialog box, 196
operating systems
  device drivers, 691
  domain names, 692
  down levels, 693
  HAL, 696
  processors, adding, 97
  servers, selecting, 98
OperatorBox_OnChange subroutine (VBScript), 476
operators (VBScript), 451-455
  addition, 451
  AND, 452
  Boolean, 452
  comparison, 454
  division, 451
  equivalence, 454
  exponential, 451
  greater than, 455
  greater than or equal to, 455
  integer-division, 452
  less than, 454
  less than or equal to, 455
  MOD, 452
  multiplication, 451
  NOT, 453
  object-reference, 454
  OR, 453
  string-concatenation, 452
  subtraction, 451
  unequal, 454
  XOR, 453
option overlays, 215
<OPTION> HTML tag, 739
  Internet Explorer, 757
Options command (Tools menu), 203, 402

Options command (View
  menu), 169, 174
Options dialog box, 179,
  402
Options menu commands
  Alert, 637
  Chart, 628, 631
  Data From, 632
  Global, 226
  Preferences, 244
  Read Only Mode, 765
  Update Now, 629, 631,
    634
OR operator (VBScript),
  453
order forms, 615
ordering, 37, 615
  databases, 615
organizations
  ISPs, 19-20
  ordering, 37
  publishing, 36
Other Requested Methods
  counter, 665
output
  addresses, 697
  BIOS, 689
  I/O buses, 697
  see also I/O
<OVERLAY> HTML tag,
  740
overlays (DHCP), 215
Owner command (Security
  menu), 286, 767

P

P-nodes, 211
<P> HTML tag, 317, 740
  Internet Explorer, 757
  Word Internet Assistant,
    760
Pacific Bell, 15
packet-switched network
  protocols, 5
packets
  IP, enabling, 112
  routing, 5-6
  wrappers, 5
Page Faults/sec counter,
  649, 651
Page Locks - Exclusive
  counter, 681
Page Locks - Shared
  counter, 681
Page Locks - Total
  counter, 681
Page Locks - Update
  counter, 681
pages
  attributes, 325-326
  Web pages, defining
    special characters, 749,
    754
Pages/sec counter, 649,
  651
paging files, 701
paint method, 539
painting Java applets,
  539-541
  reading fonts, 541
  setting current font,
    539-540
  writing text, 540-541
paragraphs
  aligning, 319
  HTML document
    attributes, 318-320
<PARAM> HTML tag,
  546, 740
parameters, 701
  IDC, 603-604
  Java applets, 535-536
  keywords, 699
  pull partners, 242
  push partners, 243
  SQL Server (Web
    Assistant), 616
  switches, 707

parity, 87, 702
  striped sets, 706
parsers (HTML), 315
partitioning, 702
  boot, 689
  disks, 59
  extended, 695
  NTFS, installing IIS, 143
  primary, 703
  systems, 708
  tables, 702
  volumes, 700, 702, 711
partners (export paths),
  695
Password Authentication
  option (WWW
  Publishing Service
  properties sheet), 141
Password option
  FTP Publishing Service
    properties sheet, 152
  Gopher Publishing
    Service properties
    sheet, 157
  WWW Publishing
    Service properties
    sheet, 140
Password parameter
  (IDC), 605
Password Uniqueness
  option (Account Policy
  dialog box), 278
passwords, 276
  accounts, 140, 152, 157
  dbWeb, 560
  domains, 66
  one-time passwords
    (OTPs) Web site, 499
  Web Assistant, 616
PATH INFO extension,
  607
Path to client stub
  property (dbWeb), 559

Index

Path to HTML dir property (dbWeb), 559
PATH TRANSLATED extension, 607
PATH_INFO CGI environment variable, 500
PATH_TRANSLATED CGI environment variable, 500
Pause Service command (Properties menu), 137
pausing (Internet Service Manager), 137
PCI (Peripheral Component Interconnect), 77, 81
   servers, 81
   VLBs, 80
PCMCIA (Personal Computer Memory Card Industry Association), 81
PDCs (primary domain controllers), 98, 702-703
performance counters
   FTP, 665-666
   Gopher, 666-667
   HTTP, 663-665
   IIS, 662-663
Performance Monitor, 624
   alerts
      creating, 635-640
      object counters, 638-640
   bottlenecks
      networks, 659
      processors, 645
   charts, creating, 626-629
   counters, 624
      instances, 634
   disk-intensive applications, 656-657
   events, 624, 631
   instances, 624
   logs
      creating, 630
      updating, 631, 634
   objects, 701
   performance tuning, 642-643
   processor-intensive applications, 646, 648
   reports
      creating, 632-634
      saving, 634
   SQL Server counters, 677-682
   toolbar, 625
   views, 624
      Alert, 635
      Chart, 626
      Log, 630
      Report, 633
      saving, 629
   WINS (object counters), 250
performance tuning, 642-643
Peripheral Component Interconnect (PCI), 77, 81
Perl
   CGI Perl scripts, 503-504
      Internet resources, 504-506
   Hello World! CGI scripts, 507-509
   mailing lists (listing), 504
   Web sites, 504
Perl for Windows NT Web site, 503
permissions, 702
   access rights, 686
   assigning to databases, 161
   auditing, 300
   deleting, 286
   directories, 282
      attributes, 283-284
      setting, 280-287
   files, 282
      attributes, 283-284
      setting, 280-287
   granting, 127
Permissions command (Object menu), 161
Permissions command (Security menu), 767
Permissions command (Users menu), 126
Permissions menu commands (Security), 283
<PERSON> HTML tag, 740
Personal Computer Memory Card Industry Association (PCMCIA), 81
PersonaNonGrata (registry keys), 254
physical drives (Performance Monitor), 657
Physical I/O counter, 681
pictures
   3D (Web 3D), 380-381
   Internet Explorer properties sheets, 175
   snapshots, 380
pipes, 702
   named, 700
PLACE.DOM configuration file, 256, 258-260
placing IIS installation, 104-106
Plain Old Telephone System (POTS), 14

plain text, encrypting, 288
<PLAINTEXT> HTML tag, 323, 741
   Internet Explorer, 757
Point-to-Point Protocol (PPP), 125, 702
policies
   audits, 688
   security, auditing, 299
   user accounts, configuring, 277-278
Policies menu commands
   Account, 277
   Audit, 298
   Auditing, 300
   User Rights, 276
Policy dialog box, 276
Policy menu commands (Audit), 688
Pool Nonpaged Bytes counter, 653
Pool Nonpaged Failures counter, 659
Pool Paged Bytes counter, 653
Pool Paged Failures counter, 659
ports
   changing the default port
      FrontPage Server, 341
      IP, 294
      firewalls, 272
      mappers, 296
Post Requests counter, 665
PostMaster Web site, 41
POTS (Plain Old Telephone System), 14
PowerPoint
   slide shows, converting into HTML, 374-376
   Web publishing, 372-375
      Internet Assistant for PowerPoint, installing, 373

PowerPoint Web site, 373
PPP (Point-to-Point Protocol), 125, 702
PPTP packets, configuring servers, 291
<PRE WIDTH> HTML tag
   Internet Explorer, 757
   Word Internet Assistant, 760
<PRE> HTML tag, 323, 741
   Internet Explorer, 757
   Word Internet Assistant, 760
preemptive multitasking, 690, 702
Preferences command (Edit menu), 556, 558
Preferences command (Options menu), 244
Preferences dialog box, 242
preventing Internet auto-replies, 202
primary domain controllers (PDCs), 67, 98, 702-703
   synchronizing, 693
primary partitions, 703
Primary Rate Interfaces (PRIs), 16
primary WINS servers, 111
Print Manager, 62
Print Subtree command (Registry menu), 766
printers, auditing, 688
printing TCP/IP, 108
printing TCP/IP service, installing, 118-119
PriorityClassHigh (registry keys), 252
PRIs (Primary Rate Interfaces), 16
Private keyword (VBScript), 461

privileges, 703
   rights, 705
   SIDs, 686
   WWW sites, 149-150
procedures (stored), 617
Process Manager, 53
processes, 50, 703
   batch, 689
   impersonations, 697
   objects, 708
   terminated, 708
   threads, 708
   tracking, 299
processing queries (URLs), 412
processor-intensive applications, 646, 648
   starting, 648
Processor queue length counter, 644
processors
   adding, 97, 648
   bottlenecks
      finding, 643-648
      Performance Monitor, 645
   I/O, selecting buses, 78-82
   object counters, 644-645
   RISC, 77
   upgrading, 648
   Windows NT Server, 77-78
products, selling, 26-27
profile properties (ODBC data sources), 563-564
profiles, 64
   users, 710
      mandatory, 700
programming
   ISAPI, 33-34
   languages
      JavaScript, 698
      VBScript, 710

object-oriented, 526
TAPI, 50
Programs option (Internet Explorer properties sheets), 183
Project Manager command (File menu), 422
Project Manager dialog box, 422
Project Manager Links dialog box, 422
properties
configuration, installing RAS, 124
database schemas, 567-569
dbWeb
Administrator, 556-558
schema, 557
servers, 558-561
defining HTML documents, 411-414
directories (WWW publishing services), 142-143
forms
delete, 584-585, 587
freeforms, 580-583
HTML, 587-589
insert, 584-587
tabular, 577-580
update, 584-587
ODBC data sources (profiles), 563-564
QBE, 573-577
RAS, 123
scopes, 226-227
snapshots, 386
traps, configuring SNMP, 117
WWW publishing services, configuring, 149-150

Properties command (File menu), 194
Properties dialog box, 185, 574
Properties menu commands, 137
Pause Service, 137
Service Properties, 139, 150, 156
properties sheets
Bindings, 94-95
forms
delete, 585-587
freeforms, 582-583
insert, 585-587
tabular, 579-580
update, 585-587
FTP publishing services, 151-152
Gopher publishing services, 156-157
Internet Explorer, 174
QBE, 575, 577
WWW publishing services, 140-141
proportional fonts, 317
protected registry keys, 763
protecting
clients from viruses, 203-204
e-mail messages, 202-203
networks
firewalls, 271
NTFS, 279-280
servers (Exchange Server), 200
user accounts, 276
protocols
DHCP, 63, 106, 206, 215, 693
B-nodes, 210
client configurations, 213-220

client reservations, 231-232
clients, 228-230
compacting databases, 232
configuring scopes, 225
creating new scope options, 227-228
database backups, 212
databases, 232
deleting scopes, 225
designing, 207
H-nodes, 211
installing, 112-114, 209
lease expirations, 213
M-nodes, 211
P-nodes, 211
properties of scopes, 226-227
rebinding, 215
renewals, 215
routers, 213
scopes, 214
servers, 212
static IP addresses, 212
subnets, 223
WINS configurations, 210
DNS, 295
errors, 196
fingering, 295
firewalls, 272
frame protocols, configuring, 787
FTP, 294, 695
Gopher, 295
HTTP, 32, 335, 697
HTTPS, 697
ICMP, 294
IP, 6, 698
MBONE, 294
NBF protocol configurations (registry keys), 787-790

network security, 274-275
NFS, 297
NNTP, 296, 701
NTP, 296
packet-switched network, 5
PPP, 702
rebinding, 215
RIPs, 107, 705
routes, 705
SLIP, 706
SMTP, 706
SNMP, 107, 295-296, 706
TCP, 6, 294, 709
TCP/IP, 30, 209, 294, 708
  installing, 108-112
Telnet, 294
UDP, 710
WAIS, 296
WINS, 234
  disabling, 96
WWW, 295
see also DHCP; FTP; HTTP; IP; PPP; SLIP; TCP/IP
providers, *see* **ISPs**
proxy agents, 270-271, 712
network security, 273-274
WINS, 236-239
proxy servers, 177-178
Proxy Settings dialog box, 178
Public keyword (VBScript), 461
publicizing Web site newsgroups, 40, 42
Publish Document command (File menu), 422

publishing
catalogs, 23-24
documents, 422
Internet, 36-39
intranets, 36-39
newsgroups, 42
text, 24-25
Publishing Directories dialog box, 131
publishing services
FTP
  configuring, 150-152
  configuring directories, 153-155
  configuring messages, 152-153
  creating virtual directories, 154
  home directories, 155
  properties sheet, 151-152
  troubleshooting, 152
Gopher
  configuring, 156-157
  configuring directories, 158-159
  configuring properties sheets, 156-157
  creating virtual directories, 158-159
WWW
  configuring, 139-141
  configuring properties, 149-150
  creating virtual servers, 145-147
  creating virtual directories, 144-145
  directories, 142
  log activity, configuring, 148
  properties of directories, 142-143

pull partners, 239
parameters, 242
WINS servers, 239
Pull Properties dialog box, 247
pull<IPAddress>MemberPrec (registry keys), 254
push partners, 239
parameters, 243
WINS servers, 239
Push Properties dialog box, 247

Q

<Q> HTML tag, 741
QBE (Query By Example)
columns, 574
properties, 573-577
properties sheet, 575, 577
queries, 596
building, 617
dbWeb columns, 566
freeform text, 617
processing URLs, 412
SQL, 706
stored procedures, 617
Queries/sec object counter, 251
QUERY STRING extension, 607
QUERY_STRING CGI environment variable, 501
Queue Length counter, 660

R

RAID (Redundant Array of Inexpensive Disks), 76
drives, selecting, 91
hardware, 91-92
hot swapping, 91

RAM (random access memory), 703
Randomize statement (VBScript), 461
ranges, selecting object counters, 628
RAS (Remote Access Server), 105, 107, 120, 126, 704
  adapters, adding, 121
  Administrator, 62
  buffers (FIFO), 120
  configuring, 126
  connections, monitoring, 127-128
  installing, 120
    adapters, 121
    configuration properties, 124
    modems, 123-125
    properties, 123
    servers, 122, 125
  Internet, 128-129
  modems, selecting, 122
  UARTs, 120
  Windows 95, 120
  Windows NT Workstation, 120
RAS Server Protocol Configuration dialog box, 287
rating systems (Internet Explorer), 185-186
ray-traced images, 386
Read Only Mode command (Options menu), 765
Read option (permissions), 281
read-only bits, 703
read-only memory, *see* ROM
ReadClient function (ISAs), 432, 437

reading fonts, 541
realistic with shadows, 386
rebinding, 208
  DHCP, 215
records
  auditing, 688
  databases, troubleshooting, 569
  DNS, 259-260
  SOA, 259
recovering infected systems, 268-270
rectangles, drawing, 540
ReDim statement (dynamic arrays), 456
Redundant Array of Inexpensive Disks (RAID), 76
RefreshInterval (registry keys), 253
REG BINARY data type, 764
REG DWORD data type, 764
REG EXPAND SZ data type, 764
REG MULTI SZ data type, 764
REG SZ data type, 764
registering domain names, 17
Registration Details dialog box, 396
registrations (WINS clients), 235
registry, 703
  hives, 696
Registry Editor, 233
  Administrative Tools group, 762
  data types, 764
  INI files, 762
  keys, creating, 765

  troubleshooting, 252, 762
  windows, 764
Registry Key Auditing dialog box, 767
registry keys, 704, 767, 786, 794-797
  creating, 765
  DHCP servers, 233-234
  files, 763
  FTP, 773
  Gopher, 774
  IIS, 769-770
  memory, 790-793
  Netlogon, 782-785
  protected, 763
  servers, 251-254, 774-779
  system service configuration, 768-769
  WINS, configuring, 253-254
  workstations, 779-781
  WWW, 770-773
Registry menu commands, 766
relationships (trust), 66, 709
  domains, 72
relay hosts, 193, 198
Releases/sec object counter, 251
Rem statement (VBScript), 461
Remote Access Server (RAS) Administrator, 62
Remote Access Setup dialog box, 124, 287-288
Remote Access Software (RAS), 704
REMOTE ADDR extension, 607
REMOTE HOST extension, 608

Remote Procedure Calls
(RPCs), 53, 704
REMOTE USER
    extension, 608
REMOTE_ADDR CGI
    environment variable,
    501
REMOTE_HOST CGI
    environment variable,
    501
REMOTE_IDENT CGI
    environment variable,
    501
REMOTE_USER CGI
    environment variable,
    501
removing
    viruses, 268-269
    WINS servers, 246
renderings
    images, 385
    three-dimensional
        objects, 381
    see also drawing
renewals, 236
    DHCP, 215
repaint method, 543
Repair Disk utility, 768
replicating databases
    (DHCP servers), 212
Replication Interval option
    (Preferences dialog box),
    246
Replication Partners
    command (Server menu),
    246
Replication Partners dialog
    box, 246
Report command (View
    menu), 632
Report view (Performance
    Monitor), 625, 633

reports
    creating, 632-634
    saving, 634
    viewing, 625
REQUEST METHOD
    extension, 608
REQUEST_METHOD
    CGI environment
    variable, 502
requests for comments
    (RFCs), 704
RequiredParameters
    parameter (IDC), 605
requirements
    IIS preinstallation
        requirements, 106-112
    service providers, 12-13
reservations (DHCP
    clients), 231
resolving WINS names,
    234
restarting audits, 299
Restore command
    (Registry menu), 766
restricting Internet access
    rights, 201-202
revision levels, 705
RFC 931 Web site, 501
RFCs (requests for com-
    ments), 206, 704
    DHCP routers, 210
Right function (VBScript),
    470
rights, 705
    access rights, 686
    users, auditing, 298
RIP (Routing for the
    Internet Protocol), 107,
    705
    installing, 115
RISC (Reduced Instruction
    Set Computer), 77
RLL (Run Length
    Limited), 82

Rnd function (VBScript),
    470
robust, 48
ROM (read-only memory),
    703
root directories, 705
routable IP addresses, 39
routers, 12, 14, 705
    DHCP, 210, 213
        RFCs, 210
    networks, 112
routines (APIs), 687
routing packets, 5-6
Routing Protocol for the
    Internet Protocol (RIP),
    705
RPCs (remote procedure
    calls), 53, 704
    bindings, 704
    connections, 704
    endpoints, 704
    Exchange Server, 200
    protocol sequences, 704
    servers, 704
RplOnlyWCnfPnrs
    (registry keys), 253
RSAC (Recreational
    Software Advisory
    Council), 185
RSet statement (VBScript),
    461
RTrim function
    (VBScript), 468
Run Length Limited
    (RLL), 82
run method (Java applet
    threads), 543

S

<S> HTML tag, 321, 742
    Internet Explorer, 757
SAM (security accounts
    manager), 705

Index

SAM registry key, 763
<SAMP> HTML tag, 742
   Internet Explorer, 757
   Word Internet Assistant, 760
Sausage Software Web site, 394
Save As command (Log menu), 307
Save As dialog box, 307
Save Chart Settings command (File menu), 629
Save command (File menu), 588
Save Key command (Registry menu), 766
Save Log Setting As command (File menu), 632
Save Report Settings As command (File menu), 634
Save Subtree command (Registry menu), 766
Save Workspace command (File menu), 629
saving
   logs, 632
   Performance Monitor views, 629
   reports, 634
scalability, 49
scales (object counters), 628
Scene menu commands (Generate Snapshot), 385
Scheduling dialog box, 618
Schema Name dialog box, 568
schema properties (dbWeb), 557

schemas
   constraints, 570-573
   database properties, 567-569
   dbWeb databases, 564
   forms
      delete, 584-587
      insert, 584-587
      update, 584-587
   freeform form properties, 580-583
   HTML form properties, 587-589
   joins, 570-573
   QBE properties, 573-577
   tables, 570
   tabular form properties, 577-580
Scope command (DHCP Options menu), 226
Scope menu commands
   Activate, 225
   Active Leases, 230, 232
   Add Reservations, 231
   Create, 223
   Deactivate, 225
   Delete, 225
   DHCP Options, 213
scopes
   configurations, adding, 228
   configuring, 225-227
      creating new options, 227-228
   creating, 223-225
   deleting, 223, 225
   DHCP, 221-222
   DHCP client reservations, adding, 231
   ID, 112
   IP addresses, 207
   properties, 226-227

<SCRIPT LANGUAGE=VBS> tag, 447
SCRIPT NAME extension, 608
SCRIPT_NAME CGI environment variable, 502
scripting browsers, 268
scripts
   autorun, 396
   CGI
      basic functions, 493-496
      basic operations, 494-496
      duplicating, 497
      Hello World!, 506-510
      Hello World! in C, 509-510
      Hello World! in Perl, 507-509
      processing time, 497
      security, 497-504
   CGI C scripts, 505
   CGI Perl, 503-504
      Internet resources, 504
   FrontPage Editor Web page design, 356-357
SCSI (small computer systems interface), 59, 83-84, 88-89
search pages, configuring Internet Explorer, 172-173
searchable indexes in HTML documents, 412
Searches Sent counter, 667
SearchGuestBook.HTX file, 611
Second function (VBScript), 470
secondary WINS Server, 111

secrets, 705
sectors
  boot viruses, 265
  clusters, 690
Secure Socket Layer (SSL), 26-27, 705
security
  ACLs, 686
  administrative alerts, 687
  Alerter Service, 687
  anonymous-level security tokens, 687
  auditing
    directories, 299-302
    files, 299-302
  browsers, 267-268
  C2-level, 689
  CGI, 497-504
    controlling access to CGI directories, 498
    transmitting sensitive data, 498
    validating users, 498-499
  descriptors, 705
  Dial-Up Networking, 287-290
  domains, 692
  e-mail messages, protecting, 202-203
  encrypting plain text, 288
  events
    archiving, 306-307
    components, 304
    filtering, 305-306
    viewing, 304-305
  Exchange Server, 200-204
    denial of service, 201
  guard-page protection, 696
  IIS, 104

Internet, 39, 104, 181, 264
  applications, 264-265
  challenge-response authentication mechanisms, 276
  configuring user accounts, 276-277
  Dial-Up Networking, 287-290
  documents, 264-265
  enabling audits, 297-299
  encrypting, 276
  firewalls, 270-273
  NTFS, 279-280
  preventing auto-replies, 202
  proxy agents, 270-271
  recovering infected systems, 268-270
  restricting access rights, 201-202
  trojan horses, 265-267
  viruses, 265-267
Internet Explorer, 181-183
intranets, 39
Java, 527
logs, 302
LSA, 700
network adapters, 96
networks
  protocols, 274-275
  proxy agents, 273-274
NTFS, 57, 279-280
passwords, 157
  accounts, 152
permissions, 702
policies, auditing, 299
privileges, 703
revision levels, 705
SAM, 705
SID, 686

SSL, 705
tokens, 705
user accounts, 275-277
  passwords, 276
viruses
  protecting, 203-204
  removing, 269
Windows NT, 49
Windows NT Server, 275
workgroups, 65
Security Accounts Manager (SAM), 705
Security Add dialog box, 293
Security command (Permissions menu), 283
Security Identifiers (SIDs), 705
Security menu commands
  Auditing, 298, 767
  Choose Permissions, 283
  Owner, 286, 767
  Permissions, 767
Security Reference Manager, 53
SECURITY registry key, 763
security tokens, 686
segments, 96
Select Components to Install dialog box, 397
Select Computer command (Registry menu), 766
Select Destination Directory dialog box, 397
Select Directory dialog box, 144, 146, 155
Select Folder dialog box, 397
Select Hypertext Target dialog box, 416
Select Network Adapter dialog box, 121

Select Network Protocol dialog box, 109
Select Network Service dialog box, 114
Select Picture dialog box, 400
<SELECT> HTML tag, 742
  Internet Explorer, 757
selecting
  alerts, 636
  drives (RAID), 91
  fonts for Java applets, 535
  I/O buses, 78-82
  modems, 122
  object counters (ranges), 628
  servers, 98
selling products, 26-27
semaphores, 705
sending e-mail, 127, 190
Sending option (Internet Explorer properties sheets), 183
Serial Line Internet Protocol (SLIP), 125, 706
Server dialog box, 100
Server Manager, 137
  domains, 62
Server menu commands
  Add, 222
  Add WINS Server, 241
  Communications Ports, 127
  Configuration, 242, 253
  Delete WINS Server, 241
  Replication Partners, 246
server message blocks (SMBs), 706
SERVER NAME extension, 608
SERVER PORT extension, 608

SERVER PORT SECURE extension, 608
SERVER PROTOCOL extension, 608
Server service, 93
SERVER SOFTWARE extension, 608
Server/Configuration dialog box, 668
SERVER_NAME CGI environment variable, 502
SERVER_PORT CGI environment variable, 502
SERVER_PROTOCOL CGI environment variable, 502
SERVER_SOFTWARE CGI environment variable, 502
servers, 31, 66-67
  applications, 206, 690
  clients, 109
  configuring PPTP packets, 291
  connecting, 137
  database models, 31
  dbWeb
    internal properties, 559
    properties, 558-561
  DHCP, 212, 215
    adding, 222
    backups, 212
    registry keys, 233-234
    replications, 212
    subnets, 223
  DHCP Manager, 221-222
  Dial-Up Networking, 692
  DNS, 83, 214, 254
    designing, 254
    records, 258-259

domains
  authenticating, 98
  single models, 68
Exchange Server, 190
  RPCs, 200
  security, 200-204
FrontPage, 340
  Administrator, 341-345
  changing the default port, 341
FTP publishing services, 31, 33
FTP Server, connecting to the Internet, 12
Gopher publishing services, 12, 31, 33
hosting ISPs, 17
HTTP (ISAs), 431
IIS, 30
  installing, 105, 129-132
ISAPI, 33-34
ISAs, 431, 439-440, 442
multihomed, 291
PCI, 81
proxy, 177-178
RAS, installing, 122, 125
Registry Editor, 764
registry keys, 774-779
RPCs, 704
SQL Server, logging site activity, 159-161
tuning, 642
virtual, 17, 142
  creating, 145-147
Windows NT
  buses, 82
  design models, 51-54
  disk subsystems, 82-84
  hardware, 77
  performance, 85
  selecting, 98

servers

UNLEASHED

Windows NT Server, 48
  compatibility, 50
  configuring firewalls, 290-297
  IIS, 11-12, 76
  integratability, 51
  multithreading, 50
  processors, 77-78
  robust, 48
  security, 275
WINS, 249
  adding, 241, 246
  databases, 249-250
  deleting, 239
  Internet, 249
  multihomed, 249
  primary, 111
  pull partners, 239
  push partners, 239
  registry keys, 251-254
  secondary, 111
WWW, 31, 711
  HTTP, 32
  publishing services, 32
WWW Server,
  connecting to the Internet, 11
ServerSupportFunction function (ISAs), 432, 438-439
Service Administrator option (Gopher Publishing Service properties sheet), 157
Service dialog box, 199
Service Properties command (Properties menu), 139, 150, 156
service providers, 4
  56KB leased lines, 14
  bandwidths, 15-16
  frame relay, 14
  ISDNs, 16-17
  requirements, 12-13
  see also ISPs

Service view, 139
Services command (Computer menu), 137
Set statement (VBScript), 462
Set Up Files dialog box, 391
setFont method, 539-540
setup wizards (dbWeb), 551
Sex option (Internet Explorer properties sheets), 186
SGML (Standard Generalized Markup Language), 313
  errors, 314
  tags, 314
Sgn function (VBScript), 470
sharepoints, 706
shareware (HotDog Pro), 394
Shiloh Consulting Web site, 40
shortcut keys
  applications, customizing HotDog Pro, 401-402
  creating, 401
  HotDog Pro, customizing, 399
Shortcut Keys command (Tools menu), 401
shutdowns, auditing, 299
SIDs (Security Identifiers), 686, 705
Sign-In-IDC.HTX file, 609, 611
Sign-In-IDC.IDC file source code, 602-603
signing Internet Explorer, 166
Simple Calculator Web page, 474

Simple Mail Transfer Protocol (SMTP), 706
Simple Network Management Protocol (SNMP), 107, 706
Simple TCP/IP, installing, 118
Sin function (VBScript), 470
single disk subsystems, 85-87
single domains, 68
Single System Images (SSIs), 706
Site Services Account dialog box, 192
sites
  Exchange Server, connecting, 199-200
  FTP site security, 264
  interactive, 524
  Internet Service Manager, 137-138
  logging activity, 147-149
  Web sites, 618
    access rights, 149-150
    Authentication Server protocol, 501
    backgrounds, 381
    bandwidths, 381
    building databases, 159-161
    C CGI programs, 505
    CGI Perl scripts, 504
    CorelWEB.GALLERY, 389-390
    CorelWEB.Transit, 391-392
    dbWeb, 550
    designing, 380
    Digital Alta Vista, 41
    directories, 41-42
    displaying images, 331
    Excite, 41

*Haynes & Company,
    40*
HTML tags, 714
*Internet Assistant for
    Access, 376*
*Internet Assistant for
    Excel, 369*
*Internet Assistant for
    Microsoft PowerPoint,
    373*
*Internet Assistant for
    Word, 363*
*Internet Explorer rating
    systems, 185-186*
*logging activity with
    SQL Server, 159-161*
Merit Network Inc., 9
*Microsoft Access
    Internet tools, 376*
Microsoft Excel, 369
*Microsoft FrontPage,
    338*
Microsoft Office, 362
*Microsoft Office
    Internet tools, 362*
*Microsoft PowerPoint,
    373*
*Multimedia Marketing
    Group, 42*
*one-time passwords
    (OTPs), 499*
*Open Market
    Commercial Sites
    Index, 41*
Perl, 504
*Perl for Windows NT,
    503*
PostMaster, 41
publicizing, 40
ray-traced, 386
*realistic with shadows,
    386*
rendering images, 385
RFC 931, 501
Sausage Software, 394
security, 267-268
Shiloh Consulting, 40
snapshot properties, 386
solid models, 386
sounds, 175
Submit It, 41
Web 3D, 380-383
*Web.Designer,
    387-389*
*Webaholics Top 50
    Links, 41*
whitepapers, 40
WinZip, 503
wireframes, 386
*Yellow Pages of the
    Entire United States,
    42*
Size counter, 682
**Skeleton.C source code
    listing, 440**
**Skeleton.DEF source code
    listing, 442**
**Skeleton.H source code
    listing, 440**
**slide shows (Microsoft
    PowerPoint, converting
    into HTML), 374-376**
**SLIP (Serial Line Internet
    Protocol), 125, 706**
**small computer systems
    interface (SCSI), 83**
<SMALL> HTML tag, 743
**SMBs (Server Message
    Blocks), 706**
**SMDS (Switched
    Multimegabit Data
    Service), 15, 105**
**SMP (symmetric multi-
    processing), 707**
**SMTP (Simple Mail
    Transfer Protocol), 706**
    addresses, 197
    Exchange Server, 190
    IMC, 200
**SMTP Properties dialog
    box, 197**
**Snapshot Animation
    Settings dialog box, 386**
snapshots, 380
    exporting, 381
    properties, 386
**SNMP (Simple Network
    Management Protocol),
    107, 295-296, 706**
    configuring traps
        properties, 117
    installing, 116-118
    WINS, configuring, 114
snooping (data), 181
**SOA record (start of
    authoritative), 259**
software
    configurations, 98-101
    HotDog Pro, 394
    RAS, 704
**SOFTWARE registry key,
    764**
solid models, 386
**Sort by Comment
    command (View menu),
    138**
**Sort by Server command
    (View menu), 138**
**Sort by Service command
    (View menu), 138**
**Sort by State command
    (View menu), 138**
sound sites, 175
**Sounds option (Internet
    Explorer properties
    sheets), 175**
source code
    Sign-In-IDC.IDC file,
        602-603
    Skeleton.C listing, 440
    Skeleton.DEF listing, 442
    Skeleton.H listing, 440
**source IP address firewalls,
    272**

source IP port firewalls, 272
<SPAN> HTML tag, 743
SPAP (Standard Internet Encryption Method), 288
Special Access dialog box, 287
special characters
 defining, 749, 754
 inserting, 415
Special Characters command (View menu), 415
Special Directory Access dialog box, 285
Special Directory Access option (Permissions), 281-282
Special File Access dialog box, 286
Special File Access option (Permissions), 281-282
speed of buses, 79
spell checker (HotDog Pro), 395
spreadsheets in Excel, 370-373
SQL (Structured Query Language), 706
SQL Server
 configuring, 668, 670-676
 dbWeb, creating guest books, 590
 logging site activity, 159-161
 Performance Monitor counters, 677-682
 Web Assistant, 614-620
 parameters, 616
SQL Server Web Assistant File Option dialog box, 618

SQL Server Web Assistant Formatting dialog box, 619
SQL Server Web Assistant Scheduling dialog box, 618
SQLStatement parameter (IDC), 605
Sqr function (VBScript), 470
SRAM (Static Random Access Memory), 89
SSIs (Single System Images), 706
SSLs (Secure Socket Layer), 26-27, 276, 705
standalones, 706
Standard Generalized Markup Language (SGML), 313
Standard Internet Encryption Method (SPAP), 288
standard link HTML documents, 413
Start menu commands (Accessories), 289
start method Java applet threads, 542
Start of Authoritative (SOA), 259
Start Service command (Properties menu), 137
start time option (Preferences dialog box), 246
starting
 HotDog Pro, 396-398
 Internet Service Manager, 137
 processor-intensive applications, 648

statements
 import, importing Java classes, 533-534
 ReDim (dynamic arrays), 456
 VBScript
  Call, 455
  Dim, 455
  Do...Loop, 457
  Erase, 457
  Exit, 457
  Exit For, 458
  Exit Function, 459
  Function, 459
  If...Then...Else, 459
  Let, 460
  loop, 457
  LSet, 460
  Mid, 460
  Next, 458
  On Error Resume Next, 461
  Randomize, 461
  Rem, 461
  RSet, 461
  Set, 462
  Step, 458
  Sub, 459, 462
static arrays, declaring with Dim statement, 456
static IP addresses, 212
Static keyword (VBScript), 462
static mappings (WINS), 248
Static Mappings command (Mappings menu), 248
Static Mappings dialog box, 248
Static Random Access Memory (SRAM), 89
static Web pages, 24

system service configuration (registry keys)

Index

status codes
  HSE STATUS ERROR, 435
  HSE STATUS PENDING, 435
  HSE STATUS SUCCESS, 435
  HSE STATUS SUCCESS AND KEEP CONN, 435
Step statement (VBScript), 458
stop method (Java applet threads), 542
Stop Service command (Properties menu), 137
stopping Internet Service Manager, 137
stored procedures (queries), 617
storing clusters, 690
Str function (VBScript), 470
StrComp function (VBScript), 471
<STRIKE> HTML tag, 321, 743
  Internet Explorer, 757
  Word Internet Assistant, 760
String function (VBScript), 471
string-concatenation operator (VBScript), 452
strings
  concatenating (VBScript), 449
  converting to numbers (Java applets), 537
  length, 537-538
  substrings, 537-538
  testing Java applets, 536-537

striped sets, 706
  disk bottlenecks, 657
  parity, 706
striping with parity, 692
  drives, 87
<STRONG> HTML tag, 320, 743
  Internet Explorer, 757
  Word Internet Assistant, 760
Structured Query Language (SQL), 706
Sub statement (VBScript), 459, 462
<SUB> HTML tag, 744
subdirectories, creating, 144
subkeys
  Clone, 699
  creating, 765
Submit It Web site, 41
subnets, 706
  default gateways, 691
  DHCP servers, 223
  DNS (lookup files), 258
  IP addresses, 223
  masks, 213
    adding to network adapters, 147
  networks (address class), 686
  WINS (proxy agents), 238-239
subroutines (VBScript)
  About dialog box, 475
  AddDigit, 478
  BtnDelete_OnClick, 477
  BtnEvaluate_OnClick, 477
  BtnHello, 448
  BtnHello_OnClick, 448
  BtnTime_OnClick, 449
  HotSpot, 486

  ImageMapGraphic_MouseMove, 486
  OperatorBox_OnChange, 476
substring method, 538
subtraction operator (VBScript), 451
Successful Queries/sec object counter, 251
Successful Releases/sec object counter, 251
<SUP> HTML tag, 744
support services
  Internet, 21-23
  ISPs, 19
swap files, 701
Sweeper (ActiveX), 34
Switch to Alert View option (Alert Options dialog box), 637
Switched Multimegabit Data Service (SMDS), 15
switches, 5, 707
  ApplicationName, 49
  wrappers, 5
symmetric multiprocessing (SMP), 50, 60, 707
synchronizing domains, 693
syntax, 707
  command-line programs (IPCONFIG), 228
System calls/sec counter, 644
system data sources, creating, 563
System Data Sources dialog box, 561
system files, 707
SYSTEM registry key, 764
system service configurartion (registry keys), 768-769

853

system-information messages, 694
SYSTEM.MDB files, 232-233
systems
    accessing, 297
    auditing, 299
    configuring, enabling audits, 297-299
    infected systems, recovering, 268-270
    logs, 302
    memory upgrades, 89-91
    object counters, 653
    partitioning, 708
Systems Settings Change dialog box, 167

T

T connectors, 708
<TAB> HTML tag, 744
tabbed tables, displaying, 317-318
table cells, formatting, 367
Table command (Insert menu), 419
Table Locks - Exclusive counter, 680
Table Locks - Total counter, 680
<TABLE> HTML tag, 332, 744
    Internet Explorer, 757
tables
    column headers, 333
    constraints, 572
    creating with HTML tags, 332-333
    dbWeb (database schema), 565
    FrontPage Editor Web page design, 354-355

    inserting into documents, 418-420
    joins, 571
    partitions, 702
    schema, 570
    tabbed, displaying, 317-318
tabular form properties sheets, 579-580
Tag Information command (Edit menu), 416
tags (HTML), 313, 329, 714
    <A>, 333, 715-716
    <ABBREV>, 716
    <ACRONYM>, 716
    <ADDRESS>, 329, 717
    <APPLET>, 527, 546, 717-718
    <AREA>, 718
    <AU>, 718
    <B>, 718
    <BANNER>, 719
    <BASE>, 719
    <BASEFONT>, 719
    <BDO>, 720
    <BGSOUND>, 326, 720
    <BIG>, 720
    <BLINK>, 720
    <BLOCKQUOTE>, 329, 721
    <BODY>, 326, 721-722
    <BOLD>, 314

, 722
    browsers, 322
    <CAPTION>, 722
    <CENTER>, 320, 722
    <CITE>, 321, 723
    <CODE>, 321, 723
    <COL>, 723
    <COLGROUP>, 724
    creating tables, 332-333
    <CREDIT>, 724
    <DD>, 328, 724

    <DEL>, 725
    <DFN>, 725
    <DIR>, 327, 725
    <DIV>, 726
    <DL>, 328, 726
    <DT>, 328, 726
    <EM>, 320, 726
    <EMBED>, 727
    <FIG>, 727
    <FN>, 727
    <FONT>, 322, 728
    <FORM>, 728
    <FRAME>, 728
    <FRAMESET>, 729
    <H1>, 324, 729
    <H2>, 730
    <H3>, 730
    <H4>, 730
    <H5>, 730
    <H6>, 731
    <H7>, 324
    <HEAD>, 731
    <HPn>, 731
    <HR>, 329, 732
    <HTML>, 732
    <I>, 320, 732
    <IMG>, 330, 732-733
    <INPUT>, 733
    <INS>, 734
    inserting into documents, 415-417
        Tags dialog box, 415-416
    <ISINDEX>, 734
    <KBD>, 321, 734
    <LANG>, 734
    <LH>, 735
    <LI>, 735
    <LINK>, 735
    <LISTING>, 323, 736
    <MAP>, 736
    <MARQUEE>, 736-737
    <MENU>, 327, 737
    <META>, 737

<TEXT AREA> HTML tag | Index

<NEXTID>, 737
<NOBR>, 738
<NOEMBED>, 738
<NOFRAMES>, 738
<NOTE>, 739
<OL>, 739
<OPTION>, 739
<OVERLAY>, 740
<P>, 317, 740
<PARAM>, 546, 740
<PERSON>, 740
<PLAINTEXT>, 323, 741
<PRE>, 323, 741
<Q>, 741
<S>, 321, 742
<SAMP>, 742
<SCRIPT LANGUAGE=VBS>, 447
<SELECT>, 742
<SMALL>, 743
<SPAN>, 743
<STRIKE>, 321, 743
<STRONG>, 320, 743
<SUB>, 744
<SUP>, 744
<TAB>, 744
<TABLE>, 332, 744
<TBODY>, 745
<TD>, 332, 745
<TEXTAREA>, 746
<TFOOT>, 746
<TH>, 332, 746
<THEAD>, 747
<TITLE>, 747
<TR>, 332, 747
<TT>, 321, 747
<U>, 748
<UL>, 748
<VAR>, 748
VBScript program definitions, 446

<WBR>, 749
Web site, 714
Word Internet Assistant, 758-760
<XMP>, 749
Tags command (View menu), 415
Tags dialog box, 415-416
Tan function (VBScript), 471
tapes (family sets), 695
TAPI, 50
Task Manager, 650
<TBODY> HTML tag, 745
TCP (Transmission Control Protocol), 6, 294, 709
TCP/IP (Transmission Control Protocol/Internet Protocol), 6, 30, 108, 708
   address class, 686
   addresses, 207
   configuring, 207
   dbWeb, 553
   DNS configurations, 110
   installing printing options, 118-119
   multihomed, 700
   printing, 108
   printing services, configuring, 119
   protocols, 294
      installing, 108-112
   simple installing, 118
   WINS configurations, 111
TCP/IP Properties dialog box, 147, 292
TCP/IP Security dialog box, 293
<TD> HTML tag, 332, 745

TDI (Transport Driver Interface), 709
technical support
   Internet, 21-23
   ISPs, 19
Telephone Application Programming, 50
telnet, 294, 335
Template from Document command (Tools menu), 421
Template parameter (IDC), 605
templates
   creating from HTML documents, 421
   FrontPage editor Web page design, 358-359
   home pages, creating with Web 3D, 383-387
   HotDog Pro, 410
   HTML, creating, 606-612, 614
terminated processes, 708
testing
   ISAPI, 430
   strings (Java applets), 536-537
text
   encrypting, 288
   entering documents, 414-415
   HTML documents, 413
      attributes, 320, 322
   publishing, 24-25
   special colors, creating HTML documents with Microsoft Word, 364-365
   writing Java applets, 540-541
text option, 529
<TEXTAREA> HTML tag, 746

<TFOOT> HTML tag, 746
<TH> HTML tag, 332, 746
<THEAD> HTML tag, 747
theft of e-mail messages, 202-203
themes, 421
third-party ISAPI applications, 430
threads, 50, 708
    defined, 534
    Executive, 693-694
    impersonations, 697
    Java applets, 542-544
        exception handling, 543-544
        run method, 543
        start method, 542
        stop method, 542
    multithreading, 700
three-dimensional objects
    CorelWEB.GALLERY, 389-390
    CorelWEB.Transit, 391-392
    home pages, creating with Web 3D, 383-387
    renderings, 381
    Web 3D, 380-383
    Web.Designer, 387-389
tiled backgrounds, 325
Time dialog box (VBScript), 449
Time function (VBScript), 471
timeout errors, 197
TimeSerial function (VBScript), 471
timeslices, 709
TimeValue function (VBScript), 471
<TITLE> HTML tag, 747
    Internet Explorer, 757
    Word Internet Assistant, 760

titles
    documents, 412
    HTML documents, 316
tokens
    access, 686
    anonymous-level security, 687
    security, 686, 705
TombstoneInterval (registry keys), 253
TombstoneTimeout (registry keys), 253
toolbars (Performance Monitor), 625
Tools menu commands
    Customize Button Bar, 400
    Options, 203, 402
    Shortcut Keys, 401
    Template from Document, 421
Total Allowed Async I/O Requests counter, 663
Total Anonymous Users counter, 665-667
Total Blocked Async I/O Requests counter, 663
Total Blocking Locks counter, 680
Total Demand Locks counter, 680
Total Exclusive Locks counter, 680
Total NonAnonymous Users counter, 665-667
Total Number of Conflicts/sec object counter, 251
Total Number of Registrations/sec object counter, 251
Total Number of Renewals/sec object counter, 251

Total Rejected Async I/O Requests counter, 663
Total Shared Locks counter, 680
<TR> HTML tag, 332, 747
tracking
    IP addresses, 10
    processes, 299
transmissions, 8
Transport Driver Interface (TDI), 709
transporting networks, 701
traps, 709
traps properties, configuring SNMP, 117
trees, *see* directory trees
Trim function (VBScript), 468
trojan horses, 265-267
troubleshooting
    backgrounds, 381
    Basic option (WWW Publishing Service properties sheet), 141
    buses, 79
    databases, 569
    disk bottlenecks, 656
    disk striping with parity, 87
    e-mail
        addresses, 196
        message conversions, 196
    flames, 201
    FTP, 106
        publishing services, 152
    graphics, 329
    HTML tags (headers), 325
    I/O buses, 82
    Internet messages, 201
    memory, 653
    permissions (No Access option), 280
    protocols, 196

Index

Registry Editor, 252, 762
registry keys, 763
timeout errors, 197
viruses, 203-204
TrueType fonts, creating HTML documents with Microsoft Word, 365
trust relationships, 66, 709
domains, 72
truth table for VBScript equivalence operator, 454
<TT> HTML tag, 321, 747
Internet Explorer, 757
Word Internet Assistant, 760
tuning
performance, 642-643
servers, 642
tutorial (HotDog Pro), 397-398

U

<U> HTML tag, 748
Internet Explorer, 757
Word Internet Assistant, 760
UARTs (universal asynchronous receiver transmitters), 120
UBound function (VBScript), 471
UCase function (VBScript), 472
UDP (User Datagram Protocol), 710
<UL> HTML tag, 748
Internet Explorer, 757
Word Internet Assistant, 760
unary minus operator (VBScript), 451
UNC (universal naming convention), 709

unequal operator (VBScript), 454
uniform resource locators, *see* **URLs**
uninterruptible power supply, 60
Unique Conflicts/sec object counter, 251
unique identifier handles, 696
Unique Registrations/sec object counter, 251
Unique Renewals/sec object counter, 251
universal asynchronous receiver transmitters (UARTs), 120
universal naming convention (UNC), 709
universal resource identifiers, *see* **URIs**
Universally Unique Identifiers (UUIDs), 710
unloading DLLs, 429
UNMAPPED REMOTE extension, 608
Update Count option (Preferences dialog box), 246
update forms
properties, 584-587
properties sheets, 585-587
Update Now command (Options menu), 629, 631, 634
Update Time option (Alert Options dialog box), 638
updating
counters, 626
logs, 631, 634
upgrades
caches, 648
hardware, 89

memory, 89-91
processors, 648
URIs (universal resource identifiers), 709
URL extension, 608
URLs (uniform resource locators), 4, 710
addresses, 412
Internet Explorer, 175
processing queries, 412
usage counter, 652
Usage Peak counter, 652
User Connections counter, 680
User Datagram Protocol (UDP), 710
USER extension, 608
user management (Windows NT), 63-65
User Manager for Domains, 63
User Profile Editor, 64
Username option
FTP Publishing Service properties sheet, 151
Gopher Publishing Service properties sheet, 157
WWW Publishing Service properties sheet, 140
UserName parameter (IDC), 605
users
accessing systems, 297
accounts
configuring policies, 277-278
displaying, 284
protecting, 276
security, 275-277
auditing, 298
CGIs, validating, 498-499
disconnecting, 127

IDs (dbWeb), 560
keywords, 412
profiles, 64, 710
  mandatory, 700
rights, auditing, 298
WINS releases, 236
Users menu commands (Permissions), 126
Users Must Log On in Order to Change Password (Account Policy dialog box), 278
UseSelfFndPnrs (registry keys), 252
utilities
Repair Disk, 768
TCP/IP, installing, 108-112
UUIDs (Universally Unique Identifiers), 710

V

Val function (VBScript), 472
validating caches, 245
Value Bar option (Chart Options dialog box), 629
value entries, 710
<VAR> HTML tag, 748
Internet Explorer, 757
Word Internet Assistant, 760
variables (CGI environment variables), 499-503
accessing variables
  C program, 511-512
  Perl script, 512-522
AUTH_TYPE, 499
CONTENT_LENGTH, 499

CONTENT_TYPE, 499
GATEWAY_INTERFACE, 500
HTTP_ACCEPT, 500
HTTP_USER_AGENT, 500
PATH_INFO, 500
PATH_TRANSLATED, 500
QUERY_STRING, 501
REMOTE_ADDR, 501
REMOTE_HOST, 501
REMOTE_IDENT, 501
REMOTE_USER, 501
REQUEST_METHOD, 502
SCRIPT_NAME, 502
SERVER_NAME, 502
SERVER_PORT, 502
SERVER_PROTOCOL, 502
SERVER_SOFTWARE, 502
variant variables with Dim statement, 456
VarType function (VBScript), 472
vBNS, 7
VBScript, 446, 710
applications
  function and control structure examples, 473-488
  Hello World!, 447-450
control structures, 455
  For Each...Next, 458
  For...Next, 458
  While...Wend, 463
Date dialog box, 449
error checking, 475
functions, 463-473
Hello World! Web page example, 449

keywords
  Nothing, 462
  Private, 461
  Public, 461
  Static, 462
labeling images, 484
operators, 451-455
statements
  Call, 455
  Dim, 455
  Do...Loop, 457
  Erase, 457
  Exit, 457
  Exit For, 458
  Exit Function, 459
  Function, 459
  If...Then...Else, 459
  Let, 460
  loop, 457
  LSet, 460
  Mid, 460
  Next, 458
  On Error Resume Next, 461
  Randomize, 461
  Rem, 461
  RSet, 461
  Set, 462
  Step, 458
  Sub, 459, 462
strings, concatenating, 449
subroutines
  About dialog box, 475
  AddDigit, 478
  BtnDelete_OnClick, 477
  BtnEvaluate_OnClick, 477
  HotSpot, 486
  ImageMapGraphic_MouseMove, 486
  OperatorBox_OnChange, 476
Time dialog box, 449

Index

VBScript information Web site, 446
VDM (Virtual DOS Machine), 711
verifying links with FrontPage, 349
VerifyInterval (registry keys), 254
Vertical Grid option (Chart Options dialog box), 629
Vertical Labels option (Chart Options dialog box), 629
Vertical Maximum option (Chart Options dialog box), 629
video, inserting, 366
video local buses (VLBs), 80
Video option (Internet Explorer properties sheets), 175
View menu commands
　Alerts, 635
　All Events, 306
　Chart, 626
　Database, 244
　Display Binary Data, 767
　Filter Events, 305
　Find Key, 767
　FTP, 139
　Gopher, 139
　Log, 630
　Options, 169, 174
　Report, 632
　Sort by Comment, 138
　Sort by Server, 138
　Sort by Service, 138
　Sort by State, 138
　Special Characters, 415
　Tags, 415
　WWW, 139

viewing
　alerts, 625
　charts, 625
　events, 304-305
　reports, 625
Viewing option (Internet Explorer properties sheets), 183
views
　Alert, 635
　Chart, 626
　Log, 630
　Performance Monitor, 624
　　Report, 633
　　saving, 629
　Service, 139
　sites, managing, 138-139
violations (access rights), 686
Violence option (Internet Explorer properties sheets), 186
virtual address space, 687
Virtual Bytes Peak counter, 654
virtual device drivers, 710
virtual directories, 142
　creating, 144-145, 154, 158-159
Virtual DOS Machine (VDM), 711
virtual memory, 711
　paging files, 701
　swap files, 701
Virtual Memory dialog box, 99-100
Virtual Memory Manager, 54
　guard-page protection, 696
virtual private networks (VPNs), 290
virtual servers, 17, 142
　creating, 145-147

viruses, 265-267
　boot sectors, 265
　clients, 203-204
　infected systems, recovering, 268-270
　macros, 266
　removing, 268-269
　Windows NT, 266
visited links (HTML documents), 414
Visual C++ (Windows NT Server), 52
VLBs (video local buses), 80
volumes, 711
　mounting, 700
VPNs (virtual private networks), 290

W

WAIS, 296, 335
WANs (wide area networks), 32, 711
　RAS, 120
Warn Before Sending Over An Open Connection option (Internet Explorer properties sheets), 183
Warn Before Viewing Over An Open Connection option (Internet Explorer properties sheets), 183
warning messages, 694
<WBR> HTML tag, 749
　Internet Explorer, 758
Web 3D, 380-383
　home pages, creating, 383-387
Web Assistant
　launching, 616
　passwords, 616
　SQL Server, 614-620
　　parameters, 616

Web browsers (HotJava), 526
Web pages
  designing (FrontPage Editor), 350-359
    document attributes, 350-351
    frames, 351-353
    FrontPage scripts, 356-357
    tables, 354-355
    templates, 358-359
  Hello World! VBScript example, 449
  Java applets
    code for Marquee applet, 530-533
    compiling, 544-545
    creating, 528-544
    embedding in HTML, 545-546
    importing classes, 533-534
    initializing, 535-538
    painting, 539-541
    parameters for Marquee applet, 529-530
    threads, 542-544
  Microsoft VBScript, 446
  Simple Calculator, 474
Web publishing
  Access, 375-378
    databases, 376-378
    Internet Assistant for Access, installing, 376
  Excel, 368-372
    Internet Assistant for Excel, installing, 369-370
    publishing spreadsheets, 370-373
  Office, 362-378
  PowerPoint, 372-375
    converting a PowerPoint slide show into HTML, 374-376
    Internet Assistant for PowerPoint, installing, 373
  Word, 362-368
    Internet Assistant for Word, installing, 363
Web, *see* **WWW**
Web sites
  Authentication Server protocol, 501
  C CGI programs, 505
  CGI Perl scripts, 504
  Internet Assistant for Access, 376
  Internet Assistant for Excel, 369
  Internet Assistant for Microsoft PowerPoint, 373
  Internet Assistant for Word, 363
  Microsoft Access Internet tools, 376
  Microsoft Excel, 369
  Microsoft FrontPage, 338
  Microsoft Office, 362
  Microsoft Office Internet tools, 362
  Microsoft PowerPoint, 373
  Microsoft VBScript information, 446
  one-time passwords (OTPs), 499
  Perl, 504
  Perl for Windows NT, 503
  RFC 931, 501
  WinZip, 503
Web.Designer, 387-389
Webaholics Top 50 Links Web site, 41
Weekday function (VBScript), 473
Welcome dialog box, 399
Welcome messages, 153
Welcome to HotDog! dialog box, 398
well-known endpoints, 704
when log file size option (Log to File radio button), 148
While...Wend control structure (VBScript), 463
whitepapers Web site, 40
wide area networks (WANs), 32, 711
wildcards (*) notation, 533
WINDBG.EXE file, 711
Windows 95 (RAS), 120
Windows Internet Name Service, *see* **WINS**
Windows NT, 54, 56
  BIOS, 49
  compression support, 57
  computer management, 61-63
  Configuration Manager, 53
  controllers, 66-67
    backup domain, 67
    domains, 67
  DHCP Manager, 63
  disk duplexing, 58, 60
  disk mirroring, 58-59
  disk striping with parity, 58, 60
  domains, 65-66
    master models, 69-72
    single models, 68
    trust relationships, 72
  environmental subsystems, 54-56

Event Viewer, 61, 302-303
fault tolerant, 49
fault-tolerant capabilities, 58-61
File Manager, 62
FTP Server publishing services, 33
Gopher Server publishing services, 33
I/O Manager, 54
IIS, 76
Internet Server Manager, 62
Local IPC Manager, 53
Logon Script, 64
network adapters, 60
NTFS, 57
Object Manager, 52
Print Manager, 62
Process Manager, 53
RAS Administrator, 62
scalability, 49
security, 49
Security Reference Manager, 53
Server Manager domains, 62
servers, 66-67
   FTP, 31
   Gopher, 31
   WWW, 31
software configurations, 98-101
symmetric multiprocessing, 50, 60
TCP/IP, 30
uninterruptible power supply, 60
user management, 63-65
User Manager for Domains, 63
User Profile Editor, 64
user profiles, 64

Virtual Memory Manager, 54
viruses, 266
WINS Manager, 63
workgroups, 65-66
   security, 65
WWW Server publishing services, 32
Windows NT Challenge/ Response option (WWW Publishing Service properties sheet), 141
Windows NT Server, 48, 65
buses, 82
CD-ROMs, adding, 84
compatibility, 50
configuring firewalls, 290-297
design models, 51-54
disk striping with parity, troubleshooting, 87
disk subsystems, 82-84
   multiple, 87-88
   SCSI, 88-89
   single, 85-87
EIDE, 83
hardware, 77
   upgrades, 89
IDE, 83
IIS, 11-12
integratability, 51
memory upgrades, 89-91
multithreading, 50
network adapters, adding, 92-97
performance, 85
processors, 77-78
   adding, 97
RAS, 105
robust, 48
security, 275
selecting, 98
Windows NT Setup dialog box, 109

Windows NT System Debugger (NTSD), 707
Windows NT Task Manager, 650
Windows NT Workstation (RAS), 120
Windows on Win32 (WOW), 55
Windows Registry Editor, 764
Windows Resolution, enabling DNS, 111
WINS (Windows Internet Name Service), 63, 107, 206, 711
addresses, mapping, 235
clients, 238, 248-249
   registrations, 235
configurations, 210
configuring
   SNMP, 114
   WINS Manager, 241-247
databases, compacting, 249
designing, 235-236
DHCP, 214, 254-255
domains, 236
installing, 114, 236-241
Internet, 249
names, resolving, 234
NetBIOS, 234
non-WINS clients (subnet networks), 238
Performance Monitor, 250
protocols, disabling, 96
proxy agents, 236-239, 712
pull partners, 239
push partners, 239
renewals, 215
servers
   adding, 241, 246
   deleting, 239

multihomed, 249
primary, 111
registry keys, 253-254
secondary, 111
static mappings, 248
TCP/IP, 111
user releases, 236
WINS Manager, 63
configuring, 241-247
WINS Server Configuration dialog box, 242, 253
WinZip Web site, 503
wireframes, 386
images, 381-382
wizards
dbWeb setup, 551
Install New Modem, 122
Word Internet Assistant (HTML tags), 758-760
Work Item Shortages counter, 660
workgroups, 65-66
security, 65
Windows NT, 65
Working Set counter, 654
Working Set Peak counter, 654
working sets, 712
Workstation service, 93
workstations
registry keys, 779-781
standalones, 706
World Wide Web, *see* **WWW**
WOW (Windows on Win32), 55-56
wrappers, 5
WriteClient function (ISAs), 432, 437-438

writing Java applets, 528-544
code for Marquee applet, 530-533
parameters for Marquee applet, 529-530
text, 540-541
WWW (World Wide Web), 4, 295, 712
advertising, 18
browsers, 32, 711
configuring Internet Explorer, 168
HotJava, 526
HTML documents, 315
HTML tags, 322
installing Internet Explorer, 167-168
Internet Explorer, 166, 173-175, 187-188
Internet Explorer colors, 175
Internet Explorer, configuring character sets, 184-185
Internet Explorer, displaying Web pages, 174
security, 267-268
directories, 41-42
graphics, inserting, 329-332
HTML documents, 313
logging site activity, 147-149
SQL Server, 159-161
pages
creating forms, 597-598
creating input forms, 598-602
defining special characters, 749, 754

DSN, 597
dynamic, 24, 596
ODBC, 597
static, 24
WYSIWYG editor, 597
publishing services
configuring, 139-141
configuring properties, 149-150
creating virtual directories, 144-145
creating virtual servers, 145-147
directories, 142
log activity, configuring, 148
properties of directories, 142-143
registry keys, 770-773
security, recovering infected systems, 268-270
servers, 711
sites, 618
access rights, 149-150
backgrounds, 381
bandwidths, 381
CorelWEB.GALLERY, 389-390
CorelWEB.Transit, 391-392
dbWeb, 550
designing, 380
Digital Alta Vista, 41
displaying images, 331
Excite, 41
Haynes & Company, 40
HTML tags, 714
Internet Explorer rating systems, 185-186
Merit Network Inc., 9
Multimedia Marketing Group, 42

Open Market Commercial Sites Index, 41
PostMaster, 41
publicizing, 40
ray-traced, 386
realistic with shadows, 386
rendering images, 385
Sausage Software, 394
security, 267-268
Shiloh Consulting, 40
snapshot properties, 386
solid models, 386
sounds, 175
Submit It, 41
Web 3D, 380-383
Web.Designer, 387-389
Webaholics Top 50 Links, 41
whitepapers, 40
wireframes, 386
Yellow Pages of the Entire United States, 42
WWW command (View menu), 139
WWW Server, 31
   HTTP, 32
   Internet, connecting to, 11
   publishing services, 32
WWW Service Properties dialog box, 142, 148-149
WWW Service Properties for *ComputerName* dialog box, 139
WWW Site Properties dialog box, 149
WYSIWYG (What-You-See-Is-What-You-Get), 597

X-Y-Z

<XMP> HTML tag, 749
   Internet Explorer, 758
XOR operator (VBScript), 453

Yahoo!, 41
Year function (VBScript), 473
Yellow Pages of the Entire United States Web site, 42

A VIACOM SERVICE

The Information SuperLibrary™

| Bookstore | Search | What's New | Reference | Software | Newsletter | Company Overviews |

| Yellow Pages | Internet Starter Kit | HTML Workshop | Win a Free T-Shirt! | Macmillan Computer Publishing | Site Map | Talk to Us |

CHECK OUT THE BOOKS IN THIS LIBRARY.

You'll find thousands of shareware files and over 1600 computer books designed for both technowizards and technophobes. You can browse through 700 sample chapters, get the latest news on the Net, and find just about anything using our massive search directories.

All Macmillan Computer Publishing books are available at your local bookstore.

We're open 24-hours a day, 365 days a year.

You don't need a card.

We don't charge fines.

And you can be as **LOUD** as you want.

The Information SuperLibrary
http://www.mcp.com/mcp/   ftp.mcp.com

Windows NT 4 Web Development

—Sanjaya Hettihewa

Windows NT and Microsoft's newly developed Internet Information Server are making it easier and more cost-effective to set up, manage, and administer a good Web site. Because the Windows NT environment is relatively new, there are few books on the market that adequately discusses its full potential. *Windows NT 4 Web Development* addresses that potential by providing information on all key aspects of server setup, maintenance, design, and implementation, and covers Java, JavaScript, Internet Studio, and VBScript.

Price: $59.99 USA/$84.95 CDN   User Level: Accomplished–Expert
ISBN: 1-57521-089-4   744 pages

Microsoft BackOffice Administrator's Survival Guide

—Arthur Knowles

This all-in-one reference focuses on what Microsoft BackOffice is and how it is used in the real world. It includes all the fundamental concepts required for daily maintenance and troubleshooting, and explains the more arcane aspects of managing the BackOffice. *Microsoft BackOffice Administrator's Survival Guide* uses step-by-step written procedures interspersed with figures captured from the actual tools. Its CD-ROM includes product demos, commercial and shareware utilities, and technical notes.

Price: $59.99 USA/$81.95 CDN   User Level: Accomplished–Expert
ISBN: 0-672-30849-5   1,008 pages

Building an Intranet with Windows NT 4

—Scott Zimmerman & Tim Evans

This hands-on guide teaches readers how to set up and maintain an efficient intranet with Windows NT. It comes complete with a selection of the best software for setting up a server, creating content, and for developing Intranet applications. The CD-ROM includes a complete Windows NT intranet toolkit with a full-featured Web server, Web content development tools, and ready-to-use intranet applications.

Price: $49.99 USA/$70.95 CDN   Casual–Accomplished
ISBN: 1-57521-137-8   608 pages

CGI Developer's Guide

—Eugene Eric Kim

This book is one of the first books to provide comprehensive information on developing with CGI (the Common Gateway Interface). It covers many of the aspects of CGI, including interactivity, performance, portability, and security. After reading this book, the reader will be able to write robust, secure, and efficient CGI programs. Readers will master forms, image maps, dynamic displays, database manipulation, and animation. The CD-ROM includes source code, sample utilities, and Internet tools.

Price: $45.00 USA/$63.95 CDN   Accomplished–Expert
ISBN: 1-57521-087-8   578 pages

Windows NT 4 Server Unleashed

—Jason Garms

The Windows NT Server has been gaining tremendous market share over Novell, and the new upgrade—which includes a Windows 95 interface—is sure to add momentum to its market drive. *Windows NT 4 Server Unleashed* is written to meet that growing market. It provides information on disk and file management, integrated networking, BackOffice integration, and TCP/IP protocols. This book focuses on using Windows NT as an Internet server, and also covers security issues and Macintosh support. The CD-ROM includes source code from the book and valuable utilities.

Price: $49.99 USA/$70.95 CDN   Accomplished–Expert
ISBN: 0-672-30933-5   1,100 pages

Teach Yourself VBScript in 21 Days

—Keith Brophy & Tim Koets

Readers learn how to use VBScript to create living, interactive Web pages. This unique scripting language from Microsoft is taught with clarity and precision, providing the reader with the best and latest information on this popular language. The book covers VBScript's animation, interaction, and mathematical abilities, as well as advanced OLE object techniques. The CD-ROM contains all the source code from the book and examples of third-party software.

Price: $39.99 USA/$56.95 CDN   New–Casual
ISBN: 1-57521-120-3   550 pages

Java Developer's Guide

—Jamie Jaworski

Java is one of the major growth areas for developers on the World Wide Web. It brings with it the ability to download and run small applications called applets from a Web server. *Java Developer's Guide* teaches developers everything they need to know to effectively develop Java applications. This book also explores new technology and future trends of Java development. The CD-ROM includes source code from the book and valuable utilities.

Price: $49.99 USA/$67.99 CDN   Accomplished–Expert
ISBN: 1-57521-069-X   768 pages

Presenting ActiveX

—Warren Ernst & John J. Kottler

This book provides a hands-on glimpse of Microsoft's new ActiveX technologies and describes the roles existing Microsoft technologies play in this new architecture. *Presenting ActiveX* teaches how ActiveX will let Web publishers and developers add "active" elements to their Web pages and Web applications. The CD-ROM contains source code from the book and powerful ActiveX utilities.

Price: $29.99 USA/$42.95 CDN   Casual–Accomplished
ISBN: 1-57521-156-4   300 pages

sams.net

Add to Your Sams.net Library Today with the Best Books for Internet Technologies

ISBN	Quantity	Description of Item	Unit Cost	Total Cost
1-57521-089-4		Windows NT 4 Web Development (book/CD-ROM)	$59.99	
0-672-30849-5		Microsoft BackOffice Administrator's Survival Guide (book/CD-ROM)	$59.99	
1-57521-137-8		Building an Intranet with Windows NT 4 (book/CD-ROM)	$49.99	
1-57521-087-8		CGI Developer's Guide (book/CD-ROM)	$45.00	
0-672-30933-5		Windows NT 4 Server Unleashed (book/CD-ROM)	$55.00	
1-57521-041-X		The Internet Unleashed 1996 (book/CD-ROM)	$49.99	
1-57521-140-8		Microsoft FrontPage Unleashed (book/CD-ROM)	$49.99	
1-57521-149-1		Laura Lemay's Web Workshop: Microsoft FrontPage (book/CD-ROM)	$39.99	
1-57521-092-4		Web Page Wizardry: Wiring Your Site for Sound and Action (book/CD-ROM)	$39.99	
1-57521-051-7		Web Publishing Unleashed (book/CD-ROM)	$49.99	
1-57521-120-3		Teach Yourself VBScript in 21 Days (book/CD-ROM)	$39.99	
1-57521-156-4		Presenting ActiveX (book/CD-ROM)	$35.00	
1-57521-069-X		Java Developer's Guide (book/CD-ROM)	$49.99	
		Shipping and Handling: See information below.		
		TOTAL		

Shipping and Handling: $4.00 for the first book, and $1.75 for each additional book. If you need to have it NOW, we can ship product to you in 24 hours for an additional charge of approximately $18.00, and you will receive your item overnight or in two days. Overseas shipping and handling adds $2.00. Prices subject to change. Call between 9:00 a.m. and 5:00 p.m. EST for availability and pricing information on latest editions.

201 W. 103rd Street, Indianapolis, Indiana 46290

1-800-428-5331 — Orders   1-800-835-3202 — FAX   1-800-858-7674 — Customer Service

Book ISBN 1-57521-109-2

What's on the Disc

The companion CD-ROM contains software developed by the authors, plus an assortment of third-party tools and product demos. The disc is designed to be explored using a CD-ROM Menu program. Using the Menu program, you can view information concerning products and companies and install programs with a single click of the mouse. To run the Menu program, follow these steps:

Windows 3.1 and Windows NT Installation Instructions:

1. Insert the CD-ROM into your CD-ROM drive.
2. From File Manager or Program Manager, choose Run from the File menu.
3. Type <drive>\setup and press Enter, where <drive> corresponds to the drive letter of your CD-ROM. For example, if your CD-ROM is drive D:, type D:\SETUP and press Enter.

Windows 95 Installation Instructions

1. Insert the CD-ROM into your CD-ROM drive.
2. If Windows 95 is installed on your computer and you have the AutoPlay feature enabled, the Menu program starts automatically whenever you insert the disc into your CD-ROM drive.
3. If AutoPlay is not enabled, choose Setup from the CD drive, using Explorer.

NOTE

For best results, set your monitor to display between 256 and 64,000 colors. A screen resolution of 640×480 pixels is also recommended. If necessary, adjust your monitor settings before using the CD-ROM.